CW01667503

PHILIP'S

MODERN SCHOOL ATLAS

GEORGE PHILIP

In Association with Heinemann Educational

George Philip Ltd.
59 Grosvenor Street
London W1X 9DA

Heinemann Educational
Halley Court Jordan Hill
Oxford OX2 8EJ

ASTRONOMICAL GEOGRAPHY

THE SOLAR SYSTEM

The Solar System is a tiny part of one of the countless galaxies that make up the Universe. It consists of the Sun at the centre with nine planets and various moons, comets, dust particles and gases revolving around it. All the planets revolve around the Sun in the same direction, anti-clockwise when viewed from the Northern Heavens, and almost in the same plane.

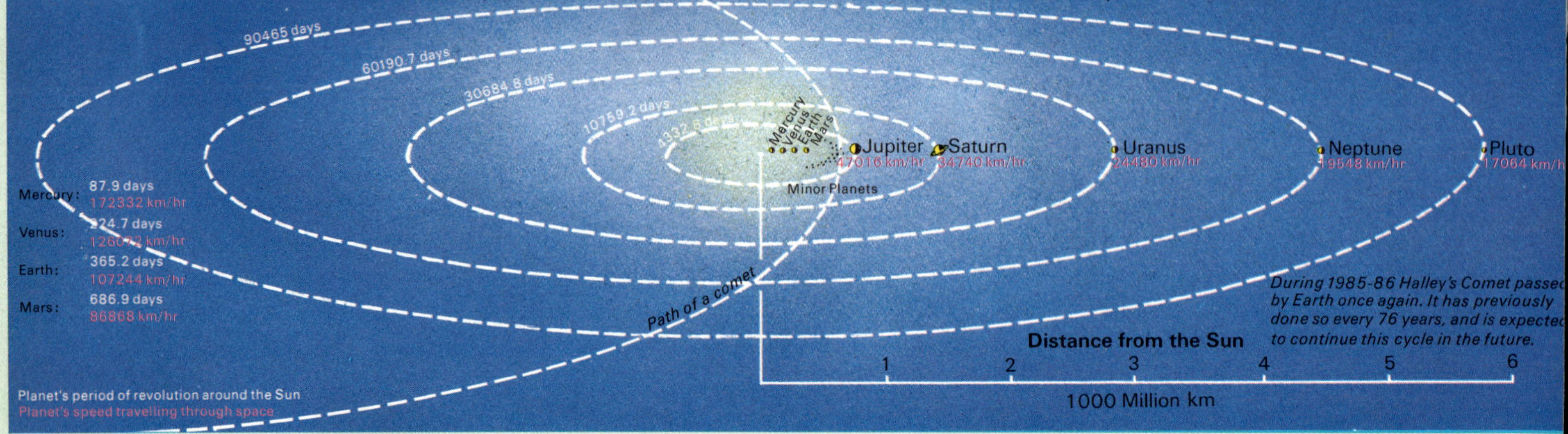

During 1985-86 Halley's Comet passed by Earth once again. It has previously done so every 76 years, and is expected to continue this cycle in the future.

THE PLANETS IN RELATION TO THEIR SIZE

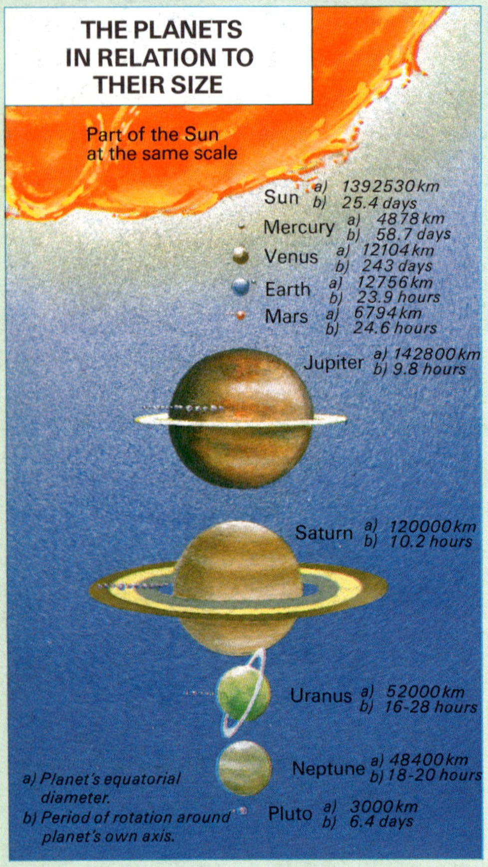

a) Planet's equatorial diameter.
b) Period of rotation around planet's own axis.

ECLIPSES

When the Moon passes between the Earth and the Sun it blots out the sunlight over part of the Earth's surface. This is called a partial eclipse of the Sun.

When the Earth passes between the Moon and the Sun it casts a shadow over the whole surface of the Moon. This is a total eclipse of the Moon.

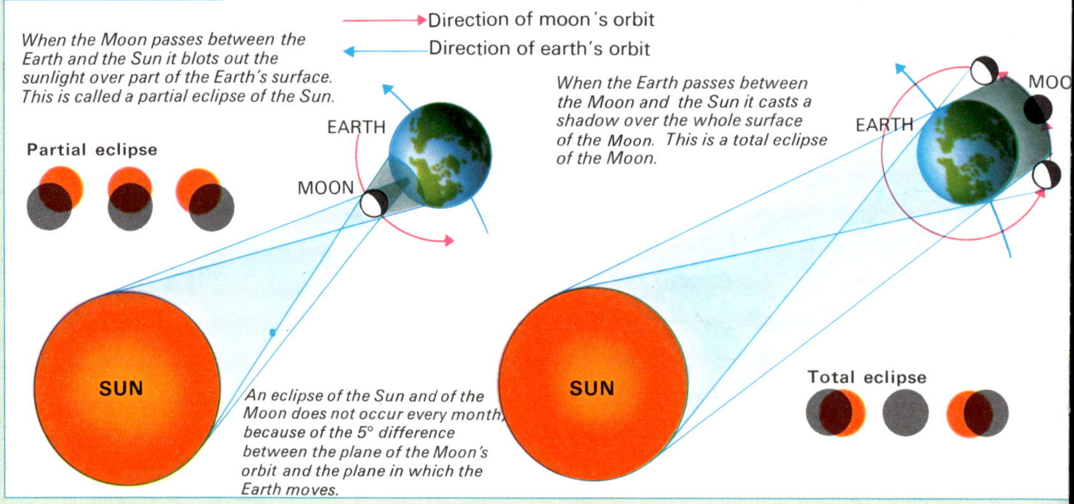

An eclipse of the Sun and of the Moon does not occur every month because of the 5° difference between the plane of the Moon's orbit and the plane in which the Earth moves.

TIDES

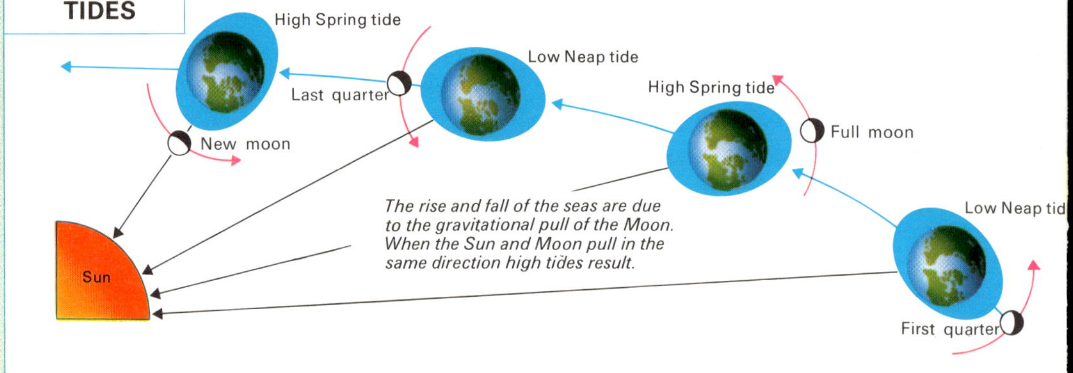

The rise and fall of the seas are due to the gravitational pull of the Moon. When the Sun and Moon pull in the same direction high tides result.

THE PHASES OF THE MOON

The Moon, like the planets, has no light of its own and shines only by reflecting sunlight.

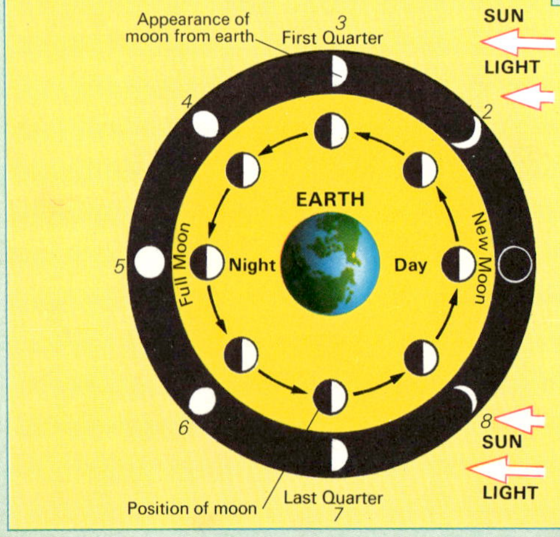

The Moon rotates on its own axis in just over 27 days, which is the same as its period of revolution around the Earth, so that it always presents the same face (hemisphere) to us. Because the Earth has moved on its own orbital plane around the Sun, while the Moon is revolving around it, the time from one full Moon to the next is 29½ days.

THE SEASONS

The earth revolves around the sun once a year in an anti-clockwise direction. The earth is tilted at an angle of 66½ degrees to the plane of its orbit and always points into space in the same direction. In June the northern hemisphere is tilted towards the sun and it is the northern summer – days are longer and it is generally warmer. The southern hemisphere is pointing away from the sun. It is cooler and the days are shorter – the southern winter. In December the reverse is the case.

Equinox – One of the two times in the year when day and night are of equal length, owing to the Sun being overhead at the Equator.

Solstice – One of the two times in the year, midway between the two equinoxes, when the Sun is overhead at one of the Tropics (Cancer or Capricorn) and is at its highest latitude from the Equator (23½° North or South).

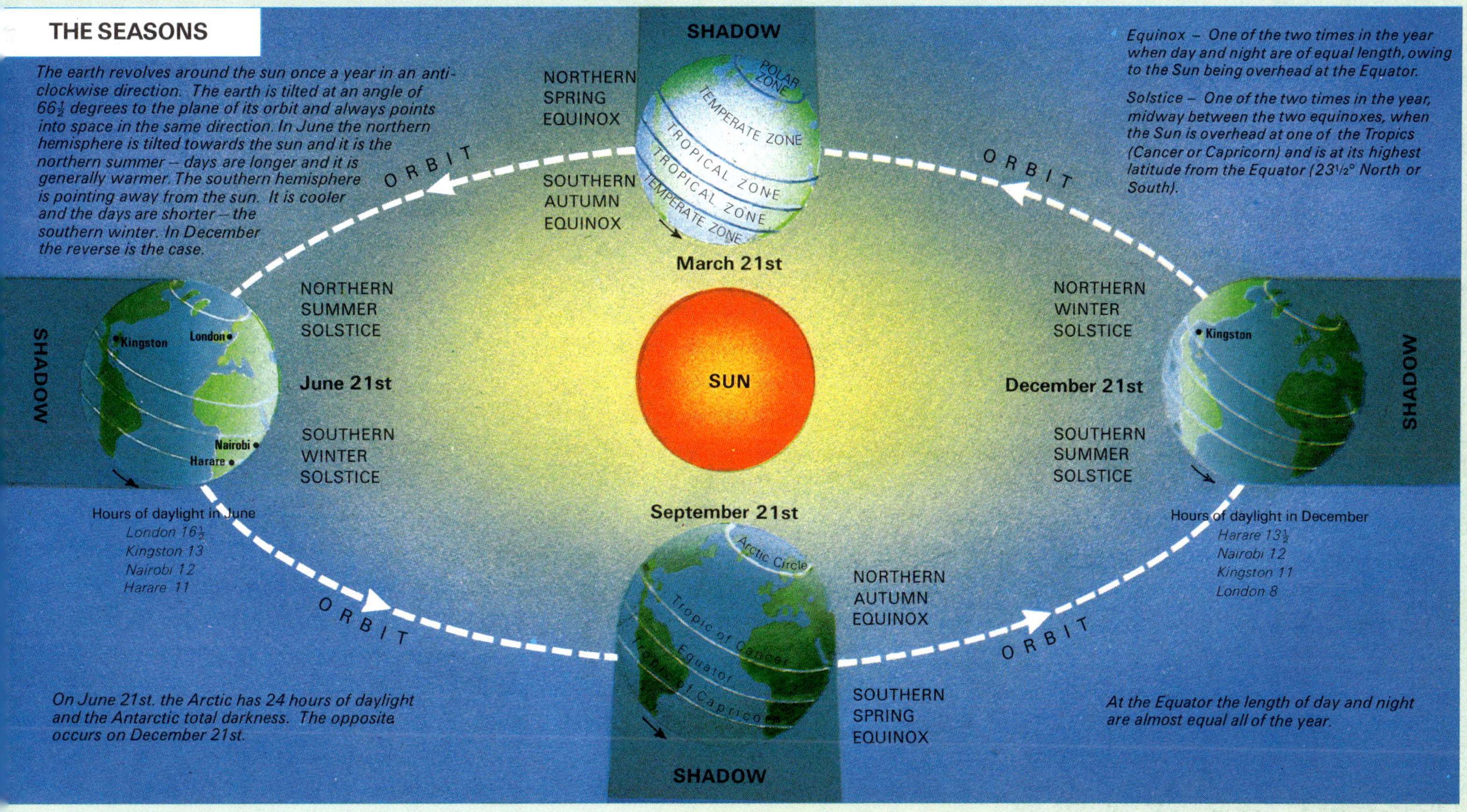

On June 21st. the Arctic has 24 hours of daylight and the Antarctic total darkness. The opposite occurs on December 21st.

At the Equator the length of day and night are almost equal all of the year.

LENGTH OF DAY AND NIGHT ON THE EARTH

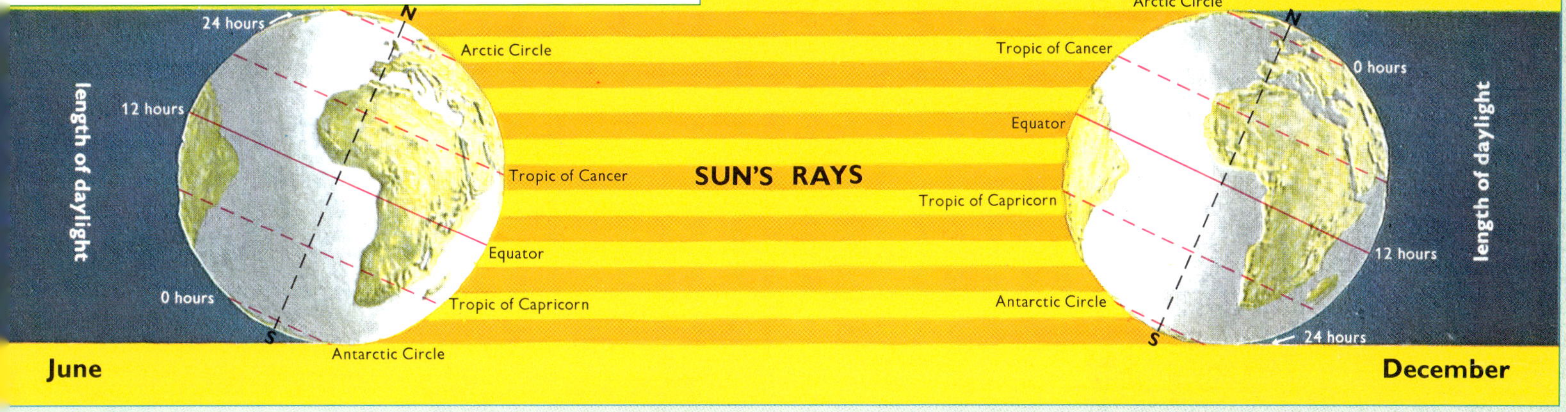

TIME

The Year *– the time taken by the Earth to revolve around the Sun, or 365¼ days.*

The Month *– the approximate time taken by the Moon to revolve around the Earth. The twelve months of the year in fact vary from 28 (29 in a Leap Year) to 31 days.*

The Week *– an artificial period of 7 days, not based on astronomical time.*

The Day *– the time taken by the Earth to complete one rotation on its axis.*

The Hour *– 24 hours make one day. Usually the day is divided into hours A.M. (ante meridiem or before noon) and P.M. (post meridiem or after noon), although most timetables now use the 24-hour system, from midnight to midnight, for example, 1p.m. = 13.00 hours.*

SUNRISE AND SUNSET

From the diagrams below it is possible to find out the time of sunrise or sunset on a given date and for latitudes between 60°N and 60°S.

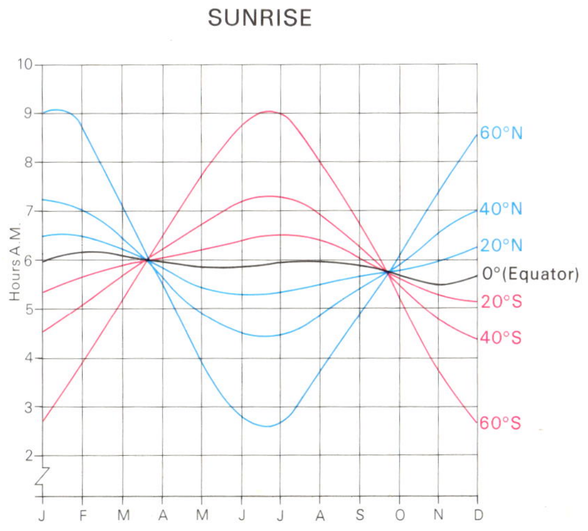

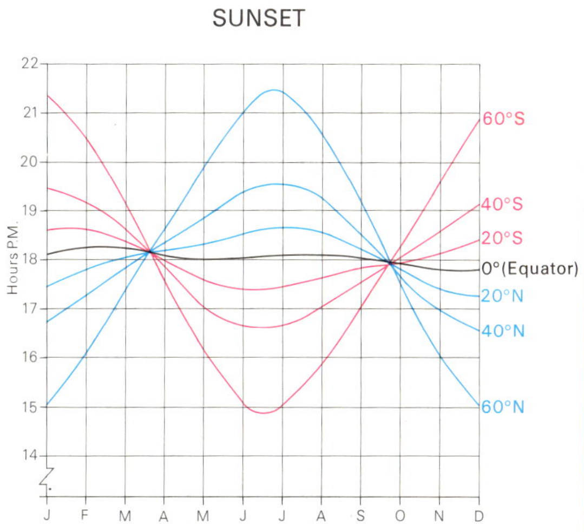

PHILIP'S

MODERN SCHOOL ATLAS

KEY TO MAP SYMBOLS

SETTLEMENTS

PARIS   Berne   Livorno   Brugge   *Algeciras*   *Fréjus*   *Oberammergau*   *Thira*

Settlement symbols and type styles vary according to the scale of each map and indicate the importance of towns on the map rather than specific population figures

∴ Ruins or Archæological Sites   Wells in Desert

ADMINISTRATION

International Boundaries

International Boundaries (Undefined or Disputed)

Internal Boundaries

National Parks

Country Names

NICARAGUA

Administrative Area Names

KENT

CALABRIA

International boundaries show the *de facto* situation where there are rival claims to territory

COMMUNICATIONS

Principal Roads

Other Roads

Trails and Seasonal Roads

Passes

Airfields

Principal Railways

Railways Under Construction

Other Railways

Railway Tunnels

Principal Canals

PHYSICAL FEATURES

Perennial Streams

Intermittent Streams

Perennial Lakes

Intermittent Lakes

Swamps and Marshes

Permanent Ice and Glaciers

▲ 8848 Elevations in metres

▼ 8050 Sea Depths in metres

1134 Height of Lake Surface Above Sea Level in metres

ELEVATION AND DEPTH TINTS

Height of Land Above Sea Level   Land Below Sea Level   Depth of Sea

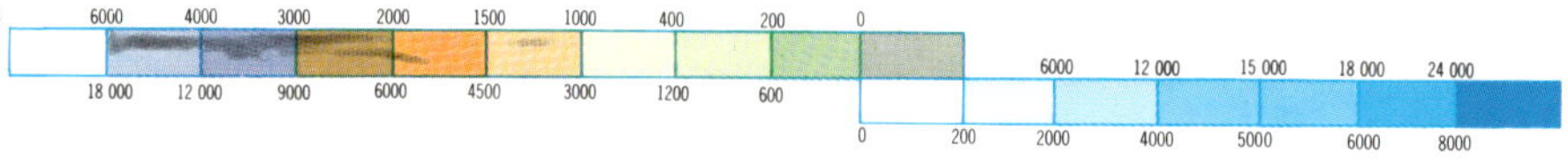

Some of the maps have different contours to highlight and clarify the principal relief features

KEY TO COLOUR CODING

The atlas is divided into four sections for ease of use.

- BRITISH ISLES
- EUROPE, ASIA, OCEANIA, AFRICA, NORTH AMERICA & SOUTH AMERICA
- THE WORLD
- INDEX

Eighty-eighth Edition

ISBN 0 540 05669 3 Paperback Edition
ISBN 0 540 05668 5 Hardback Edition

Edited by B.M. Willett, B.A., Cartographic Editor, George Philip Limited

Printed in Great Britain by Butler and Tanner Limited, Frome

CONTENTS

FRONT ENDPAPER: *astronomical geography*

BRITISH ISLES

- *physical* 1:4M — 4
- *administrative* 1:4M — 5
- *climate* — 6
- *transport* — 7
- *population* — 8
- *agriculture* — 9
- *energy and industry* — 10
- *employment, leisure and trade* — 11
- *climate graphs* — 12-13
- SOUTH & SOUTH-EAST ENGLAND 1:1M — 14-15
- SOUTH-WEST ENGLAND 1:1M — 16
- WALES 1:1M — 17
- NORTHERN ENGLAND 1:1M — 18-19
- SCOTLAND - SOUTH: 1:1M — 20-21
- SCOTLAND - NORTH: 1:1M — 22-23
- IRELAND 1:1,25M — 24-25

EUROPE

- *physical* 1:20M — 26
- *political* 1:20M — 27
- *climate and natural vegetation* 1:40M — 28
- *economic* 1:20M — 29
- EUROPEAN THEMES — 30-31
- *statistics* — 32-33
- FRANCE & WESTERN EUROPE 1:4M — 34-35
- LOW COUNTRIES AND LOWER RHINE 1:2M — 36
- SPAIN & PORTUGAL 1:5M — 37
- MEDITERRANEAN LANDS 1:10m — 38-39
- ITALY & THE BALKANS 1:5M — 40-41
- CENTRAL EUROPE 1:5M — 42-43
- SCANDINAVIA & THE BALTIC LANDS 1:6M — 44-45
- EUROPEAN RUSSIA & TURKEY 1:10M — 46-47
- SOVIET UNION 1:20M — 48-49

ASIA

- *physical* 1:50M — 50
- *political* 1:50M — 51
- *climate and natural vegetation* 1:100M — 52
- *economic* 1:50M — 53
- ASIA & OCEANIA: *statistics* — 54-55
- SOUTH-WEST ASIA 1:15M — 56-57
  - THE HOLY LAND 1:1,5M
- SOUTH ASIA 1:10M — 58-59
- CHINA & KOREA 1:15M — 60-61
- JAPAN 1:7,5M — 62
- SOUTH-EAST ASIA 1:15M — 63
- PACIFIC OCEAN 1:54M — 64-65

AUSTRALIA AND NEW ZEALAND

- AUSTRALIA 1:12M — 66-67
- *climate and natural vegetation* 1:60M — 68
- *economic* 1:20M — 69
- SOUTH-EAST AUSTRALIA 1:4,5M — 70
- NEW ZEALAND 1:6M — 71

AFRICA

- *physical* 1:40M — 72
- *political* 1:40M — 73
- *climate and natural vegetation* 1:80M — 74
- *economic* 1:40M — 75
- *statistics* — 76-77
- NORTHERN AFRICA 1:15M — 78-79
- CENTRAL & SOUTHERN AFRICA 1:15M — 80-81

NORTH AMERICA

- *physical* 1:35M — 82
- *political* 1:35M — 83
- *climate and natural vegetation* 1:70M — 84
- *economic* 1:32M — 85
- NORTH & SOUTH AMERICA: *statistics* — 86-87
- CANADA 1:15M — 88-89
  - ALASKA 1:30M
- UNITED STATES 1:12M — 90-91
  - HAWAIIAN ISLANDS 1:10M
- THE ST. LAWRENCE & NORTH-EAST UNITED STATES 1:6M — 92-93
- MEXICO, CENTRAL AMERICA & THE WEST INDIES 1:15M — 94-95
  - JAMAICA, TRINIDAD & TOBAGO, LEEWARD & WINDWARD ISLANDS 1:5M

SOUTH AMERICA

- *physical* 1:30M — 96
- *political* 1:30M — 97
- *climate and natural vegetation* 1:70M — 98
- *economic* 1:30M — 99
- SOUTH AMERICA - NORTH 1:16M — 100-101
- SOUTH AMERICA - SOUTH 1:16M — 102
- POLAR REGIONS 1:50M — 103

THE WORLD

- *temperature and ocean currents* — 104
- *pressure, winds and annual precipitation* — 105
- *climate statistics* — 106-109
- *climatic regions, soils and vegetation* — 110-111
- *structure, volcanoes and earthquakes* — 112-113
- *environmental issues* — 114-115
- *physical* 1:80M — 116-117
- *political* 1:80M — 118-119
- *population of countries* — 120
- *population of cities* — 121
- *population distribution* — 122-123
- *population trends* — 124-125
- *quality of life I* — 126-127
- *quality of life II* — 128-129
- *agriculture* — 130-131
- *minerals and energy* — 132-133
- *trade and communications* — 134-135
- *languages and religion* — 136
- *international organisations* — 137
- *time and distance* — 138-139

- INDEX: *guide to use* — 140
- INDEX — 141-161
- BACK ENDPAPER: *map projections*

Publisher's Note *The maps of the Soviet Union and Yugoslavia show the situation at the time of going to press in December, 1991. Extra maps of the Republics and Nationalities of the Soviet Union and the Republics and Ethnic Groups of Yugoslavia are provided on p. 161.*

BRITISH ISLES: *physical*

Projection: Conical with two standard parallels

1:4 000 000

50 0 50 100 150 km

The DISTRICTS of Northern Ireland have been numbered and can be identified by reference to this table.
1 Londonderry 14 Craigavon
2 Limavady 15 Armagh
3 Coleraine 16 Newry & Mourne
4 Ballymoney 17 Banbridge
5 Moyle 18 Down
6 Larne 19 Lisburn
7 Ballymena 20 Antrim
8 Magherafelt 21 Newtownabbey
9 Cookstown 22 Carrickfergus
10 Strabane 23 North Down
11 Omagh 24 Ards
12 Fermanagh 25 Castlereagh
13 Dungannon 26 Belfast
ORKNEY
Kirkwall
HIGHLAND
SHETLAND
Lerwick
WESTERN ISLES
Stornoway
HIGHLAND
Inverness
GRAMPIAN
Aberdeen
SCOTLAND
TAYSIDE
Dundee
FIFE
Glenrothes
CENTRAL
Stirling
Edinburgh
LOTHIAN
Glasgow
STRATHCLYDE
Newtown St. Boswells
BORDERS
DUMFRIES AND GALLOWAY
Dumfries
NORTHUMBERLAND
Morpeth
Newcastle
TYNE AND WEAR
Durham
Carlisle
CUMBRIA
DURHAM
CLEVELAND
Middlesbrough
Northallerton
NORTH YORKSHIRE
ISLE OF MAN
Douglas
ATLANTIC OCEAN
North Channel
NORTH SEA
IRISH SEA
Lifford
DONEGAL
Londonderry
Antrim
NORTHERN IRELAND
Tyrone
Fermanagh
Armagh
Down
Belfast
Sligo
SLIGO
LEITRIM
Monaghan
MONAGHAN
Carrick-on-Shannon
Cavan
CAVAN
Dundalk
LOUTH
MAYO
Castlebar
ROSCOMMON
Roscommon
Longford
LONGFORD
Mullingar
WESTMEATH
An Uaimh (Navan)
MEATH
DUBLIN
Dublin
GALWAY
Galway
Tullamore
OFFALY
KILDARE
Naas
IRELAND
Port Laoise
LAOIS
CLARE
Ennis
Wicklow
WICKLOW
Carlow
CARLOW
Limerick
LIMERICK
Kilkenny
KILKENNY
TIPPERARY
Clonmel
WEXFORD
Wexford
Tralee
KERRY
WATERFORD
Waterford
CORK
Cork
St. George's Channel
CELTIC SEA
LANCASHIRE
Preston
WEST YORKSHIRE
Wakefield
HUMBERSIDE
Beverley
GREATER MANCHESTER
Manchester
Barnsley
SOUTH YORKSHIRE
MERSEYSIDE
Liverpool
ENGLAND
Lincoln
LINCOLNSHIRE
Caernarfon
Mold
CLWYD
Chester
CHESHIRE
DERBYSHIRE
Matlock
NOTTINGHAMSHIRE
Nottingham
GWYNEDD
Stafford
STAFFORDSHIRE
Shrewsbury
SHROPSHIRE
Leicester
LEICESTERSHIRE
NORFOLK
Norwich
WEST MIDLANDS
Birmingham
WALES
POWYS
Llandrindod Wells
HEREFORD AND WORCESTER
Worcester
Warwick
WARWICKSHIRE
NORTHAMPTONSHIRE
Northampton
CAMBRIDGESHIRE
Cambridge
SUFFOLK
Ipswich
Bedford
BEDFORDSHIRE
DYFED
Carmarthen
Gloucester
GLOUCESTERSHIRE
Oxford
OXFORDSHIRE
Aylesbury
BUCKINGHAMSHIRE
Hertford
HERTFORDSHIRE
ESSEX
Chelmsford
WEST GLAMORGAN
Swansea
MID GLAMORGAN
GWENT
Cwmbran
Cardiff
SOUTH GLAMORGAN
Bristol
AVON
WILTSHIRE
Trowbridge
Reading
BERKSHIRE
GREATER LONDON
Kingston
Maidstone
SURREY
KENT
SOMERSET
Taunton
HAMPSHIRE
Winchester
WEST SUSSEX
Chichester
EAST SUSSEX
Lewes
DEVON
Exeter
DORSET
Dorchester
Newport
ISLE OF WIGHT
CORNWALL
Truro
ENGLISH CHANNEL
FRANCE
Norwich Administrative headquarters
MERSEYSIDE Metropolitan counties
Antrim Former Northern Ireland counties
Projection: Conical with two standard parallels
West from Greenwich 0 East from Greenwich
1:4 000 000
50 0 50 100 150 km

BRITISH ISLES: *climate*

January Temperature

Actual surface temperature

°C: 7, 6, 5, 4, 3, 2, 1, 0

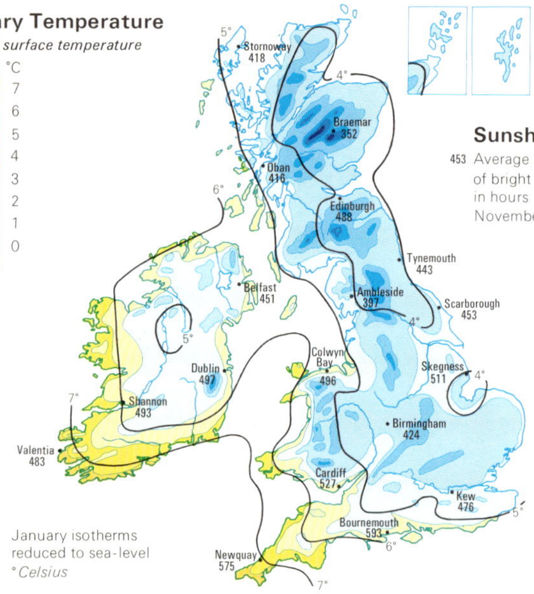

Sunshine

453 Average duration of bright sunshine in hours November - April

—— January isotherms reduced to sea-level °*Celsius*

July Temperature

Actual surface temperature

°C: 17, 16, 15, 14, 13, 12, 11, 10

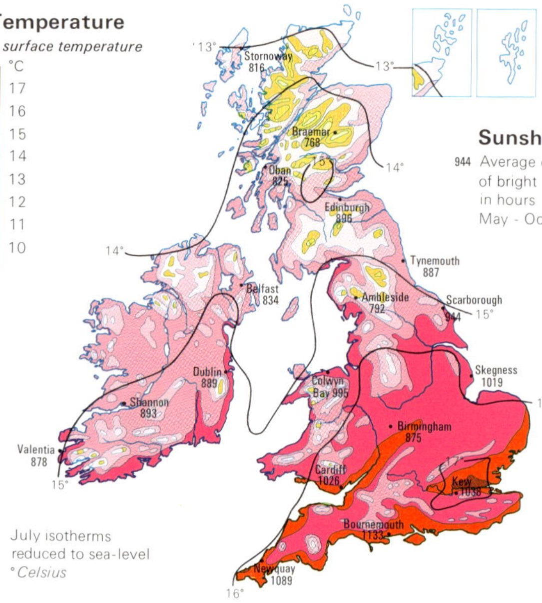

Sunshine

944 Average duration of bright sunshine in hours May - October

—— July isotherms reduced to sea-level °*Celsius*

Annual Rainfall

mm: 2500, 2000, 1500, 1000, 750, 625

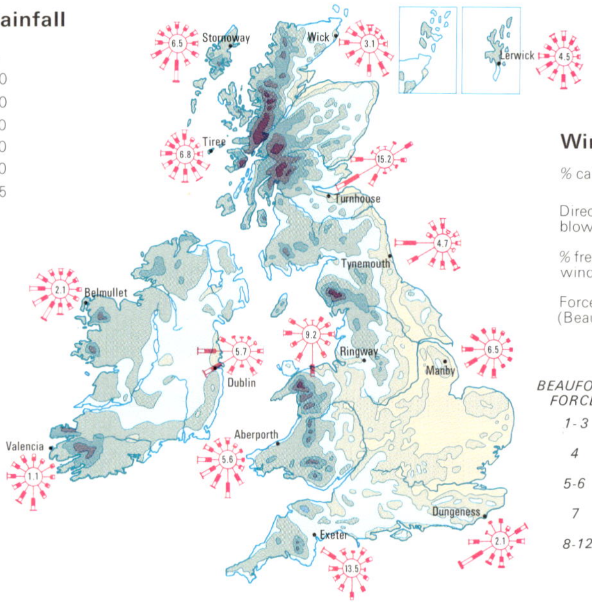

Wind

% calms in a year

Direction the wind blows from

% frequency of wind from a direction

Force of wind (Beaufort scale)

BEAUFORT FORCE	SPEED (K.P.H.)	CATEGORY
1-3	1-20	Light breeze
4	21-29	Moderate breeze
5-6	30-50	Fresh to strong wind
7	51-61	Moderate gale
8-12	over 62	Gale, storm or hurricane

Snow

Average number of mornings with snow cover per year

- more than 50
- 20-50
- 15-20
- 10-15
- 5-10
- less than 5

(after Manley, 1970)

Frost

—5— Mean length of frost free period in months

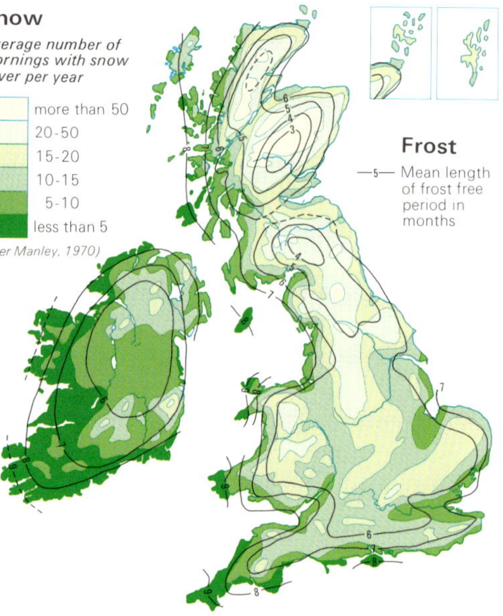

Variability of Rain

The percentage frequency with which rainfall varies from the normal rainfall regime in an area: the higher the percentage figure, the more variable the rainfall.

- over 20%
- 18-20%
- 16-18%
- 14-16%
- 12-14%
- 10-12%
- under 10%

(after Gregory, 1955)

Rainfall is least variable in the wetter northern and western areas and most variable in the drier eastern and southern areas

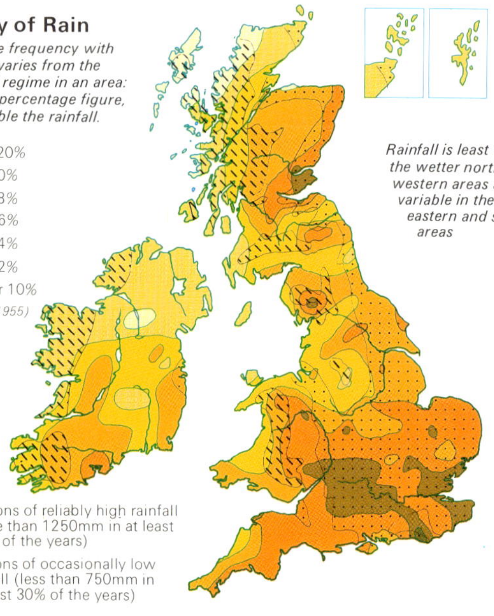

Regions of reliably high rainfall (more than 1250mm in at least 70% of the years)

Regions of occasionally low rainfall (less than 750mm in at least 30% of the years)

Synoptic Chart for a Typical Winter Depression

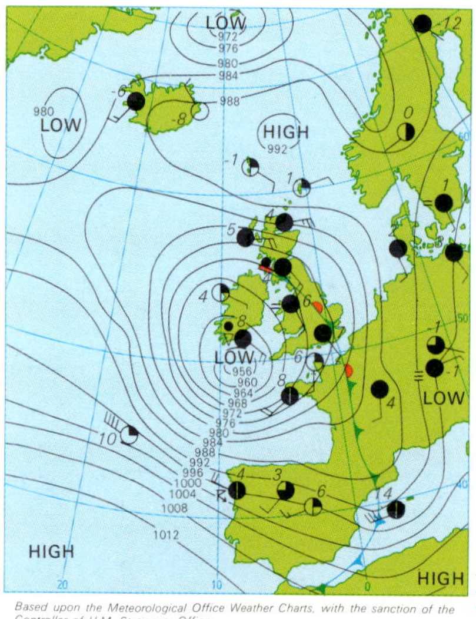

Based upon the Meteorological Office Weather Charts, with the sanction of the Controller of H.M. Stationery Office

HOUR OF OBSERVATION
06h00 GREENWICH MEAN TIME

PRESSURE

Isobars are drawn at intervals of 4 mb.

WIND

Arrows fly with the wind. A full length feather represents 18 k.p.h. and a short feather 9 k.p.h. A solid pennant represents 90 k.p.h. Calm is indicated by a circle outside the weather symbol

TEMPERATURE

Given in °C and is shown on the charts by a figure alongside the station circle.

CLOUD SYMBOLS

- Clear sky
- Sky ⅛ covered
- Sky ²⁄₈ covered
- Sky ⅜ covered
- Sky ⁴⁄₈ covered
- Sky ⅝ covered
- Sky ⁶⁄₈ covered
- Sky ⅞ covered
- Sky ⁸⁄₈ covered
- Sky obscured

WEATHER SYMBOLS

- Rain
- Drizzle
- Snow
- Rain and Snow
- Hail
- Shower
- Thunderstorm
- Fog
- Mist

FRONTS

- Warm front on the surface
- Cold front on the surface
- Occluded front

Roads and Ferry Routes

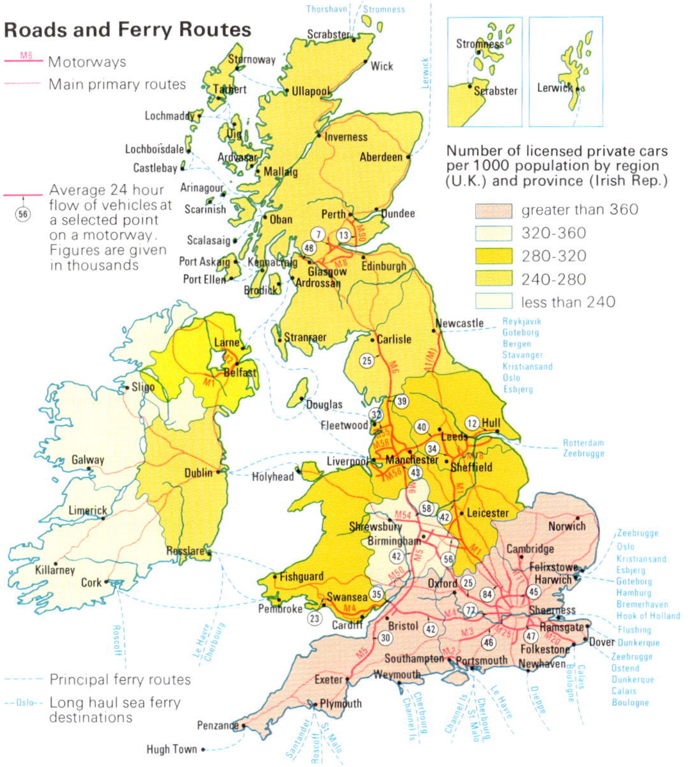

Railways

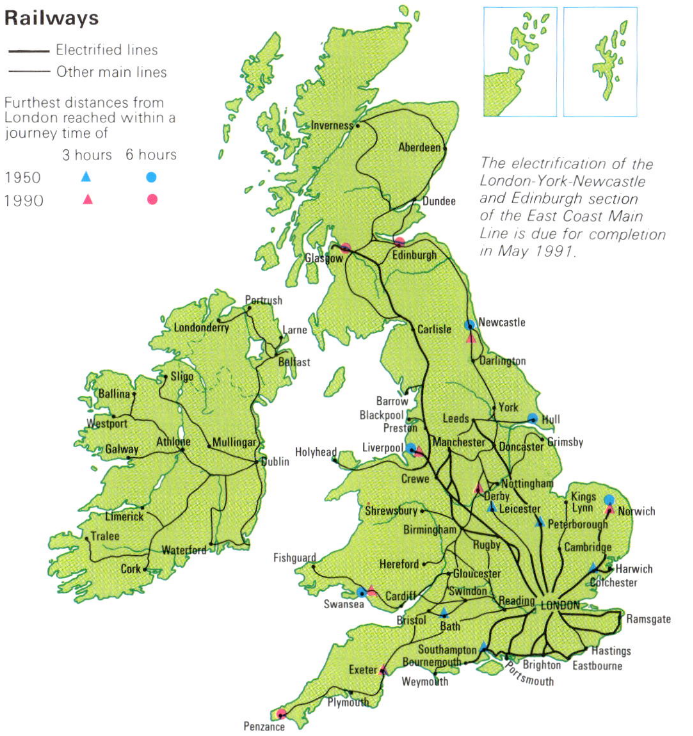

Means of Transportation Within the U.K.

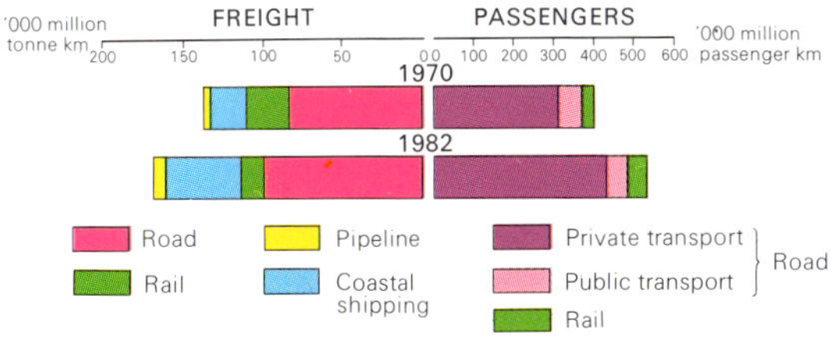

(Air transport accounted for only 2000 million passenger km in 1970 and 3000 million in 1982)

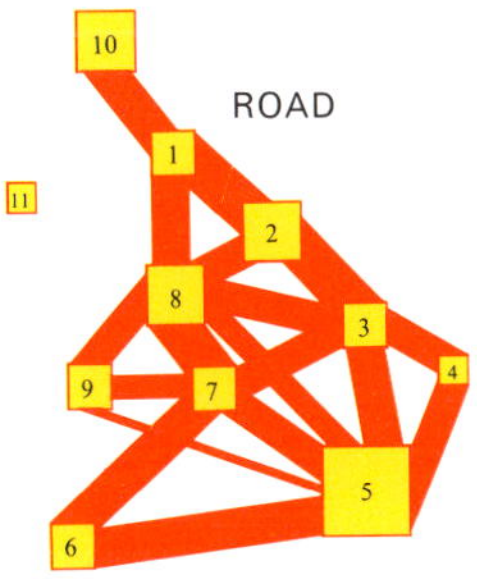

Regional Freight Movement

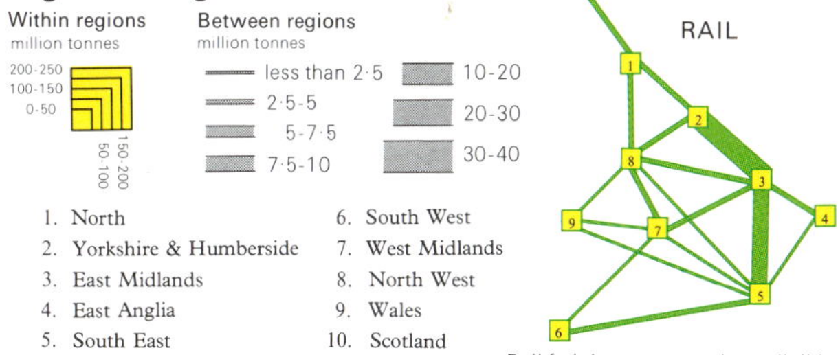

1. North
2. Yorkshire & Humberside
3. East Midlands
4. East Anglia
5. South East
6. South West
7. West Midlands
8. North West
9. Wales
10. Scotland
11. Northern Ireland

Rail freight movement is negligible within Northern Ireland

Ports

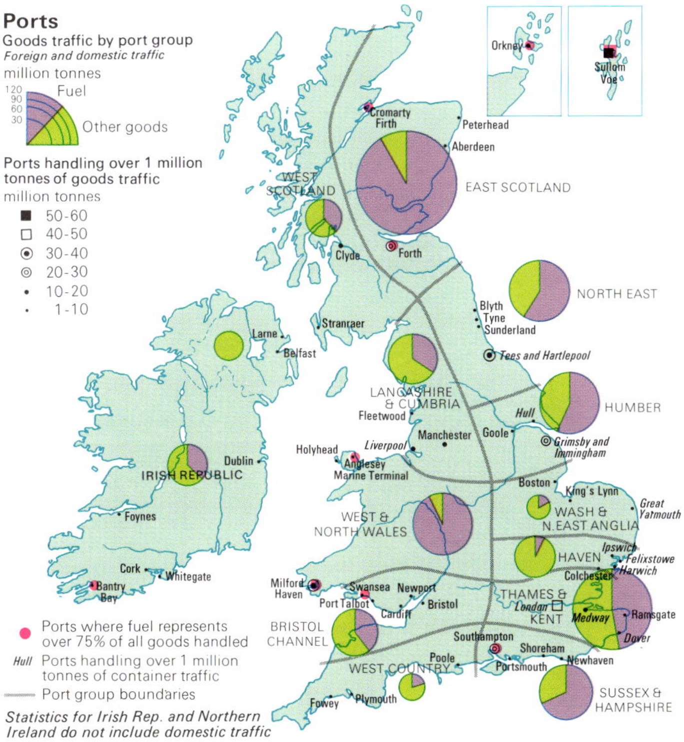

Statistics for Irish Rep. and Northern Ireland do not include domestic traffic

Airports

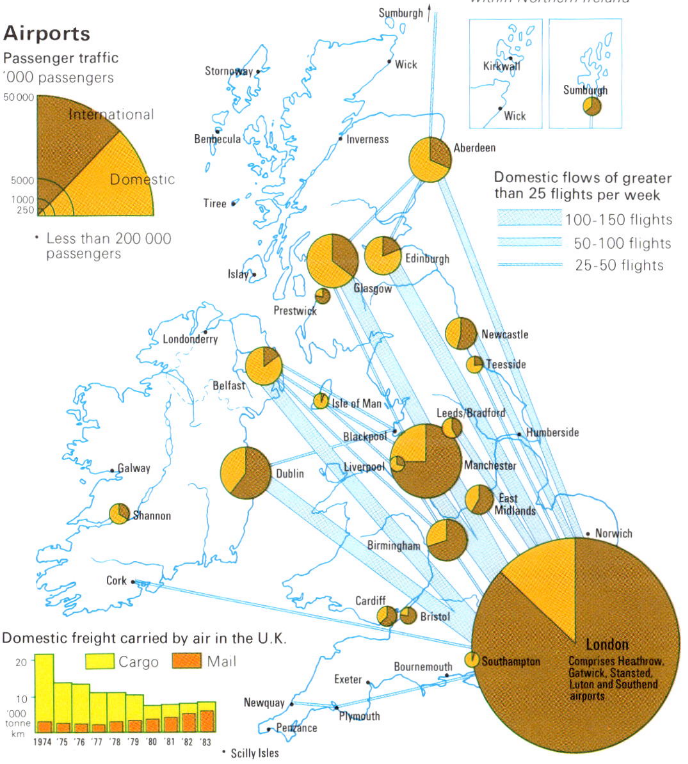

BRITISH ISLES: *population*

Population Density and Principal Towns

1:8 500 000

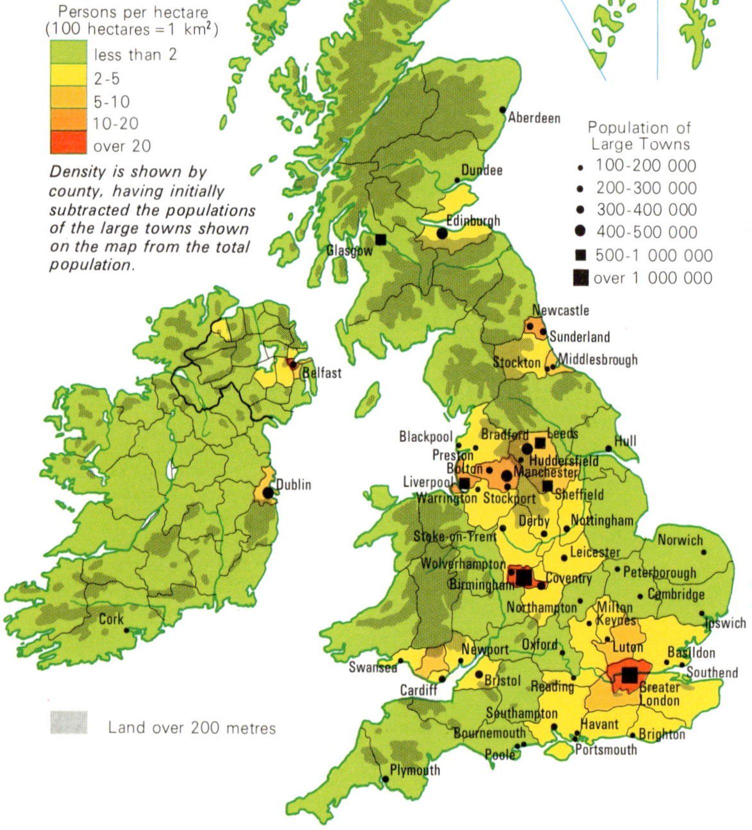

Population Change 1961-1981

1:8 500 000

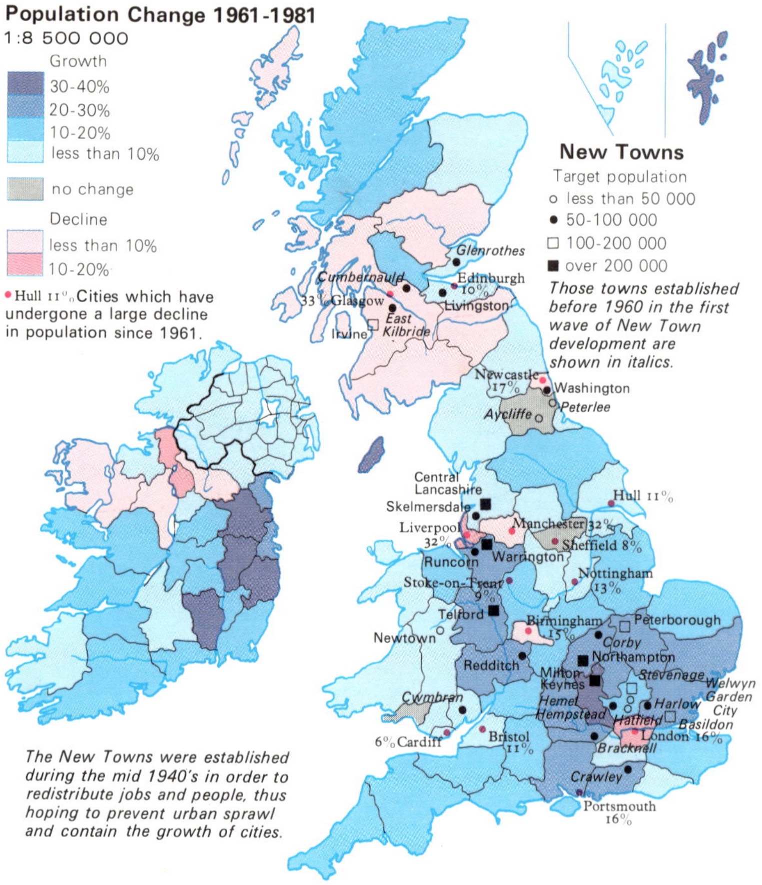

Dependency Ratio

1:10 000 000

The dependency ratio is the number of people aged under 15 years plus those of retiring age (60 and over for females, 65 and over for males) per 100 people of working age.

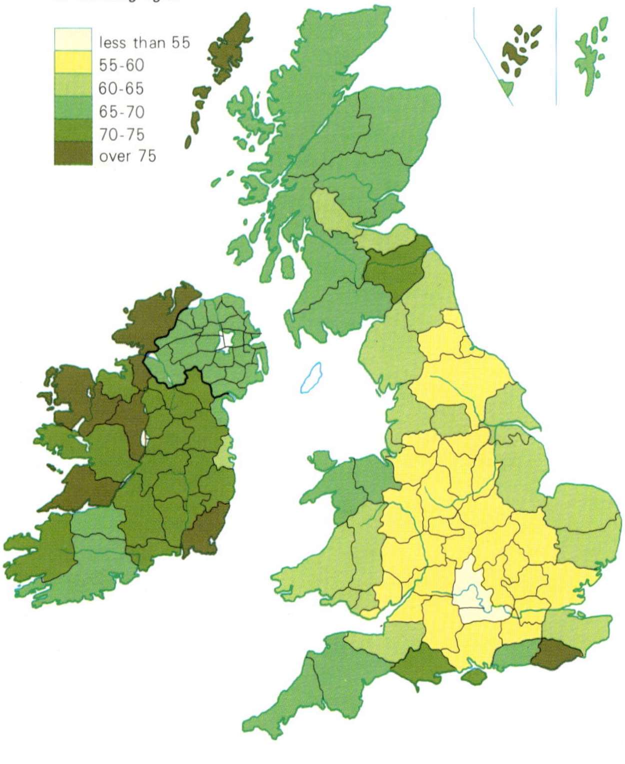

Age Structure of the U.K. in 1901, 1983 and Projected to 2051.

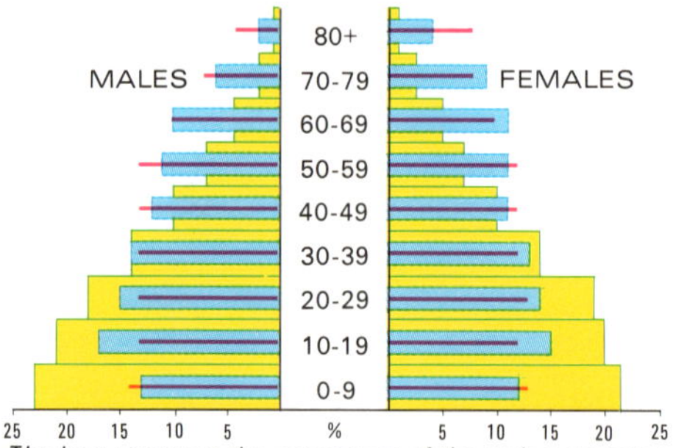

The bars represent the percentage of the male population and the percentage of the female population in the age group shown. 1901 [yellow] 1983 [blue] 2051 [red line]

Age Group Distribution Within the Population of the U.K.

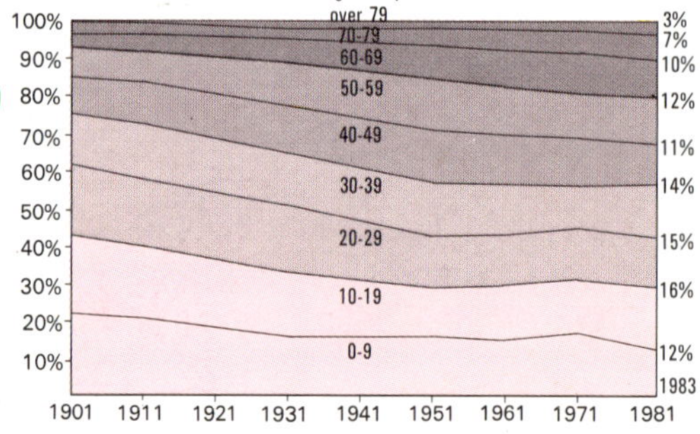

U.K. Vital Statistics, 1900-2000

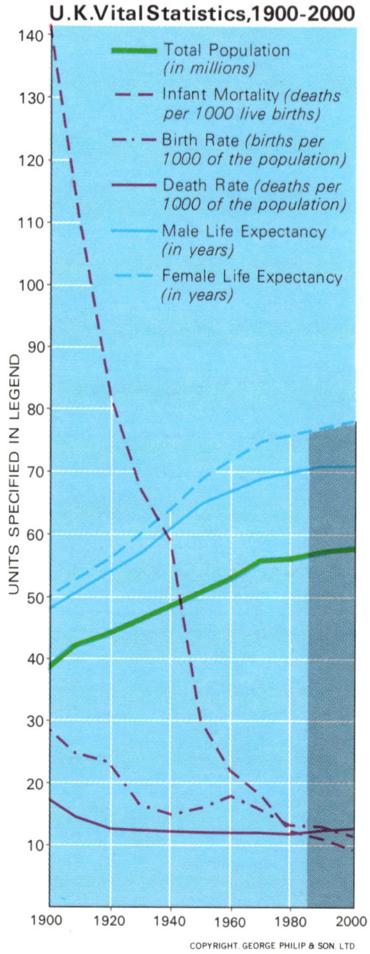

Agricultural Land Use Capability

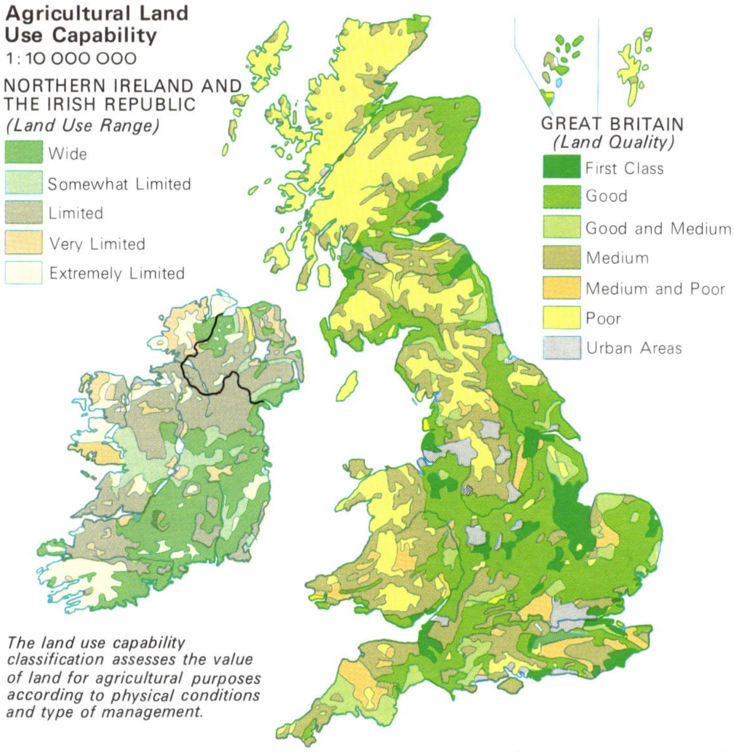

The land use capability classification assesses the value of land for agricultural purposes according to physical conditions and type of management.

Leading Agricultural Enterprises

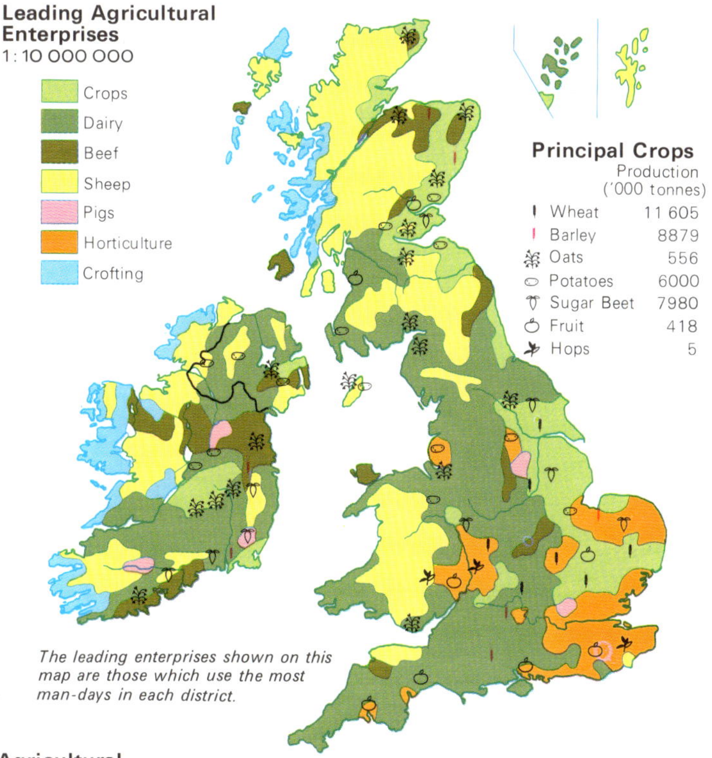

The leading enterprises shown on this map are those which use the most man-days in each district.

Yield of Selected Crops in the U.K.

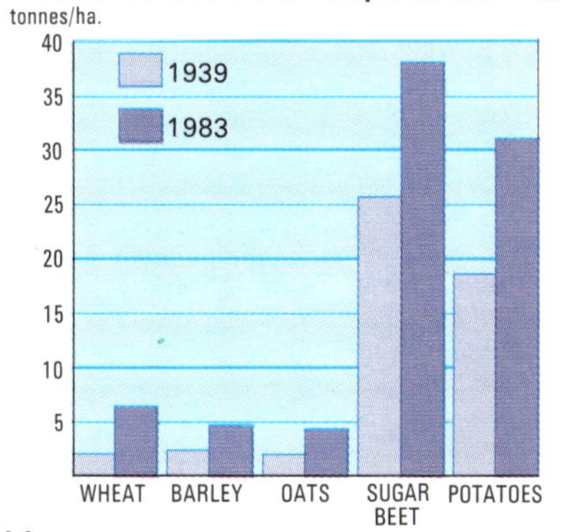

Number and Size of Agricultural Holdings in the U.K.

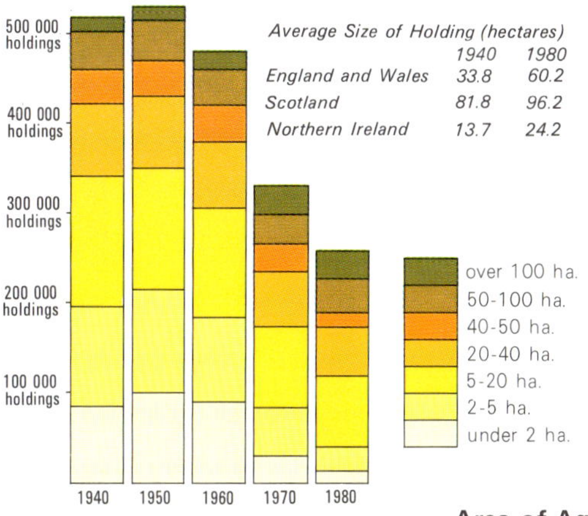

Self-Sufficiency of the U.K. in Agricultural Production

(home production given as a percentage of total consumption)

PRODUCT	1969	1977	1987
Wheat	42%	61%	79%
Barley	90%	121%	114%
Potatoes	91%	95%	95%
Sugar	33%	40%	53%
Cheese	45%	67%	67%
Butter	12%	40%	63%
Beef	77%	72%	99%
Pork	101%	62%	127%
Poultry	100%	100%	98%

Fishing

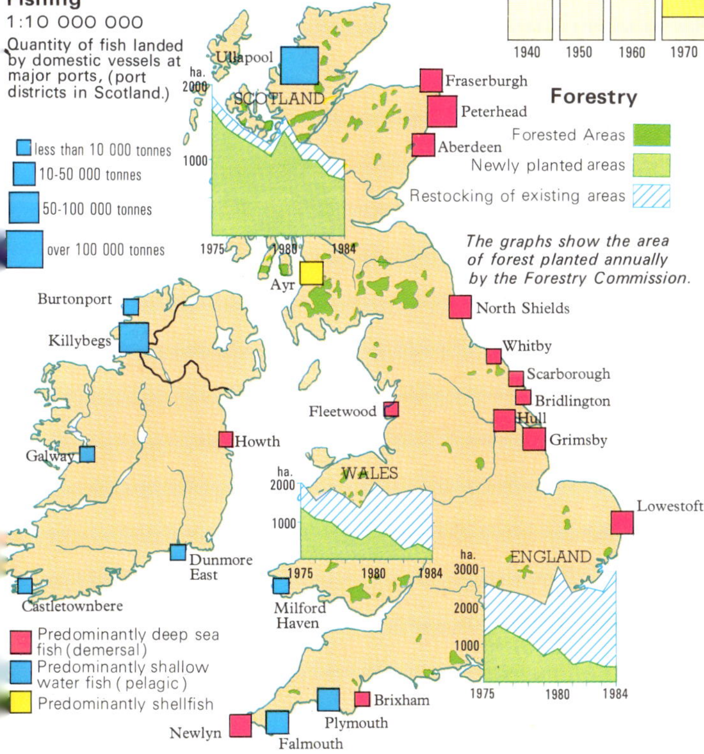

Area of Agricultural Land Under Selected Enterprises

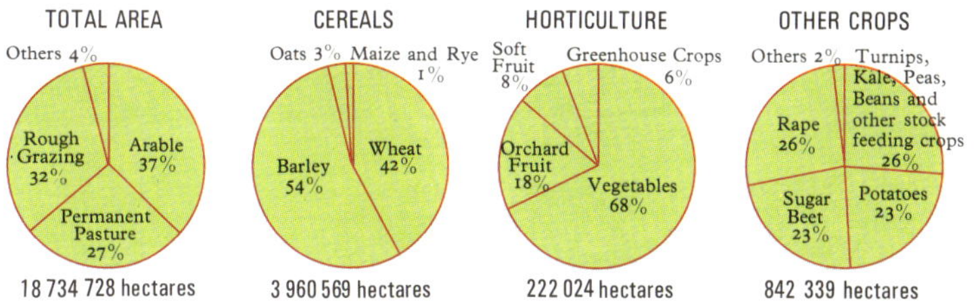

Quantity of Fish Landed by British Vessels in all Fishing Areas

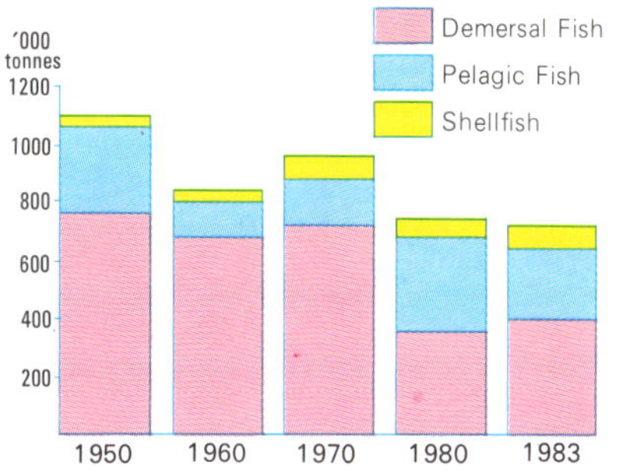

Number and Size of Livestock Holdings in the U.K.

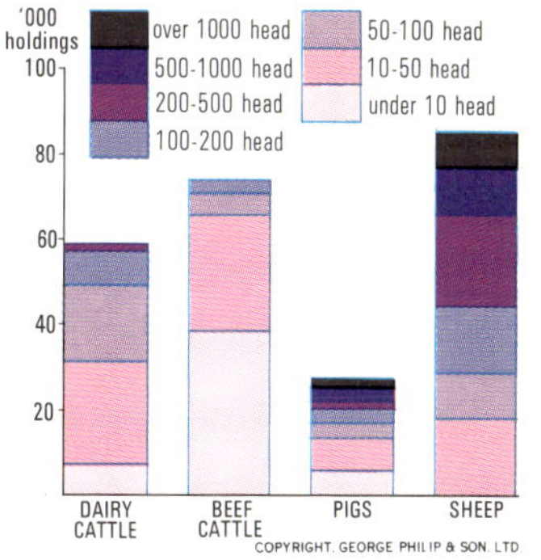

Coal and Power 1:8 500 000

Coalfields 1988-89	Saleable Output (million tonnes)	Output per Manshift (tonnes)
1 Scottish	1.9	10.1
2 North East	10.3	18.7
3 North West	9.8	24.2
4 South Wales	5.0	15.3
5 North Yorkshire	16.1	29.9
6 South Yorkshire	13.3	17.6
7 Nottinghamshire	17.2	17.2
8 Kent	0.4	14.1
9 Central	10.8	16.9

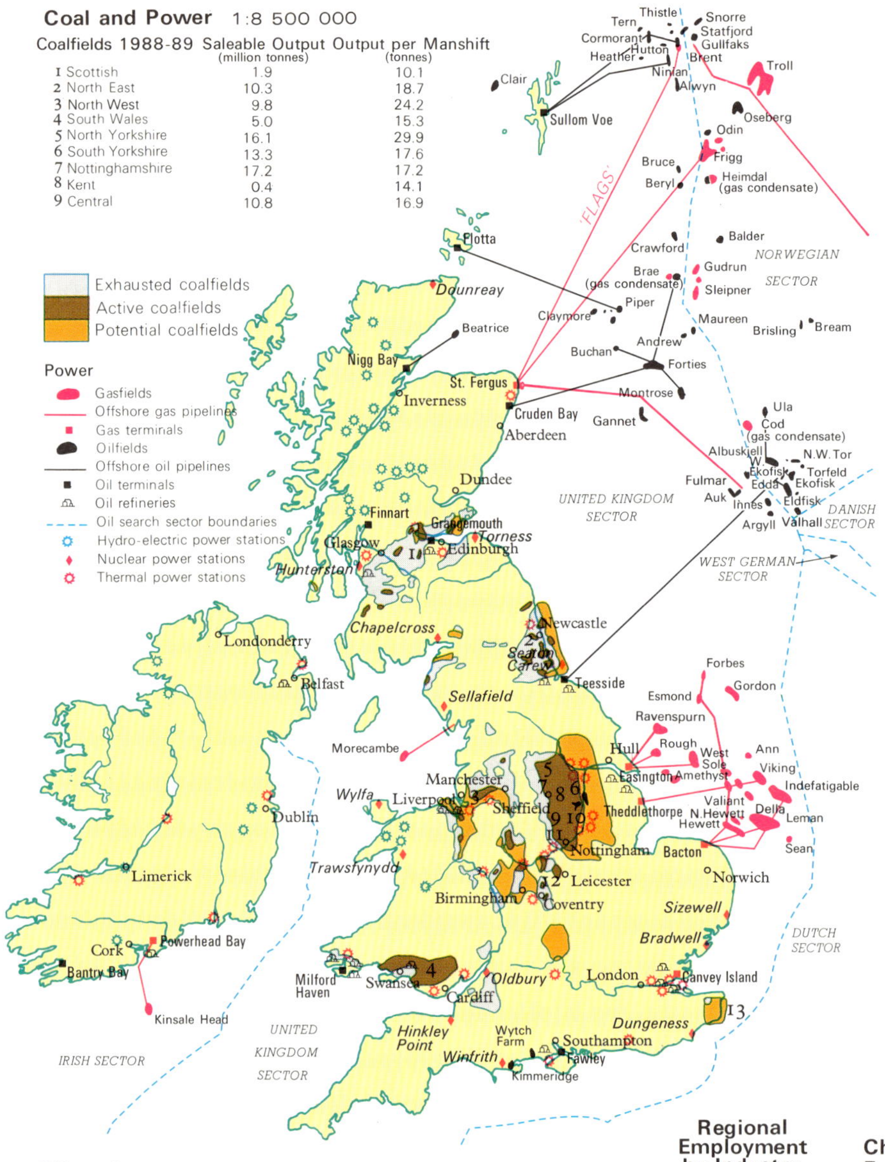

Production of Primary Fuels in the U.K.

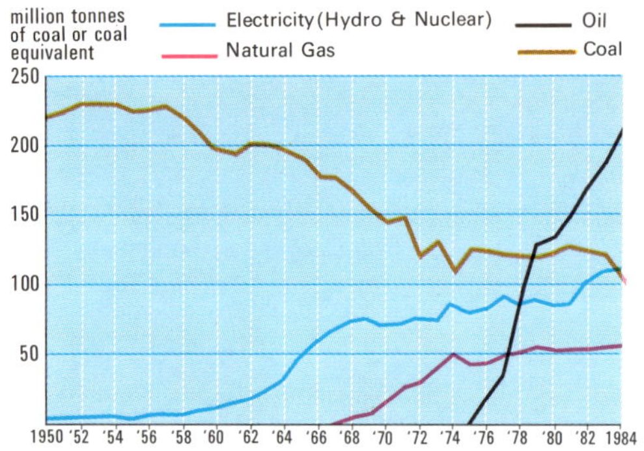

Consumption of Primary Fuels in the U.K.

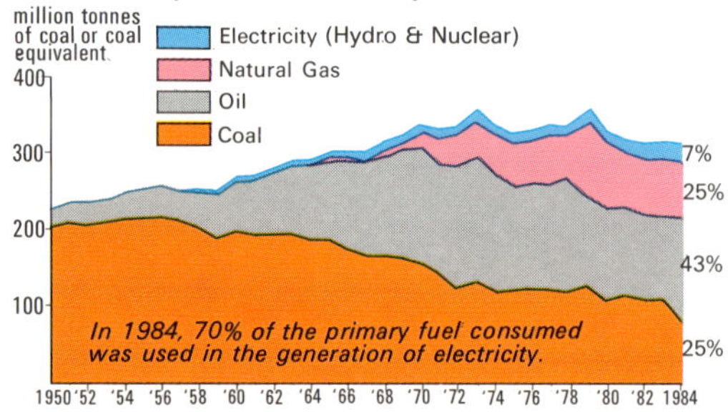

Coal Consumption in the U.K.

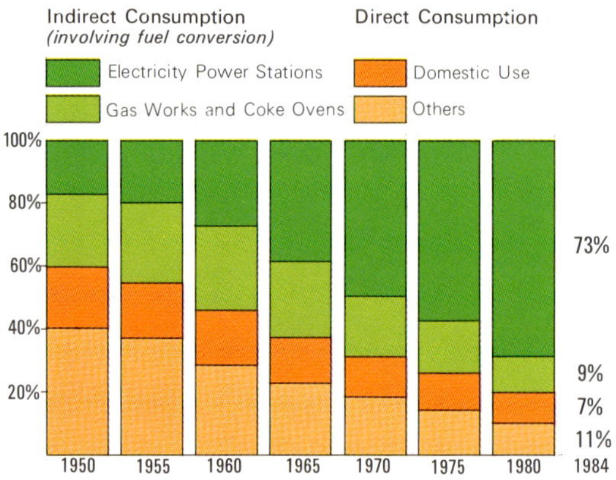

Minerals 1:10 000 000

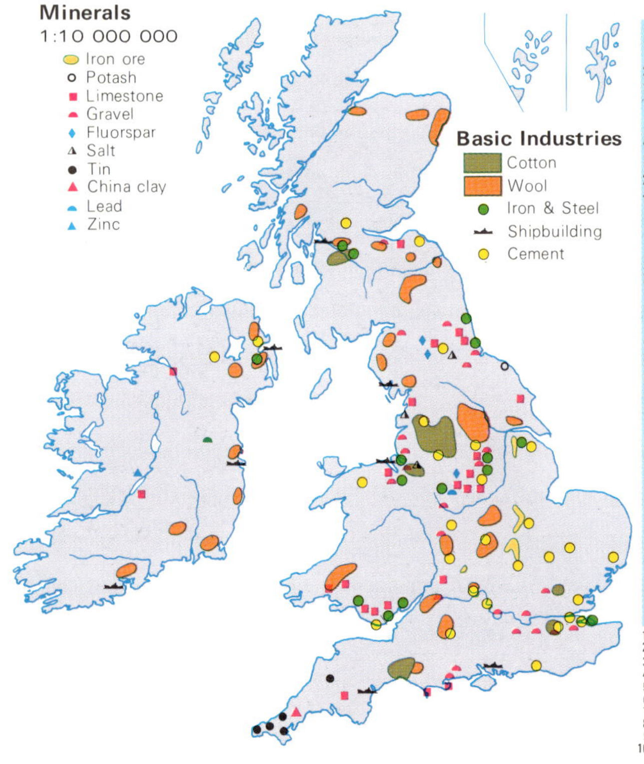

Regional Employment by Industry

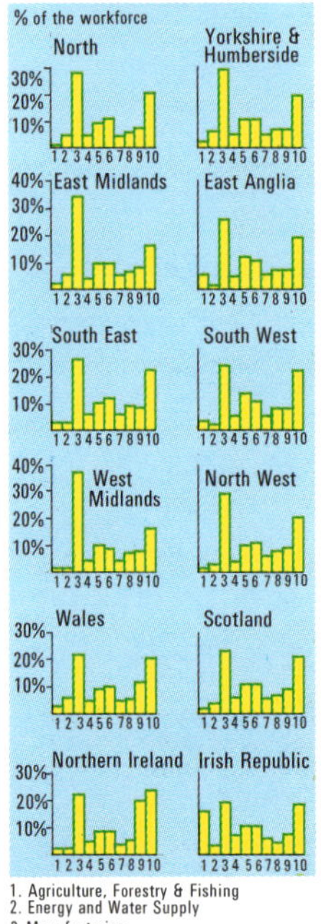

1. Agriculture, Forestry & Fishing
2. Energy and Water Supply
3. Manufacturing
4. Construction
5. Wholesale Distribution, Hotels & Catering
6. Retail Distribution
7. Transport and Communications
8. Banking, Insurance and Finance
9. Public Administration and Defence
10. Education, Health and Other Services

Change in Manufacturing Employment by County 1961-1981

1:10 000 000

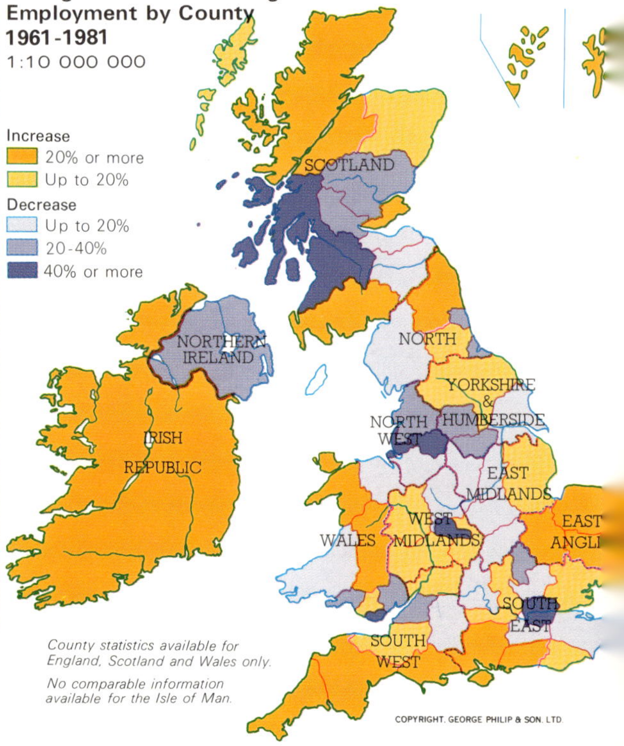

County statistics available for England, Scotland and Wales only.

No comparable information available for the Isle of Man.

EMPLOYMENT

Employment in the U.K. by Industry

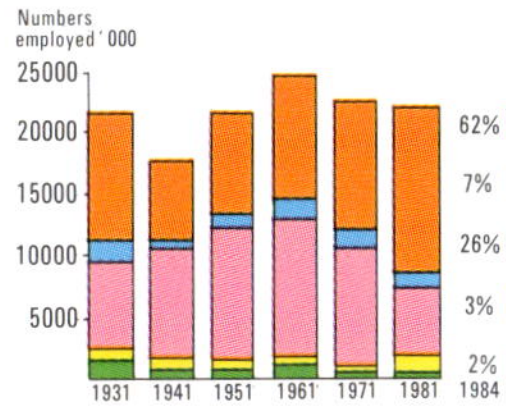

Employment by County

£ Over 75% employed in Services

Over 30% employed in Manufacturing

Over 5% employed in Agriculture

County statistics available for England, Scotland and Wales only.

UNEMPLOYMENT

1:10 000 000

Unemployment Rate by County, 1985

- over 20%
- 16-20%
- 12-16%
- 8-12%
- less than 8%

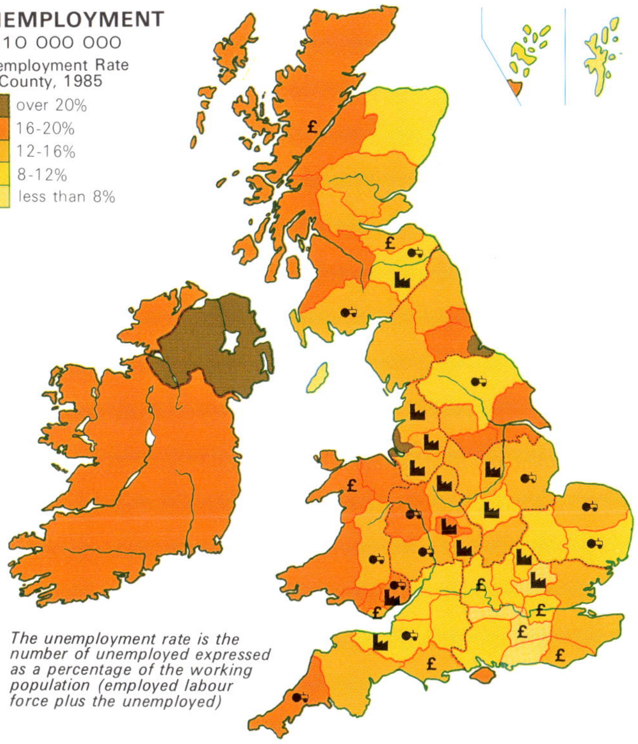

The unemployment rate is the number of unemployed expressed as a percentage of the working population (employed labour force plus the unemployed)

Leisure

1:8 500 000

- National Parks
- National Park Direction Areas (Scotland)
- National Forest Parks
- Areas of Outstanding Natural Beauty (England & Wales)
- National Scenic Areas (Scotland)
- Coastal Conservation Zones (Scotland)
- Heritage Coasts (England & Wales)
- Long Distance Footpaths
- Navigable Waterways
- Canals

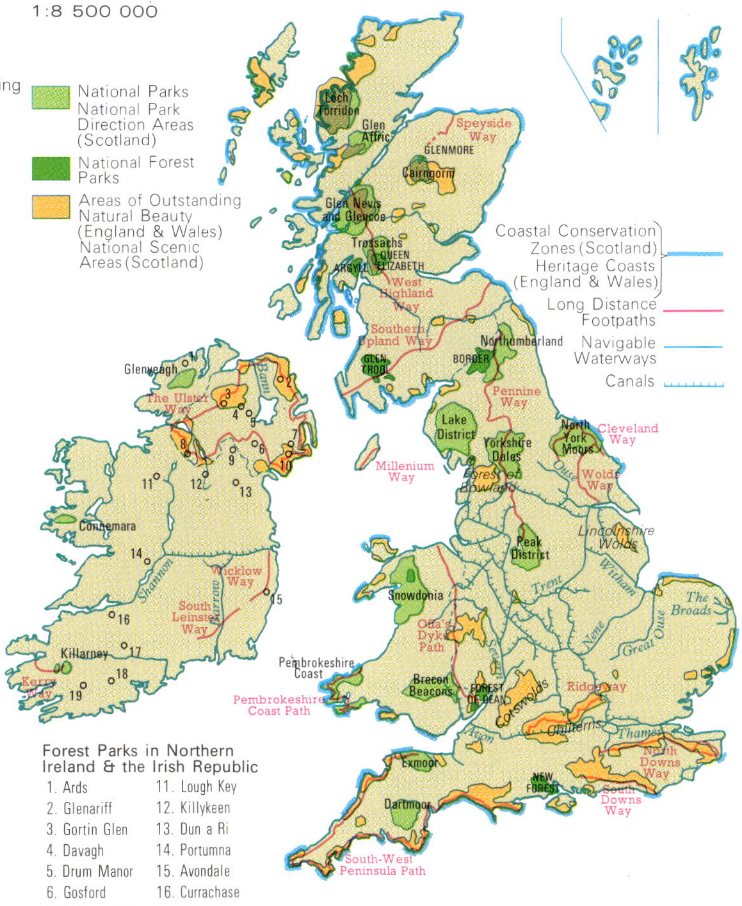

Forest Parks in Northern Ireland & the Irish Republic

1. Ards
2. Glenariff
3. Gortin Glen
4. Davagh
5. Drum Manor
6. Gosford
7. Castlewellan
8. Florence Court
9. Rossmore
10. Tollymore
11. Lough Key
12. Killykeen
13. Dun a Ri
14. Portumna
15. Avondale
16. Currachase
17. Doneraile
18. Farran
19. Gougane Barra

Top Ten Trading Partners with the U.K. by Value of Goods

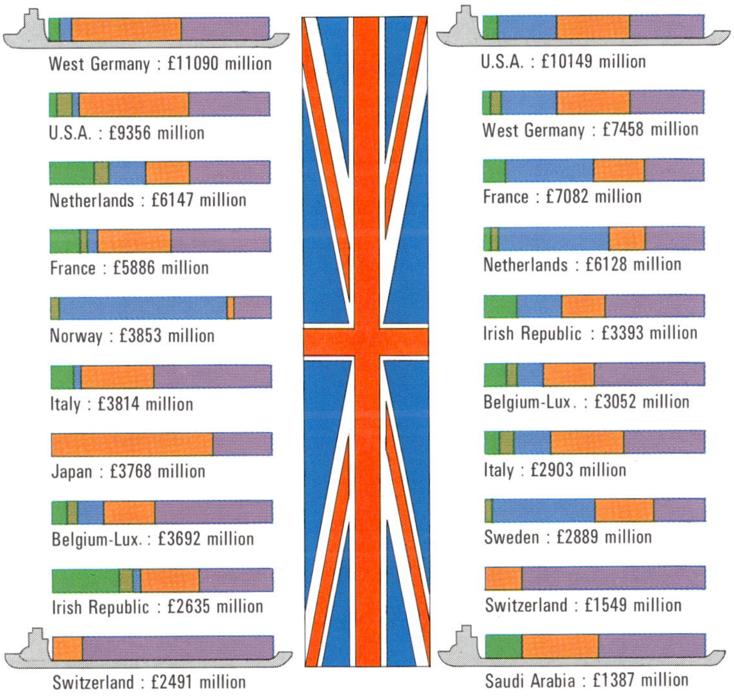

Food and drink · Raw materials · Fuel · Machinery and equipment · Manufactured goods

U.K. Trade by Country Group and Commodity Type

(percentages are given by value of trade)

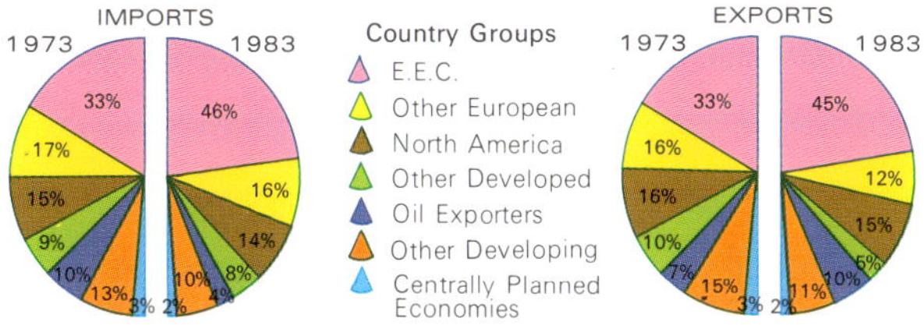

Country Groups
- E.E.C.
- Other European
- North America
- Other Developed
- Oil Exporters
- Other Developing
- Centrally Planned Economies

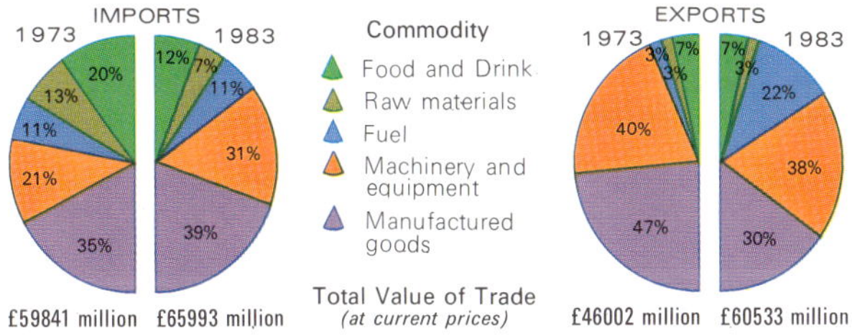

Commodity
- Food and Drink
- Raw materials
- Fuel
- Machinery and equipment
- Manufactured goods

Total Value of Trade *(at current prices)*

Balance of Payments (£ million)

		1967	1977	1987
CREDITS	Visibles *(Exports)*	5241	31682	79422
	Invisibles	3310	21351	80010
	Total	8551	53033	159432
DEBITS	Visibles *(Imports)*	5840	34006	89584
	Invisibles	2992	19177	72352
	Total	8832	53183	161936
BALANCE		−281	−150	−2504

Visible trade involves transactions of goods while invisible trade involves transactions of money and services.

BRITISH ISLES: *climate graphs*

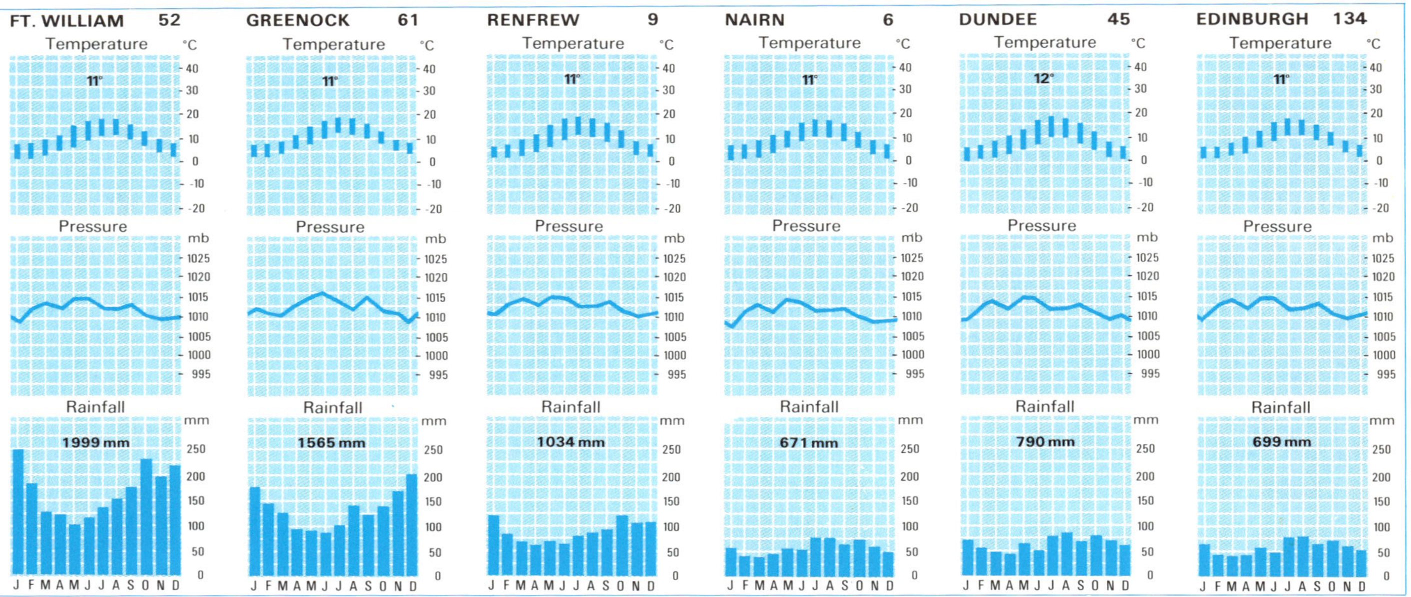

The climate graphs should be used in conjunction with the maps illustrating the climate of the British Isles on page 6. The stations have been selected to show climatic variations throughout the British Isles. On each graph the name of the station is followed by its height in metres above sea level, so that comparisons between stations can be made allowing for elevation. Temperature is shown by a bar, the top of the bar representing the mean monthly maximum and the bottom of the bar the mean monthly minimum temperature. A mid point between these is the mean monthly temperature; the mean annual range of temperature (in degrees Celsius) is given above the graph. The line on the pressure graphs shows the mean monthly pressure (in millibars and reduced to sea level). The rainfall graphs show the average monthly rainfall and above them is given the average total annual rainfall (in millimetres).

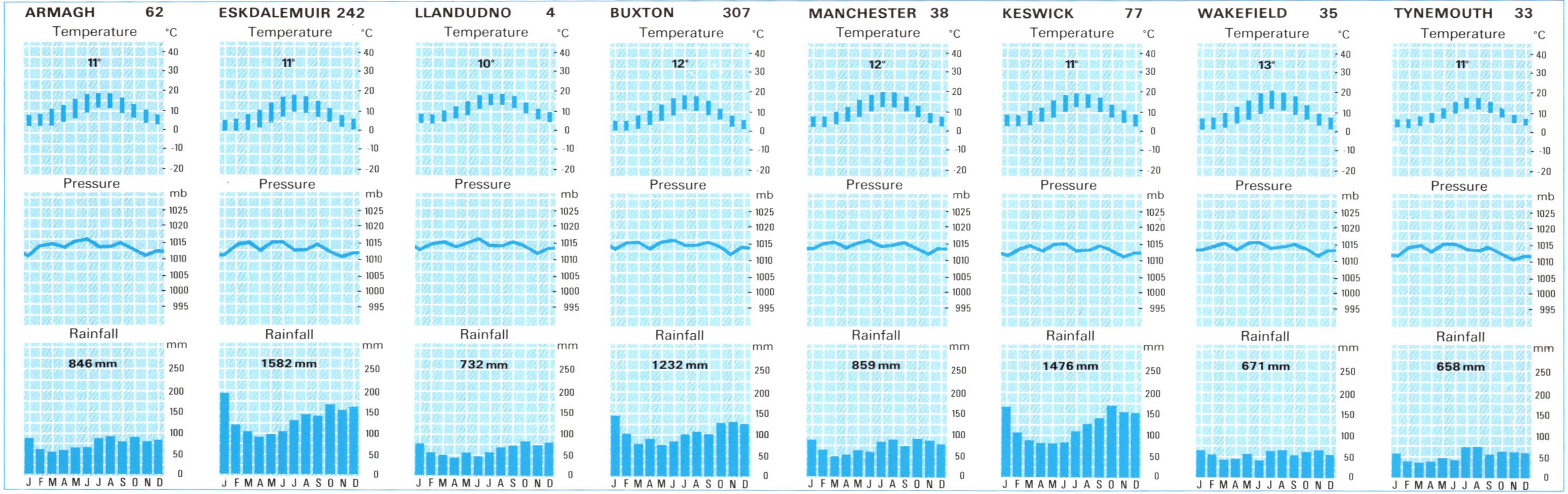

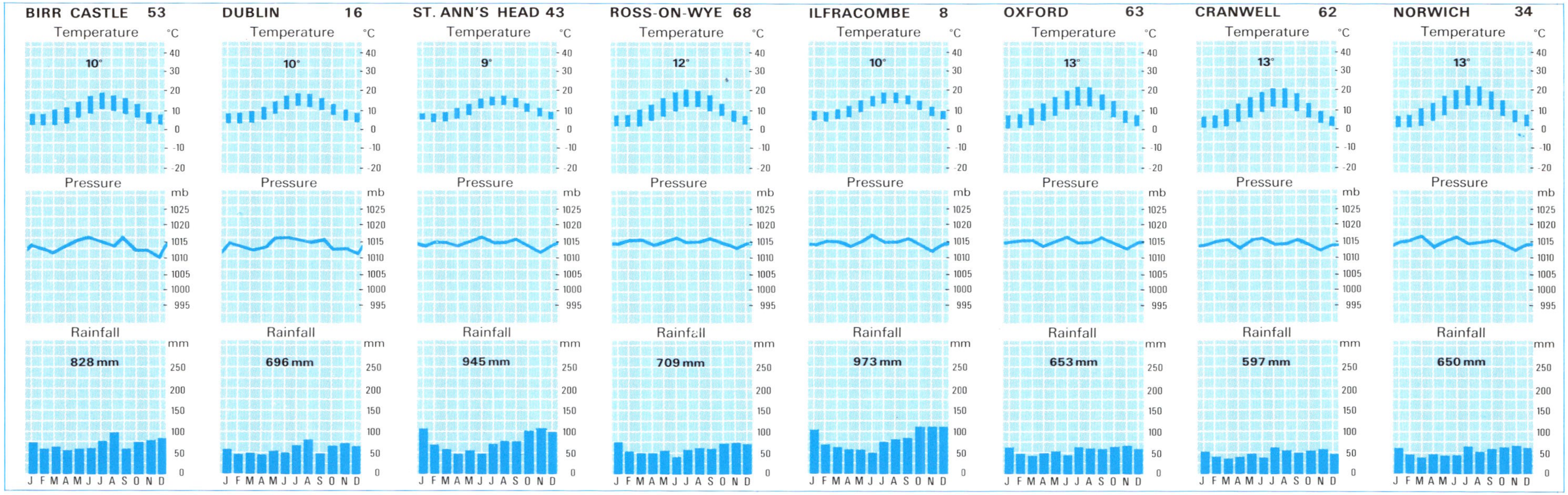
BIRR CASTLE 53
Temperature °C
10°
Pressure mb
Rainfall mm
828 mm
DUBLIN 16
10°
696 mm
ST. ANN'S HEAD 43
9°
945 mm
ROSS-ON-WYE 68
12°
709 mm
ILFRACOMBE 8
10°
973 mm
OXFORD 63
13°
653 mm
CRANWELL 62
13°
597 mm
NORWICH 34
13°
650 mm
J F M A M J J A S O N D

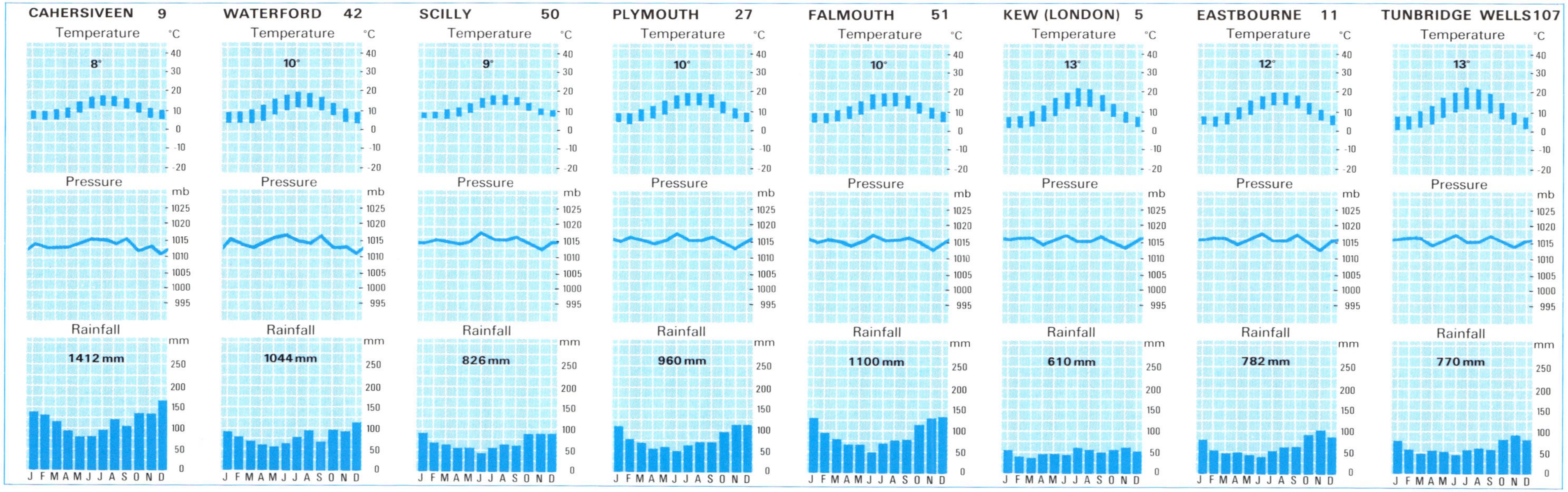
CAHERSIVEEN 9
Temperature °C
8°
Pressure mb
Rainfall mm
1412 mm
WATERFORD 42
10°
1044 mm
SCILLY 50
9°
826 mm
PLYMOUTH 27
10°
960 mm
FALMOUTH 51
10°
1100 mm
KEW (LONDON) 5
13°
610 mm
EASTBOURNE 11
12°
782 mm
TUNBRIDGE WELLS 107
13°
770 mm
J F M A M J J A S O N D

Oswestry
Shrewsbury
Telford
Stafford
STAFFORDSHIRE
Burton upon Trent
Swadlincote
Loughborough
Coalville
Cannock
Lichfield
Tamworth
Welshpool
Newtown
Wellington
Dawley
Wolverhampton
Walsall
Sutton Coldfield
Wednesbury
West Bromwich
Dudley
Smethwick
BIRMINGHAM
Solihull
Nuneaton
Hinckley
Bedworth
COVENTRY
Rugby
Kenilworth
Warwick
Royal Leamington Spa
SHROPSHIRE
Bridgnorth
Kidderminster
Stourbridge
Halesowen
Bromsgrove
Redditch
Droitwich
Worcester
HEREFORD AND WORCESTER
Great Malvern
Evesham
WARWICKSHIRE
Stratford-upon-Avon
Banbury
Leominster
Hereford
Ledbury
Ross-on-Wye
Tewkesbury
Cheltenham
Gloucester
Charlton Kings
Chipping Norton
GLOUCESTERSHIRE
Stroud
Cirencester
Witney
Oxford
Abingdon
Didcot
Wantage
Wallingford
Swindon
Newbury
Hungerford
Marlborough
Chippenham
Calne
Devizes
Trowbridge
WILTSHIRE
Salisbury Plain
Andover
Basingstoke
Salisbury
Winchester
HAMPSHIRE
Romsey
Eastleigh
SOUTHAMPTON
Portsmouth
Ryde
Newport
Cowes
ISLE OF WIGHT
Ventnor
The Needles
St. Catherine's Pt.
Lymington
Christchurch
Bournemouth
Poole
Wareham
Swanage
Weymouth
I. of Portland
Dorchester
DORSET
Bridport
Lyme Regis
Sidmouth
Exmouth
Exeter
Crediton
Tiverton
DEVON
Taunton
Wellington
Bridgwater
Bridgwater Bay
Minehead
Exmoor
Brendon Hills
Quantock Hills
SOMERSET
Yeovil
Sherborne
Shaftesbury
Blandford Forum
Wimborne Minster
Crewkerne
Chard
Ilminster
Glastonbury
Street
Wells
Shepton Mallet
Frome
Mendip Hills
Westbury
Warminster
Bath
BRISTOL
Keynsham
Kingswood
Weston-super-Mare
Clevedon
Portishead
Avonmouth
Bristol Channel
CARDIFF
Penarth
Barry
Newport
Caerphilly
Pontypridd
Bridgend
Port Talbot
Swansea
Neath
Maesteg
Porthcawl
Merthyr Tydfil
Ebbw Vale
Abergavenny
Monmouth
Chepstow
Pontypool
Cwmbran
Brecon
Black Mountains
Llandovery
Builth Wells
Llandrindod Wells
Rhayader
Knighton
Ludlow
Church Stretton
Long Mynd
Wenlock Edge
Clee Hills
POWYS
DYFED
Mynydd Eppynt
Machynlleth
Dolgellau
GWYNEDD
Llanidloes
GWENT
MID GLAMORGAN
SOUTH GLAMORGAN
WEST GLAMORGAN
Tenbury
Bromyard
Severn
Thames
Avon
Wye
Cotswold Hills
Vale of White Horse
Berkshire Downs
Marlborough Downs
Vale of Pewsey
Cranborne Chase
Blackmoor Vale
Dorset Downs
Blackdown Hills
Polden Hills
Chesil Beach
The Solent
Southampton Water
New Forest
Projection: Conical with two standard parallels
1:1 000 000
10 0 10 20 30 40 km
m
800
600
400
200
100
0
50

Based upon the Ordnance Survey Map with the permission of the Controller of Her Majesty's Stationery Office.

Based upon the Ordnance Survey Map with the permission of the Controller of Her Majesty's Stationery Office. Crown Copyright Reserved.

1:1 000 000

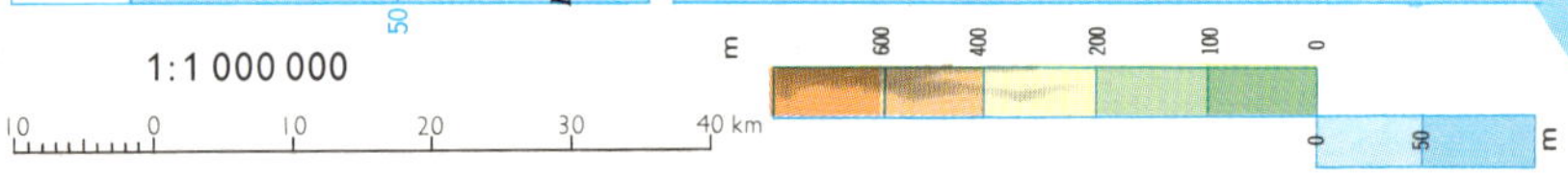

Projection: Conical with two standard parallels

West from Greenwich

1:1 000 000

60' 50' 40' 30' 20' 10' 0'

10 0 10 20 30 40 km

NORTHERN ENGLAND

1:1 000 000

10 0 10 20 30 40 km

Based upon the Ordnance Survey Map with the permission of the Controller of Her Majesty's Stationery Office. Crown Copyright Reserved.

Pt. of Ardnamurchan
Ardnamurchan
Sunart
Coll
Tiree
Hynish B.
Passage of Tiree
Treshnish Isles
Gometra
Ulva
Staffa
Tobermory
L. Frisa
L. Tuath
Morvern
Sd. of Mull
Mull
Loch Linnhe
Lismore
Kerrera
Oban
L. na Keal
L. Scridain
Ross of Mull
Iona
L. Buie
Firth of Lorn
L. Spelve
Seil
Luing
Garvellachs
Scarba
G. of Corryvreckan
Torran Rocks
Dubh Artach
Colonsay
Oronsay
Passage of Oronsay
ATLANTIC
OCEAN
L. Leven
Kinlochleven
Glen Coe
Rannoch Moor
L. Laidon
L. Tulla
Glen Lyon
Glen Etive
Loch Etive
Glen Orchy
Dalmally
Tyndrum
Crianlarich
Ben Lui
B. Cruachan
L. Awe
L. Avich
Kilmelford
Inveraray
L. Fyne
L. Voil
L. Katrine
The Trossachs
L. Lomond
B. Lomond
L. Eck
L. Long
L. Goil
Arrochar
Tarbet
Helensburgh
Alexandria
Dumbarton
Gourock
Greenock
Port Glasgow
Dunoon
Rothesay
Bute
Kyles of Bute
GLASGOW
Paisley
Renfrew
Clydebank
Milngavie
Johnstone
Barrhead
Largs
Cumbrae Is.
Millport
Kilbirnie
Beith
Stewarton
Kilwinning
Kilmarnock
Irvine
Saltcoats
Ardrossan
Stevenston
West Kilbride
Troon
Prestwick
Ayr
Heads of Ayr
Maybole
Girvan
Ailsa Craig
334
Lendalfoot
Bennane Hd.
Ballantrae
Carrick
L. Doon
Crinan Can.
Lochgilphead
Ardrishaig
L. Craignish
L. Melfort
Jura
Sound of Jura
Paps of Jura
784
L. Tarbert
Rubha a'Mhail
Ardnave Pt.
Port Askaig
Sound of Islay
Islay
Bridgend
Bowmore
Port Charlotte
L. Indaal
Portnahaven
Laggan B.
Port Ellen
The Oa
Mull of Oa
Ardbeg
Ardmore Pt.
Gigha I.
L. Caolisport
Knapdale
Tarbert
Kintyre
Kilbrannan Sound
Skipness
Sd. of Bute
Arran
Goat Fell
874
Brodick
Lamlash
Holy I.
Pladda
Firth of Clyde
Carradale
Campbeltown
Machrihanish
Southend
Mull of Kintyre
Sanda I.
Inishtrahull
Malin Hd.
Malin Pen.
Inishowen
Lough Foyle
Moville
Londonderry
LONDONDERRY
Limavady
Coleraine
Portstewart
Portrush
Giants Causeway
Benbane Hd.
Bushmills
Ballycastle
Rathlin
Ballycastle B.
Fair Hd.
Ballymoney
Mountains of Antrim
Cushendall
Red B.
Garron Pt.
ANTRIM
NORTHERN
ULSTER
IRELAND
Sperrin Mts.
Ballymena
Larne
Larne Lough
Island Magee
Black Hd.
Whitehead
Carrickfergus
Belfast Lough
Bangor
Copeland I.
Donaghadee
Newtownards
Holywood
BELFAST
Newtownabbey
Antrim
Lough Neagh
Cookstown
Dungannon
Omagh
TYRONE
NORTH CHANNEL
Corsewall Pt.
Milleur Pt.
Kirkcolm
Stranraer
Loch Ryan
The Rhins
Portpatrick
Port Logan
Mull of Galloway
Drummore
Luce Bay
Glenluce
Newton Stewart
Wigtown
Whithorn
Burrow Hd.
Galloway
m
1000
800
600
400
200
100
0
50
100
m
56
55
6
5
Projection: Conical with two standard parallels
West from Greenwich

1:1 000 000

10 0 10 20 30 40 km

Based upon the Ordnance Survey Map with the permission of the Controller of Her Majesty's Stationery Office. Crown Copyright Reserved.

SHETLAND ISLANDS
on same scale
Herma Ness
Haroldswick
Unst
Balta
Bluemull Sd.
Baltasound
Cullivoe
Uyeasound
Mu Ness
Ramna Stacks
Whale Firth
Point of Fethaland
Fetlar
North Roe
The Faither
Yell
Ronas Hill
450
Colgrave Sd.
The Snap
Esha Ness
Burravoe
Hillswick
Lunna Ness
St. Magnus Bay
SHETLAND
Skaw Taing
Out Skerries
Muckle Roe
Brae
Papa Stour
Whalsay
Sd. of Papa
The Haa
Sandness
S.Nesting Bay
Walls
Vaila
Gruting Voe
Score Hd.
Lerwick
I. of Noss
Scalloway
Bressay
Hamnavoe
West Burra
Bard Hd.
Cliff Sound
Bressay Sd.
Kettla Ness
Helli Ness
Hoswick
Mousa
St. Ninian's I.
Scousburgh
Fitful Hd.
Boddam
B. of Quendale
Sumburgh Hd.
Butt of Lewis
Port of Ness
South Dell
Ness
Borve
Cellar Hd.
Barvas
North Tolsta
Tolsta Hd.
Shawbost
Carloway
Back
Broad Bay
Tiumpan Hd.
Great Bernera
Gallan Hd.
291
Newmarket
Stornoway
Melbost
Portaguiran
Eye Peninsula
Bayble
Callanish
L. Roag
Uig
Lewis
Chicken Hd.
Aird Brenish
575
Gisla
Lochs
Crossbost
Loch Langavat
Balallan
Cromore
Erisort
Park
Kinloch
Gravir
Kebock Hd.
Scarp
Husinish
Husinish Pt.
N.Harris
Ardvourlie Castle
799
571
Beinn Mhor
L. Shell
Taransay
W. L. Tarbert
Ardhasig
L. Seaforth
Sd. of Shiant
Shiant Is.
Sd. of Taransay
Toe Hd.
Tarbert
Harris
Scalpay
WESTERN
E. L. Tarbert
Scarastavore
S.Harris
Leverburgh
Pabbay
Sd. of Pabbay
Berneray
Sound of Harris
Rodel
Renish Pt.
Haskeir Is.
Griminish Pt.
Sollas
ISLES
Rubha Hunish
Kilmaluag
North Uist
Lochmaddy
L. Maddy
Vaternish Pt.
Sound of Monach
Paible
Clachan
L. Eport
Uig
Loch Snizort
Rona
Monach Is.
Baleshare
Carinish
347
Eaval
Dunvegan Head
Waternish
Trotternish
Grimsay
Stein
Ronay
The Storr
719
Benbecula
Gramisdale
Milovaig
Lephin
Ardivachar Pt.
L. Bee
Dunvegan
Roskhill
Portree
Raasay
Wiay
Bagh nam Faoileann
488
Bracadale
Colbost
Crowlin Is.
Howmore
South Uist
Hecla
606
L. Bracadale
L. Harport
Fernilea
Carbost
Drynoch
Skye
Sligachan
Scalpay
Rubha Ardvule
620
B. Mhor
L. Eynort
Minginish
Cuillin Hills
1009
Bla Bheinn
928
Glenbrittle
Broadford
Daliburgh
Lochboisdale
L. Boisdale
Rubh'an Dunain
Soay Sd.
Soay
Elgol
L. Scavaig
L. Eishort
Sound of Barra
Sd. of Eriskay
Eriskay
Cuillin Sound
Canna
Sanday
Sd. of Canna
Kinloch
Greian Hd.
Barra
384
Castlebay
Bruernish Pt.
Rhum
810
Pt. of Sleat
Vatersay
Sound of Rhum
Eigg
Sandray
394
Pabbay
Sd. of Eigg
Mingulay
Muck
Berneray
Barra Head
241
Pt. of Ardnamurchan
Sorisdale
Coll
Clabhach
Arinagour
Caliach Pt.
Tobermory
Calgary
Dervaig
Coloes
Treshnish Isles
L. Frisa
Tiree
Scarinish
Hynish B.
Passage of Tiree
L. Tuath
Hynish
Outer Hebrides
Inner Hebrides
Little Minch
North Minch
Inner Sound
Sound of Raasay
C. Wrath
L. Inchard
L. Laxford
Handa I.
Scourie
Eddrachillis Bay
Pt. of Stoer
Drumbeg
Quinag
Stoer
Assynt
Enard Bay
Lochinver
Rhu Coigach
Summer Isles
Lurgainn
L. Broom
Gruinard B.
Greenstone Pt.
Ullapool
Mellon Charles
Aultbea
An Teallach
1062
L. Ewe
L. na Sealga
Melvaig
Poolewe
Fionn Loch
Longa I.
L. Gairloch
Gairloch
Henderson
Kerrysdale
Talladale
981
Slioch
L. Maree
Kinlochewe
L. Fannich
L. Torridon
1053
Torridon
Fasag
Achnasheen
Shieldaig
Achnashellach
Applecross Forest
Applecross
Carron
Monar Forest
L. Monar
1052
Lochcarron
L. Kishorn
Toscaig
Stromemore
Plockton
Stromeferry
Mullardoch
L. Carron
Kyle of Lochalsh
Kyleakin
Auchtertyre
Dornie
L. Alsh
Carn Eige
1182
Glenelg
The Saddle
1010
Glen Shiel
Eileann Iarmain
Teangue
Armadale
Ardvasar
L. Hourn
Sound of Sleat
L. Quoich
Ladhar B.
1019
Knoydart
Inverie
L. Nevis
Mallaig
Morar
1040
Sgurr na Ciche
Loch Morar
L. Arkaig
Arisaig
Sd. of Arisaig
983
Culvain
Lochailort
Glenfinnan
Caledonian Canal
Kinlocheil
Shona I.
L. Moidart
Moidart
Kinlochmoidart
882
L. Eil
Loch Shiel
Ardnamurchan
Kilchoan
Mingary
527
Salen
Sunart
888
Strontian
Ardgour
Corran
L. Sunart
Drimnin
Morvern
Lochaline
Sd. of Mull
Salen
Kingairloch
Loch Linnhe
Lismore I.
North Ballachulish
South Ballachulish
Portnacroish
Loch Etive
Projection: Conical with two standard parallels
m
1000
800
600
400
200
100
0
50
100
m

1:1 000 000

10 0 10 20 30 40 km

Based upon the Ordnance Survey Map with the permission of the Controller of Her Majesty's Stationery Office. Crown Copyright Reserved.

DISTRICTS IN NORTHERN IRELAND
1 Londonderry
2 Limavady
3 Coleraine
4 Ballymoney
5 Moyle
6 Larne
7 Ballymena
8 Magherafelt
9 Cookstown
10 Strabane
11 Omagh
12 Fermanagh
13 Dungannon
14 Craigavon
15 Armagh
16 Newry and Mourne
17 Banbridge
18 Down
19 Lisburn
20 Antrim
21 Newtownabbey
22 Carrickfergus
23 North Down
24 Ards
25 Castlereagh
26 Belfast
NORTHERN IRELAND
ULSTER
CONNACHT

LEINSTER
MUNSTER
ATLANTIC
OCEAN
KILKENNY
WEXFORD
WICKLOW
KILDARE
OFFALY
LAOIS
TIPPERARY
WATERFORD
LIMERICK
CLARE
CORK
KERRY
Galway Bay
Aran Is.
Shannon
Mouth of the Shannon
Limerick
Cork
Waterford
Wexford
Kilkenny
Tralee
Killarney
Cork Harbour
Waterford Harbour
Wexford Harbour
Dungarvan Harbour
Youghal Bay
Kinsale Harbour
Bantry Bay
Dingle Bay
Kenmare R.
Macgillycuddy's Reeks
Knockmealdown Mts.
Galty Mts.
Silver Mine Mts.
Slieve Bloom Mts.
Fastnet Rock
C. Clear
Projection: Conical with two standard parallels
1:1 250 000
West from Greenwich

NORWEGIAN SEA
ATLANTIC OCEAN
NORTH SEA
BALTIC SEA
BLACK SEA
CASPIAN SEA
MEDITERRANEAN SEA
ADRIATIC SEA
Tyrrhenian Sea
Ionian Sea
Aegean Sea
Ligurian Sea
White Sea
Bay of Biscay
English Channel
Irish Sea
G. of Bothnia
G. of Finland
G. of Riga
G. of Lions
Sea of Azov
Skagerrak
Kattegat
Str. of Gibraltar
Str. of Otranto
Str. of Bonifacio
Str. of Messina
Str. of Kerch
Bosporus
S. of Marmara
Iceland
British Isles
Great Britain
Ireland
Faroe Is.
Shetland Is.
Orkney Is.
Hebrides
Scandinavia
Lapland
Finland
Kola Peninsula
Kanin Peninsula
Jutland
Lofoten
Vesterålen
North Cape
Nordkinn
Brittany
Iberian Peninsula
Old Castile
New Castile
Andalusia
Sierra Morena
Sa. Nevada
Cantabrian Mts.
Pyrenees
Central Massif
Alps
Dinaric Alps
Apennines
Carpathians
Transylvanian Alps
Balkans
Balkan Peninsula
Rhodope
Pindus
Morea
Plain of Hungary
Wallachia
Pripyat Marshes
Ukraine
Crimea
Central Russian Uplands
Volga Uplands
Obshchiy Syrt
Ural Mountains
Caucasus
Anatolia
Taurus
Cyprus
Crete
Sicily
Sardinia
Corsica
Balearic Is.
Malta
Calabria
Atlas
Plateau of the Shotts
Maritime Atlas
Er Rif
Harz
Erz Geb.
Sudetes
Vosges
Black For.
Ardennes
Jura
Bohemian For.
Moravian Heights
Bakony For.
Cevennes
Volga
Don
Dnepr (Dnieper)
Dnestr (Dniester)
Danube
Wisła (Vistula)
Odra (Oder)
Elbe
Weser
Rhine
Rhône
Seine
Loire
Garonne
Douro
Tagus
Guadalquivir
Po
Tiber
Ural
Pechora
Mezen
N. Dvina
Onega
L. Onega
L. Ladoga
Rybinsk Res.
Tsimlyansk Res.
Vänern
Vättern
Mälaren
Gotland
Tisza
Sava
Drava
Prut
Bug
Niemen
Kuban
Terek
Manych
Rion
Euphrates
Tigris
L. Van
L. Urmia
Aras
Kama
Oka
Neva
Ob
Mt. Blanc 4807
Elbrus 5633
Mt. Ararat 5165
Mt. Etna 3263
Vesuvius 1277
Gran Sasso 2914
Pico de Aneto 3404
Mulhacén 3478
Mt. Dore 1886
Snowdon 1085
Ben Nevis 1343
Galdhøpiggen 2469
Kebnekaise 2123
Vatna Jökull 2119
Harz 1142
Ida 1756
Cyprus 1951
C. Matapan
C. Finisterre
C. da Roca
C. St. Vincent
C. Trafalgar
C. Spartel
C. Bon
C. Blanco
C. Clear
Land's End
Arctic Circle
Netherlands
Heligoland
Dogger Bank
Fisher Bank
Rockall
VIKING
FORTIES
FISHER
GERMAN BIGHT
HUMBER
THAMES
DOVER
WIGHT
PORTLAND
PLYMOUTH
LUNDY
FASTNET
SOLE
FINISTERRE
BISCAY
SHANNON
ROCKALL
MALIN
HEBRIDES
BAILEY
SOUTH EAST ICELAND
FAEROES
FAIR ISLE
CROMARTY
FORTH
TYNE
DOGGER
IRISH SEA
NORTH UTSIRE
SOUTH UTSIRE
Projection: Bonne West from Greenwich 0 East from Greenwich
Sea areas named in ROCKALL weather forecasts
1:20 000 000
200 0 200 400 600 800 km
m 4000 2000 1000 400 200 0
0 200 2000 4000 m

The maps of the Soviet Union and Yugoslavia show the situation at the time of going to press in December, 1991. Extra maps of the Republics and Nationalities of the Soviet Union and the Republics and Ethnic Groups of Yugoslavia are provided on p. 161.

1:20 000 000

200 0 200 400 600 800 km

Projection: Bonne West from Greenwich East from Greenwich

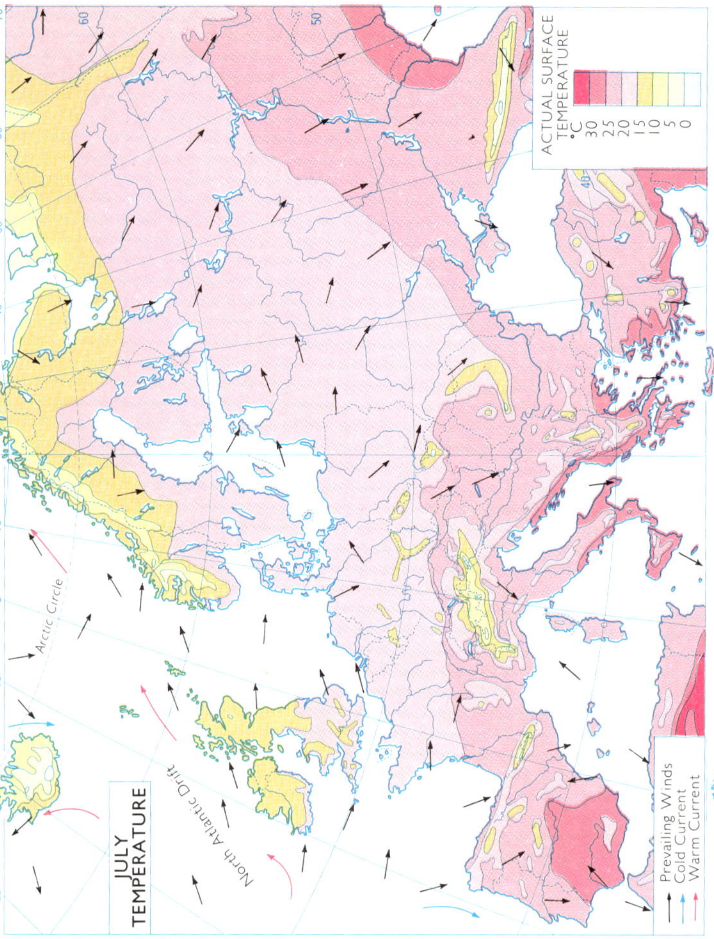
JULY TEMPERATURE
ACTUAL SURFACE TEMPERATURE
°C
30
25
20
15
10
5
0
Prevailing Winds
Cold Current
Warm Current
North Atlantic Drift
Arctic Circle

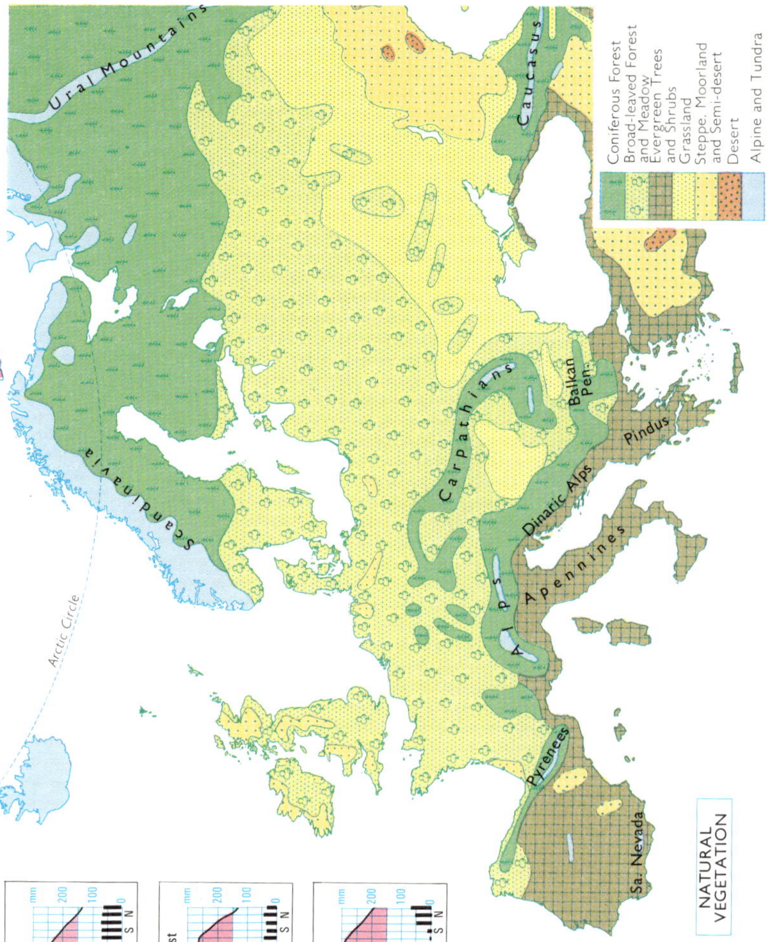
NATURAL VEGETATION
Coniferous Forest
Broad-leaved Forest and Meadow
Evergreen Trees and Shrubs
Grassland
Steppe, Moorland and Semi-desert
Desert
Alpine and Tundra
Ural Mountains
Caucasus
Carpathians
Balkan Pen.
Pindus
Dinaric Alps
Apennines
Alps
Pyrenees
Sa. Nevada
Scandinavia
Arctic Circle

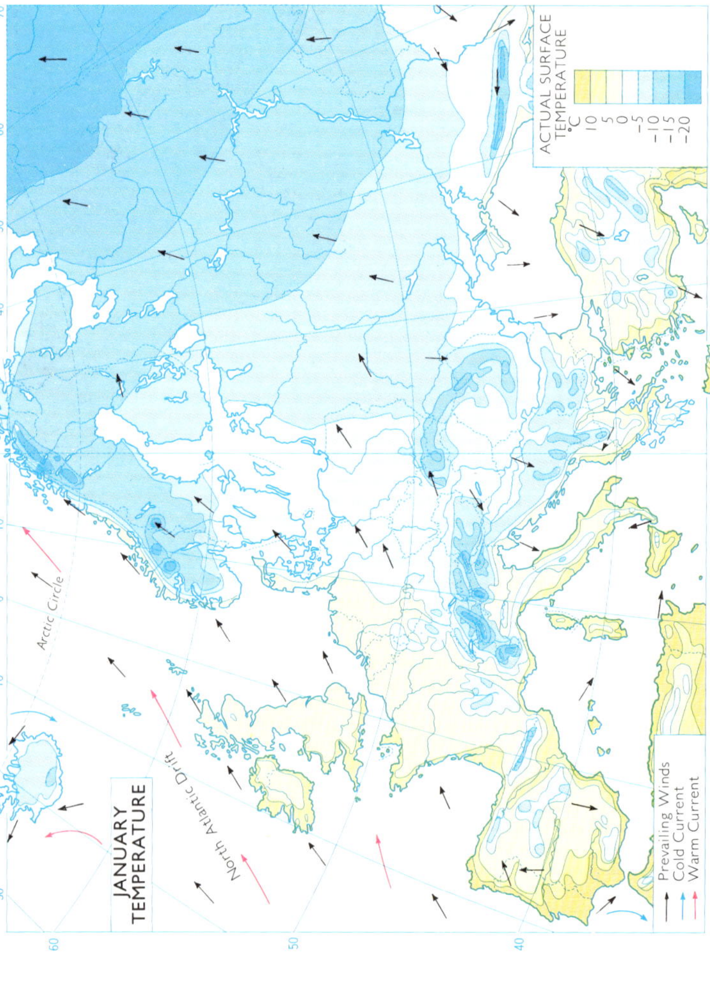
JANUARY TEMPERATURE
ACTUAL SURFACE TEMPERATURE
°C
10
5
0
-5
-10
-15
-20
Prevailing Winds
Cold Current
Warm Current
North Atlantic Drift
Arctic Circle

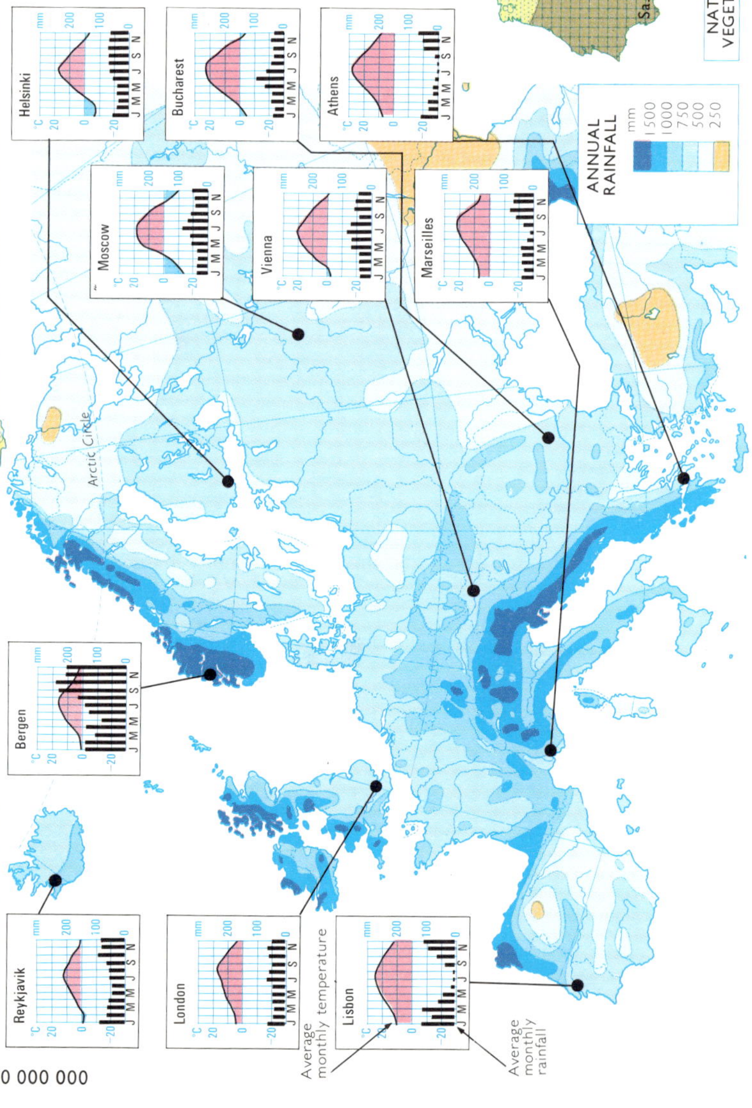
ANNUAL RAINFALL
mm
1500
1000
750
500
250
Helsinki
Bucharest
Athens
Moscow
Vienna
Marseilles
Bergen
Reykjavik
London
Lisbon
Average monthly temperature
Average monthly rainfall
Arctic Circle

1 : 40 000 000

1:20 000 000

200 0 200 400 600 800 km

DENSITY OF POPULATION

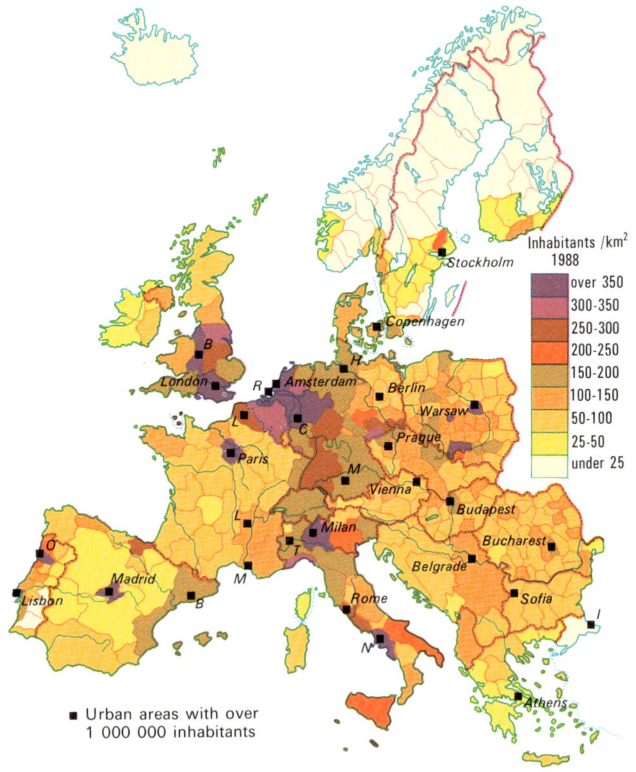

POPULATION CHANGE

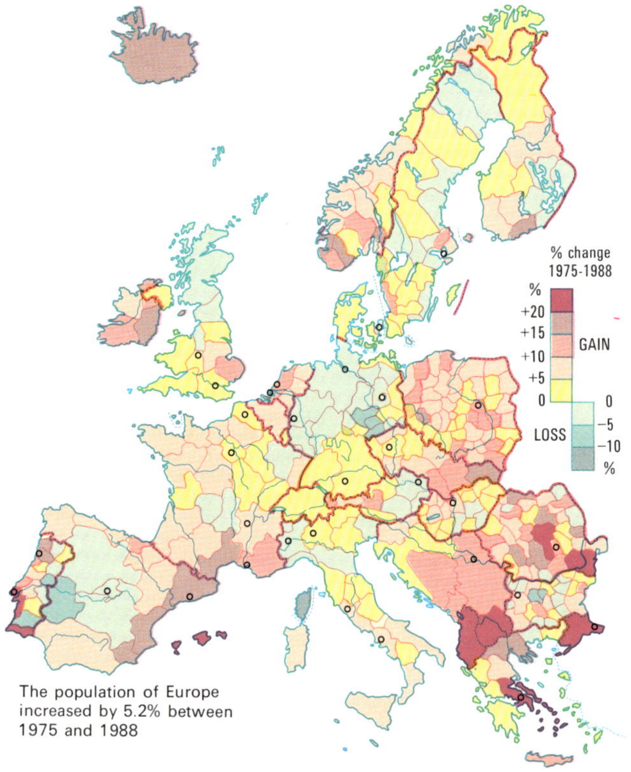

The population of Europe increased by 5.2% between 1975 and 1988

UNEMPLOYMENT

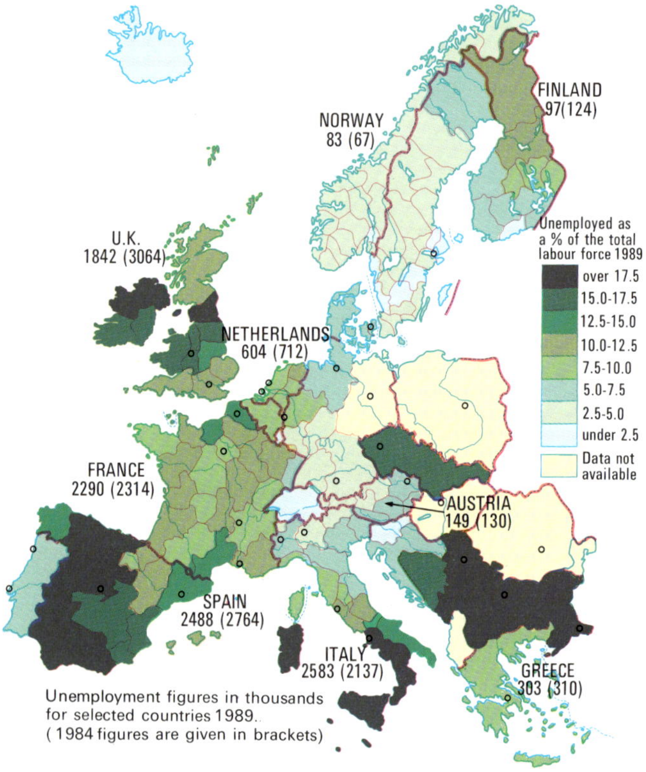

Unemployment figures in thousands for selected countries 1989. (1984 figures are given in brackets)

IMPORTANCE OF AGRICULTURE

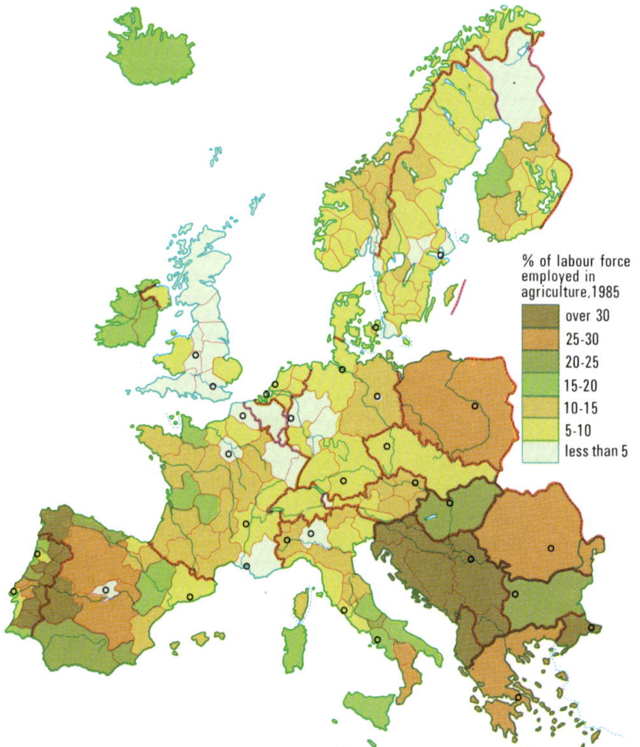

The maps of the Soviet Union and Yugoslavia show the situation at the time of going to press in December, 1991. Extra maps of the Republics and Nationalities of the Soviet Union and the Republics and Ethnic Groups of Yugoslavia are provided on p. 161.

STANDARDS OF LIVING

Gross Domestic Product (GDP) is a measure of a country's total production of goods and services.

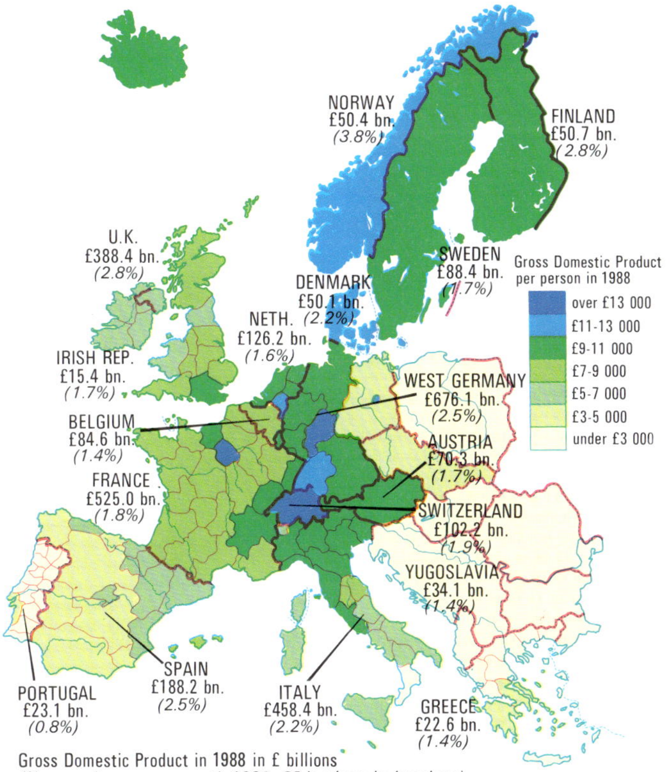

Gross Domestic Product in 1988 in £ billions
(% annual average growth 1980–88 is given in brackets)

ENERGY CONSUMPTION

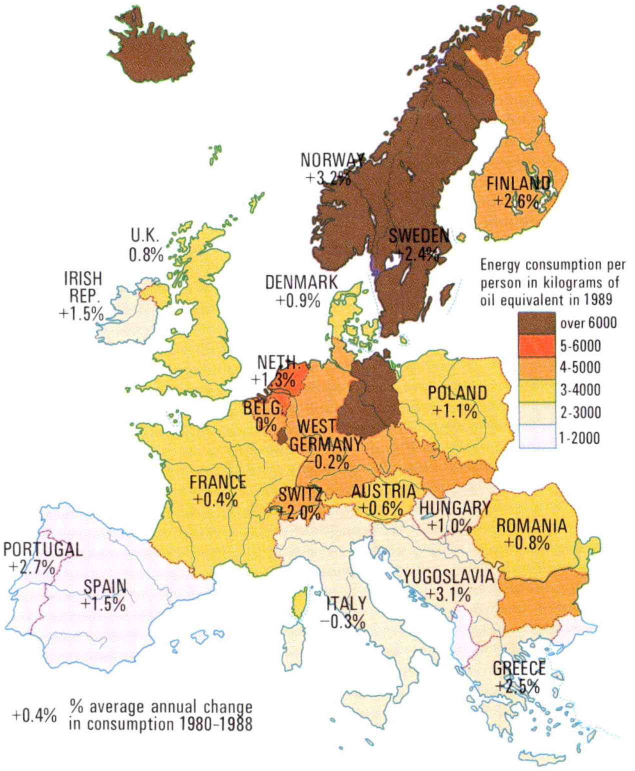

TRADE ORGANISATIONS

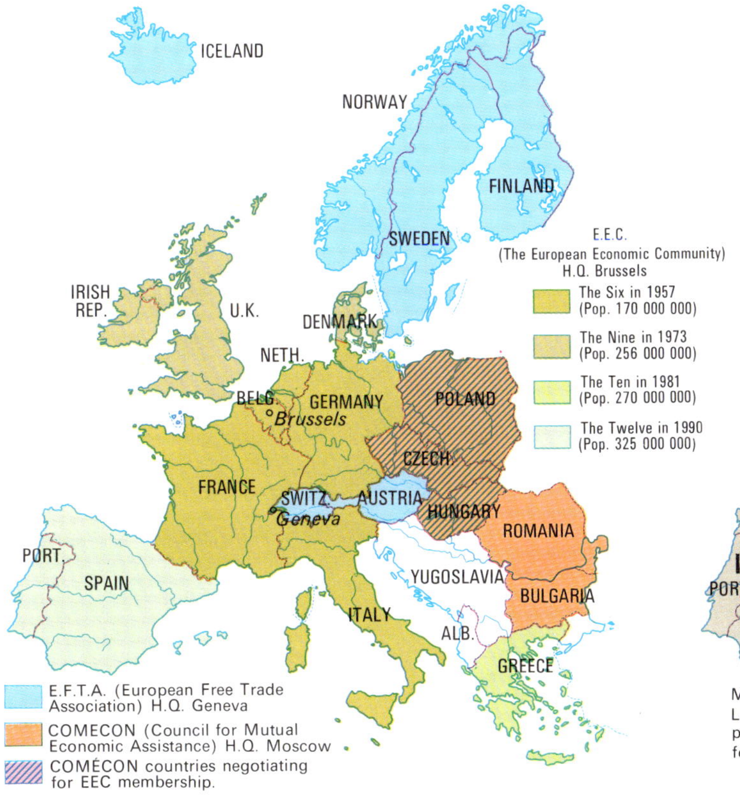

East Germany became a part of the E.E.C. with the German unification on 3rd October 1990.

TRANSPORT

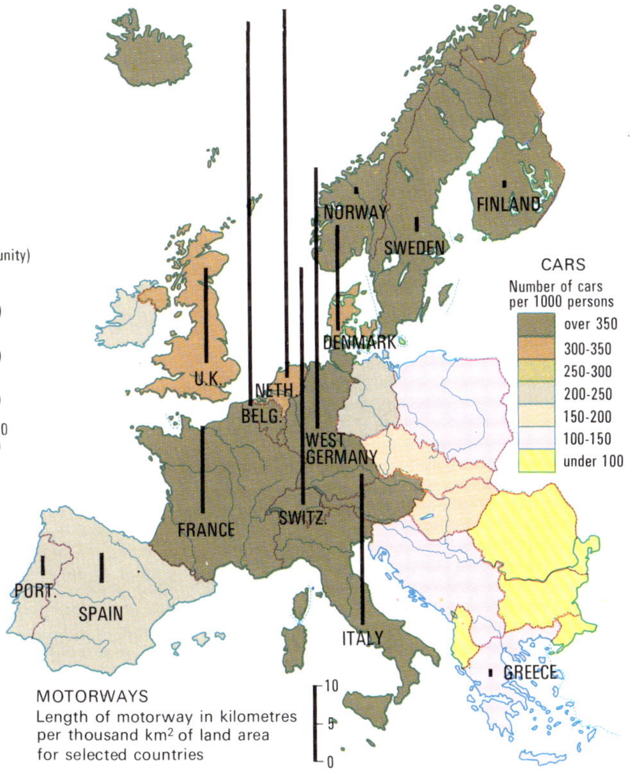

	Population								Land			Agriculture		
	Total	Density	Birth Rate	Death Rate	Life Expectancy	Growth 1965-80	Growth 1980-88	Urban	Area	Arable	Forest	Agricultural Population	Index of Production	Food Intake
	th.	persons per km²	per th. popn.	per th. popn.	yrs.	av. % per annum	av. % per annum	%	th. km²	th. km²	th. km²	% of total popn.	1979-81 = 100	calories per day
Albania	3145	117	26	6	72	2.5	2.1	35	27	7	11	51	111	2726
Austria	7563	91	12	11	74	0.3	0	57	83	15	32	7	105	3428
Belgium *	9867	329	12	11	75	0.3	0	97	30	8	7	2	116	3679
Bulgaria	8995	81	13	12	72	0.5	0.2	70	111	41	39	13	103	3663
Czechoslovakia	15610	125	14	11	71	0.5	0.3	68	125	51	46	10	125	3465
Denmark	5133	122	12	12	76	0.5	0	86	42	26	5	5	120	3633
Finland	4944	16	12	10	76	0.3	0.4	60	305	24	232	9	103	3122
France	55873	102	14	9	77	0.7	0.5	74	546	195	147	6	104	3336
Germany, East	16665	157	13	13	73	−0.2	−0.1	78	106	49	30	9	116	3791
Germany, West	61049	250	11	11	75	0.3	−0.1	86	244	75	73	4	112	3528
Greece	10030	77	11	10	76	0.7	0.5	61	131	39	26	26	104	3688
Hungary	10604	115	12	13	70	0.4	−0.1	59	92	53	17	13	105	3569
Iceland	249	3	17	7	77	0.8	1.1	90	100	0.1	1	8	106	3142
Ireland	3574	52	17	9	74	1	0.6	58	69	10	3	15	105	3632
Italy	57470	196	10	9	77	0.6	0.2	68	294	122	67	8	100	3523
Luxembourg *	371	143	12	10	74	0.9	0.2	83	3	0.6				
Malta	345	1150	15	8	73	0.2	−0.9	87	0.3	0.1	0	4	111	2682
Netherlands	14760	434	13	8	77	0.9	0.5	88	34	9	3	4	115	3326
Norway	4205	14	14	11	77	0.6	0.3	74	308	9	83	6	112	3223
Poland	37873	124	16	10	72	0.8	0.8	61	305	147	87	23	109	3336
Portugal	10162	111	12	9	74	0.6	0.3	32	92	28	36	19	107	3151
Romania	23052	100	16	11	70	1	0.4	49	230	107	63	23	114	3373
Spain	38997	78	11	8	77	1	0.5	77	499	204	157	12	114	3359
Sweden	8357	20	13	12	77	0.5	0.1	84	412	30	280	4	93	3064
Switzerland	6545	164	12	9	77	0.5	0.3	61	40	4	11	5	111	3437
United Kingdom	57019	236	14	11	75	0.2	0.2	92	242	70	23	2	106	3256
Yugoslavia	23552	92	15	9	72	0.9	0.7	48	255	78	93	25	103	3563
U.S.S.R.	285659	13	20	10	69	0.9	0.9	68	22272	2325	9440	15	118	3440

* Many figures for Luxembourg included in Belgium.

Population. This is the United Nation's estimate for the mid-year 1988 (thousands)

Population Density. This is the quoted population total divided by the quoted land area (persons per square kilometre).

Birth Rates and Death Rates. These are the registered or United Nation's estimated rates per thousand population.

Life Expectancy. This figure indicates the number of years that a child born today can expect to live if the levels of death of today last throughout its life. The figure is the average of that for men and women. The figure for women is usually higher than that for men (U.K. Male 75, female 78 years).

Population Growth. This shows the average annual percentage change in population for two periods, 1965–1980 and 1980–1988.

Urbanization. This is the percentage of the total population living in urban areas. The definition of urban is that of the individual nation and usually includes quite small towns.

Land Area. This is the total area of the country minus the area covered by major lakes and rivers (thousand square kilometres).

Arable Land and Permanent Crops. This excludes fallow land but includes temporary pasture (thousand square kilometres).

Forest and Woodland. This includes natural and planted woodland and land recently cleared of timber which will be replanted (thousand square kilometres).

Agricultural Population. This is the percentage of the economically active population working in agriculture. It also includes those people working in forestry, hunting and fishing.

Index of Agricultural Production. The base period for this index is 1979–1981 and it shows the level of production in each country in 1988 in comparison with that of the earlier period. Only edible crops and meat are included.

Food Intake. The figures are the average intake per person in calories per day for the year 1986.

Trade		Education		Health	Energy	Consumer Price Index	G.N.P.		G.D.P.		Loans & Debt		
Imports	Exports	Primary	Secondary					Growth per capita	Part formed by Agric.	Part formed by Indust.			
US$ per capita	US$ per capita	% of age group	% of age group	Popn. per doctor	Consumption in kg of oil equiv. per capita	1980 = 100	US$ per capita	% per year 1965-88	%	%	end 1987 US$ millions	as % of G.N.P.	
	159	96	70		1178		900						Albania
4315	3592	100	79	388	3465	133	11980	3.1	3	37	302	0.2	Austria
8371	8407	96	96	331	4844	146	11480	2.6	2	31	592	0.4	* Belgium
1843	1915	100	100	277	4705		6295	3.1	15	62			Bulgaria
1554	1477	97	37	277	4954	111	8280	2.3	7	61			Czechoslovakia
4936	4811	98	100	399	3887	165	14930	1.9	5	29	922	0.9	Denmark
4017	4053	100	100	443	5581	170	14470	3.2	7	35	610	0.6	Finland
2819	2561	100	95	320	3729	172	12790	2.7	4	31	6959	0.7	France
1727	1792	100	78	439	6031		9800	3	13	66			Germany, East
3724	4812	97	72	377	4531	122	14400	2.5	2	38	4700	0.4	Germany, West
1347	649	100	88	351	1971	416	4020	3.1	16	29	23120	0.1	Greece
929	903	98	70	307	3062	184	2240	3.8	15	40	18957	79	Hungary
6321	5719	99	95	435	6884	1050	20160	2.4	10	16			Iceland
3809	4468	100	96	676	2503	195	6120	2	10	37	57	0.2	Ireland
2127	2029	97	76	234	2676	222	10350	2.7	4	34	2615	0.4	Italy
		100	74	552	11330	142	22600	1.7	3	29			* Luxembourg
3299	1751	97	75	879	1501	103	5050	2.7	4	29			Malta
6187	9293	100	100	450	5198	135	11860	2.1	4	30	2231	1	Netherlands
5369	5101	98	97	451	8932	192	17190	3.5	4	35	988	1	Norway
286	322	100	80	487	3386	928	1930	3.4	13	49	42135	58	Poland
1322	902	100	52	412	1322	381	2830	3.2	9	40	18245	63	Portugal
496	544	97	79	567	3464		5200	4.3	15		6662	5	Romania
1257	874	100	98	317	1939	214	6010	2.3	6	37			Spain
4861	5303	99	83	387	6453	177	15500	1.8	3	35	1534	0.9	Sweden
7725	6930	100		696	4105	128	21330	1.4	2	21	615	0.3	Switzerland
2708	2300	100	85	611	3805	160	10420	1.7	2	38	2615	0.3	United Kingdom
533	494	95	82	549	2115	2891	2480	3.7	11	43	23518	41	Yugoslavia
336	378	100	99	270	5006	108	7120	2.5	20	45			U.S.S.R.

Andorra, Land 0.5/Popn. 51; Faeroe Is. 1.4/46; Gibraltar 0.01/30; Liechtenstein 0.2/28; Monaco 0.0015/27; San Marino 0.06/23; Svalbard 62/4.

Trade. The trade figures are for the year 1988. The total trade figures have been divided by the population and are a measure of the country's external trade (U.S. $ per capita).

Education. The ages of primary school are taken to be 6–11 years and secondary school 12–17 years. The percentage of total school age group in this type of education is shown.

Energy. All forms of energy have been converted to their equivalent in oil. Firewood and other traditional forms used in developing countries are not included and so the energy consumption in those countries is understated (kilograms of oil equivalent per capita).

Consumer Price Index. The base year is 1980 which is 100 and the level of consumer prices in 1987 or 1988 are shown in relation to the base year. It is a measure of inflation.

G.N.P. (Gross National Product) This figure is an estimate of the average production per person measured in U.S. dollars and for 1988. The G.N.P. measures the value of goods and services produced in a country, plus the balance, positive or negative, of income from abroad, for example investments, interest on capital, money returned from foreign labour, etc. The rate of change is the average annual percentage change during the period 1965–1988 in the G.N.P. The G.D.P. (Gross Domestic Product) is the G.N.P. minus the foreign balances. The adjoining two columns show the percentage contribution to the G.D.P. made by the agricultural and mining and manufacturing sectors.

Loans and Debts. This figure in millions of U.S. dollars shows the external public debt ar the end of 1988. This is then shown as a percentage of the annual G.N.P. The figures in red show official development assistance made by the developed countries and also as a percentage of the donor country's G.N.P.

To convert from square kilometres (km^2) to square miles multiply by 0.39
To convert from kilograms to pounds multiply by 2.2

FRANCE AND WESTERN EUROPE

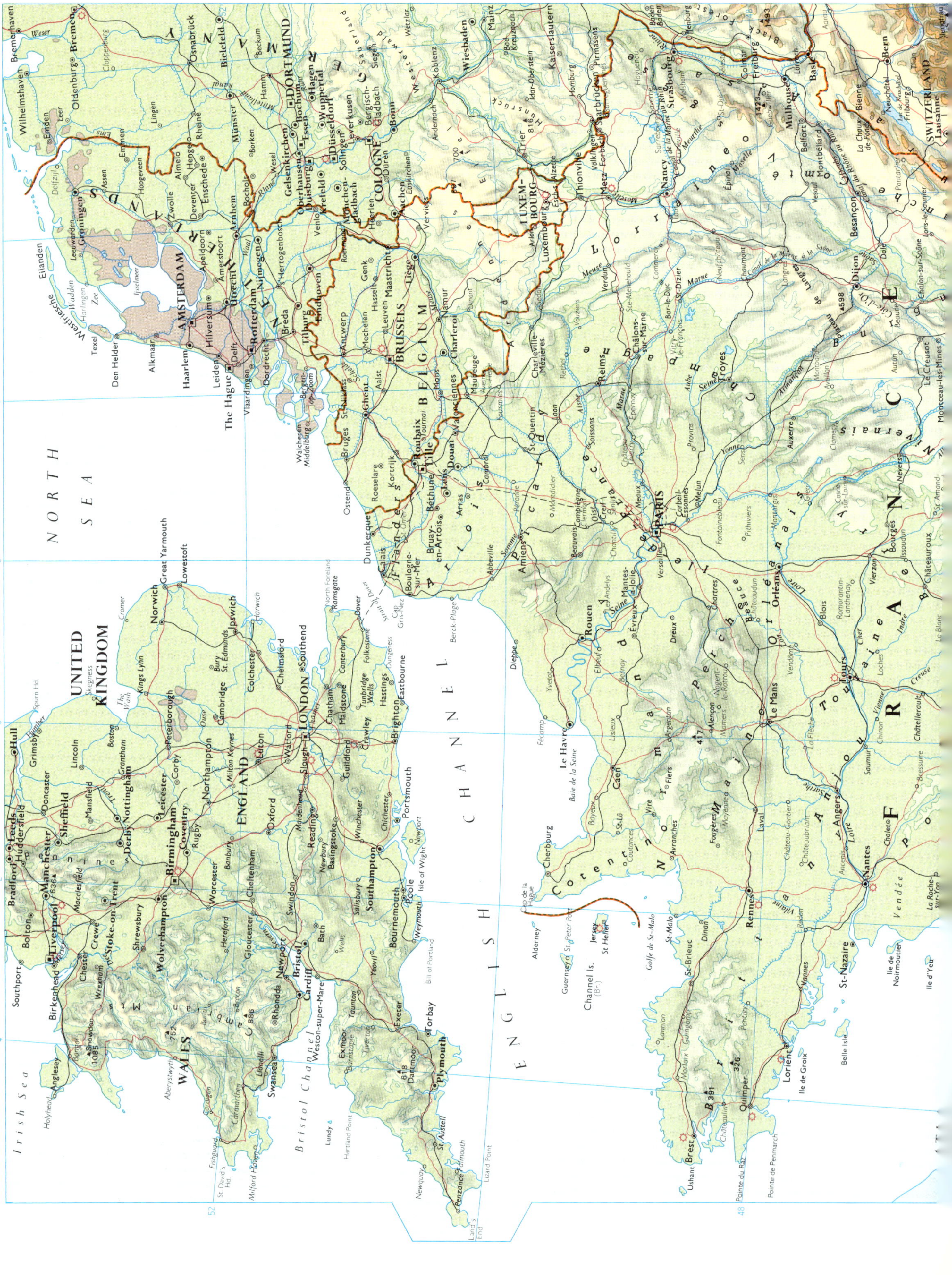

Projection: Conical with two standard parallels

LOW COUNTRIES AND LOWER RHINE

Projection: Conical with two standard parallels

East from Greenwich

1:2 000 000

10 0 10 20 30 40 50 60 70 80 km

1:5 000 000

50 0 50 100 150 200 km

Projection: Conical with two standard parallels

MEDITERRANEAN LANDS

The maps of the Soviet Union and Yugoslavia show the situation at the time of going to press in December, 1991. Extra maps of the Republics and Nationalities of the Soviet Union and the Republics and Ethnic Groups of Yugoslavia are provided on p. 161.

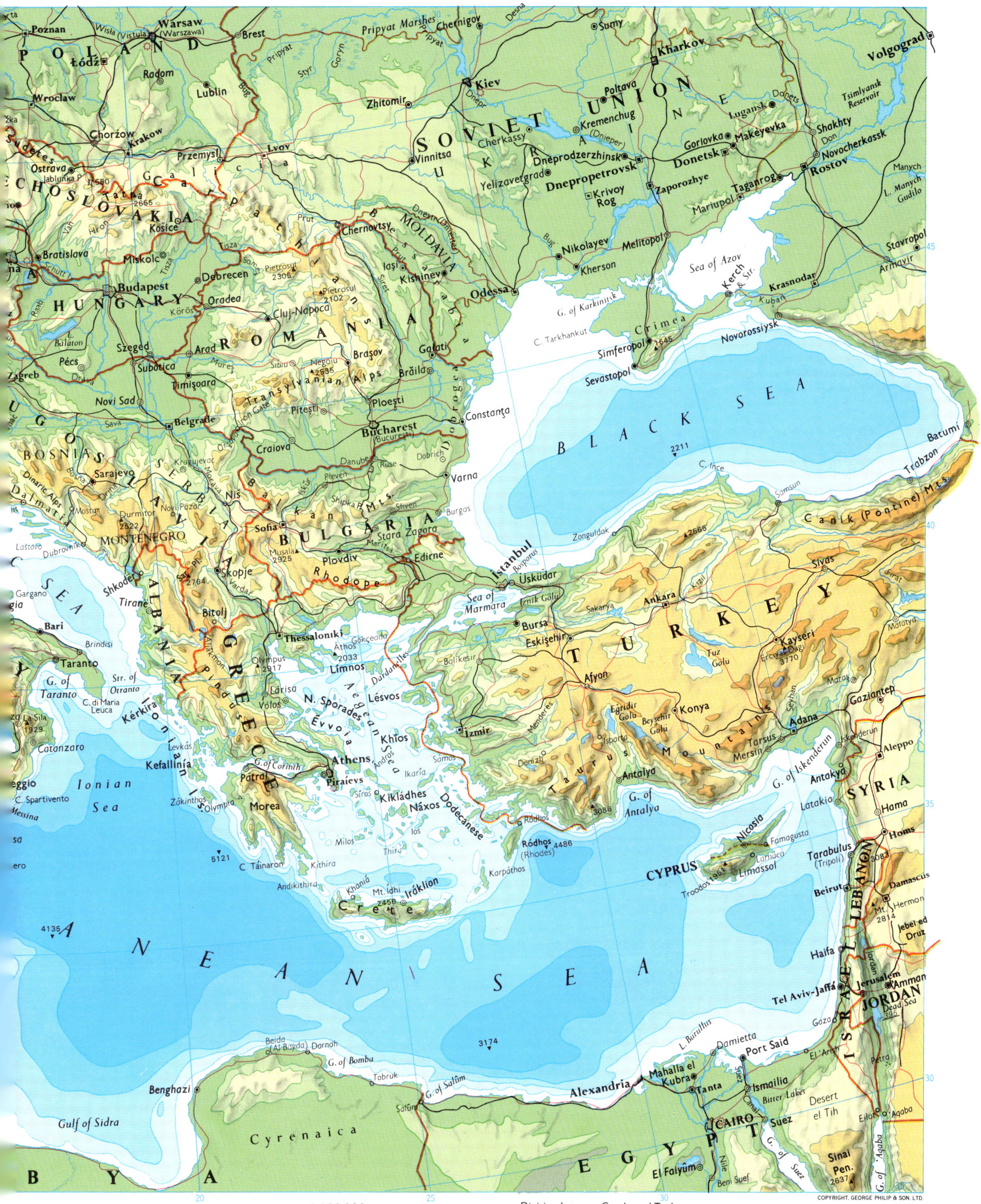

1:10 000 000

100 0 100 200 300 400 km

Division between Greeks and Turks in Cyprus; Turks to the North.

The maps of the Soviet Union and Yugoslavia show the situation at the time of going to press in December, 1991. Extra maps of the Republics and Nationalities of the Soviet Union and the Republics and Ethnic Groups of Yugoslavia are provided on p. 161.

SOVIET UNION
ROMANIA
Transylvania
Carpathians
Transylvanian Alps
Banat
Wallachia
Dobrogea
YUGOSLAVIA
SERBIA
MONTENEGRO
MACEDONIA
ALBANIA
BULGARIA
Balkan Mountains
Rhodope Mountains
TURKEY
GREECE
THESSALY
EPIRUS
Pindus Mts.
PELOPONNESE
THRACE
Anatolia
BLACK SEA
AEGEAN SEA
IONIAN SEA
MEDITERRANEAN SEA
Str. of Otranto
Sea of Marmara
Bosporus
Dardanelles (Hellespont)
KIKLÁDHES (Cyclades)
DODECANESE
CRETE
Hódmezővásárhely
Szeged
Subotica
Pécs
Szekszárd
Baja
Arad
Timişoara
Kikinda
Sombor
Osijek
Novi Sad
Zrenjanin (Petrovgrad)
Pančevo
Belgrade (Beograd)
Smederevo
Tuzla
Sarajevo
Kragujevac
Cacak
Krusevac
Niš
Leskovac
Pristina
Mostar
Dubrovnik
Titograd (Podgorica)
Pec
Prizren
Tetovo
Skopje
Kumanovo
Shkodër
Durrës
Tirane
Elbasan
Korce
Vlöre
Berat
Bitola (Monastir)
Prilep
Florina
Kastoria
Kozáni
Véroia
Edhessa
Thessaloniki
Sérrai
Dráma
Kavála
Xánthi
Komotini
Alexandroúpolis
Larisa
Volos
Trikkala
Ioánnina
Lamia
Préveza
Kerkira (Corfu)
Levkás (Sta. Maura)
Kefallinía (Cephalonia)
Zákinthos
Patrai
Athens (Athinai)
Piraievs (Piraeus)
Kórinthos
Tripolis
Kalamata
Spárti
Návplion
Pírgos
Olympia
Iráklion (Candia)
Khaniá
Alba-Iulia
Sibiu
Deva
Braşov (Orasul Stalin)
Sfântu Gheorghe
Focşani
Galati
Braila
Izmail
Tulcea
Buzău
Ploeşti
Pitesti
Tîrgovişte
Rîmnicu Vîlcea
Tîrgu-Jiu
Turnu-Severin
Iron Gate
Craiova
Slatina
Bucharest (Bucureşti)
Giurgiu
Călărasi
Constanţa
Trajan's Wall
Silistra
Tutrakan
Ruse (Ruschuk)
Vidin
Oryakhovo
Somovit
Svishtov
Pleven
Dobrich (Tolbukhin)
Sumen (Kolarovgrad)
Varna
C. Kaliakra
Burgas
Sliven
Yambol
Gabrovo
Shipka P.
Stara Zagora
Sofia
Pernik
Kyustendil
Trajan's Gate
Pazardzhik
Plovdiv
Khaskovo
Musala 2925
Vezhen 2198
Edirne
Istanbul
Üsküdar
Marmara
Bandirma
Bursa
Gelibolu (Gallipoli)
Canakkale
Troy
Balikesir
Ayvalik
Manisa
Izmir (Smyrna)
Aydin
Mugla
Bodrum
Kos
Rodhos (Rhodes)
Karpathos
Kasos
Thasos
Samothráki
Gökçeada
Límnos
Lésvos
Khíos (Chios)
Samos
Ikaria
Pátmos
Kalimnos
Évvoia (Euboea)
N. Sporades
Skiros
Ándros
Tínos
Míkonos
Síros
Kéa
Kíthnos
Sérifos
Sífnos
Mílos
Páros
Náxos
Amorgós
Thíra
Kíthira (Cerigo)
Andikíthira
Mt. Áthos 2033
Olympus 2917
Óssa
Parnassós 2457
Mt. Idhi 2456
Lévka Óri 2452
C. Matapan
C. Malea
G. of Thessaloniki
G. of Corinth
G. of Patrai
G. of Aiyina
G. of Argolis
G. of Lakonia
G. of Messini
Kiparissia G.
G. of Saros
G. of Edremit
G. of Izmir
G. of Kerme
G. of Mandalya
Danube
Drava
Sava
Morava
Vardar
Struma
Maritsa
Tundzha
Olt
Mureş
Siret
Prut
Ida 1766
Brindisi
Lecce
Otranto
C. St. Maria di Leuca
Istranca Mts.
Dhidhimotikhon
1:5 000 000
50 0 50 100 150 200 km
East from Greenwich

NORTH SEA
BALTIC
Frisian Islands
Heligoland
Heligoland Bay
Flensburg
SCHLESWIG-HOLSTEIN
Kiel
Kiel Bay
Kiel Canal
Lolland
Falster
Fehmarn Belt
Fehmarn
Gedser
Lübeck Bay
Warnemünde
Sassnitz
Rügen
Stralsund
Rostock
Lübeck
Wilhelmshaven
Cuxhaven
Bremerhaven
Altona
Hamburg
Schwerin
Emden
Leeuwarden
Groningen
Den Helder
IJssel L.
Alkmaar
North Sea Canal
Haarlem
Zaandam
NETHERLANDS
Amsterdam
The Hague
Hook of Holland
Leiden
Utrecht
Apeldoorn
Enschede
Rotterdam
Dordrecht
Arnhem
Nijmegen
Waal
Maas
's Hertogenbosch
Flushing
Zeebrugge
Ostend
Bruges
Ghent
Antwerp
Tilburg
Eindhoven
FLANDERS
Kortrijk
Tourcoing
Roubaix
Lille
Brussels
Mechelen
Leuven
Maastricht
BELGIUM
Liège
Namur
Mons
Charleroi
Douai
Valenciennes
Cambrai
Meuse
Ardennes
LUX.
Luxembourg
St. Quentin
Charleville-Mézières
Laon
Aisne
Reims
Thionville
Metz
Épernay
Châlons sur Marne
LORRAINE
Nancy
Bar-le-Duc
St. Dizier
Aube
Troyes
CHAMPAGNE
Chaumont
Épinal
Vosges
Colmar
ALSACE
Strasbourg
Mulhouse
Belfort
Basle
Langres
Plateau de Langres
Saône
Dijon
Dôle
Besançon
FRANCHE-COMTÉ
Montbéliard
Jura
Doubs
Chalon sur Saône
Mâcon
Côte d'Or
BURGUNDY
Lyons
Rhône
Vienne
St. Étienne
Chambéry
Annecy
SAVOIE
Isère
Grenoble
DAUPHINÉ
Valence
Mt. Pelvoux
Montélimar
Gap
Durance
Mt. Viso
Nîmes
Avignon
Arles
PROVENCE
Verdon
Aix
Marseilles
Grasse
Nice
Cannes
Monaco & Monte Carlo
Maritime Alps
Col di Tenda
Digne
Cuneo
FRANCE
Oldenburg
Bremen
LOWER SAXONY
Lüneburg Heath
Aller
Weser
Elbe
Ems
Osnabrück
Münster
Teutoburger Wald
Herford
Bielefeld
Hanover
Hildesheim
Hameln
Brunswick
Wolfsburg
Salzgitter
Magdeburg
Halberstadt
Brocken
Harz Mts.
NORTH RHINE-WESTPHALIA
Lippe
Oberhausen
Duisburg
Gelsenkirchen
Hamm
Dortmund
Bochum
Essen
Hagen
Krefeld
M. Gladbach
Wuppertal
Remscheid
Düsseldorf
RHINE
Cologne
Aachen
Bonn
Siegen
Rothaar G.
Paderborn
Göttingen
Kassel
Eder
Fulda
Werra
Sieg
Westerwald
Koblenz
Eifel
Hunsrück
Taunus
Wiesbaden
Frankfurt
Offenbach
Mainz
Vogels Berg
Rhön
PALATINATE
Worms
Trier
Saar
Kaiserslautern
SAAR
Saarbrücken
Ludwigshafen
Mannheim
Darmstadt
Spessart
Würzburg
Heidelberg
Karlsruhe
Heilbronn
BADEN
Neckar
Pforzheim
Stuttgart
WÜRTTEMBERG
Black Forest
Freiburg
Danube
Ulm
Jura
Schaffhausen
Bamberg
Erlangen
Fürth
Nuremberg
Regensburg
BAVARIA
Ingolstadt
Augsburg
Lech
Iller
Isar
Amper
Munich
Rosenheim
Passau
Inn
Fichtel Geb.
Naab
Bohemian Forest
Halle
Saale
Leipzig
SAXONY
Erfurt
Gotha
Jena
Gera
Thuringian Forest
Reichenbach
Zwickau
Chemnitz (Karl Marx Stadt)
Plauen
Erz Gebirge (Ore Mts.)
Dresden
Dessau
Mulde
GERMANY
BRANDENBURG
Havel
Spandau
Charlottenburg
BERLIN
Potsdam
Brandenburg
Spree
Frankfurt
Cottbus
L. Müritz
Neu Brandenburg
Haff
Szczecin (Stettin)
Stargard Szczeciński
Oder
Koszalin
Słupsk
Piła
Noteć (Netze)
Gorzów Wielkopolski
Warta (Warthe)
Poznań
Zielona Góra
Bóbr
Leszno
Głogów
Lubin
Legnica
Görlitz
Neisse
Liberec
Jelenia Góra
Riesen G. (Giant Mts.)
Sněžka
Wałbrzych
Sudetes
Highlands
Ústí nad Labem
Most
Ohře
Lausitz Geb.
Cheb
Kladno
Prague (Praha)
Labe (Elbe)
Pardubice
Hradec Králové
Plzeň (Pilsen)
BOHEMIA
Vltava
Sázava
Moravian Hts.
CZECHOSLOVAKIA
Olomouc
Brno (Brünn)
Jihlava
České Budějovice
Linz
Steyr
Enns
Welser
UPPER AUSTRIA
LOWER AUSTRIA
Krems
St. Pölten
Vienna (Wien)
Wiener Neustadt
Semmering
Neusiedler See
BURGENLAND
Szombathely
Salzburg
SALZBURG
Innsbruck
TYROL
Brenner P.
Gross Glockner
STYRIA
Graz
Mur
Drava
CARINTHIA
Klagenfurt
Villach
Karawanken
Carnic Alps
AUSTRIA
Maribor
Zalaegerszeg
Varaždin
Celje
SLOVENIA
Ljubljana
Zagreb
CROATIA
Sava
Kupa
Karlovac
Sisak
Julian Alps
Triglav
Udine
FRIULI-VENEZIA GIULIA
Trieste
Istria
Rijeka
Krk
Cres
Lošinj
Pula
Pag
Dugi Otok
Velebit Planina
Kapela
Una
Sana
Zadar
Dinara Pla.
Troglav
Bregenz
VORARLBERG
Arlberg P.
LIECHTENSTEIN
St. Gallen
Winterthur
Zürich
Zug
Schwyz
Luzern
Aarau
Solothurn
Biel
Neuchâtel
Bern
Fribourg
SWITZERLAND
Lausanne
Montreux
Geneva
L. Geneva
Interlaken
St. Gotthard P.
Simplon P.
Rhine
Chur
Engadin
Bernina
Matterhorn
Mt. Blanc
Gt. St. Bernard P.
Lit. St. Bernard P.
Aosta
VALLE D'AOSTA
Gran Paradiso
Graian Alps
Turin
PIEDMONT
Asti
Alessandria
Tanaro
Savona
Genoa (Genova)
Gulf of Genoa
RIVIERA
LIGURIA
Ticino
Novara
Lugano
Maggiore
L. Como
Como
Milan
Bergamo
LOMBARDY
Brescia
Adda
Pavia
Piacenza
Cremona
Po
Garda
Mantua (Mantova)
Ortles
Stelvio P.
Bolzano
TRENTINO-ALTO ADIGE
Adamello
Trento
Dolomites
Marmolada
Adige
Vicenza
Verona
VENETO
Treviso
Piave
Padua (Padova)
Venice (Venezia)
Gulf of Venice
Ferrara
Parma
Reggio
Modena
Trebbia
P. dei Giovi
EMILIA-ROMAGNA
Apennines
Mte. Cimone
Bologna
Reno
La Spezia
Pistoia
Prato
Florence (Firenze)
Lucca
Pisa
Ravenna
Forlì
Rubicone
Rimini
San Marino
Pesaro
ADRIATIC SEA
ITALY
Projection: Conical with two standard parallels
East from Greenwich

The maps of the Soviet Union and Yugoslavia show the situation at the time of going to press in December, 1991. Extra maps of the Republics and Nationalities of the Soviet Union and the Republics and Ethnic Groups of Yugoslavia are provided on p. 161.

1:5 000 000

50 0 50 100 150 200 km

SCANDINAVIA AND THE BALTIC LANDS

The maps of the Soviet Union and Yugoslavia show the situation at the time of going to press in December, 1991. Extra maps of the Republics and Nationalities of the Soviet Union and the Republics and Ethnic Groups of Yugoslavia are provided on p. 161.

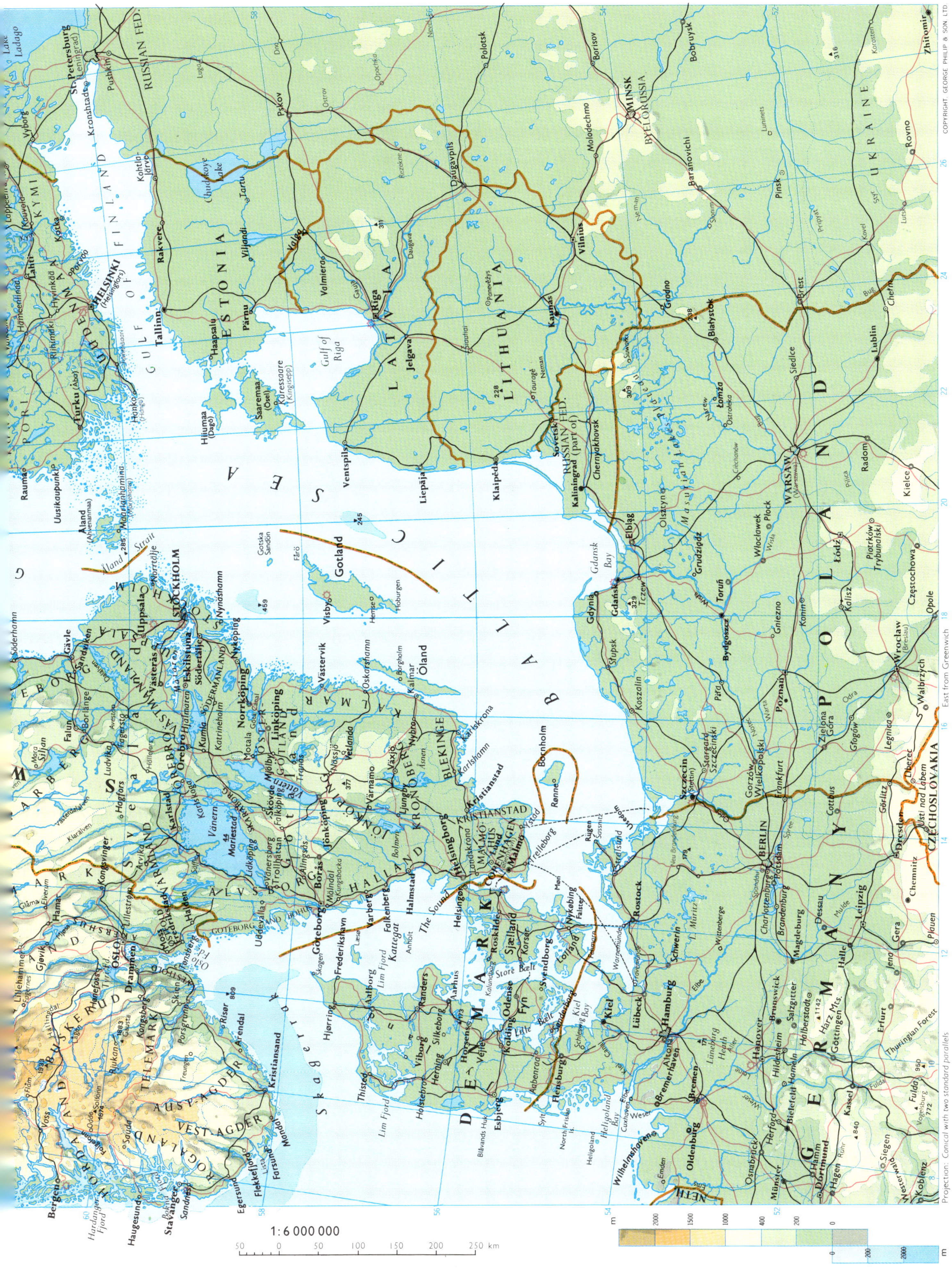

STOCKHOLM
HELSINKI (Helsingfors)
St. Petersburg (Leningrad)
Tallinn
Riga
Vilnius
MINSK
WARSAW (Warszawa)
BERLIN
OSLO
COPENHAGEN (København)
Hamburg
Göteborg
Gdańsk
Kaliningrad (part of RUSSIAN FED.)
ESTONIA
LATVIA
LITHUANIA
BYELORUSSIA
UKRAINE
POLAND
GERMANY
DENMARK
RUSSIAN FED.
CZECHOSLOVAKIA
BALTIC SEA
GULF OF FINLAND
Gulf of Riga
Skagerrak
Kattegat
The Sound
Gotland
Öland
Bornholm
Saaremaa (Ösel)
Hiiumaa (Dagö)
Vänern
Vättern
Lake Ladoga
Chudskoye Lake
Åland Strait
Gdansk Bay
Masurian Lakes
Lübeck
Rostock
Kiel
Szczecin (Stettin)
Poznań
Wrocław (Breslau)
Łódź
Toruń
Bydgoszcz
Białystok
Grodno
Brest
Lublin
Kaunas
Klaipėda
Liepāja
Ventspils
Daugavpils
Pärnu
Tartu
Pskov
Malmö
Helsingborg
Kristianstad
Kalmar
Visby
Uppsala
Västerås
Örebro
Norrköping
Linköping
Jönköping
Borås
Halmstad
Ålborg
Århus
Odense
Esbjerg
Kristiansand
Drammen
Bergen
Stavanger
Dresden
Leipzig
Magdeburg
Hanover
Bremen
Projection: Conical with two standard parallels
East from Greenwich
COPYRIGHT GEORGE PHILIP & SON LTD
1:6 000 000
50 0 50 100 150 200 250 km

The maps of the Soviet Union and Yugoslavia show the situation at the time of going to press in December, 1991. Extra maps of the Republics and Nationalities of the Soviet Union and the Republics and Ethnic Groups of Yugoslavia are provided on p. 161.

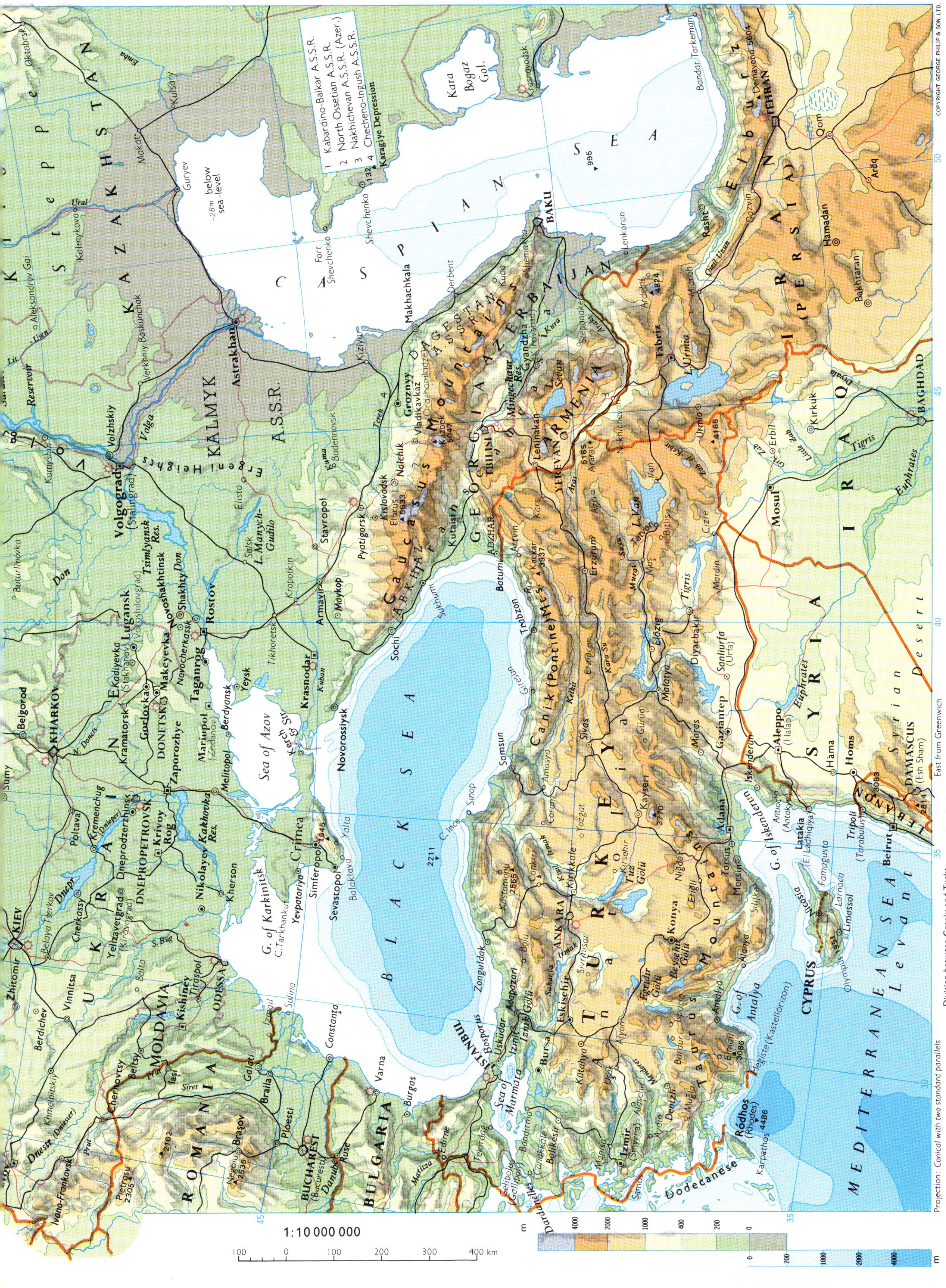

1:10 000 000
100 0 100 200 300 400 km
m
4000
2000
1000
400
200
0
200
1000
2000
4000
1 Kabardino-Balkar A.S.S.R.
2 North Ossetian A.S.S.R.
3 Nakhichevan A.S.S.R. (Azer.)
4 Checheno-Ingush A.S.S.R.
-132 Karagiye Depression
Projection: Conical with two standard parallels
Division between Greeks and Turks in Cyprus, Turks to the North
A.S.S.R. = Autonomous Republic
East from Greenwich
COPYRIGHT GEORGE PHILIP & SON, LTD.
CASPIAN SEA
BLACK SEA
MEDITERRANEAN SEA
Levant
Sea of Azov
Sea of Marmara
Kara Bogaz Gol.
KAZAKHSTAN
UKRAINE
MOLDAVIA
ROMANIA
BULGARIA
TURKEY
GEORGIA
ARMENIA
AZERBAIJAN
DAGESTAN A.S.S.R.
KALMYK A.S.S.R.
IRAN (PERSIA)
IRAQ
SYRIA
LEBANON
CYPRUS
Caucasus Mountains
Taurus Mountains
Canik (Pontine) Mts.
Anatolia
Elburz
Syrian Desert
Yergeni Heights
Crimea
Dodecanese
KIEV
KHARKOV
DNEPROPETROVSK
DONETSK
ODESSA
Volgograd (Stalingrad)
Astrakhan
Rostov
TBILISI
YEREVAN
BAKU
TEHRAN
BAGHDAD
DAMASCUS (Esh Sham)
Beirut
ANKARA
ISTANBUL
BUCHAREST (Bucureşti)
Izmir (Smyrna)
Aleppo (Halab)
Tabriz
Mosul
Hamadan
Trabzon
Samsun
Sevastopol
Simferopol
Novorossiysk
Krasnodar
Stavropol
Groznyy
Makhachkala
Guryev
Batumi
Sukhumi
Erzurum
Sivas
Kayseri
Konya
Adana
Diyarbakir
Kirkuk
Erbil
Homs
Hama
Latakia
Tripoli
Nicosia
Rodhos (Rhodes)
Constanţa
Varna
Burgas
Edirne
Bursa
Eskişehir
Kishinev
Nikolayev
Kherson
Zaporozhye
Taganrog
Mariupol (Zhdanov)
Lugansk
Sochi
Kutaisi
Rasht
Ardabil
Qom
Demavend 5604
Elbrus 5633
Ararat 5165
Euphrates
Tigris
Volga
Don
Dnepr
Ural
Danube
L. Van
L. Urmia
Sevan
Bosporus
Dardanelles

SOVIET UNION

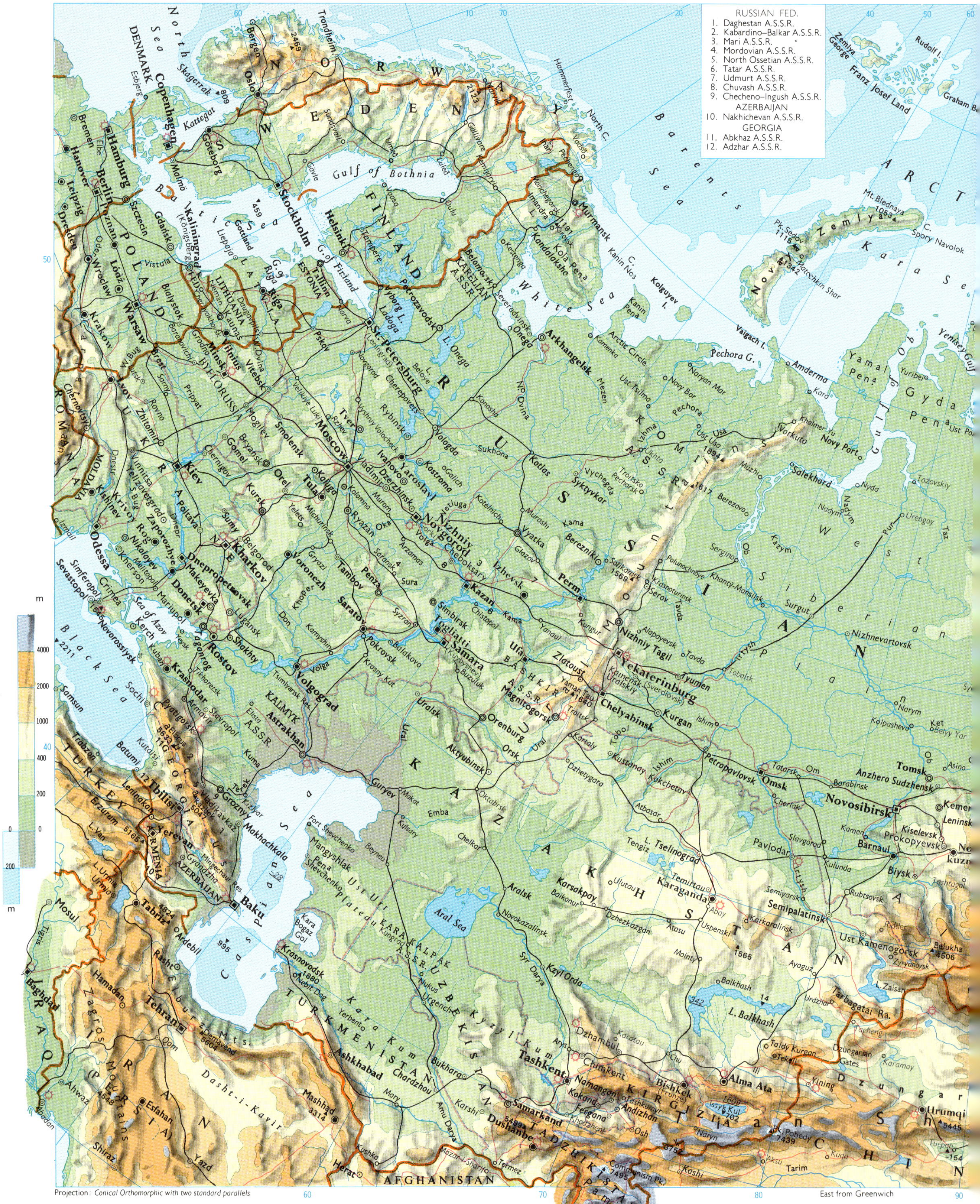

The maps of the Soviet Union and Yugoslavia show the situation at the time of going to press in December, 1991. Extra maps of the Republics and Nationalities of the Soviet Union and the Republics and Ethnic Groups of Yugoslavia are provided on p. 161.

Chukchi Sea
C. Dezhneva (East C.)
St. Lawrence I. (U.S.A.)
Gulf of Anadyr
Wrangel I.
East Siberian Sea
De Long Is.
New Siberia
Faddeyev I.
New Siberian Is.
Medvezhi Is.
Komsomolets I.
October Revolution I.
Severnaya Zemlya
Bolshevik I.
Boris Vilkitski Str.
OCEAN
Laptev Sea
Kotelny I.
Lyakhov Is.
Bolshoi I.
Dimitri Laptev Str.
Chukot Range
Koryak Range
Byrranga Mts.
Taimyr
L. Taimyr
Begichev I.
Nordvik
Tiksi
Sredne Kolymsk
Kolyma
Gizhiga
Penzhina G.
Gizhiga G.
Shelekhov Gulf
Bering Sea
Komandorskiye Is.
Kamchatka Pen.
Sredinnyy Ra.
Petropavlovsk-Kamchatskiy
Verkhoyansk
Verkhoyansk Range
Cherskiy Ra.
Kolyma Ra.
Magadan
Okhotsk
Sea of Okhotsk
Khatanga
Norilsk
Central Siberian Plateau
Arctic Circle
Yakutsk
Vilyuysk
Lena
Aldan
Olekminsk
Mirnyy
Dzhugdzhur Ra.
Ayan
Shantar Is.
Sakhalin Str.
Nikolayevsk
Sakhalin
Sovetskaya Gavan (Soviet Harbour)
Yuzhno-Sakhalinsk
Kuril Islands
Stanovoy Ra.
Yablonovyy Ra.
Kirensk
Bratsk
Krasnoyarsk
Eastern Sayan
Western Sayan
Irkutsk
Angarsk
Ulan Ude
Chita
Baikal
BURYAT A.S.S.R.
Komsomolsk
Khabarovsk
Sikhote Alin
Birobidzhan
Blagoveshchensk
Great Khingan
Qiqihar
Harbin
Vladivostok
Nakhodka
Hokkaido
Sapporo
Hakodate
Honshū
Niigata
Kanazawa
Sea of JAPAN
Manzhouli
Hulun Nur
Hentiyn Nuruu
Ulan Bator (Ulaanbaatar)
MONGOLIA
GOBI
INNER MONGOLIA
Manchuria
Changchun
Jilin
Shenyang (Mukden)
Fushun
Anshan
Dalian
Pyongyang
NORTH KOREA
Wŏnsan
Chongjin
Seoul
SOUTH KOREA
Pusan
Peking
Baotou
Hami
Boundaries of A.S.S.R. (Autonomous Republics)
1:20 000 000
200 0 200 400 600 800 km

ARCTIC OCEAN
PACIFIC OCEAN
INDIAN OCEAN
Caspian Sea
Black Sea
Mediterranean Sea
Red Sea
Arabian Sea
Bay of Bengal
South China Sea
East China Sea
Sea of Japan
Sea of Okhotsk
Bering Sea
Laptev Sea
Kara Sea
Barents Sea
Aral Sea
Yellow Sea
Himalaya
Plateau of Tibet
Kunlun Shan
Tian Shan
Altai
Ural Mountains
West Siberian Plain
Central Siberian Plateau
Verkhoyansk Range
Plateau of Mongolia
Plateau of Iran
Arabia
India
Deccan
Sumatra
Borneo
Java
Philippine Is.
Formosa
Korea
Honshu
Hokkaido
Sakhalin
Kamchatka Peninsula
Ceylon
Western Ghats
Eastern Ghats
Scandinavia
Libyan Desert
Equator
Tropic of Cancer
Arctic Circle
East from Greenwich
Projection: Bonne
1: 50 000 000
500 0 500 1000 1500 2000 km

East from Greenwich

Peking Capital Cities

Projection: Bonne

1:50 000 000

500 0 500 1000 1500 2000 km

The maps of the Soviet Union and Yugoslavia show the situation at the time of going to press in December, 1991. Extra maps of the Republics and Nationalities of the Soviet Union and the Republics and Ethnic Groups of Yugoslavia are provided on p. 161.

ASIA: *climate and natural vegetation*

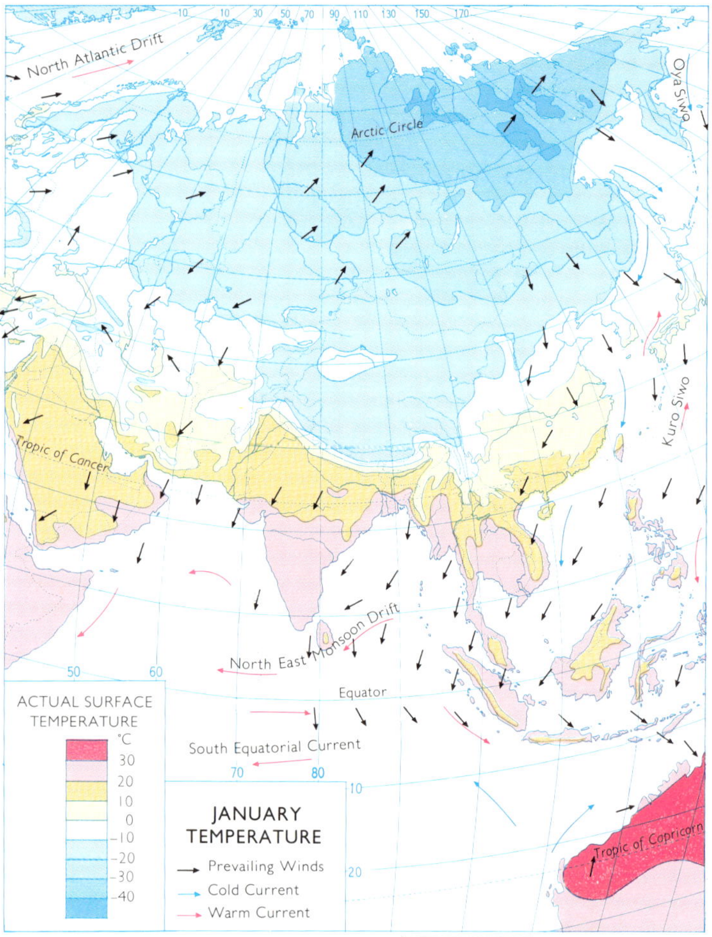

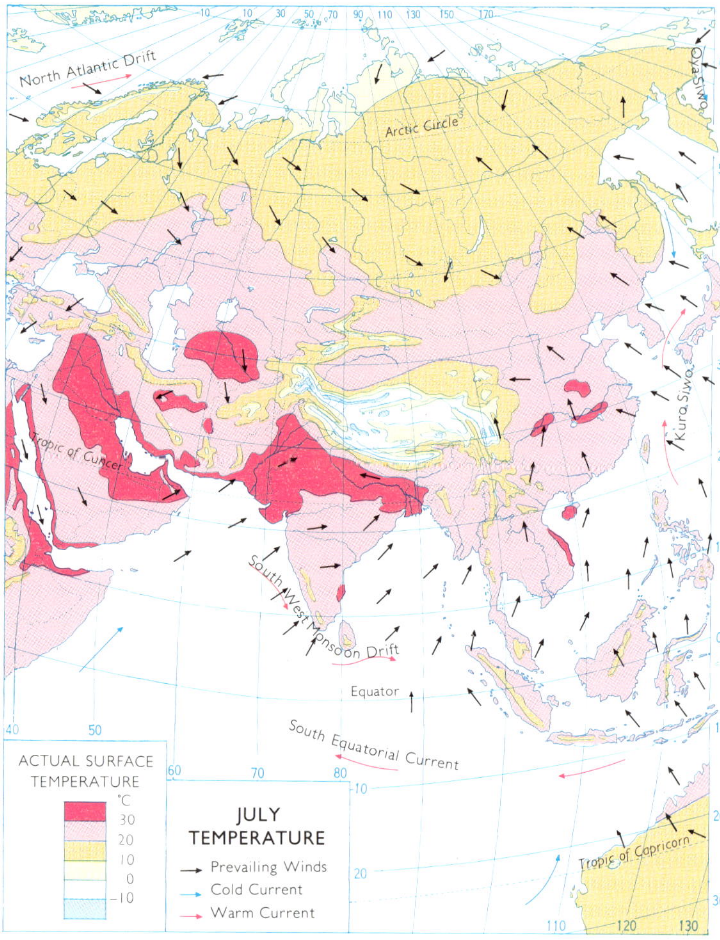

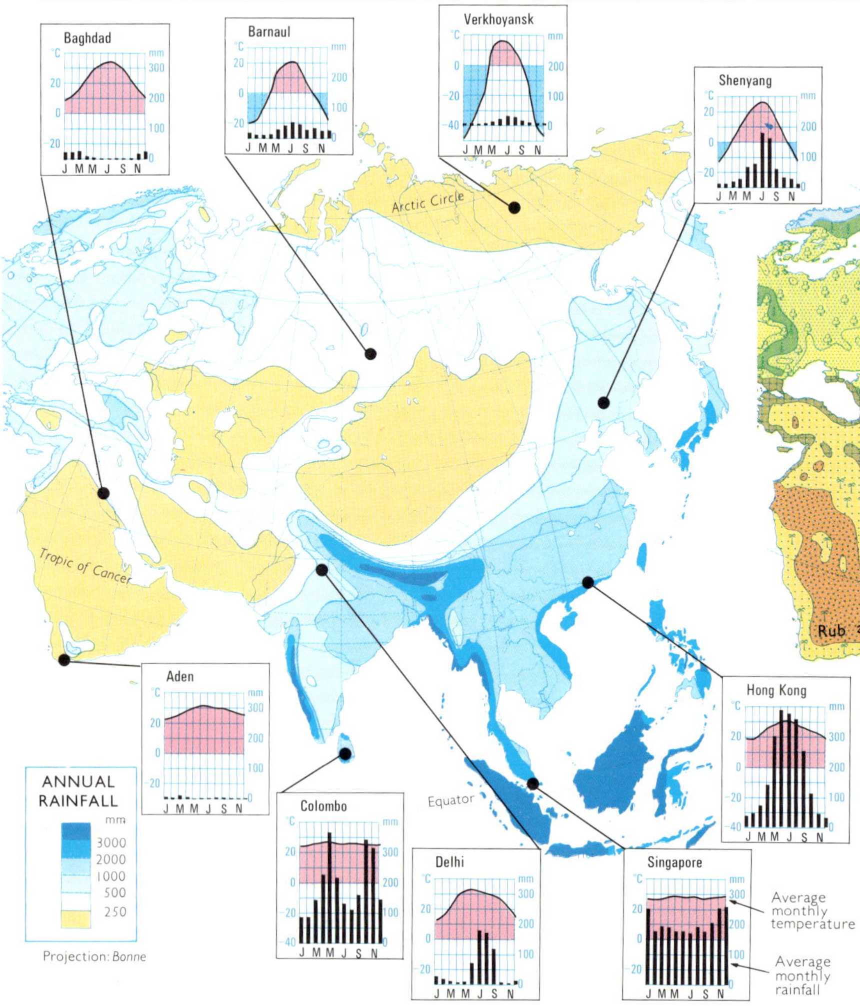

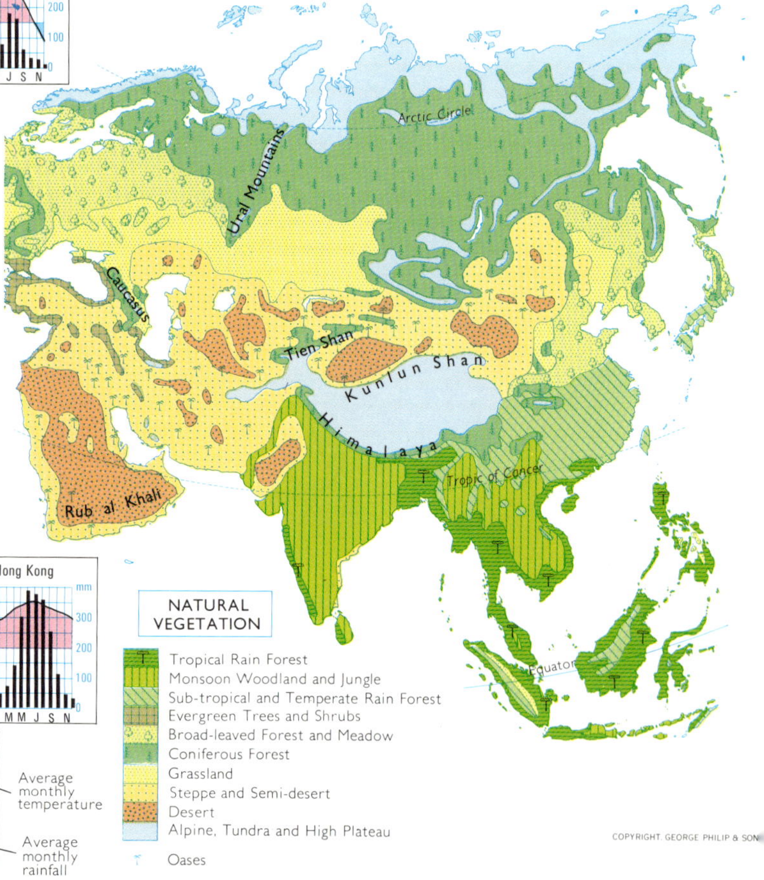

1 : 100 000 000

Arctic Circle
Tropic of Cancer
Equator
Stockholm
Warsaw
Moscow
Urals
Kuzbas
Donbas
Istanbul
Beirut
Kirkuk
Tehrān
Tashkent
Delhi
Calcutta
Rangoon
Bangkok
Ho Chi Minh City
Singapore
Manila
Hong Kong
Chungking
Daye
Peking
Tokyo
LAND USE
Arable land
Arable land with permanent pasture
Fruit trees, vineyards and plantations
Permanent pasture
Woods and forests
Rough grazing
Rough grazing with trees
Non-productive land
LIVESTOCK
Cattle
Sheep
MINERALS
Asbestos
Bauxite
Copper
Diamonds
Gold
Iron ore
Lead
Lead and Zinc
Mica
Silver
Tin
Zinc
Sb Antimony
Cr Chrome
Co Cobalt
Mg Magnesium
Mn Manganese
Hg Mercury
Ni Nickel
Ti Titanium
POWER
Coalfields
Gasfields
Oilfields
Hydro-electric power
CROPS
Bananas
Barley
Citrus fruits
Coffee
Cotton
Date palms
Groundnuts
Maize
Millet
Potatoes
Rice
Rubber
Soybeans
Sugar beet
Sugar cane
Tea
Tobacco
Vines
Wheat
Principal fishing areas
LAND USE (million hectares)
Arable land and permanent crops 713.6
Permanent pasture 911.7
Woods and forests 1 523.6
Other land 1 754.9
Total land area 4 903.8 million hectares
East from Greenwich
1:50 000 000
500 0 500 1000 1500 2000 km

	Population								Land			Agriculture		
	Total	Density	Birth Rate	Death Rate	Life Expectancy	Growth 1965-80	Growth 1980-88	Urban	Area	Arable	Forest	Agricultural Population	Index of Production	Food Intake
	th.	persons per km²	per th. popn.	per th. popn.	yrs.	av. % per annum	av. % per annum	%	th. km²	th. km²	th. km²	% of total popn.	1979-81 = 100	calories per day
Afghanistan	15513	24	48	22	37	2.4	2.6	22	648	81	19	57	99	2055
Bangladesh	115244	130	42	12	51	2.7	2.8	13	134	92	21	71	109	1927
Burma (Myanmar)	40162	61	31	10	60	2.3	2.2	24	658	101	324	49	146	2609
Cambodia	7869	45	41	17	48	0.3	2.9	12	177	31	134	71	173	2276
China	1083889	116	21	7	70	2.2	1.2	38	9326	970	1166	70	140	2630
Cyprus	686	76	19	8	76		1.1	53	9	2	1	22	96	3378
Hong Kong	5674	5674	13	5	76	2.1	1.5	93	1	0.1	0.1	1	60	2859
India	813990	274	32	11	58	2.3	2.1	27	2973	1689	671	68	133	2238
Indonesia	174832	97	27	11	61	2.3	2.1	27	1812	212	1215	51	138	2579
Iran	48555	30	43	12	63	3.2	3	53	1636	148	180	30	121	3313
Iraq	17657	41	43	8	64	3.4	3.6	72	434	55	19	23	136	2932
Israel	4444	222	23	7	76	2.8	1.7	91	20	4	1	5	115	3061
Japan	122433	330	11	6	78	1.2	0.6	77	371	47	251	8	102	2864
Jordan	3937	41	46	7	66	2.6	3.7	66	97	4	0.7	7	158	2991
Korea, North	21877	182	29	5	69	2.7	2.5	67	120	24	90	36	132	3151
Korea, South	42593	435	16	6	70	1.9	1.4	69	98	21	65	28	112	2907
Laos	3879	17	41	16	49	1.4	2.4	17	231	9	130	73	132	2391
Lebanon	2827	283	29	8	67	1.6	−0.01	83	10	3	0.8	11	129	2995
Malaysia	16921	51	29	6	70	2.5	2.6	40	329	44	196	35	165	2730
Mongolia	2086	1	39	8	64	3	2.9	51	1565	13	152	33	119	2807
Nepal	18053	132	40	15	51	2.4	2.7	9	137	23	23	92	125	2052
Pakistan	105677	136	33	8	55	3.1	3.1	31	779	208	31	51	140	2315
Philippines	59686	200	33	8	64	2.9	2.4	41	298	79	110	48	109	2372
Saudi Arabia	14016	7	42	8	64	4.6	3.7	75	2150	12	12	42	332	3004
Singapore	2639	4398	20	5	73	1.6	1.1	100	0.6	0.03	0.03	1	91	2840
Sri Lanka	16565	255	21	6	71	1.8	1.5	21	65	19	18	52	100	2401
Syria	11667	63	44	7	65	3.4	3.6	51	184	56	5	26	126	3260
Taiwan	19673	547	16	5	73		1.5	72	36	9	2	26	104	
Thailand	54469	106	22	7	65	2.7	1.9	21	512	201	144	66	120	2331
Turkey	53772	70	28	8	64	2.4	2.3	47	771	279	202	51	119	3229
Vietnam	66682	205	32	10	66	3.1	2.6	21	325	65	130	63	136	2297
Yemen, North	8742	45	48	16	46	2.8	2.7	23	195	14	16	65	132	2318
Yemen, South	2339	7	47	16	51	2	2.9	42	333	1	15	34	108	2299
U.S.S.R. †														
Oceania														
Australia	16506	2	15	7	76	1.8	1.4	86	7618	471	1060	6	114	3326
New Zealand	3623	14	17	8	75	1.3	1	84	269	5	73	10	93	3463
Papua New Guinea	3804	8	35	12	54	2.3	2.7	15	452	4	383	70	121	2205

† See statistics table for Europe.

Population. This is the United Nation's estimate for the mid-year 1988 (thousands)

Population Density. This is the quoted population total divided by the quoted land area (persons per square kilometre).

Birth Rates and Death Rates. These are the registered or United Nation's estimated rates per thousand population.

Life Expectancy. This figure indicates the number of years that a child born today can expect to live if the levels of death of today last throughout its life. The figure is the average of that for men and women. The figure for women is usually higher than that for men (U.K. Male 75, female 78 years).

Population Growth. This shows the average annual percentage change in population for two periods, 1965–1980 and 1980–1988.

Urbanization. This is the percentage of the total population living in urban areas. The definition of urban is that of the individual nation and usually includes quite small towns.

Land Area. This is the total area of the country minus the area covered by major lakes and rivers (thousand square kilometres).

Arable Land and Permanent Crops. This excludes fallow land but includes temporary pasture (thousand square kilometres).

Forest and Woodland. This includes natural and planted woodland and land recently cleared of timber which will be replanted (thousand square kilometres).

Agricultural Population. This is the percentage of the economically active population working in agriculture. It also includes those people working in forestry, hunting and fishing.

Index of Agricultural Production. The base period for this index is 1979–1981 and it shows the level of production in each country in 1988 in comparison with that of the earlier period. Only edible crops and meat are included.

Food Intake. The figures are the average intake per person in calories per day for the year 1986.

Trade		Education		Health	Energy	Consumer Price Index	G.N.P.		G.D.P.		Loans & Debt		
Imports	Exports	Primary	Secondary					Growth per capita	Part formed by Agric.	Part formed by Indust.			
US$ per capita	US$ per capita	% of age group	% of age group	Popn. per doctor	Consumption in kg of oil equiv. per capita	1980 = 100	US$ per capita	% per year 1965-88	%	%	end 1987 US$ millions	as % of G.N.P.	
91	36	18	6	6419	71				69	14			Afghanistan
150	62	60	18	6731	47	199	160	0.3	47	13	9432	49	Bangladesh
16	5	100	24	3743	73	190	200	2.3	51	10	4386	46	Burma (Myanmar)
					59				41	17			Cambodia
40	36	100	42	1000	525		290	5.2	31	49	27919	7	China
		99	90	746	1599	148	6260		7	16	1439	35	Cyprus
8541	8543	100	69	1075	1525	180	8070	6.2	0	29			Hong Kong
23	15	92	35	2521	208	201	300	1.8	30	30	41694	16	India
83	98	100	41	9464	216	199	450	4.5	26	33	47562	59	Indonesia
377	417	100	18	2780	955				26	36			Iran
420	511	99	52	1806	732				18	46			Iraq
3217	1907	99	79	345	1965	46447	6800	2.5	5	21	26332	87	Israel
1192	1870	100	96	663	3232	116	15760	4.2	3	41			Japan
684	236	99	79	1139	750	134	1560		9	28	3585	67	Jordan
				420	2165								Korea, North
961	1107	94	95	1166	1475	160	2690	6.4	11	43	23907	14	Korea, South
18	8	94	19	1362	37		170				833	165	Laos
665	209	100	56	667	871				9	12	496		Lebanon
739	1055	100	54	1935	771	130	1810	4.1	20	31	19377	56	Malaysia
		100	92	104	1181								Mongolia
32	8	79	25	30230	23	204	160	0.5	57	14	1060	34	Nepal
55	39	52	24	2941	207	129	350	2.5	23	28	13072	37	Pakistan
120	95	100	68	6700	241	289	590	1.7	24	33	23710	60	Philippines
1460	1650	71	44	688	3292	95	6200	4	4	50			Saudi Arabia
12308	10834	100	71	1309	4436	118	7940	7.2	1	38			Singapore
126	84	100	66	5516	160	234	400	3	27	27	3956	56	Sri Lanka
218	116	100	60	1309	900	538	1640	3.3	27	19	4678	24	Syria
1754	2721	100	95	1016	73	174			6	40			Taiwan
238	214	99	29	6294	330	139	850	3.9	17	23	17685	31	Thailand
263	190	100	44	1381	763	528	1210	2.6	17	36	30697	42	Turkey
28	16	100	43	995	88		300		29	17			Vietnam
150	2	79	15	6268	100		590		28	17	2166	39	Yemen, North
620	175	66	19	4344	707		420		16	23	1689	171	Yemen, South
													† U.S.S.R.
													Oceania
1776	1532	100	96	436	4821	176	11100	1.8	4	33	501	0.3	Australia
2002	1982	100	84	576	4211	245	7750	0.9	8	31	84	0.5	New Zealand
321	308	60	11	6160	229	158	700	0.8	34	26	2218	64	Papua New Guinea

Bahrain, Land 0.6/Popn. 445; Bhutan 47/1370; Brunei 5.3/235; Kuwait 17.8/1919; Macau 0.02/429; Maldives 0.3/200; Oman 212.5/1402; Qatar 11/332; U.A.E. 83.6/1500.
American Samoa 0.2/36; Cocos Is. 0.01/0.6; Cook Is. 0.2/20; Fed. States of Micronesia 0.7/90; Fiji 18.3/722; Fr. Polynesia 3.7/179; Guam 0.6/128; Kiribati 0.7/66; Nauru 0.02/8; New Caledonia 18.8/158; Niue I. 0.26/2; Norfolk I. 0.036/2; Northern Marianas 0.5/17; Palau 0.5/12; Samoa 2.9/163; Solomon Is. 27.5/293; Tokelau 0.01/2; Tonga 0.7/100; Tuvalu 0.2/8; Vanuatu 14.8/150; Wallis & Futuna 0.2/14.

Trade. The trade figures are for the year 1988. The total trade figures have been divided by the population and are a measure of the country's external trade (U.S. $ per capita).

Education. The ages of primary school are taken to be 6–11 years and secondary school 12–17 years. The percentage of total school age group in this type of education is shown.

Energy. All forms of energy have been converted to their equivalent in oil. Firewood and other traditional forms used in developing countries are not included and so the energy consumption in those countries is understated (kilograms of oil equivalent per capita).

Consumer Price Index. The base year is 1980 which is 100 and the level of consumer prices in 1987 or 1988 are shown in relation to the base year. It is a measure of inflation.

G.N.P. (Gross National Product) This figure is an estimate of the average production per person measured in U.S. dollars and for 1988. The G.N.P. measures the value of goods and services produced in a country, plus the balance, positive or negative, of income from abroad, for example investments, interest on capital, money returned from foreign labour, etc. The rate of change is the average annual percentage change during the period 1965–1988 in the G.N.P. The G.D.P. (Gross Domestic Product) is the G.N.P. minus the foreign balances. The adjoining two columns show the percentage contribution to the G.D.P. made by the agricultural and mining and manufacturing sectors.

Loans and Debts. This figure in millions of U.S. dollars shows the external public debt ar the end of 1988. This is then shown as a percentage of the annual G.N.P. The figures in red show official development assistance made by the developed countries and also as a percentage of the donor country's G.N.P.

To convert from square kilometres (km^2) to square miles multiply by 0.39
To convert from kilograms to pounds multiply by 2.2

SOUTH-WEST ASIA

The maps of the Soviet Union and Yugoslavia show the situation at the time of going to press in December, 1991. Extra maps of the Republics and Nationalities of the Soviet Union and the Republics and Ethnic Groups of Yugoslavia are provided on p. 161.

1:15 000 000

100 0 100 200 300 400 500 600 km

SOVIET UNION
UZBEK
TURKMENISTAN
TADZHIKISTAN
CHINA
Tashauz
Samarkand
Bukhara
Dushanbe
Amu Darya
Pamir
Kashmir
Srinagar
Chardzhou
Karshi
Termez
Kerki
Kara Kum
Ashkhabad
Mary
Mazar-i-Sharif
Maimana
Hindu Kush
Kabul
Jalalabad
Peshawar
Rawalpindi
Islamabad
Nishapur
Mashhad
Sabzawar
Herat
AFGHANISTAN
Ghazni
Bannu
Kohat
Sialkot
Lahore
Chenab
Gunabad
Farah
Daulatabad
Qandahar
Multan
Dera Ismail Khan
Sandeman
Birjand
Girishk
Helmand
Registan
Quetta
Pishin
Bolan Pass
Sibi
Dera Ghazi Khan
Bahawalpur
Sutlej
INDIA
Neh
Hamun-i-Helmand
Zabul
Khash
Kalat
Jacobabad
Sukkur
Kerman
Saguch
3994
Dasht-i-Lut
Zahidan
Lodis
Kuh-i-Taftan
4042
Saidabad
4419
Bam
PAKISTAN
Shikarpur
Larkana
Nawabshah
Indus
Panjgur
Bela
Hyderabad
Karachi
Khanu
Bampur
Minab
Bandar Abbas
Qishm
Fanuch
Makran
Pasni
Kuhran
2163
Str. of Hormuz
Sharja
2057
Jask
Chahbar
Gwadar
Gulf of Oman
Abu Dhabi
As Sohar
Al Khabura
Matrah
Muscat
Tropic of Cancer
J. ash Sham
3019
Izki
Sur
Ras al Hadd
Arabian Sea
OMAN
W. Andam
Al Khalaf
Dawwah
Al Masira
Gulf of Masira
Ras al Madraka
Sauqra Bay
Dhofar
1678
Kuria Muria Is.
Marbat
Socotra (Yemen)
The Brothers

BEIRUT (Bayrut)
Djounie (Juniyah)
J. Sannini
2628
Ba'labakk (Baalbek)
Bikfaiya
Zahlah
Lebanon Mts.
Anti Lebanon
2462
Aley
Zabdani
Beka'a Valley
Saydā (Sidon)
Bisri
Jezzine
Damascus (Esh Sham)
LEBANON
Hermon
2814
Qatana
Dareiya
Kiswe
Nabatiye el Tahta
Litani
Al Khiyam
Tyre (Sur)
Tibnin
Qiryat Shemona
SYRIA
Al Qunaytirah
Sanamein
Nahariya
Me'ona
1208
Acre
B. of Haifa
GALILEE
Tsefat (Safad)
Capernaum
L. Kinneret (Sea of Galilee)
-209
Haifa
Qiryat Yam
Qiryat Ata
Migdal
Tiberias
Tirat Karmel
546
Mt. Carmel
Nazareth
Yarmuk
Dar'a
Daliyat el Karmel
Plain of Esdraelon
Afula
515
Taiyiba
Irbid
Ramtha
Megiddo
Umm el Fahm
Caesarea
Pardes Hanna
Hadera
Janin
Beit Shean
SAMARIA
Yabis
1198
Jebel 'Ajlun
1247
Ajlun
Jarash
Netanya
Tul Karm
Tubas
940
881
Nabulus
Jacob's Well
Zarqa
Ra'anana
Herzliya
Kefar Sava
Shilo
Damiya
Az Zarqa
TEL AVIV-JAFFA
Petah Tiqva
Ramat Gan
Holon
Bat Yam
Rishon Le-Zion
1016
1113
As Salt
Lod (Lydda)
Ramla
Rehovot
Ram Allah
Wadi es Sir
Amman
Na'ur
Jericho
Hussein B.
JORDAN
Ashdod
Yavne
Gedera
Jerusalem
Qumran
802
Ashqelon
Bethlehem
JUDAEA
Madaba
Heidan
Shiqma
Qiryat Gat
1020
Hebron (El Khalil)
Dhiban
Gaza (Ghazzah)
Gaza Strip
Mujib
Dead Sea
-395
Khan Yūnis
Rafah
Az Zuhiriyah
Mishmar Ha Negev
Masada
Al Mazra
Habesor
Beersheba
Arad
Wilderness of Judaea
Qatrana
Al Karak
ISRAEL
EGYPT
Dimona
716
Qeziot
NEGEV
THE HOLY LAND
Armistice boundaries between Arab States and Israel, 1949-1974
1:1 500 000
10 0 10 20 30 40 50 km
East from Greenwich
COPYRIGHT GEORGE PHILIP & SON LTD.

Projection: Conical with two standard parallels

CHINESE REPUBLIC
TIBET
QINGHAI
SICHUAN
YUNNAN
Xil Shan
Bayan Har Shan
Tanglha Range
Nganglong Kangri
Nyenchen Tanglha Range
Lhasa
Yarlung Zangbo Jiang
Xigazê
Gyangzê
Nam Co
Siling Co
Gyaring Co
Gyaring Hu
Ngoring Hu
Dogai Coring
Maqên Gangri
6282
Maqên
Yushu
Tang Pass
5180
Dêngqên
Qamdo
Baiyu
Garzê
Salween
Mekong
Yangtze
Zhongdian
Gerze
Coqên
Tangra Yumco
Xainza
Lhünzhub
7088
Lhari
Bomi
7756
Mapam Yumco
Burang
Namja Pass
4944
7059
Zhongba
Saga
Maquan
Gya Pass
5602
Lhazê
Gamba
Lhünzê
Comai
Cona
7554
7314
8013
Mustang
Muktinath
Dhaulagiri
8221
Himalaya
NEPAL
Siwalik Range
Katmandu
Lalitapur
Mt Everest
8848
Kanchenjunga
8598
SIKKIM
Gangtok
Darjeeling
BHUTAN
Punakha
Thimbu
ARUNACHAL PRADESH
Subansiri
Dibrugarh
North Lakhimpur
Sibsagar
Jorhat
Brahmaputra
Patkai Bum
Hukawng Valley
Kumon Bum
KACHIN STATE
Myitkyina
Hpungan Pass
3072
Putao
Chaukan Pass
2432
Bumhpa Bum
3411
Thala Pass
5881
Zayu
5500
Lijiang
ASSAM
Tezpur
Nowgong
Barpeta
Gauhati
Alipur Duar
Cooch Behar
Dhubri
NAGALAND
Kohima
3824
Mokokchung
MEGHALAYA
Shillong
Tura
1412
1924
Barail Range
Silchar
Sylhet
MANIPUR
Imphal
Chindwin
Homalin
Thaungdut
Mangin Range
Indaw
Shwegu
Bhamo
Tengchong
Baoshan
Xiaguan
Tropic of Cancer
Lashio
Namtu
Hsenwi
2299
Mawlaik
Kalewa
Irrawaddy
Shwebo
Mandalay
Monywa
Sagaing
Myingyan
Meiktila
Maymyo
SHAN STATE
Keng Tung
Mong Hsu
Taunggyi
Inle Lake
2519
Mong Nai
Mong Ton
Chiang Rai
BURMA
KAYAH
Loi-kaw
Mae Hong Son
2163
Chiengmai
Lamphun
Lampang
THAILAND (SIAM)
2576
Taungoo
2620
KAWTHOOLEI
Salween
Tak (Raheng)
Dawna Range
Moulmein
Thaton
Pa-an
2080
Kalegauk I.
Ye
Tavoy
Moscos Islands
Gulf of Martaban
Rangoon
Pegu
Pegu Yoma
Prome
Pyu
Thayetmyo
Magwe
Yenangyaung
Minbu
Arakan Yoma
Henzada
Myanaung
Gwa
Bassein
Insein
Pyapon
Yandoon
Myaungmya
Mouths of the Irrawaddy
C. Negrais
Preparis I. (Burma)
Gt. Coco Island (Burma)
Taungup
Ramree I.
Cheduba I.
Arakan Coast
Sittwe (Akyab)
Ponnyadaung
CHINS DIVISION
Mt Victoria
3053
Haka
Falam
2704
Tiddim
MIZORAM
Aijal
Karnaphuli Res.
Chittagong
Cox's Bazar
Rangamati
TRIPURA
Agartala
Comilla
BANGLADESH
DACCA
Dhaka
Narayanganj
Chandpur
Madaripur
Barisal
Noakhali
Khulna
Jessore
Kushtia
Pabna
Rajshahi
Bogra
Mymensingh
Jamalpur
Dinajpur
Saidpur
Rangpur
Jalpaiguri
Siliguri
Kishanganj
Purnea
Katihar
Balurghat
English Bazar
Berhampore
Krishnanagar
Durgapur
Asansol
Burdwan
WEST BENGAL
Bhatpara
Serampore
Haora
CALCUTTA
Kharagpur
Midnapore
Sundarbans
Hooghly
Mouths of the Ganges
Haringhata R.
Subarnarekha
Balasore
Cuttack
Bhubaneswar
Puri
Chilka Lake
Brahmani
Mahanadi
ORISSA
Sambalpur
Hirakud Dam
1187
Raurkela
Jamshedpur
Ranchi
Purulia
Bankura
Chakradharpur
Dhanbad
1366
Giridih
Hazaribagh
Ramgarh
Lohardaga
1225
Ambikapur
BIHAR
Bhagalpur
Monghyr
Jamalpur
Deoghar
Gaya
Patna
Arrah
Bihar
Chapra
Muzaffarpur
Darbhanga
Motihari
Bettiah
Gandak
Siwan
Gorakhpur
Basti
Ghaghara
Azamgarh
Faizabad
Gonda
Bahraich
Balrampur
Lucknow
Rae Bareli
Fatehpur
Jaunpur
Ghazipur
Varanasi (Banaras)
Mirzapur
Allahabad
Rewa
Satna
Aurangabad
Dehri
UTTAR PRADESH
MADHYA PRADESH
Bilaspur
Korba
Raigarh
Raipur
Durg
Dhamtari
Kawardha
Bolangir
Berhampur
1501
Jeypore
Jagdalpur
1240
Bobbili
Vizianagram
Vishakhapatnam
Anakapalle
Eastern Ghats
Northern Circars
1680
Rajahmundry
Godavari Point
Kakinada (Cocanada)
Vijayawada
Bhimavaram
Machilipatnam (Bandar)
1001
BAY OF BENGAL
INDIAN OCEAN
East from Greenwich
1:10 000 000
100 0 100 200 300 400 km
COPYRIGHT: GEORGE PHILIP & SON LTD

CHINA AND KOREA

Projection: Bonne

East from Greenwich

The maps of the Soviet Union and Yugoslavia show the situation at the time of going to press in December, 1991. Extra maps of the Republics and Nationalities of the Soviet Union and the Republics and Ethnic Groups of Yugoslavia are provided on p. 161.

Lake Baykal
Chita
Ulan Ude
Yablonovyy Range
Nerchinsk
Borzya
Argun
Manzhouli
Hulun Nur
Hailar
Buir Nur
Choybalsan
Kerulen
Oroqen Zizhiqi
Nenjiang
Bei'an
Butha Qi
Qiqihar
Nen
Anda
Suihua
Yichun
Hegang
Jiamusi
Shuangyashan
Svobodny
Amur
Blagoveshchensk
Aihui
Little Khingan Mts.
Chegdomyn
Komsomolsk
Aleksandrovsk
L. Bolon
Birobidzhan
Khabarovsk
Bikin
Sikhote Alin Ra.
Poronaysk
C. Terpeniya
Sakhalin
Yuzhno-Sakhalinsk
La Perouse Str.
Wakkanai
Asahigawa
2290
Hokkaido
Kushiro
Otaru
SAPPORO
C. Erimo
Hakodate
Tsugaru Strait
Aomori
Hachinohe
Morioka
Akita
Sendai
Sado
Niigata
Koriyama
Utsunomiya
Toyama
Kanazawa
TOKYO
KAWASAKI
YOKOHAMA
NAGOYA
Fuji-san
3776
Yokosuka
KYOTO
KOBE
OSAKA
Sakai
Shizuoka
Hamamatsu
Wakayama
Okayama
Hiroshima
Shikoku
Kochi
Matsuyama
Shimonoseki
KITAKYUSHU
FUKUOKA
Sasebo
Nagasaki
Kumamoto
Kyushu
Kagoshima
Tanega
Honshu
JAPAN
SEA OF JAPAN
HEILONGJIANG
Great Khingan Mts.
Horqin Youyi Qianqi
HARBIN
Manchuria
Mishan
Jixi
Lake Khanka
Mudanjiang
Ussuriysk
Tao'an
JILIN
CHANGCHUN
Jilin
Shuangliao
Vladivostok
Nakhodka
Songhua Lake
Yanji
Tongliao
Siping
Liaoyuan
Chongjin
2744
FUSHUN
Mukden
SHENYANG
Tonghua
Benxi
Liaoyang
ANSHAN
Yalu
NORTH
Hungnam
Wonsan
Dandong
KOREA
Korea Bay
YONGYANG
Kaesong
SEOUL
Haeju
INCHON
SOUTH
Taejon
TAEGU
PUSAN
Masan
Kwangju
1915
Cheju Do
1950
Korea Str.
Saynshand
Dzamin Üüd
Erenhot
Abagnar Qi
INNER MONGOLIA
1949
LIAONING
Chifeng
Fuxin
Chaoyang
Jinzhou
Yingkou
G. of Liaodong
Liaodong Pen.
DALIAN
(Lüda)
Hohhot
Jining
Zhangjiakou
Xuanhua
Datong
Chengde
Qinghuangdao
PEKING
(Beijing)
Tangshan
TIENTSIN (Tianjin)
Cangzhou
G. of Chihli
(Bo Hai)
Baoding
HEBEI
3058
TAIYUAN
Shijiazhuang
Yangquan
Yuci
SHANXI
Fenyang
Changzhi
Handan
Anyang
Dezhou
Huang He
JINAN
Weifang
Zibo
Ye Xian
Yantai
Weihai
SHANDONG
QINGDAO
YELLOW SEA
Tai'an
Jining
Xinxiang
Lianyungang
Tongchuan
Luoyang
Kaifeng
Grand Canal
Sanmenxia
ZHENGZHOU
HENAN
Shangqiu
Xuzhou
Qingjiang
Pingdingshan
Nanyang
Shangshui
Hongze Hu
JIANGSU
Bengbu
Zhumadian
Han Shui
Huainan
NANKING
(Nanjing)
Zhenjiang
Changzhou
Nantong
Xiangfan
Hefei
Wuxi
Suzhou
SHANGHAI
Dabie Shan
ANHUI
Wuhu
HUBEI
WUHAN
Tongling
Yichang
Anqing
Hangzhou
Hangzhou Wan
Shashi
Huangshi
Tunxi
Shaoxing
Ningbo
Jiujiang
ZHEJIANG
Changde
Dongting Hu
Poyang L.
Jingdezhen
Jinhua
Yiyang
Nanchang
Shangrao
HUNAN
Changsha
JIANGXI
Wuyi Shan
2120
Wenzhou
Xiangtan
Zhuzhou
Shaoyang
Jian
Nanping
Hengyang
Sanming
Fuzhou
Ganzhou
FUJIAN
Nan Ling
Quanzhou
Shaoguan
Zhangzhou
Xiamen
(Amoy)
Mei Xian
Chao'an
Wuzhou
GUANGDONG
CANTON
(Guangzhou)
Shantou
Foshan
Jiangmen
HONG KONG (Br.)
Macau
(Port.)
Maoming
Zhanjiang
Hainan Str.
Haikou
HAINAN
1879
EAST CHINA SEA
Amami-ō-Shima
Ryukyu Islands
Okinawa
Naha
Sakashima Gunto
Chilung
TAIPEI
Taichung
Formosa Strait
Chiai
Yu Shan
3997
TAIWAN
Tainan
KAOHSIUNG
Tropic of Cancer
PACIFIC OCEAN
Batan Is.
Babuyan Is.
SOUTH CHINA SEA
COPYRIGHT GEORGE PHILIP & SON LTD
1:15 000 000
100 0 100 200 300 400 500 600 km

SEA OF JAPAN
PACIFIC OCEAN
Sea of Okhotsk
CHINA
NORTH KOREA
SOUTH KOREA
HOKKAIDO
HONSHU
SHIKOKU
KYUSHU
Lake Khanka
Mudanjiang
Spassk-Dalni
Dalnegorsk
Sikhote Alin
Ussuriysk
Yanji
Vladivostok
Nakhodka
Petra Velikogo Bay
Chongjin
Tanchon
Ullung Do
Samchok
Pusan
Korea Strait
Tsushima
Tsushima Strait
Iki
Rebun
Rishiri
Wakkanai
Teshio
Otoineppu
Monbetsu
Nemuro Str.
Rumoi
Shibetsu
Kitami
Abashiri
Daisetsu 2290
Asahigawa
Nemuro
Otaru Bay
C. Kamui
Otaru
Iwamisawa
Obihiro
Kushiro
Sapporo
Tomakomai
2052
Setana
Uchiura Bay
Muroran
Mombetsu
Urakawa
Okushiri
Esashi
Hakodate
C. Yesan
C. Erimo
Matsumae
Tsugaru Strait
C. Shiriya
Mutsu
Aomori
Hirosaki
Hachinohe
Odate
Noshiro
C. Oga
Iwate 2041
Akita
Morioka
Miyako
Omono
Hanamaki
Kitakami
Ichinoseki
Sakata
Tsuruoka
Mogami
Ishinomaki
Yamagata
Sendai
Sado
Niigata
Shibata
Yonezawa
Agano
Fukushima
Bandai 1819
C. Suzu
Nagaoka
Aizuwakamatsu
Koriyama
Tajima
Toyama Bay
Takada
Iwaki
Nanao
Nikko
Takaoka
Toyama
Nagano
Hitachi
Kanazawa
Shinano
Maebashi
Kiryu
Utsunomiya
Matsumoto
Ueda
Tochigi
Mito
Takasaki
Oki Is.
Fukui
Takayama
Omiya
Tsuchiura
Ontake 3063
Kawagoe
Tone
Kawaguchi
Ichikawa
Choshi
C. Kyo
Wakasa Bay
Tsuruga
Tenryu
Kofu
Tokyo
Kawasaki
C. Hino
Matsue
Tottori
Maizuru
Kiso
Yokohama
Chiba
Izumo
Yonago
Biwa
Gifu
Fuji-San 3776
Yokosuka
Tsuyama
Ichinomiya
Fujisawa
Hamada
Himeji
Amagasaki
Kyoto
Otsu
Nagoya
Numazu
Okazaki
Shimizu
Masuda
Okayama
Kurashiki
Kobe
Yokkaichi
Shizuoka
Ito
Tateyama
Fukuyama
Akashi
Osaka
Tsu
Hamamatsu
O-Shima
Hiroshima
Hagi
Sakai
Nara
Toyohashi
Ise-Wan
Kure
Shimonoseki
Tokuyama
Takamatsu
Kishiwada
Wakayama
Ube
Inland Sea
Tokushima
Kii Channel
Suo Bay
Niihama
Fukuoka
Kitakyushu
Matsuyama
Kurume
Shingu
Sasebo
Omuta
Beppu
Yawatahama
Kochi
C. Shio
Kuju 1787
Oita
Uwajima
C. Muroto
Nagasaki
Fukue
Kumamoto
Bungo Channel
C. Ashizuri
Hachijo
Yatsushiro
Amakusa
Nobeoka
Aoga
Sendai
Miyazaki
Kagoshima
Miyakonojo
Kanoya
Osumi Channel
Osumi Islands
Tanega
Kuchinoerabu-Jima
Yaku
Tokara Channel
Nakano
Suwanose
Tokara Ch.
Yaku
Nakano
Suwanose
Ryukyu Islands
Okinawa-Shoto
Amami
Tokuno
Okinoerabu
Okinawa
Kerama
Naha
PACIFIC OCEAN
7507
Miyako
Yaeyama
Ishigaki
Iriomote
RYUKYU ISLANDS
Continuation southwards in same scale
m
1500
1000
400
200
0
200
m
Projection: Bonne
East from Greenwich
COPYRIGHT GEORGE PHILIP & SON LTD
1:7 500 000
50 0 50 100 150 200 250 300 km

PHILIPPINES
LUZON
MANILA
Quezon City
Mindanao
SULU SEA
CELEBES SEA
MOLUCCA SEA
BANDA SEA
FLORES SEA
CERAM SEA
SOUTH CHINA SEA
M A L A Y S I A
PENINSULAR MALAYSIA
SARAWAK
SABAH (NORTH BORNEO)
B O R N E O
K A L I M A N T A N
SULAWESI (CELEBES)
Halmahera
Moluccas
I N D O N E S I A
SUMATRA
J A V A
JAKARTA
SURABAYA
BANDUNG
Lesser Sunda Islands
Timor
Flores
Sumba
Bali
Lombok
Sumbawa
JAVA SEA
Greater Sunda Islands
SINGAPORE
THAILAND (SIAM)
BANGKOK
CAMBODIA (KAMPUCHEA)
Phnom Penh
LAOS
VIETNAM
HO CHI MINH CITY (SAIGON)
Da Nang
BURMA
Gulf of Thailand
Strait of Malacca
Makasar Str.
Karimata Str.
INDIAN OCEAN
Palawan
Mindoro
Panay
Samar
Leyte
Cebu
Negros
Kuching
Pontianak
Banjarmasin
Balikpapan
Samarinda
Kota Kinabalu
Bandar Seri Begawan
Medan
Padang
Palembang
Kuala Lumpur
Ipoh
George Town
Kuantan
Manado
Ujung Pandang
Kendari
Ambon
Kupang
Denpasar
Semarang
Yogyakarta
Malang
Bogor
Teluk Betung
Bengkulu
Siberut
Nias
Simeulue
Bangka
Belitung Is.
Natuna Is.
Anambas Is.
Spratly I.
Paracel Islands
1:15 000 000
100 0 100 200 300 400 500 600 km
Projection: Mercator
East from Greenwich
COPYRIGHT GEORGE PHILIP & SON, LTD

PACIFIC OCEAN

ALASKA
Bristol Bay
Gulf of Alaska
Prince of Wales I.
Prince Rupert
Queen Charlotte Is.
Juneau
6050
Kitimat
CANADA
NORTH AMERICA
Rocky Mountains
Edmonton
Calgary
Regina
Winnipeg
L. Winnipeg
Hudson Bay
Labrador
GREENLAND
C. Farewell
NORTH
Newfoundland
St. Lawrence
Quebec
Montréal
Pr. Edward I.
Saint John
Ottawa
Toronto
L. Huron
L. Superior
Michigan
L. Ontario
L. Erie
Buffalo
Boston
C. Sable
NEW YORK
Philadelphia
Baltimore
Washington
Pittsburgh
Detroit
Cincinnati
Vancouver
Vancouver I.
Victoria
Seattle
Portland
Missouri
Minneapolis
CHICAGO
Boise
Snake
Salt Lake City
Denver
Kansas
St. Louis
C. Mendocino
San Francisco
4418
Colorado
UNITED STATES
Oklahoma
Memphis
Appalachian Mts.
Mississippi
Atlanta
ATLANTIC
C. Hatteras
Los Angeles
San Diego
Dallas
Jacksonville
Bermuda (U.K.)
Ciudad Juarez
Houston
New Orleans
San Antonio
6741
6225
Sierra Madre
Gulf of California
MEXICO
Monterrey
Gulf of Mexico
Miami
Florida Strait
BAHAMAS
OCEAN
Hawaiian Is. (U.S.)
Ridge
Honolulu
Oahu
Hawaii
Tropic of Cancer
Havana
CUBA
Yucatan Channel
Mérida
West Indies
Hispaniola
DOM. REP.
9200
HAITI
7680
JAMAICA
Kingston
PUERTO RICO
Leeward Is.
Revilla Gigedo Is. (Mexico)
Guadalajara
México
Puebla
5700
Acapulco
BELIZE
ston I. (U.S.)
IFIC
Caribbean Sea
HONDURAS
GUATEMALA
Guatemala
Salvador
EL SALVADOR
NICARAGUA
Managua
CENTRAL AMERICA
San José
COSTA RICA
PANAMA
Colón
Panama
Canal
Barranquilla
Maracaibo
Caracas
Orinoco
VENEZUELA
BARBADOS
Windward Is.
TRINIDAD & TOBAGO
Clipperton I. (Fr.)
Christmas Island Ridge
Palmyra Is. (U.S.)
Teraina
Tabuaeran
Kiritimati
Jarvis I. (U.S.)
EAN
Equator
Cocos I.
Medellín
Bogota
Cali
COLOMBIA
Quito
ECUADOR
Galápagos (Ecuador)
Guayaquil
Manaus
Amazon
Iquitos
C. Pariñas
BRAZIL
SOUTH
AMERICA
Malden I.
Starbuck I.
nix Is.
Marquesas Is.
Tongareva
Penrhyn Is.
Manihiki
Vostok I.
Caroline I.
Flint I.
Suwarrow Is.
East Pacific Ridge
Trujillo
PERU
Lima
6369
Cuzco
L. Titicaca
Illampu & Ancohuma
6550
La Paz
BOLIVIA
Arequipa
6866
Peru-Chile Trench
Leeward Is.
Society Is.
Tuamotu Archipelago
Cook Islands (N.Z.)
Windward Is.
Tahiti
FRENCH POLYNESIA
Manuae
Austral
Tuamotu Ridge
Rarotonga
Iquique
Chile
8050
Antofagasta
PARAGUAY
Tropic of Capricorn
Pitcairn I. (U.K.)
Ducie I (U.K.)
Tubuai Is. (Austral Is.)
Seamount Chain
Rapa Iti
Sala-y-Gomez (Chile)
Easter Is. (Chile)
San Félix (Chile)
San Ambrosio (Chile)
Asunción
Tucumán
Pto. Alegre
Andes
Arch. de Juan Fernández (Chile)
6860
Córdoba
Rosario
URUGUAY
Valparaíso
Santiago
Buenos Aires
Montevideo
Río de la Plata
Pacific-Antarctic Ridge
Chile Rise
Concepción
ARGENTINA
Patagonia
SOUTH
ATLANTIC
OCEAN
Chonos Arch.
G. of Penas
6212
Falkland Is. (U.K.)
Punta Arenas
Str. of Magellan
Tierra del Fuego
C. Horn
South Georgia
West from Greenwich
COPYRIGHT. GEORGE PHILIP & SON. LTD.

1:54 000 000

Java Trench
6389
TIMOR SEA
Ashmore Reef
Scott Reef
Bonaparte Archipelago
Rowley Shoals
INDIAN OCEAN
Croker
Coboure Pen.
Melville I.
Bathurst I.
Van Diemen Gulf
Clarence Str.
P. Darwin
Darwin
Crocodile Is.
Arnhem
Arnhem Land
Rum Jungle
Anson B.
Batchelor
Daly
Katherine
Roper
Mataranka
Birdum
C. Londonderry
C. Bougainville
Admiralty G.
Cambridge G.
Joseph Bonaparte Gulf
Drysdale
Wyndham
Kununurra
Victoria
Mt. Hann
776
Collier B.
King Sd.
C. Levêque
Lacepede Is.
Kimberley
L. Argyle
Ord
Durack Range
King Leopold Ras.
Mt. Ord
1007
Derby
Broome
Roebuck B.
Fitzroy
Fitzroy Crossing
Hall's Creek
Gordon Downs
Wave Hill
Newcastle Waters
L. Woods
Barkly
Tanami Desert
Tennant Creek
Sturt
NORTHERN TERRITORY
Gregory Lake
Hordern Hills
Murchison Ra.
Davenport Ra.
Eighty Mile Beach
P. Hedland
Mount Goldsworthy
De Grey
Great Sandy Desert
Dampier Archipelago
Karratha
C. Dampier
Roebourne
Barrow I.
Marble Bar
Pilbara
Throssell Ra.
L. Dora
Mt. Singleton
808
Sandover
Reynolds Ra.
998
Nullagine
L. Mackay
Mt. Ziel
1510
Macdonnell Ras.
Alice Springs
L. Macdonald
N.W. Cape
Exmouth
Learmonth
Exmouth G.
Onslow
Fortescue
Hamersley Ra.
Mt. Bruce
1235
Tom Price
Ophthalmia Ra.
Robertson Ra.
L. Disappointment
James Ra.
Hugh
Finke
Palmer
Ashburton
Paraburdoo
Mount Whaleback
Newman
Gibson Desert
Rawlinson Ra.
L. Amadeus
Mt. Olga
1069
Ayers Rock
868
WESTERN AUSTRALIA
L. McLeod
Lyons
Mt. Augustus
1105
Blackstone Ra.
Musgrave Ranges
1549
Mt. Woodroffe
Hamilton
Alberga
Geographe Chan.
Carnarvon
Gascoyne
Wooramel
Robinson Ra.
Peak Hill
L. Carnegie
L. Wells
661
Everard Ras.
Oodnadatta
Shark B.
Denham
Dirk Hartog
Wiluna
Meekatharra
Murchison
L. Yeo
Warrina
L. Austin
Sandstone
Great Victoria Desert
Laverton
Coober Pedy
Stuart
Tallering Peak
453
Mt. Magnet
Leonora
L. Carey
L. Minigwal
SOUTH AUSTRALIA
Houtman Abrolhos
Northampton
Mullewa
L. Barlee
L. Ballard
Menzies
Ooldea
Tarcoola
Geraldton
L. Monger
L. Moore
Dongara
Darling Range
Bonnie Rock
Kanowna
Kalgoorlie-Boulder
Rawlinna
Deakin
Nullarbor Plain
L. Everard
Bencubbin
Coolgardie
L. Lefroy
Hampton Tableland
Penong
Ceduna
L. Gairdner
Nukey
Southern Cross
L. Cowan
Eyre
Head of Bight
C. Adieu
Swan
Northam
Kellerberrin
The Johnston Lakes
Norseman
L. Dundas
Nuyts Archipelago
Streaky B.
Perth
Fremantle
Kwinana
York
Great Australian Bight
Anxious B.
Eyre Pen.
Pinjarra
Narrogin
Esperance
C. Pasley
Coffin B. Penin.
Port Lincoln
Bunbury
Collie
Wagin
Archipelago of the Recherche
Geographe B.
Katanning
Busselton
Bridgetown
Stirling Ra.
Augusta
Manjimup
Mt Barker
C. Knob
C. Leeuwin
Albany
Flinders B.
m
2000
1500
1000
400
200
0
200
2000
4000
6000
m
115
120
125
130
135
15
20
25
30
35
Projection: Bonne
East from Greenwich

AUSTRALASIA POLITICAL
1:80 000 000
INDONESIA
IRIAN JAYA
PAPUA NEW GUINEA
INDIAN OCEAN
WESTERN AUSTRALIA
NORTHERN TERRITORY
QUEENSLAND
SOUTH AUSTRALIA
NEW SOUTH WALES
VICTORIA
TASMANIA
AUSTRALIA
Darwin
Perth
Adelaide
Melbourne
Canberra
Sydney
Brisbane
Rockhampton
Townsville
Cairns
Hobart
Newcastle
Alice Springs
Mt. Isa
Broken Hill
Geraldton
Great Australian Bight
Arafura Sea
Timor Sea
Coral Sea
Tasman Sea
PACIFIC OCEAN
Tropic of Capricorn
Vanuatu
Fiji
Suva
Nouvelle Calédonie
Nouméa
Auckland
Wellington
Christchurch
Dunedin
NEW ZEALAND
International Date Line
Gulf of Carpentaria
Groote Eylandt
Wessel Is.
C. Arnhem
Nhulunbuy
Edward Pellew Group
Mornington I.
Wellesley Is.
Bentinck I.
Prince of Wales I.
Banks I.
C. York
Endeavour Str.
Shelburne B.
C. Grenville
Cape York Peninsula
Albatross B.
Weipa
Coen
Coleman
Princess Charlotte B.
C. Melville
Osprey Rf.
C. Flattery
Cooktown
Laura
Normanby
Mitchell
Gilbert
Mossman
Chillagoe
Mareeba
Cairns
Atherton
Bartle Frere
Innisfail
Normanton
Burketown
Croydon
Forsayth
Gregory Ra.
Norman
Flinders
Leichhardt
Camooweal
Kajabbi
Mount Isa
Mary Kathleen
Cloncurry
Richmond
Selwyn Range
Georgina
Dajarra
Hughenden
Winton
Great Barrier Reef
Hinchinbrook I.
Ingham
Palm Is.
Halifax B.
Townsville
C. Cleveland
Home Hill
Bowen
Charters Towers
Proserpine
Whitsunday I.
Collinsville
Mackay
Denham Ra.
Sarina
Broad Sd.
Belyando
Isaac
Peak Ra.
Clermont
Emerald
Great Dividing Range
QUEENSLAND
Longreach
Barcaldine
Alpha
Diamantina
Thomson
Bedourie
Eyre Cr.
Barcoo
Blackall
Yaraka
Windorah
Warrego Ra.
Drummond Ra.
Mackenzie
Mt. Morgan
Rockhampton
Yeppoon
Keppel B.
Gladstone
Biloela
Curtis I.
Dawson
Expedition Ra.
Townshend I.
Swain Rfs.
Saumarez Rf.
CORAL SEA ISLANDS TERRITORY
Lihou Reef & Cays
Îles Chesterfield
Kenn Reef
Bellona Rfs.
Bird I.
Cato I.
Tropic of Capricorn
Birdsville
L. Yamma Yamma
Cooper Creek
Warburton
Grey Range
Quilpie
Bulloo
Charleville
Mitchell
Roma
Maranoa
Balonne
Miles
Bundaberg
Hervey Bay
Sandy C.
Fraser I.
Maryborough
Gympie
Nambour
Kingaroy
Dalby
Moonie
Toowoomba
Ipswich
BRISBANE
Gold Coast
Warwick
Murwillumbah
Thargomindah
Cunnamulla
St. George
Dirranbandi
Goondiwindi
Macintyre
Gwydir
Moree
Lismore
Casino
Tenterfield
Clarence
Grafton
Glen Innes
Inverell
New England Range
Armidale
Coffs Harbour
Macleay
L. Eyre (North)
L. Eyre (South)
L. Gregory
L. Blanche
L. Frome
L. Torrens
Strzelecki Cr.
Tibooburra
Paroo
Warrego
Bourke
Barwon
Walgett
Narrabri
Bogan
Macquarie
Coonamble
Liverpool Plains
Gunnedah
Tamworth
Liverpool Ra.
Taree
Port Macquarie
Barrington Tops
Muswellbrook
Singleton
Cessnock
Maitland
Newcastle
Hawkesbury R.
SYDNEY
Port Jackson
Liverpool
Wollongong
Shellharbour
Jervis B.
Batemans B.
Tasman Sea
NEW SOUTH WALES
Broken Hill
Barrier Ra.
Wilcannia
Darling
Menindee
Cobar
Nyngan
Narromine
Dubbo
Mudgee
Orange
Bathurst
Lithgow
Penrith
Condobolin
Parkes
Forbes
Hillston
Lachlan
Griffith
Hay
Murrumbidgee
Cowra
Young
Cootamundra
Junee
Bowral
Goulburn
Canberra
Queanbeyan
Tumut
Leeton
Wagga Wagga
Riverina
Deniliquin
Albury
Hume
Murray
Mildura
Wentworth
Renmark
Balranald
Ouyen
Swan Hill
Kerang
Flinders Ranges
St. Mary Pk.
Leigh Creek
Quorn
Port Augusta
Peterborough
Jamestown
Burra
Port Pirie
Kadina
Yorke Penin.
G. St. Vincent
Adelaide
Elizabeth
Murray Bridge
Victor Harbor
Encounter B.
Kingston S.E.
Naracoorte
Bordertown
Horsham
Wimmera
Stawell
Ararat
Hamilton
Millicent
Mt. Gambier
Discovery B.
C. Bridgewater
Portland
Warrnambool
C. Otway
Colac
Geelong
Ballarat
Port Phillip B.
MELBOURNE
Maryborough
Castlemaine
Bendigo
Shepparton
Benalla
Wangaratta
Mt. Bogong
Australian Alps
Mt. Kosciusko
Cooma
Bega
Bombala
Snowy
Gippsland
Moe
Sale
Morwell
Ninety Mile Beach
Pt. Hicks
C. Howe
VICTORIA
CAP. TERR.
Bass Strait
King I.
Flinders I.
Furneaux Group
C. Grim
Devonport
Burnie
Ulverstone
Scottsdale
Launceston
Ben Lomond
Mt. Ossa
Queenstown
Macquarie Harb.
New Norfolk
Hobart
Glenorchy
Tasman Penin.
Storm B.
Bruny I.
S.E. Cape
TASMANIA
on same scale
COPYRIGHT GEORGE PHILIP & SON, LTD
1:12 000 000
100 0 100 200 300 400 500 km

AUSTRALIA AND NEW ZEALAND: *climate and natural vegetation*

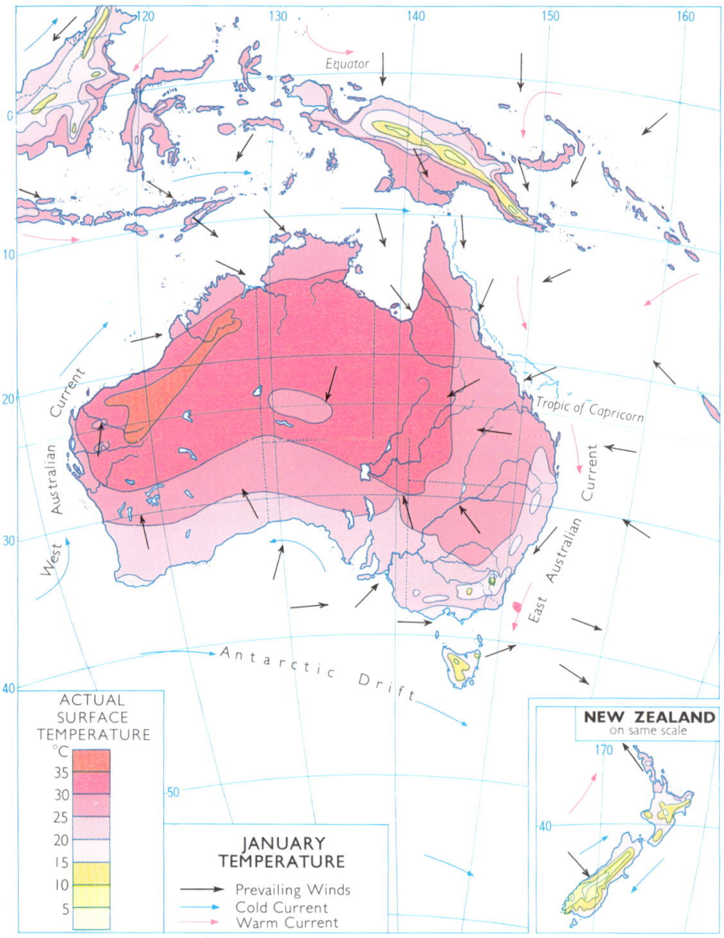

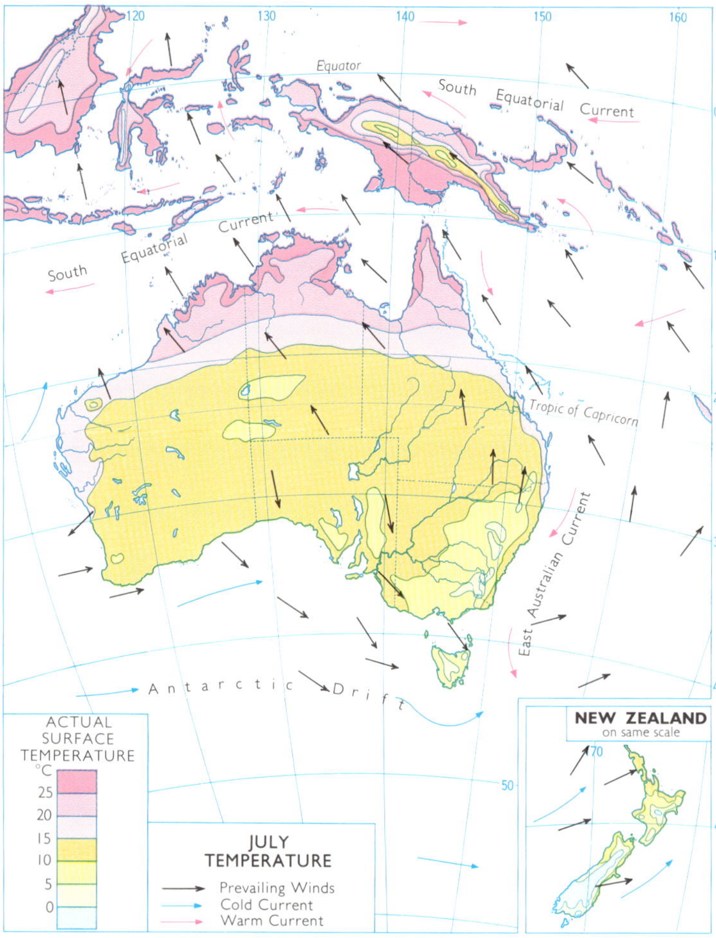

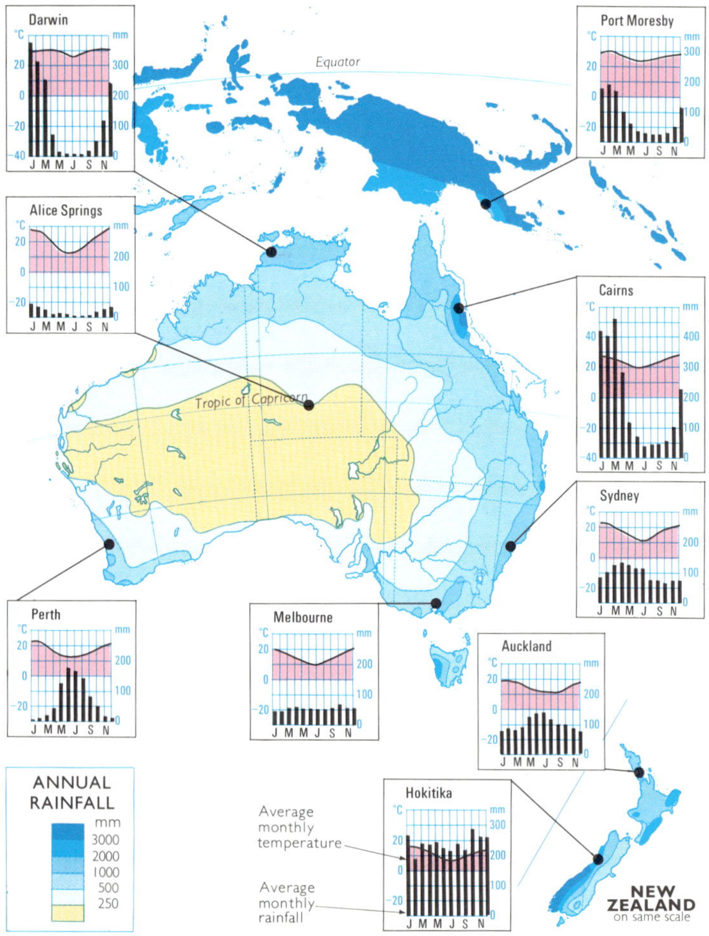

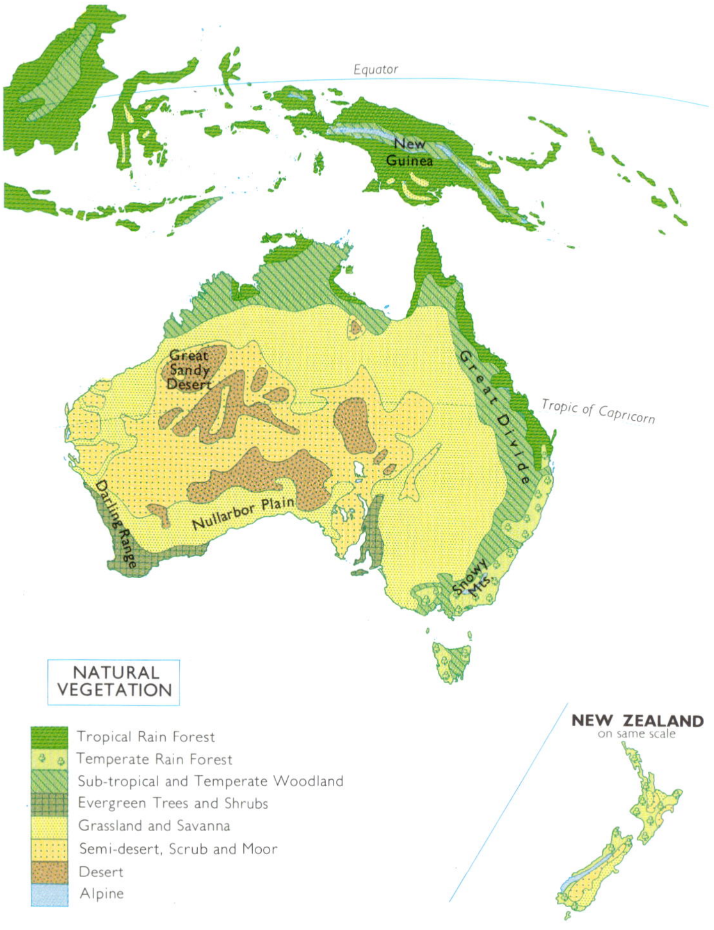

1:60 000 000

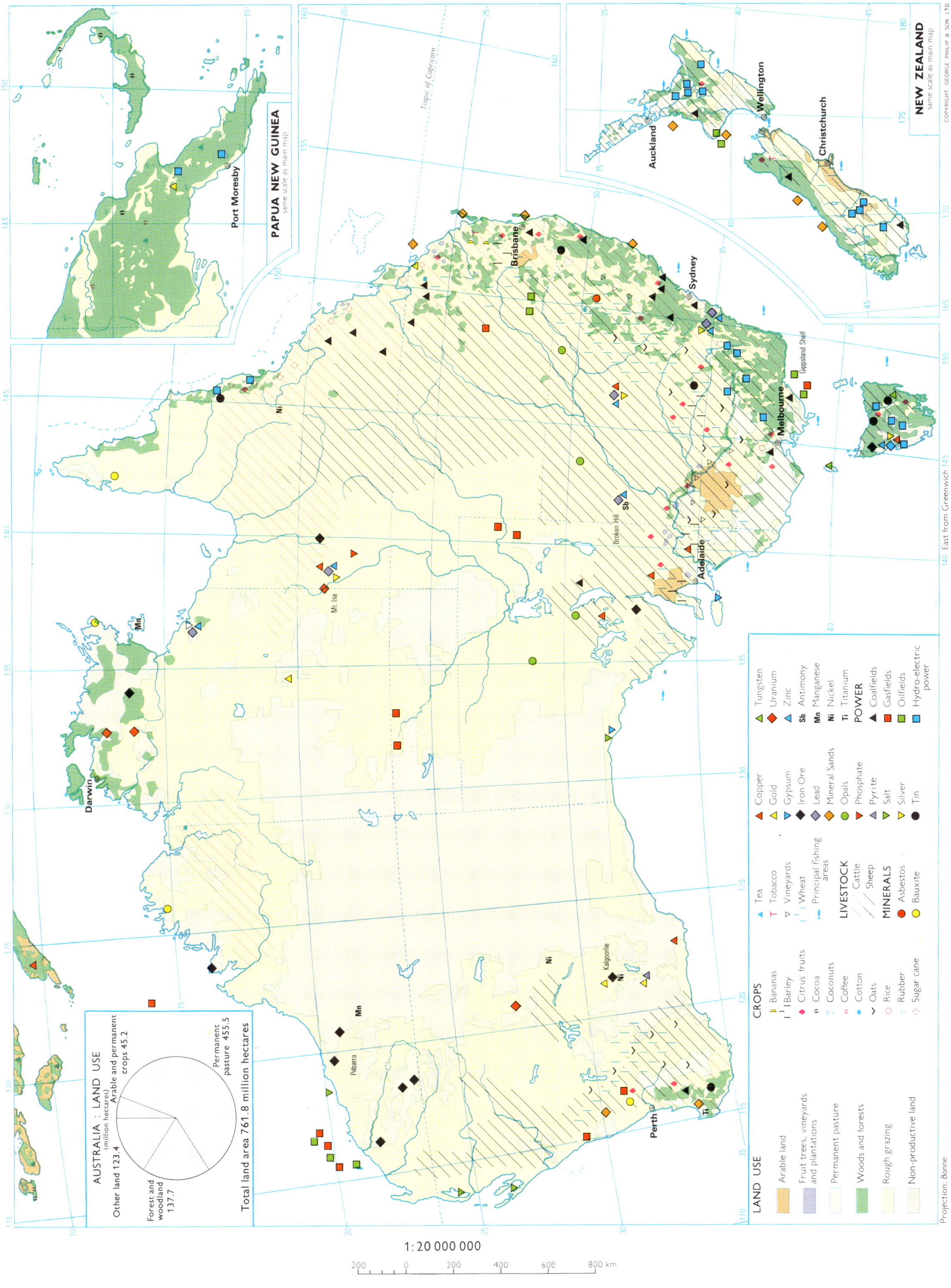

PAPUA NEW GUINEA
same scale as main map
Port Moresby
NEW ZEALAND
same scale as main map
Auckland
Wellington
Christchurch
COPYRIGHT GEORGE PHILIP & SON, LTD
Darwin
Brisbane
Sydney
Melbourne
Adelaide
Perth
Broken Hill
Mt. Isa
Kalgoorlie
Pilbarra
Gippsland Shelf
Tropic of Capricorn
East from Greenwich
AUSTRALIA : LAND USE
(million hectares)
Arable and permanent crops 45.2
Permanent pasture 455.5
Forest and woodland 137.7
Other land 123.4
Total land area 761.8 million hectares
LAND USE
Arable land
Fruit trees, vineyards and plantations
Permanent pasture
Woods and forests
Rough grazing
Non-productive land
CROPS
Bananas
Barley
Citrus fruits
Cocoa
Coconuts
Coffee
Cotton
Oats
Rice
Rubber
Sugar cane
Tea
Tobacco
Vineyards
Wheat
Principal fishing areas
LIVESTOCK
Cattle
Sheep
MINERALS
Asbestos
Bauxite
Copper
Gold
Gypsum
Iron Ore
Lead
Mineral Sands
Opals
Phosphate
Pyrite
Salt
Silver
Tin
Tungsten
Uranium
Zinc
Sb Antimony
Mn Manganese
Ni Nickel
Ti Titanium
POWER
Coalfields
Gasfields
Oilfields
Hydro-electric power
Projection: Bonne
1:20 000 000
200 0 200 400 600 800 km

SOUTH-EAST AUSTRALIA

1:4 500 000

25 0 25 50 75 100 125 150 175 200 km

m 2000 1500 1000 400 200 0

0 200 2000 4000 m

Projection: Albers' Equal Area with two standard parallels

NEW ZEALAND & DEPENDENCIES
1:60 000 000
0 500 1000 1500 km
New Zealand Territory
Self-governing Territory
Tokelau or Union Group
WESTERN SAMOA
Savaii
Upolu
AMERICAN SAMOA
Pukapuka (Danger)
Rakahanga
Manihiki
Tongareva (Penrhyn) I.
Nassau
Suwarrow
Northern Group
Cook Is.
Îles de la Société
Palmerston Atoll
Aitutaki
Lower Group
Mitiaro
Atiu
Mauke
Rarotonga
Mangaia
Niue
Rotuma (Fiji)
Vanua Levu
FIJI
Viti Levu
Fiji Is.
Lau or Eastern Group
TONGA (Friendly Is.)
Tropic of Capricorn
PACIFIC OCEAN
Raoul (Sunday) I.
Macauley
Curtis
Kermadec Is.
Three Kings Is.
Auckland
NORTH I.
Cook Strait
NEW ZEALAND
Wellington
Christchurch
SOUTH I.
Dunedin
Chatham Is.
Bounty Is.
Tasman Sea
Stewart I.
Snares
Antipodes Is.
Campbell I.
Auckland Is.
Macquarie I. (Austr.)
SOUTHERN OCEAN
Three Kings Is.
North C.
C. Maria van Diemen
Houhora
Doubtless Bay
Mangonui
Kaitaia
Opua
C. Brett
Rawene
Kaikohe
Hikurangi
NORTHLAND
Whangarei
Dargaville
Waipu
Bream Hd.
Gt. Barrier I.
Kaipara Harb.
C. Colville
Hauraki Gulf
Helensville
Coromandel
Takapuna
Devonport
CENTRAL AUCKLAND
AUCKLAND
Onehunga
Manukau
Thames
Pukekohe
NORTH ISLAND
Waiuku
Waikato
Paeroa
Waihi
Te Aroha
Huntly
Mt. Maunganui
Bay of Plenty
C. Runaway
Raglan
Tauranga
Cambridge
Hamilton
SOUTH AUCKLAND
BAY OF PLENTY
Whakatane
Opotiki
East C.
Hikurangi 1754
Raukumara Ra.
Te Awamutu
Putaruru
Rotorua
L. Rotorua
Kawerau
Tokoroa
Murupara
Te Kuiti
EAST COAST
North Taranaki Bight
Waitara
New Plymouth
L. Taupo
Taupo
Taumarunui
Gisborne
TARANAKI
Inglewood
Mt. Egmont 2518
C. Egmont
Opunake
Stratford
Eltham
Ruapehu 2797
Raetihi
Ohakune
Waiouru
Kaimanawa
Mahia Peninsula
Wairoa
Hawke Bay
Napier
Hastings
C. Kidnappers
HAWKE'S BAY
Ruahine Ra.
Hawera
Patea
South Taranaki Bight
Taihape
Wanganui
Marton
Feilding
Waipawa
Waipukurau
Dannevirke
Palmerston N.
Foxton
Woodville
Pahiatua
Levin
Otaki
Tararua Ra.
WELLINGTON
Masterton
Carterton
Martinborough
Wairarapa
Porirua
Up. Hutt
Lr. Hutt
Eastbourne
WELLINGTON
PACIFIC OCEAN
C. Farewell
Golden Bay
D'Urville I.
Collingwood
Takaka
Tasman Bay
Tasman Mts.
Motueka
Nelson
Richmond
Karamea Bight
Picton
Blenheim
Cook Strait
TASMAN SEA
Westport
Lyell Ra.
MARLBOROUGH
Rotoroa
Tapuaenuku 2885
Mt. Travers 2338
Reefton
Spenser Mts.
Kaikoura Ra.
Clarence
Kaikoura
Runanga
Greymouth
L. Brunner
Waiau
Hokitika
CANTERBURY
Hurunui
Waipara
Arthur's Pass
Pegasus Bay
Oxford
Rangiora
Colerige
Waimakariri
New Brighton
Christchurch
Riccarton
Lyttelton
Banks Peninsula
Akaroa
Westland Bight
SOUTH ISLAND
Westland
Mt. Cook 3764
Southern Alps
Methven
Canterbury Plains
L. Ellesmere
Ashburton
Rakaia
Tekapo
Fairlie
Pukaki
Rangitata
Temuka
Timaru
Canterbury Bight
Mt. Aspiring 3027
L. Wanaka
L. Hawea
Ohau
Milford Sd.
Mt. Earnslaw 2819
Wanaka
Dunstan Mts.
Waitaki
Kurow
Waimate
Queenstown
Cromwell
Alexandra
Kakanui Mts.
Oamaru
Secretary I.
Doubtful Sd.
Wakatipu
Kingston
L. Te Anau
L. Manapouri
Eyre Mts.
Garvie Mts.
OTAGO
Roxburgh
Palmerston
Port Chalmers
Dunedin
Mosgiel
C. Saunders
Resolution I.
Mossburn
Clutha
SOUTHLAND
Kelso
St. Kilda
Winton
Gore
Mataura
Milton
Balclutha
Tuatapere
Nugget Pt.
Riverton
Invercargill
Bluff
Foveaux Str.
Ruapuke I.
Oban
Stewart I.
Port Pegasus
S.W. Cape
Projection: Conical with two standard parallels
1:6 000 000
50 0 50 100 150 200 250 km
SAMOA ISLANDS
1:12 000 000
WESTERN SAMOA
Savai'i
Apia
Upolu
AMERICAN SAMOA
Pago Pago
Tutuila
Manua Is.
Rose I.
Futuna (Fr.)
Niuafo'ou (Tonga)
Thikombia
Lambasa
Vanua Levu
FIJI
Taveuni
Vanua Balavu
Yasawa Group
Koro
Fiji Is.
Lautoka
Nandi
Viti Levu 1323
Levuka
Ovalau
Suva
Gau
Koro Sea
Lakemba
Lau or Eastern Group
Moala
Kandavu
Vatoa
Vava'u
TONGA
Tonga (Friendly) Is.
Tofua I.
Ha'apai Group
Nuku'alofa
Tongatapu
FIJI AND TONGA ISLANDS
1:12 000 000
100 0 100 200 300 km
m
4000
3000
2000
1000
400
200
0
200
m
COPYRIGHT. GEORGE PHILIP & SON. LTD.

AFRICA: *physical*

Projection: *Zenithal Equidistant*

West from Greenwich | East from Greenwich

1: 40 000 000

400 0 400 800 1200 1600 km

UNITED KINGDOM
London
NETH.
BELG.
GERMANY
POLAND
Warsaw
Prague
CZECHOSLOVAKIA
Kiev
Volgograd
Paris
Vienna
AUSTRIA
HUNGARY
SWITZ.
FRANCE
Bay of Biscay
ATLANTIC
OCEAN
Aral Sea
Caspian Sea
ROMANIA
Odessa
YUGOSLAVIA
Adriatic Sea
ITALY
Corsica
Black Sea
BULGARIA
Istanbul
PORTUGAL
Madrid
SPAIN
Lisbon
Rome
ALB.
Baku
Ankara
Sardinia
GREECE
TURKEY
Mediterranean
Athens
Sicily
MALTA
Tunis
Algiers
Annaba
Constantine
Oran
Gibraltar (Br.)
Tetouan
Madeira (Port.)
Casablanca
Rabat
Fès
MOROCCO
Marrakesh
TUNISIA
Sfax
Chott Djerid
Tripoli
Misratah
Benghazi
Crete
CYPRUS
Aleppo
Mosul
Tehran
SYRIA
LEB.
Damascus
Baghdad
Esfahan
Euphrates
IRAN
Tigris
Tel Aviv-Jaffa
Jerusalem
ISRAEL
JORDAN
Syrian Desert
IRAQ
Alexandria
Port Said
Suez
Basra
KUWAIT
CAIRO
El Faiyum
Canary Is. (Sp.)
ALGERIA
Ghadames
Dra
El Aaiun
In Salah
LIBYA
EGYPT
Asyut
Nile
The Gulf
Bahrain
QATAR
WESTERN SAHARA
Dakhla
Marzuq
SAUDI
Riyadh
Medina
Tropic of Cancer
Al Jawf
Aswan
Red Sea
ARABIA
F'Dérik
Sahara
Mecca
Jedda
Wadi-Halfa
Ras Nouadhibou (Cap Blanc)
MAURITANIA
Nouakchott
Pt. Sudan
Tombouctou (Timbuktu)
Agades
Atbara
NIGER
CHAD
Kassala
Eritrea
Mesewa
Asmera
YEMEN
St. Louis
C. Vert
Dakar
Senegal
SENEGAL
GAMBIA
Banjul
GUINEA-BISSAU
Bissau
MALI
Niger
Niamey
Omdurman
Khartoum
SUDAN
Wad Medani
El Fasher
El Obeid
Socotra (Yemen)
G. of Aden
Ras Asir (C. Guardafui)
BURKINA FASO
Ouagadougou
Bamako
Kano
L. Chad
Abéché
Ndjamena (Ft. Lamy)
Maiduguri
White Nile
Blue Nile
L. Tana
DJIBOUTI
Djibouti
Berbera
GUINEA
Bobo-Dioulasso
Kaduna
NIGERIA
Chari
Conakry
Freetown
SIERRA LEONE
BENIN
Abuja
Benue
Addis Ababa
Harer
Malakal
ETHIOPIA
LIBERIA
Monrovia
IVORY COAST
Bouake
Kumasi
GHANA
TOGO
Lomé
Ibadan
Lagos
Enugu
Wau
Bel Jebel
Shaballe
Abidjan
Accra
Porto-Novo
Port Harcourt
CAMEROON
CENTRAL AFRICAN REPUBLIC
Oubangi
SOMALI REP.
Sekondi-Takoradi
Bight of Benin
Bioko
Douala
Yaoundé
Bangui
L. Turkana
EQUATORIAL GUINEA
Rio Muni
Zaïre (Congo)
L. Mobutu Sese Seko
Mogadishu (Mogadiscio)
Gulf of Guinea
SAO TOMÉ & PRINCIPE
Libreville
Kisangani
UGANDA
Kampala
KENYA
Juba
Equator
C. Lopez
GABON
Mbandaka
L. Edward
L. Victoria
Kisumu
Nairobi
Kismayu
Annobon
CONGO
ZAÏRE
Lualaba
L. Kivu
Kigali
RWANDA
Mwanza
Tana
INDIAN
Bujumbura
BURUNDI
Brazzaville
Kinshasa
Kasai
Mombasa
Pointe Noire
CABINDA
Zaïre
Matadi
Kananga
TANZANIA
L. Tanganyika
Dodoma
Zanzibar
Dar-es-Salaam
Cuango
OCEAN
Ascension (Br.)
Luanda
L. Mweru
Aldabra Is.
Likasi
L. Nyasa (L. Malawi)
Ruvuma
C. Delgado
COMOROS
ANGOLA
Lubumbashi
MALAWI
Antsiranana
Lobito
Huambo
Ndola
Lilongwe
ZAMBIA
MOZAMBIQUE
Mozambique
Mahajanga
ATLANTIC
Namibe
Lusaka
Zambezi
Blantyre
Mozambique Channel
St. Helena (Br.)
Cunene
Cubango
Livingstone
Harare
C. Fria
ZIMBABWE
Toamasina
Beira
Antananarivo
MADAGASCAR
MAURITIUS
OCEAN
NAMIBIA
Windhoek
BOTSWANA
Bulawayo
Réunion (Fr.)
Fianarantsoa
Walvis Bay (South Africa)
Limpopo
Tropic of Capricorn
Gaborone
TRANSVAAL
Pretoria
Johannesburg
Mbabane
SWAZILAND
Maputo
Vaal
ORANGE FREE STATE
Orange
Kimberley
Bloemfontein
NATAL
Maseru
LESOTHO
SOUTH AFRICA
Durban
CAPE PROVINCE
East London
Cape Town
C. of Good Hope
C. Agulhas
Port Elizabeth
Nairobi Capital Cities
Projection: Zenithal Equidistant.
West from Greenwich
East from Greenwich
COPYRIGHT GEORGE PHILIP & SON LTD
1:40 000 000
400 0 400 800 1200 1600 km

AFRICA: *climate and natural vegetation*

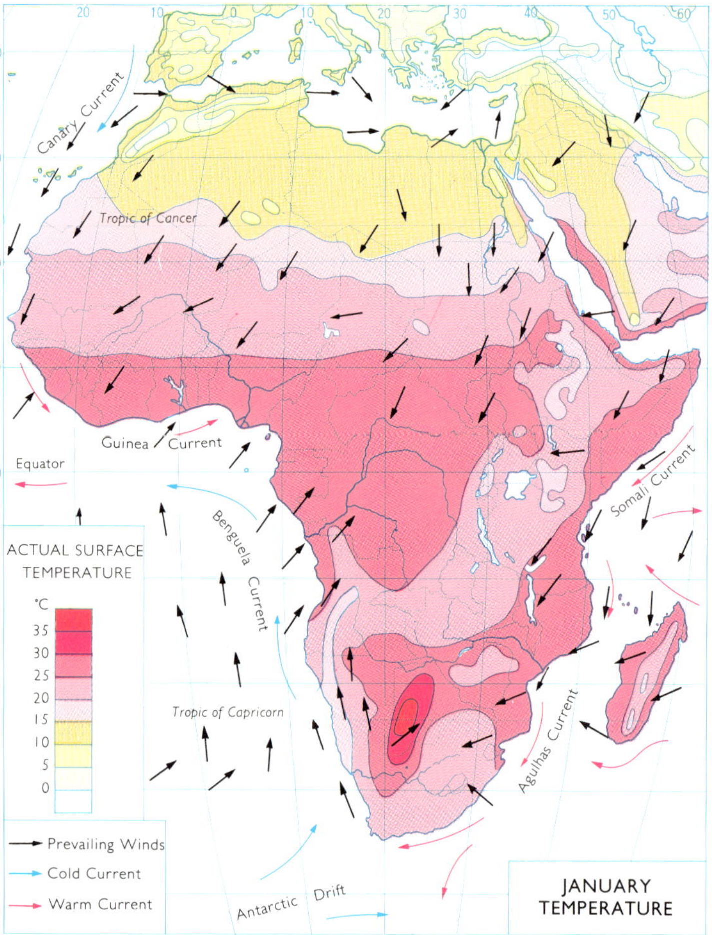

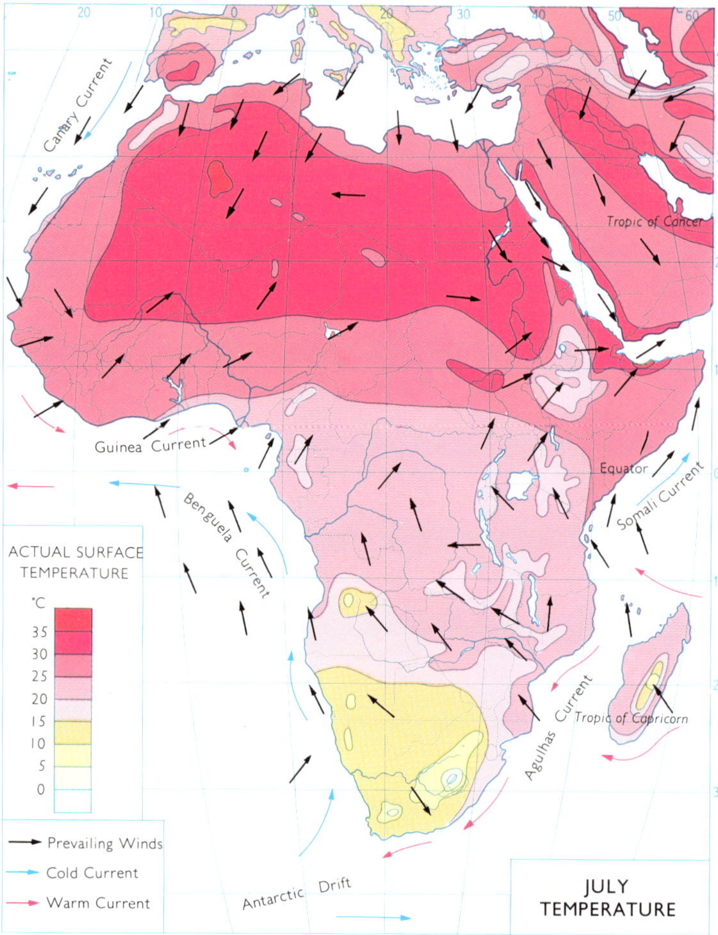

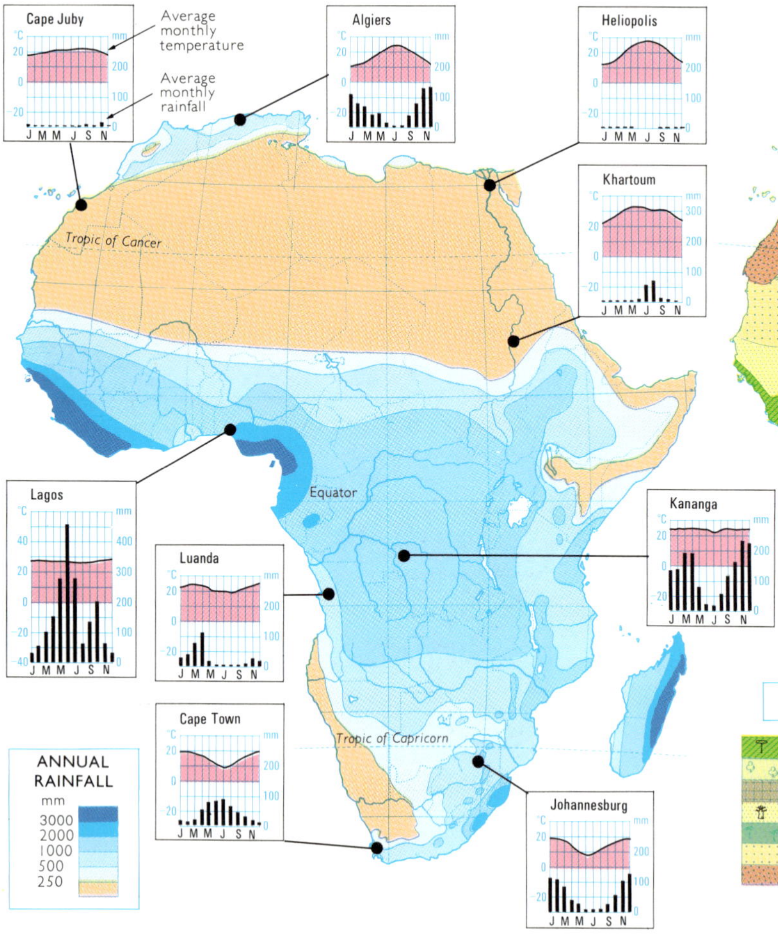

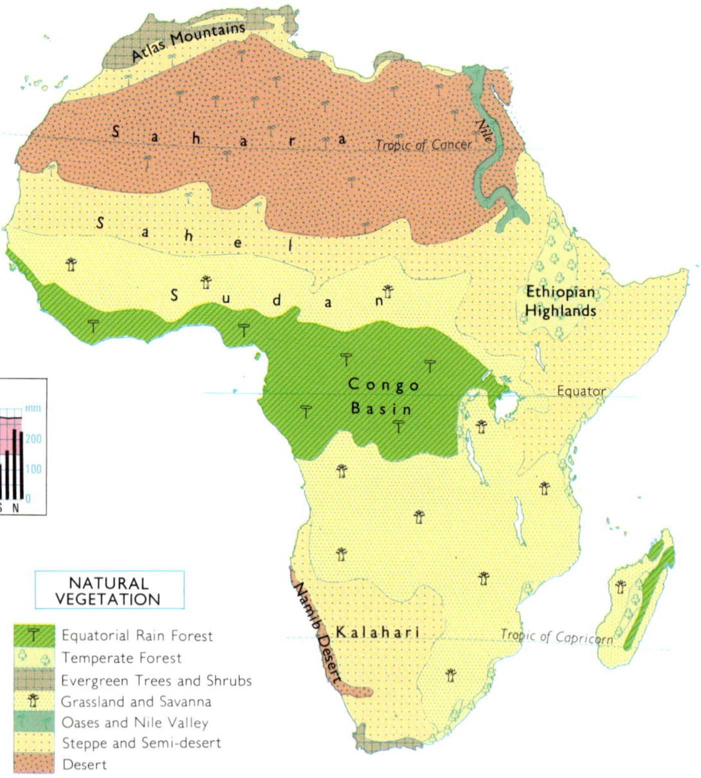

Projection: *Sanson-Flamsteed's Sinusoidal*

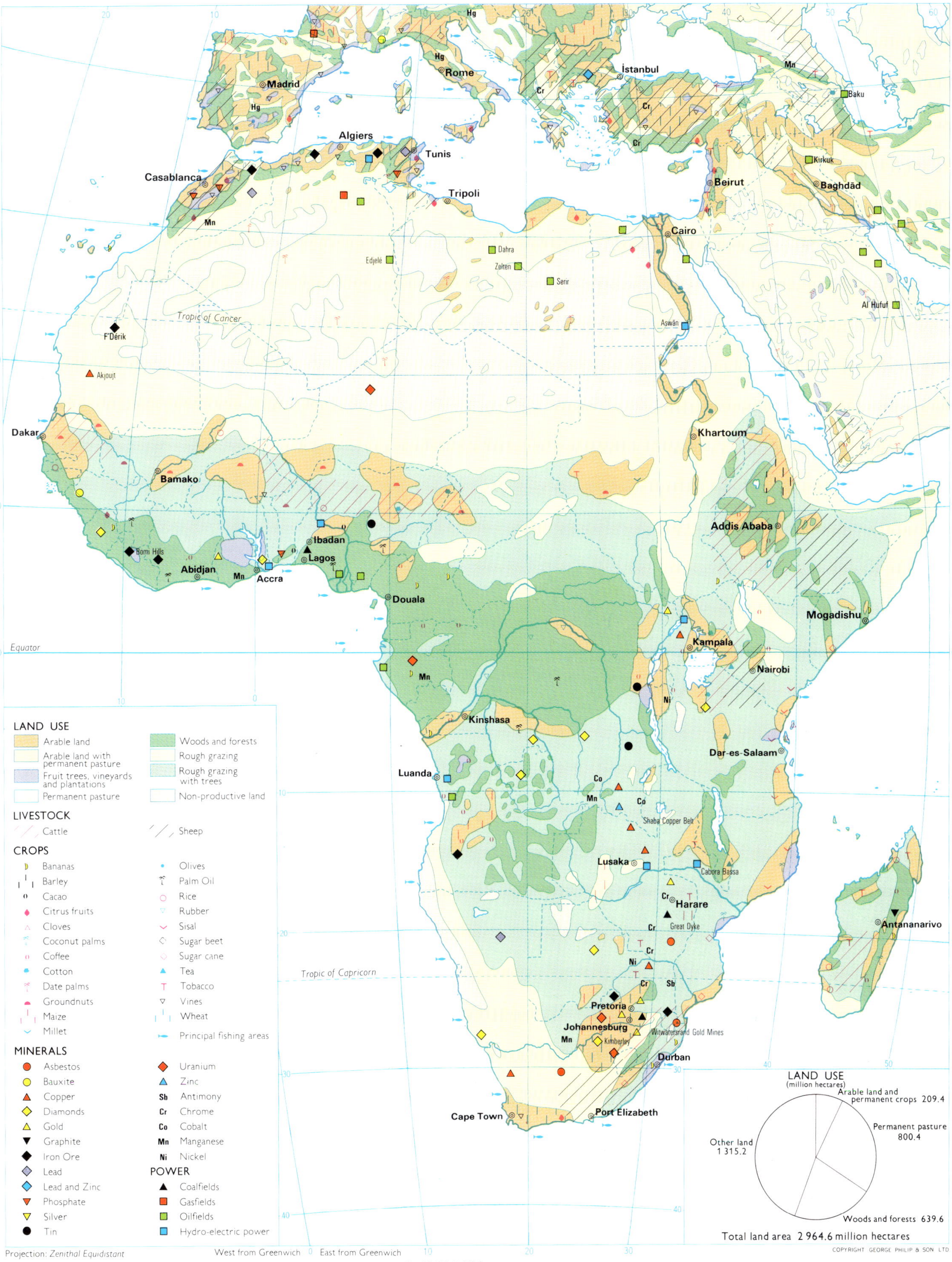

1: 40 000 000

400 0 400 800 1200 1600 km

	Population								Land			Agriculture		
	Total	Density	Birth Rate	Death Rate	Life Expectancy	Growth 1965-80	Growth 1980-88	Urban	Area	Arable	Forest	Agricultural Population	Index of Production	Food Intake
	th.	persons per km^2	per th. popn.	per th. popn.	yrs.	av. % per annum	av. % per annum	%	th. km^2	th. km^2	th. km^2	% of total popn.	1979-81 = 100	calories per day
Algeria	23805	10	40	9	63	3.1	3.1	44	2382	75	47	25	121	2715
Angola	9421	8	47	20	45	2.8	2.5	25	1247	36	531	71	104	1969
Benin	4454	40	51	19	51	2.7	3.2	39	111	18	36	64	143	2184
Botswana	1164	2	47	12	68	3.5	3.3	21	585	14	10	65	100	2201
Burkina Faso	8546	31	47	19	47	2	2.6	8	274	31	68	85	148	2139
Burundi	5149	198	46	17	49	1.9	2.9	7	26	13	0.7	92	128	2343
Cameroon	11213	24	42	16	57	2.7	3.2	46	469	70	249	64	118	2028
Central Africa	2794	4	44	20	48	1.8	2.5	45	623	20	358	66	101	1949
Chad	5399	4	44	20	46	2	2.4	30	1259	32	130	77	127	1717
Congo	2100	6	44	17	59	2.7	3.4	41	342	7	212	60	116	2619
Egypt	51447	52	41	9	61	2.4	2.7	48	995	26	0.03	42	148	3342
Ethiopia	46144	42	44	24	48	2.7	2.5	12	1101	139	451	76	108	1749
Gabon	1077	4	39	16	53	3.5	3.9	43	258	5	200	70	112	2521
Gambia	822	82	47	21	44	2.6	3.3	21	10	2	2	82	131	2251
Ghana	14040	61	44	13	54	2.2	3.5	32	230	29	83	52	142	1759
Guinea	6641	27	47	22	42	1.9	2.4	24	246	16	100	76	109	1777
Guinea-Bissau	940	34	41	20	40	1.4	1.9	27	28	3	11	80	155	2505
Ivory Coast	11587	36	51	14	53	4.2	4.2	44	318	36	64	59	131	2562
Kenya	23021	40	54	12	56	3.6	4.2	22	569	24	37	78	125	2060
Lesotho	1673	56	41	12	56	2.3	2.7	19	30	3	0	82	108	2303
Liberia	2401	25	45	13	55	3	3.3	42	96	4	21	71	120	2381
Libya	4249	2	38	9	61	4.6	4.3	67	1760	22	7	13	126	3601
Madagascar	11259	19	46	14	54	2.5	3.3	23	582	31	147	78	117	2440
Malawi	8155	87	49	25	46	2.9	3.8	13	94	24	43	78	108	2310
Mali	7989	7	47	20	47	2.1	2.4	19	1220		85	82	135	2074
Mauritania	1907	2	46	19	46	2.3	2.6	38	1030	2	150	66	112	2322
Morocco	23920	54	35	10	61	2.5	2.7	47	446	85	52	39	150	2915
Mozambique	14967	19	45	19	48	2.5	2.7	23	784	31	149	83	103	1595
Namibia	1262	2	44	12	57		3.2	51	823	7	184	37	126	2197
Niger	6998	6	51	21	45	2.7	3	18	1267	35	25	89	124	2432
Nigeria	110131	121	50	16	52	2.5	3.4	33	911	313	143	66	126	2146
Rwanda	6657	266	51	17	49	3.3	3.3	7	25	11	5	92	97	1830
Senegal	7154	37	46	19	48	2.5	2.9	37	192	52	59	79	127	2350
Sierra Leone	3938	55	48	23	42	2	2.4	26	72	18	21	65	108	1855
Somalia	5882	9	51	20	47	2.7	2.9	36	627	9	88	72	131	2135
South Africa	33938	28	32	10	61	2.4	2.3	57	1221	132	45	15	104	2924
Sudan	23776	10	45	16	50	3	3.1	21	2376	125	468	64	128	2208
Swaziland	737	43	47	13	56		3.4	26	17	2	1	69	127	2553
Tanzania	24739	28	51	14	53	3.3	3.5	29	886	52	424	82	116	2192
Togo	3362	62	45	14	53	3	3.4	24	54	14	14	71	111	2207
Tunisia	7796	50	28	7	66	2.1	2.5	54	155	47	6	27	110	2994
Uganda	16195	81	50	15	51	2.9	3.2	10	200	67	57	82	108	2344
Zaire	33615	15	46	14	53	2.8	3.1	38	2268	67	1753	68	120	2164
Zambia	7486	10	51	14	54	3.1	3.6	53	741	52	292	70	126	2137
Zimbabwe	9257	24	42	10	63	3.1	3.6	26	387	28	199	70	123	2132

For explanations and metric/imperial conversion note see the statistics tables for Europe, Asia or the Americas.

Trade		Education		Health	Energy	Consumer Price Index	G.N.P.		G.D.P.		Loans & Debt		
Imports	Exports	Primary	Secondary					Growth per capita	Part formed by Agric.	Part formed by Indust.			
US$ per capita	US$ per capita	% of age group	% of age group	Popn. per doctor	Consumption in kg of oil equiv. per capita	1980 = 100	US$ per capita	% per year 1965-88	%	%	end 1987 US$ millions	as % of G.N.P.	
295	343	95	54	2327	1003	153	2680	3.2	12	42	18574	34	Algeria
72	195	93	13	17784	203			–4.8	10	39			Angola
94	38	65	16	15937	46		310	0.2	46	14	907	51	Benin
		100	31	6910	429	189	1050	8.9	3	57	518		Botswana
63	24	35	6	57183	18	139	190	1.6	38	25	825	44	Burkina Faso
40	16	59	4	21120	20	166	250	1.6	59	14	745	68	Burundi
193	153	100	23	13990	144	203	970	3.8	24	31	3002	23	Cameroon
67	47	66	13	23067	30	140	330	–0.3	41	13	573	51	Central Africa
30	26	43	6	38358	18	160	150	–2	43	18	280	35	Chad
271	421	100	52	8138	223	178	870	4.2	12	33	694	171	Congo
164	78	87	66	786	588	118	680	3.5	21	25	39338	104	Egypt
25	9	36	12	77356	21	127	130	0.1	42	18	2526	46	Ethiopia
776	1193	100	27	2793	1121	168	2700	1.1	11	14	1893	55	Gabon
168	140	75	20	11688	68	331			28	7	283	99	Gambia
60	75	63	35	14894	129	1583	390	–1.6	51	16	2390	46	Ghana
56	70	29	9	57390	59		350		40	22	1678	75	Guinea
78	26	60	11	7262	37						351	271	Guinea-Bissau
187	257	78	20	15234	172	154	740	1	36	25	12632	127	Ivory Coast
76	42	94	20	10101	99	233	330	1.9	31	19	5178	61	Kenya
		100	22	18614	10	287	370	4.7	21	28	373	101	Lesotho
87	160	66	20	9240	169	129	450	–1.6	37	28	1618		Liberia
1148	2524	100	87	694	2674		5460	–2.3	2	65			Libya
34	28	100	36	10002	39	416	210	–1.8	43	16	3235	172	Madagascar
34	32	64	4	11564	40	337	160	1.4	37	18	1228	85	Malawi
56	27	22	7	23487	24	230	210	1.6	54	12	1924	99	Mali
249	224	46	15	12113	113	480	440	–0.4	37	22	1931	193	Mauritania
177	117	79	34	4749	242	179	610	1.8	19	31	19500	103	Morocco
32	6	82	7	37949	86		170		50	12			Mozambique
		100	45										Namibia
60	52	29	6	38775	42	130	260	–2.2	34	24	1561	65	Niger
71	67	92	29	7978	133	274	370	1.1	30	43	29721	98	Nigeria
53	18	67	3	34681	42	145	300	1.6	37	23	565	26	Rwanda
164	90	55	13	13445	155	178	520	–0.6	22	27	3290	66	Senegal
34	30	58	17	13626	77	3952	300	0.2	45	19	659		Sierra Leone
77	16	20	12	16089	81	1113	290	0.3	65	9	1733	173	Somalia
431	591	100	39	1906	2465	299	1890	0.6	6	44			South Africa
29	20	50	20	10108	58	598	330	–0.5	37	15	8468	96	Sudan
		100	43	18848	291	253	790		21	20			Swaziland
47	14	69	3	26552	35	643	180	–0.4	61	8	4316	151	Tanzania
124	88	100	21	8724	52	144	290	0	29	18	1042	85	Togo
388	276	100	39	2154	496	191	1180	3.6	18	32	6012	60	Tunisia
29	20	58	8	21903	26	11644	260	–2.7	76	5	1256	23	Uganda
34	47	76	22	13041	73	1714	150	–2.4	32	33	7211	111	Zaire
100	116	100	19	7102	380	846	250	–2.1	12	36	4330	144	Zambia
114	147	100	46	7188	512	255	580	0.9	11	43	2537	40	Zimbabwe

Cape Verde, Land 4.0/Popn. 359; Comoros 2.2/434; Djibouti 22/484; Eq. Guinea 28/300; Mauritius 1.9/1056; Reunion 2.5/575; St. Helena 0.3/6; Sao Tome 0.9/115; Seychelles 0.3/67; Western Sahara 266/180.

NORTH ATLANTIC
OCEAN
6578
Madeira (Port.)
Funchal
Canary Is. (Span.)
Lanzarote
Fuerteventura
Palma
Tenerife
Sta. Cruz
Gomera
Hierro
Gran Canaria
Las Palmas
SPAIN
Málaga
Cádiz
Str. of Gibraltar
Gibraltar (Br.)
Ceuta (Sp.)
Tangier
Tétouan
Melilla (Sp.)
Ksar er Kebir
Kenitra
Salé
Rabat
CASABLANCA
El Jadida
Ras Beddouza (C. Cantin)
Settat
Khouribga
Safi
Essaouira
Marrakesh
Fès
Meknès
Taza
Oujda
MOROCCO
Middle Atlas
High Atlas
Beni Mellal
Er Rachidia
Toubkal 4165
C. Rhir
Agadir
Taroudant
Anti Atlas
Ifni
Dra
Figuig
Béchar
Abadla
Beni Abbès
Tlemcen
Oran
Sidi Bel Abbès
Mostaganem
Mascara
Saïda
Tiaret
Mécheria
Ch. ech Chergui
El Bayadh
2235
Saharan Atlas
Djelfa
Laghouat
ALGIERS (Alger)
Blida
Médéa
Ech Cheliff
Tizi-Ouzou
Bejaia
Sétif
Ch. el Hodna
Constantine
Skikda
Annaba (Bône)
Batna
Biskra
Bou Saâda
Tébessa
Kairouan
Gafsa
Gabès
Chott Djerid
El Oued
Touggourt
Ghardaïa
Ouargla
El Goléa
Hassi Inifel
Ghadames
Timimoun
ALGERIA
Plateau du Tademait
Adrar
In Salah
Bordj Omar Driss
Bj. Fly Ste. Marie
Zaouiet Reggane
Tindouf
C. Juby
Tarfaya (Villa Bens)
El Aaiun
C. Bojador
WESTERN SAHARA
Bir Mogrein (Ft. Trinquet)
Dakhla
Pta. Durnford
Fderik
Zouérate
Nouadhibou (Port Etienne)
Atar
Chinguetti
Akjoujt
C. Timris
Nouakchott
Tidjikdja
Moudjeria
Boutilimit
Boghé
Kaédi
Kiffa
M'bout
Sélibaby
Néma
MAURITANIA
El Djouf
Erg Chech
Tanezrouft
Poste Maurice Cortier (Bidon 5)
TRANS SAHARAN MOTOR ROUTE
Tessalit
Adrar
Mabrouk
Araouane
Kidal
Bamba
Bourem
Tombouctou (Timbuktu)
Goundam
Gao
Ansongo
Ménaka
MALI
Nioro
Nara
Sokolo
Diéma
Mopti
Douentza
Djenné
Kolokani
Ségou
San
Kita
Bamako
Koulikoro
Koutiala
Bougouni
Sikasso
Siguiri
Ilizi
Arak
Bj.-in-Eker
Idelès
Djanet
Ahaggar
Tahat 2918
Tamanrasset
Iférouane
Tamgak Mts.
Aïr (Azbine)
1900
Agadès
NIGER
Tahoua
Filingué
Madaoua
Birni Nkonni
Maradi
Zinder
Tanout
Niamey
Dosso
Tera
Dori
BURKINA FASO
Ouahigouya
Kaya
Ouagadougou
Koudougou
Dédougou
Fada N'Gourma
Tenkodogo
Bobo-Dioulasso
Banfora
Gaoua
Black Volta
St. Louis
Louga
Linguéré
Thiès
Diourbel
C. Vert
DAKAR
Kaolack
SENEGAL
Kayes
Tambacounda
GAMBIA
Banjul
Georgetown
Kolda
Ziguinchor
GUINEA-BISSAU
Bissau
Bafatá
Bissagos Is.
Fouta Djalon
Labé
Boké
Télimélé
Pita
Kindia
Dubréka
Conakry
GUINEA
Kankan
Faranah
Kissidougou
Guékédou
1948
SIERRA LEONE
Makeni
Magburaka
Freetown
Bo
Kenema
Sherbro I.
Bonthe
LIBERIA
Monrovia
Buchanan
Greenville
C. Palmas
Nzérékoré
Odienné
Korhogo
IVORY COAST
Man
Séguéla
Katiola
Bouaké
Danané
Daloa
Gagnoa
Dimbokro
Agboville
Abidjan
Grand Bassam
San Pedro
Sassandra
Bondoukou
Bolgatanga
Wa
Tamale
GHANA
Lake Volta
Sunyani
Kumasi
Koforidua
Oda
Nkawkaw
Accra
Tema
Winneba
Cape Coast
Tarkwa
Sekondi-Takoradi
C. Three Points
Bawku
Mango
TOGO
Sokodé
Kpalimé
Atakpamé
Lomé
Keta
Ho
BENIN
Natitingou
Kandi
Parakou
Abomey
Cotonou
Porto Novo
Bight of Benin
Birnin-Kebbi
Gaya
Argungu
Sokoto
Gusau
Gummi
Katsina
Kano
Nguru
Hadejia
Azare
Potiskum
Zaria
Kaduna
Bauchi
Jos
Kontagora
Kainji Dam
Minna
Bida
Abuja
NIGERIA
Ilorin
Ogbomosho
Oshogbo
Iwo
Ife
Ibadan
Abeokuta
LAGOS
Ijebu Ode
Akure
Owo
Benin City
Lokoja
Lafia
Shendam
Wukari
Makurdi
Benue
Enugu
Onitsha
Warri
Aba
Port Harcourt
Calabar
Niger Delta
Bamenda
Foumban
Nkongsamba
4070
Cameroon Pk.
Limbe
Douala
Sanaga
Rey Malabo
Bioko
EQUATORIAL GUINEA
CAMEROON
TUNISIA
Niger
Senegal
Bafing
Gambia
Sassandra
Projection: Sanson Flamsteed's Sinusoidal
West from Greenwich
East from Greenwich
m
4000
3000
2000
1500
1000
400
200
0
200
m

1:15 000 000

100 0 100 200 300 400 500 600 km

CENTRAL AND SOUTHERN AFRICA

MADAGASCAR
On same scale as General Map
COPYRIGHT, GEORGE PHILIP & SON, LTD
INDIAN OCEAN
ATLANTIC OCEAN
Mozambique Channel
SOUTH AFRICA
BOTSWANA
ZIMBABWE
MOZAMBIQUE
ZAMBIA
MALAWI
NAMIBIA (SOUTH WEST AFRICA)
LESOTHO
SWAZILAND
TRANSVAAL
ORANGE FREE STATE
NATAL
CAPE PROVINCE
Kalahari
Namib
Great Karoo
Caprivi Strip
Okavango Swamps
Etosha Pan
Tropic of Capricorn
East from Greenwich
Projection: Sanson Flamsteed's Sinusoidal
Antananarivo (Tananarive)
Toamasina
Mahajanga
Fianarantsoa
Antsirabe
Toliara
Antsiranana
Maputo (Lourenço Marques)
Beira
Quelimane
Inhambane
Harare (Salisbury)
Bulawayo
Lusaka
Gaborone
Windhoek
Walvis Bay
Swakopmund
Lüderitz
Pretoria
JOHANNESBURG
Soweto
Bloemfontein
Kimberley
Durban
Pietermaritzburg
Maseru
East London
Port Elizabeth
CAPE TOWN
C. of Good Hope
Lobito
Benguela
Huambo
Lubango
1:15 000 000
100 0 100 200 300 400 500 600 km
m
6000
4000
3000
2000
1500
1000
400
200
0
200

1: 35 000 000

400 0 400 800 1200 km

Projection: Bonne

1:35 000 000

400 0 400 800 1200 km

NORTH AMERICA: *climate and natural vegetation*

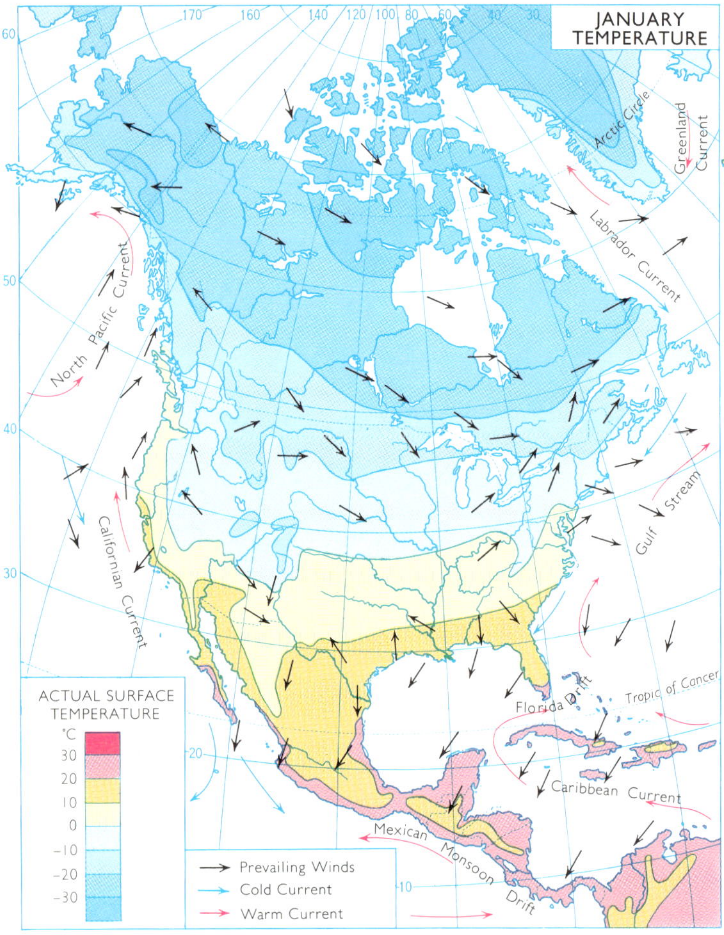

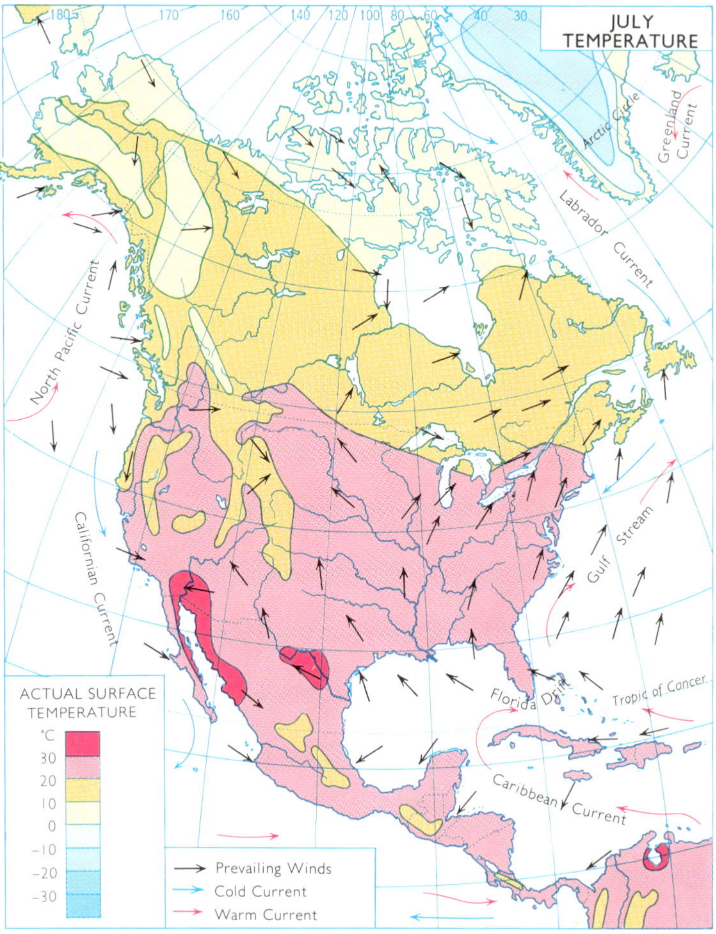

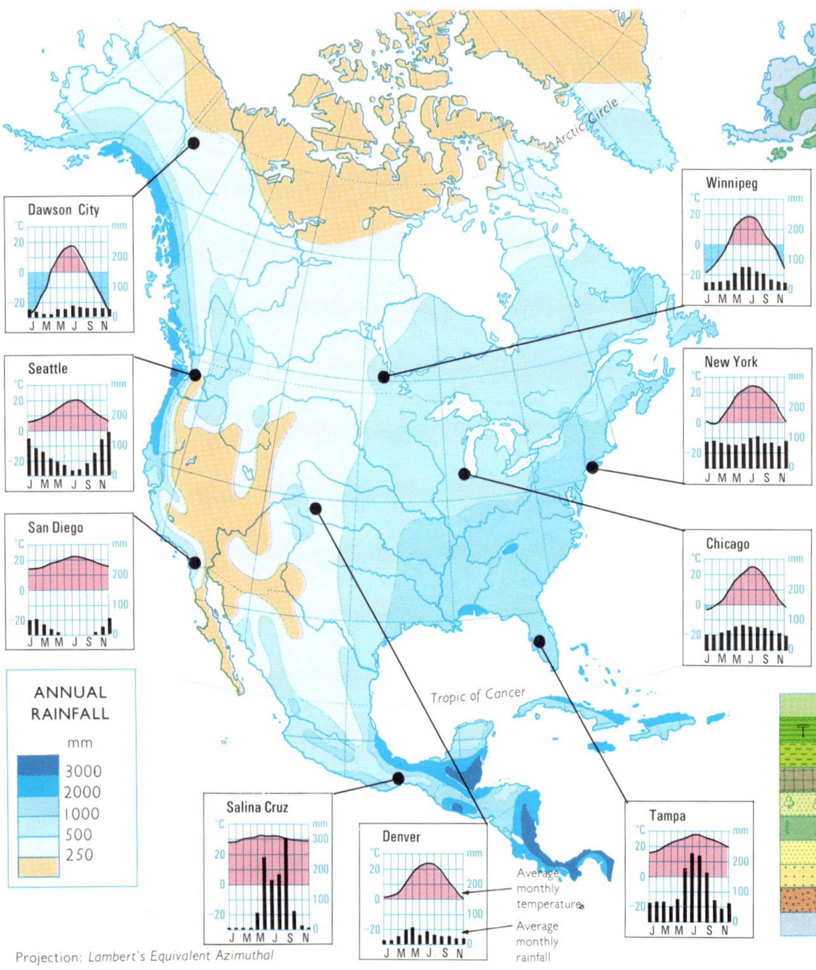

Projection: *Lambert's Equivalent Azimuthal*

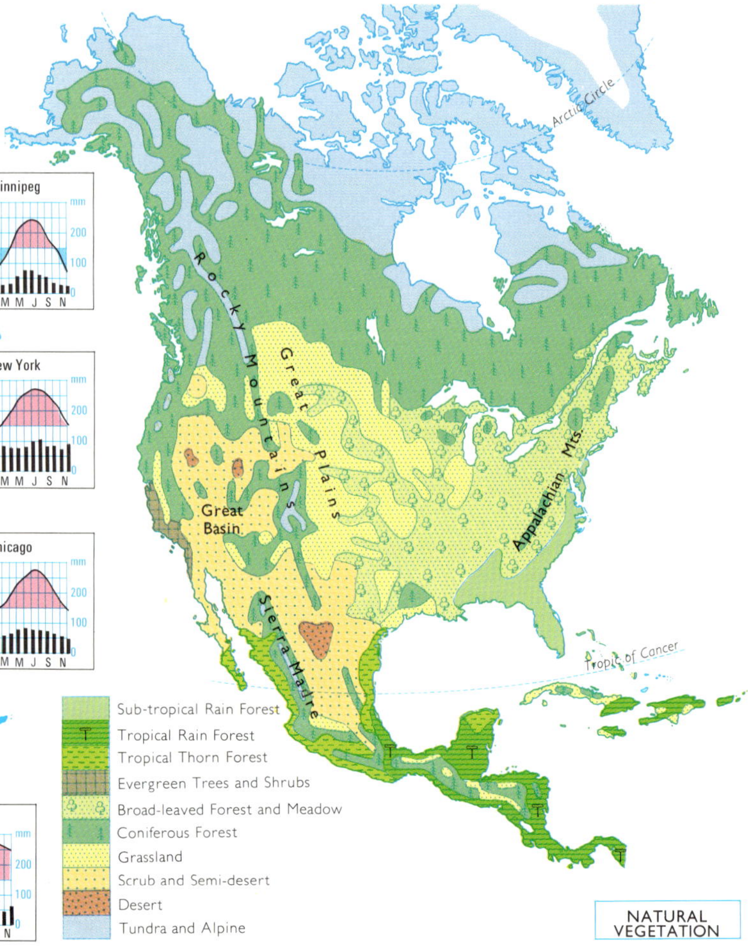

Projection: *Polyconic*

1:32 000 000

400 0 400 800 1200 km

	Population								Land			Agriculture		
	Total	Density	Birth Rate	Death Rate	Life Expectancy	Growth 1965-80	Growth 1980-88	Urban	Area	Arable	Forest	Agricultural Population	Index of Production	Food Intake
	th.	persons per km²	per th. popn.	per th. popn.	yrs.	av. % per annum	av. % per annum	%	th. km²	th. km²	th. km²	% of total popn.	1979-81 = 100	calories per day
Bahamas	242	24	18	6	70		2	75	10	0.1	3	7		2699
Barbados	254	633	15	9	75		0.3	44	0.4	0.3	0	8	75	3020
Canada	26104	3	14	7	77	1	1	76	9221	460	3540	4	100	3462
Costa Rica	2670	52	29	4	74	2.6	2.3	45	51	5	16	26	108	2803
Cuba	10394	92	18	7	75	1.5	0.9	75	111	33	33	21	110	3122
Dominican Rep.	6859	134	31	7	66	2.9	2.4	58	48	15	6	39	110	2477
El Salvador	5056	234	36	9	63	2.7	1.4	44	21	7	1	39	98	2160
Guadaloupe	338	185	19	7	74		0.5	48	2	0.4	0.7	11	120	2512
Guatemala	8688	76	39	6	62	2.8	2.9	33	108	19	40	53	120	2307
Haiti	6254	191	34	13	55	2	1.8	29	28	9	0.5	66	103	1902
Honduras	4837	40	40	8	64	3.2	3.6	42	112	18	18	57	114	2068
Jamaica	2429	216	22	5	74	1.5	1.4	51	11	3	2	28	110	2590
Martinique	330	298	19	6	74		0.2	75	1	0.2	0.3	9	127	2673
Mexico	83593	41	29	5	69	3.1	2.2	71	1923	247	441	32	112	3132
Nicaragua	3623	28	42	10	64	3.1	3.4	58	119	13	37	41	86	2495
Panama	2315	29	25	4	72	2.6	2.1	54	76	6	40	27	111	2446
Puerto Rico	3376	393	19	7	75		0.6	74	9	1	2	3	98	
Trinidad and Tobago	1241	236	27	7	70	1.3	1.6	67	5	1	2	8	81	3082
U.S.A.	245871	26	16	9	75	1	1	74	9167	1899	2652	3	92	3645
Argentina	31506	11	21	8	71	1.6	1.4	85	2737	358	595	11	108	3210
Bolivia	6917	6	47	5	53	2.5	2.7	50	1084	34	558	43	117	2143
Brazil	144369	16	29	6	65	2.4	2.2	75	8457	775	5579	26	132	2656
Chile	12760	16	22	6	72	1.8	1.7	85	749	56	87	14	124	2579
Colombia	30007	28	29	5	66	2.2	1.9	69	1039	53	512	30	120	2543
Ecuador	10154	35	35	5	65	3.1	2.8	55	277	27	118	33	116	2058
Guyana	1006	5	28	7	70			35	197	5	164	24	80	2359
Paraguay	4042	10	35	3	67	2.8	3.2	46	397	22	156	47	150	2853
Peru	20681	16	35	9	62	2.8	2.2	69	1280	37	692	36	126	2246
Surinam	429	2	28	7	67		2.6	48	161	0.7	149	17	112	2524
Uruguay	3004	17	18	10	71	0.4	0.5	85	174	14	7	14	108	2648
Venezuela	18759	20	28	4	70	3.5	2.8	83	882	39	311	12	114	2494

Population. This is the United Nation's estimate for the mid-year 1988 (thousands)

Population Density. This is the quoted population total divided by the quoted land area (persons per square kilometre).

Birth Rates and Death Rates. These are the registered or United Nation's estimated rates per thousand population.

Life Expectancy. This figure indicates the number of years that a child born today can expect to live if the levels of death of today last throughout its life. The figure is the average of that for men and women. The figure for women is usually higher than that for men (U.K. Male 75, female 78 years).

Population Growth. This shows the average annual percentage change in population for two periods, 1965–1980 and 1980–1988.

Urbanization. This is the percentage of the total population living in urban areas. The definition of urban is that of the individual nation and usually includes quite small towns.

Land Area. This is the total area of the country minus the area covered by major lakes and rivers (thousand square kilometres).

Arable Land and Permanent Crops. This excludes fallow land but includes temporary pasture (thousand square kilometres).

Forest and Woodland. This includes natural and planted woodland and land recently cleared of timber which will be replanted (thousand square kilometres).

Agricultural Population. This is the percentage of the economically active population working in agriculture. It also includes those people working in forestry, hunting and fishing.

Index of Agricultural Production. The base period for this index is 1979–1981 and it shows the level of production in each country in 1988 in comparison with that of the earlier period. Only edible crops and meat are included.

Food Intake. The figures are the average intake per person in calories per day for the year 1986.

Trade		Education		Health	Energy	Consumer Price Index	G.N.P.		G.D.P.		Loans & Debt		
Imports	Exports	Primary	Secondary					Growth per capita	Part formed by Agric.	Part formed by Indust.			
US$ per capita	US$ per capita	% of age group	% of age group	Popn. per doctor	Consumption in kg of oil equiv. per capita	1980 = 100	US$ per capita	% per year 1965-88	%	%	end 1987 US$ millions	as % of G.N.P.	
6673	6814	99	99	1050	2390	148	10570	–0.5	4	12	189	7	Bahamas
2752	2657	100	94	1300	1410	159	5990	2.3	6	13			Barbados
3547	3558	100	100	510	9690	162	15160	2.7	3	35	2340	0.5	Canada
516	433	100	42	960	470	703	1610	1.5	18	29	4100	67	Costa Rica
732	520	100	89	720	1420		1400		4	43			Cuba
260	104	100	47	1760	450	269	730	2.3	17	30	2609	53	Dominican Rep.
193	125	70	24	2830	170	391	860	–0.4	14	22	1762	39	El Salvador
4902	781	100	34	1020	930	174	4330	4.7	7	7			Guadaloupe
170	125	76	20	2180	190	202	950	1.2	25	16	2187	30	Guatemala
60	42	78	18	7180	50	141	360	0.5	32	17	713	29	Haiti
185	171	100	36	1510	200	148	810	0.7	22	24	2410	53	Honduras
497	267	100	58	2060	1090	284	940	–1.5	6	41	3322	99	Jamaica
6455	1130	100	47	900	950	183	4270	3.3	6	5			Martinique
152	250	100	55	1240	1600	9907	1830	2.5	9	34	90938	49	Mexico
255	83	98	42	1500	310		830	–2.5	21	34	5343	198	Nicaragua
539	154	100	59	980	640	119	2240	2.4	9	18	3722	68	Panama
		100	78	800	2210	124	5540	0.8	2	41			Puerto Rico
982	1178	95	76	960	7590	233	4210	1.3	4	39	1154	24	Trinidad and Tobago
1718	1027	100	100	470	9490	144	18350	1.5	2	30	12170	0.25	U.S.A.
185	202	100	74	370	1740	2.6 mill	2390	0.1	13	43	55709	63	Argentina
112	82	87	37	1540	340	9.1 mill	580	–0.5	24	24	4769	107	Bolivia
115	182	100	36	1080	760	53000	2020	4.1	11	38	100781	26	Brazil
315	399	100	70	1230	920	431	1310	0.2	6	31	15448	70	Chile
141	167	100	56	1190	780	526	1240	2.7	19	35	15851	41	Colombia
222	199	100	55	830	660	731	1040	3.2	16	31	9438	85	Ecuador
219	209	90	55	9600	650	209	410	–0.2	20	15			Guyana
297	236	99	30	1460	250	334	990	3.4	27	26	2246	50	Paraguay
146	126	100	65	1040	520	85519	1470	0.2	11	33	11049	45	Peru
1879	1935	100	51	1725	1370	255	2450	3.4	9	21			Surinam
379	396	100	71	510	610	2978	2190	1.4	15	40	3090	41	Uruguay
465	563	100	46	700	3380	159	3230	–0.9	6	38	31326	53	Venezuela

Antigua & Barbuda, Land 0.4/Popn. 82; Belize 23/145; Bermuda 0.05/55; Br. Virgin Is. 0.2/13; Cayman Is. 0.3/24; Dominica 0.8/94; Greenland 342/54; Grenada 0.3/92; Montserrat 0.1/12; Netherlands Antilles 1/189; St. Christopher-Nevis 0.4/44; St. Lucia 0.6/147; St. Pierre & M. 0.2/6; St. Vincent 0.3/113; Turks & Caicos Is. 0.4/11; U.S. Virgin Is. 0.3/110.
Falkland Is. 12/2; Fr. Guiana 89/91.

Trade. The trade figures are for the year 1988. The total trade figures have been divided by the population and are a measure of the country's external trade (U.S. $ per capita).

Education. The ages of primary school are taken to be 6–11 years and secondary school 12–17 years. The percentage of total school age group in this type of education is shown.

Energy. All forms of energy have been converted to their equivalent in oil. Firewood and other traditional forms used in developing countries are not included and so the energy consumption in those countries is understated (kilograms of oil equivalent per capita).

Consumer Price Index. The base year is 1980 which is 100 and the level of consumer prices in 1987 or 1988 are shown in relation to the base year. It is a measure of inflation.

G.N.P. (Gross National Product) This figure is an estimate of the average production per person measured in U.S. dollars and for 1988. The G.N.P. measures the value of goods and services produced in a country, plus the balance, positive or negative, of income from abroad, for example investments, interest on capital, money returned from foreign labour, etc. The rate of change is the average annual percentage change during the period 1965–1988 in the G.N.P. The G.D.P. (Gross Domestic Product) is the G.N.P. minus the foreign balances. The adjoining two columns show the percentage contribution to the G.D.P. made by the agricultural and mining and manufacturing sectors.

Loans and Debts. This figure in millions of U.S. dollars shows the external public debt ar the end of 1988. This is then shown as a percentage of the annual G.N.P. The figures in red show official development assistance made by the developed countries and also as a percentage of the donor country's G.N.P.

To convert from square kilometres (km^2) to square miles multiply by 0.39
To convert from kilograms to pounds multiply by 2.2

CANADA

PACIFIC OCEAN
ALASKA
YUKON TERRITORY
NORTHWEST TERRITORIES
INUVIK
FORT SMITH
KITIKMEOT
KEEWATIN
BRITISH COLUMBIA
ALBERTA
SASKATCHEWAN
MANITOBA
CANADA
UNITED STATES
WASHINGTON
MONTANA
NORTH DAKOTA
SOUTH DAKOTA
MINNESOTA
NEBRASKA
WYOMING
Anchorage
Fairbanks
Seward
Valdez
Cordova
Yukon
Tanana
Wrangell Mts.
Mt. Sanford 4940
Mt. St. Elias 5489
Mt. Logan 6050
St. Elias Mts.
Whitehorse
Yakutat
Mt. Fairweather 4663
Chichagof I.
Sitka
Baranof I.
Skagway
Juneau
Wrangell
Pr. of Wales I.
Dixon Entrance
Pr. Rupert
Queen Charlotte Is.
Hecate Str.
Q. Charlotte Sd.
Vancouver I.
Juan de Fuca Str.
C. Flattery
Nanaimo
Victoria
VANCOUVER
SEATTLE
Tacoma
Spokane
Old Crow
Dawson
Klondike
Mackenzie Mountains
Mayo
Pelly
Inuvik
Arctic Red R.
Mackenzie
Peel
Ft. Good Hope
Norman Wells
Franklin Mts.
Gt. Bear
Gt. Bear Lake
Echo Bay
Anderson
Horton
C. Bathurst
Amundsen Gulf
Banks Island
Prince Albert Pen.
Victoria Island
Wollaston Pen.
Dolphin & Union Str.
Coppermine
Coronation Gulf
Kent Pen.
Cambridge Bay
Queen Maud Gulf
Bathurst Inlet
King William I.
Boothia Peninsula
Chantrey Inlet
Adelaide Pen.
Melville Sound
Viscount
Prince of Wales Island
M'Clintock Channel
Franklin Str.
Somerset Island
Lac la Martre
Yellowknife
Great Slave L.
Ft. Simpson
Liard
Trout L.
Hay River
Pine Point
Ft. Smith
de Gras
Aylmer
Clinton Golden L.
Back
L. Garry
Fort Reliance
Dubawnt L.
Dubawnt
Baker L.
Baker Lake
Chesterfield I.
Wholdaia L.
Kasba L.
Nueltin L.
Eskimo Pt.
Uranium City
Lake Athabasca
Athabasca
Fort McMurray
Wollaston L.
Cree L.
Seal
Churchill
C. Churchill
Reindeer Lake
Lynn Lake
Southern Indian L.
Churchill L.
Nelson
Thompson
Caribou Mts.
Peace
Ft. Vermilion
Ft. Nelson
Ft. St. John
Dawson Creek
Grande Prairie
Peace R.
Lesser Slave L.
Smoky
Skeena
Stikine
Cassiar Mountains
Dease L.
Alaska Highway
Churchill Pk.
Rocky Mountains
Babine L.
Stuart L.
Prince George
Cariboo Mts.
Quesnel
Fraser
Mt. Waddington 3994
Coast Mts.
Mt. Robson 3954
Yellowhead P.
Edmonton
Leduc
Wetaskiwin
Camrose
Red Deer
Kicking Horse P.
Banff
Calgary
Drumheller
Kamloops
Vernon
Kelowna
Penticton
Trail
Selkirk Mts.
Kootenay L.
Crowsnest P.
Lethbridge
Medicine Hat
Swift Current
Brooks
Lac la Biche
Lloydminster
N. Battleford
Prince Albert
Saskatoon
Biggar
Melfort
N. Saskatchewan
S. Saskatchewan
Moose Jaw
Regina
Melville
Yorkton
Weyburn
Estevan
L. la Ronge
Flin Flon
Sherridon
The Pas
Cedar Lake
Winnipegosis
Dauphin
L. Manitoba
Lake Winnipeg
Norway Ho.
Gods L.
Island L.
Sandy L.
Red L.
Lac Seul
Kenora
L. of the Woods
Fort Frances
Brandon
Portage la Prairie
Selkirk
Winnipeg
St. Boniface
Souris
Minot
Havre
Milk
Fort Peck
Missouri
Yellowstone
Grand Forks
Fargo
Moorhead
Jamestown
Bismarck
Red
Red Lake
Bemidji
Hibbing
Duluth
Brainerd
Superior
St. Cloud
Aberdeen
Minneapolis
St. Paul
Pierre
Rapid City
Black Hills 2207
Cheyenne
White
Niobrara
Powder
Sioux Falls
Mankato
Rochester
Des Moines
Mason City
Sioux City
Fort Dodge
Omaha
Grand Island
Platte
North Platte
Cedar Rapids
Waterloo
Projection: Bonne
ALASKA
1:30 000 000
0 200 400 600 km
Chukot Sea
Chukot Ra.
Anadyr
Koryak Ra.
Provideniya
Gulf of Anadyr
Bering Strait
Nome
Seward Pen.
Kotzebue
Baird Mts.
Brooks Range
Prudhoe Bay
Barrow
Norton Sound
St. Lawrence I. (U.S.)
St. Matthew I.
Nunivak I.
Kuskokwim Bay
Bristol Bay
Alaska Peninsula
Kodiak I.
Unimak I.
Unalaska I.
Umnak I.
Aleutian Is.
Andreanof Is.
Rat Is.
Near Is.
Pribilof Is.
BERING SEA
Alaska Range
Mt. McKinley 6194
Anchorage
Homer
Cook Inlet
Valdez
Cordova
Fairbanks
Dawson
Whitehorse
Juneau
Sitka
Wrangell
Ketchikan
Chichagof I.
Alexander Archipelago
Prince of Wales I.
Prince Rupert
Graham I.
Queen Charlotte Is.
GULF OF ALASKA
PACIFIC OCEAN
West from Greenwich
m
3000
2000
1500
1000
400
200
0
200
2000
m

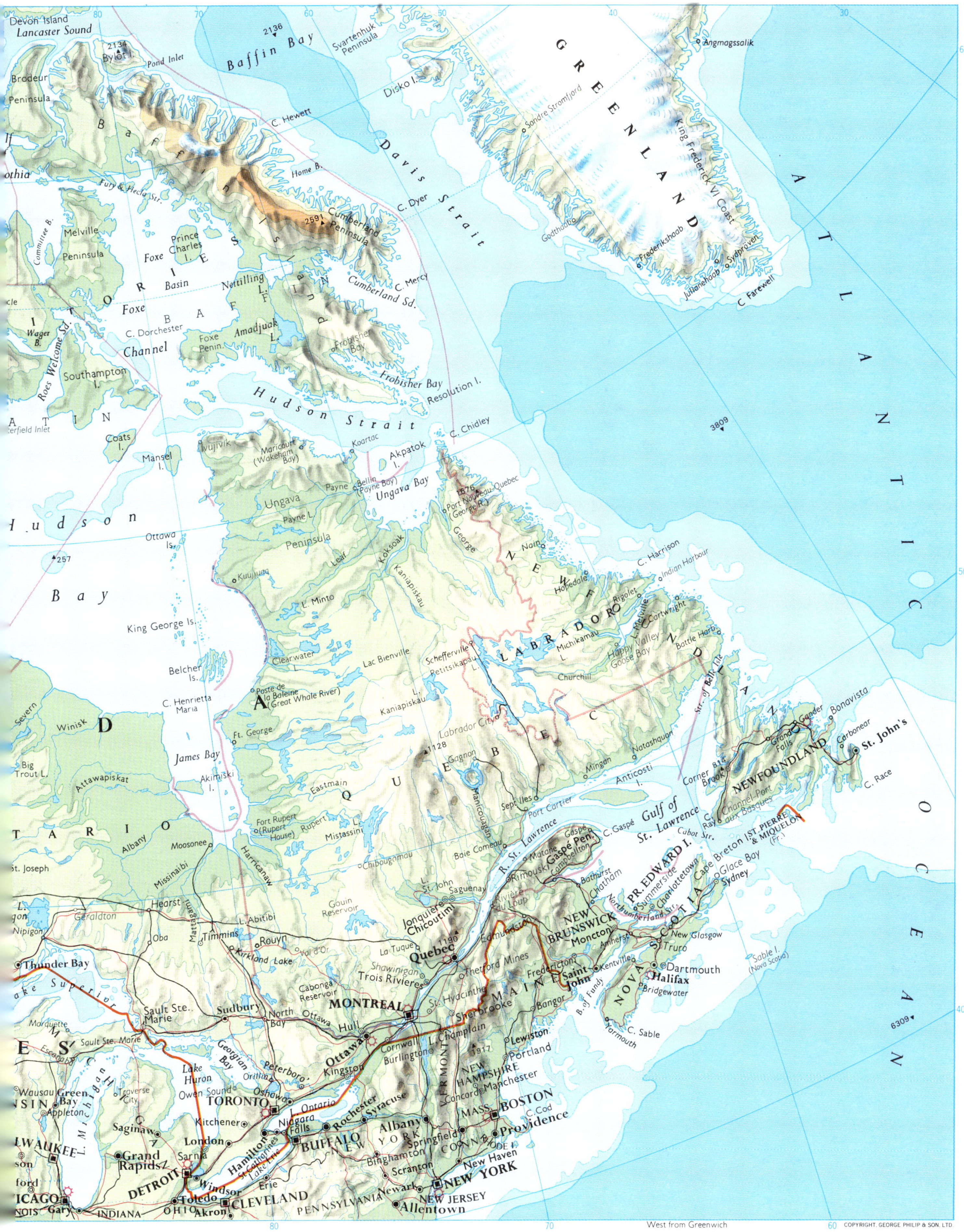

1:15 000 000

100 0 100 200 300 400 500 600 km

Projection: Albers' Equal Area with two standard parallels

West from Greenwich

1:12 000 000

100 0 100 200 300 400 500 km

Projection: Albers' Equal Area with two standard parallels

1:6 000 000

50 0 50 100 150 200 250 km

Projection: Bonne

1:15 000 000

100 0 100 200 300 400 500 600 km

SOUTH AMERICA: *physical*

Projection: *Lambert's Equivalent Azimuthal*

1: 30 000 000

200 0 200 400 600 800 1000 km

Projection: *Lambert's Equivalent Azimuthal*

West from Greenwich

BUENOS AIRES Capital Cities

1:30 000 000

200 0 200 400 600 800 1000 km

SOUTH AMERICA: *climate and natural vegetation*

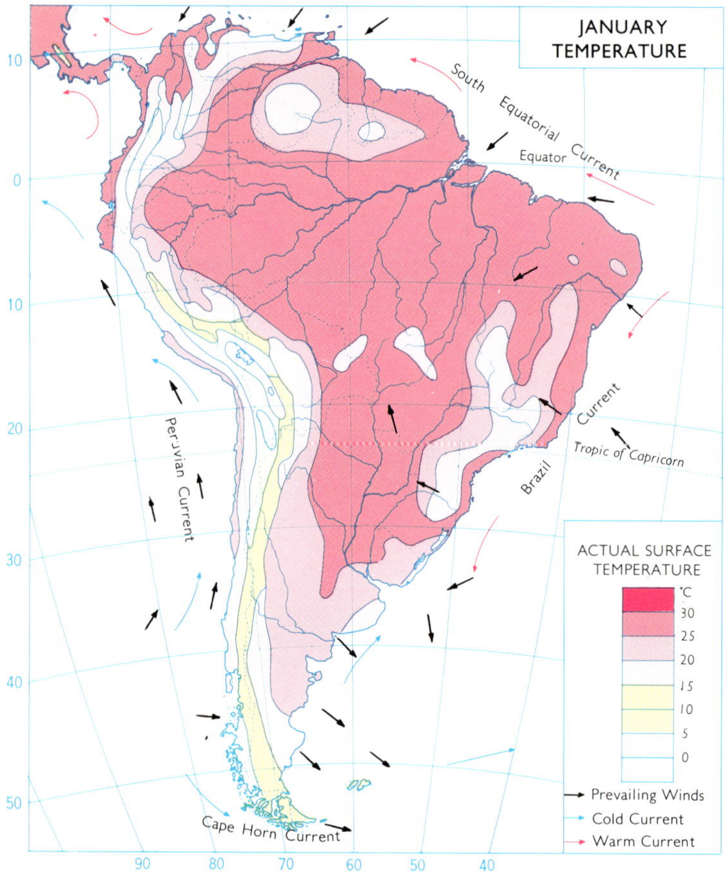

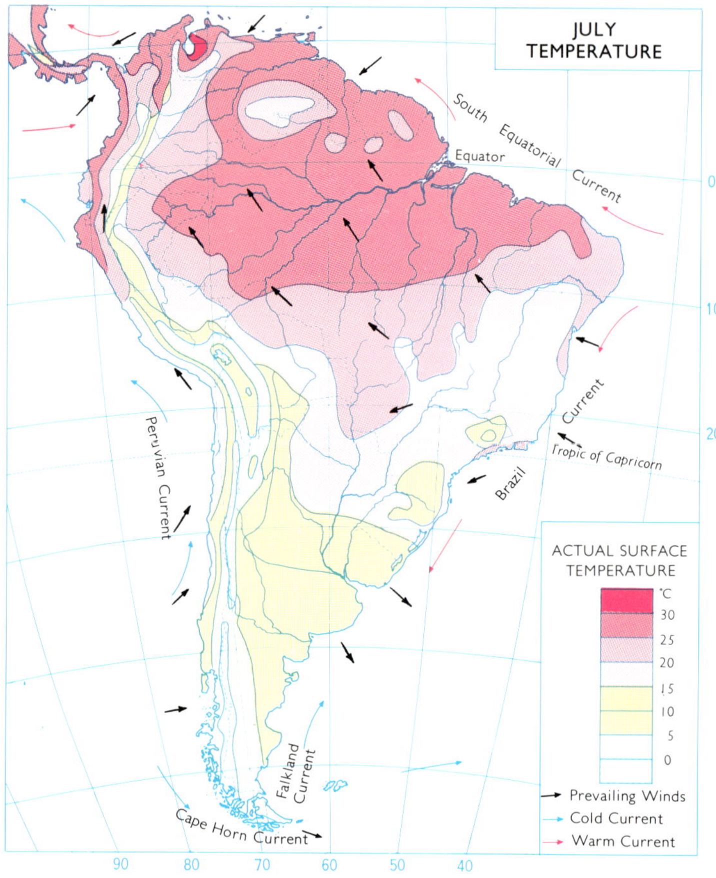

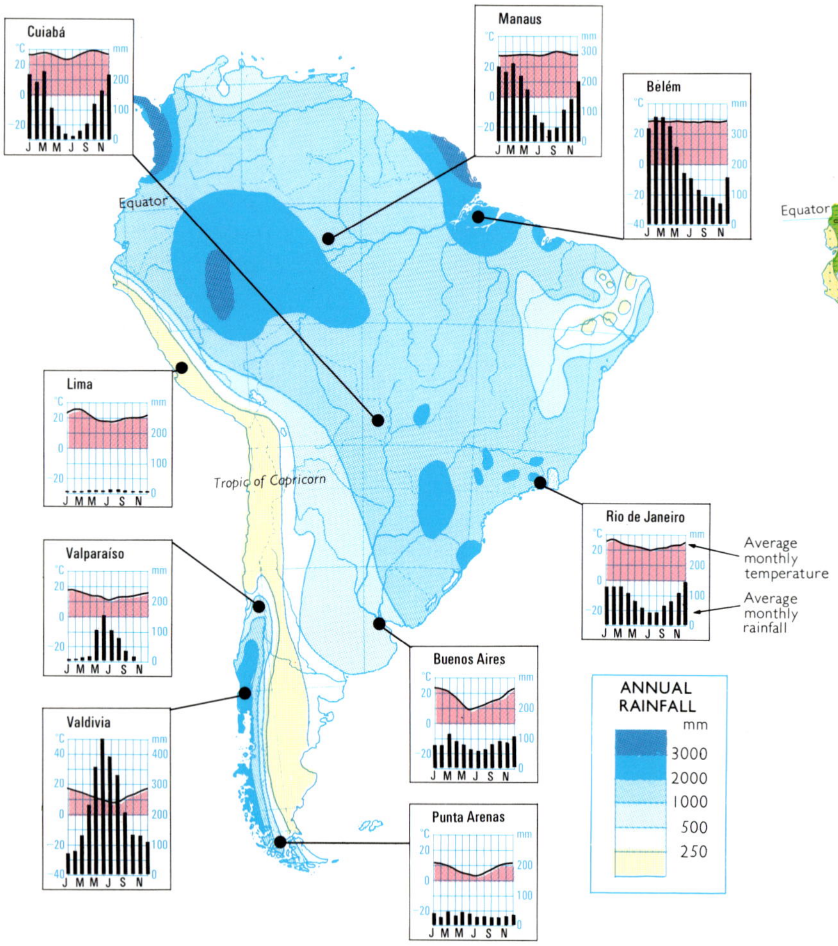

Projection: *Lambert's Equivalent Azimuthal*

1: 30 000 000

200 0 200 400 600 800 1000 km

Projection: Sanson-Flamsteed's Sinusoidal

1:16 000 000

200 100 0 200 400 600 km

Projection: *Sanson-Flamsteed's Sinusoidal*

West from Greenwich

1:16 000 000

200 100 0 200 400 600 km

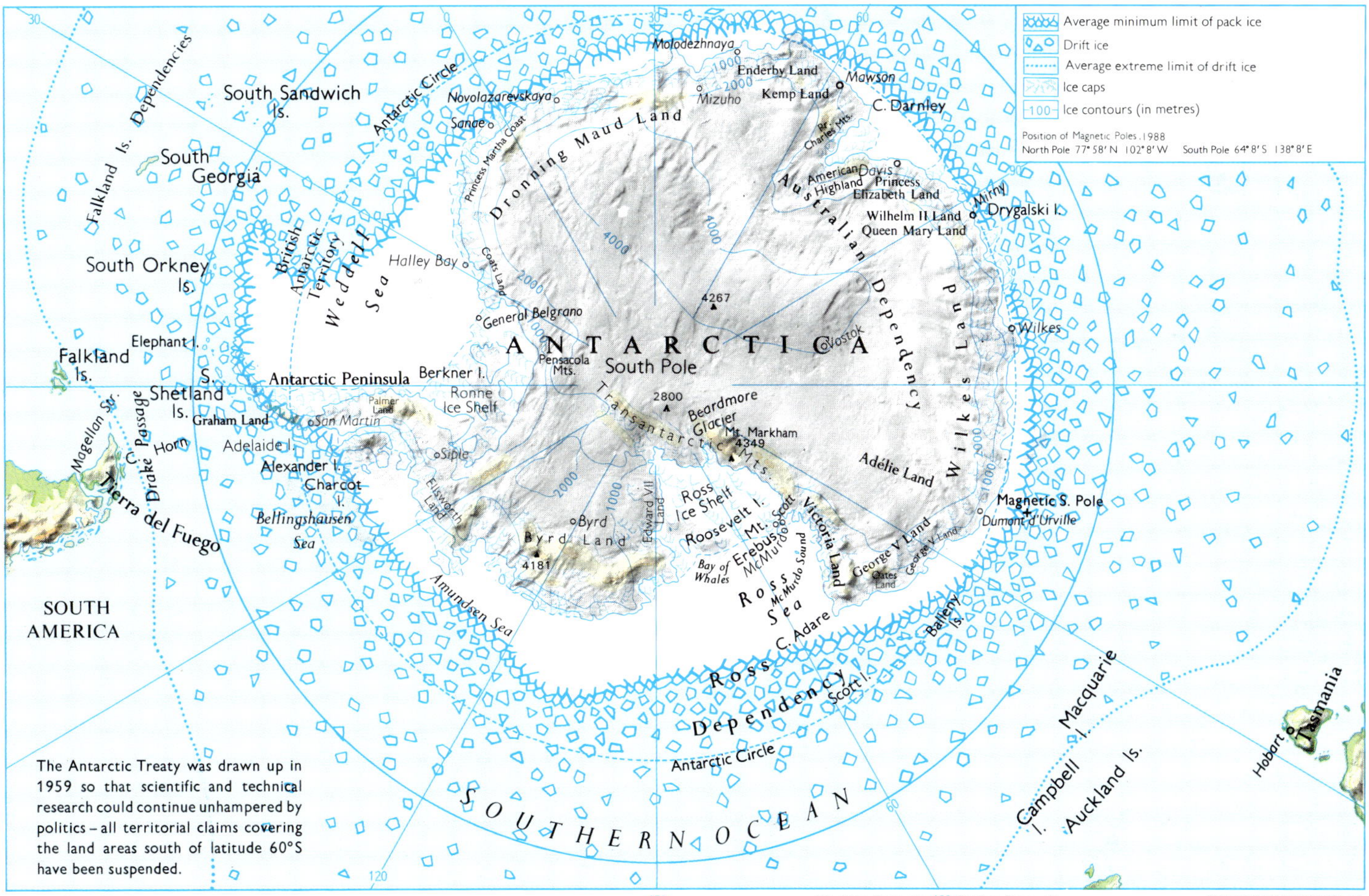

The Antarctic Treaty was drawn up in 1959 so that scientific and technical research could continue unhampered by politics – all territorial claims covering the land areas south of latitude 60°S have been suspended.

Projection: *Zenithal Equidistant*

West from Greenwich 180 East from Greenwich

1:50 000 000

500 0 500 1000 1500 2000 km

January Temperature and Ocean Currents
(Northern Hemisphere—Winter)

ACTUAL SURFACE TEMPERATURE
°C
30
20
10
0
−10
−20
−30
−40

Warm Current
Cold Current

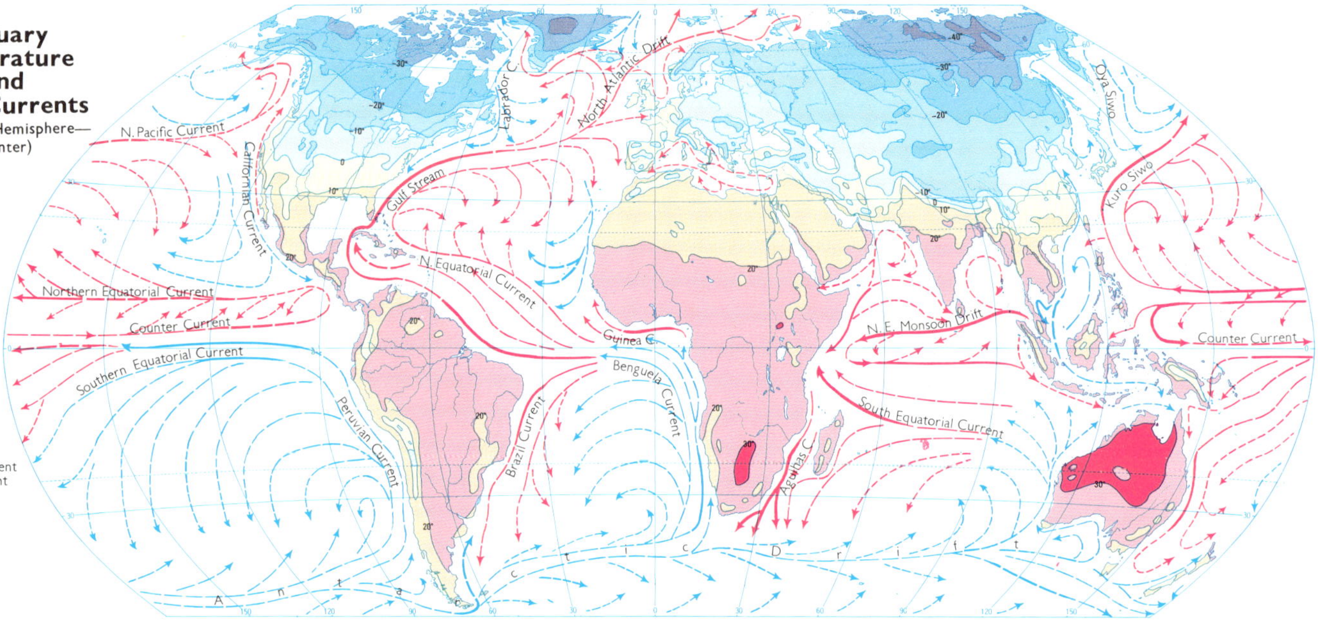

July Temperature and Ocean Currents
(Northern Hemisphere—Summer)

ACTUAL SURFACE TEMPERATURE
°C
30
20
10
0
−10

Warm Current
Cold Current

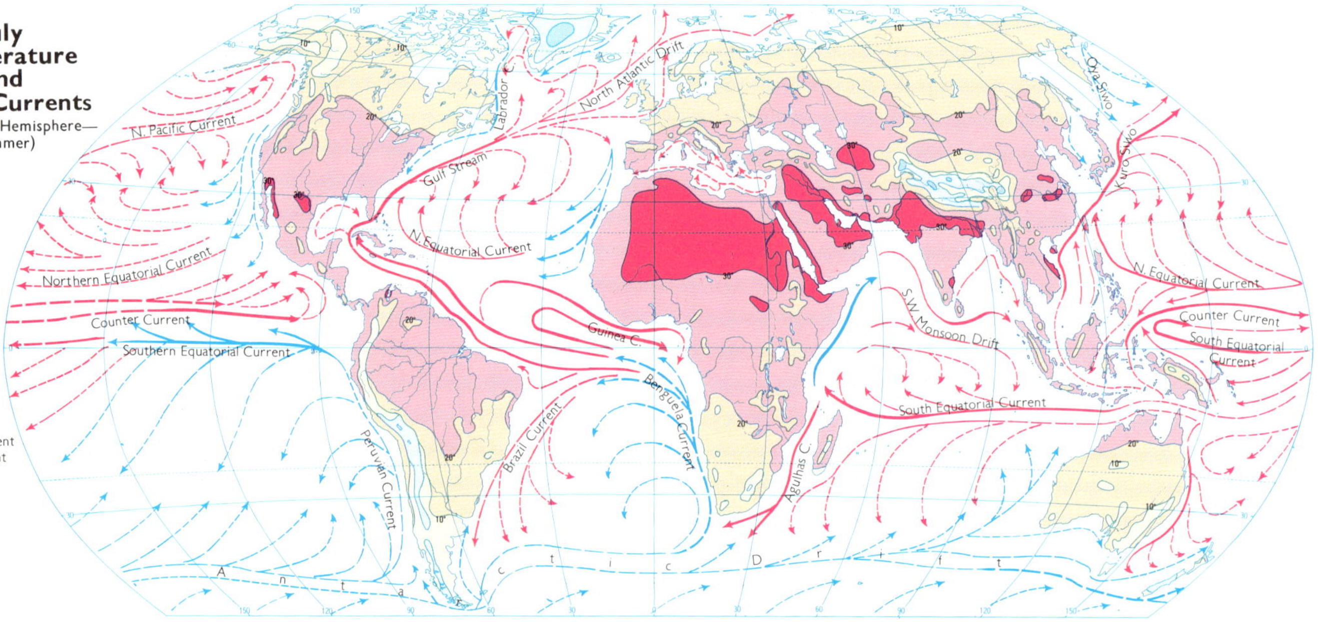

Annual Range of Temperature

°C
60
50
40
30
20
10
5
0

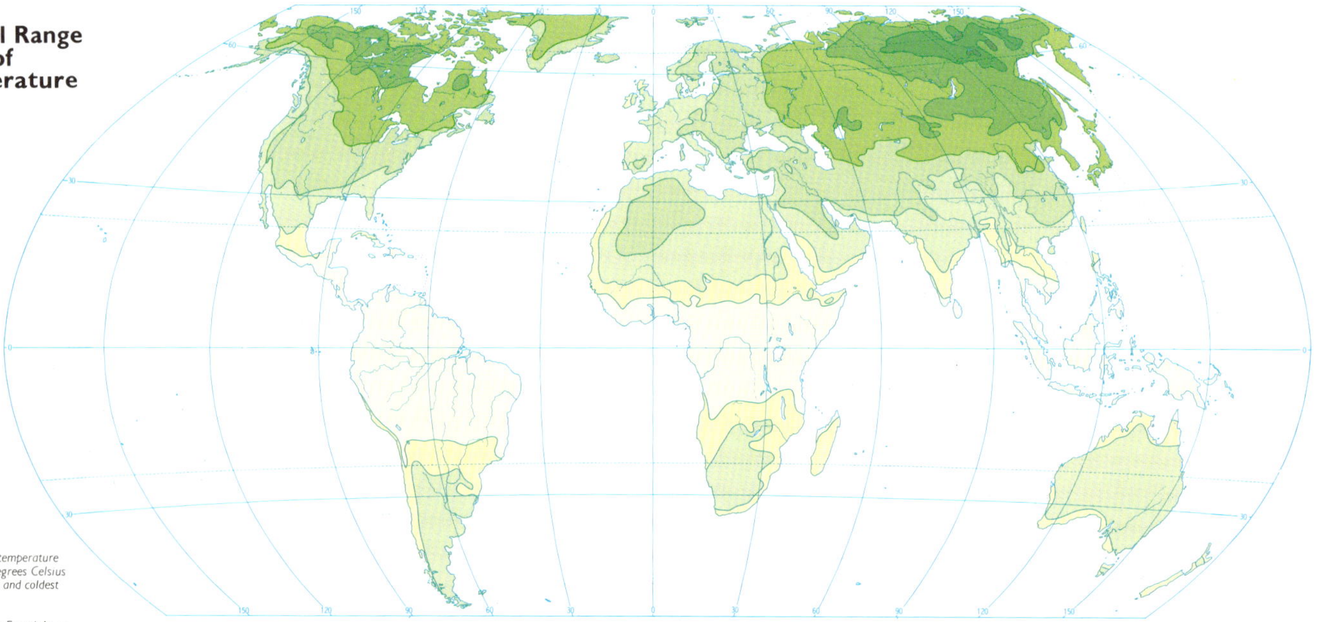

The annual range of temperature is the difference in degrees Celsius between the warmest and coldest months of the year.

Projection: *Hammer Equal Area*

1:190 000 000

January Pressure and Winds

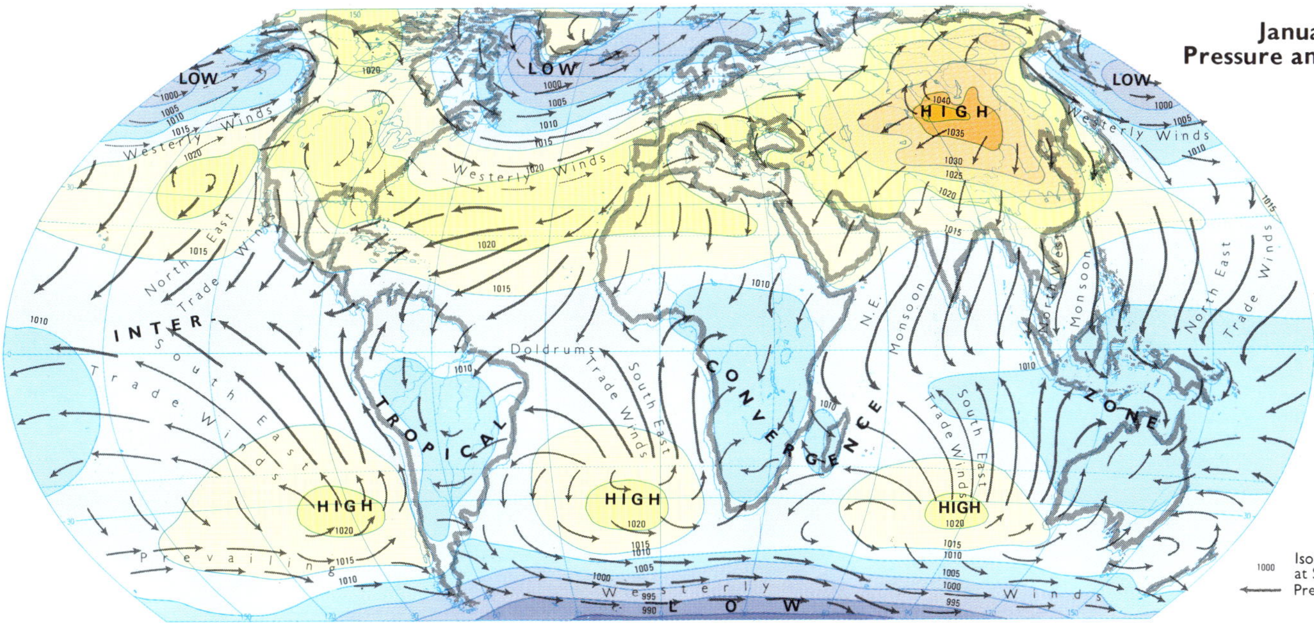

mb: 1040, 1035, 1030, 1025, 1020, 1015, 1010, 1005, 1000, 995, 990

1000 Isobars in millibars at Sea Level

Prevailing Winds

July Pressure and Winds

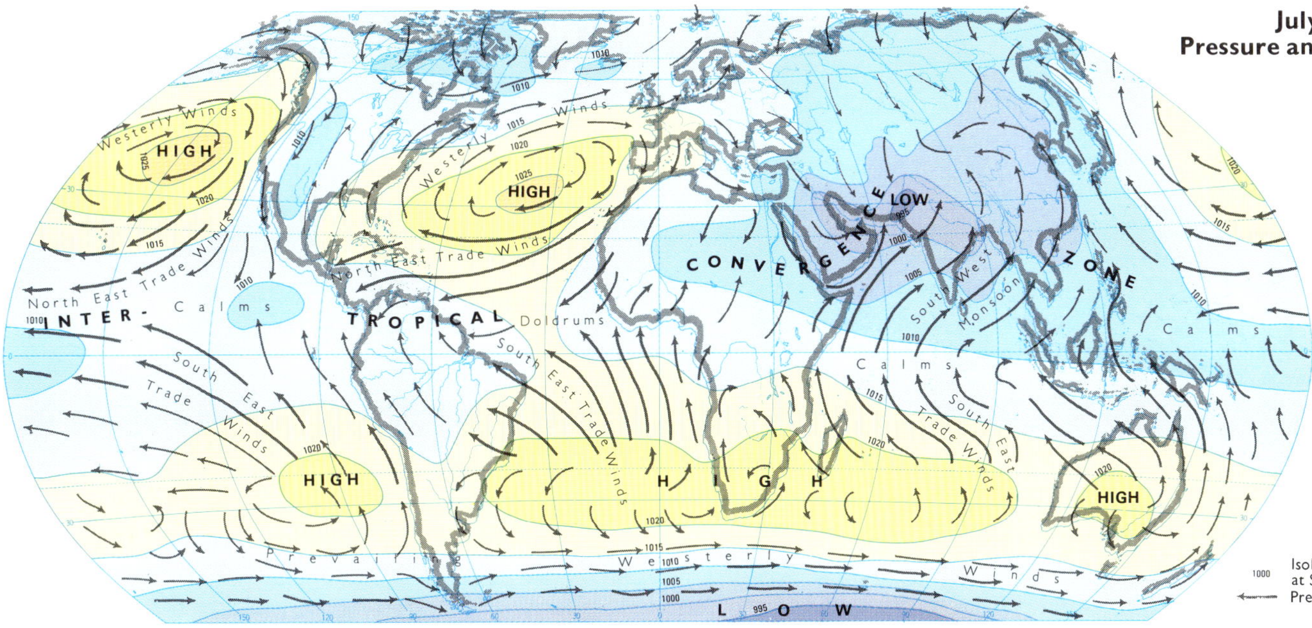

mb: 1025, 1020, 1015, 1010, 1005, 1000, 995

1000 Isobars in millibars at Sea Level

Prevailing Winds

Annual Precipitation

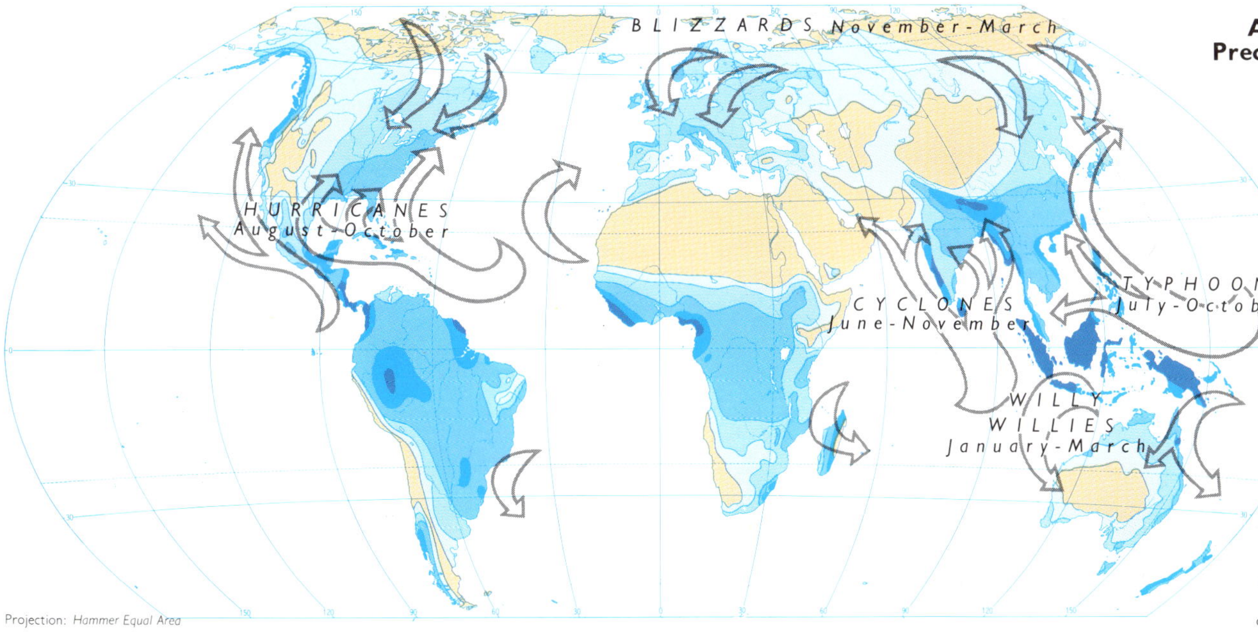

mm: 3000, 2000, 1000, 500, 250

Paths of tropical storms and winter blizzards

Projection: *Hammer Equal Area*

1:190 000 000

These four pages give temperature and precipitation statistics for over 80 stations, which are arranged by listing the continents and the places within each continent in alphabetical order. The elevation of each station, in metres above mean sea level, is stated beneath its name. The average monthly temperature, in degrees Celsius, and the average monthly precipitation, in millimetres, are given. To the right, the average yearly rainfall, the average yearly temperature, and the annual range of temperature (the difference between the warmest and the coldest months) are also stated.

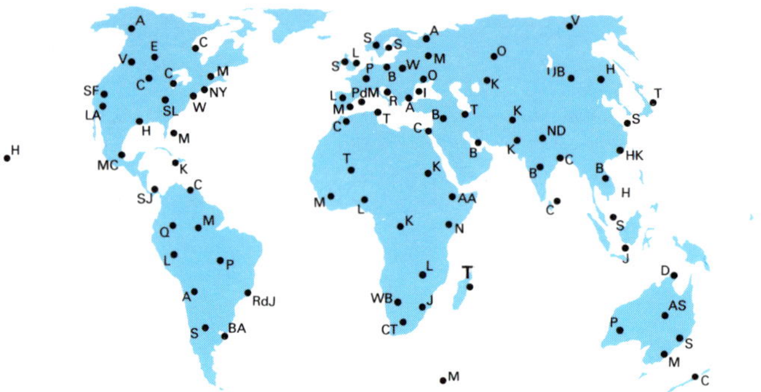

AFRICA

Station		Jan.	Feb.	Mar.	Apr.	May	June	July	Aug.	Sept.	Oct.	Nov.	Dec.	Year	Annual Range
Addis Ababa, Ethiopia															
	Precipitation	<3	3	25	135	213	201	206	239	102	28	<3	0	1 151	
2 450 m	*Temperature*	19	20	20	20	19	18	18	19	21	22	21	20	20	4
Cairo, Egypt															
	Precipitation	5	5	5	3	3	<3	0	0	<3	<3	3	5	28	
116 m	*Temperature*	13	15	18	21	25	28	28	28	26	24	20	15	22	15
Cape Town, South Africa															
	Precipitation	15	8	18	48	79	84	89	66	43	31	18	10	508	
17 m	*Temperature*	21	21	20	17	14	13	12	13	14	16	18	19	17	9
Casablanca, Morocco															
	Precipitation	53	48	56	36	23	5	0	<3	8	38	66	71	404	
50 m	*Temperature*	13	13	14	16	18	20	22	23	22	19	16	13	18	10
Johannesburg, South Africa															
	Precipitation	114	109	89	38	25	8	8	8	23	56	107	125	709	
1 665 m	*Temperature*	20	20	18	16	13	10	11	13	16	18	19	20	16	10
Khartoum, Sudan															
	Precipitation	<3	<3	<3	<3	3	8	53	71	18	5	<3	0	158	
390 m	*Temperature*	24	25	28	31	33	34	32	31	32	32	28	25	29	9
Kinshasa, Zaïre															
	Precipitation	135	145	196	196	158	8	3	3	31	119	221	142	1 354	
325 m	*Temperature*	26	26	27	27	26	24	23	24	25	26	26	26	25	4
Lagos, Nigeria															
	Precipitation	28	46	102	150	269	460	279	64	140	206	69	25	1 836	
3 m	*Temperature*	27	28	29	28	28	26	26	25	26	26	28	28	27	4
Lusaka, Zambia															
	Precipitation	231	191	142	18	3	<3	<3	0	<3	10	91	150	836	
1 277 m	*Temperature*	21	22	21	21	19	16	16	18	22	24	23	22	21	8
Monrovia, Liberia															
	Precipitation	31	56	97	216	516	973	996	373	744	772	236	130	5 138	
23 m	*Temperature*	26	26	27	27	26	25	24	25	25	25	26	26	26	3
Nairobi, Kenya															
	Precipitation	38	64	125	211	158	46	15	23	31	53	109	86	958	
1 820 m	*Temperature*	19	19	19	19	18	16	16	16	18	19	18	18	18	3
Tananarive, Madagascar															
	Precipitation	300	279	178	53	18	8	8	10	18	61	135	287	1 356	
1 372 m	*Temperature*	21	21	21	19	18	15	14	15	17	19	21	21	19	7
Timbuktu, Mali															
	Precipitation	<3	<3	3	<3	5	23	79	81	38	3	<3	<3	231	
301 m	*Temperature*	22	24	28	32	34	35	32	30	32	31	28	23	29	13
Tunis, Tunisia															
	Precipitation	64	51	41	36	18	8	3	8	33	51	48	61	419	
66 m	*Temperature*	10	11	13	16	19	23	26	27	25	20	16	11	18	17
Walvis Bay, South Africa															
	Precipitation	<3	5	8	3	3	<3	<3	3	<3	<3	<3	<3	23	
7 m	*Temperature*	19	19	19	18	17	16	15	14	14	15	17	18	18	5

AMERICA, NORTH

Station		Jan.	Feb.	Mar.	Apr.	May	June	July	Aug.	Sept.	Oct.	Nov.	Dec.	Year	Annual Range
Anchorage, Alaska, U.S.A.															
	Precipitation	20	18	15	10	13	18	41	66	66	56	25	23	371	
40 m	*Temperature*	–11	–8	–5	2	7	12	14	13	9	2	–5	–11	2	25
Cheyenne, Wyo., U.S.A.															
	Precipitation	10	15	25	48	61	41	53	41	31	25	13	13	376	
1 871 m	*Temperature*	–4	–3	1	5	10	16	19	19	14	7	1	–2	7	23
Chicago, Ill., U.S.A.															
	Precipitation	51	51	66	71	86	89	84	81	79	66	61	51	836	
251 m	*Temperature*	–4	–3	2	9	14	20	23	22	19	12	5	–1	10	27
Churchill, Man., Canada															
	Precipitation	15	13	18	23	32	44	46	58	51	43	39	21	402	
13 m	*Temperature*	–28	–26	–20	–10	–2	6	12	11	5	–2	–12	–22	–7	40

		Jan.	Feb.	Mar.	Apr.	May	June	July	Aug.	Sept.	Oct.	Nov.	Dec.	Year	Annual range
Edmonton, Alta., Canada															
	Precipitation	25	19	19	22	43	77	89	78	39	17	16	25	466	
676 m	*Temperature*	– 15	– 10	– 5	4	11	15	17	16	11	6	– 4	– 10	3	32
Honolulu, Hawaii, U.S.A.															
	Precipitation	104	66	79	48	25	18	23	28	36	48	64	104	643	
12 m	*Temperature*	23	18	19	20	22	24	25	26	26	24	22	19	22	8
Houston, Tex., U.S.A.															
	Precipitation	89	76	84	91	119	117	99	99	104	94	89	109	1 171	
12 m	*Temperature*	12	13	17	21	24	27	28	29	26	22	16	12	21	17
Kingston, Jamaica															
	Precipitation	23	15	23	31	102	89	38	91	99	180	74	36	800	
34 m	*Temperature*	25	25	25	26	26	28	28	28	27	27	26	26	26	3
Los Angeles, Calif., U.S.A.															
	Precipitation	79	76	71	25	10	3	< 3	< 3	5	15	31	66	381	
95 m	*Temperature*	13	14	14	16	17	19	21	22	21	18	16	14	17	9
Mexico City, Mexico															
	Precipitation	13	5	10	20	53	119	170	152	130	51	18	8	747	
2 309 m	*Temperature*	12	13	16	18	19	19	17	18	18	16	14	13	16	7
Miami, Fla., U.S.A.															
	Precipitation	71	53	64	81	173	178	155	160	203	234	71	51	1 516	
8 m	*Temperature*	20	20	22	23	25	27	28	28	27	25	22	21	24	8
Montreal, Que., Canada															
	Precipitation	72	65	74	74	66	82	90	92	88	76	81	87	946	
57 m	*Temperature*	– 10	– 9	– 3	– 6	13	18	21	20	15	9	2	– 7	6	31
New York, N.Y., U.S.A.															
	Precipitation	94	97	91	81	81	84	107	109	86	89	76	91	1 092	
96 m	*Temperature*	–1	–1	3	10	16	20	23	23	21	15	7	2	8	24
St. Louis, Mo., U.S.A.															
	Precipitation	58	64	89	97	114	114	89	86	81	74	71	64	1 001	
173 m	*Temperature*	0	1	7	13	19	24	26	26	22	15	8	2	14	26
San Francisco, Calif., U.S.A.															
	Precipitation	119	97	79	38	18	3	< 3	< 3	8	25	64	112	561	
16 m	*Temperature*	10	12	13	13	14	15	15	15	17	16	14	11	14	7
San José, Costa Rica															
	Precipitation	15	5	20	46	229	241	211	241	305	300	145	41	1 798	
1 146 m	*Temperature*	19	19	21	21	22	21	21	21	21	20	20	19	20	2
Vancouver, B.C., Canada															
	Precipitation	154	115	101	60	52	45	32	41	67	114	150	182	1113	
14 m	*Temperature*	3	5	6	9	12	15	17	17	14	10	6	4	10	14
Washington, D.C., U.S.A.															
	Precipitation	86	76	91	84	94	99	112	109	94	74	66	79	1 064	
22 m	*Temperature*	1	2	7	12	18	23	25	24	20	14	8	3	13	24

AMERICA, SOUTH

		Jan.	Feb.	Mar.	Apr.	May	June	July	Aug.	Sept.	Oct.	Nov.	Dec.	Year	Annual range
Antofagasta, Chile															
	Precipitation	0	0	0	< 3	< 3	3	5	3	< 3	3	< 3	0	13	
94 m	*Temperature*	21	21	20	18	16	15	14	14	15	16	18	19	17	7
Buenos Aires, Argentina															
	Precipitation	79	71	109	89	76	61	56	61	79	86	84	99	950	
27 m	*Temperature*	23	23	21	17	13	9	10	11	13	15	19	22	16	14
Caracas, Venezuela															
	Precipitation	23	10	15	33	79	102	109	109	107	109	94	46	836	
1 042 m	*Temperature*	19	19	20	21	22	21	21	21	21	21	20	20	21	3
Lima, Peru															
	Precipitation	3	< 3	< 3	< 3	5	5	8	8	8	3	3	< 3	41	
120 m	*Temperature*	23	24	24	22	19	17	17	16	17	18	19	21	20	8
Manaus, Brazil															
	Precipitation	249	231	262	221	170	84	58	38	46	107	142	203	1 811	
44 m	*Temperature*	28	28	28	27	28	28	28	28	29	29	29	28	28	2
Paraná, Brazil															
	Precipitation	287	236	239	102	13	< 3	3	5	28	127	231	310	1 582	
260 m	*Temperature*	23	23	23	23	23	21	21	22	24	24	24	23	23	3
Quito, Ecuador															
	Precipitation	99	112	142	175	137	43	20	31	69	112	97	79	1 115	
2 879 m	*Temperature*	15	15	15	15	15	14	14	15	15	15	15	15	15	1
Rio de Janeiro, Brazil															
	Precipitation	125	122	130	107	79	53	41	43	66	79	104	137	1 082	
61 m	*Temperature*	26	26	25	24	22	21	21	21	21	22	23	25	23	5
Santiago, Chile															
	Precipitation	3	3	5	13	64	84	76	56	31	15	8	5	358	
520 m	*Temperature*	21	20	18	15	12	9	9	10	12	15	17	19	15	12

ASIA

		Jan.	Feb.	Mar.	Apr.	May	June	July	Aug.	Sept.	Oct.	Nov.	Dec.	Year	Annual range
Bahrain															
	Precipitation	8	18	13	8	< 3	0	0	0	0	0	18	18	81	
5 m	*Temperature*	17	18	21	25	29	32	33	34	31	28	24	19	26	16
Bangkok, Thailand															
	Precipitation	8	20	36	58	198	160	160	175	305	206	66	5	1 397	
2 m	*Temperature*	26	28	29	30	29	29	28	28	28	28	26	25	28	5
Beirut, Lebanon															
	Precipitation	191	158	94	53	18	3	< 3	< 3	5	51	132	185	892	
34 m	*Temperature*	14	14	16	18	22	24	27	28	26	24	19	16	21	14
Bombay, India															
	Precipitation	3	3	3	< 3	18	485	617	340	264	64	13	3	1 809	
11 m	*Temperature*	24	24	26	28	30	29	27	27	27	28	27	26	27	6
Calcutta, India															
	Precipitation	10	31	36	43	140	297	325	328	252	114	20	5	1 600	
6 m	*Temperature*	20	22	27	30	30	30	29	29	29	28	23	19	26	11
Colombo, Sri Lanka															
	Precipitation	89	69	147	231	371	224	135	109	160	348	315	147	2 365	
7 m	*Temperature*	26	26	27	28	28	27	27	27	27	27	26	26	27	2
Harbin, China															
	Precipitation	5	5	10	23	43	94	112	104	46	33	8	5	488	
160 m	*Temperature*	–18	–15	–5	6	13	19	22	21	14	4	–6	–16	3	40
Ho Chi Minh City, Vietnam															
	Precipitation	15	3	13	43	221	330	315	269	335	269	114	56	1 984	
9 m	*Temperature*	26	27	29	30	29	28	28	28	27	27	27	26	28	4
Jakarta, Indonesia															
	Precipitation	300	300	211	147	114	97	64	43	66	112	142	203	1 798	
8 m	*Temperature*	26	26	27	27	27	27	27	27	27	27	27	26	27	1
Hong Kong															
	Precipitation	33	46	74	137	292	394	381	361	257	114	43	31	2 162	
33 m	*Temperature*	16	15	18	22	26	28	28	28	27	25	21	18	23	13
Kabul, Afghanistan															
	Precipitation	31	36	94	102	20	5	3	3	< 3	15	20	10	338	
1 815 m	*Temperature*	–3	–1	6	13	18	22	25	24	20	14	7	3	12	28
Karachi, Pakistan															
	Precipitation	13	10	8	3	3	18	81	41	13	< 3	3	5	196	
4 m	*Temperature*	19	20	24	28	30	31	30	29	28	28	24	20	26	12
New Delhi, India															
	Precipitation	23	18	13	8	13	74	180	172	117	10	3	10	640	
218 m	*Temperature*	14	17	23	28	33	34	31	30	29	26	20	15	25	20
Shanghai, China															
	Precipitation	48	58	84	94	94	180	147	142	130	71	51	36	1 135	
7 m	*Temperature*	4	5	9	14	20	24	28	28	23	19	12	7	16	24
Singapore															
	Precipitation	252	173	193	188	173	173	170	196	178	208	254	257	2 413	
10 m	*Temperature*	26	27	28	28	28	28	28	27	27	27	27	27	27	2
Tehran, Iran															
	Precipitation	46	38	46	36	13	3	3	3	3	8	20	31	246	
1 220 m	*Temperature*	2	5	9	16	21	26	30	29	25	18	12	6	17	28
Tokyo, Japan															
	Precipitation	48	74	107	135	147	165	142	152	234	208	97	56	1 565	
6 m	*Temperature*	3	4	7	13	17	21	25	26	23	17	11	6	14	23
Ulan Bator, Mongolia															
	Precipitation	< 3	< 3	3	5	10	28	76	51	23	5	5	3	208	
1 325 m	*Temperature*	–26	–21	–13	–1	6	14	16	14	8	–1	–13	–22	–3	42

AUSTRALIA, NEW ZEALAND and ANTARCTICA

		Jan.	Feb.	Mar.	Apr.	May	June	July	Aug.	Sept.	Oct.	Nov.	Dec.	Year	Annual range
Alice Springs, Australia															
	Precipitation	43	33	28	10	15	13	8	8	8	18	31	38	252	
579 m	*Temperature*	29	28	25	20	15	12	12	14	18	23	26	28	21	17
Christchurch, New Zealand															
	Precipitation	56	43	48	48	66	66	69	48	46	43	48	56	638	
10 m	*Temperature*	16	16	14	12	9	6	6	7	9	12	14	16	11	10
Darwin, Australia															
	Precipitation	386	312	254	97	15	3	< 3	3	13	51	119	239	1 491	
30 m	*Temperature*	29	29	29	29	28	26	25	26	28	29	30	29	28	5
Mawson, Antarctica															
	Precipitation	11	30	20	10	44	180	4	40	3	20	0	0	362	
14 m	*Temperature*	0	–5	–10	–14	–15	–16	–18	–18	–19	–13	–5	–1	–11	18

		Jan.	Feb.	Mar.	Apr.	May	June	July	Aug.	Sept.	Oct.	Nov.	Dec.	Year	Annual Range
Melbourne, Australia															
	Precipitation	48	46	56	58	53	53	48	48	58	66	58	58	653	
35 m	*Temperature*	20	20	18	15	13	10	9	11	13	14	16	18	15	11
Perth, Australia															
	Precipitation	8	10	20	43	130	180	170	149	86	56	20	13	881	
60 m	*Temperature*	23	23	22	19	16	14	13	13	15	16	19	22	18	10
Sydney, Australia															
	Precipitation	89	102	127	135	127	117	117	76	73	71	73	73	1 181	
42 m	*Temperature*	22	22	21	18	15	13	12	13	15	18	19	21	17	10

EUROPE and U.S.S.R.

		Jan.	Feb.	Mar.	Apr.	May	June	July	Aug.	Sept.	Oct.	Nov.	Dec.	Year	Annual Range
Archangel, U.S.S.R.															
	Precipitation	31	19	25	29	42	52	62	56	63	63	47	41	530	
13 m	*Temperature*	–16	–14	–9	0	7	12	15	14	8	2	–4	–11	0	31
Athens, Greece															
	Precipitation	62	37	37	23	23	14	6	7	15	51	56	71	402	
107 m	*Temperature*	10	10	12	16	20	25	28	28	24	20	15	11	18	18
Berlin, Germany															
	Precipitation	46	40	33	42	49	65	73	69	48	49	46	43	603	
55 m	*Temperature*	–1	0	4	9	14	17	19	18	15	9	5	1	9	20
Istanbul, Turkey															
	Precipitation	109	92	72	46	38	34	34	30	58	81	103	119	816	
114 m	*Temperature*	5	6	7	11	16	20	23	23	20	16	12	8	14	18
Kazalinsk, U.S.S.R.															
	Precipitation	10	10	13	13	15	5	5	8	8	10	13	15	125	
63 m	*Temperature*	–12	–11	–3	6	18	23	25	23	16	8	–1	–7	7	37
Lisbon, Portugal															
	Precipitation	111	76	109	54	44	16	3	4	33	62	93	103	708	
77 m	*Temperature*	11	12	14	16	17	20	22	23	21	18	14	12	17	12
London, U.K.															
	Precipitation	54	40	37	37	46	45	57	59	49	57	64	48	593	
5 m	*Temperature*	4	5	7	9	12	16	18	17	15	11	8	5	11	14
Málaga, Spain															
	Precipitation	61	51	62	46	26	5	1	3	29	64	64	62	474	
33 m	*Temperature*	12	13	15	17	19	29	25	26	23	20	16	13	18	17
Moscow, U.S.S.R.															
	Precipitation	39	38	36	37	53	58	88	71	58	45	47	54	624	
156 m	*Temperature*	–13	–10	–4	6	13	16	18	17	12	6	–1	–7	4	31
Odessa, U.S.S.R.															
	Precipitation	57	62	30	21	34	34	42	37	37	13	35	71	473	
64 m	*Temperature*	–3	–1	2	9	15	20	22	22	18	12	9	1	10	25
Omsk, U.S.S.R.															
	Precipitation	15	8	8	13	31	51	51	51	28	25	18	20	318	
85 m	*Temperature*	–22	–19	–12	–1	10	16	18	16	10	1	–11	–18	–1	40
Palma de Mallorca, Spain															
	Precipitation	39	34	51	32	29	17	3	25	55	77	47	40	449	
10 m	*Temperature*	10	11	12	15	17	21	24	25	23	18	14	11	17	15
Paris, France															
	Precipitation	56	46	35	42	57	54	59	64	55	50	51	50	619	
75 m	*Temperature*	3	4	8	11	15	18	20	19	17	12	7	4	12	17
Rome, Italy															
	Precipitation	71	62	57	51	46	37	15	21	63	99	129	93	744	
17 m	*Temperature*	8	9	11	14	18	22	25	25	22	17	13	10	16	17
Shannon, Irish Republic															
	Precipitation	94	67	56	53	61	57	77	79	86	86	96	117	929	
2 m	*Temperature*	5	5	7	9	12	14	16	16	14	11	8	6	10	11
Stavanger, Norway															
	Precipitation	93	56	45	70	49	84	93	118	142	129	125	126	1 130	
85 m	*Temperature*	1	1	3	6	10	13	15	15	13	9	6	3	8	14
Stockholm, Sweden															
	Precipitation	43	30	25	31	34	45	61	76	60	48	53	48	554	
44 m	*Temperature*	–3	–3	–1	5	10	15	18	17	12	7	3	0	7	21
Verkhoyansk, U.S.S.R.															
	Precipitation	5	5	3	5	8	23	28	25	13	8	8	5	134	
100 m	*Temperature*	–50	–45	–32	–15	0	12	14	9	2	–15	–38	–48	–17	64
Warsaw, Poland															
	Precipitation	27	32	27	37	46	69	96	65	43	38	31	44	555	
110 m	*Temperature*	–3	–3	2	7	14	17	19	18	14	9	3	0	8	22

CLIMATES

after Köppen

Climatic group		Climate	Temperature	Rainfall
A TROPICAL RAINY CLIMATES	**Af**	RAIN-FOREST CLIMATE	All mean monthly temperatures above 18°C	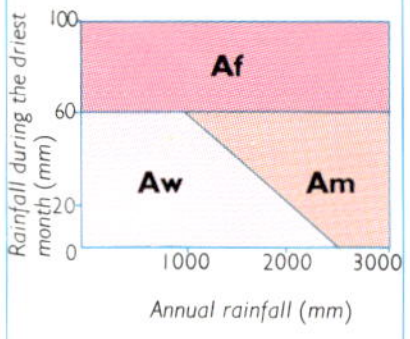
	Am	MONSOON CLIMATE		
	Aw	SAVANNA CLIMATE		
B DRY CLIMATES	**BS**	STEPPE CLIMATE	Mean annual temperature; **h** = above 18°C; **k** = below 18°C	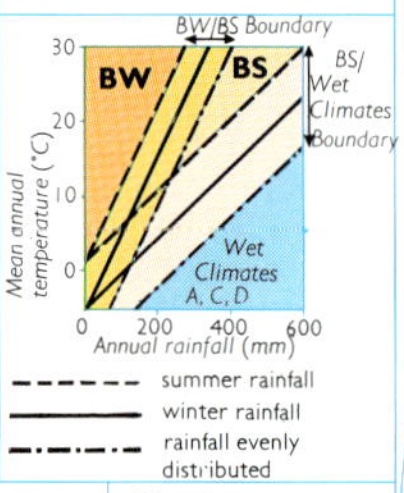
	BW	DESERT CLIMATE		
C WARM TEMPERATE RAINY CLIMATES	**Cw**	DRY WINTER CLIMATE	Mean temperature of the coldest month between −3°C to 18°C. **a** Mean temperature of hottest month above 22°C, and with more than 4 months of over 10°C	**w** dry winter. Rainfall of the driest month of the cold season is one-tenth or less of the rainfall of the wettest month of the hot season
	Cs	DRY SUMMER CLIMATE (Mediterranean)	**b** Mean temperature of hottest month below 22°C and with more than 4 months of over 10°C	**s** dry summer. Rainfall of the driest month of the hot season is less than one-third of the rainfall of the wettest month of the cold season and less than 40mm.
	Cf	CLIMATE WITH NO DRY SEASON		
D COLD TEMPERATE RAINY CLIMATES	**Dw**	DRY WINTER CLIMATE	Mean temperature of the coldest month below −3°C. **c** Mean temperature of hottest month below 22°C, but with less than 4 months of over 10°C	**f** with no dry season. Rainfall does not correspond to w or s climates
	Df	CLIMATE WITH NO DRY SEASON	**d** Mean temperature of hottest month below 22°C, and of the coldest month below −38°C	
E POLAR CLIMATES	**ET**	TUNDRA CLIMATE	Mean temperature of the hottest month below 10°C. Mean temperature of the hottest month between 0°C and 10°C	**H** More than 1500m above sea level
	EF	PERPETUAL FROST	Mean temperature of the hottest month between 0°C and 10°C	

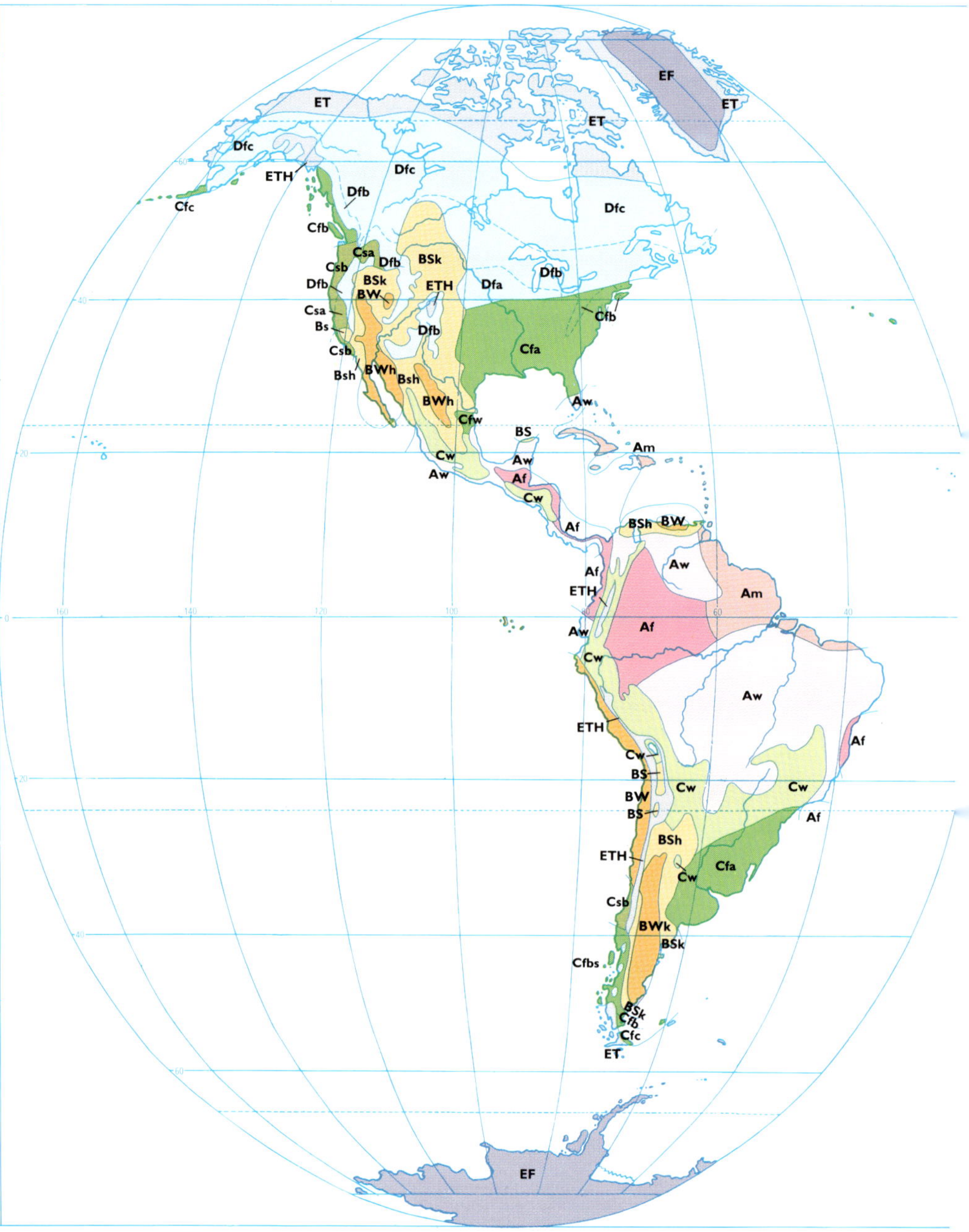

SOIL REGIONS

1:240 000 000

after Glinka, Stremme, Marbut, and others

- Tundra Soil
- Podzols
- Brown Forest Soil
- Lightly leached Dry Forest Soil
- Red and yellow Sub-tropical Forest Soil
- Reddish Savanna Soil and Tropical Red Earths
- Laterites
- Chernozem
- Degraded Chernozem
- Black Savanna Soil
- Chestnut Steppe Soil
- Grey, light brown and red brown Desert Steppe Soils
- Alluvium
- Mountain and High Plateau Soils
- Oases Soil
- Tropical and Mangrove Swamp

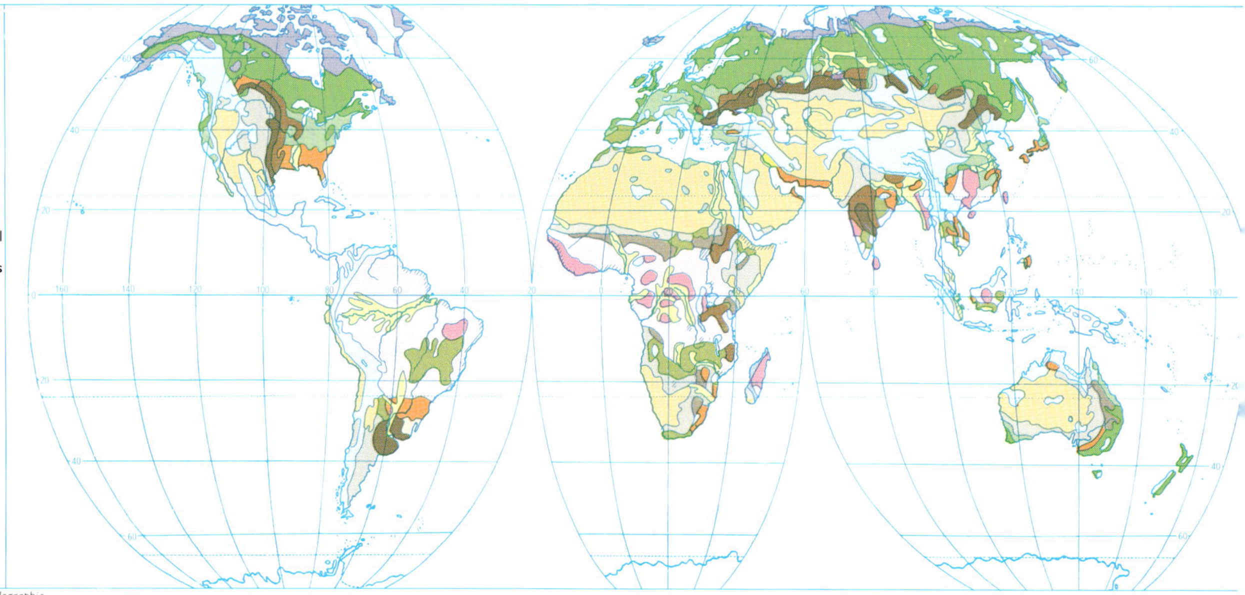

Projection: *Interrupted Mollweide's Homolographic*

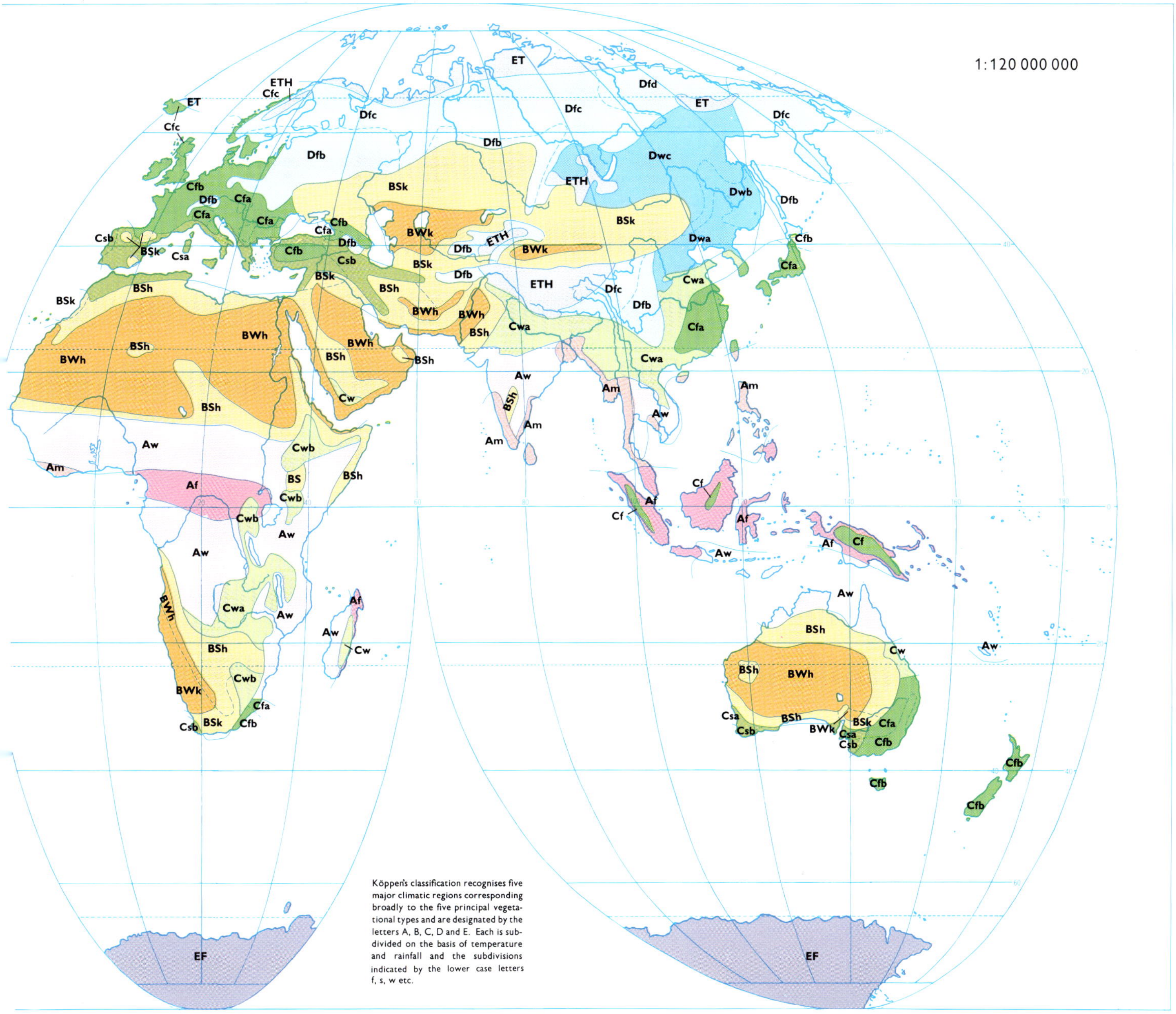

Köppen's classification recognises five major climatic regions corresponding broadly to the five principal vegetational types and are designated by the letters A, B, C, D and E. Each is subdivided on the basis of temperature and rainfall and the subdivisions indicated by the lower case letters f, s, w etc.

NATURAL VEGETATION

1:240 000 000

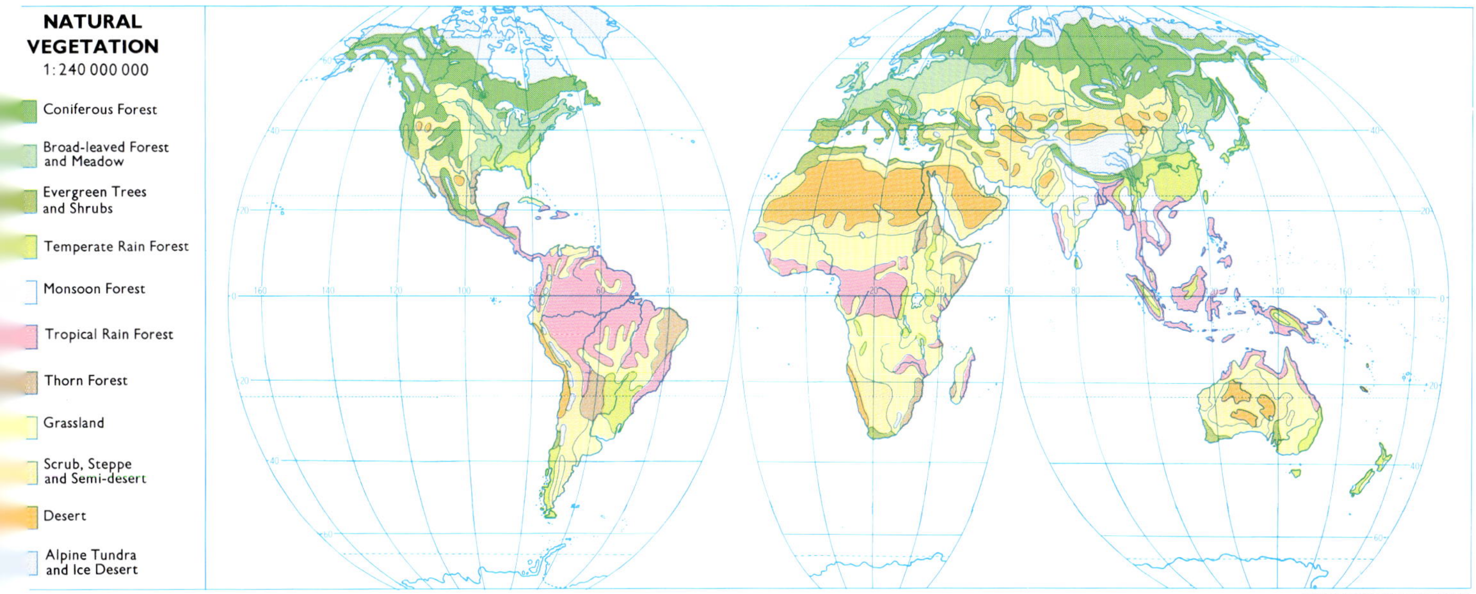

STRUCTURE

1:95 000 000

Structural Regions of the Land

- Pre-Cambrian shields
- Sedimentary cover on Pre-Cambrian shields
- Palæozoic (Caledonian and Hercynian) folding
- Sedimentary cover on Palæozoic folding
- Mesozoic folding
- Sedimentary cover on Mesozoic folding
- Cainozoic folding
- Sedimentary cover on Cainozoic folding
- Intensive Mesozoic and Cainozoic vulcanism
- Oceanic-type crust raised above sea level

Structural Regions of the Oceans

- Regions of continental-type crust
- Limit of continental shelf
- Oceanic marginal troughs
- Mid-oceanic volcanic ridges
- Rift valleys in mid-oceanic ridges
- Principal faults
- Frontal line of overthrust folds

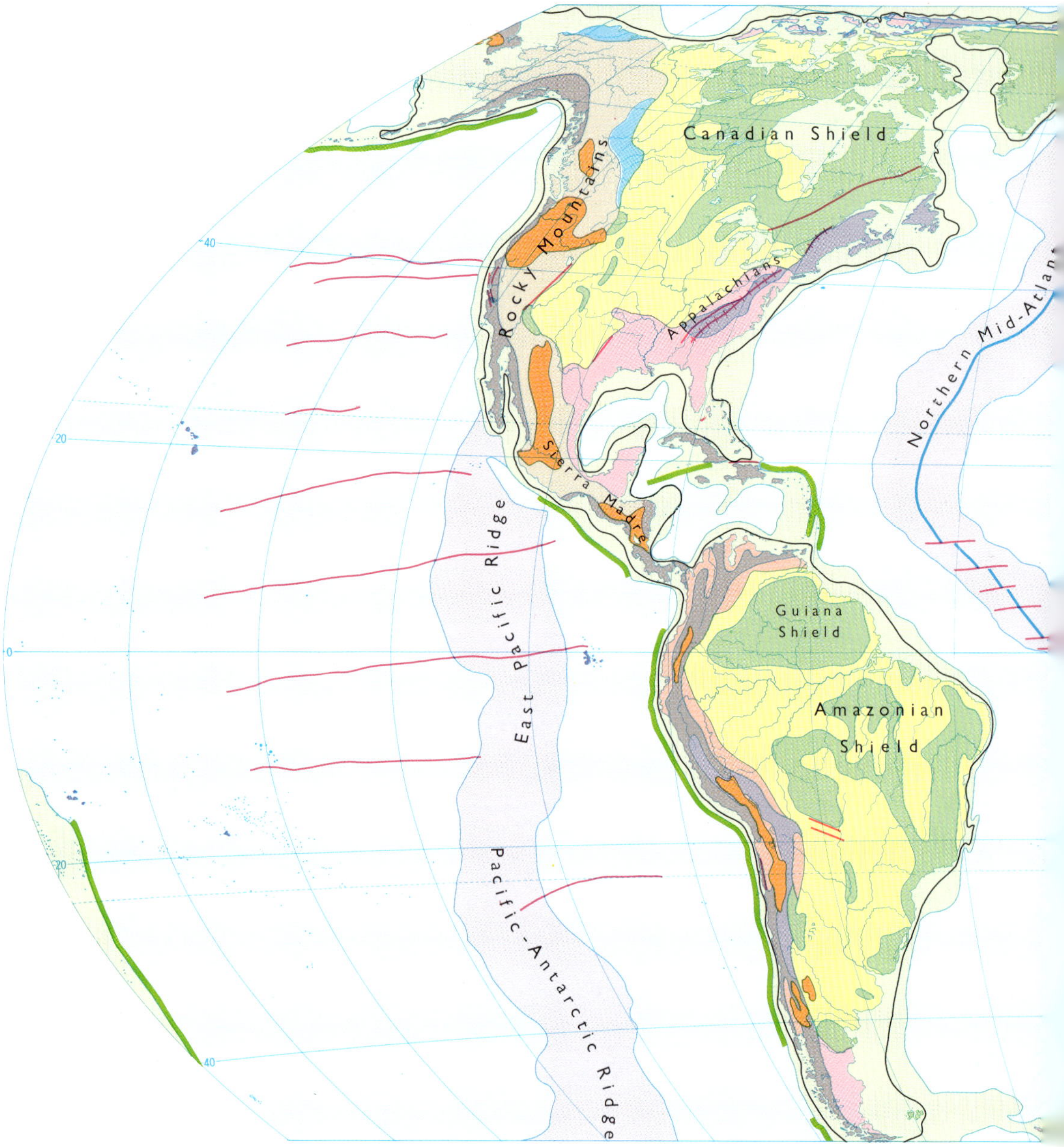

GEOLOGICAL TIME SCALE

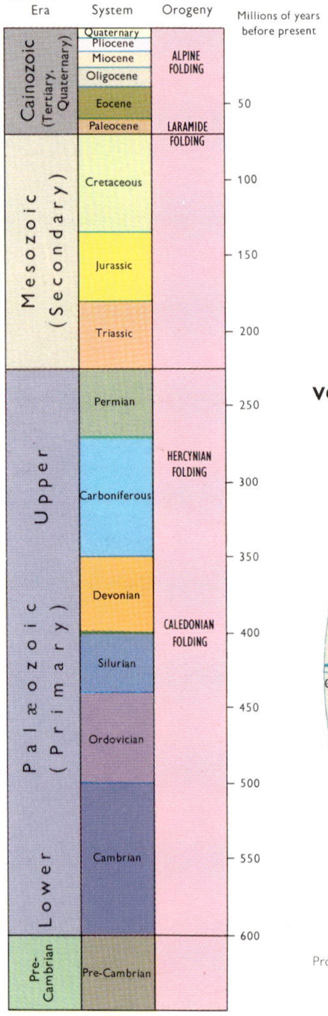

VOLCANOES

Equatorial Scale 1:280 000

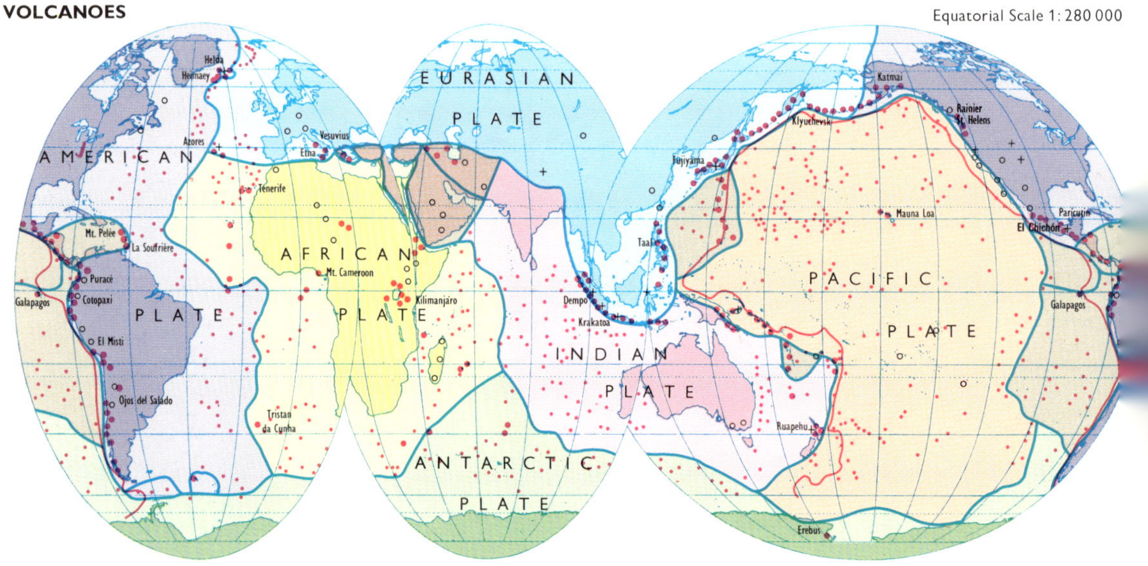

Projection: *Interrupted Mollweide's Homolographic*

- Land volcanoes active since 1700
- Land volcanoes inactive since 1700
- Submarine volcanoes
- Geysers
- Plate boundaries
- Andesite line (boundary be[tween] sial continental crust and oceanic crust in the Pacifi[c])

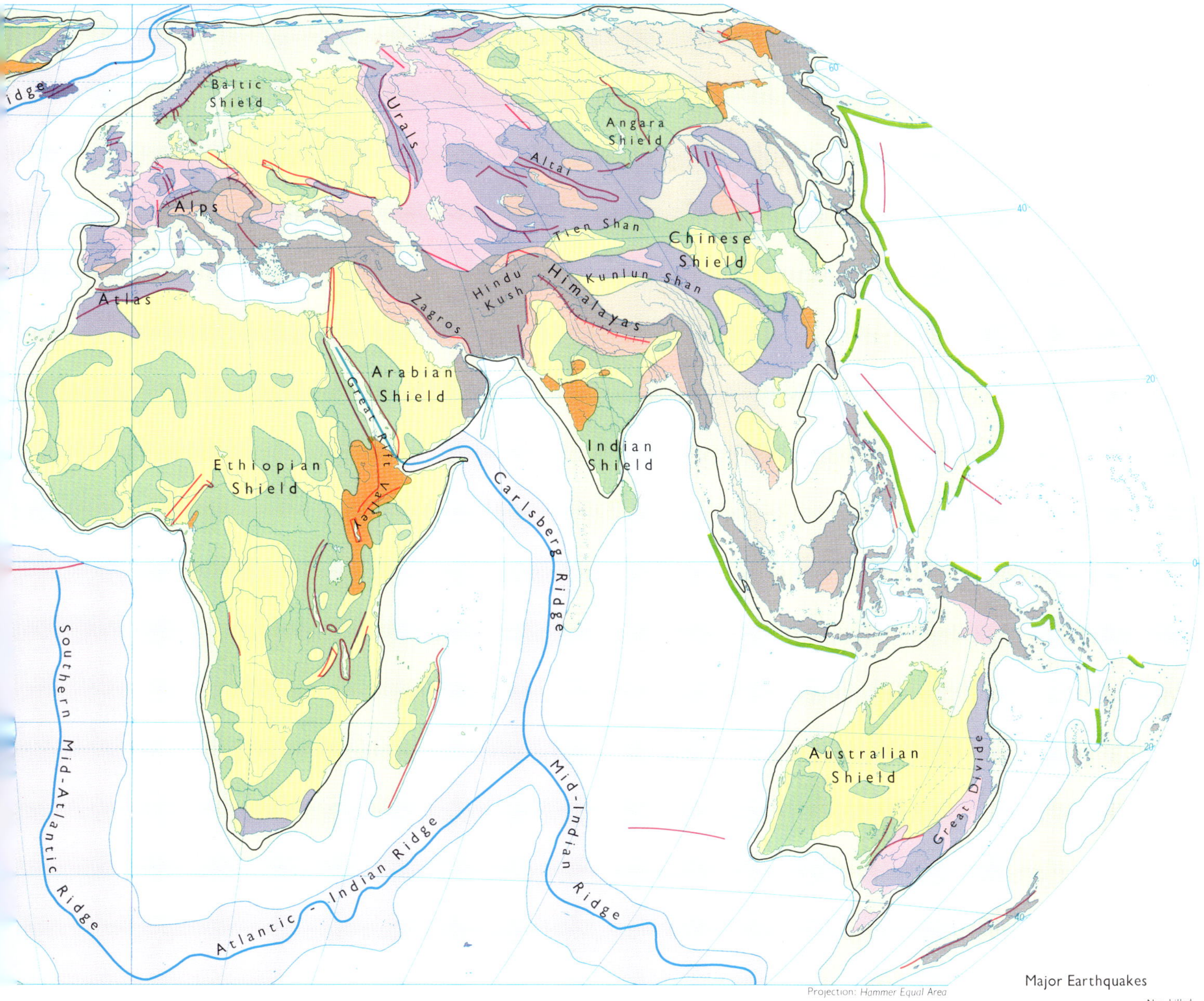

Projection: *Hammer Equal Area*

ARTHQUAKES

Equatorial Scale 1: 280 000 000

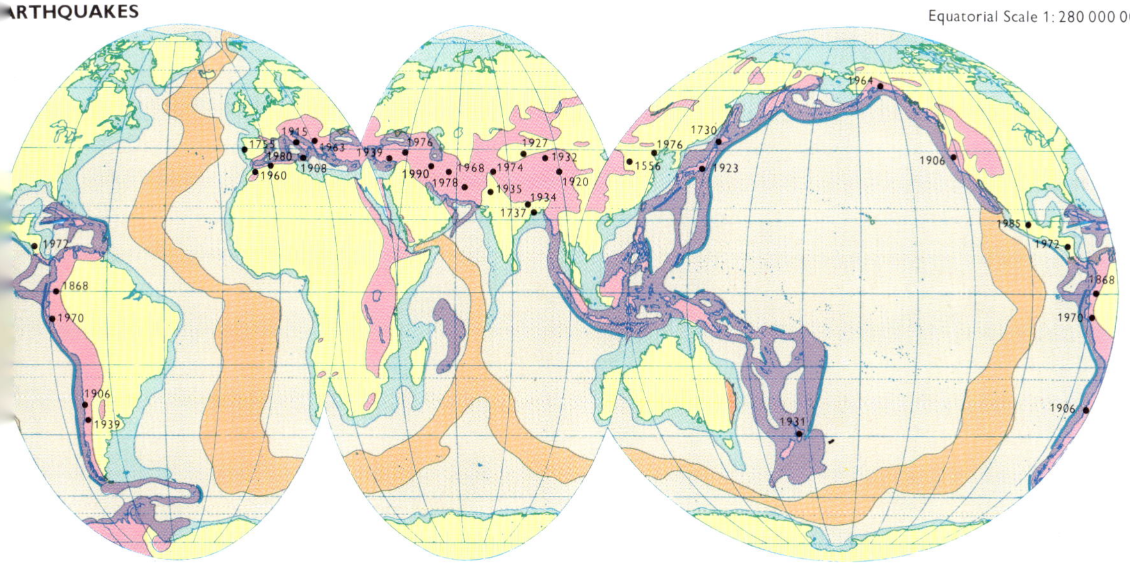

06 Principal earthquakes and their dates

— Oceanic marginal troughs

Mobile land areas

Submarine zones of mobile land areas

Stable land platforms

Submarine extensions of stable land platforms

Mid-oceanic volcanic ridges

Oceanic platforms

Major Earthquakes

		Nos. killed
1556	Shaanxi, China	830 000
1730	Hokkaido, Japan	137 000
1737	Calcutta, India	300 000
1755	Lisbon, Portugal	60 000
1868	Ecuador and N. Peru	40 000
1906	Valparaiso, Chile	22 000
1906	San Francisco, U.S.A.	450
1908	Messina, Italy	77 000
1915	Avezzano, Italy	30 000
1920	Gansu, China	180 000
1923	Yokohama, Japan	143 000
1927	Nan Shan, China	200 000
1931	Napier, N. Zealand	250
1932	Gansu, China	70 000
1934	Nepal	11 700
1935	Quetta, Pakistan	30 000
1939	Erzincan, Turkey	30 000
1960	Agadir, Morocco	12 000
1963	Skopje, Yugoslavia	1000
1964	Anchorage, Alaska	100
1968	N.E. Iran	12 000
1970	N. Peru	67 000
1972	Managua, Nicaragua	7 000
1974	N. Pakistan	10 000
1976	Tangshan, China	650 000
1978	Tabas, Iran	11 000
1980	El Asnam, Algeria	20 000
1985	Mexico	10 000
1988	Armenia	55 000
1990	N. Iran	50 000

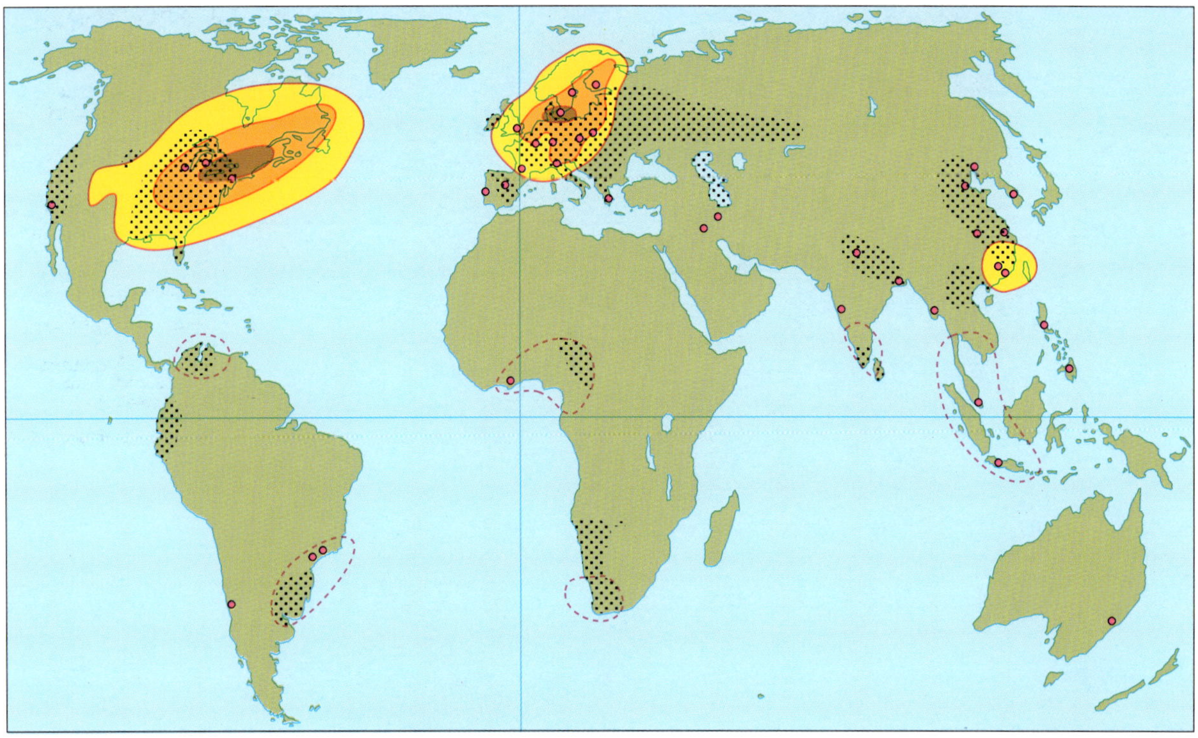

ACID RAIN

Acid rain is caused by high levels of sulphur and nitroge in the atmosphere. They combine with water vapour and oxygen to form acids (H_2SO_4 and HNO_3) which fall as precipitation.

Main areas of sulphu and nitrogen emissio (from the burning of fossil fuels)

Major cities with high levels of air pollution (including sulphur an nitrogen emissions)

Areas of acid deposition

(pH numbers measure acidity: normal rain is pH 5.6)

pH less than 4.0 (most acidic)

pH 4.0 - 4.5

pH 4.5 - 5.0

Potential problem areas

GLOBAL WARMING

Global warming is caused by high levels of carbon dioxide and other gases in the atmosphere (the Greenhouse Effect). It is estimated that by 2020 the world could be approximately 1.3°C warmer than now.

Carbon dioxide (CO_2) emissions in tonnes per person per year

Over 10 tonnes

5 - 10 tonnes

1 - 5 tonnes

Under 1 tonne

Coastal areas vulnerable to rising sea levels caused by global warming

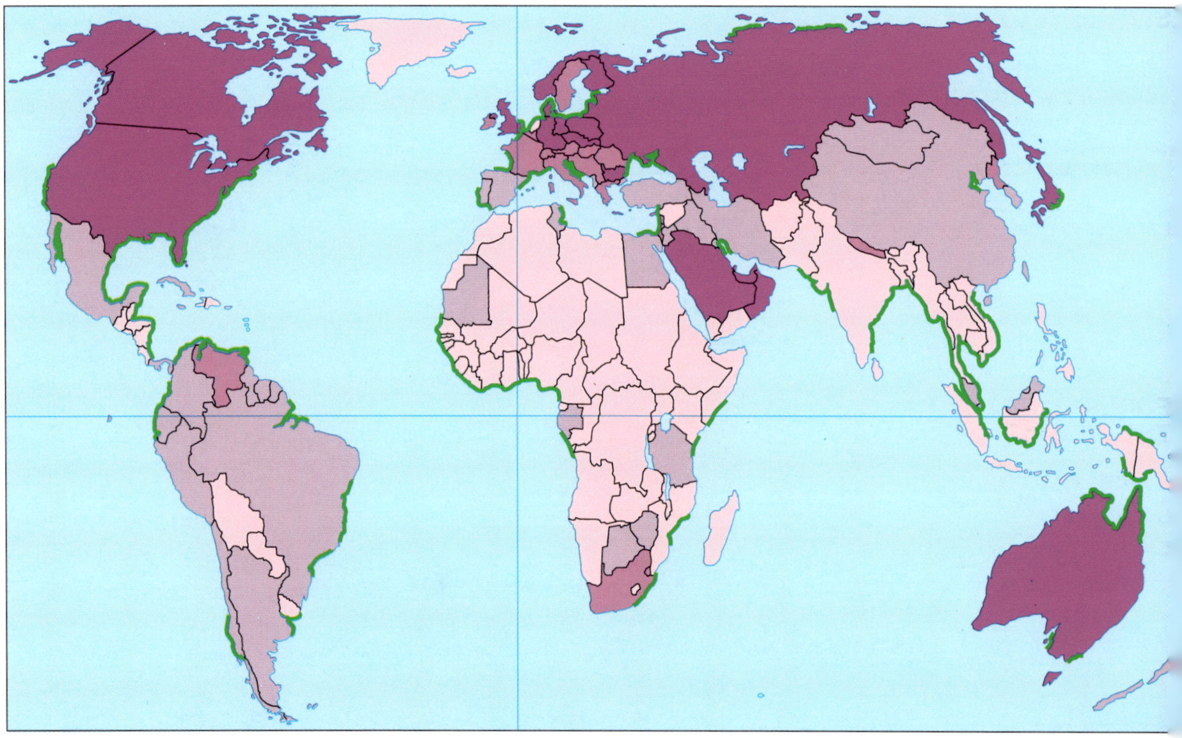

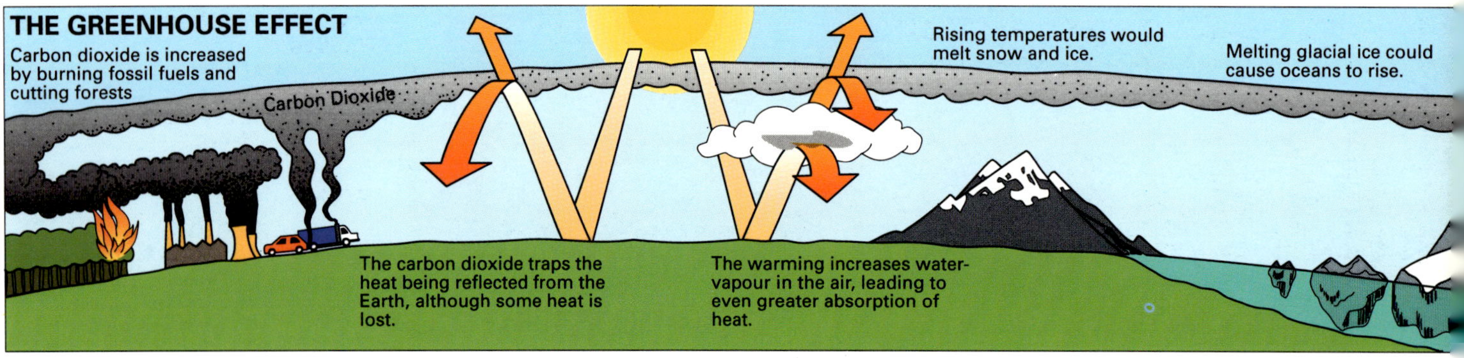

WATER POLLUTION

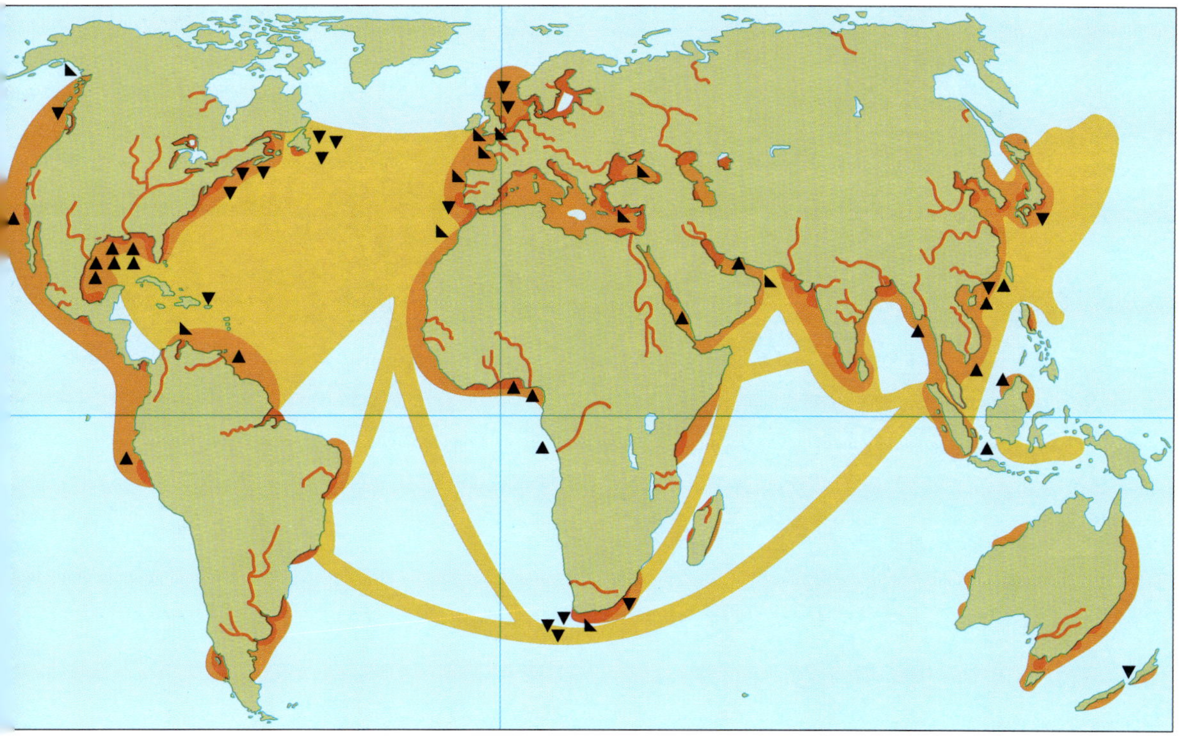

Severely polluted sea areas and lakes

Other polluted sea areas and lakes

Sea areas of frequent oil pollution from shipping

Major oil tanker spills

Major oil rig blow-outs

Offshore dumpsites for industrial and municipal waste

Severely polluted rivers

SERTIFICATION

Existing deserts

eas with a high risk of desertification

as with a moderate k of desertification

FORESTATION THE TROPICS

Former areas of rainforest

Existing rainforest

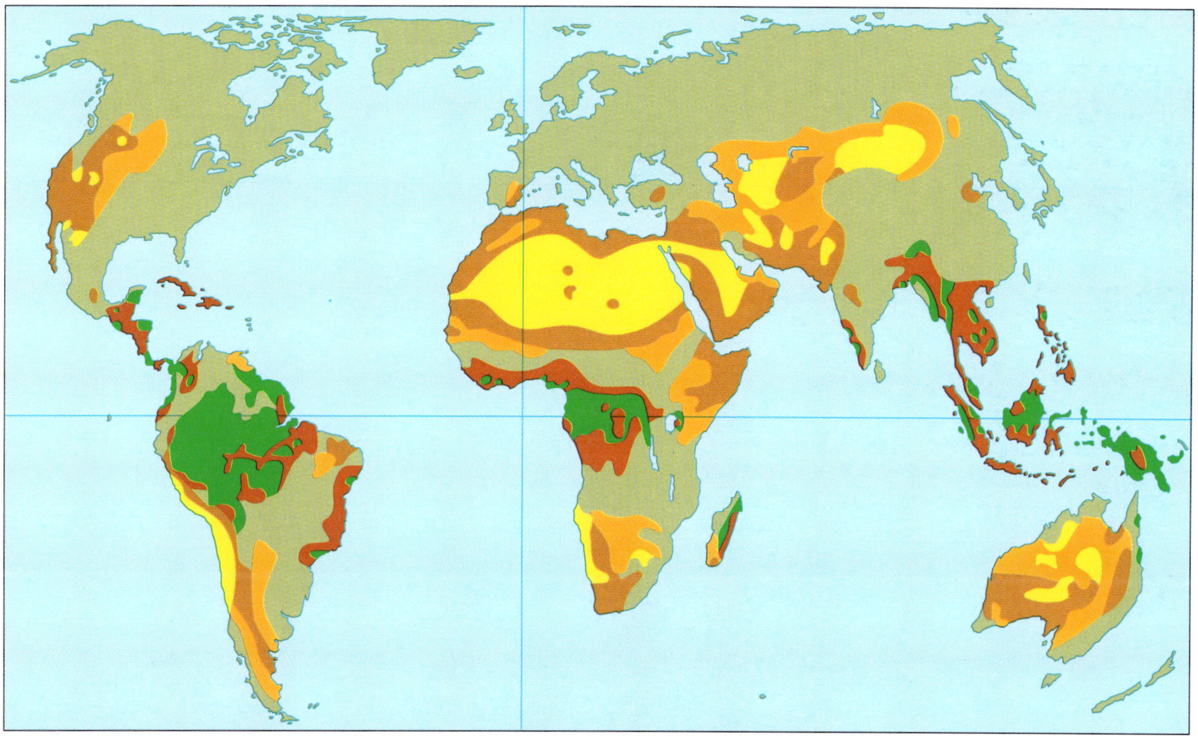

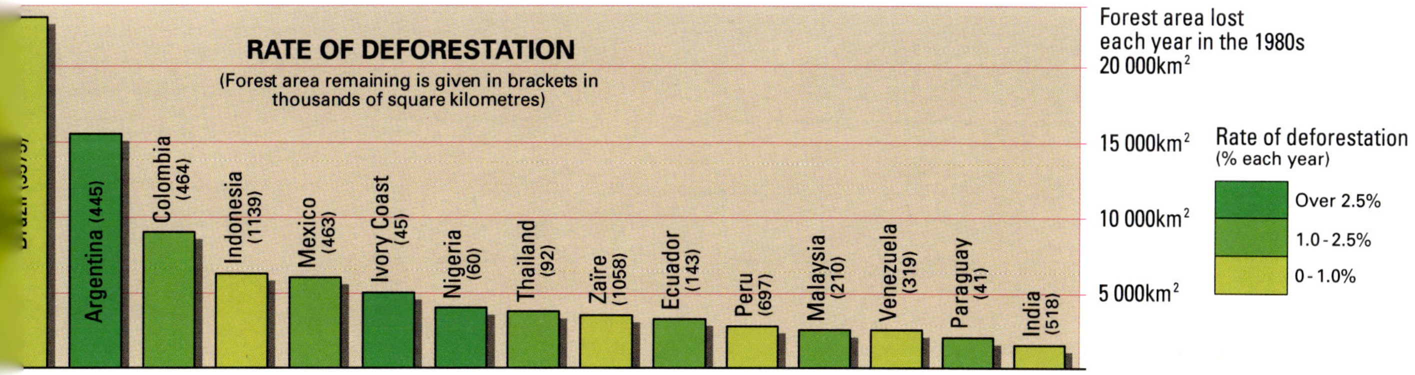

Projection: Hammer Equal Area

HEIGHT OF LAND
in metres
Above 6 000
4 000–6 000
2 000–4 000
1000–2 000
200–1000
0–200
Below Sea-Level
DEPTH OF SEA
in metres
0–200
200–4000
4000–8000
Below 8000
A R C T I C O C E A N
New Siberian Is.
Severnaya Zemlya
Novaya Zemlya
albard
N. Cape
Scandinavia
Baltic Sea
L. Ladoga
North European Plain
Rhine
Alps
Blanc 4810
Carpathians
Danube
Don
Volga
Apennines
Balkan Pen.
Black Sea
Caucasus
Elbrus 5633
Caspian Sea
Aral Sea
Anatolia
Elburz Mts.
Mediterranean Sea
Ural Mts.
Ob
West Siberian Plain
Siberia
Yenisey
Lr. Tunguska
Angara
Irtysh
Lena
Aldan
Stanovoy Ra.
Sea of Okhotsk
Sakhalin
L. Baikal
Amur
Sayan Mts.
Altai
L. Balkhash
Syr Darya
Amu Darya
Tian Shan
Gobi
Huang
Nan Shan
Pamirs
Hindu Kush
Karakoram
Kunlun
Plateau of Tibet
Himalaya
Mt. Everest 8848
Sulaiman Ra.
Indus
Thar Desert
Ganges
Yangtze
Salween
Mekong
Tigris
Euphrates
The Gulf
Sea of Japan
Hokkaido
Honshu
Mt. Fuji 3776
North China Plain
Yellow Sea
East China Sea
Taiwan
PACIFIC OCEAN
Hainan
South China Sea
Philippine Is.
Mariana Is.
Guam
Wake I.
Marshall Is.
Caroline Islands
Gilbert Is.
Nauru
Libyan Desert
Nile
Red Sea
Arabia
Rub 'al Khali
Hoggar
Tibesti
Sahara
L. Chad
White Nile
Blue Nile
Ethiopian Highlands
Socotra
C. Guardafui
Arabian Sea
W. Ghats
Deccan
E. Ghats
Bay of Bengal
C. Comorin
Ceylon
Str. of Malacca
Sumatra
Kinabalu 4101
Borneo
Celebes Sea
Celebes
Moluccas
Java Sea
Java
Sunda Is.
Banda Sea
Timor
New Guinea
Bismarck Arch.
Solomon Is.
Ellice Is.
Cameroon Pk. 4070
Uele
(Congo)
Zaire
L. Turkana
Mt. Kenya 5199
L. Victoria
Kilimanjaro 5895
L. Tanganyika
Kasai
L. Malawi
Zambezi
Cubango
Kalahari Desert
Orange
Drakensberg
C. of Good Hope
INDIAN OCEAN
Seychelles
Comoro Is.
Mozambique Chan.
Madagascar
Mauritius
Réunion
Cocos or Keeling Is.
Torres Str.
C. York
Coral Sea
Gt. Barrier Reef
New Hebrides
Fiji Is.
New Caledonia
Hamersley Ra.
Macdonnell Ra.
Great Victoria Desert
Great Dividing Range
Darling
Murray
C. Leeuwin
Great Australian Bight
Australian Alps
Mt. Kosciusko 2230
Bass Str.
Tasmania
North I.
New Zealand
Mt. Cook 3764
South I.
Crozet Is.
Kerguelen Is.
SOUTHERN OCEAN
Queen Maud Land
Enderby Land
Queen Mary Coast
Wilkes Land
Adélie Land
South Magnetic Pole
Victoria Land
from Greenwich

1:80 000 000

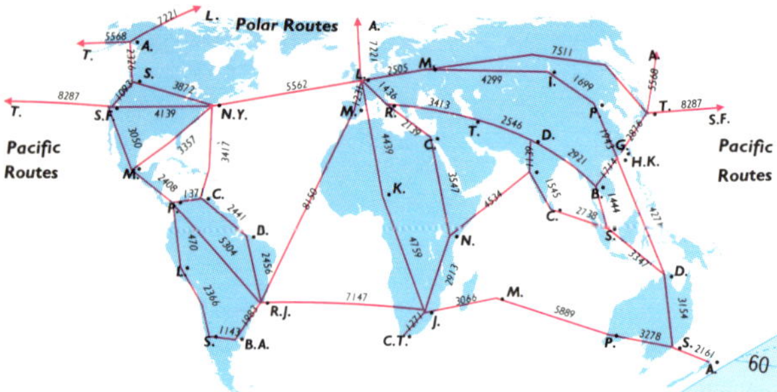

Principal Air Routes
Distances in km

The maps of the Soviet Union and Yugoslavia show the situation at the time of going to press in December, 1991. Extra maps of the Republics and Nationalities of the Soviet Union and the Republics and Ethnic Groups of Yugoslavia are provided on p. 161.

Projection: Hammer Equal Area

Principal Sea Routes
Distances in km

1:80 000 000

Country	Area in thousands of square km.	Population in thousands	Density of population per sq. km.	Capital Population in thousands
Afghanistan	652	15 510	28	Kābul (1 127)
Albania	29	3 140	108	Tiranë (216)
Algeria	2 382	23 840	10	Algiers (1 722)
Angola	1 247	9 480	8	Luanda (1 200)
Argentina	2 767	31 960	12	Buenos Aires (10 728)
Australia	7 687	16 530	2	Canberra (286)
Austria	84	7 600	92	Vienna (1 531)
Bangladesh	144	104 530	780	Dhaka (3 459)
Belgium	31	9 920	325	Brussels (970)
Belize	23	170	7	Belmopan (4)
Benin	113	4 450	40	Porto-Novo (208)
Bhutan	47	1 450	31	Thimphu (60)
Bolivia	1 099	6 990	6	Sucre (87)
				La Paz (993)
Botswana	582	1 210	2	Gaborone (111)
Brazil	8 512	144 430	17	Brasilia (1 577)
Brunei	6	240	45	Bandar Seri Begawan (58)
Bulgaria	111	8 990	81	Sofia (1 129)
Burkina Faso	274	8 510	31	Ouagadougou (375)
Burma (Myanmar)	677	39 970	61	Rangoon (2 459)
Burundi	28	5 150	198	Bujumbura (273)
Cambodia (Kampuchea)	181	7 870	44	Phnom Penh (500)
Cameroon	475	10 670	23	Yaoundé (654)
Canada	9 976	25 950	3	Ottawa (819)
Central African Rep.	623	2 770	4	Bangui (597)
Chad	1 284	5 400	4	Ndjamena (512)
Chile	757	12 750	17	Santiago (4 318)
China	9 597	1 104 000	118	Peking (9 750)
Colombia	1 139	30 240	29	Bogotá (3 975)
Congo	342	1 890	6	Brazzaville (596)
Costa Rica	51	2 850	56	San José (245)
Cuba	111	10 400	94	Havana (2 059)
Cyprus	9	690	75	Nicosia (165)
Czechoslovakia	128	15 620	125	Prague (1 211)
Denmark	43	5 130	122	Copenhagen (1 344)
Djibouti	23	380	17	Djibouti (290)
Dominican Republic	49	6 870	143	Santo Domingo (1 313)
Ecuador	284	10 200	37	Quito (1 110)
Egypt	1 001	51 900	52	Cairo (6 325)
El Salvador	21	5 110	243	San Salvador (884)
Equatorial Guinea	28	420	15	Rey Malabo (37)
Ethiopia	1 222	47 880	43	Addis Ababa (1 465)
Fiji	18	730	40	Suva (71)
Finland	338	4 950	16	Helsinki (987)
France	552	55 870	102	Paris (8 510)
French Guiana	90	86	1	Cayenne (38)
Gabon	268	1 090	4	Libreville (350)
Gambia, The	11	810	81	Banjul (146)
Germany	357	77 672	217	Bonn (291)
				Berlin (3 102)
Ghana	239	14 130	61	Accra (965)
Greece	132	10 010	76	Athens (3 027)
Greenland	2 176	54	0.2	Godthaab (11)
Guatemala	109	8 680	80	Guatemala (1 300)
Guinea	246	5 070	21	Conakry (705)
Guinea-Bissau	36	940	34	Bissau (125)
Guyana	215	1 010	5	Georgetown (188)
Haiti	28	5 520	197	Port-au-Prince (738)
Honduras	112	4 800	43	Tegucigalpa (598)
Hong Kong	1	5 680	5 680	Hong Kong (1 176)
Hungary	93	10 600	115	Budapest (2 105)
Iceland	103	250	3	Reykjavík (93)
India	3 288	786 600	268	Delhi (5 729)
Indonesia	1 905	174 950	97	Jakarta (6 503)
Iran	1 648	52 520	32	Tehrān (6 043)
Iraq	438	17 660	41	Baghdād (4 649)
Irish Republic	70	3 540	51	Dublin (921)
Israel	21	4 430	222	Jerusalem (483)
Italy	301	57 440	195	Rome (2 817)
Ivory Coast	322	11 610	37	Abidjan (1 850)
				Yamoussoukro (120)
Jamaica	11	2 450	223	Kingston (525)
Japan	378	122 610	330	Tōkyō (11 829)
Jordan	89	3 940	41	'Ammān (834)
Kenya	580	23 880	42	Nairobi (1 200)
Korea, North	121	21 900	183	Pyŏngyang (2 639)
Korea, South	99	41 970	428	Seoul (9 646)
Kuwait	18	1 960	109	Kuwait (189)
Laos	237	3 870	17	Vientiane (377)
Lebanon	10	2 830	285	Beirut (702)
Lesotho	30	1 680	56	Maseru (109)
Liberia	111	2 510	26	Monrovia (425)
Libya	1 760	4 230	2	Tripoli (980)
Luxembourg	3	368	142	Luxembourg (77)
Madagascar	587	11 240	19	Antananarivo (703)
Malawi	118	7 750	82	Lilongwe (99)
Malaysia	330	16 920	51	Kuala Lumpur (938)
Mali	1 240	8 920	7	Bamako (419)
Malta	0.3	345	1 150	Valletta (101)
Mauritania	1 026	1 920	2	Nouakchott (500)
Mauritius	2	1 100	579	Port Louis (139)
Mexico	1 958	82 730	43	Mexico City (18 748)
Mongolia	1 565	2 090	1	Ulan Bator (500)
Morocco	447	23 910	54	Rabat (893)
Mozambique	802	14 930	19	Maputo (883)
Namibia	824	1 760	2	Windhoek (115)
Nepal	141	18 230	133	Katmandu (235)
Netherlands	37	14 760	434	Amsterdam (1 031)
New Zealand	269	3 290	13	Wellington (325)
Nicaragua	130	3 620	30	Managua (615)
Niger	1 267	6 690	5	Niamey (399)
Nigeria	924	105 470	116	Lagos (1 097)
				Abuja
Norway	324	4 200	14	Oslo (643)
Oman	212	1 380	7	Muscat (80)
Pakistan	796	105 410	124	Islamabad (204)
Panama	77	2 320	31	Panamá (625)
Papua New Guinea	463	3 560	8	Port Moresby (152)
Paraguay	407	4 040	10	Asunción (708)
Peru	1 285	21 260	17	Lima (4 605)
Philippines	300	58 720	197	Manila (1 728)
Poland	313	37 860	120	Warsaw (1 671)
Portugal	92	10 410	113	Lisbon (1 612)
Puerto Rico	9	3 291	370	San Juan (1 816)
Romania	238	23 050	100	Bucharest (1 976)
Rwanda	26	6 750	270	Kigali (157)
Saudi Arabia	2 150	14 020	7	Riyadh (667)
Senegal	197	7 110	37	Dakar (1 382)
Sierra Leone	72	3 950	55	Freetown (470)
Singapore	0.6	2 650	4 417	Singapore (2 600)
Somali Republic	638	4 760	11	Mogadishu (1 000)
South Africa	1 221	33 750	28	Pretoria (739)
				Cape Town (1 491)
Spain	505	39 050	78	Madrid (3 101)
Sri Lanka	66	16 590	255	Colombo (1 412)
Sudan	2 506	23 800	10	Khartoum (476)
Surinam	163	386	3	Paramaribo (151)
Swaziland	17	740	44	Mbabane (38)
Sweden	450	8 440	20	Stockholm (1 471)
Switzerland	41	6 540	164	Bern (300)
Syria	185	11 340	62	Damascus (1 219)
Taiwan	36	19 800	550	Taipei (2 637)
Tanzania	945	24 000	27	Dodoma (85)
Thailand	513	54 540	107	Bangkok (5 468)
Togo	57	3 250	60	Lomé (366)
Trinidad and Tobago	5	1 240	244	Port of Spain (60)
Tunisia	164	7 810	50	Tunis (774)
Turkey	779	52 420	68	Ankara (2 252)
U.S.S.R.	22 402	283 680	13	Moscow (8 816)
Uganda	236	17 190	86	Kampala (458)
United Arab Emirates	84	1 500	18	Abu Dhabi (243)
United Kingdom	245	57 080	236	London (6 767)
U.S.A.	9 373	246 330	27	Washington (3 563)
Uruguay	177	3 060	18	Montevideo (1 248)
Venezuela	912	18 750	21	Caracas (3 185)
Vietnam	330	64 230	180	Hanoi (2 571)
Western Samoa	2.8	168	58	Apia (34)
Yemen, North	195	7 530	38	Sana' (278)
Yemen, South	333	2 510	8	Aden (264)
Yugoslavia	256	23 560	92	Belgrade (1 088)
Zaïre	2 345	33 460	15	Kinshasa (2 654)
Zambia	753	7 530	10	Lusaka (819)
Zimbabwe	391	8 880	23	Harare (681)

The population figures used are from censuses or more recent estimates and are given in thousands for towns and cities over 500,000 (over 1,000,000 in Brazil, China, India, Japan, U.S.A. and U.S.S.R.) Where possible the population of the metropolitan area is given e.g. Greater London, Greater New York etc.

AFRICA

ALGERIA (1983)
- Algiers 1 722
- Oran 664

ANGOLA (1988)
- Luanda 1 200

CAMEROON (1986)
- Douala 1 030
- Yaoundé 654

CENTRAL AFRICAN REPUBLIC (1988)
- Bangui 597

CHAD (1986)
- Ndjamena 512

CONGO (1985)
- Brazzaville 596

EGYPT (1986)
- Cairo 6 325
- Alexandria 2 893
- El Giza 1 671
- Shubra el Kheima 533

ETHIOPIA (1985)
- Addis Ababa 1 465

GHANA (1984)
- Accra 965

GUINEA (1983)
- Conakry 705

IVORY COAST (1982)
- Abidjan 1 850
- Bouaké 640

KENYA (1986)
- Nairobi 1 200

LIBYA (1982)
- Tripoli 980
- Benghazi 650

MADAGASCAR (1986)
- Antananarivo 703

MAURITANIA (1985)
- Nouakchott 500

MOROCCO (1982)
- Casablanca 2 158
- Rabat-Salé 893
- Fès 548

MOZAMBIQUE (1986)
- Maputo 883

NIGERIA (1983)
- Lagos 1 097
- Ibadan 1 060
- Ogbomosho 527

SENEGAL (1985)
- Dakar 1 382

SOMALI REP. (1986)
- Mogadishu 1 000

SOUTH AFRICA (1980)
- Johannesburg 1 726
- Cape Town 1 491
- Durban 961
- Pretoria 739
- Port Elizabeth 585

SUDAN (1983)
- Omdurman 526

TANZANIA (1985)
- Dar-es-Salaam 1 096

TUNISIA (1984)
- Tunis 774

ZAÏRE (1984)
- Kinshasa 2 654
- Lubumbashi 543

ZAMBIA (1987)
- Lusaka 819

ZIMBABWE (1983)
- Harare 681

ASIA

AFGHANISTAN (1982)
- Kābul 1 127

BANGLADESH (1982)
- Dacca 3 459
- Chittagong 1 388
- Khulna 623

BURMA (MYANMAR) (1983)
- Rangoon 2 459
- Mandalay 533
- Phnom Penh 500

CHINA (1986)
- Shanghai 12 320
- Beijing 9 750
- Tianjin 5 459
- Shenyang 4 285
- Wuhan 3 493
- Guangzhou 3 359
- Chongqing 2 832
- Harbin 2 668
- Chengdu 2 642
- Xi'an 2 387
- Zibo 2 329
- Nanchang 2 289
- Nanjing 2 289
- Lupanshui 2 247
- Taiyuan 1 929
- Changchun 1 908
- Dalian 1 682
- Zhaozhuang 1 612
- Zhengzhou 1 610
- Kunming 1 516
- Jinan 1 464
- Tangshan 1 410
- Guiyang 1 403
- Lanzhou 1 391
- Linyi 1 385
- Pingxiang 1 305
- Qiqihar 1 301
- Anshan 1 298
- Qingdao 1 273
- Xintao 1 272
- Hangzhou 1 271
- Fushun 1 270
- Yancheng 1 265
- Yulin 1 255
- Dongguang 1 230
- Chao'an 1 227
- Xiaogan 1 219
- Fuzhou, Fujian 1 205
- Suining 1 195
- Changsha 1 193
- Shijiazhuang 1 187
- Jilin 1 169
- Xintai 1 167
- Puyang 1 125
- Baotou 1 119
- Bozhou 1 112
- Zhongshan 1 073
- Luoyang 1 063
- Laiwu 1 054
- Leshan 1 039
- Ürümqi 1 038
- Ningbo 1 033
- Datong 1 020
- Huainan 1 019
- Heze 1 017
- Handan 1 014
- Linhai 1 012
- Macheng 1 010
- Changshu 1 004

HONG KONG (1986)
- Kowloon 2 302
- Hong Kong 1 176
- Tsuen Wan 654

INDIA (1981)
- Calcutta 9 194
- Bombay 8 243
- Delhi 5 729
- Madras 4 289
- Bangalore 2 922
- Ahmadabad 2 548
- Hyderabad 2 546
- Pune 1 686
- Kanpur 1 639
- Nagpur 1 302
- Jaipur 1 015
- Lucknow 1 008

INDONESIA (1980)
- Jakarta 6 503
- Surabaya 2 028
- Bandung 1 462
- Medan 1 379
- Semarang 1 026
- Palembang 787
- Ujung Pandang 709
- Malang 512

IRAN (1986)
- Tehrān 6 043
- Mashhad 1 464
- Esfahān 987
- Tabrīz 971
- Shirāz 848
- Ahvāz 580
- Bākhtarān 561
- Qom 543

IRAQ (1985)
- Baghdād 4 649
- Basra 617
- Mosul 571

JAPAN (1985)
- Tōkyō 11 829
- Yokohama 2 993
- Ōsaka 2 636
- Nagoya 2 116
- Sapporo 1 543
- Kyōto 1 479
- Kobe 1 411
- Fukuoka 1 160
- Kawasaki 1 089
- Kitakyūshū 1 056
- Hiroshima 1 044

JORDAN (1986)
- 'Ammān 834

KOREA, NORTH (1984)
- Pyŏngyang 2 639
- Hamhung 775
- Chongjin 754
- Chinnamp'o 691
- Sinŭiju 500

KOREA, SOUTH (1985)
- Seoul 9 646
- Pusan 3 517
- Taegu 2 031
- Inchŏn 1 387
- Kwangju 906
- Taejon 866
- Ulsan 551

LEBANON (1980)
- Beirut 702

MALAYSIA (1980)
- Kuala Lumpur 938

MONGOLIA (1988)
- Ulan Bator 500

PAKISTAN (1981)
- Karachi 5 181
- Lahore 2 953
- Faisalabad 1 104
- Rawalpindi 795
- Hyderabad 752
- Multan 722
- Gujranwala 659
- Peshawar 556

PHILIPPINES (1984)
- Manila 1 728
- Quezon City 1 326
- Cebu 552
- Caloocan 524

SAUDI ARABIA (1974)
- Riyadh 667
- Jedda 561

SINGAPORE (1987)
- Singapore 2 600

SRI LANKA (1985)
- Colombo 1 412

SYRIA (1986)
- Damascus 1 219
- Aleppo 1 191

TAIWAN (1987)
- Taipei 2 637
- Kaohsiung 1 343
- Taichung 715
- Tainan 657
- Panchiao 506

THAILAND (1982)
- Bangkok 5 468

TURKEY (1985)
- İstanbul 5 495
- Ankara 2 252
- İzmir 1 490
- Adana 776
- Bursa 614

VIETNAM (1979)
- Ho Chi Minh City 3 420
- Hanoi 2 571
- Haiphong 1 279

EUROPE

AUSTRIA (1984)
- Vienna 1 531

BELGIUM (1988)
- Brussels 970

BULGARIA (1987)
- Sofia 1 129

CZECHOSLOVAKIA (1989)
- Prague 1 211

DENMARK (1988)
- Copenhagen 1 344

FINLAND (1988)
- Helsinki 987

FRANCE (1982)
- Paris 8 510
- Lyons 1 170
- Marseilles 1 080
- Lille 935
- Bordeaux 628
- Toulouse 523

GERMANY (1986-7)
- Berlin 3 102
- Hamburg 1 571
- Munich 1 275
- Cologne 914
- Essen 615
- Frankfurt 592
- Dortmund 568
- Stuttgart 565
- Düsseldorf 561
- Leipzig 552
- Bremen 522
- Dresden 520
- Duisburg 515
- Hanover 506

GREECE (1981)
- Athens 3 027
- Thessaloníki 871

HUNGARY (1988)
- Budapest 2 105

IRISH REPUBLIC (1986)
- Dublin 921

ITALY (1987)
- Rome 2 817
- Milan 1 479
- Naples 1 201
- Turin 1 025
- Palermo 729
- Genoa 722

NETHERLANDS (1988)
- Rotterdam 1 036
- Amsterdam 1 031
- The Hague 680
- Utrecht 521

NORWAY (1988)
- Oslo 643

POLAND (1988)
- Warsaw 1 671
- Łodz 845
- Kraków 745
- Wrocław 640
- Poznań 586

PORTUGAL (1981)
- Lisbon 1 612
- Oporto 1 315

ROMANIA (1985)
- Bucharest 1 976

SPAIN (1987)
- Madrid 3 101
- Barcelona 1 704
- Valencia 732
- Seville 655
- Zaragoza 575
- Málaga 566

SWEDEN (1988)
- Stockholm 1 471
- Göteborg 720

SWITZERLAND (1986)
- Zürich 840

U.S.S.R. (1987)
- Moscow 8 816
- Leningrad 4 948
- Kiev 2 544
- Tashkent 2 124
- Baku 1 741
- Kharkov 1 587
- Minsk 1 543
- Gorki 1 425
- Novosibirsk 1 423
- Sverdlovsk 1 331
- Kuybyshev 1 280
- Tbilisi 1 194
- Dnepropetrovsk 1 182
- Yerevan 1 168
- Odessa 1 141
- Omsk 1 134
- Chelyabinsk 1 119
- Alma-Ata 1 108
- Ufa 1 092
- Donetsk 1 090
- Perm 1 075
- Kazan 1 068
- Rostov 1 004

UNITED KINGDOM (1985)
- London 6 767
- Birmingham 1 007
- Glasgow 734
- Liverpool (1981) 510

YUGOSLAVIA (1981)
- Belgrade 1 088
- Zagreb 650

NORTH AMERICA

CANADA (1986)
- Toronto 3 427
- Montréal 2 921
- Vancouver 1 381
- Ottawa 819
- Edmonton 785
- Calgary 671
- Winnipeg 625
- Québec 603
- Hamilton 557

CUBA (1987)
- Havana 2 059

DOMINICAN REP. (1981)
- Santo Domingo 1 313

EL SALVADOR (1983)
- San Salvador 884

GUATEMALA (1983)
- Guatemala 1 300

HAITI (1984)
- Port-au-Prince 738

HONDURAS (1986)
- Tegucigalpa 598

JAMAICA (1982)
- Kingston 525

MEXICO (1986)
- Mexico 18 748
- Guadalajara 2 587
- Monterrey 2 335
- Puebla 1 218
- León 947
- Torreón 730
- San Luis Potosi 602
- Ciudad Juárez 596
- Mérida 580
- Culiacán Rosales 560
- Mexicali 511

NICARAGUA (1981)
- Managua 615

PANAMA (1984)
- Panama 625

PUERTO RICO (1984)
- San Juan 1 816

UNITED STATES (1987)
- New York 17 968
- Los Angeles 13 075
- Chicago 8 111
- San Francisco 5 878
- Philadelphia 5 833
- Detroit 4 611
- Boston 4 059
- Dallas 3 655
- Houston 3 635
- Washington 3 563
- Miami 2 912
- Cleveland 2 766
- Atlanta 2 561
- St. Louis 2 438
- Pittsburgh 2 316
- Minneapolis-St. Paul 2 295
- Seattle 2 285
- Baltimore 2 280
- San Diego 2 201
- Tampa 1 914
- Phoenix 1 885
- Denver 1 847
- Cincinnati 1 690
- Milwaukee 1 552
- Kansas City (Mo.) 1 518
- Portland (Or.) 1 364
- New Orleans 1 334
- Norfolk 1 309
- Columbus (Oh.) 1 299
- Sacramento 1 291
- San Antonio 1 275
- Indianapolis 1 213
- Buffalo 1 187
- Charlotte 1 065

OCEANIA

AUSTRALIA (1986)
- Sydney 3 431
- Melbourne 2 942
- Brisbane 1 171
- Perth 1 025
- Adelaide 993

NEW ZEALAND (1988)
- Auckland 842

SOUTH AMERICA

ARGENTINA (1985)
- Buenos Aires 10 728
- Córdoba 1 055
- Rosario 1 016
- Mendoza 668
- La Plata 611
- San Miguel de Tucumán 571

BOLIVIA (1985)
- La Paz 993

BRAZIL (1985)
- São Paulo 10 099
- Rio de Janeiro 5 615
- Belo Horizonte 2 122
- Salvador 1 811
- Fortaleza 1 589
- Brasilia 1 577
- Nova Iguaçu 1 325
- Recife 1 290
- Curitiba 1 285
- Pôrto Alegre 1 275
- Belém 1 221

CHILE (1985)
- Santiago 4 318

COLOMBIA (1985)
- Bogotá 3 975
- Medellin 1 419
- Cali 1 324
- Barranquilla 897

ECUADOR (1982)
- Guayaquil 1 301
- Quito 1 110

PARAGUAY (1983)
- Asunción 708

PERU (1988)
- Lima 4 605
- Arequipa 592

URUGUAY (1985)
- Montevideo 1 248

VENEZUELA (1986)
- Caracas 3 185
- Maracaibo 1 261
- Valencia 1 089
- Maracay 826
- Barquisimento 696

AGE DISTRIBUTION PYRAMIDS

The bars represent the percentage of the total population (males plus females) in the age group shown. Males are on the left, females on the right.

1990 2020

World

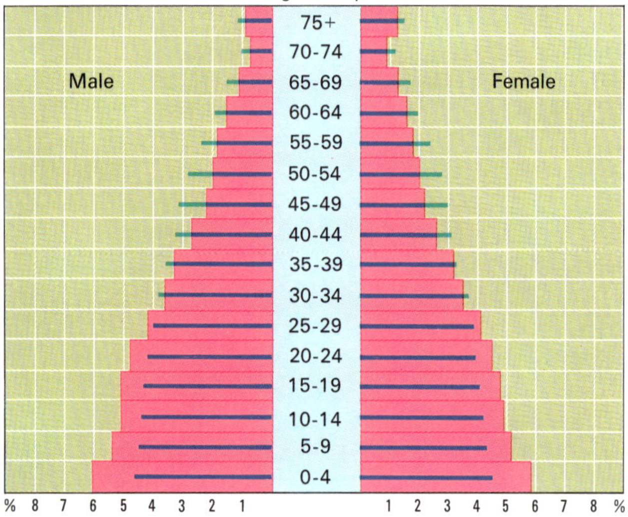

Developed Countries

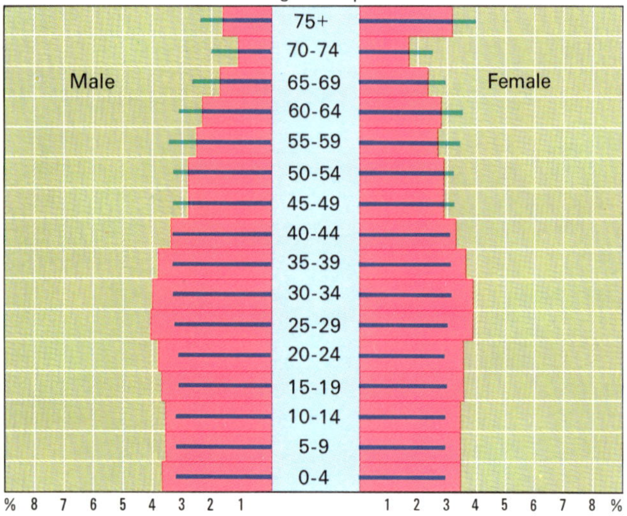

Less Developed Countries

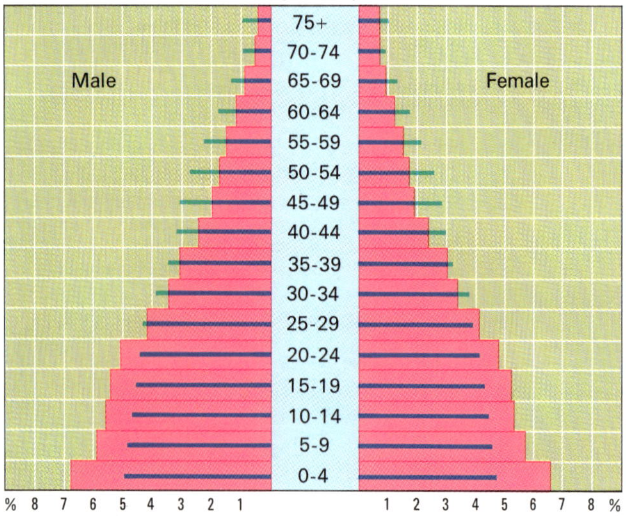

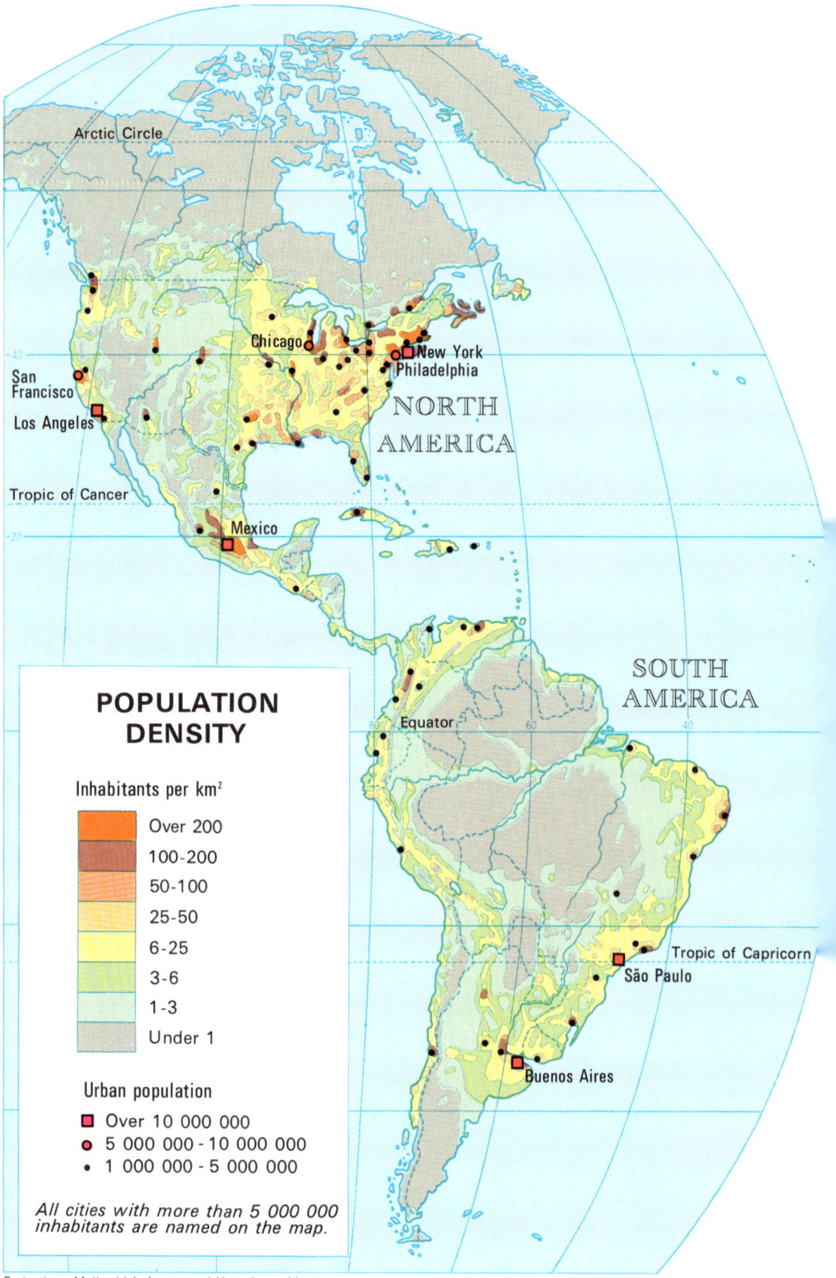

Projection : *Mollweide's Interrupted Homolographic*

POPULATION CHANGE 1930-2020

Population totals are in millions

Figures in italics represent the percentage average annual increase for the period shown

	1930	*1930–1960*	1960	*1960–1990*	1990	*1990–2020*	2020
World	2013	*1.4%*	3019	*1.9%*	5292	*1.4%*	8062
Africa	155	*2.0%*	281	*2.8%*	648	*2.7%*	1441
North America	135	*1.3%*	199	*1.1%*	276	*0.6%*	327
Latin America*	129	*1.8%*	218	*2.4%*	448	*1.6%*	719
Asia	1073	*1.5%*	1669	*2.1%*	3108	*1.4%*	4680
Europe	355	*0.6%*	425	*0.5%*	498	*0.1%*	514
Oceania	10	*1.4%*	16	*1.7%*	27	*1.1%*	37
U.S.S.R.	176	*0.7%*	214	*1.0%*	288	*0.6%*	343

* *South America plus Central America, Mexico and the West Indies*

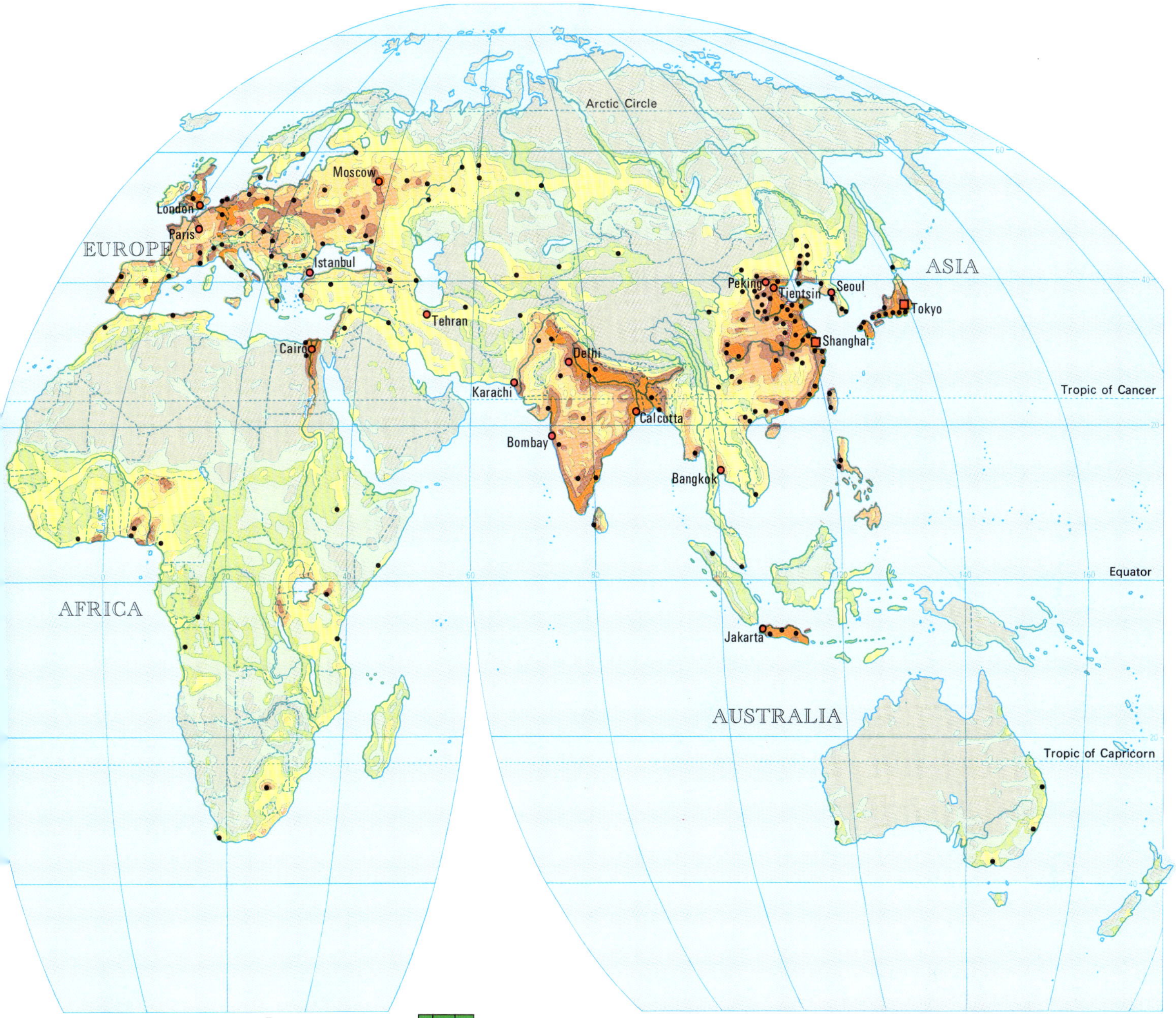

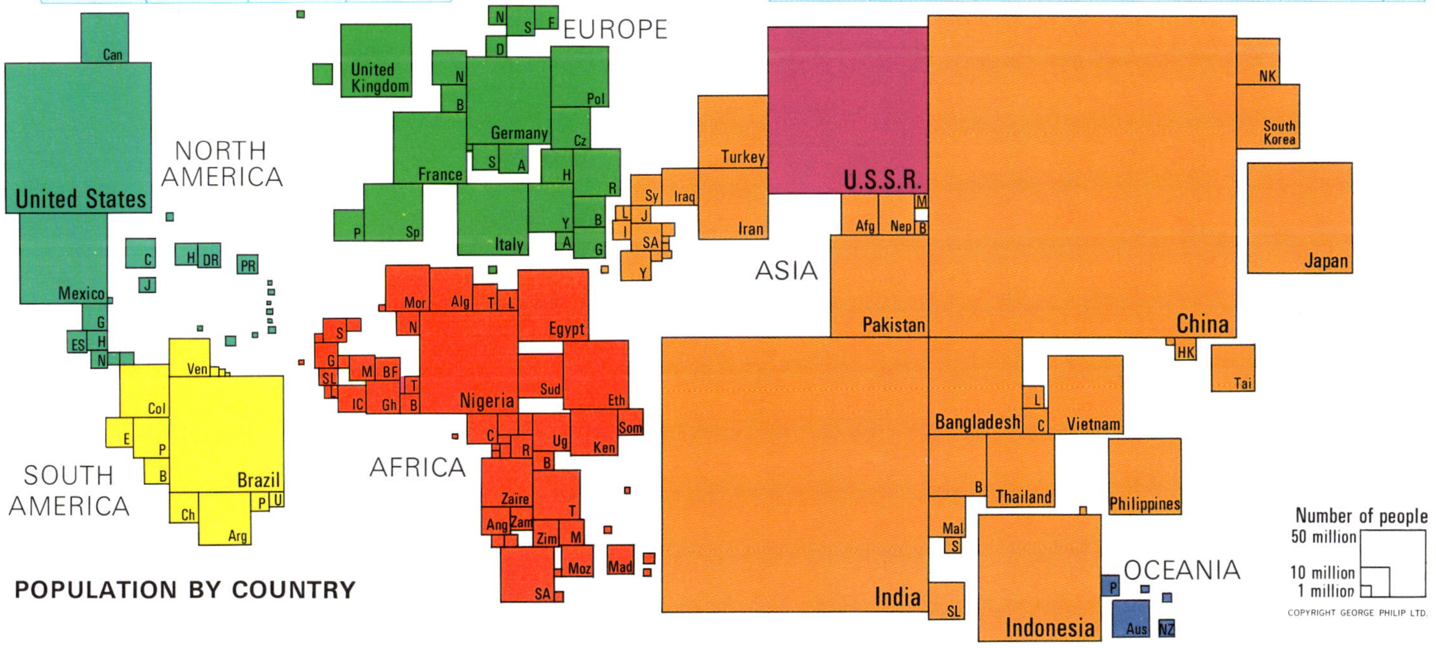

POPULATION BY COUNTRY

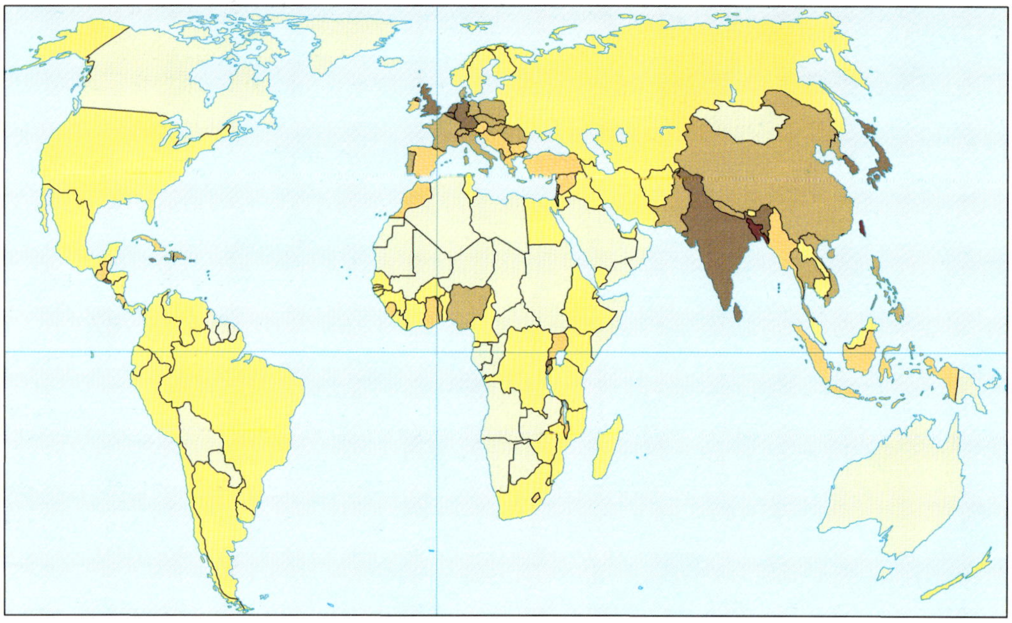

POPULATION DENSITY BY COUNTRY

Density of people per square kilometre

- Over 500 people per km²
- 200-500 people per km²
- 100-200 people per km²
- 50-100 people per km²
- 10-50 people per km²
- Under 10 people per km²

Top 5 countries		Bottom 5 countries	
Macau	19 600 per km²	Greenland	0.2 per km²
Hong Kong	5 533 per km²	Western Sahara	0.6 per km²
Singapore	4 310 per km²	French Guiana	0.9 per km²
Bangladesh	751 per km²	Mongolia	1.2 per km²
Taiwan	532 per km²	Mauritania	1.9 per km²

U.K. 235 per km²

POPULATION CHANGE 1986-2000

Expected percentage population change between 1986 and 2000

- Over 60% population gain
- 40-60% population gain
- 20-40% population gain
- 0-20% population gain
- No change or population loss

Top 5 countries		Bottom 5 countries	
Haiti	+84%	Andorra	−15%
Kenya	+82%	Switzerland	−10%
El Salvador	+77%	Oman	−5%
Jordan	+75%	Sweden	−4%
Tanzania	+74%	West Germany	−2%

U.K. − 0.9%

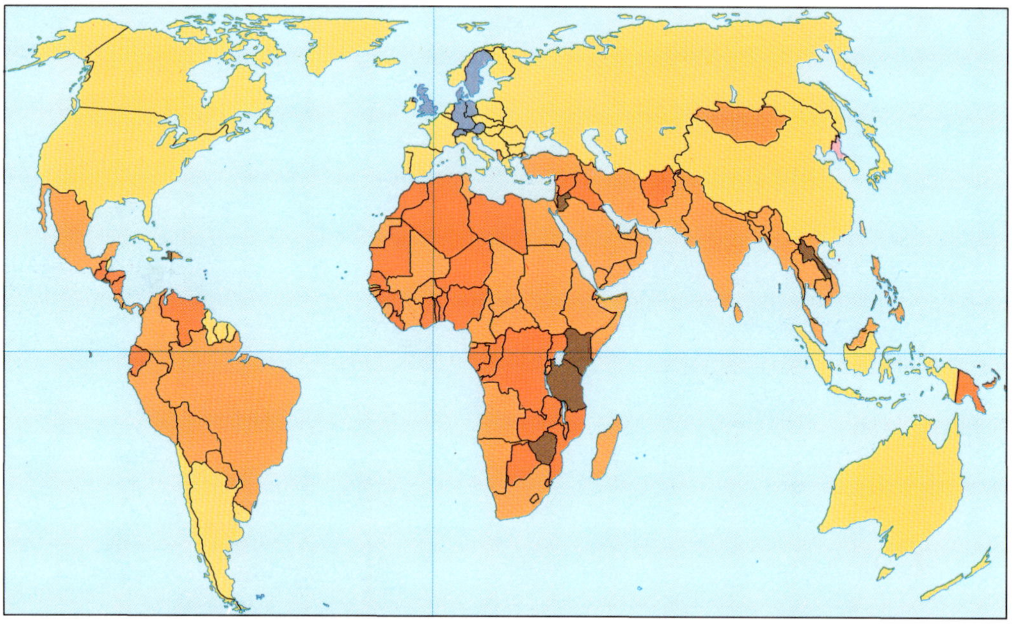

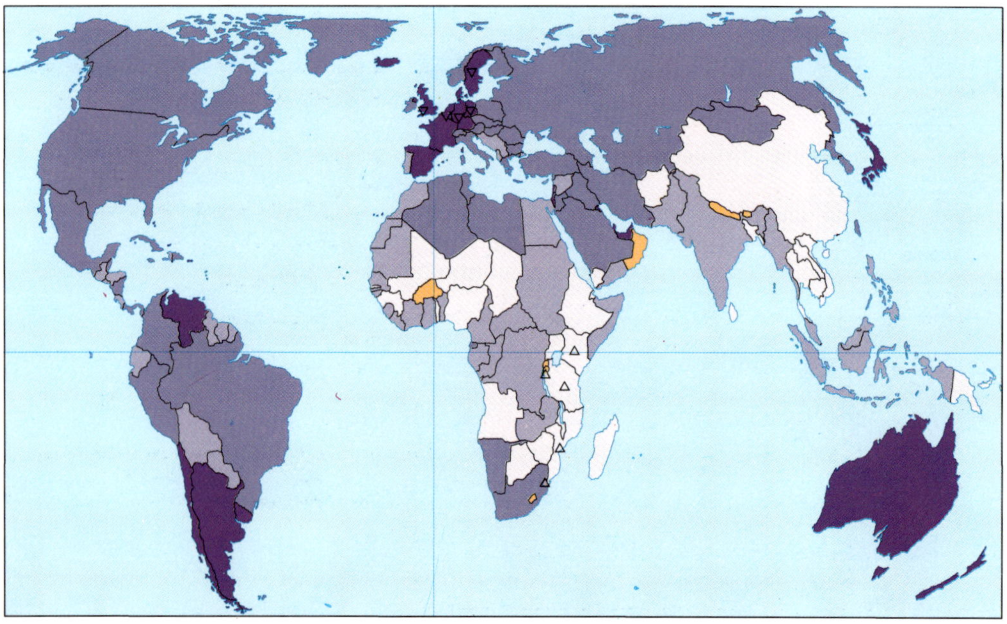

URBAN POPULATION

Percentage of total population living in towns and cities

- Over 75% urban
- 50-75% urban
- 25-50% urban
- 10-25% urban
- Under 10% urban

Most urbanized 1990		Least urbanized 1990	
Singapore	100%	Bhutan	5%
Belgium	97%	Burundi	7%
Kuwait	96%	Rwanda	8%
Hong Kong	93%	Burkina Faso	9%
U.K.	93%	Nepal	10%

△ Fastest urbanization per annum		▽ Slowest urbanization per annum	
Tanzania	+9.6%	Sweden	+0.1%
Mozambique	+9.0%	West Germany	+0.1%
Burundi	+8.3%	Belgium	+0.2%
Swaziland	+8.0%	U.K.	+0.3%
Kenya	+7.8%	East Germany	+0.3%

CHILD MORTALITY

The number of babies who die under the age of one, per 1000 births

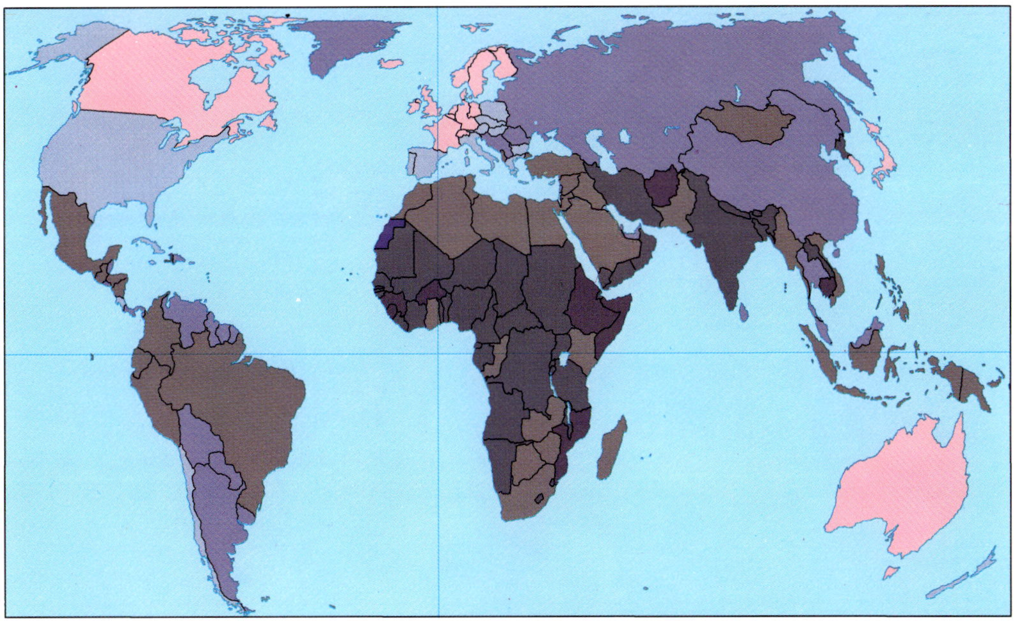

- Over 150 deaths per 1000 births
- 100-150 deaths per 1000 births
- 50-100 deaths per 1000 births
- 20-50 deaths per 1000 births
- 10-20 deaths per 1000 births
- Under 10 deaths per 1000 births

Highest child mortality		Lowest child mortality	
Mozambique	172 deaths	Iceland	3 deaths
Afghanistan	171 deaths	Japan	5 deaths
Mali	168 deaths	Sweden	6 deaths
Ethiopia	153 deaths	Finland	6 deaths
Sierra Leone	153 deaths	Switzerland	7 deaths

U.K. 8 deaths

LIFE EXPECTANCY

Average expected lifespan in years

- Over 70 years
- 60-70 years
- 50-60 years
- 40-50 years
- Below 40 years

Highest life expectancy		Lowest life expectancy	
Japan	77.3 years	Burkina Faso	31.6 years
Iceland	77.1 years	Chad	32.0 years
Sweden	76.9 years	Sierra Leone	34.0 years
Netherlands	76.3 years	Cent. African Rep.	34.5 years
Switzerland	76.1 years	Gabon	35.0 years

U.K. 75 years

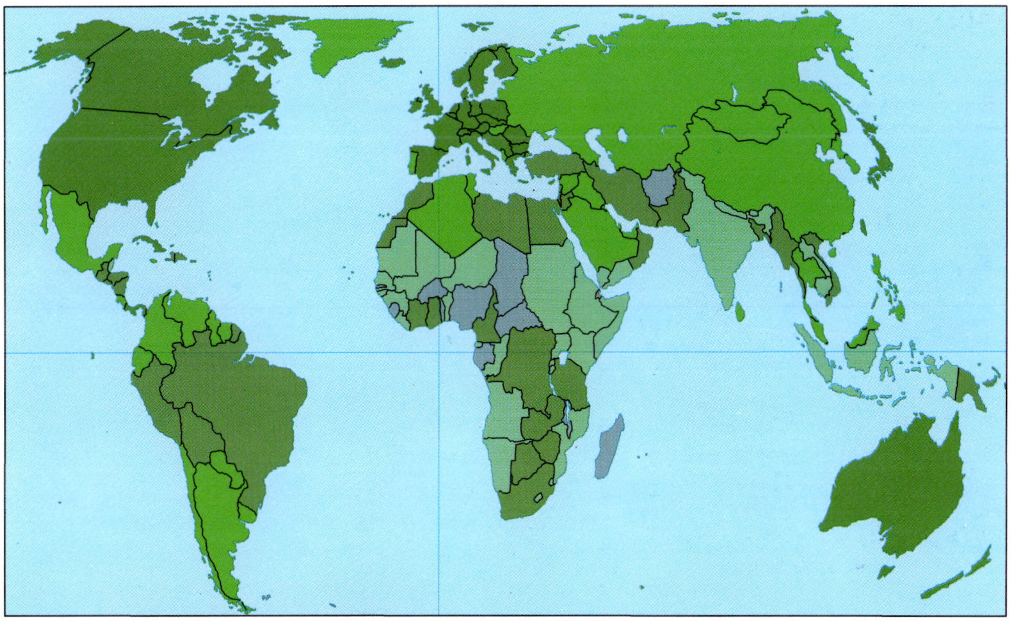

FAMILY SIZE

The average number of children a woman can expect to bear during her lifetime

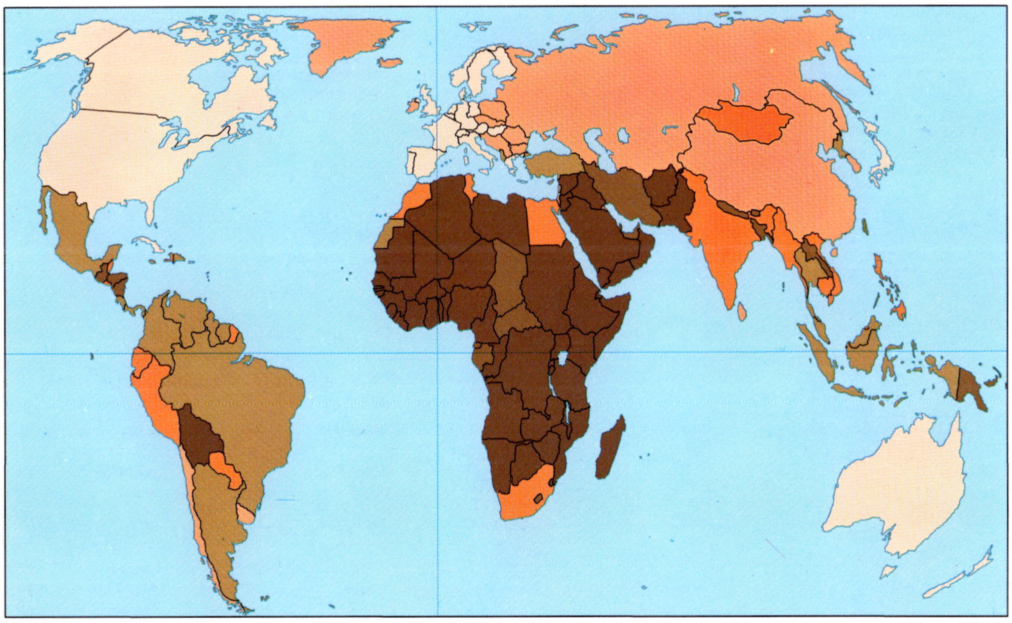

- 6 children or more
- 5 children or more
- 4 children or more
- 3 children or more
- 2 children or more
- 1 child

In the U.K. the average family size is 1.8 children per family, whilst in Kenya the average size is 5 children.

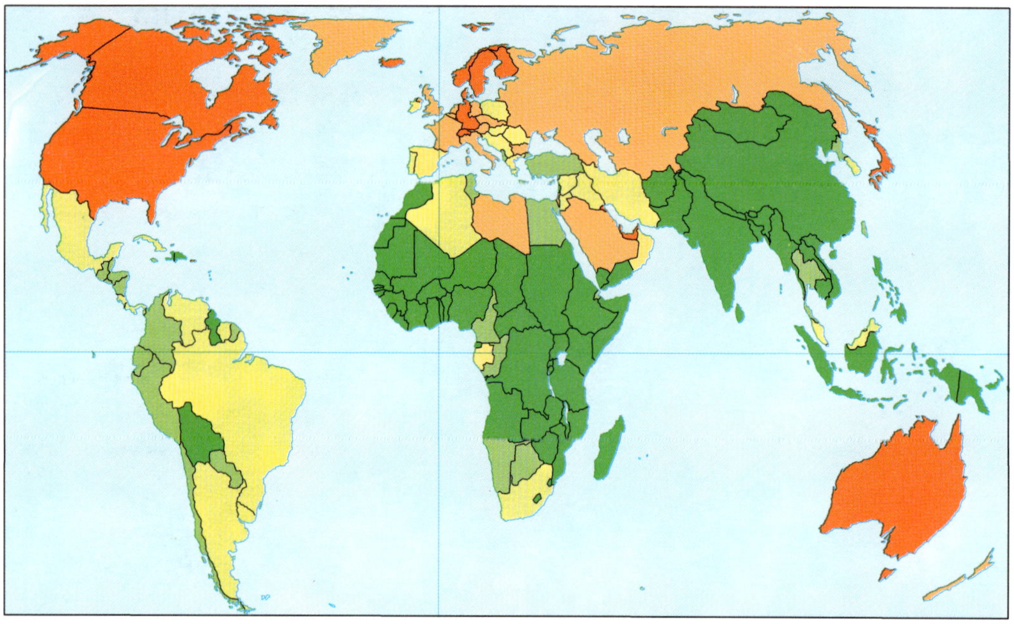

WEALTH

The value of total production divided by population (The Gross National Product per capita)

- Over 400% of World average
- 200-400% of World average
- 100-200% of World average

World average wealth per person £1991

- 50-100% of World average
- 25-50% of World average
- Under 25% of World average

Richest 5 countries 1988		Poorest 5 countries 1988	
Switzerland	£15 075	Mozambique	£55
Japan	£11 635	Ethiopia	£66
Iceland	£11 148	Bhutan	£87
Norway	£11 071	Chad	£87
U.S.A.	£10 938	Malawi	£90

U.K. £7 078

AID

Aid provided or received, divided by total population (3 years average 1985-7)

PROVIDERS
- Over £100 per person
- 10-£100 per person
- Under £10 per person

No aid given or received

RECEIVERS
- Under £10 per person
- 10-£100 per person
- Over £100 per person

Top 5 providers 1988		Top 5 receivers 1988	
Norway	£130	Israel	£507
Sweden	£100	Botswana	£224
Denmark	£99	Jordan	£198
Netherlands	£84	Papua N. Guinea	£192
Saudi Arabia	£83	Mauritania	£173

U.K. £26

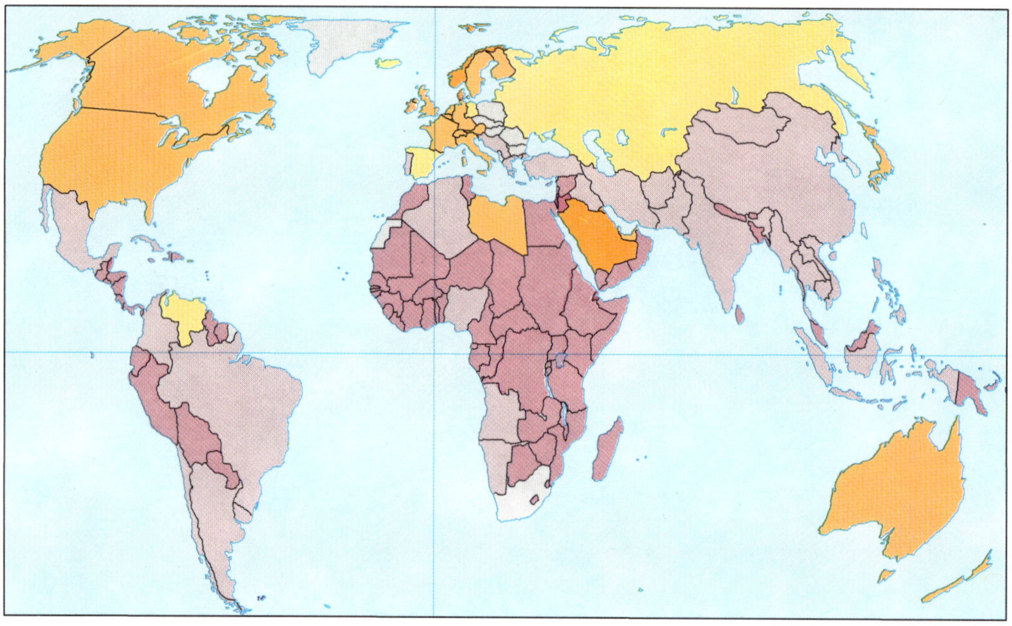

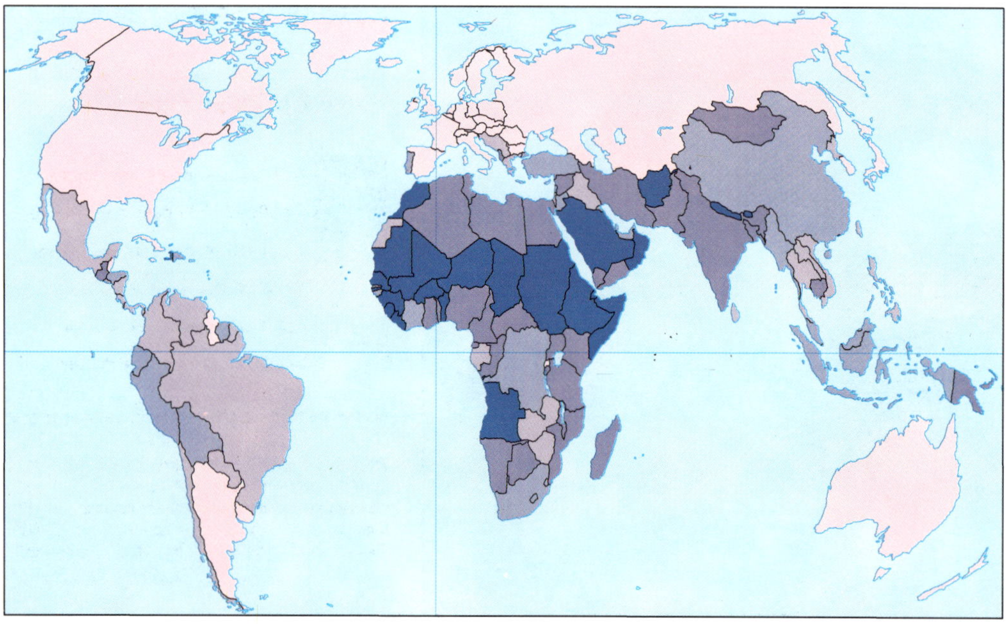

ILLITERACY

Percentage of total population unable to read or write

- Over 75% of population illiterate
- 50-75% of population illiterate
- 25-50% of population illiterate
- 10-25% of population illiterate
- Under 10% of population illiterate

5 most illiterate countries		5 least illiterate countries	
Somalia	88%	Iceland	0.1%
Niger	86%	U.S.S.R.	0.2%
Burkina Faso	86%	Tonga	0.4%
Mali	83%	U.S.A.	0.5%
Mauritania	83%	Barbados	0.7%

U.K. 1%

THE IMPORTANCE OF AGRICULTURE

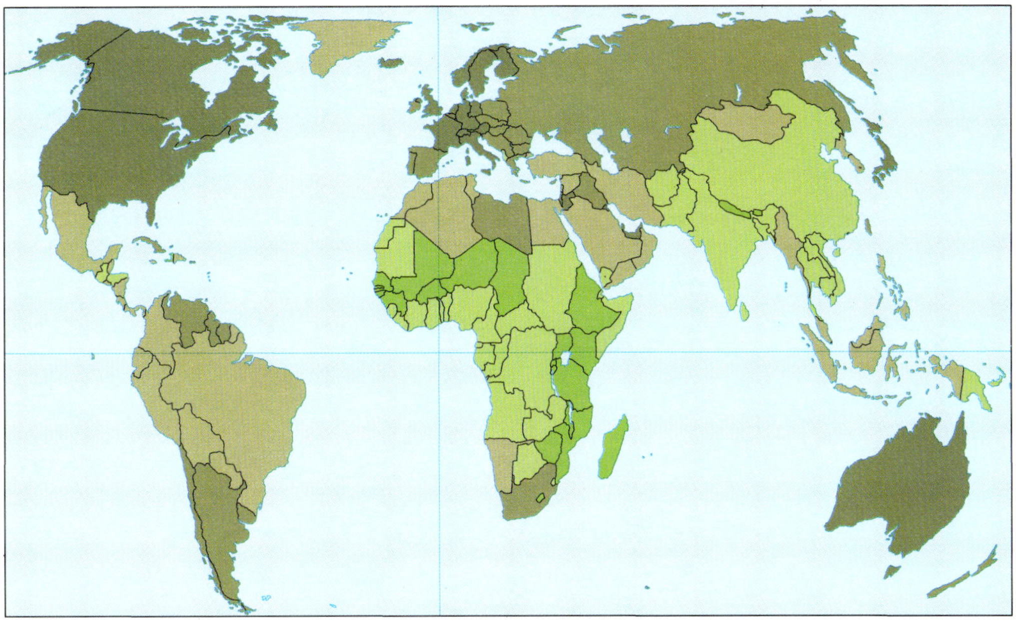

The percentage of the total population who depend on agriculture

- Over 75% dependent
- 50-75% dependent
- 25-50% dependent
- 10-25% dependent
- Under 10% dependent

Top 5 countries		Bottom 5 countries	
Burundi	92%	Singapore	1.2%
Rwanda	92%	Kuwait	1.4%
Bhutan	91%	Hong Kong	1.5%
Nepal	91%	Qatar	1.8%
Burkina Faso	90%	U.K.	2.2%

DAILY FOOD CONSUMPTION

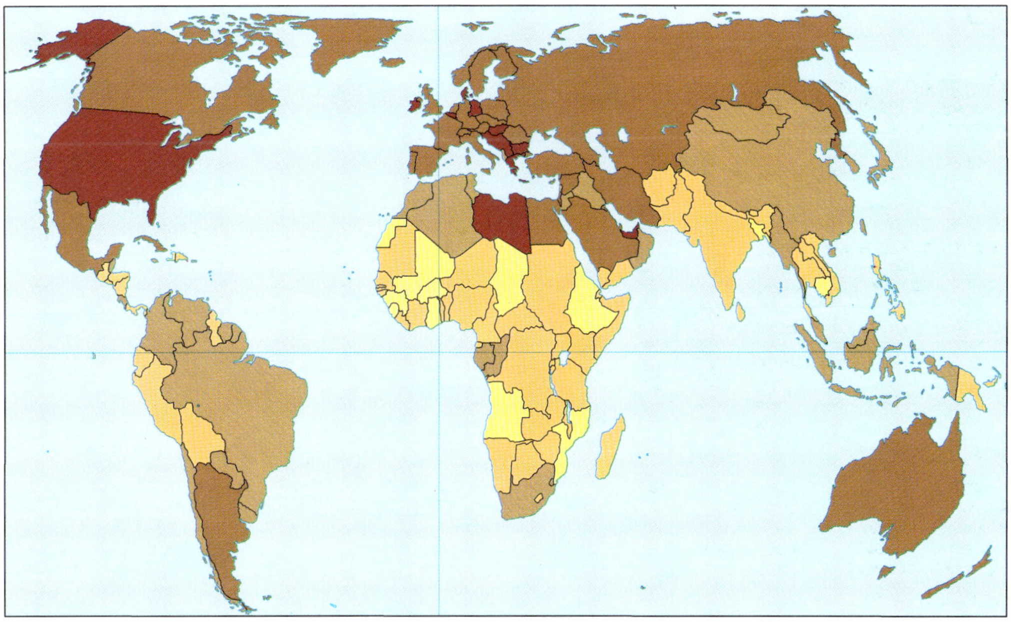

Average daily food intake in Kilocalories* per person

- Over 3 500 K. cal per person
- 3 000-3 500 K. cal per person
- 2 500-3 000 K. cal per person
- 2 000-2 500 K. cal per person
- Under 2 000 K. cal per person

A unit of the energy value of food

Top 5 countries 1988		Bottom 5 countries 1988	
E Germany	3 814K. cal	Central Africa	1 040K. cal
U.A.E.	3 733K. cal	Mozambique	1 595K. cal
Greece	3 688K. cal	Chad	1 717K. cal
U.S.A.	3 645K. cal	Ethiopia	1 749K. cal
Bulgaria	3 642K. cal	Ghana	1 759K. cal

U.K. 3 256K. cal

HEALTH CARE

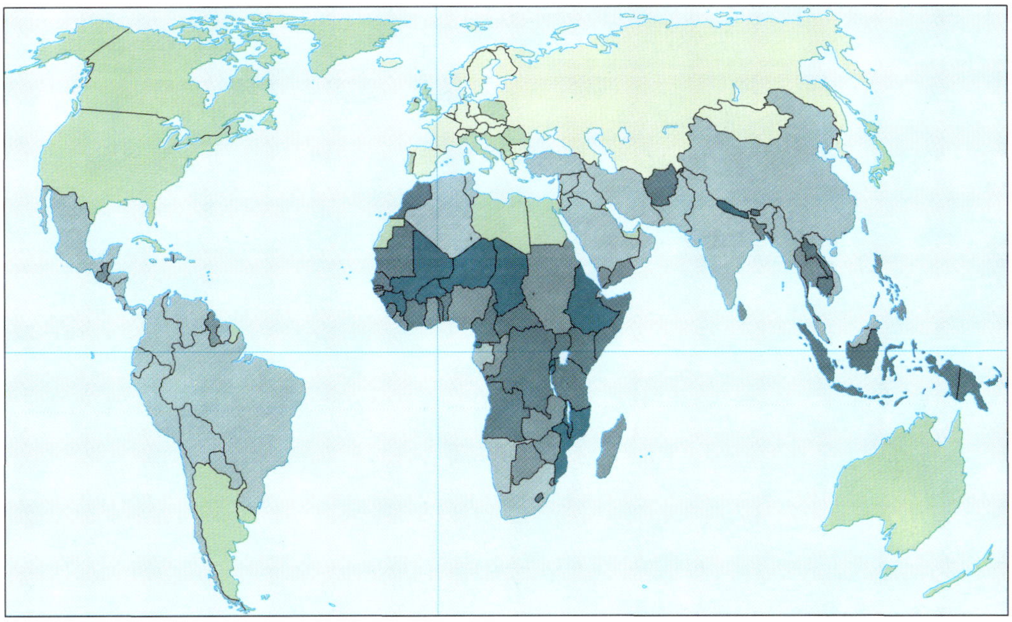

Number of people per doctor

- Over 25 000 people per doctor
- 10 000-25 000 people per doctor
- 5 000-10 000 people per doctor
- 1 000- 5 000 people per doctor
- 500-1 000 people per doctor
- Under 500 people per doctor

Most people per doctor 1988		Fewest people per doctor 1988	
Ethiopia	77 356	Italy	234
Guinea	57 390	U.S.S.R.	270
Burkina Faso	57 183	Czechoslovakia	277
Niger	38 775	Bulgaria	277
Chad	38 358	Hungary	307

U.K. 611

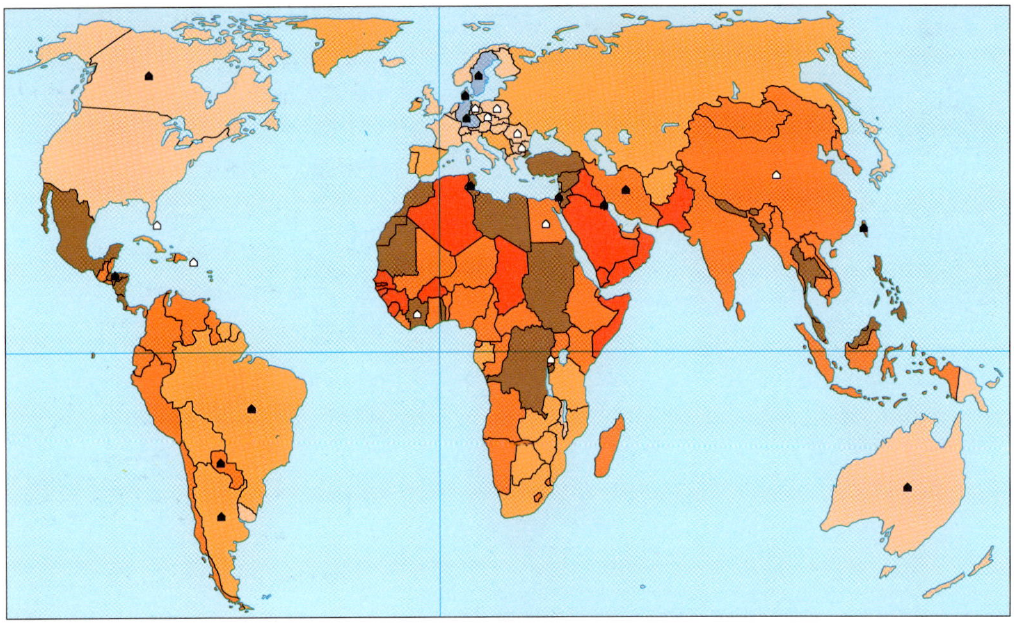

HOUSING

Number of people per household
(latest available year)

- Over 6 people per household
- 6 people per household
- 5 people per household
- 4 people per household
- 3 people per household
- Under 3 people per household

Expenditure on housing and energy as a percentage of total consumer spending

- Over 20% spent
- Under 5% spent

WATER SUPPLY

Percentage of total population with access to safe drinking water
(latest available year)

- Over 90% with safe water
- 75-90% with safe water
- 60-75% with safe water
- 45-60% with safe water
- 30-45% with safe water
- Under 30% with safe water

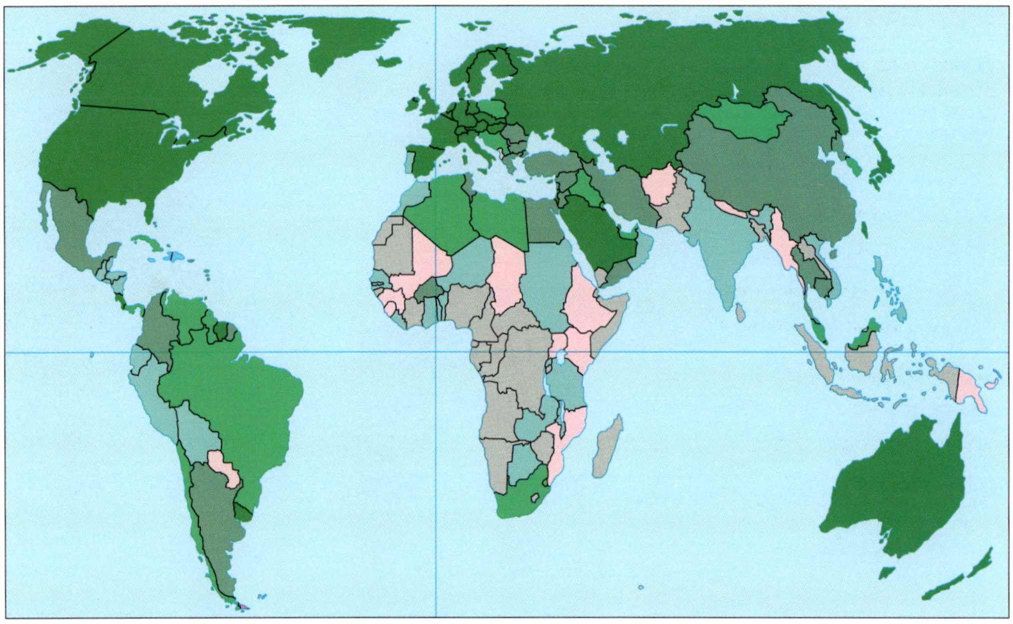

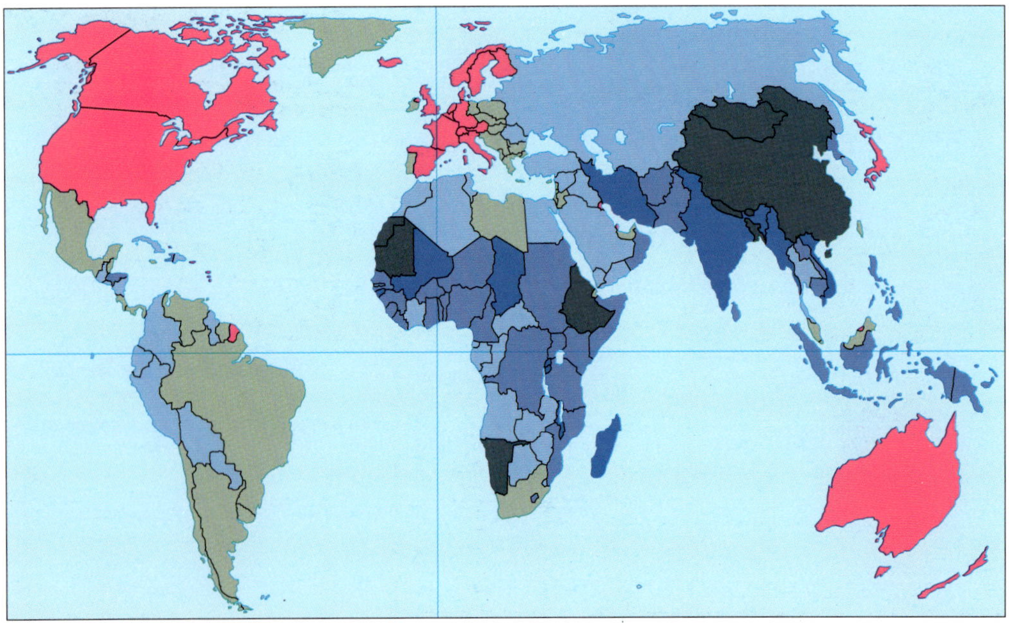

CAR OWNERSHIP

Number of people per car
(latest available year)

- Over 1000 people per car
- 500-1000 people per car
- 100-500 people per car
- 25-100 people per car
- 5-25 people per car
- Under 5 people per car

Most people per car		Most cars (millions)	
China	4300	U.S.A.	140.7
Mauritania	3400	Japan	30.8
Bangladesh	2053	W. Germany	29.2
Nepal	2000	France	27.0
Togo	1237	Italy	23.5

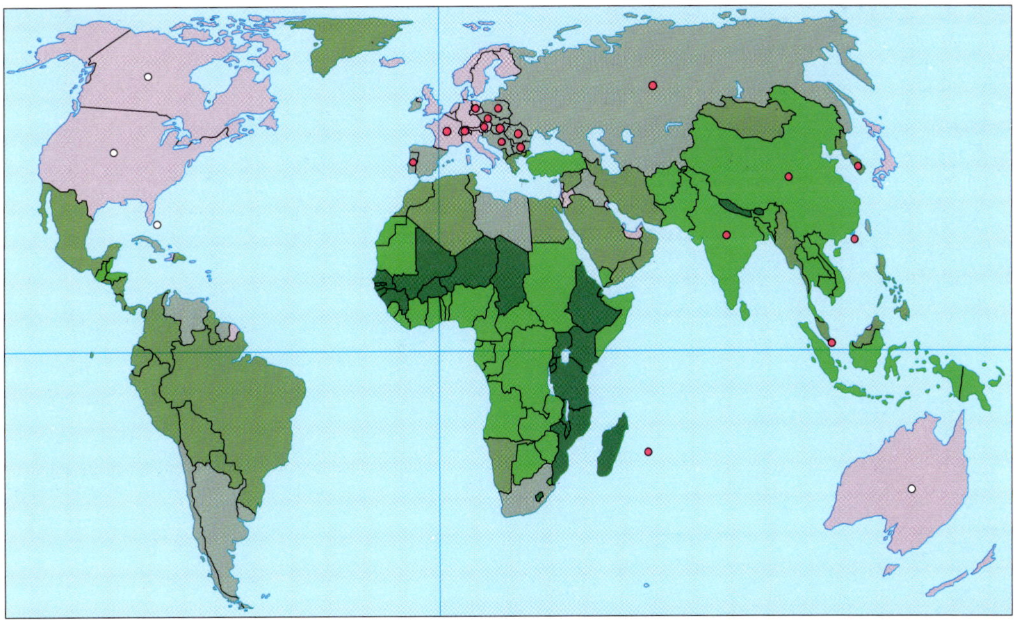

TYPE OF WORK

Percentage of total workforce employed in agriculture* (latest available year)

- Over 75% in agriculture
- 50-75% in agriculture
- 25-50% in agriculture
- 10-25% in agriculture
- Under 10% in agriculture

- Over 25% of total workforce employed in manufacturing
- Over 75% of total workforce employed in service industries (work in offices, shops, tourism, transport, construction and government)

* Includes forestry and fishing

WOMEN IN THE WORKFORCE

Working women as a percentage of the total workforce (latest available year)

- Over 40% are women
- 30-40% are women
- 20-30% are women
- 10-20% are women
- Under 10% are women

Most women in the workforce		Fewest women in the workforce	
Burundi	48%	U.A.E.	6%
U.S.S.R.	48%	Saudi Arabia	7%
Mozambique	48%	Bangladesh	7%
Tanzania	48%	Qatar	7%
Benin	48%	Algeria	8%

U.K. 39%

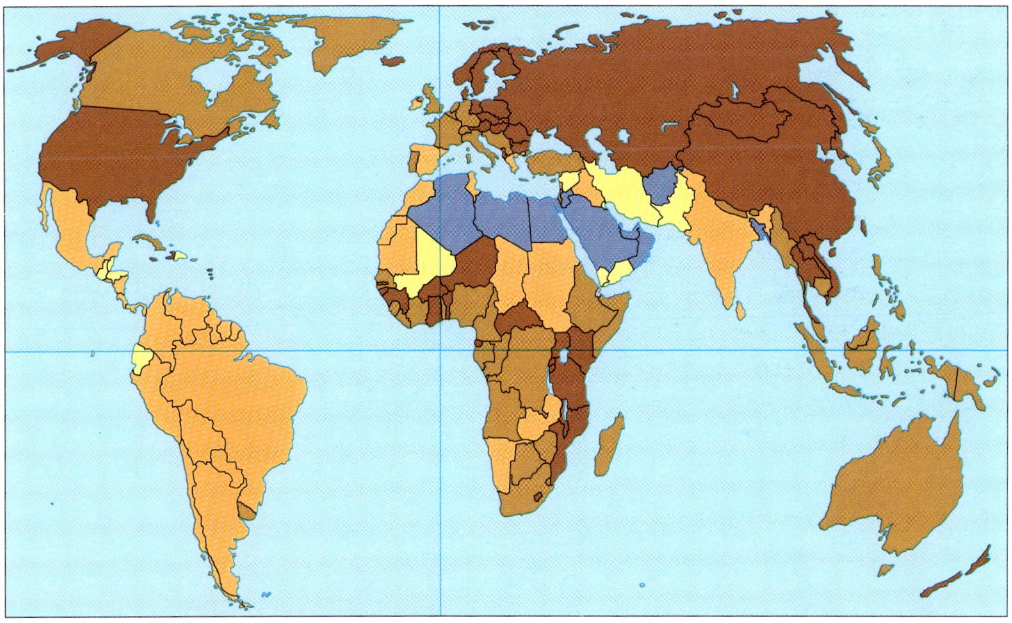

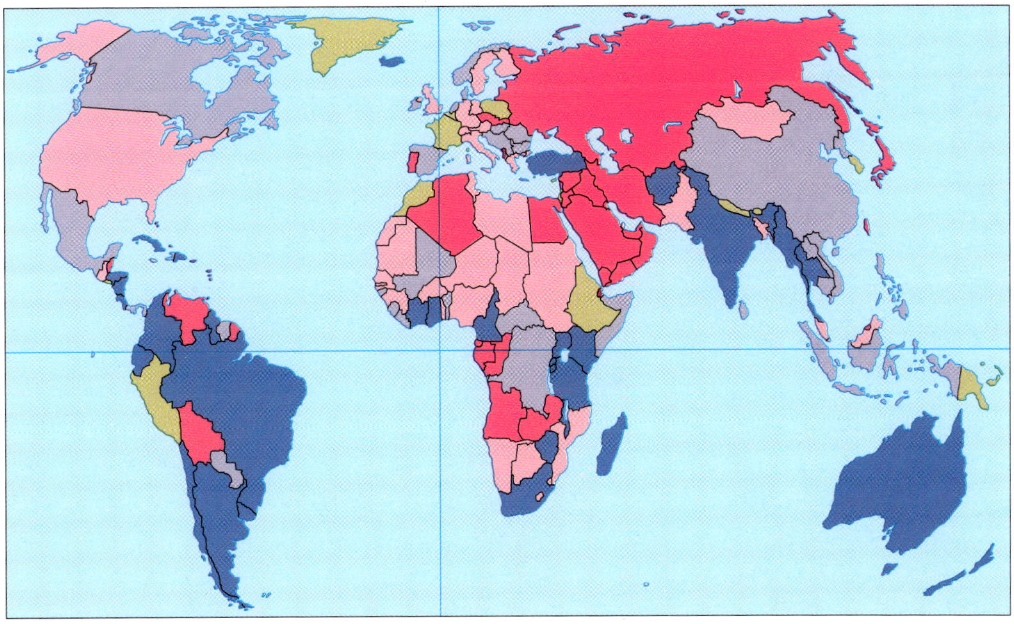

SELF SUFFICIENCY IN FOOD

Balance of trade in food products as a percentage of total trade in food products 1988

- Over 50% surplus
- 10-50% surplus
- 10% either side
- 10-50% deficit
- Over 50% deficit

Wheat

The most important grain crop in the temperate regions though it is also grown in a variety of climates e.g. in Monsoon lands as a winter crop.

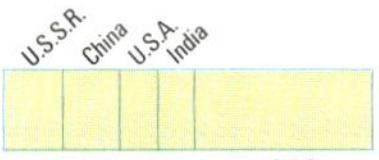

World production 1989
537.3 million tonnes

Oats

Widely grown in temperate regions with the limit fixed by early autumn frosts. Mainly fed to cattle. The best quality oats are used for oatmeal, porridge and breakfast foods.

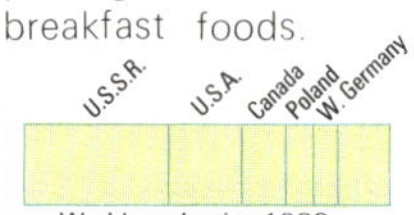

World production 1989
42.6 million tonnes

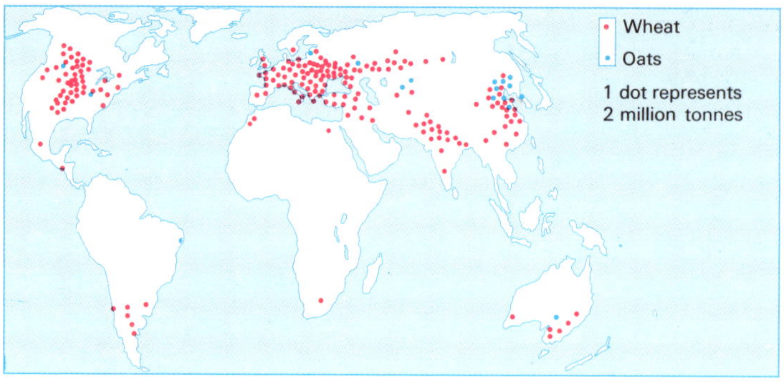

Rye

The hardiest of cereals and more resistant to cold, pests and disease than wheat. An important foodstuff in Central and E. Europe and the U.S.S.R.

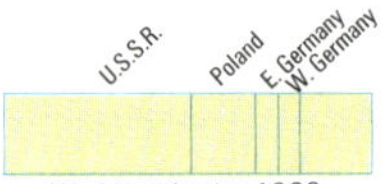

World production 1989
33 million tonnes

Maize (or Corn)

Needs plenty of sunshine, summer rain or irrigation and frost free for 6 months. Important as animal feed and for human food in Africa, Latin America and as a vegetable and breakfast cereal.

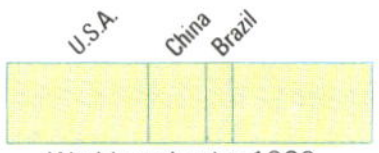

World production 1989
470.6 million tonnes

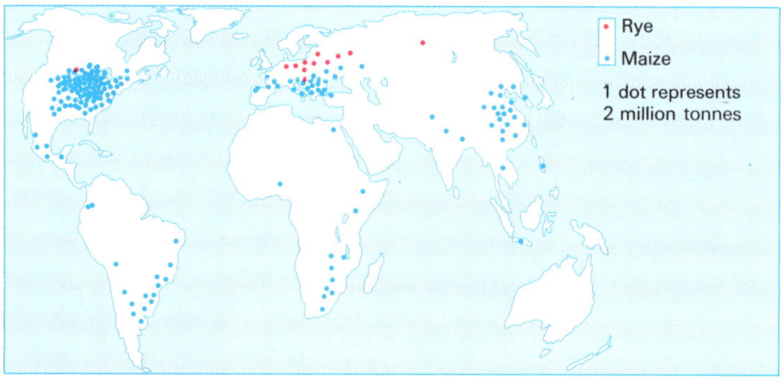

Barley

Has the widest range of cultivation requiring only 8 weeks between seed time and harvest. Used mainly as animal-feed and by the malting industry.

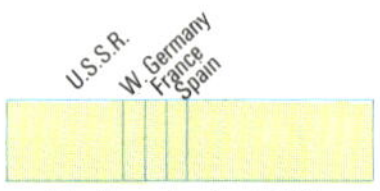

World production 1989
171.3 million tonnes

Rice

The staple food of half the human race. The main producing areas are the flood plains and hill terraces of S. and E. Asia where water is abundant in the growing season.

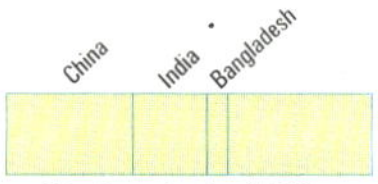

World production 1989
506.9 million tonnes

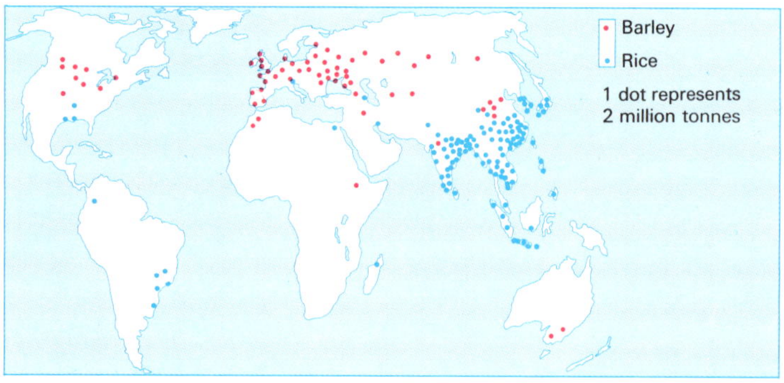

Millets

The name given to a number of related members of the grass family, of which sorghum is one of the most important. They provide nutritious grain.

World production 1989
88.7 million tonnes

Potatoes

An important food crop though less nutritious weight for weight than grain crops. Requires a temperate climate with a regular and plentiful supply of rain.

World production 1989
279.4 million tonnes

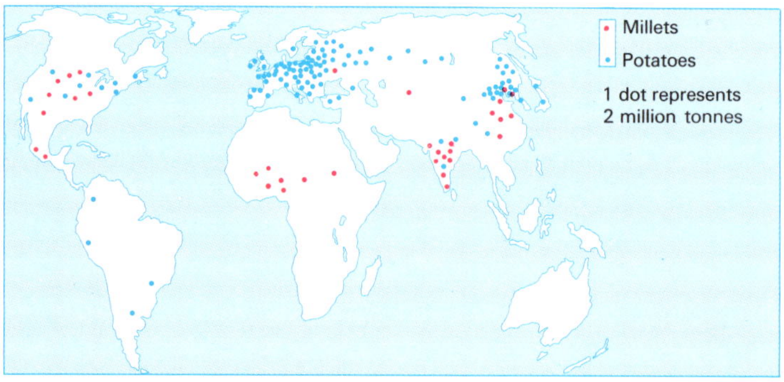

Vegetable oilseeds and oils

Despite the increasing use of synthetic chemical products and animal and marine fats, vegetable oils extracted from these crops grow in quantity, value and importance. Food is the major use- in margarine and cooking fats.

Groundnuts are also a valuable subsistence crop and the meal is used as animal feed. Soya-bean meal is a growing source of protein for humans and animals. The Mediterranean lands are the prime source of olive oil.

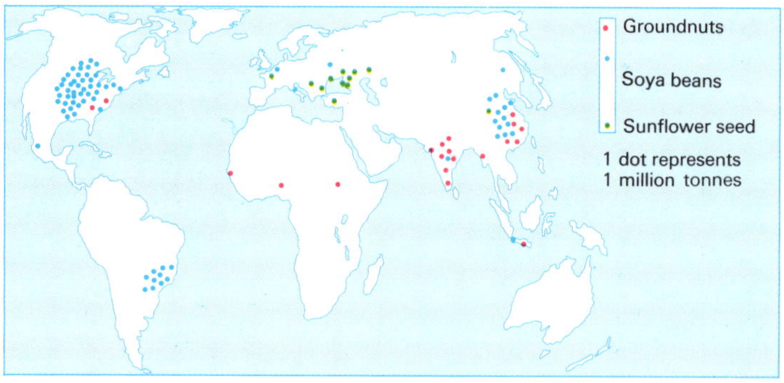

Tea and cacao

Tea requires plentiful rainfall and well-drained, sloping ground, whereas cacao prefers a moist heavy soil. Both are grown mainly for export.

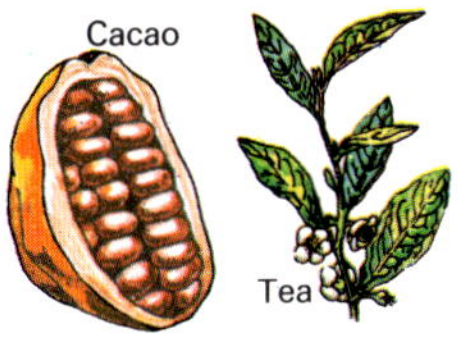

Coffee

Prefers a hot climate, wet and dry seasons and an elevated location. It is very susceptible to frost, drought and market fluctuations.

World production 1989
5.7 million tonnes

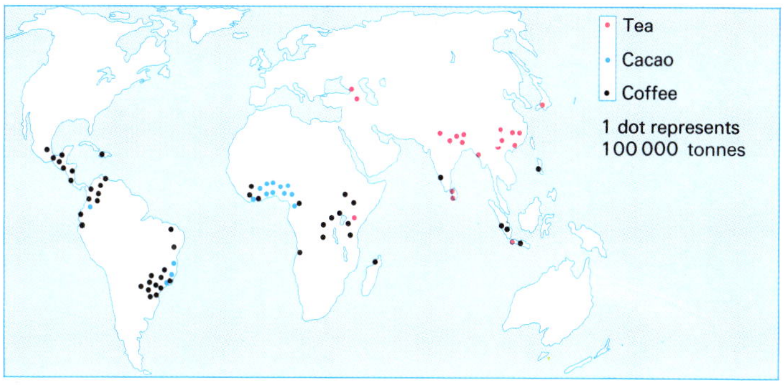

Sugar beet

Requires a deep, rich soil and a temperate climate. Europe produces over 90 % of the world's beets mainly for domestic consumption.

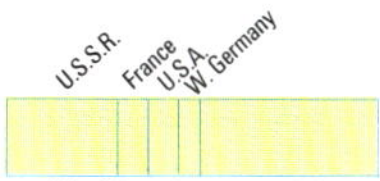

World production 1989
296.2 million tonnes

Sugar cane

Also requires deep and rich soil but a tropical climate. It produces a much higher yield per hectare than beet and is grown primarily for export.

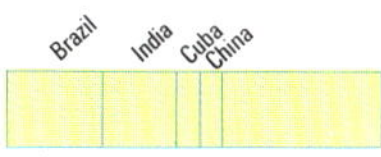

World production 1989
1002.5 million tonnes

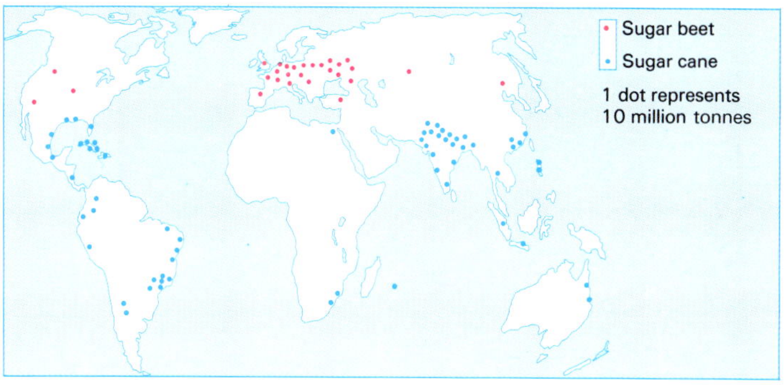

Fruit

With the improvements in canning, drying and freezing, and in transport and marketing, the international trade and consumption of deciduous and soft fruits, citrus fruits and tropical fruits has greatly increased. Recent developments in the use of the peel will give added value to some of the fruit crops.

Fish

Commercial fishing requires large shoals of fish of one species within reach of markets. Freshwater fishing is also important. A rich source of protein, fish will become an increasingly valuable food source.

World catch 1987
92.7 million tonnes

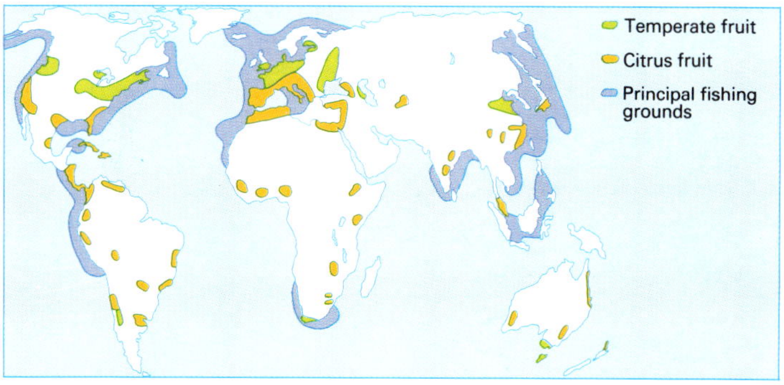

Beef cattle

Australia, New Zealand and Argentina provide the major part of international beef exports. Western U.S.A. and Europe have considerable production of beef for their local high demand.

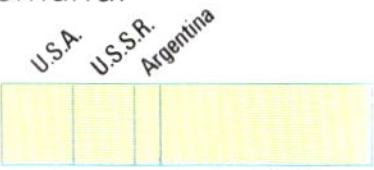

World production 1989
50.8 million tonnes

Dairy cattle

The need of herds for a rich diet and for nearby markets result in dairying being characteristic of densely-populated areas of the temperate zones - U.S.A., N.W. Europe, and S.E. Australia.

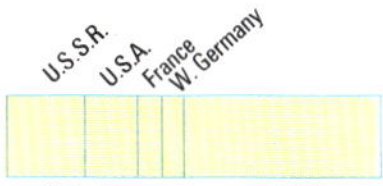

World production 1989
473.8 million tonnes

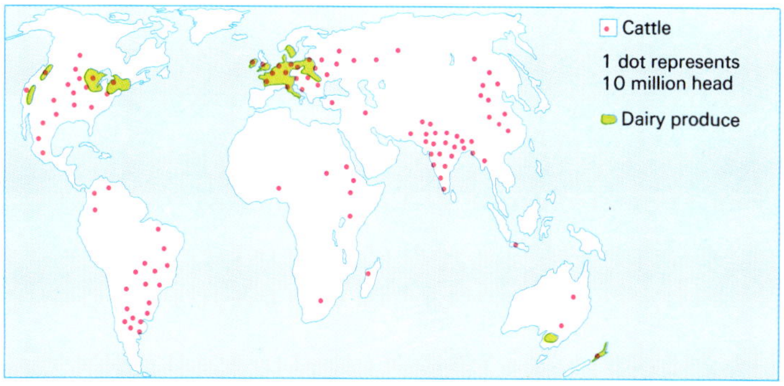

Sheep

Raised mostly for wool and meat, their skins and the cheese from their milk are important products in some countries. The merino yields a fine wool and crossbreeds are best for meat.

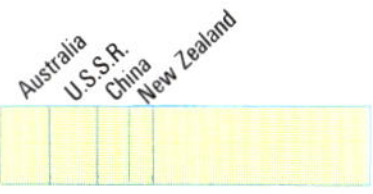

World production 1989
1178 million head

Pigs

Can be reared in most climates from monsoon to cool temperate. They are abundant in China, the Corn Belt of the U.S.A. N.W. and C. Europe, Brazil and U.S.S.R.

World production 1989
67.2 million tonnes

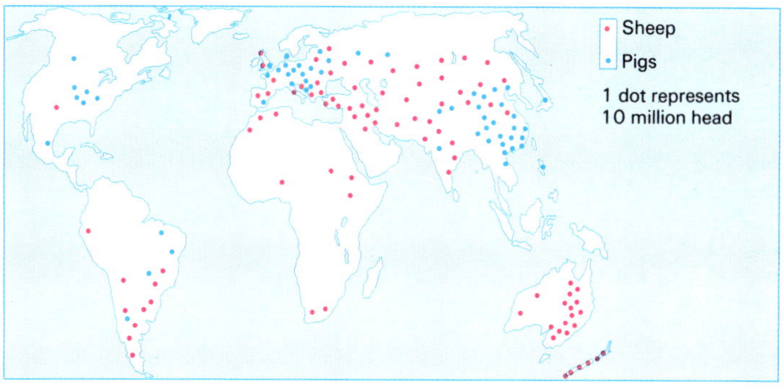

Some countries are highly dependent upon minerals. The following are dependent on metals and minerals for over 50% of the value of their exports: Zambia 93%, New Caledonia 81%, Zaire 55%.

● Iron Fe ■ Nickel Ni ◗ Chrome Cr ▲ Manganese Mn ▽ Gold Au ◠ Silver Ag ◆ Diamonds

Top 5 producers for each mineral with percentage of World production 1989

Iron		Nickel		Chrome		Manganese		Gold		Silver		Diamonds	
U.S.S.R.	29%	U.S.S.R.	30%	South Africa	35%	U.S.S.R.	40%	South Africa	30%	Mexico	16%	Australia	38%
China	17%	Canada	27%	U.S.S.R.	27%	South Africa	15%	U.S.S.R.	14%	U.S.A.	14%	Zaïre	20%
Brazil	16%	Australia	10%	Albania	7%	Brazil	11%	U.S.A.	13%	Peru	14%	Botswana	15%
Australia	11%	New Caledonia	8%	India	7%	Gabon	10%	Australia	10%	U.S.S.R.	11%	U.S.S.R.	12%
U.S.A.	6%	Cuba	6%	Zimbabwe	5%	China	7%	Canada	8%	Canada	10%	South Africa	9%

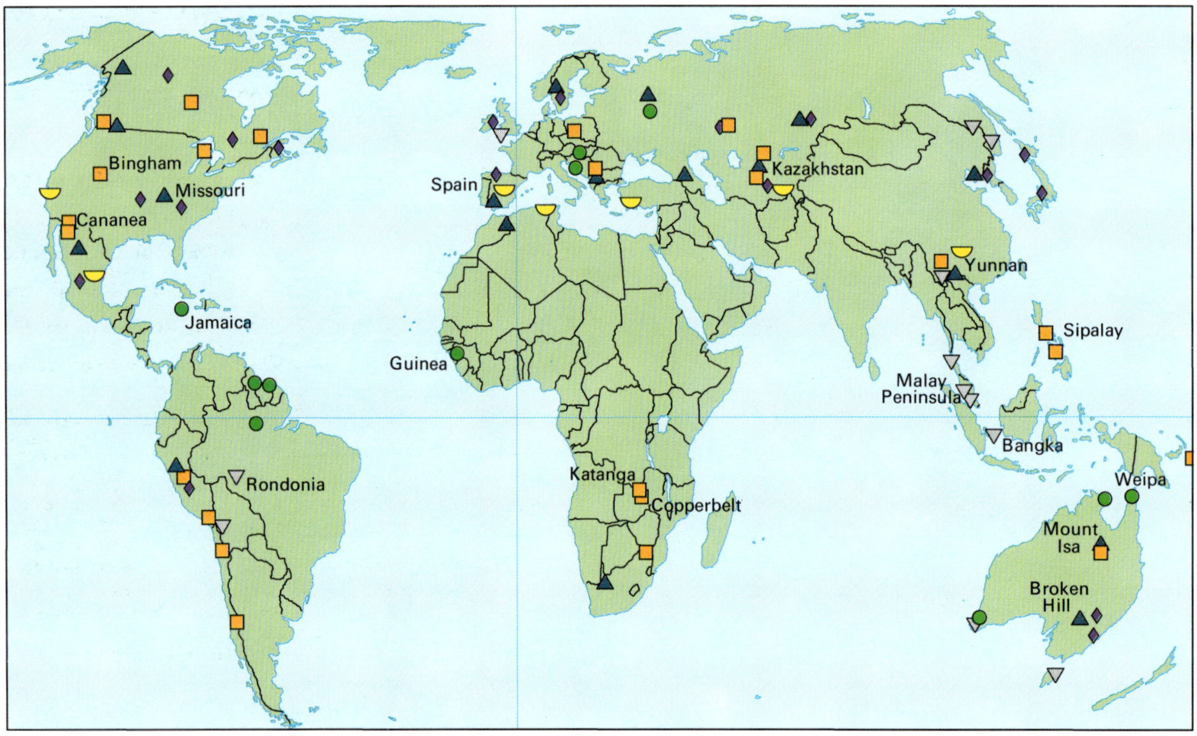

■ Copper Cu ▲ Lead Pb ● Bauxite Al ▽ Tin Sn ◆ Zinc Zn ◡ Mercury Hg

Top 5 producers for each mineral with percentage of World production 1989

Copper		Lead		Bauxite		Tin		Zinc		Mercury	
Chile	19%	Australia	16%	Australia	38%	Brazil	23%	Canada	19%	U.S.S.R.	28%
U.S.A.	18%	U.S.S.R.	15%	Guinea	17%	Malaysia	15%	U.S.S.R.	13%	Spain	26%
Canada	9%	U.S.A.	14%	Jamaica	9%	Indonesia	15%	Australia	12%	China	15%
U.S.S.R.	8%	Canada	9%	Brazil	8%	China	13%	Peru	9%	Algeria	13%
China	6%	China	9%	U.S.S.R.	7%	U.S.S.R.	7%	China	7%	Mexico	6%

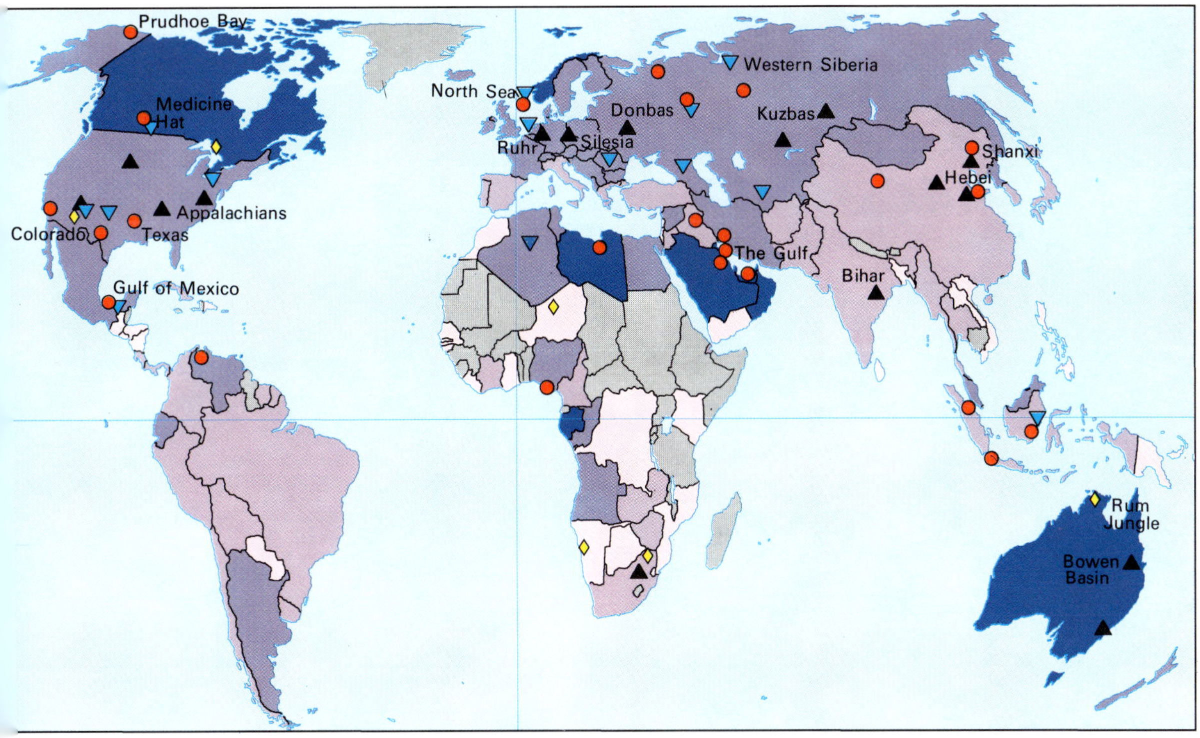

ENERGY PRODUCTION

Primary energy production expressed as kg of coal per person

- Over 10 000 kg per person
- 1000-10 000 kg per person
- 100-1000 kg per person
- 10-100 kg per person
- Under 10 kg per person

Primary energy sources include coal, lignite, peat, oil, natural gas, plus hydro-, nuclear and geothermally generated electricity.

In developing countries traditional fuels are still very important. Sometimes called biomass fuels, they include wood, charcoal and dried dung. The pie graph for Nigeria at the foot of the page shows their importance to even the eleventh highest oil producer in the World.

Oil ▽ Natural Gas ▲ Coal and Lignite ◇ Uranium *(the fuel used to generate nuclear power)*

Top 5 producers for each primary energy source with percentage of World production 1989

Oil		*Natural Gas*		*Coal*		*Lignite*		*Uranium*		*Nuclear Power*		*Hydro-Electricity*	
S.S.R.	20%	U.S.S.R.	38%	China	30%	East Germany	20%	Canada	23%	U.S.A.	32%	U.S.A.	14%
S.A.	14%	U.S.A.	26%	U.S.A.	19%	U.S.A.	19%	U.S.S.R.	13%	France	13%	Canada	12%
udi Arabia	8%	Canada	5%	U.S.S.R.	16%	U.S.S.R.	11%	East Germany	12%	Japan	10%	U.S.S.R.	11%
n	5%	Netherlands	3%	India	6%	West Germany	7%	U.S.A.	10%	West Germany	7%	Brazil	9%
xico	5%	Algeria	2%	Poland	6%	Czechoslovakia	6%	Australia	7%	Canada	4%	China	6%

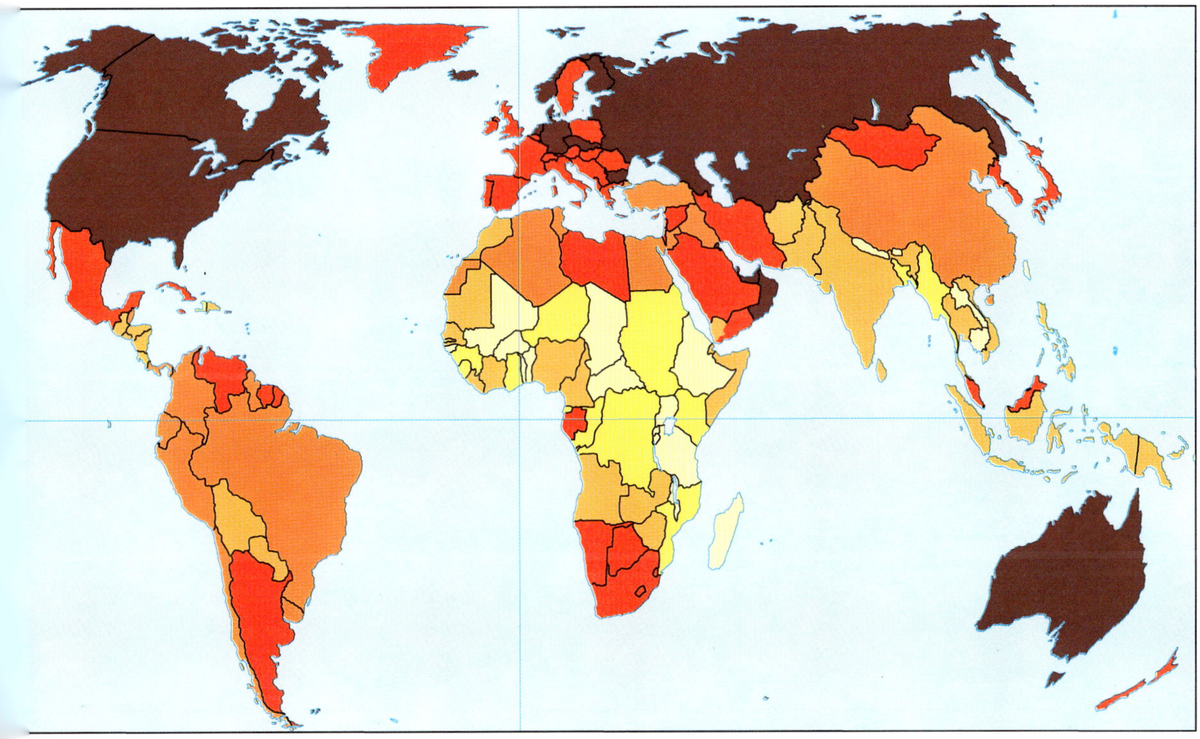

ENERGY CONSUMPTION

Primary energy consumption expressed as kg of coal per person

- Over 5 000 kg per person
- 1000-5 000 kg per person
- 500-1 000 kg per person
- 100-500 kg per person
- 50-100 kg per person
- Under 50 kg per person

Energy consumption by continent 1989

		(Change 1988-9)
North America	27.7%	*(+1.4%)*
Asia	23.0%	*(+6.3%)*
Europe	22.3%	*(−0.6%)*
U.S.S.R.	17.3%	*(−0.0%)*
South America	5.7%	*(+4.1%)*
Africa	2.7%	*(+2.1%)*
Australasia	1.3%	*(+8.7%)*

World total 12 019.9 million tonnes

TYPE OF ENERGY CONSUMED BY SELECTED COUNTRIES

- Coal and Lignite
- Oil
- Natural Gas
- Electricity
- Traditional Fuels

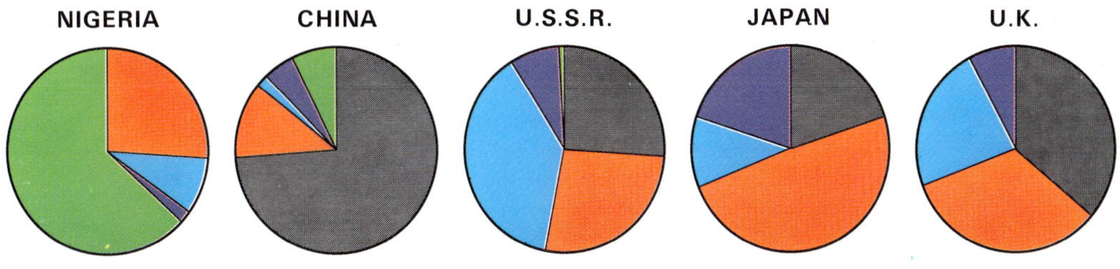

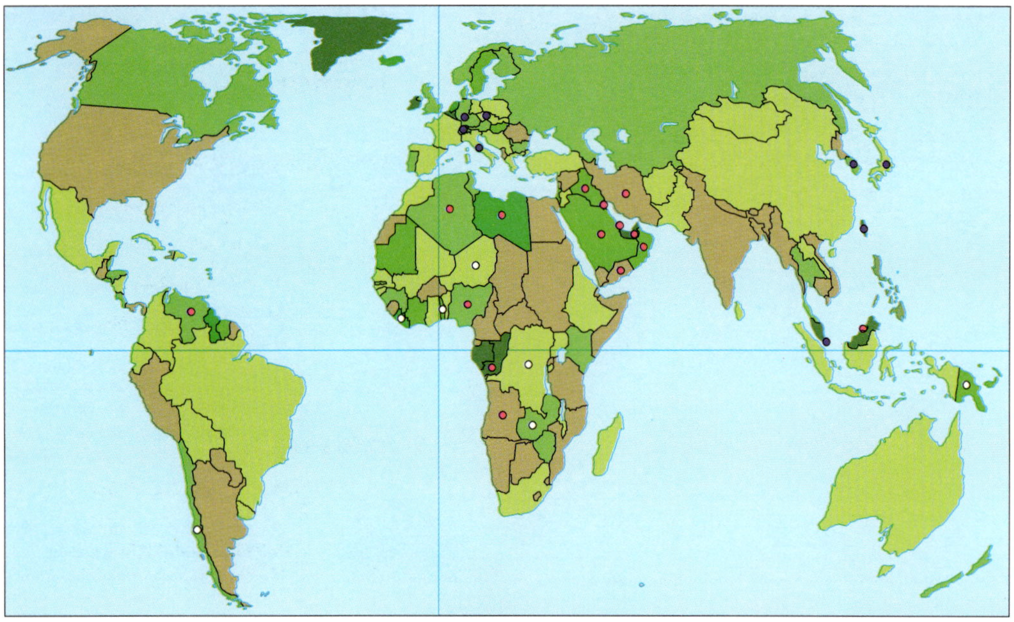

DEPENDENCE ON TRADE

Value of exports as a percentage of G.D.P. (Gross Domestic Product) 1988

- Over 50% G.D.P.
- 40-50% G.D.P.
- 30-40% G.D.P.
- 20-30% G.D.P.
- 10-20% G.D.P.
- Under 10% G.D.P.

- Most dependent on industrial exports (over 75% of total exports)
- Most dependent on fuel exports (over 75% of total exports)
- Most dependent on metal and mineral exports (over 75% of total exports)

BALANCE OF TRADE

Value of exports in proportion to the value of imports 1988

Exports exceed imports by:

- More than 50%
- 10-50%
- 10% either side
- 10-50%
- More than 50%

Imports exceed exports by:

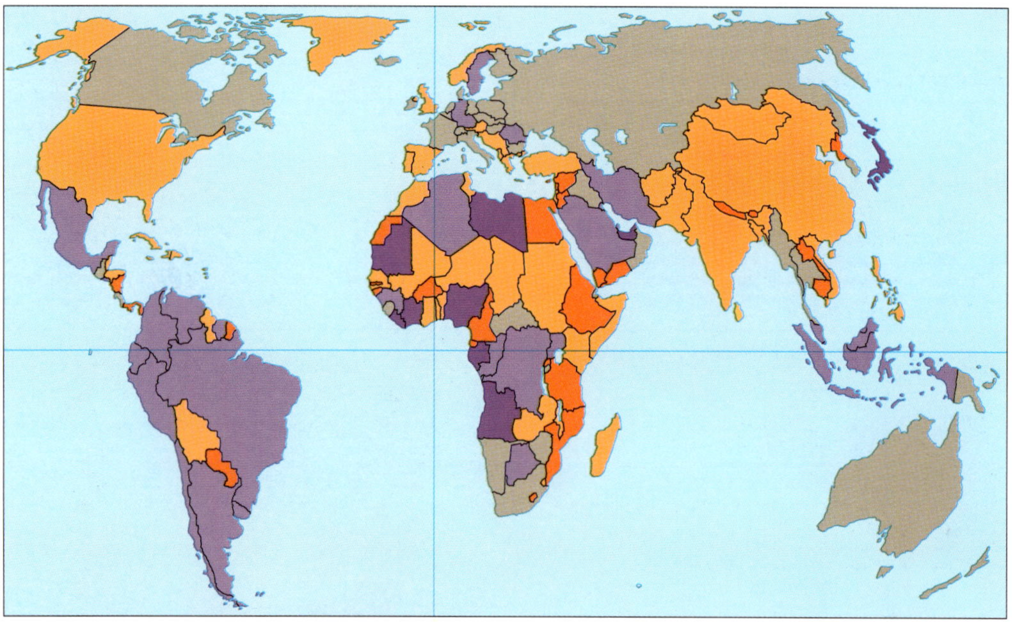

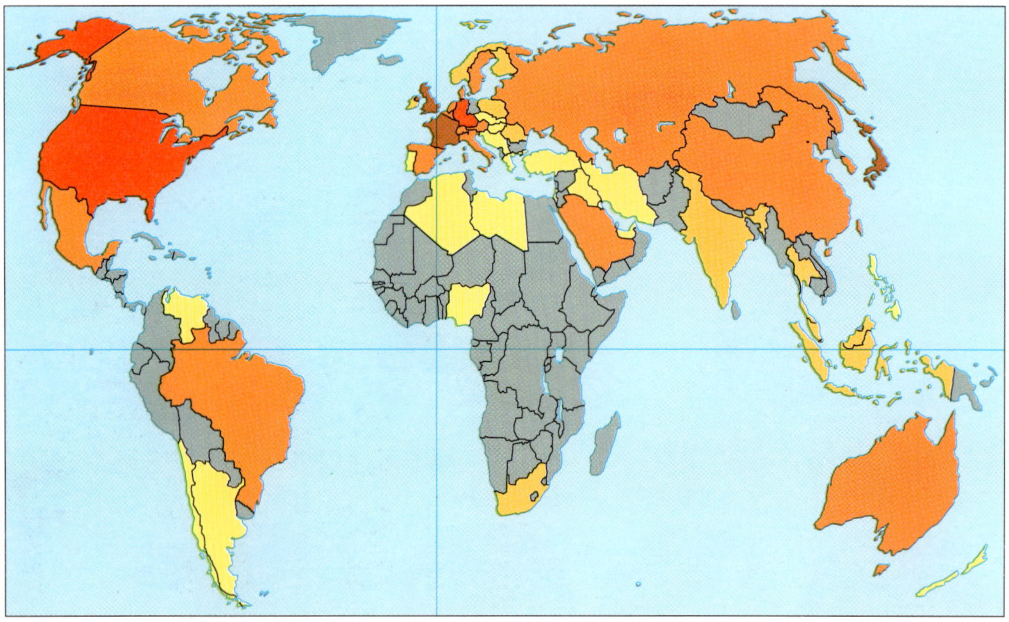

SHARE OF WORLD TRADE

Percentage share of total world exports by value 1988

- Over 10% of world trade
- 5-10% of world trade
- 1-5% of world trade
- 0.5-1% of world trade
- 0.25-0.5% of world trade
- Under 0.25% of world trade

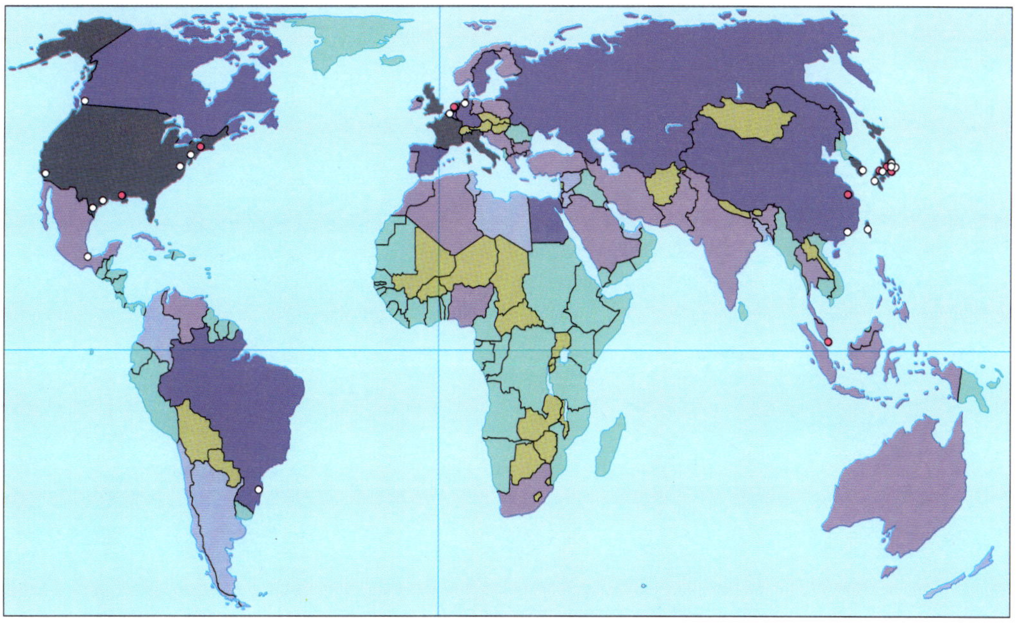

SHIPPING

Freight unloaded in millions of tonnes 1988

- Over 100 million tonnes
- 50 - 100 million tonnes
- 10 - 50 million tonnes
- 5 - 10 million tonnes
- Under 5 million tonnes
- Land-locked countries

Major Seaports

- Handling over 100 million tonnes p.a.
- Handling 50-100 million tonnes p.a.

AIR TRAVEL

Passenger kilometres flown 1988*

- Over 100 000 million
- 50 000 - 100 000 million
- 10 000 - 50 000 million
- 1 000 - 10 000 million
- 500 - 1 000 million
- Under 500 million

Major airports (handling over 20 million passengers in 1988)

* Passenger kilometres are the number of passengers (international and domestic) multiplied by the distance flown by each passenger from the airport of origin.

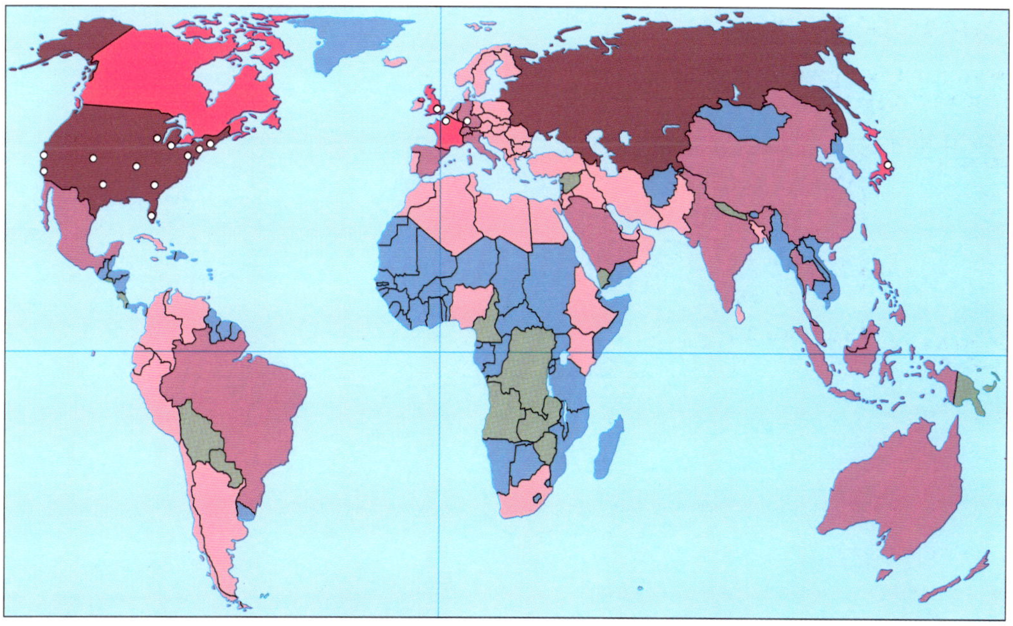

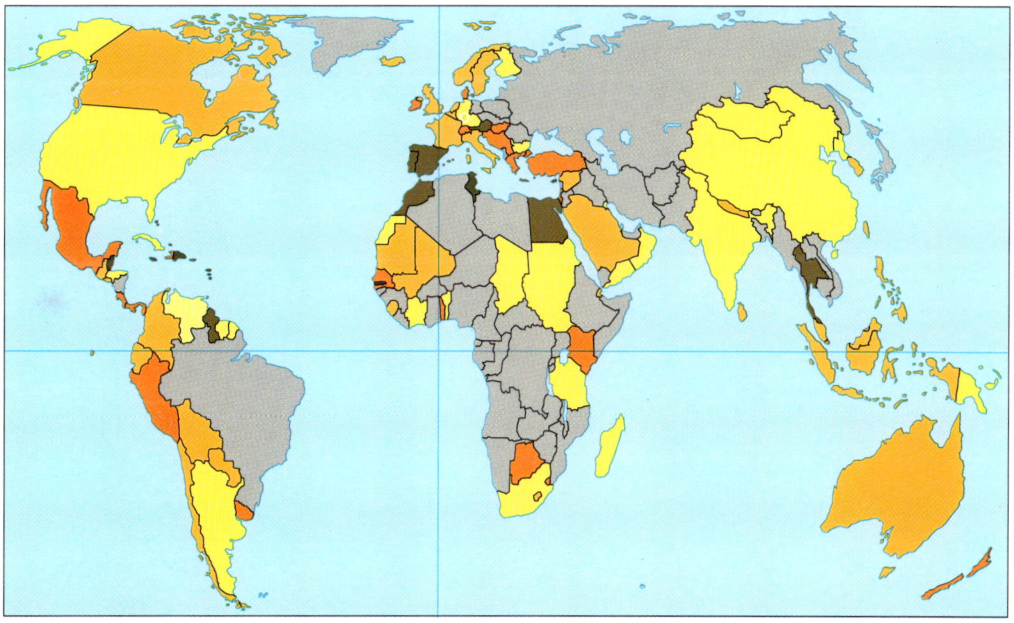

TOURISM

Tourism receipts as a percentage of G.N.P. (Gross National Product) 1988

- Over 10% of G.N.P. from tourism
- 5 - 10% of G.N.P. from tourism
- 2.5 - 5% of G.N.P. from tourism
- 1 - 2.5% of G.N.P. from tourism
- 0.5 - 1% of G.N.P. from tourism
- Under 0.5% of G.N.P. from tourism

Largest percentage share of total world spending on tourism 1988	
West Germany	16%
U.S.A.	14%
U.K.	8%
Japan	7%
France	6%

Largest percentage share of total world receipts from tourism 1988	
U.S.A.	10%
Spain	9%
Italy	8%
France	8%
U.K.	6%

THE WORLD: *languages and religion*

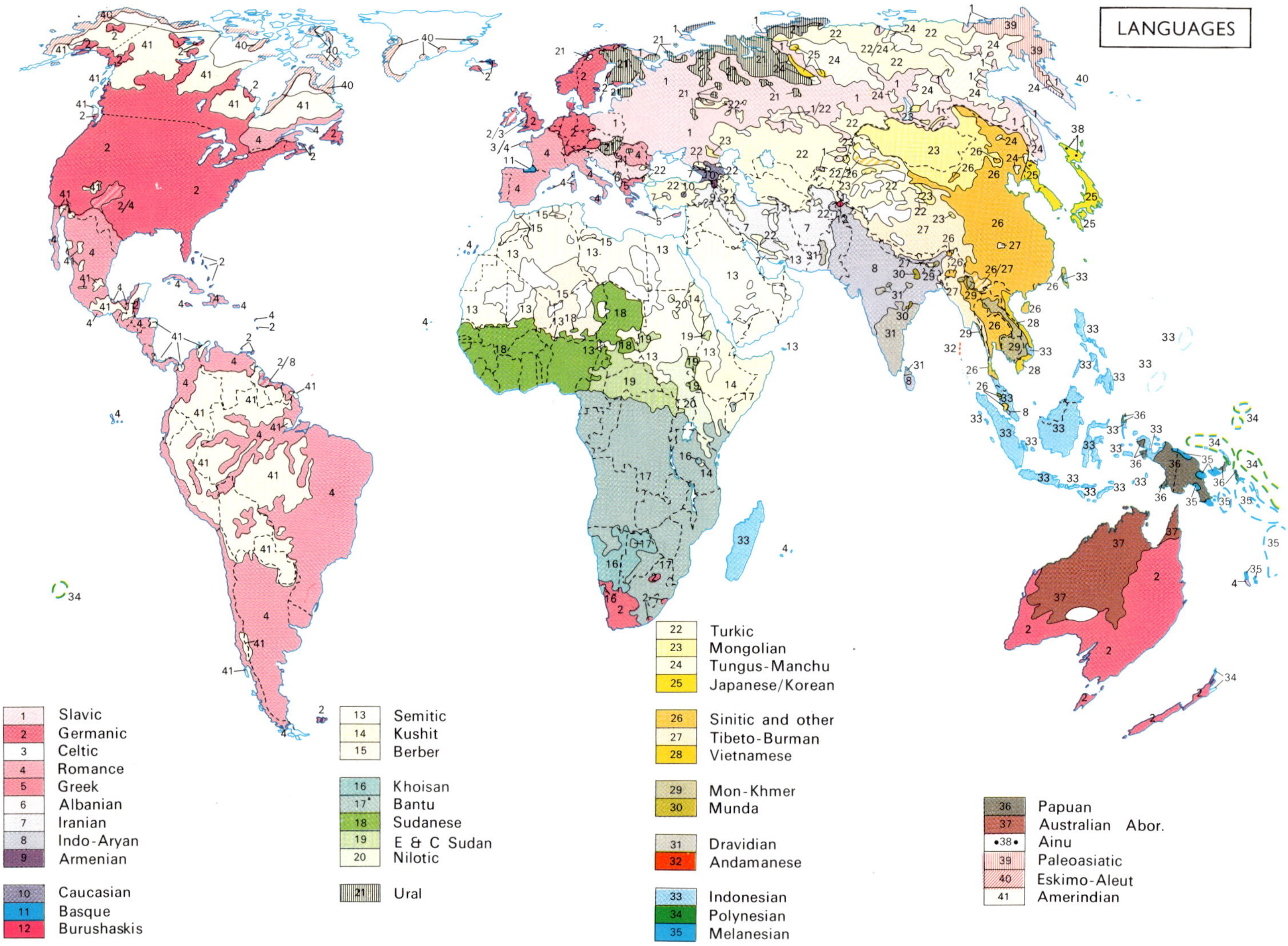

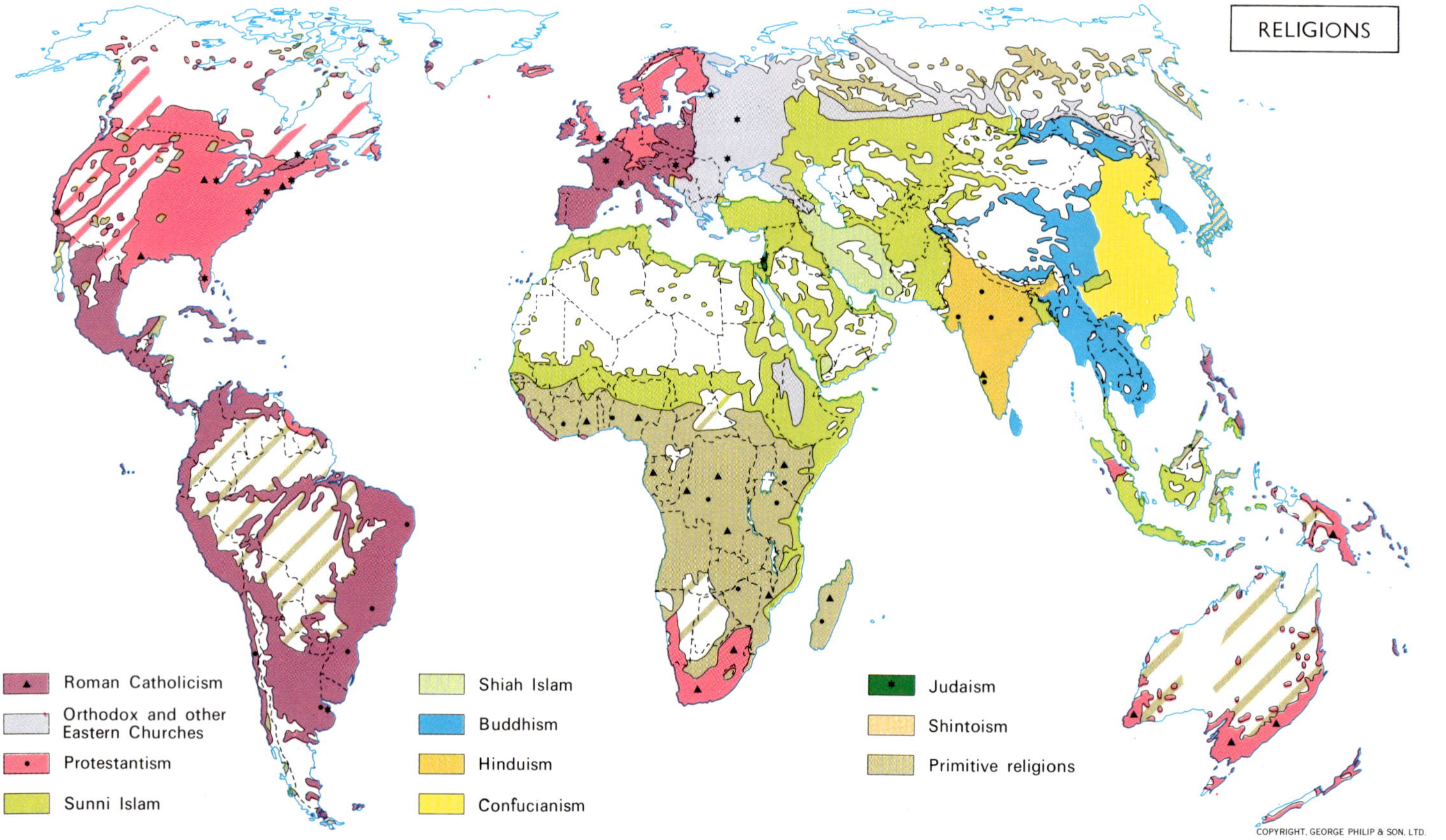

1:105 000 000

UNITED NATIONS

Created in 1945 to promote peace and cooperation and based in New York, the United Nations is the world's largest international organisation, with 159 members and an annual budget of over two billion US dollars. Each member of the General Assembly has one vote, while the permanent members of the 15-nation Security Council - USA, USSR, China, UK and France - hold a veto. The Economic and Social Council comprises 54 members responsible for economic, social, cultural, educational, health and related matters. The Secretariat is the UN's chief administrative arm; the only territory now administered by the Trusteeship Council is Belau (by the USA). The UN has 24 specialised agencies - based in Canada, France, Switzerland and Italy as well as the USA - which help members in fields such as economic development (UNDP), education (UNESCO), agriculture (FAO) and medicine (WHO).

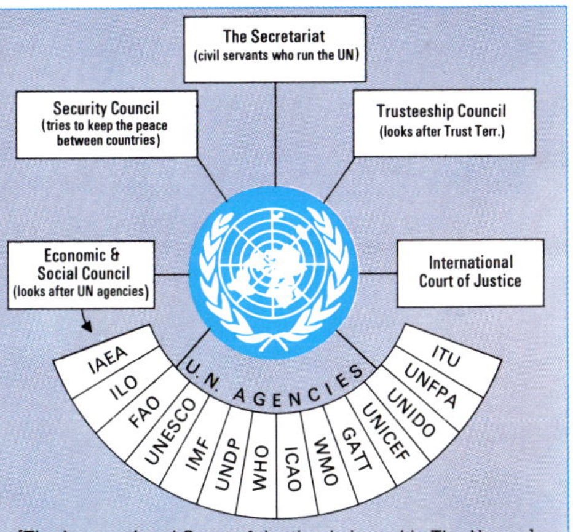

[The International Court of Justice is based in The Hague]

Membership: There are 17 independent states who are not members of the UN - Andorra, Estonia, Kiribati, Latvia, Liechtenstein, Lithuania, Micronesia, N. Korea, S. Korea, Monaco, Nauru, San Marino, Switzerland, Taiwan, Tonga, Tuvalu and Vatican City. The UN's 159 members include two who are not independent nations - the Soviet republics of Byelorussia and Ukraine. There were 51 members in 1945. Official languages are Chinese, English, French, Russian, Spanish and Arabic.
Funding: The UN budget for 1988-1989 was US $ 1,788,746,000. Contributions are assessed by members' ability to pay, with the maximum 25% of the total, the minimum 0.01%. Contributions for 1988-1989 were: USA 25%, Japan 11.38%, USSR 9.99%, W. Germany 8.08%, France 6.25%, UK 4.86%, Italy 3.99%, Canada 3.09%, Spain 1.95%, Netherlands 1.65% (others 23.75%).
Peacekeeping: The UN has been involved in 18 peacekeeping operations worldwide since 1945, five of which (Afghanistan/Pakistan, Iran/Iraq, Angola, Namibia and Honduras) were initiated in 1988-1989. In June 1991 UN personnel totalling over 11,000 were working in eight separate areas.

EFTA: European Free Trade Association (formed in 1960). Portugal left the 'Seven' in 1989 to join the EEC.
ACP: African-Caribbean-Pacific (1963).
OIEC: Organisation for International Economic Cooperation (1991). It was formed from the defunct Communist trade bloc COMECON.

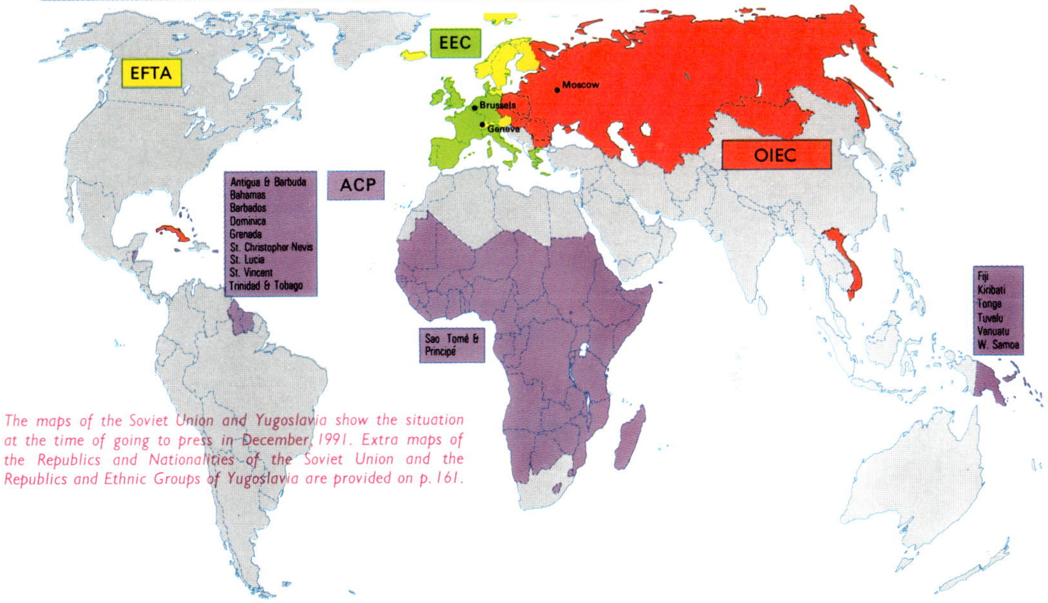

The maps of the Soviet Union and Yugoslavia show the situation at the time of going to press in December 1991. Extra maps of the Republics and Nationalities of the Soviet Union and the Republics and Ethnic Groups of Yugoslavia are provided on p. 161.

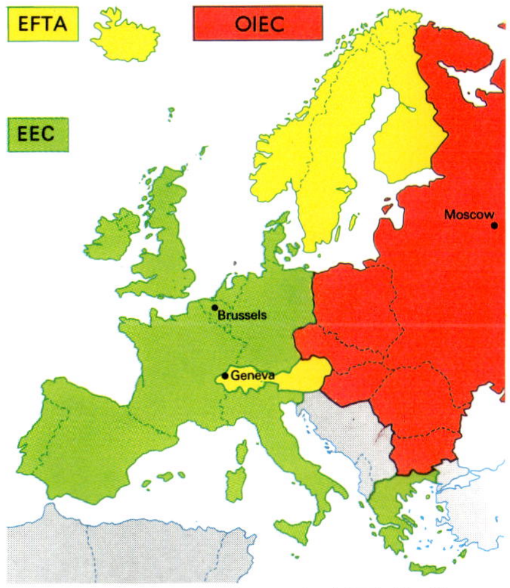

EEC: European Economic Community (1957). The 'Common Market' aims to integrate economies, coordinate social developments and bring about political union. Members of what is now the world's biggest market share agricultural and industrial policies and tariffs on trade.

NATO: North Atlantic Treaty Organisation (formed 1949). It continues after 1991 despite the winding up of the Warsaw Pact.
OAU: Organisation of African Unity (1963). Its 52 members represent over 90% of Africa's population.
ASEAN: Association of South-East Asian Nations (1967).
OAS: Organisation of American States (1949). It aims to promote social and economic cooperation between developed countries of North America and eveloping nations of Latin America.
LAIA: Latin American Integration Association (1980).
OECD: Organisation for Economic Cooperation and Development (1961). The 24 major Western free-market economies plus Yugoslavia as associate member.
COMMONWEALTH: The Commonwealth of Nations evolved from the British Empire; it comprises 18 nations recognising the British monarch as head of state and 32 with their own heads of state.
OPEC: Organisation of Petroleum Exporting Countries (1960). It controls about three-quarters of the world's oil supply.

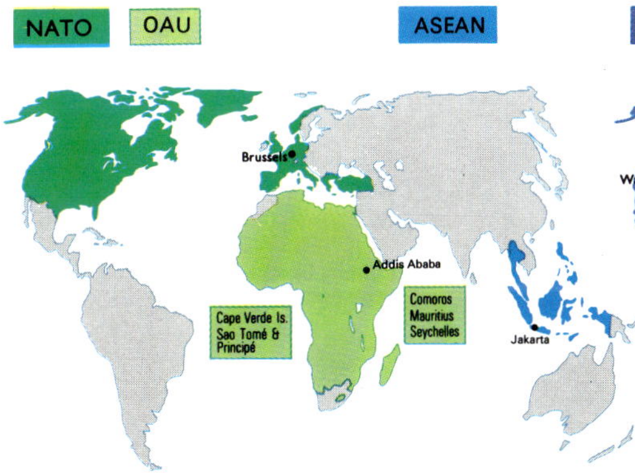

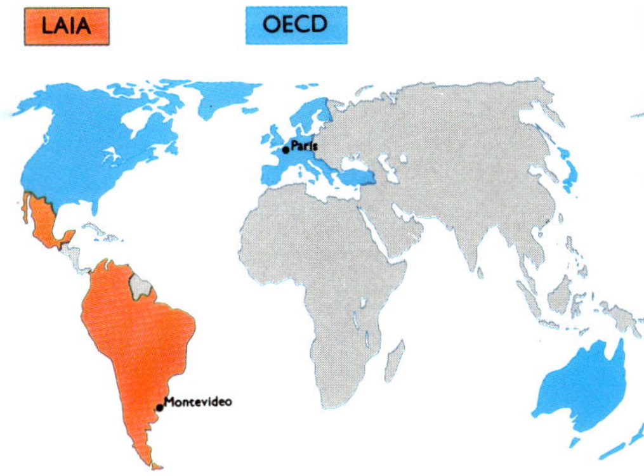

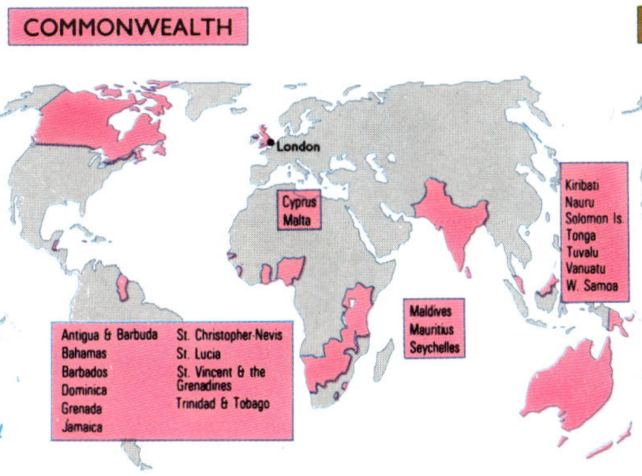

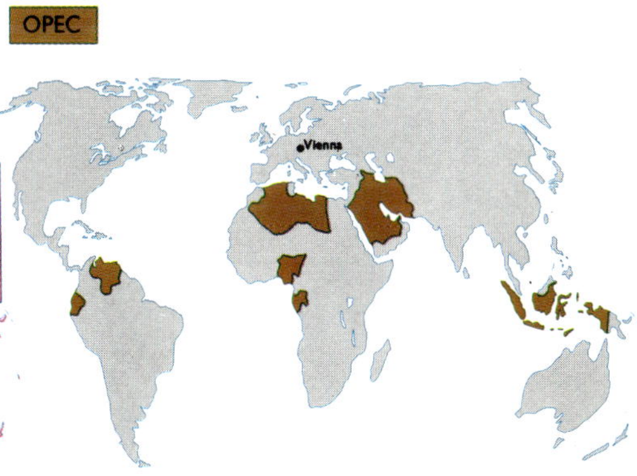

THE WORLD: *time and distance*

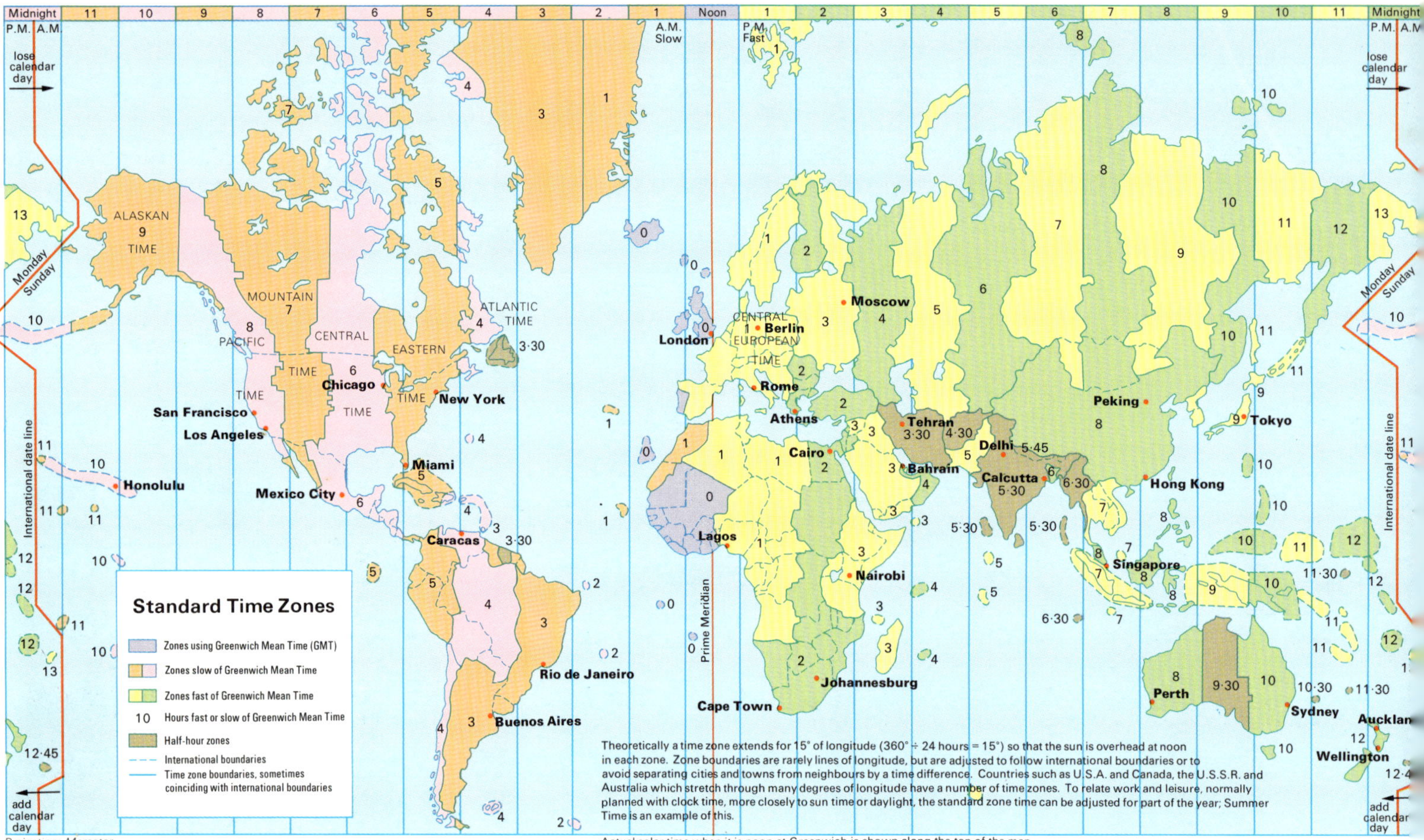

Theoretically a time zone extends for 15° of longitude (360° ÷ 24 hours = 15°) so that the sun is overhead at noon in each zone. Zone boundaries are rarely lines of longitude, but are adjusted to follow international boundaries or to avoid separating cities and towns from neighbours by a time difference. Countries such as U.S.A. and Canada, the U.S.S.R. and Australia which stretch through many degrees of longitude have a number of time zones. To relate work and leisure, normally planned with clock time, more closely to sun time or daylight, the standard zone time can be adjusted for part of the year; Summer Time is an example of this.

Projection: *Mercator*

Actual solar time when it is noon at Greenwich is shown along the top of the map

Mexico City
19 26N 99 4W

London
51 28N 0 27W

These circular maps are drawn on an Azimuthal Equidistant projection with its origin, its centre, at the city shown. The whole world is shown and so there are some strange distortions of the coastline at the edges, for example, in that of Singapore. The principal property of the projection is that all distances measured through the centre of the circle are true to scale, and so a straight line passing from the centre to any other point is a great circle and shows the shortest distance between the cities. Also that line is correct for direction/bearing and shows the great circle flight path.

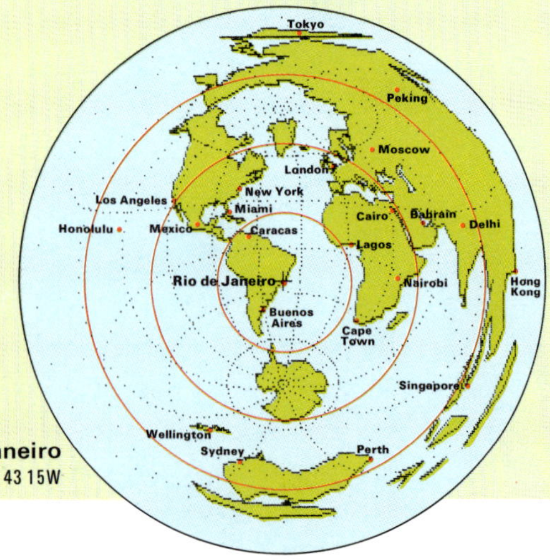

Rio de Janeiro
22 50S 43 15W

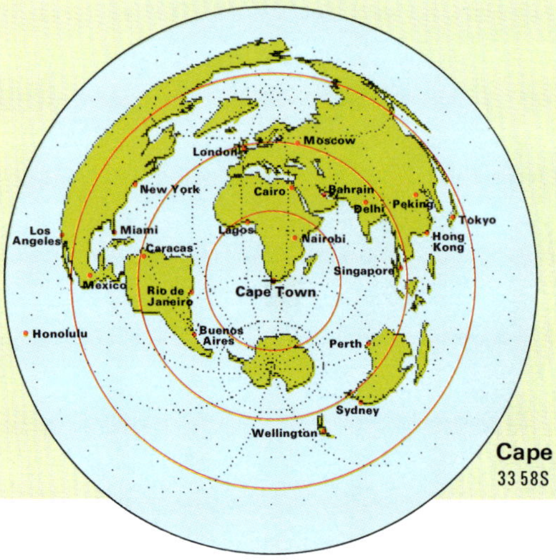

Cape Town
33 58S 18 36E

These distances are in kilometres and are the great circle distances between the cities (international airports). Great circle distances are the shortest distances between two points on the globe. They are the normal flight paths for aircraft where they are free from the restrictions of air corridors or national airspace.

	Bahrain	Buenos Aires	Cairo	Cape Town	Caracas	Delhi	Hong Kong	Honolulu	Lagos	London	Los Angeles	Mexico	Miami	Moscow	Nairobi	New York	Peking	Perth	Rio de Janeiro	Singapore	Sydney	Tokyo
Buenos Aires	13 291																					
Cairo	1 927	11 845																				
Cape Town	7 496	6 880	7 246																			
Caracas	12 121	5 124	10 200	10 254																		
Delhi	2 618	15 784	4 400	9 278	14 186																	
Hong Kong	6 387	18 442	8 121	11 852	16 340	3 768																
Honolulu	13 882	12 158	14 195	18 555	9 671	11 984	8 911															
Lagos	5 454	7 932	3 926	4 783	7 722	8 071	11 832	16 286														
London	5 089	11 128	3 528	9 672	7 465	6 726	9 637	11 617	4 998													
Los Angeles	13 210	9 854	12 206	16 067	5 813	12 863	11 634	4 105	12 408	8 752												
Mexico	13 962	7 391	12 360	13 701	3 572	14 651	12 121	6 096	11 043	8 898	2 498											
Miami	12 182	7 113	10 441	12 334	2 190	13 495	14 430	7 806	9 045	7 102	3 759	2 050										
Moscow	3 466	13 488	2 909	10 150	9 900	4 359	7 148	11 289	6 250	2 505	9 748	10 682	9 191									
Nairobi	3 398	10 413	3 542	4 096	11 545	5 413	8 750	17 255	3 828	6 835	15 560	14 812	12 771	6 365								
New York	10 613	8 526	9 009	12 551	3 402	11 747	12 956	8 000	8 437	5 535	3 968	3 361	1 751	7 476	11 828							
Peking	6 180	19 273	7 526	12 956	14 356	3 804	1 985	8 124	11 452	8 146	10 030	12 426	12 475	5 789	9 217	10 971						
Perth	9 467	12 562	11 256	8 684	17 610	7 874	6 030	10 886	12 517	14 495	14 986	16 247	18 281	12 236	8 889	18 699	8 000					
Rio de Janeiro	11 462	1 990	9 897	6 080	4 522	14 054	17 688	13 330	6 022	9 248	10 132	7 659	6 713	11 528	8 937	7 724	17 306	13 527				
Singapore	6 319	15 860	8 246	9 650	18 332	4 148	2 581	10 789	11 149	10 867	14 099	16 593	16 951	8 437	7 446	15 330	4 489	3 909	15 729			
Sydney	12 502	11 760	14 391	10 982	15 341	10 424	7 370	8 163	15 514	17 005	12 052	12 973	15 012	14 501	12 125	16 001	8 956	3 274	13 512	6 294		
Tokyo	8 271	18 338	9 552	14 710	14 154	5 852	2 874	6 185	13 475	9 584	8 806	11 304	11 991	7 487	11 243	10 869	2 089	7 896	18 557	5 300	7 809	
Wellington	14 678	9 943	16 503	11 287	13 119	12 647	9 424	7 508	16 047	18 816	10 787	11 099	13 054	16 547	13 643	14 406	10 782	5 246	11 865	8 521	2 226	9 258

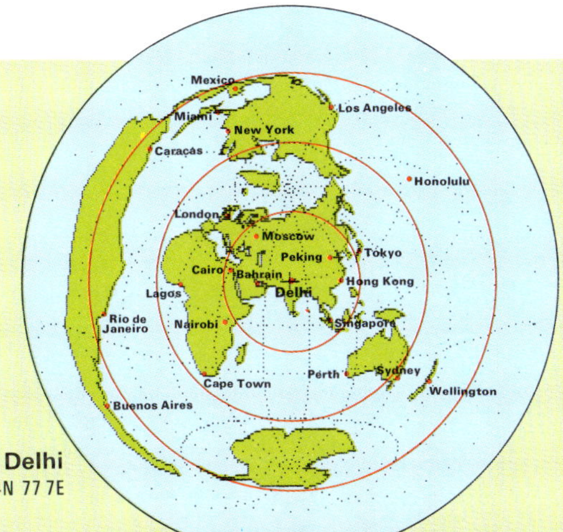

Delhi
28 34N 77 7E

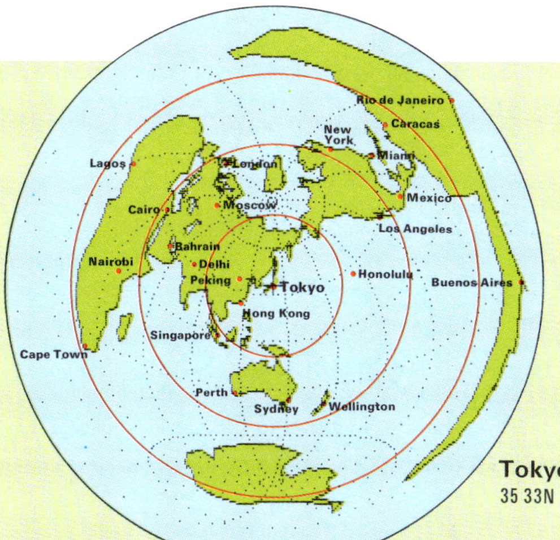

Tokyo
35 33N 139 46E

The three circles are drawn at radius 5 000, 10 000 and 15 000 km from the central city

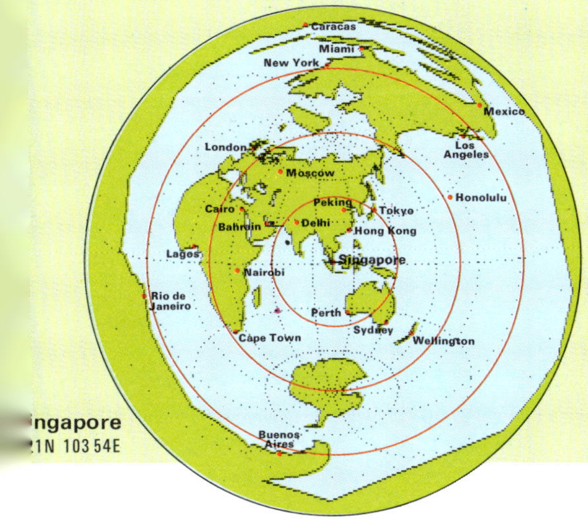

Singapore
1 21N 103 54E

• Cities shown on the distance table

The co-ordinates given are for the airport of each city

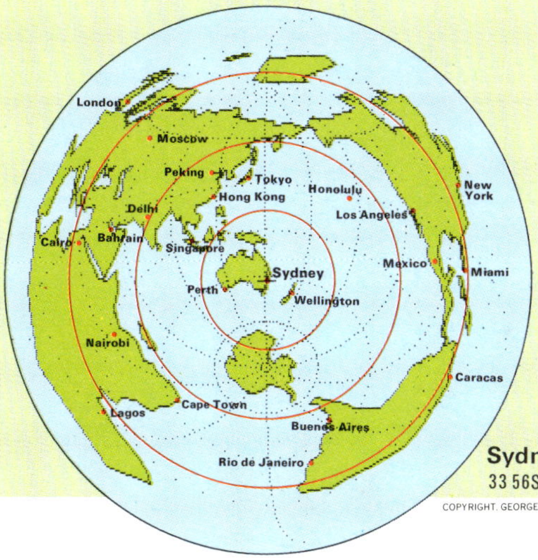

Sydney
33 56S 151 10E

INDEX: *guide to use*

The number in bold type which follows each name in the index refers to the number of the page where that feature or place will be found.

The geographical co-ordinates which follow the place name are sometimes only approximate but are close enough for the place name to be located.

An open square □ signifies that the name refers to an administrative division of a country while a solid square ■ follows the name of a country.

Rivers have been indexed to their mouth or to their confluence.

The alphabetical order of names composed of two or more words is governed primarily by the first word and then by the second. This is an example of the rule:

West Wyalong
West Yorkshire
Westbourne
Westbury
Westbury-on-Severn
Western Australia

Names composed of a proper name (Gibraltar) and a description (Strait of) are positioned alphabetically by the proper name. All river names are followed by ~→. If the same word occurs in the name of a town and a geographical feature, the town name is listed first followed by the name or names of the geographical features.

Names beginning with M', Mc are all indexed as if they were spelled Mac.

If the same place name occurs twice or more in the index and the places are in different countries they will be followed by the country names and the latter in alphabetical order.

Sydney, Australia
Sydney, Canada

In the index each placename is followed by its geographical co-ordinates which allow the reader to find the place on the map. These co-ordinates give the latitude and longitude of a particular place.

The latitude (or parallel) is the distance of a point north or south of the Equator measured as an angle with the centre of the earth. The Equator is latitude 0°, the North Pole is 90°N and the South Pole 90°S. On a globe the lines could be drawn as concentric circles parallel to the Equator, decreasing in diameter from the Equator until they become a point at the Poles. On the maps these lines of latitude are usually represented as lines running across the map from East to West in smooth curves. They are numbered on the sides of the map; north of the Equator the numbers increase northwards, to the south they increase southwards. The degree interval between them depends on the scale of the map. On a large scale map (for example, 1:2 000 000) the interval is one degree, but on a small scale (for example 1:50 000 000) it will be ten degrees.

Lines of longitude (or meridians) cut the latitude lines at right angles on the globe and intersect with one another at the Poles. Longitude is measured by the angle at the centre of the earth between it and the meridian of origin which runs through Greenwich (0°). It may be a measurement East or West of this line and from 0° to 180° in each direction. The longitude line of 180° runs North – South through the Pacific Ocean. On a particular map the interval between the lines of longitude is always the same as that between the lines of latitude and normally they are drawn vertically. They are numbered in the top and bottom margins and a note states East or West from Greenwich.

The unit of measurement for latitude and longitude is the degree and it is subdivided into 60 minutes. An index entry states the position of a place in degrees and minutes, a space being left between the degrees and minutes. The latitude is followed by N(orth) or S(outh) and the longitude by E(ast) or W(est).

The diagram illustrates how the reader has to estimate the required distance from the nearest line of latitude or longitude. In the diagram there is one degree, or 60 minutes between the lines and so to find the position of Calais an estimate has to be made, 57 parts of 60 north of the 50 degree latitude line and 50 parts of 60, or 50 minutes east of the one degree longitude line.

Where the map is smaller in scale it is more difficult to calculate the position of a place because there are five or ten degree intervals between the lines.

Scale 1:2 000 000

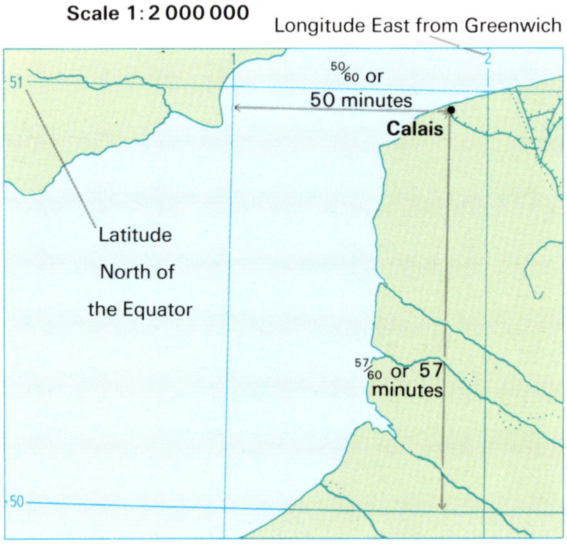

Calais 34 50 57 N 1 50 E
page latitude longitude

The following is a list of the principal abbreviations used in the Index.

A.S.S.R. – Autonomous Soviet Socialist Republic
Afg. – Afghanistan
Afr. – Africa
Alb. – Albania
Alg. – Algeria
Am. – America
Ant. – Antarctica
Arch. – Archipelago
Arg. – Argentina
Atl. Oc. – Atlantic Ocean
B. – Bay
B. Faso – Burkina Faso
Barb. – Barbados
Berm. – Bermuda
Bol. – Bolivia
Bots. – Botswana
Bulg. – Bulgaria
Bur. – Burma
C. – Cape (Cap, Cabo)
C.A.R. – Central African Republic
C.R. – Costa Rica
Cam. – Cameroon
Carib. – Caribbean Sea
Chan. – Channel
Col. – Colombia
Cont. – Continent
Cr. – Creek
Cur. – Curaçao
Dom. – Dominica
Dom. Rep. – Dominican Republic
E. – East
Eq. Guin. – Equatorial Guinea
Eth. – Ethiopia
Falk. – Falkland Is.
Fr. – France
Fr. G. – French Guiana
G. – Gulf (Golf, Golfo)
Ga. – Georgia
Ger. – Germany
Gr. – Great
Green. – Greenland
Gren. – Grenada
Guad. – Guadeloupe
Guat. – Guatemala
Guin. – Guinea
Guy. – Guyana
Hond. – Honduras
Hr. – Harbour
Hts. – Heights
I. – Island (Isle, Ile, Isla)
Ill. – Illinois
Ind. – Indies
Kor. – Korea
Kuw. – Kuwait
L. – Lake (Lac, Loch, Lough, Lago)
Leb. – Lebanon
Les. – Lesotho
Lib. – Liberia
Mart. – Martinique
Mass. – Massachusetts
Maurit. – Mauritania
Minn. – Minnesota
Miss. – Mississippi
Mong. – Mongolia
Mor. – Morocco
Mt. – Mountain (Mount, Mont, Monte, Monti, Montana)
N. – North
N. Cal. – New Caledonia
Nam. – Namibia
Nic. – Nicaragua
Nig. – Nigeria
Nor. – Norway
Oc. – Oceania
P.N.G. – Papua New Guinea
P.R. – Puerto Rico
Pac. Oc. – Pacific Ocean
Pan. – Panama
Par. – Paraguay
Pen. – Peninsula
Pk. – Peak
Pt. – Point (Pointe, Punta)
Ra. – Range
Rom. – Romania
S. – South
S. Oc. – Southern Ocean
Sd. – Sound
Sene. – Senegal
Si. Arab. – Saudi Arabia
Som. – Somalia
St. L. – St. Lucia
Str. – Strait
Swaz. – Swaziland
Tanz. – Tanzania
U.A.E. – United Arab Emirates
Ven. – Venezuela
W. – West
Yem. – Yemen
Zam. – Zambia
Zim. – Zimbabwe

The maps of the Soviet Union and Yugoslavia show the situation at the time of going to press in December, 1991. Extra maps of the Republics and Nationalities of the Soviet Union and the Republics and Ethnic Groups of Yugoslavia are provided on p. 161.

A

Aachen, *Ger.* 36 50 47N 6 4 E
Aalborg, *Den.* 45 57 2N 9 54 E
Aalst, *Belg.* 36 50 56N 4 2 E
Aarhus, *Den.* 45 56 8N 10 11 E
Ābādān, *Iran* 56 30 22N 48 20 E
Abbey Town, *U.K.* 18 54 50N 3 18W
Abbots Bromley, *U.K.* 14 52 50N 1 52W
Abbots Langley, *U.K.* 15 51 43N 0 25W
Abbotsbury, *U.K.* 14 50 40N 2 36W
Abéché, *Chad* 79 13 50N 20 35 E
Aberaeron, *U.K.* 17 52 15N 4 16W
Aberdare, *U.K.* 17 51 43N 3 27W
Aberdeen, *U.K.* 23 57 9N 2 6W
Aberdour, *U.K.* 21 56 2N 3 18W
Aberdovey, *U.K.* 17 52 33N 4 3W
Aberfeldy, *U.K.* 23 56 37N 3 50W
Aberfoyle, *U.K.* 20 56 10N 4 23W
Abergavenny, *U.K.* 17 51 49N 3 1W
Abergele, *U.K.* 17 53 17N 3 35W
Aberlady, *U.K.* 21 56 0N 2 51W
Abernethy, *U.K.* 21 56 19N 3 18W
Aberporth, *U.K.* 17 52 8N 4 32W
Abersoch, *U.K.* 17 52 50N 4 30W
Abersychan, *U.K.* 17 51 44N 3 3W
Abertillery, *U.K.* 17 51 44N 3 9W
Aberystwyth, *U.K.* 17 52 25N 4 6W
Abidjan, *Ivory C.* 78 5 26N 3 58W
Abingdon, *U.K.* 14 51 40N 1 17W
Abington, *U.K.* 21 55 30N 3 42W
Aboyne, *U.K.* 23 57 4N 2 48W
Abū Dhabī, *U.A.E.* 57 24 28N 54 36 E
Acapulco, *Mex.* 94 16 51N 99 56W
Accra, *Ghana* 78 5 35N 0 6W
Accrington, *U.K.* 18 53 46N 2 22W
Achill Hd., *Ire.* 24 53 59N 10 15W
Achill I., *Ire.* 24 53 58N 10 5W
Achinsk, *U.S.S.R.* 49 56 20N 90 20 E
Achnasheen, *U.K.* 22 57 35N 5 5W
Acklins I., *Baham.* 95 22 30N 74 0W
Acle, *U.K.* 15 52 38N 1 32 E
Aconcagua, Cerro, *Arg.* 102 32 39S 70 0W
Acre, *Isr.* 57 32 55N 35 4 E
Acton Burnell, *U.K.* 14 52 37N 2 41W
Adamaoua Plateau, *Cam.* 80 7 20N 12 20 E
Adam's Bridge, *Sri L.* 58 9 15N 79 40 E
Adana, *Turk.* 47 37 0N 35 16 E
Adapazarı, *Turk.* 47 40 48N 30 25 E
Addis Ababa, *Eth.* 79 9 2N 38 42 E
Addlestone, *U.K.* 15 51 22N 0 30W
Adelaide, *Austral.* 67 34 52S 138 30 E
Adélie Land, *Ant.* 103 68 0S 140 0 E
Aden, *S. Yem.* 56 12 45N 45 0 E
Aden, G. of, *Asia* 56 13 0N 50 0 E
Adirondack Mts., *U.S.A.* 93 44 0N 74 15W
Admiralty Is., *P.N.G.* 64 2 0S 147 0 E
Adrar, *Alg.* 78 27 51N 0 11W
Adriatic Sea, *Europe* 40 43 0N 16 0 E
Adwick le Street, *U.K.* 19 53 35N 1 12W
Ægean Sea, *Europe* 41 37 0N 25 0 E
Afghanistan ■, *Asia* 57 33 0N 65 0 E
Agadès, *Niger* 78 16 58N 7 59 E
Agadir, *Mor.* 78 30 28N 9 35W
Agartala, *India* 59 23 50N 91 23 E
Agra, *India* 58 27 17N 77 58 E
Agrigento, *It.* 40 37 19N 13 33 E
Aguascalientes, *Mex.* 94 21 53N 102 12W
Ahmadabad, *India* 58 23 0N 72 40 E
Ahvāz, *Iran* 56 31 20N 48 40 E
Ahvenanmaa = Åland, *Fin.* 45 60 15N 20 0 E
Ailsa Craig, *U.K.* 20 55 15N 5 7W
Ainsdale, *U.K.* 18 53 37N 3 2W
Airdrie, *U.K.* 21 55 53N 3 57W
Aire →, *U.K.* 19 53 42N 0 55W
Aisgill, *U.K.* 18 54 23N 2 21W
Aix-en-Provence, *Fr.* 35 43 32N 5 27 E
Ajaccio, *Fr.* 35 41 55N 8 40 E
Akashi, *Jap.* 62 34 45N 135 0 E
Akita, *Jap.* 62 39 45N 140 7 E
Akranes, *Ice.* 44 64 19N 21 58W
Akron, *U.S.A.* 92 41 7N 81 31W
Aktyubinsk, *U.S.S.R.* 47 50 17N 57 10 E
Akure, *Nig.* 78 7 15N 5 5 E
Akureyri, *Ice.* 44 65 40N 18 6W
Al Ḥudaydah, *Yem.* 56 14 50N 43 0 E
Al Hūfuf, *Si. Arab.* 56 25 25N 49 45 E
Al Jawf, *Si. Arab.* 56 29 55N 39 40 E
Al Qaṭīf, *Si. Arab.* 56 26 35N 50 0 E
Al Qunaytirah, *Syria* 57 32 55N 35 45 E
Alabama □, *U.S.A.* 91 33 0N 87 0W
Åland, *Fin.* 45 60 15N 20 0 E
Alaska □, *U.S.A.* 88 65 0N 150 0W
Alaska, G. of, *Pac. Oc.* 88 58 0N 145 0W
Alaska Pen., *U.S.A.* 88 56 0N 160 0W
Alaska Range, *U.S.A.* 88 62 50N 151 0W
Alba Iulia, *Rom.* 43 46 8N 23 39 E
Albacete, *Sp.* 37 39 0N 1 50W
Albania ■, *Europe* 41 41 0N 20 0 E
Albany, *Austral.* 66 35 1S 117 58 E
Albany, *Ga., U.S.A.* 91 31 40N 84 10W
Albany, *N.Y., U.S.A.* 93 42 35N 73 47W
Albany →, *Canada* 89 52 17N 81 31W
Alberta □, *Canada* 88 54 40N 115 0W
Albrighton, *U.K.* 14 52 38N 2 17W
Albuquerque, *U.S.A.* 90 35 5N 106 47W
Albury, *Austral.* 70 36 3S 146 56 E
Alcalá de Henares, *Sp.* 37 40 28N 3 22W
Alcester, *U.K.* 14 52 13N 1 52W
Aldan →, *U.S.S.R.* 49 63 28N 129 35 E
Aldborough, *U.K.* 19 54 6N 1 21W
Aldbourne, *U.K.* 14 51 28N 1 38W
Aldbrough, *U.K.* 19 53 50N 0 7W
Aldeburgh, *U.K.* 15 52 9N 1 35 E
Alderbury, *U.K.* 14 51 4N 1 45W
Alderley Edge, *U.K.* 18 53 18N 2 15W
Alderney, *U.K.* 34 49 42N 2 12W
Aldershot, *U.K.* 15 51 15N 0 43W
Aldingham, *U.K.* 18 54 8N 3 3W
Aleppo, *Syria* 56 36 10N 37 15 E
Alessándria, *It.* 40 44 54N 8 37 E
Ålesund, *Nor.* 44 62 28N 6 12 E
Aleutian Is., *Pac. Oc.* 88 52 0N 175 0W
Alexander Arch., *U.S.A.* 88 57 0N 135 0W
Alexandria, *Egypt* 79 31 0N 30 0 E
Alexandria, *U.K.* 20 55 59N 4 40W
Alexandria, *U.S.A.* 91 31 20N 92 30W
Alford, *Grampian, U.K.* 23 57 13N 2 42W
Alford, *Lincs., U.K.* 19 53 16N 0 10 E
Alfreton, *U.K.* 19 53 6N 1 22W
Alfriston, *U.K.* 15 50 48N 0 10 E
Algarve, *Port.* 37 36 58N 8 20W
Algeciras, *Sp.* 37 36 9N 5 28W
Algeria ■, *Africa* 78 35 10N 3 11 E
Algiers, *Alg.* 78 36 42N 3 8 E
Alicante, *Sp.* 37 38 23N 0 30W
Alice Springs, *Austral.* 66 23 40S 133 50 E
Aligarh, *India* 58 27 55N 78 10 E
Alkmaar, *Neth.* 36 52 37N 4 45 E
Allahabad, *India* 59 25 25N 81 58 E
Allegheny Mts., *U.S.A.* 92 38 0N 80 0W
Allen →, *U.K.* 21 54 53N 2 13W
Allen, Bog of, *Ire.* 25 53 15N 7 0W
Allen, L., *Ire.* 24 54 12N 8 5W
Allendale, *U.K.* 21 54 55N 2 15W
Allenheads, *U.K.* 21 54 49N 2 12W
Allentown, *U.S.A.* 93 40 36N 75 30W
Alloa, *U.K.* 21 56 7N 3 49W
Allonby, *U.K.* 18 54 45N 3 27W
Alma Ata, *U.S.S.R.* 48 43 15N 76 57 E
Almelo, *Neth.* 36 52 22N 6 42 E
Almería, *Sp.* 37 36 52N 2 27W
Almond →, *U.K.* 21 56 27N 3 27W
Almondsbury, *U.K.* 14 51 33N 2 34W
Aln →, *U.K.* 21 55 27N 1 32W
Alness, *U.K.* 23 57 41N 4 15W
Alnmouth, *U.K.* 21 55 24N 1 37W
Alnwick, *U.K.* 19 55 25N 1 42W
Alphen, *Neth.* 36 51 29N 4 58 E
Alphington, *U.K.* 16 50 41N 3 32W
Alps, *Europe* 42 47 0N 8 0 E
Alrewas, *U.K.* 14 52 43N 1 44W
Alsager, *U.K.* 18 53 7N 2 20W
Alston, *U.K.* 18 54 48N 2 26W
Altai Mts., *Asia* 60 46 40N 92 45 E
Altarnun, *U.K.* 16 50 35N 4 30W
Altay, *China* 60 47 48N 88 10 E
Alton, *U.K.* 15 51 8N 0 59W
Altoona, *U.S.A.* 92 40 32N 78 24W
Altrincham, *U.K.* 18 53 25N 2 21W
Altun Shan, *China* 60 38 30N 88 0 E
Alva, *U.K.* 21 56 9N 3 49W
Alvechurch, *U.K.* 14 52 22N 1 58W
Alwinton, *U.K.* 21 55 20N 2 7W
Alyth, *U.K.* 23 56 38N 3 15W
Amadjuak L., *Canada* 89 65 0N 71 8W
Amagasaki, *Jap.* 62 34 42N 135 20 E
Amarillo, *U.S.A.* 90 35 14N 101 46W
Amazon →, *S. Am.* 100 0 5S 50 0W
Amazonas □, *Brazil* 101 4 0S 62 0W
Amble, *U.K.* 21 55 20N 1 36W
Ambleside, *U.K.* 18 54 26N 2 58W
Ambon, *Indon.* 63 3 35S 128 20 E
American Samoa ■, *Pac. Oc.* 65 14 20S 170 40W
Amersfoort, *Neth.* 36 52 9N 5 23 E
Amersham, *U.K.* 15 51 40N 0 38W
Amesbury, *U.K.* 14 51 10N 1 46W
Amiens, *Fr.* 34 49 54N 2 16 E
Amlwch, *U.K.* 17 53 24N 4 21W
'Ammān, *Jord.* 57 31 57N 35 52 E
Ammanford, *U.K.* 17 51 48N 4 0W
Amoy = Xiamen, *China* 61 24 25N 118 4 E
Ampleforth, *U.K.* 19 54 13N 1 8W
Ampthill, *U.K.* 15 52 3N 0 30W
Amravati, *India* 58 20 55N 77 45 E
Amritsar, *India* 58 31 35N 74 57 E
Amsterdam, *Neth.* 36 52 23N 4 54 E
Amudarya →, *U.S.S.R.* 48 43 40N 59 0 E
Amundsen Gulf, *Canada* 88 71 0N 124 0W
Amundsen Sea, *Ant.* 103 72 0S 115 0W
Amur →, *U.S.S.R.* 49 52 56N 141 10 E
An Nafūd, *Si. Arab.* 56 28 15N 41 0 E
An Najaf, *Iraq* 56 32 3N 44 15 E
An Uaimh, *Ire.* 24 53 39N 6 40W
Anadyr, G. of, *U.S.S.R.* 49 64 0N 180 0 E
Anaheim, *U.S.A.* 90 33 50N 118 0W
Anápolis, *Brazil* 101 16 15S 48 50W
Anatolia, *Turk.* 47 38 0N 30 0 E
Ancaster, *U.K.* 19 52 59N 0 32W
Ancholme →, *U.K.* 19 53 42N 0 32W
Anchorage, *U.S.A.* 88 61 10N 149 50W
Ancona, *It.* 40 43 37N 13 30 E
Ancrum, *U.K.* 21 55 31N 2 35W
Anda, *China* 61 46 24N 125 19 E
Andalusia, Reg., *Sp.* 37 37 35N 5 0W
Andaman Is., *India* 51 12 30N 92 30 E
Anderlecht, *Belg.* 36 50 50N 4 19 E
Andes, *S. Am.* 96 20 0S 68 0W
Andhra Pradesh □, *India* 58 16 0N 79 0 E
Andizhan, *U.S.S.R.* 48 41 10N 72 0 E
Andorra ■, *Europe* 35 42 30N 1 30 E
Andover, *U.K.* 14 51 13N 1 29W
Andreanof Is., *Pac. Oc.* 88 52 0N 178 0W
Andreas, *U.K.* 18 54 23N 4 25W
Ándria, *It.* 40 41 13N 16 17 E
*Andropov, *U.S.S.R.* 46 58 5N 38 50 E
Andros I., *Baham.* 95 24 30N 78 0W
Angara →, *U.S.S.R.* 49 58 30N 97 0 E
Angarsk, *U.S.S.R.* 49 52 30N 104 0 E
Angers, *Fr.* 34 47 30N 0 35W
Anglesey, *U.K.* 17 53 17N 4 20W
Angmagssalik, *Green.* 89 65 40N 37 20W
Angmering, *U.K.* 15 50 48N 0 28W
Angola ■, *Africa* 81 12 0S 18 0 E
Angoulême, *Fr.* 35 45 39N 0 10 E
Anguilla, *W. Ind.* 94 18 14N 63 5W
Angus, Braes of, *U.K.* 23 56 51N 3 10W
Anhui □, *China* 61 32 0N 117 0 E
Anjou, *Fr.* 34 47 20N 0 15W
Ankara, *Turk.* 47 40 0N 32 54 E
Ann Arbor, *U.S.A.* 92 42 17N 83 45W
Annaba, *Alg.* 78 36 50N 7 46 E
Annalee →, *Ire.* 24 54 3N 7 15W
Annan, *U.K.* 21 55 0N 3 17W
Annan →, *U.K.* 21 54 58N 3 18W
Annandale, *U.K.* 21 55 10N 3 25W
Annecy, *Fr.* 35 45 55N 6 8 E
Annfield Plain, *U.K.* 19 54 52N 1 45W
Annobón, *Atl. Oc.* 73 1 25S 5 36 E
Anshan, *China* 61 41 5N 122 58 E
Anshun, *China* 60 26 18N 105 57 E
Anstey, *U.K.* 14 52 41N 1 14W
Anstruther, *U.K.* 21 56 14N 2 40W
Antalya, *Turk.* 47 36 52N 30 45 E
Antananarivo, *Madag.* 81 18 55S 47 31 E
Antarctic Pen., *Ant.* 103 67 0S 60 0W
Antarctica, *Cont.* 103 90 0S 0 0 E
Anticosti, I. d', *Canada* 93 49 30N 63 0W
Antigua & Barbuda ■, *W. Ind.* 94 17 20N 61 48W
Antofagasta, *Chile* 102 23 50S 70 30W
Antony, *U.K.* 16 50 22N 4 13W
Antrim, *U.K.* 24 54 43N 6 13W
Antrim □, *U.K.* 24 54 55N 6 20W
Antrim, Mts. of, *U.K.* 24 54 57N 6 8W
Antsiranana, *Madag.* 81 12 25S 49 20 E
Antwerp, *Belg.* 36 51 13N 4 25 E
Anyang, *China* 61 36 5N 114 21 E
Anzhero-Sudzhensk, *U.S.S.R.* 48 56 10N 86 0 E
Aomori, *Jap.* 62 40 45N 140 45 E
Apeldoorn, *Neth.* 36 52 13N 5 57 E
Apennines, *It.* 40 44 20N 10 20 E
Appalachian Mts., *U.S.A.* 91 38 0N 80 0W
Appleby, *U.K.* 18 54 35N 2 29W
Appledore, *Devon, U.K.* 16 51 3N 4 12W
Appledore, *Kent, U.K.* 15 51 2N 0 47 E
Arabia, *Asia* 50 25 0N 45 0 E
Arabian Desert, *Egypt* 79 26 0N 33 30 E
Arabian Sea, *Ind. Oc.* 50 16 0N 65 0 E
Aracaju, *Brazil* 101 10 55S 37 4W
Araçatuba, *Brazil* 101 21 10S 50 30W
Arad, *Rom.* 43 46 10N 21 20 E
Arafura Sea, *E. Ind.* 64 9 0S 135 0 E
Aragón □, *Sp.* 37 41 25N 1 0W
Araguaia →, *Brazil* 101 5 21S 48 41W
Arakan Yoma, *Burma* 59 20 0N 94 40 E
Aral Sea, *U.S.S.R.* 48 44 30N 60 0 E
Aralsk, *U.S.S.R.* 48 46 50N 61 20 E
Aran I., *Ire.* 24 55 0N 8 30W
Aran Is., *Ire.* 25 53 5N 9 42W
Arapiraca, *Brazil* 101 9 45S 36 39W
Ararat, *Austral.* 70 37 16S 143 0 E
Arbroath, *U.K.* 23 56 34N 2 35W
Arctic Ocean, *Arctic* 103 78 0N 160 0W
Arctic Red River, *Canada* 88 67 15N 134 0W
Ardbeg, *U.K.* 20 55 38N 6 6W
Ardchyle, *U.K.* 20 56 26N 4 24W
Ardee, *Ire.* 24 53 51N 6 32W
Ardennes, *Belg.* 36 50 0N 5 10 E
Ardentinny, *U.K.* 20 56 3N 4 56W
Ardgour, *U.K.* 22 56 45N 5 25W
Ardingly, *U.K.* 15 51 3N 0 3W
Ardlui, *U.K.* 20 56 19N 4 43W
Ardmore Pt., *U.K.* 20 55 40N 6 0W
Ardnamurchan, Pt. of, *U.K.* 22 56 44N 6 14W
Ardnave Pt., *U.K.* 20 55 54N 6 20W
Ardrishaig, *U.K.* 20 56 0N 5 27W
Ardrossan, *U.K.* 20 55 39N 4 50W
Ards □, *U.K.* 24 54 35N 5 30W
Ards Pen., *U.K.* 24 54 30N 5 25W
Ardvasar, *U.K.* 22 57 5N 5 52W
Arendal, *Nor.* 45 58 28N 8 46 E
Arequipa, *Peru* 100 16 20S 71 30W
Argentina ■, *S. Am.* 102 35 0S 66 0W
Argyll, *U.K.* 20 56 14N 5 10W
Arica, *Chile* 100 18 32S 70 20W
Arima, *Trin. & Tob.* 94 10 38N 61 17W
Arinagour, *U.K.* 20 56 38N 6 31W
Arisaig, *U.K.* 22 56 55N 5 50W
Arizona □, *U.S.A.* 90 34 20N 111 30W
Arkaig, L., *U.K.* 22 56 58N 5 10W
Arkansas □, *U.S.A.* 91 35 0N 92 30W
Arkansas →, *U.S.A.* 91 33 48N 91 4W
Arkhangelsk, *U.S.S.R.* 46 64 40N 41 0 E
Arkle →, *U.K.* 18 54 25N 1 55W
Arklow, *Ire.* 25 52 48N 6 10W
Arles, *Fr.* 35 43 41N 4 40 E
Arlon, *Belg.* 36 49 42N 5 49 E
Armadale, *U.K.* 21 55 54N 3 42W
Armagh, *U.K.* 24 54 22N 6 40W
Armagh □, *U.K.* 24 54 18N 6 37W
Armenia, *Col.* 100 4 35N 75 45W
Armenia □, *U.S.S.R.* 47 40 0N 41 0 E
Armidale, *Austral.* 67 30 30S 151 40 E
Arnhem, *Neth.* 36 51 58N 5 55 E
Arnhem Land, *Austral.* 66 13 10S 134 30 E
Arnold, *U.K.* 19 53 0N 1 8W
Arnside, *U.K.* 18 54 12N 2 49W
Arran, *U.K.* 20 55 34N 5 12W
Arras, *Fr.* 34 50 17N 2 46 E
Arrochar, *U.K.* 20 56 12N 4 45W
Arrow, L., *Ire.* 24 54 3N 8 20W
Arun →, *U.K.* 15 50 48N 0 33W
Arunachal Pradesh □, *India* 59 28 0N 95 0 E
Arundel, *U.K.* 15 50 52N 0 32W
Arusha, *Tanz.* 80 3 20S 36 40 E
As Salt, *Jord.* 57 32 2N 35 43 E
As Summān, *Si. Arab.* 56 25 0N 47 0 E
Asahigawa, *Jap.* 62 43 46N 142 22 E
Asansol, *India* 59 23 40N 87 1 E
Ascension I., *Atl. Oc.* 118 8 0S 14 15W
Ascot, *U.K.* 15 51 24N 0 41W
Asfordby, *U.K.* 15 52 45N 0 57W
Ash, *Kent, U.K.* 15 51 17N 1 16 E
Ash, *Surrey, U.K.* 15 51 14N 0 43W
Ashbourne, *U.K.* 19 53 2N 1 44W
Ashburton, *N.Z.* 71 43 53S 171 48 E
Ashburton, *U.K.* 16 50 31N 3 45W
Ashburton →, *Austral.* 66 21 40S 114 56 E
Ashby-de-la-Zouch, *U.K.* 14 52 45N 1 29W
Ashchurch, *U.K.* 14 52 0N 2 7W
Ashdown Forest, *U.K.* 15 51 4N 0 2 E
Ashford, *Derby, U.K.* 19 53 13N 1 43W
Ashford, *Kent, U.K.* 15 51 8N 0 53 E
Ashington, *U.K.* 21 55 12N 1 35W
Ashkhabad, *U.S.S.R.* 48 38 0N 57 50 E
Ashq'elon, *Isr.* 57 31 42N 34 35 E
Ashton-in-Makerfield, *U.K.* 18 53 29N 2 39W
Ashton-under-Lyne, *U.K.* 18 53 30N 2 8W
Ashurstwood, *U.K.* 15 51 6N 0 2 E
Ashwater, *U.K.* 16 50 43N 4 18W
Ashwick, *U.K.* 14 51 13N 2 31W
'Asīr □, *Si. Arab.* 56 18 40N 42 30 E
Asir, Ras, *Som.* 73 11 55N 51 10 E
Askrigg, *U.K.* 18 54 19N 2 6W
Aslackby, *U.K.* 19 52 53N 0 23W
Asmera, *Eth.* 79 15 19N 38 55 E
Aspatria, *U.K.* 18 54 45N 3 20W
Assam □, *India* 59 26 0N 93 0 E
Assen, *Neth.* 36 53 0N 6 35 E
Assynt, L., *U.K.* 22 58 25N 5 15W
Asti, *It.* 40 44 54N 8 11 E
Aston Clinton, *U.K.* 15 51 48N 0 44W
Astrakhan, *U.S.S.R.* 47 46 25N 48 5 E
Astwood Bank, *U.K.* 14 52 15N 1 55W
Asunción, *Par.* 102 25 10S 57 30W
Aswân, *Egypt* 79 24 4N 32 57 E
Atacama, Desierto de, *Chile* 102 24 0S 69 20W
Atbara, *Sudan* 79 17 42N 33 59 E
Athabasca, L., *Canada* 88 59 15N 109 15W
Athboy, *Ire.* 24 53 37N 6 55W
Athenry, *Ire.* 25 53 18N 8 45W
Athens, *Greece* 41 37 58N 23 46 E
Atherstone, *U.K.* 14 52 35N 1 32W
Atherton, *U.K.* 18 53 32N 2 30W
Athínai = Athens, *Greece* 41 37 58N 23 46 E
Athlone, *Ire.* 24 53 26N 7 57W
Atholl, Forest of, *U.K.* 23 56 51N 3 50W
Athy, *Ire.* 25 53 0N 7 0W
Atlanta, *U.S.A.* 91 33 50N 84 24W
Atlantic City, *U.S.A.* 93 39 25N 74 25W
Atlantic Ocean 118 0 0 20 0W
Atlas Mts., *Mor.* 72 32 30N 5 0W
Attleborough, *U.K.* 15 52 32N 1 1 E
Auchencairn, *U.K.* 21 54 51N 3 52W
Auchinleck, *U.K.* 20 55 28N 4 18W
Auchterarder, *U.K.* 21 56 18N 3 43W
Auchterderran, *U.K.* 21 56 8N 3 16W
Auchtermuchty, *U.K.* 21 56 18N 3 15W
Auchtertyre, *U.K.* 22 57 17N 5 35W
Auckland, *N.Z.* 71 36 52S 174 46 E
Audlem, *U.K.* 18 52 59N 2 31W
Aughnacloy, *U.K.* 24 54 25N 6 58W
Augsburg, *Ger.* 42 48 22N 10 54 E
Augusta, *U.S.A.* 91 33 29N 81 59W
Aurangabad, *India* 58 19 50N 75 23 E
Aurora, *U.S.A.* 92 41 42N 88 12W
Austin, *U.S.A.* 90 30 20N 97 45W
Australia ■, *Oc.* 66 23 0S 135 0 E
Australian Alps, *Austral.* 70 36 30S 148 30 E
Australian Cap. Terr. □, *Austral.* 70 35 30S 149 0 E
Austria ■, *Europe* 42 47 0N 14 0 E
Auxerre, *Fr.* 34 47 48N 3 32 E

* Renamed Rybinsk

Avebury, *U.K.* 14 51 25N 1 52W
Avellino, *It.* 40 40 54N 14 46 E
Aveton Gifford, *U.K.* 16 50 17N 3 51W
Avich, L., *U.K.* 20 56 17N 5 25W
Aviemore, *U.K.* 23 57 11N 3 50W
Avignon, *Fr.* 35 43 57N 4 50 E
Ávila, *Sp.* 37 40 39N 4 43W
Avoca, *Ire.* 25 52 52N 6 13W
Avon □, *U.K.* 14 51 30N 2 40W
Avon →, *Avon, U.K.* 14 51 30N 2 43W
Avon →, *Hants., U.K.* 14 50 44N 1 45W
Avon →, *Warwick, U.K.* 14 52 0N 2 9W
Avonmouth, *U.K.* 14 51 30N 2 42W
Awe, L., *U.K.* 20 56 15N 5 15W
Axbridge, *U.K.* 14 51 17N 2 50W
Axe →, *U.K.* 14 51 17N 2 52W
Axe Edge, *U.K.* 18 53 14N 1 59W
Axholme, Isle of, *U.K.* 19 53 30N 0 55W
Axminster, *U.K.* 16 50 47N 3 1W
Axmouth, *U.K.* 16 50 43N 3 2W
Ayers Rock, *Austral.* 66 25 23S 131 5 E
Aylesbury, *U.K.* 15 51 48N 0 49W
Aylesford, *U.K.* 15 51 18N 0 29 E
Aylsham, *U.K.* 15 52 48N 1 16 E
Aynho, *U.K.* 14 51 59N 1 15W
Ayr, *U.K.* 20 55 28N 4 37W
Ayr →, *U.K.* 20 55 29N 4 40W
Ayr, Heads of, *U.K.* 20 55 25N 4 43W
Ayre, Pt. of, *U.K.* 18 54 27N 4 21W
Aysgarth, *U.K.* 18 54 18N 2 0W
Ayton, *Borders, U.K.* 21 55 51N 2 6W
Ayton, *N. Yorks., U.K.* 19 54 15N 0 29W
Az Zarqā, *Jord.* 57 32 5N 36 4 E
Azores, *Atl. Oc.* 118 38 44N 29 0W
Azov Sea, *U.S.S.R.* 47 46 0N 36 30 E
Azuero, Pen. de, *Pan.* 95 7 30N 80 30W

B

Bābol, *Iran* 56 36 40N 52 50 E
Bacabal, *Brazil* 101 4 15S 44 45W
Bacău, *Rom.* 43 46 35N 26 55 E
Back, *U.K.* 22 58 17N 6 20W
Bacolod, *Phil.* 63 10 40N 122 57 E
Bacton, *U.K.* 15 52 50N 1 29 E
Bacup, *U.K.* 18 53 42N 2 12W
Badajoz, *Sp.* 37 38 50N 6 59W
Badalona, *Sp.* 37 41 26N 2 15 E
Baffin B., *Canada* 89 72 0N 64 0W
Baffin I., *Canada* 89 68 0N 75 0W
Bagenalstown = Muine Bheag, *Ire.* 25 52 42N 6 57W
Baggy Pt., *U.K.* 16 51 11N 4 12W
Baghdād, *Iraq* 56 33 20N 44 30 E
Bagshot, *U.K.* 15 51 22N 0 41W
Bahamas ■, *Atl. Oc.* 95 24 0N 75 0W
Bahawalpur, *Pak.* 58 29 24N 71 40 E
Bahía = Salvador, *Brazil* 101 13 0S 38 30W
Bahía Blanca, *Arg.* 102 38 35S 62 13W
Bahrain ■, *Asia* 56 26 0N 50 35 E
Baia Mare, *Rom.* 43 47 40N 23 35 E
Baildon, *U.K.* 19 53 52N 1 46W
Baile Atha Cliath = Dublin, *Ire.* 24 53 20N 6 18W
Bain →, *U.K.* 19 53 10N 0 15W
Bainbridge, *U.K.* 18 54 18N 2 7W
Bakersfield, *U.S.A.* 90 35 25N 119 0W
Bakewell, *U.K.* 19 53 13N 1 40W
Bākhtarān, *Iran* 56 34 23N 47 0 E
Baku, *U.S.S.R.* 47 40 25N 49 45 E
Bala, *U.K.* 17 52 54N 3 36W
Bala, L. = Tegid, L., *U.K.* 17 52 53N 3 38W
Balallan, *U.K.* 22 58 5N 6 35W
Balaton, *Hung.* 43 46 50N 17 40 E
Balbeggie, *U.K.* 21 56 26N 3 19W
Balboa, *Pan.* 94 9 0N 79 30W
Balbriggan, *Ire.* 24 53 35N 6 10W
Balderton, *U.K.* 19 53 3N 0 46W
Baldock, *U.K.* 15 51 59N 0 11W
Balearic Is., *Sp.* 37 39 30N 3 0 E
Balfron, *U.K.* 20 56 4N 4 20W
Bali □, *Indon.* 63 8 20S 115 0 E
Balikesir, *Turk.* 47 39 35N 27 58 E
Balikpapan, *Indon.* 63 1 10S 116 55 E
Balkan Mts., *Bulg.* 41 43 15N 23 0 E
Balkan Pen., *Europe* 26 42 0N 22 0 E
Balkhash, L., *U.S.S.R.* 48 46 0N 74 50 E
Ballachulish, *U.K.* 22 56 40N 5 10W
Ballantrae, *U.K.* 20 55 6N 5 0W
Ballarat, *Austral.* 70 37 33S 143 50 E
Ballasalla, *U.K.* 18 54 7N 4 36W
Ballater, *U.K.* 23 57 2N 3 2W
Ballaugh, *U.K.* 18 54 20N 4 32W
Ballina, *Mayo, Ire.* 24 54 7N 9 10W
Ballina, *Tipp., Ire.* 25 52 49N 8 27W
Ballinasloe, *Ire.* 25 53 20N 8 12W
Ballinrobe, *Ire.* 24 53 36N 9 13W
Ballinskelligs B., *Ire.* 25 51 46N 10 11W
Balloch, *U.K.* 20 56 0N 4 35W
Ballycastle, *U.K.* 24 55 12N 6 15W
Ballyclare, *U.K.* 24 54 46N 6 0W
Ballymena, *U.K.* 24 54 53N 6 18W
Ballymena □, *U.K.* 24 54 53N 6 18W
Ballymoney, *U.K.* 24 55 5N 6 30W
Ballymoney □, *U.K.* 24 55 5N 6 23W
Ballynahinch, *U.K.* 24 54 24N 5 55W
Ballyshannon, *Ire.* 24 54 30N 8 10W
Balmaclellan, *U.K.* 21 55 6N 4 5W
Balmoral, *U.K.* 23 57 3N 3 13W
Balquhidder, *U.K.* 20 56 22N 4 22W
Balsas →, *Mex.* 94 17 55N 102 10W
Baltic Sea, *Europe* 45 56 0N 20 0 E
Baltimore, *Ire.* 25 51 29N 9 22W
Baltimore, *U.S.A.* 92 39 18N 76 37W
Baluchistan □, *Pak.* 58 27 30N 65 0 E
Balurghat, *India* 59 25 15N 88 44 E
Balvicar, *U.K.* 20 56 17N 5 38W
Bamako, *Mali* 78 12 34N 7 55W
Bamberg, *Ger.* 42 49 54N 10 53 E
Bamburgh, *U.K.* 21 55 36N 1 42W
Bamenda, *Cam.* 80 5 57N 10 11 E
Bamford, *U.K.* 19 53 21N 1 41W
Bampton, *Devon, U.K.* 16 50 59N 3 29W
Bampton, *Oxon., U.K.* 14 51 44N 1 33W
Banaras = Varanasi, *India* 59 25 22N 83 0 E
Banbridge, *U.K.* 24 54 21N 6 17W
Banbridge □, *U.K.* 24 54 21N 6 16W
Banbury, *U.K.* 14 52 4N 1 21W
Banchory, *U.K.* 23 57 3N 2 30W
Banda Aceh, *Indon.* 63 5 35N 95 20 E
Banda Sea, *Indon.* 63 6 0S 130 0 E
Bandār 'Abbās, *Iran* 57 27 15N 56 15 E
Bandar Seri Begawan, *Brunei* 63 4 52N 115 0 E
Bandon, *Ire.* 25 51 44N 8 45W
Bandon →, *Ire.* 25 51 40N 8 41W
Bandundu, *Zaïre* 80 3 15S 17 22 E
Bandung, *Indon.* 63 6 54S 107 36 E
Banff, *U.K.* 23 57 40N 2 32W
Bangalore, *India* 58 12 59N 77 40 E
Bangka, Selat, *Indon.* 63 2 30S 105 30 E
Bangkok, *Thai.* 63 13 45N 100 35 E
Bangladesh ■, *Asia* 59 24 0N 90 0 E
Bangor, *N. Ireland, U.K.* 24 54 40N 5 40W
Bangor, *Wales, U.K.* 17 53 13N 4 9W
Bangor, *U.S.A.* 93 44 48N 68 42W
Bangui, *C.A.R.* 80 4 23N 18 35 E
Banham, *U.K.* 15 52 27N 1 3 E
Banjarmasin, *Indon.* 63 3 20S 114 35 E
Banjul, *Gambia* 78 13 28N 16 40W
Bankend, *U.K.* 21 55 2N 3 31W
Bankfoot, *U.K.* 21 56 30N 3 31W
Banks I., *Canada* 88 73 15N 121 30W
Banks Pen., *N.Z.* 71 43 45S 173 15 E
Bann →, *Down, U.K.* 24 54 30N 6 31W
Bann →, *Londonderry, U.K.* 24 55 10N 6 34W
Bannockburn, *U.K.* 21 56 5N 3 55W
Bantry, *Ire.* 25 51 40N 9 28W
Bantry, B., *Ire.* 25 51 35N 9 50W
Banwell, *U.K.* 14 51 19N 2 51W
Baoding, *China* 61 38 50N 115 28 E
Baoji, *China* 60 34 20N 107 5 E
Baotou, *China* 61 40 32N 110 2 E
Barbados ■, *W. Ind.* 94 13 0N 59 30W
Barcaldine, *Austral.* 67 23 43S 145 6 E
Barcelona, *Sp.* 37 41 21N 2 10 E
Bardney, *U.K.* 19 53 13N 0 19W
Bardsey I., *U.K.* 17 52 46N 4 47W
Bareilly, *India* 58 28 22N 79 27 E
Barents Sea, *Arctic* 48 73 0N 39 0 E
Barford, *U.K.* 14 52 15N 1 35W
Bargoed, *U.K.* 17 51 42N 3 22W
Barham, *U.K.* 15 51 12N 1 10 E
Bari, *It.* 40 41 6N 16 52 E
Bari Doab, *Pak.* 58 30 20N 73 0 E
Barisal, *Bangla.* 59 22 45N 90 20 E
Barisan Mts., *Indon.* 63 3 30S 102 15 E
Barking, *U.K.* 15 51 31N 0 10 E
Barkly Tableland, *Austral.* 67 17 50S 136 40 E
Barlborough, *U.K.* 19 53 17N 1 17W
Barlby, *U.K.* 19 53 48N 1 3W
Barletta, *It.* 40 41 20N 16 17 E
Barmby Moor, *U.K.* 19 53 55N 0 47W
Barmoor Castle, *U.K.* 21 55 38N 2 0W
Barmouth, *U.K.* 17 52 44N 4 3W
Barnard Castle, *U.K.* 18 54 33N 1 55W
Barnaul, *U.S.S.R.* 48 53 20N 83 40 E
Barnet, *U.K.* 15 51 37N 0 15W
Barnetby le Wold, *U.K.* 19 53 34N 0 24W
Barnoldswick, *U.K.* 18 53 55N 2 11W
Barnsley, *U.K.* 19 53 33N 1 29W
Barnstaple, *U.K.* 16 51 5N 4 3W
Barnstaple B., *U.K.* 16 51 5N 4 25W
Baroda = Vadodara, *India* 58 22 20N 73 10 E
Barquísimeto, *Ven.* 100 10 4N 69 19W
Barr, *U.K.* 20 55 13N 4 44W
Barra, *U.K.* 22 57 0N 7 30W
Barra, Sd. of, *U.K.* 22 57 4N 7 25W
Barra Hd., *U.K.* 22 56 47N 7 40W
Barrancabermeja, *Col.* 100 7 0N 73 50W
Barranquilla, *Col.* 100 11 0N 74 50W
Barrhead, *U.K.* 20 55 48N 4 23W
Barrhill, *U.K.* 20 55 7N 4 46W
Barrow →, *Ire.* 25 52 10N 6 57W
Barrow-in-Furness, *U.K.* 18 54 8N 3 15W
Barrow upon Humber, *U.K.* 19 53 41N 0 22W
Barrowford, *U.K.* 18 53 51N 2 14W
Barry, *S. Glam., U.K.* 17 51 23N 3 19W
Barry, *Tayside, U.K.* 21 56 29N 2 45W
Barton, *U.K.* 19 54 28N 1 38W
Barton-upon-Humber, *U.K.* 19 53 41N 0 27W
Barvas, *U.K.* 22 58 21N 6 31W
Barwell, *U.K.* 14 52 35N 1 22W
Basildon, *U.K.* 15 51 34N 0 29 E
Basingstoke, *U.K.* 14 51 15N 1 5W
Basle, *Switz.* 42 47 35N 7 35 E
Basra, *Iraq* 56 30 30N 47 50 E
Bass Rock, *U.K.* 21 56 5N 2 40W
Bass Str., *Austral.* 67 39 15S 146 30 E
Basse-Terre, *Guad.* 94 16 0N 61 40W
Bassein, *Burma* 59 16 45N 94 30 E
Bassenthwaite, L., *U.K.* 18 54 40N 3 14W
Basseterre, *Guad.* 94 17 17N 62 43W
Bastia, *Fr.* 35 42 40N 9 30 E
Baston, *U.K.* 15 52 43N 0 19W
Bata, *Eq. Guin.* 80 1 57N 9 50 E
Batangas, *Phil.* 63 13 35N 121 10 E
Bath, *U.K.* 14 51 22N 2 22W
Bathford, *U.K.* 14 51 23N 2 18W
Bathgate, *U.K.* 21 55 54N 3 38W
Bathurst, *Austral.* 70 33 25S 149 31 E
Bathurst, *Canada* 93 47 37N 65 43W
Batley, *U.K.* 19 53 43N 1 38W
Batna, *Alg.* 78 35 34N 6 15 E
Baton Rouge, *U.S.A.* 91 30 30N 91 5W
Battle, *U.K.* 15 50 55N 0 30 E
Batumi, *U.S.S.R.* 47 41 30N 41 30 E
Bauru, *Brazil* 101 22 10S 49 0W
Bavaria □, *Ger.* 42 49 7N 11 30 E
Bawdsey, *U.K.* 15 52 1N 1 27 E
Bawtry, *U.K.* 19 53 25N 1 1W
Bayamo, *Cuba* 95 20 20N 76 40W
Bayan Har Shan, *China* 60 34 0N 98 0 E
Bayeux, *Fr.* 34 49 17N 0 42W
Baykal, L., *U.S.S.R.* 49 53 0N 108 0 E
Bayonne, *Fr.* 35 43 30N 1 28W
Beachley, *U.K.* 14 51 37N 2 39W
Beachy Head, *U.K.* 15 50 44N 0 16 E
Beaconsfield, *U.K.* 15 51 36N 0 39W
Beadnell, *U.K.* 21 55 33N 1 38W
Beagle, Canal, *S. Am.* 102 55 0S 68 30W
Beaminster, *U.K.* 14 50 48N 2 44W
Bear I., *Ire.* 25 51 38N 9 50W
Beardmore Glacier, *Ant.* 103 84 30S 170 0 E
Bearsden, *U.K.* 20 55 55N 4 21W
Bearsted, *U.K.* 15 51 15N 0 35 E
Beattock, *U.K.* 21 55 19N 3 27W
Beaufort Sea, *Arctic* 103 72 0N 140 0W
Beaulieu, *U.K.* 14 50 49N 1 27W
Beauly, *U.K.* 23 57 29N 4 27W
Beauly →, *U.K.* 23 57 26N 4 28W
Beaumaris, *U.K.* 17 53 16N 4 7W
Beaumont, *U.S.A.* 91 30 5N 94 8W
Beauvais, *Fr.* 34 49 25N 2 8 E
Bebington, *U.K.* 18 53 23N 3 1W
Beccles, *U.K.* 15 52 27N 1 33 E
Béchar, *Alg.* 78 31 38N 2 18W
Beckermet, *U.K.* 18 54 26N 3 31W
Beckfoot, *U.K.* 18 54 50N 3 25W
Beckingham, *U.K.* 19 53 24N 0 49W
Bedale, *U.K.* 19 54 18N 1 35W
Beddgelert, *U.K.* 17 53 2N 4 8W
Bedford, *U.K.* 15 52 8N 0 29W
Bedford □, *U.K.* 15 52 4N 0 28W
Bedford Level, *U.K.* 15 52 25N 0 5 E
Bedlington, *U.K.* 21 55 8N 1 35W
Bedworth, *U.K.* 14 52 28N 1 29W
Beeford, *U.K.* 19 53 58N 0 18W
Beer, *U.K.* 16 50 41N 3 5W
Beersheba, *Isr.* 57 31 15N 34 48 E
Beeston, *U.K.* 19 52 55N 1 11W
Bei'an, *China* 61 48 10N 126 20 E
Beighton, *U.K.* 19 53 21N 1 21W
Beijing = Peking, *China* 61 39 55N 116 20 E
Beira, *Mozam.* 81 19 50S 34 52 E
Beira-Baixa, *Port.* 37 40 2N 7 30W
Beirut, *Leb.* 57 33 53N 35 31 E
Beith, *U.K.* 20 55 45N 4 38W
Belau ■, *Pac. Oc.* 64 8 0N 134 0 E
Belbroughton, *U.K.* 14 52 23N 2 5W
Belcher Is., *Canada* 89 56 15N 78 45W
Belém, *Brazil* 101 1 20S 48 30W
Belfast, *U.K.* 24 54 35N 5 56W
Belfast □, *U.K.* 24 54 35N 5 56W
Belfast L., *U.K.* 24 54 40N 5 50W
Belford, *U.K.* 21 55 36N 1 50W
Belfort, *Fr.* 34 47 38N 6 50 E
Belgium ■, *Europe* 36 50 30N 5 0 E
Belgorod, *U.S.S.R.* 47 50 35N 36 35 E
Belgrade, *Yug.* 41 44 50N 20 37 E
Beliton, Is., *Indon.* 63 3 10S 107 50 E
Belize ■, *Cent. Am.* 94 17 0N 88 30W
Belize City, *Belize* 94 17 25N 88 0W
Bell Rock = Inchcape Rock, *U.K.* 21 56 26N 2 24W
Bellary, *India* 58 15 10N 76 56 E
Belle-Ile, *Fr.* 34 47 20N 3 10W
Belle Isle, Str. of, *Canada* 89 51 30N 56 30W
Belleville, *Canada* 92 44 10N 77 23W
Bellingham, *U.K.* 21 55 9N 2 16W
Belmopan, *Belize* 94 17 18N 88 30W
Belmullet, *Ire.* 24 54 13N 9 58W
Belo Horizonte, *Brazil* 101 19 55S 43 56W
Beloye More, *U.S.S.R.* 46 66 30N 38 0 E
Belper, *U.K.* 19 53 2N 1 29W
Belsay, *U.K.* 21 55 6N 1 53W
Belton, *Humberside, U.K.* 19 53 33N 0 49W
Belton, *Norfolk, U.K.* 15 52 35N 1 39 E
Belturbet, *Ire.* 24 54 6N 7 28W
Bembridge, *U.K.* 14 50 41N 1 4W
Ben Bheigeir, *U.K.* 20 55 43N 6 6W
Ben Chonzie, *U.K.* 21 56 27N 4 0W
Ben Cruachan, *U.K.* 20 56 26N 5 8W
Ben Dearg, *U.K.* 23 57 47N 4 58W
Ben Dorain, *U.K.* 20 56 30N 4 42W
Ben Hope, *U.K.* 23 58 24N 4 36W
Ben Lawers, *U.K.* 23 56 33N 4 13W
Ben Lomond, *U.K.* 20 56 12N 4 39W
Ben Lui, *U.K.* 20 56 24N 4 50W
Ben Macdhui, *U.K.* 23 57 4N 3 40W
Ben Mhor, *U.K.* 22 57 16N 7 21W
Ben More, *Central, U.K.* 20 56 23N 4 31W
Ben More, *Strathclyde, U.K.* 20 56 26N 6 2W
Ben More Assynt, *U.K.* 23 58 7N 4 51W
Ben Nevis, *U.K.* 22 56 48N 5 0W
Ben Venue, *U.K.* 20 56 13N 4 28W
Ben Vorlich, *U.K.* 20 56 22N 4 15W
Ben Wyvis, *U.K.* 23 57 40N 4 35W
Benalla, *Austral.* 70 36 30S 146 0 E
Benares = Varanasi, *India* 59 25 22N 83 0 E
Benbecula, *U.K.* 22 57 26N 7 21W
Bendigo, *Austral.* 70 36 40S 144 15 E
Beneraird, *U.K.* 20 55 4N 4 57W
Benevento, *It.* 40 41 7N 14 45 E
Bengal, Bay of, *Ind. Oc.* 59 18 0N 90 0 E
Bengbu, *China* 61 32 58N 117 20 E
Benghazi, *Libya* 79 32 11N 20 3 E
Beni Suef, *Egypt* 79 29 5N 31 6 E
Benin ■, *Africa* 78 10 0N 2 0 E
Benin, Bight of, *W. Afr.* 78 5 0N 3 0 E
Benin City, *Nig.* 78 6 20N 5 31 E
Benington, *U.K.* 19 52 59N 0 5 E
Bennane Hd., *U.K.* 20 55 9N 5 2W
Benoni, *S. Afr.* 81 26 11S 28 18 E
Benson, *U.K.* 14 51 37N 1 6W
Bentley, *Hants., U.K.* 15 51 12N 0 52W
Bentley, *S. Yorks., U.K.* 19 53 33N 1 9W
Benue →, *Nig.* 78 7 48N 6 46 E
Benxi, *China* 61 41 20N 123 48 E
Berbera, *Som.* 73 10 30N 45 2 E
Berbérati, *C.A.R.* 80 4 15N 15 40 E
Bere Alston, *U.K.* 16 50 29N 4 11W
Bere Regis, *U.K.* 14 50 45N 2 13W
Berezniki, *U.S.S.R.* 46 59 24N 56 46 E
Bérgamo, *It.* 40 45 42N 9 40 E
Bergen, *Nor.* 45 60 23N 5 20 E
Bergen-op-Zoom, *Neth.* 36 51 30N 4 18 E
Bergerac, *Fr.* 35 44 51N 0 30 E
Bergisch-Gladbach, *Ger.* 36 50 59N 7 9 E
Berhampore, *India* 59 24 2N 88 27 E
Berhampur, *India* 59 19 15N 84 54 E
Bering Sea, *Pac. Oc.* 88 58 0N 167 0 E
Bering Str., *N. Am.* 103 66 0N 170 0W
Berkeley, *U.K.* 14 51 41N 2 28W
Berkhamsted, *U.K.* 15 51 45N 0 33W
Berkshire □, *U.K.* 14 51 30N 1 20W
Berkshire Downs, *U.K.* 15 51 30N 1 30W
Berlin, *Ger.* 42 52 32N 13 24 E
Bermuda ■, *Atl. Oc.* 95 32 45N 65 0W
Bern, *Switz.* 42 46 57N 7 28 E
Berry Hd., *U.K.* 16 50 24N 3 29W
Berwick-upon-Tweed, *U.K.* 19 55 47N 2 0W
Berwyn Mts., *U.K.* 17 52 54N 3 26W
Besançon, *Fr.* 34 47 15N 6 0 E
Bethesda, *U.K.* 17 53 11N 4 3W
Bethlehem, *Jord.* 57 31 43N 35 12 E
Bethlehem, *U.S.A.* 93 40 39N 75 24W
Béthune, *Fr.* 34 50 30N 2 38 E
Betws-y-Coed, *U.K.* 17 53 4N 3 49W
Beverley, *U.K.* 19 53 52N 0 26W
Beverwijk, *Neth.* 36 52 28N 4 38 E
Bewdley, *U.K.* 14 52 23N 2 19W
Bexhill, *U.K.* 15 50 51N 0 29 E
Bexley, *U.K.* 15 51 26N 0 10 E
Béziers, *Fr.* 35 43 20N 3 12 E
Bhagalpur, *India* 59 25 10N 87 0 E
Bhatinda, *India* 58 30 15N 74 57 E
Bhatpara, *India* 59 22 50N 88 25 E
Bhavnagar, *India* 58 21 45N 72 10 E
Bhimavaram, *India* 59 16 30N 81 30 E
Bhopal, *India* 58 23 20N 77 30 E
Bhubaneshwar, *India* 59 20 15N 85 50 E
Bhutan ■, *Asia* 59 27 25N 90 30 E
Białystok, *Pol.* 43 53 10N 23 10 E
Biarritz, *Fr.* 35 43 29N 1 33W
Bibury, *U.K.* 14 51 46N 1 50W
Bicester, *U.K.* 14 51 53N 1 9W
Bicton, *U.K.* 14 52 43N 2 47W
Biddenden, *U.K.* 15 51 7N 0 40 E
Biddulph, *U.K.* 18 53 8N 2 11W
Bideford, *U.K.* 16 51 1N 4 13W
Bideford Bay, *U.K.* 16 51 5N 4 20W
Bidford on Avon, *U.K.* 14 52 9N 1 53W
Bié Plateau, *Angola* 81 12 0S 16 0 E
Biel, *Switz.* 42 47 8N 7 14 E
Bielefeld, *Ger.* 42 52 2N 8 31 E
Bigbury, *U.K.* 16 50 17N 3 52W
Bigbury B., *U.K.* 16 50 18N 3 58W
Biggar, *U.K.* 21 55 38N 3 31W
Biggleswade, *U.K.* 15 52 6N 0 16W
Bighorn Mts., *U.S.A.* 90 44 30N 107 30W
Bihar □, *India* 59 25 0N 86 0 E
Bikaner, *India* 58 28 2N 73 18 E

Bikini Atoll, *Pac. Oc.* **64** 12 0N 167 30 E
Bilbao, *Sp.* **37** 43 16N 2 56W
Billericay, *U.K.* **15** 51 38N 0 25 E
Billesdon, *U.K.* **15** 52 38N 0 56W
Billingham, *U.K.* **19** 54 36N 1 18W
Billinghay, *U.K.* **19** 53 5N 0 17W
Billings, *U.S.A.* **90** 45 43N 108 29W
Billingshurst, *U.K.* **15** 51 2N 0 28W
Bilston, *U.K.* **14** 52 34N 2 5W
Binbrook, *U.K.* **19** 53 26N 0 9W
Bingham, *U.K.* **19** 52 57N 0 55W
Binghamton, *U.S.A.* **93** 42 9N 75 54W
Bingley, *U.K.* **18** 53 51N 1 50W
Bioko, *Eq. Guin.* **80** 3 30N 8 40 E
Birch, *U.K.* **15** 51 50N 0 54 E
Birchington, *U.K.* **15** 51 22N 1 18 E
Birdlip, *U.K.* **14** 51 50N 2 7W
Birkdale, *U.K.* **18** 53 38N 3 2W
Birkenhead, *U.K.* **18** 53 24N 3 1W
Birmingham, *U.K.* **14** 52 30N 1 55W
Birmingham, *U.S.A.* **91** 33 31N 86 50W
Birr, *Ire.* **25** 53 7N 7 55W
Birtley, *Northumberland, U.K.* **21** 55 5N 2 12W
Birtley, *Tyne & Wear, U.K.* **21** 54 53N 1 34W
Bishkek, *U.S.S.R.* **48** 42 54N 74 46 E
Biscay, B. of, *Atl. Oc.* **35** 45 0N 2 0W
Bishop Auckland, *U.K.* **19** 54 40N 1 40W
Bishop's Castle, *U.K.* **14** 52 29N 3 0W
Bishop's Cleeve, *U.K.* **14** 51 56N 2 3W
Bishop's Frome, *U.K.* **14** 52 8N 2 29W
Bishops Lydeard, *U.K.* **14** 51 4N 3 12W
Bishop's Nympton, *U.K.* **16** 50 58N 3 44W
Bishop's Stortford, *U.K.* **15** 51 52N 0 11 E
Bishop's Waltham, *U.K.* **14** 50 57N 1 13W
Bishopsteignton, *U.K.* **16** 50 32N 3 32W
Bishopstoke, *U.K.* **14** 50 58N 1 19W
Biskra, *Alg.* **78** 34 50N 5 44 E
Bismarck Arch., *P.N.G.* **64** 2 30S 150 0 E
Bissau, *Guin.-Biss.* **78** 11 45N 15 45W
Bitola, *Yug.* **41** 41 5N 21 10 E
Bitton, *U.K.* **14** 51 25N 2 27W
Biysk, *U.S.S.R.* **48** 52 40N 85 0 E
Blaby, *U.K.* **14** 52 34N 1 10W
Black Combe, *U.K.* **18** 54 16N 3 20W
Black Esk →, *U.K.* **21** 55 14N 3 13W
Black Forest, Mts., *Ger.* **42** 48 0N 8 0 E
Black Hd., *U.K.* **16** 50 1N 5 6W
Black Mt. = Mynydd Du, *U.K.* **17** 51 45N 3 45W
Black Mts., *U.K.* **17** 51 52N 3 5W
Black Sea, *Europe* **47** 43 30N 35 0 E
Black Volta →, *Africa* **78** 8 41N 1 33W
Blackall, *Austral.* **67** 24 25S 145 45 E
Blackburn, *U.K.* **18** 53 44N 2 30W
Blackdown Hills, *U.K.* **14** 50 57N 3 15W
Blackford, *U.K.* **21** 56 15N 3 48W
Blackmoor Gate, *U.K.* **16** 51 9N 3 55W
Blackmoor Vale, *U.K.* **14** 50 54N 2 28W
Blackpool, *U.K.* **18** 53 48N 3 3W
Blacksod B., *Ire.* **24** 54 6N 10 0W
Blacktown, *Austral.* **70** 33 48S 150 55 E
Blackwater →, *Ire.* **25** 51 55N 7 50W
Blackwater →, *Essex, U.K.* **15** 51 44N 0 53 E
Blackwater →, *N. Ireland, U.K.* **24** 54 31N 6 35W
Blackwood, *U.K.* **21** 55 40N 3 56W
Blaenau Ffestiniog, *U.K.* **17** 53 0N 3 57W
Blaenavon, *U.K.* **17** 51 46N 3 5W
Blagdon, *U.K.* **14** 51 19N 2 42W
Blagoveshchensk, *U.S.S.R.* **49** 50 20N 127 30 E
Blair Athol, *Austral.* **67** 22 42S 147 31 E
Blair Atholl, *U.K.* **23** 56 46N 3 50W
Blairgowrie, *U.K.* **23** 56 36N 3 20W
Blakeney, *Gloucs., U.K.* **14** 51 45N 2 29W
Blakeney, *Norfolk, U.K.* **15** 52 57N 1 1 E
Blanc, Mont, *Europe* **35** 45 48N 6 50 E
Blandford Forum, *U.K.* **14** 50 52N 2 10W
Blantyre, *Malawi* **81** 15 45S 35 0 E
Blarney, *Ire.* **25** 51 57N 8 35W
Blaydon, *U.K.* **19** 54 56N 1 47W
Bleadon, *U.K.* **14** 51 18N 2 57W
Blean, *U.K.* **15** 51 18N 1 3 E
Bleasdale Moors, *U.K.* **18** 53 57N 2 40W
Blenheim, *N.Z.* **71** 41 38S 173 57 E
Bletchingdon, *U.K.* **14** 51 51N 1 16W
Bletchley, *U.K.* **15** 51 59N 0 44W
Blisworth, *U.K.* **15** 52 11N 0 56W
Blockley, *U.K.* **14** 52 1N 1 45W
Bloemfontein, *S. Afr.* **81** 29 6S 26 14 E
Blofield, *U.K.* **15** 52 38N 1 25 E
Blois, *Fr.* **34** 47 35N 1 20 E
Bloody Foreland, *Ire.* **24** 55 10N 8 18W
Bloxham, *U.K.* **14** 52 1N 1 22W
Blue Mts., *Austral.* **70** 33 40S 150 0 E
Blue Mts., *U.S.A.* **90** 45 15N 119 0W
Blue Nile →, *Sudan* **79** 12 30N 34 30 E
Blue Ridge Mts., *U.S.A.* **91** 36 30N 80 15W
Blue Stack Mts., *Ire.* **24** 54 46N 8 5W
Blumenau, *Brazil* **102** 27 0S 49 0W
Blundeston, *U.K.* **15** 52 33N 1 42 E
Blyth, *Northumberland, U.K.* **19** 55 8N 1 32W
Blyth, *Notts., U.K.* **19** 53 22N 1 2W
Blyth →, *U.K.* **21** 55 8N 1 30W
Blyth Bridge, *U.K.* **21** 55 41N 3 22W
Blyton, *U.K.* **19** 53 25N 0 42W
Bobo-Dioulasso, *B. Faso* **78** 11 8N 4 13W
Bocholt, *Ger.* **36** 51 50N 6 35 E
Bochum, *Ger.* **36** 51 28N 7 12 E
Bodenham, *U.K.* **14** 52 9N 2 41W
Bodensee, *Ger.* **42** 47 35N 9 25 E
Bodiam, *U.K.* **15** 51 1N 0 33 E
Bodinnick, *U.K.* **16** 50 20N 4 37W
Bodmin, *U.K.* **16** 50 28N 4 44W
Bodmin Moor, *U.K.* **16** 50 33N 4 36W
Bodø, *Nor.* **44** 67 17N 14 24 E
Bogan →, *Austral.* **67** 29 59S 146 17 E
Boggeragh Mts., *Ire.* **25** 52 2N 8 55W
Bognor Regis, *U.K.* **15** 50 47N 0 40W
Bogor, *Indon.* **63** 6 36S 106 48 E
Bogota, *Col.* **100** 4 34N 74 0W
Bohemian Forest, *Czech.* **42** 49 20N 13 0 E
Boise, *U.S.A.* **90** 43 43N 116 9W
Bolgatanga, *Ghana* **78** 10 44N 0 53W
Bolivia ■, *S. Am.* **100** 17 6S 64 0W
Bolivian Plateau, *S. Am.* **96** 20 0S 67 30W
Bollington, *U.K.* **18** 53 18N 2 8W
Bolney, *U.K.* **15** 50 59N 0 11W
Bologna, *It.* **40** 44 30N 11 20 E
Bolshevik, I., *U.S.S.R.* **49** 78 30N 102 0 E
Bolshezemelsk Tundra, *U.S.S.R.* **46** 67 0N 56 0 E
Bolsover, *U.K.* **19** 53 14N 1 18W
Bolt Head, *U.K.* **16** 50 13N 3 48W
Bolt Tail, *U.K.* **16** 50 13N 3 55W
Bolton, *U.K.* **18** 53 35N 2 26W
Bolton Abbey, *U.K.* **18** 53 59N 1 53W
Bolton by Bowland, *U.K.* **18** 53 56N 2 21W
Bolton le Sands, *U.K.* **18** 54 7N 2 49W
Bolungavík, *Ice.* **44** 66 9N 23 15W
Bolzano, *It.* **40** 46 30N 11 20 E
Boma, *Zaïre* **80** 5 50S 13 4 E
Bombay, *India* **58** 18 55N 72 50 E
Bonaparte Archipelago, *Austral.* **66** 14 0S 124 30 E
Bonarbridge, *U.K.* **23** 57 53N 4 20W
Bonchester Bridge, *U.K.* **21** 55 23N 2 36W
Bonchurch, *U.K.* **14** 50 36N 1 11W
Bo'ness, *U.K.* **21** 56 0N 3 38W
Bonifacio, Str. of, *Fr.* **40** 41 12N 9 15 E
Bonn, *Ger.* **36** 50 43N 7 6 E
Bonnyrigg, *U.K.* **21** 55 52N 3 8W
Boot, *U.K.* **18** 54 24N 3 18W
Boothia, Gulf of, *Canada* **89** 71 0N 90 0W
Boothia Pen., *Canada* **88** 71 0N 94 0W
Bootle, *Cumbria, U.K.* **18** 54 17N 3 24W
Bootle, *Merseyside, U.K.* **18** 53 28N 3 1W
Borås, *Swed.* **45** 57 43N 12 56 E
Bordeaux, *Fr.* **35** 44 50N 0 36W
Borders □, *U.K.* **21** 55 35N 2 50W
Bordon, *U.K.* **15** 51 6N 0 52W
Borehamwood, *U.K.* **15** 51 40N 0 15W
Boreland, *U.K.* **21** 55 12N 3 16W
Borgarnes, *Ice.* **44** 64 32N 21 55W
Borneo, *E. Ind.* **63** 1 0N 115 0 E
Bornholm, *Den.* **45** 55 10N 15 0 E
Boroughbridge, *U.K.* **19** 54 6N 1 23W
Borrowdale, *U.K.* **18** 54 31N 3 10W
Borth, *U.K.* **17** 52 29N 4 3W
Bosbury, *U.K.* **14** 52 5N 2 27W
Boscastle, *U.K.* **16** 50 42N 4 42W
Bosham, *U.K.* **15** 50 50N 0 51W
Bosporus, *Turk.* **47** 41 10N 29 10 E
Boston, *U.K.* **19** 52 59N 0 2W
Boston, *U.S.A.* **93** 42 20N 71 0W
Botany Bay, *Austral.* **70** 34 0S 151 14 E
Bothel, *U.K.* **18** 54 43N 3 16W
Bothnia, G. of, *Europe* **44** 63 0N 20 0 E
Botswana ■, *Africa* **81** 22 0S 24 0 E
Bottesford, *U.K.* **19** 52 57N 0 48W
Bottrop, *Ger.* **36** 51 34N 6 59 E
Bouaké, *Ivory C.* **78** 7 40N 5 2W
Bouar, *C.A.R.* **80** 6 0N 15 40 E
Boulogne-sur-Mer, *Fr.* **34** 50 42N 1 36 E
Bourges, *Fr.* **34** 47 9N 2 25 E
Bourgogne, *Fr.* **34** 47 0N 4 50 E
Bourke, *Austral.* **67** 30 8S 145 55 E
Bourne, *U.K.* **15** 52 46N 0 22W
Bournemouth, *U.K.* **14** 50 43N 1 53W
Bourton-on-the-Water, *U.K.* **14** 51 53N 1 45W
Bovey Tracey, *U.K.* **16** 50 36N 3 40W
Bowen, *Austral.* **67** 20 0S 148 16 E
Bowes, *U.K.* **18** 54 31N 1 59W
Bowland, Forest of, *U.K.* **18** 54 0N 2 30W
Bowmore, *U.K.* **20** 55 45N 6 18W
Bowness, *Solway, U.K.* **18** 54 57N 3 13W
Bowness, *Windermere, U.K.* **18** 54 22N 2 56W
Box, *U.K.* **14** 51 24N 2 16W
Box Hill, *U.K.* **15** 51 16N 0 16W
Boxley, *U.K.* **15** 51 17N 0 34 E
Boyle, *Ire.* **24** 53 58N 8 19W
Boyne →, *Ire.* **24** 53 43N 6 15W
Bozeat, *U.K.* **15** 52 14N 0 41W
Bracadale, L., *U.K.* **22** 57 20N 6 30W
Bracebridge Heath, *U.K.* **19** 53 13N 0 32W
Brackley, *U.K.* **14** 52 3N 1 9W
Bracknell, *U.K.* **15** 51 24N 0 45W
Braco, *U.K.* **21** 56 16N 3 55W
Bradda Hd., *U.K.* **18** 54 6N 4 46W
Bradford, *U.K.* **19** 53 47N 1 45W
Bradford-on-Avon, *U.K.* **14** 51 20N 2 15W
Brading, *U.K.* **14** 50 41N 1 9W
Bradwell-on-Sea, *U.K.* **15** 51 44N 0 55 E
Bradworthy, *U.K.* **16** 50 54N 4 22W
Braemar, *U.K.* **23** 57 2N 3 20W
Braga, *Port.* **37** 41 35N 8 25W
Brahmaputra →, *India* **59** 24 2N 90 59 E
Braich-y-pwll, *U.K.* **17** 52 47N 4 46W
Brăila, *Rom.* **43** 45 19N 27 59 E
Brailsford, *U.K.* **19** 52 58N 1 35W
Braintree, *U.K.* **15** 51 53N 0 34 E
Bramford, *U.K.* **15** 52 5N 1 6 E
Brampton, *Canada* **92** 43 45N 79 45W
Brampton, *Cambs., U.K.* **15** 52 19N 0 13W
Brampton, *Cumbria, U.K.* **18** 54 56N 2 43W
Bramshott, *U.K.* **15** 51 5N 0 47W
Brancaster, *U.K.* **15** 52 58N 0 40 E
Branco →, *Brazil* **100** 1 20S 61 50W
Brander, Pass of, *U.K.* **20** 56 25N 5 10W
Brandon, *Canada* **88** 49 50N 99 57W
Brandon, *Durham, U.K.* **19** 54 46N 1 37W
Brandon, *Suffolk, U.K.* **15** 52 27N 0 37 E
Brandon, Mt., *Ire.* **25** 52 15N 10 15W
Brandon B., *Ire.* **25** 52 17N 10 8W
Branston, *U.K.* **19** 53 13N 0 28W
Brantford, *Canada* **92** 43 10N 80 15W
Brasília, *Brazil* **101** 15 47S 47 55 E
Braşov, *Rom.* **43** 45 38N 25 35 E
Brasted, *U.K.* **15** 51 16N 0 8 E
Bratislava, *Czech.* **43** 48 10N 17 7 E
Bratsk, *U.S.S.R.* **49** 56 10N 101 30 E
Braunton, *U.K.* **16** 51 6N 4 9W
Bray, *Ire.* **25** 53 12N 6 6W
Bray, *U.K.* **15** 51 30N 0 42W
Brazil ■, *S. Am.* **101** 10 0S 50 0W
Brazilian Highlands, *Brazil* **101** 18 0S 46 30W
Brazzaville, *Congo* **80** 4 9S 15 12 E
Breadalbane, *U.K.* **20** 56 30N 4 15W
Breage, *U.K.* **16** 50 6N 5 17W
Breamish →, *U.K.* **21** 55 30N 1 55W
Brechin, *U.K.* **23** 56 44N 2 40W
Breckland, *U.K.* **15** 52 30N 0 40 E
Brecon, *U.K.* **17** 51 57N 3 23W
Brecon Beacons, *U.K.* **17** 51 53N 3 27W
Brede, *U.K.* **15** 50 56N 0 37 E
Bredon Hill, *U.K.* **14** 52 3N 2 2W
Breiðafjörður, *Ice.* **44** 65 15N 23 15W
Bremen, *Ger.* **42** 53 4N 8 47 E
Bremerhaven, *Ger.* **42** 53 34N 8 35 E
Brendon Hills, *U.K.* **14** 51 6N 3 25W
Brenner Pass, *Alps* **42** 47 0N 11 30 E
Brent, *U.K.* **15** 51 33N 0 18W
Brentwood, *U.K.* **15** 51 37N 0 19 E
Bréscia, *It.* **40** 45 33N 10 13 E
Breslau = Wrocław, *Pol.* **43** 51 5N 17 5 E
Bressay I., *U.K.* **22** 60 10N 1 5W
Brest, *Fr.* **34** 48 24N 4 31W
Brest, *U.S.S.R.* **46** 52 10N 23 40 E
Bretagne, *Fr.* **34** 48 0N 3 0W
Brewood, *U.K.* **14** 52 41N 2 10W
* Brezhnev, *U.S.S.R.* **46** 55 42N 52 19 E
Bride, *U.K.* **18** 54 24N 4 23W
Bridestowe, *U.K.* **16** 50 41N 4 7W
Bridge, *U.K.* **15** 51 14N 1 8 E
Bridge of Allan, *U.K.* **21** 56 9N 3 57W
Bridge of Earn, *U.K.* **21** 56 20N 3 25W
Bridge of Orchy, *U.K.* **20** 56 29N 4 48W
Bridge of Weir, *U.K.* **20** 55 51N 4 35W
Bridgend, *Islay, U.K.* **20** 55 46N 6 15W
Bridgend, *Mid Glam., U.K.* **17** 51 30N 3 35W
Bridgeport, *U.S.A.* **93** 41 12N 73 12W
Bridgetown, *Barb.* **94** 13 0N 59 30W
Bridgnorth, *U.K.* **14** 52 33N 2 25W
Bridgwater, *U.K.* **14** 51 7N 3 0W
Bridgwater B., *U.K.* **14** 51 15N 3 15W
Bridlington, *U.K.* **19** 54 6N 0 11W
Bridlington B., *U.K.* **19** 54 4N 0 10W
Bridport, *U.K.* **14** 50 43N 2 45W
Brierfield, *U.K.* **18** 53 49N 2 15W
Brierley Hill, *U.K.* **14** 52 29N 2 7W
Brigg, *U.K.* **19** 53 33N 0 30W
Brighouse, *U.K.* **19** 53 42N 1 47W
Brighstone, *U.K.* **15** 50 38N 1 23W
Brightlingsea, *U.K.* **15** 51 49N 1 1 E
Brighton, *U.K.* **15** 50 50N 0 9W
Brigstock, *U.K.* **15** 52 27N 0 38W
Brill, *U.K.* **14** 51 49N 1 3W
Brimfield, *U.K.* **14** 52 18N 2 42W
Bríndisi, *It.* **41** 40 39N 17 55 E
Brinklow, *U.K.* **14** 52 25N 1 22W
Brinkworth, *U.K.* **14** 51 33N 1 59W
Brisbane, *Austral.* **67** 27 25S 153 2 E
Bristol, *U.K.* **14** 51 26N 2 35W
Bristol Channel, *U.K.* **16** 51 18N 4 30W
Briston, *U.K.* **15** 52 52N 1 4 E
British Columbia □, *Canada* **88** 55 0N 125 15W
British Guiana = Guyana ■, *S. Am.* **100** 5 0N 59 0W
British Isles, *Europe* **4** 55 0N 4 0W
Briton Ferry, *U.K.* **17** 51 37N 3 50W
Brittany = Bretagne, *Fr.* **34** 48 0N 3 0W
Brixham, *U.K.* **16** 50 24N 3 31W
Brixworth, *U.K.* **15** 52 20N 0 54W
Brize Norton, *U.K.* **14** 51 46N 1 35W
Brno, *Czech.* **42** 49 10N 16 35 E
Broad B., *U.K.* **22** 58 14N 6 16W
Broad Chalke, *U.K.* **14** 51 2N 1 54W
Broad Haven, *Ire.* **24** 54 20N 9 55W
Broad Law, *U.K.* **21** 55 30N 3 22W
Broad Sd., *U.K.* **16** 49 56N 6 19W
Broadclyst, *U.K.* **16** 50 46N 3 27W
Broadford, *U.K.* **22** 57 14N 5 55W
Broadhembury, *U.K.* **16** 50 49N 3 16W
Broads, The, *U.K.* **15** 52 45N 1 30 E
Broadstairs, *U.K.* **15** 51 21N 1 28 E
Broadway, *U.K.* **14** 52 2N 1 51W
Broadwindsor, *U.K.* **14** 50 49N 2 49W
Brockenhurst, *U.K.* **14** 50 49N 1 34W
Brockton, *U.S.A.* **93** 42 25N 79 26W
Brockworth, *U.K.* **14** 51 51N 2 9W
Brodick, *U.K.* **20** 55 34N 5 9W
Broken Hill, *Austral.* **70** 31 58S 141 29 E
Bromborough, *U.K.* **18** 53 20N 3 0W
Bromfield, *U.K.* **14** 52 25N 2 45W
Bromham, *U.K.* **14** 51 23N 2 3W
Bromley, *U.K.* **15** 51 20N 0 5 E
Brompton, *U.K.* **19** 54 22N 1 25W
Bromsgrove, *U.K.* **14** 52 20N 2 3W
Bromyard, *U.K.* **14** 52 12N 2 30W
Brooks, *Canada* **88** 50 35N 111 55W
Brooks Ra., *U.S.A.* **88** 68 40N 147 0W
Broom, L., *U.K.* **22** 57 55N 5 15W
Broomfield, *U.K.* **15** 51 46N 0 28 E
Broomhill, *U.K.* **21** 55 19N 1 36W
Brora, *U.K.* **23** 58 0N 3 50W
Brora →, *U.K.* **23** 58 4N 3 52W
Broseley, *U.K.* **14** 52 36N 2 30W
Brosna →, *Ire.* **25** 53 8N 8 0W
Brothertoft, *U.K.* **19** 53 0N 0 5W
Brotton, *U.K.* **19** 54 34N 0 55W
Brough, *Cumbria, U.K.* **18** 54 32N 2 19W
Brough, *Humberside, U.K.* **19** 53 44N 0 35W
Broughton, *Borders, U.K.* **21** 55 37N 3 25W
Broughton, *Humberside, U.K.* **19** 53 33N 0 36W
Broughton, *N. Yorks., U.K.* **19** 54 26N 1 8W
Broughton, *Northants., U.K.* **15** 52 22N 0 45W
Broughton-in-Furness, *U.K.* **18** 54 17N 3 12W
Broughty Ferry, *U.K.* **21** 56 29N 2 50W
Brown Willy, *U.K.* **16** 50 35N 4 34W
Brownhills, *U.K.* **14** 52 38N 1 57W
Broxburn, *U.K.* **21** 55 56N 3 23W
Bruay-en-Artois, *Fr.* **34** 50 29N 2 33 E
Bruce, Mt., *Austral.* **66** 22 37S 118 8 E
Brue →, *U.K.* **14** 51 10N 2 59W
Bruges, *Belg.* **36** 51 13N 3 13 E
Brunei ■, *E. Ind.* **63** 4 50N 115 0 E
Brunswick, *Ger.* **42** 52 17N 10 28 E
Brunton, *U.K.* **21** 55 2N 2 6W
Brussels, *Belg.* **36** 50 51N 4 21 E
Bruton, *U.K.* **14** 51 6N 2 28W
Bryansk, *U.S.S.R.* **46** 53 13N 34 25 E
Bryher I., *U.K.* **16** 49 57N 6 21W
Brynamman, *U.K.* **17** 51 49N 3 52W
Brynmawr, *U.K.* **17** 51 48N 3 11W
Bucaramanga, *Col.* **100** 7 0N 73 0W
Buchan, *U.K.* **23** 57 32N 2 8W
Buchan Ness, *U.K.* **23** 57 29N 1 48W
Bucharest, *Rom.* **43** 44 27N 26 10 E
Buchlyvie, *U.K.* **20** 56 7N 4 20W
Buckden, *U.K.* **15** 52 17N 0 16W
Buckfastleigh, *U.K.* **16** 50 28N 3 47W
Buckhaven, *U.K.* **21** 56 10N 3 2W
Buckie, *U.K.* **23** 57 40N 2 58W
Buckingham, *U.K.* **15** 52 0N 0 59W
Buckingham □, *U.K.* **15** 51 50N 0 55W
Buckland Brewer, *U.K.* **16** 50 56N 4 14W
Buckland Newton, *U.K.* **14** 50 45N 2 25W
Buckley, *U.K.* **17** 53 10N 3 5W
Budapest, *Hung.* **43** 47 29N 19 5 E
Buddon Ness, *U.K.* **21** 56 29N 2 42W
Bude, *U.K.* **16** 50 49N 4 33W
Bude Bay, *U.K.* **16** 50 50N 4 40W
Budle B., *U.K.* **21** 55 37N 1 45W
Budleigh Salterton, *U.K.* **16** 50 37N 3 19W
Buenaventura, *Col.* **100** 3 53N 77 4W
Buenos Aires, *Arg.* **102** 34 30S 58 20W
Buffalo, *U.S.A.* **92** 42 55N 78 50W
Bug →, *Pol.* **43** 52 31N 21 5 E
Bug →, *U.S.S.R.* **47** 46 59N 31 58 E
Buglawton, *U.K.* **18** 53 12N 2 11W
Bugle, *U.K.* **16** 50 23N 4 46W
Buie L., *U.K.* **20** 56 20N 5 55W
Builth Wells, *U.K.* **17** 52 10N 3 26W
Bujumbura, *Bur.* **80** 3 16S 29 18 E
Bukavu, *Zaïre* **80** 2 20S 28 52 E
Bukhara, *U.S.S.R.* **48** 39 48N 64 25 E
Bulawayo, *Zimb.* **81** 20 7S 28 32 E
Bulford, *U.K.* **14** 51 11N 1 45W
Bulgaria ■, *Europe* **41** 42 35N 25 30 E
Bulwell, *U.K.* **19** 53 1N 1 12W
Bunbury, *Austral.* **66** 33 20S 115 35 E
Buncrana, *Ire.* **24** 55 8N 7 28W
Bundaberg, *Austral.* **67** 24 54S 152 22 E
Bundoran, *Ire.* **24** 54 24N 8 17W

* *Renamed Naberezhnyye Chelny*

Bunessan, U.K. 20 56 18N 6 15W
Bungay, U.K. 15 52 27N 1 26 E
Buntingford, U.K. 15 51 57N 0 1W
Bunwell, U.K. 15 52 30N 1 9 E
Buraydah, Si. Arab. 56 26 20N 44 8 E
Burbage, Derby, U.K. 18 53 15N 1 55W
Burbage, Leics., U.K. 14 52 31N 1 20W
Burbage, Wilts., U.K. 14 51 21N 1 40W
Burdwan, India 59 23 14N 87 39 E
Bure →, U.K. 15 52 38N 1 45 E
Burford, U.K. 14 51 48N 1 38W
Burgas, Bulg. 41 42 33N 27 29 E
Burgess Hill, U.K. 15 50 57N 0 7W
Burgh-le-Marsh, U.K. 19 53 10N 0 15 E
Burgos, Sp. 37 42 21N 3 41W
Burgundy = Bourgogne, Fr. 34 47 0N 4 50 E
Burkina Faso ■, Africa 78 12 0N 1 0W
Burley, Hants., U.K. 14 50 49N 1 41W
Burley, N. Yorks., U.K. 19 53 55N 1 46W
Burlington, U.S.A. 93 44 27N 73 14W
Burma ■, Asia 59 21 0N 96 30 E
Burnham, Essex, U.K. 15 51 37N 0 50 E
Burnham, Somerset, U.K. 14 51 14N 3 0W
Burnham Market, U.K. 15 52 57N 0 43 E
Burnie, Austral. 67 41 4S 145 56 E
Burnley, U.K. 18 53 47N 2 15W
Burnmouth, U.K. 21 55 50N 2 4W
Burntisland, U.K. 21 56 4N 3 14W
Burrelton, U.K. 21 56 30N 3 16W
Burrow Hd., U.K. 20 54 40N 4 23W
Burry Port, U.K. 17 51 41N 4 17W
Bursa, Turk. 47 40 15N 29 5 E
Burstwick, U.K. 19 53 43N 0 6W
Burton, U.K. 18 54 10N 2 43W
Burton Agnes, U.K. 19 54 4N 0 18W
Burton Bradstock, U.K. 14 50 41N 2 43W
Burton Fleming, U.K. 19 54 8N 0 20W
Burton Latimer, U.K. 15 52 23N 0 41W
Burton upon Stather, U.K. 19 53 39N 0 41W
Burton-upon-Trent, U.K. 14 52 48N 1 39W
Burundi ■, Africa 80 3 15S 30 0 E
Burwash, U.K. 15 50 59N 0 24 E
Burwell, U.K. 15 52 17N 0 20 E
Bury, U.K. 18 53 36N 2 19W
Bury St. Edmunds, U.K. 15 52 15N 0 42 E
Buryat A.S.S.R. □, U.S.S.R. 49 53 0N 110 0 E
Būshehr, Iran 56 28 20N 51 45 E
Bushey, U.K. 15 51 38N 0 20W
Bushmills, U.K. 24 55 14N 6 32W
Bute, U.K. 20 55 48N 5 2W
Bute, Kyles of, U.K. 20 55 55N 5 10W
Bute, Sd. of, U.K. 20 55 43N 5 8W
Buttermere, U.K. 18 54 32N 3 17W
Butuan, Phil. 63 8 57N 125 33 E
Buxton, U.K. 18 53 16N 1 54W
Buzău, Rom. 43 45 10N 26 50 E
Bydgoszcz, Pol. 43 53 10N 18 0 E
Byfield, U.K. 14 52 10N 1 15W
Byrd Land, Ant. 103 79 30S 125 0W
Byrrang Mts., U.S.S.R. 49 75 0N 100 0 E
Bytom, Pol. 43 50 25N 18 54 E

C

Cabimas, Ven. 100 10 23N 71 25W
Cabinda □, Angola 80 5 0S 12 30 E
Čačak, Yug. 41 43 54N 20 20 E
Cáceres, Sp. 37 39 26N 6 23W
Cachoeira do Sul, Brazil 102 30 3S 52 53W
Cader Idris, U.K. 17 52 43N 3 56W
Cádiz, Sp. 37 36 30N 6 20W
Caen, Fr. 34 49 10N 0 22W
Caenby Corner, U.K. 19 53 23N 0 32W
Caernarfon, U.K. 17 53 8N 4 17W
Caernarfon B., U.K. 17 53 4N 4 40W
Caerphilly, U.K. 17 51 34N 3 13W
Caersws, U.K. 17 52 32N 3 27W
Cagayan de Oro, Phil. 63 8 30N 124 40 E
Cágliari, It. 40 39 15N 9 6 E
Caha Mts., Ire. 25 51 45N 9 40W
Caher, Ire. 25 52 23N 7 56W
Cahersiveen, Ire. 25 51 57N 10 13W
Cahore Pt., Ire. 25 52 34N 6 11W
Caicos Is., W. Ind. 95 21 40N 71 40W
Cairn Gorm, U.K. 23 57 7N 3 40W
Cairn Table, U.K. 21 55 30N 4 0W
Cairn Toul, U.K. 23 57 3N 3 44W
Cairngorm Mts., U.K. 23 57 6N 3 42W
Cairnryan, U.K. 20 54 59N 5 0W
Cairns, Austral. 67 16 57S 145 45 E
Cairo, Egypt 79 30 1N 31 14 E
Caister-on-Sea, U.K. 15 52 38N 1 43 E
Caistor, U.K. 19 53 29N 0 20W
Caithness, Ord of, U.K. 23 58 9N 3 37W
Cajamarca, Peru 100 7 5S 78 28W
Calabar, Nig. 78 4 57N 8 20 E
Calábria □, It. 40 39 24N 16 30 E
Calais, Fr. 34 50 57N 1 50 E
Calbayog, Phil. 63 12 4N 124 38 E
Calcutta, India 59 22 36N 88 24 E
Caldbeck, U.K. 18 54 45N 3 3W
Calder →, U.K. 19 53 44N 1 21W
Calder Bridge, U.K. 18 54 27N 3 31W
Caldew →, U.K. 18 54 54N 2 59W
Caledonian Canal, U.K. 23 56 50N 5 6W
Calf of Man, U.K. 18 54 4N 4 48W
Calgary, Canada 88 51 0N 114 10W
Calgary, U.K. 20 56 34N 6 17W
Cali, Col. 100 3 25N 76 35W
Caliach Pt., U.K. 20 56 37N 6 20W
Calicut, India 58 11 15N 75 43 E
California □, U.S.A. 90 37 25N 120 0W
California, G. of, N. Am. 94 27 0N 111 0W
Callan, Ire. 25 52 33N 7 25W
Callander, U.K. 20 56 15N 4 14W
Callao, Peru 100 12 0S 77 0W
Calne, U.K. 14 51 26N 2 0W
Calshot, U.K. 14 50 49N 1 18W
Calstock, U.K. 16 50 30N 4 13W
Caltanissetta, It. 40 37 30N 14 3 E
Cam →, U.K. 15 52 21N 0 16 E
Camagüey, Cuba 95 21 20N 78 0W
Camargue, Fr. 35 43 34N 4 34 E
Cambay, G. of, India 58 20 45N 72 30 E
Camberley, U.K. 15 51 20N 0 44W
Cambo, U.K. 21 55 9N 1 57W
Cambodia ■, Asia 63 12 15N 105 0 E
Camborne, U.K. 16 50 13N 5 18W
Cambrian Mts., U.K. 17 52 25N 3 52W
Cambridge, U.K. 15 52 13N 0 8 E
Cambridge, U.S.A. 93 42 20N 71 8W
Cambridge Bay, Canada 88 69 10N 105 0W
Cambridgeshire □, U.K. 15 52 12N 0 7 E
Camden, U.K. 15 51 33N 0 10W
Camden, U.S.A. 93 39 57N 75 7W
Camel →, U.K. 16 50 28N 4 49W
Camelford, U.K. 16 50 37N 4 41W
Cameroon ■, Africa 80 6 0N 12 30 E
Campbellton, Canada 93 49 17N 54 56W
Campbelltown, Austral. 70 34 53S 138 40 E
Campbeltown, U.K. 20 55 25N 5 36W
Campeche, Mex. 94 19 50N 90 32W
Campeche, G. of, Mex. 94 19 30N 93 0W
Campina Grande, Brazil 101 7 20S 35 47W
Campinas, Brazil 102 22 50S 47 0W
Campo Grande, Brazil 101 20 25S 54 40W
Campos, Brazil 101 21 50S 41 20W
Campsie Fells, U.K. 20 56 2N 4 20W
Camrose, Canada 88 53 0N 112 50W
Can Tho, Viet. 63 10 2N 105 46 E
Canada ■, N. Am. 88 60 0N 100 0W
Canary Is., Atl. Oc. 78 29 30N 17 0W
Canaveral, C., U.S.A. 91 28 28N 80 31W
Canberra, Austral. 70 35 15S 149 8 E
Canik Mts., Turk. 47 40 30N 38 0 E
Canna, U.K. 22 57 3N 6 33W
Cannes, Fr. 35 43 32N 7 0 E
Cannington, U.K. 14 51 8N 3 4W
Cannock, U.K. 14 52 42N 2 2W
Cannock Chase, U.K. 14 52 43N 2 0W
Canonbie, U.K. 21 55 4N 2 58W
Cantabrian Mts., Sp. 37 43 0N 5 10W
Canterbury, U.K. 15 51 17N 1 5 E
Canterbury Plains, N.Z. 71 43 55S 171 22 E
Canton = Guangzhou, China 61 23 5N 113 10 E
Canton, U.S.A. 92 40 47N 81 22W
Canvey, U.K. 15 51 32N 0 35 E
Caoles, U.K. 20 56 32N 6 43W
Caolisport, Loch, U.K. 20 55 54N 5 40W
Cape Breton I., Canada 93 46 0N 60 30W
Cape Coast, Ghana 78 5 5N 1 15W
Cape Province □, S. Afr. 81 32 0S 23 0 E
Cape Town, S. Afr. 81 33 55S 18 22 E
Cape Verde Is. ■, Atl. Oc. 118 17 10N 25 20W
Cape York Peninsula, Austral. 67 12 0S 142 30 E
Capel, U.K. 15 51 8N 0 18W
Caracas, Ven. 100 10 30N 66 55W
Caratinga, Brazil 101 19 50S 42 10W
Carbost, U.K. 22 57 19N 6 21W
Cardiff, U.K. 17 51 28N 3 11W
Cardigan, U.K. 17 52 6N 4 41W
Cardigan B., U.K. 17 52 30N 4 30W
Cardington, U.K. 15 52 7N 0 23W
Carey, L., Austral. 66 29 0S 122 15 E
Caribbean Sea 95 15 0N 75 0W
Carisbrooke, U.K. 14 50 42N 1 19W
Cark, U.K. 18 54 11N 2 59W
Carleton Rode, U.K. 15 52 30N 1 6 E
Carlingford, L., Ire. 24 54 0N 6 5W
Carlisle, U.K. 18 54 54N 2 55W
Carlops, U.K. 21 55 47N 3 20W
Carlow, Ire. 25 52 50N 6 58W
Carlow □, Ire. 25 52 43N 6 50W
Carloway, U.K. 22 58 17N 6 48W
Carlton, U.K. 19 52 58N 1 6W
Carlton Colville, U.K. 15 52 27N 1 41 E
Carlton Miniott, U.K. 19 54 13N 1 22W
Carluke, U.K. 21 55 44N 3 50W
Carmarthen, U.K. 17 51 52N 4 20W
Carmarthen B., U.K. 17 51 40N 4 30W
Carnarvon, Austral. 66 24 51S 113 42 E
Carndonagh, Ire. 24 55 15N 7 16W
Carnegie, L., Austral. 66 26 5S 122 30 E
Carnforth, U.K. 18 54 8N 2 47W
Carno, U.K. 17 52 34N 3 31W
Carnoustie, U.K. 21 56 30N 2 41W
Carnsore Pt., Ire. 25 52 10N 6 20W
Carnwath, U.K. 21 55 42N 3 38W
Caroline Is., Pac. Oc. 64 8 0N 150 0 E
Carpathians, Mts., Europe 43 49 50N 21 0 E
Carpentaria, G. of, Austral. 67 14 0S 139 0 E
Carradale, U.K. 20 55 35N 5 30W
Carrauntoohill, Mt., Ire. 25 52 0N 9 49W
Carrick, U.K. 20 55 12N 4 38W
Carrick-on-Shannon, Ire. 24 53 57N 8 7W
Carrick-on-Suir, Ire. 25 52 22N 7 30W
Carrickfergus, U.K. 24 54 43N 5 50W
Carrickfergus □, U.K. 24 54 43N 5 49W
Carrickmacross, Ire. 24 54 0N 6 43W
Carron →, U.K. 22 57 30N 5 30W
Carron, L., U.K. 22 57 22N 5 35W
Carronbridge, U.K. 21 55 16N 3 46W
Carse of Gowrie, U.K. 21 56 30N 3 10W
Carsphairn, U.K. 20 55 13N 4 15W
Carstairs, U.K. 21 55 42N 3 41W
Cartagena, Col. 100 10 25N 75 33W
Cartagena, Sp. 37 37 38N 0 59W
Cartmel, U.K. 18 54 13N 2 57W
Caruaru, Brazil 101 8 15S 35 55W
Carúpano, Ven. 100 10 39N 63 15W
Casablanca, Mor. 78 33 36N 7 36W
Cascade Ra., U.S.A. 90 47 0N 121 30W
Cashel, Ire. 25 52 31N 7 53W
Casper, U.S.A. 90 42 52N 106 20W
Caspian Sea, U.S.S.R. 47 43 0N 50 0 E
Castellón □, Sp. 37 40 15N 0 5W
Castle Acre, U.K. 15 52 42N 0 42 E
Castle Cary, U.K. 14 51 5N 2 32W
Castle Donington, U.K. 14 52 50N 1 20W
Castle Douglas, U.K. 21 54 57N 3 57W
Castle Eden, U.K. 19 54 45N 1 20W
Castlebar, Ire. 24 53 52N 9 17W
Castlebay, U.K. 22 56 57N 7 30W
Castleblaney, Ire. 24 54 7N 6 44W
Castleford, U.K. 19 53 43N 1 21W
Castlereagh, Ire. 24 53 47N 8 30W
Castlereagh □, U.K. 24 54 33N 5 53W
Castlereagh →, Austral. 70 30 12S 147 32 E
Castleside, U.K. 18 54 50N 1 52W
Castleton, Derby, U.K. 19 53 20N 1 47W
Castleton, N. Yorks., U.K. 19 54 27N 0 57W
Castletown, U.K. 18 54 4N 4 40W
Castletown Bearhaven, Ire. 25 51 40N 9 54W
Castries, St. Lucia 94 14 0N 60 50W
Catánia, It. 40 37 31N 15 4 E
Catanzaro, It. 40 38 54N 16 38 E
Catcleugh, U.K. 21 55 19N 2 22W
Caterham, U.K. 15 51 16N 0 4W
Caton, U.K. 18 54 5N 2 41W
Catrine, U.K. 20 55 30N 4 20W
Catsfield, U.K. 15 50 53N 0 28 E
Catterick, U.K. 19 54 23N 1 38W
Catterick Camp, U.K. 19 54 22N 1 43W
Catton, U.K. 21 54 56N 2 16W
Caucasus, U.S.S.R. 47 43 0N 44 0 E
Caulkerbush, U.K. 21 54 54N 3 40W
Cavan, Ire. 24 54 0N 7 22W
Cavan □, Ire. 24 53 58N 7 10W
Cawood, U.K. 19 53 50N 1 7W
Cawston, U.K. 15 52 47N 1 10 E
Caxias, Brazil 101 4 55S 43 20W
Caxias do Sul, Brazil 102 29 10S 51 10W
Cayenne, Fr. G. 101 5 0N 52 18W
Ceanannus Mor, Ire. 24 53 42N 6 53W
Cebu, Phil. 63 10 18N 123 54 E
Cedar Rapids, U.S.A. 91 42 0N 91 38W
Celbridge, Ire. 25 53 20N 6 33W
Celebes = Sulawesi □, Indon. 63 2 0S 120 0 E
Celebes Sea, E. Ind. 63 3 0N 123 0 E
Cemaes Bay, U.K. 17 53 24N 4 27W
Central □, U.K. 20 56 10N 4 30W
Central African Republic ■, Africa 80 7 0N 20 0 E
Central Russian Uplands, U.S.S.R. 26 54 0N 36 0 E
Central Siberian Plateau, U.S.S.R. 49 65 0N 105 0 E
Cephalonia = Kefallinía, Greece 41 38 20N 20 30 E
Ceram, Indon. 63 3 10S 129 0 E
Ceres, U.K. 21 56 18N 2 57W
Cerignola, It. 40 41 17N 15 53 E
Cerne Abbas, U.K. 14 50 49N 2 29W
Cerrig-y-drudion, U.K. 17 53 2N 3 34W
Cessnock, Austral. 70 32 50S 151 21 E
Ceuta, Mor. 78 35 52N 5 18W
Cévennes, Fr. 35 44 10N 3 50 E
Ceylon = Sri Lanka ■, Asia 58 7 30N 80 50 E
Chacewater, U.K. 16 50 15N 5 8W
Chad ■, Africa 78 15 0N 17 15 E
Chad, L., Chad 79 13 30N 14 30 E
Chagford, U.K. 16 50 40N 3 50W
Chale, U.K. 14 50 35N 1 19W
Chalfont St. Peter, U.K. 15 51 36N 0 33W
Châlons-sur-Marne, Fr. 34 48 58N 4 20 E
Chambéry, Fr. 35 45 34N 5 55 E
Champagne, Fr. 34 48 40N 4 20 E
Champlain, L., U.S.A. 93 44 30N 73 20W
Chandigarh, India 58 30 43N 76 47 E
Chandler's Ford, U.K. 14 50 59N 1 23W
Changchun, China 61 43 58N 125 19 E
Changde, China 61 29 4N 111 35 E
Changsha, China 61 28 5N 113 1 E
Changzhou, China 61 31 47N 119 58 E
Channel Is., U.K. 34 49 30N 2 40W
Chao Phraya →, Thai. 63 13 32N 100 36 E
Chapel-en-le-Frith, U.K. 18 53 19N 1 54W
Chapel St. Leonards, U.K. 19 53 13N 0 19 E
Chard, U.K. 14 50 52N 2 59W
Chardzhou, U.S.S.R. 48 39 6N 63 34 E
Charing, U.K. 15 51 12N 0 49 E
Charlbury, U.K. 14 51 52N 1 29W
Charleroi, Belg. 36 50 24N 4 27 E
Charleston, U.S.A. 91 32 47N 79 56W
Charleville = Rath Luirc, Ire. 25 52 21N 8 40W
Charleville, Austral. 67 26 24S 146 15 E
Charleville-Mézières, Fr. 34 49 44N 4 40 E
Charlotte, U.S.A. 91 35 16N 80 46W
Charlottenburg, Ger. 42 52 31N 13 15 E
Charlottetown, Canada 93 46 14N 63 8W
Charlton Kings, U.K. 14 51 52N 2 3W
Charlwood, U.K. 15 51 8N 0 12W
Charminster, U.K. 14 50 43N 2 28W
Charmouth, U.K. 14 50 45N 2 54W
Charnwood Forest, U.K. 14 52 43N 1 18W
Charters Towers, Austral. 67 20 5S 146 13 E
Chartham, U.K. 15 51 14N 1 1 E
Chartres, Fr. 34 48 29N 1 30 E
Châteauroux, Fr. 34 46 50N 1 40 E
Chatham, U.K. 15 51 22N 0 32 E
Chattanooga, U.S.A. 91 35 2N 85 17W
Chatteris, U.K. 15 52 27N 0 3 E
Chatton, U.K. 21 55 34N 1 55W
Cheadle, Gr. Manchester, U.K. 18 53 23N 2 14W
Cheadle, Staffs., U.K. 18 52 59N 1 59W
Cheadle Hulme, U.K. 18 53 22N 2 12W
Cheboksary, U.S.S.R. 46 56 8N 47 12 E
Cheddar, U.K. 14 51 16N 2 47W
Cheddleton, U.K. 18 53 5N 2 2W
Chelmarsh, U.K. 14 52 29N 2 25W
Chelmer →, U.K. 15 51 45N 0 42 E
Chelmsford, U.K. 15 51 44N 0 29 E
Cheltenham, U.K. 14 51 55N 2 5W
Chelyabinsk, U.S.S.R. 48 55 10N 61 24 E
Chemnitz, Ger. 42 50 50N 12 55 E
Chengdu, China 60 30 38N 104 2 E
Chepstow, U.K. 17 51 38N 2 40W
Cherbourg, Fr. 34 49 39N 1 40W
Cheremkhovo, U.S.S.R. 49 53 8N 103 1 E
Cherepovets, U.S.S.R. 46 59 5N 37 55 E
Cheriton, U.K. 14 51 3N 1 9W
Cheriton Fitzpaine, U.K. 16 50 51N 3 38W
Cherkassy, U.S.S.R. 47 49 27N 32 4 E
Chernigov, U.S.S.R. 46 51 28N 31 20 E
Chernovtsy, U.S.S.R. 47 48 15N 25 52 E
Chertsey, U.K. 15 51 23N 0 30W
Cherwell →, U.K. 14 51 46N 1 18W
Chesapeake Bay, U.S.A. 92 38 0N 76 12W
Chesham, U.K. 15 51 42N 0 36W
Cheshire □, U.K. 18 53 14N 2 30W
Cheshunt, U.K. 15 51 42N 0 1W
Chesil Beach, U.K. 14 50 37N 2 33W
Chester, U.K. 18 53 12N 2 53W
Chester-le-Street, U.K. 19 54 53N 1 34W
Chesterfield, U.K. 19 53 14N 1 26W
Chesterfield Inlet, Canada 88 63 30N 90 45W
Cheviot, The, U.K. 19 55 29N 2 8W
Cheviot Hills, U.K. 19 55 20N 2 30W
Chew Magna, U.K. 14 51 21N 2 37W
Chiai, China 61 23 29N 120 25 E
Chiba, Jap. 62 35 30N 140 7 E
Chicago, U.S.A. 92 41 53N 87 40W
Chichester, U.K. 15 50 50N 0 47W
Chiclayo, Peru 100 6 42S 79 50W
Chicoutimi, Canada 93 48 28N 71 5W
Chiddingfold, U.K. 15 51 6N 0 37W
Chidley, C., Canada 89 60 23N 64 26W
Chieti, It. 40 42 22N 14 10 E
Chihli, G. of, China 61 38 30N 119 0 E
Chihuahua, Mex. 94 28 40N 106 3W
Chile ■, S. Am. 102 35 0S 72 0W
Chilham, U.K. 15 51 15N 0 59 E
Chillán, Chile 102 36 40S 72 10W
Chilpancingo, Mex. 94 17 30N 99 30W
Chiltern Hills, U.K. 15 51 44N 0 42W
Chilung, Taiwan 61 25 3N 121 45 E
Chimborazo, Ecuad. 100 1 29S 78 55W
Chimbote, Peru 100 9 0S 78 35W
Chimkent, U.S.S.R. 48 42 18N 69 36 E
China ■, Asia 60 30 0N 110 0 E
Chincha Alta, Peru 100 13 25S 76 7W
Chingola, Zam. 81 12 31S 27 53 E
Chipata, Zam. 81 13 38S 32 28 E
Chippenham, U.K. 14 51 27N 2 7W
Chipping Campden, U.K. 14 52 4N 1 48W
Chipping Norton, U.K. 14 51 56N 1 32W
Chipping Ongar, U.K. 15 51 43N 0 15 E
Chipping Sodbury, U.K. 14 51 31N 2 23W
Chirbury, U.K. 14 52 35N 3 6W
Chirnside, U.K. 21 55 47N 2 11W
Chiseldon, U.K. 14 51 30N 1 44W
Chita, U.S.S.R. 49 52 0N 113 35 E
Chittagong, Bangla. 59 22 19N 91 48 E

Chollerton, *U.K.* **21** 55 4N 2 7W
Cholsey, *U.K.* **14** 51 34N 1 10W
Chongjin, *N. Kor.* **61** 41 47N 129 50 E
Chongqing = Chungking, *China* **60** 29 35N 106 25 E
Chorley, *U.K.* **18** 53 39N 2 39W
Chorrera, La, *Pan.* **94** 8 50N 79 50W
Chorzów, *Pol.* **43** 50 18N 18 57 E
Choybalsan, *Mong.* **61** 48 4N 114 30 E
Christchurch, *N.Z.* **71** 43 33S 172 47 E
Christchurch, *U.K.* **14** 50 44N 1 33W
Chuuk, *Pac. Oc.* **64** 7 25N 151 46 E
Chudleigh, *U.K.* **16** 50 35N 3 36W
Chulmleigh, *U.K.* **16** 50 55N 3 52W
Chungking, *China* **60** 29 35N 106 25 E
Chur, *Switz.* **42** 46 52N 9 32 E
Church Stretton, *U.K.* **14** 52 32N 2 49W
Churchdown, *U.K.* **14** 51 53N 2 9W
Churchill →, *Canada* **88** 58 47N 94 12W
Cienfuegos, *Cuba* **95** 22 10N 80 30W
Cincinnati, *U.S.A.* **92** 39 10N 84 26W
Cinderford, *U.K.* **14** 51 49N 2 30W
Cirencester, *U.K.* **14** 51 43N 1 59W
Citlaltépetl, *Mex.* **94** 19 0N 97 20W
Ciudad Bolívar, *Ven.* **100** 8 5N 63 36W
Ciudad Guayana, *Ven.* **100** 8 0N 62 30W
Ciudad Juárez, *Mex.* **94** 31 40N 106 28W
Ciudad Madero, *Mex.* **94** 22 19N 97 50W
Ciudad Obregón, *Mex.* **94** 27 28N 109 59W
Ciudad Real, *Sp.* **37** 38 59N 3 55W
Ciudad Victoria, *Mex.* **94** 23 41N 99 9W
Clabhach, *U.K.* **20** 56 38N 6 36W
Clach Leathad, *U.K.* **20** 56 36N 7 52W
Clachan, *U.K.* **20** 55 45N 5 35W
Clackmannan, *U.K.* **21** 56 10N 3 50W
Clacton-on-Sea, *U.K.* **15** 51 47N 1 10 E
Cladich, *U.K.* **20** 56 21N 5 5W
Clara, *Ire.* **25** 53 20N 7 38W
Clare, *U.K.* **15** 52 5N 0 36 E
Clare □, *Ire.* **25** 52 20N 9 0W
Clare →, *Ire.* **24** 53 22N 9 5W
Clare I., *Ire.* **24** 53 48N 10 0W
Claremorris, *Ire.* **24** 53 45N 9 0W
Clarksville, *U.S.A.* **91** 36 32N 87 20W
Clatteringshaws L., *U.K.* **20** 55 3N 4 17W
Claverley, *U.K.* **14** 52 32N 2 19W
Clay Cross, *U.K.* **19** 53 11N 1 26W
Clay Hd., *U.K.* **18** 54 13N 4 23W
Claydon, *U.K.* **15** 52 6N 1 7 E
Clear, C., *Ire.* **25** 51 26N 9 30W
Clear I., *Ire.* **25** 51 26N 9 30W
Cleator Moor, *U.K.* **18** 54 30N 3 32W
Clee Hills, *U.K.* **14** 52 26N 2 35W
Cleethorpes, *U.K.* **19** 53 33N 0 2W
Cleeve Cloud, *U.K.* **14** 51 56N 2 0W
Clent, *U.K.* **14** 52 25N 2 6W
Cleobury Mortimer, *U.K.* **14** 52 23N 2 28W
Clermont-Ferrand, *Fr.* **35** 45 46N 3 4 E
Clevedon, *U.K.* **14** 51 26N 2 52W
Cleveland, *U.S.A.* **92** 41 28N 81 43W
Cleveland □, *U.K.* **19** 54 35N 1 8 E
Cleveland Hills, *U.K.* **19** 54 25N 1 11W
Clew B., *Ire.* **24** 53 54N 9 50W
Cley, *U.K.* **15** 52 57N 1 3 E
Clifden, *Ire.* **24** 53 30N 10 2W
Cliffe, *U.K.* **15** 51 27N 0 31 E
Clifford, *U.K.* **14** 52 6N 3 6W
Clipston, *U.K.* **15** 52 26N 0 58W
Clitheroe, *U.K.* **18** 53 52N 2 23W
Clonakilty, *Ire.* **25** 51 37N 8 53W
Clonakilty B., *Ire.* **25** 51 33N 8 50W
Cloncurry, *Austral.* **67** 20 40S 140 28 E
Clones, *Ire.* **24** 54 10N 7 13W
Clonmel, *Ire.* **25** 52 22N 7 42W
Closeburn, *U.K.* **21** 55 13N 3 45W
Cloughton, *U.K.* **19** 54 20N 0 27W
Clovelly, *U.K.* **16** 51 0N 4 25W
Clowne, *U.K.* **19** 53 18N 1 16W
Cluj-Napoca, *Rom.* **43** 46 47N 23 38 E
Clun, *U.K.* **14** 52 26N 3 2W
Clun Forest, *U.K.* **14** 52 27N 3 7W
Clunbury, *U.K.* **14** 52 25N 2 55W
Clwyd □, *U.K.* **17** 53 5N 3 20W
Clwyd →, *U.K.* **17** 53 20N 3 30W
Clyde →, *U.K.* **20** 55 56N 4 29W
Clyde, Firth of, *U.K.* **20** 55 20N 5 0W
Clydebank, *U.K.* **20** 55 54N 4 25W
Clydesdale, *U.K.* **21** 55 42N 3 50W
Coalbrookdale, *U.K.* **14** 52 38N 2 30W
Coalburn, *U.K.* **21** 55 35N 3 55W
Coalville, *U.K.* **14** 52 43N 1 21W
Coast Mts., *Canada* **88** 55 0N 129 0W
Coast Ranges, *U.S.A.* **90** 41 0N 123 0W
Coatbridge, *U.K.* **21** 55 52N 4 2W
Coatzacoalcos, *Mex.* **94** 18 7N 94 25W
Cóbh, *Ire.* **25** 51 50N 8 18W
Cobourg Pen., *Austral.* **66** 11 20S 132 15 E
Cochabamba, *Bol.* **100** 17 26S 66 10W
Cochin, *India* **58** 9 59N 76 22 E
Cockburnspath, *U.K.* **21** 55 56N 2 23W
Cockenzie, *U.K.* **21** 55 58N 2 59W
Cockerham, *U.K.* **18** 53 58N 2 49W
Cockermouth, *U.K.* **18** 54 40N 3 22W
Cockfield, *U.K.* **15** 52 8N 0 47 E
Cod, C., *U.S.A.* **93** 42 8N 70 10W
Coddenham, *U.K.* **15** 52 8N 1 8 E
Coffs Harbour, *Austral.* **67** 30 16S 153 5 E
Coggeshall, *U.K.* **15** 51 53N 0 41 E
Coimbatore, *India* **58** 11 2N 76 59 E
Coimbra, *Port.* **37** 40 15N 8 27W
Colac, *Austral.* **70** 38 21S 143 35 E
Colby, *U.K.* **18** 54 6N 4 42W
Colchester, *U.K.* **15** 51 54N 0 55 E
Cold Fell, *U.K.* **18** 54 54N 2 40W
Coldingham, *U.K.* **21** 55 53N 2 10W
Coldstream, *U.K.* **21** 55 39N 2 14W
Colebrooke, *U.K.* **16** 50 45N 3 44W
Coleford, *U.K.* **14** 51 46N 2 38W
Coleraine, *U.K.* **24** 55 8N 6 40W
Coleraine □, *U.K.* **24** 55 8N 6 40 E
Coleshill, *U.K.* **14** 52 30N 1 42W
Colima, *Mex.* **94** 19 14N 103 43W
Colinton, *U.K.* **21** 55 54N 3 17W
Coll, *U.K.* **20** 56 40N 6 35W
Collie, *Austral.* **66** 33 22S 116 8 E
Collier Law Pk., *U.K.* **18** 54 47N 1 59W
Collin, *U.K.* **21** 55 4N 3 30W
Collingbourne, *U.K.* **14** 51 16N 1 39W
Collooney, *Ire.* **24** 54 11N 8 28W
Colmar, *Fr.* **34** 48 5N 7 20 E
Colmonel, *U.K.* **20** 55 8N 4 55W
Colne, *U.K.* **18** 53 51N 2 11W
Colne →, *Essex, U.K.* **15** 51 55N 0 50 E
Colne →, *Herts., U.K.* **15** 51 36N 0 30W
Cologne, *Ger.* **36** 50 56N 6 58 E
Colombia ■, *S. Am.* **100** 3 45N 73 0W
Colombo, *Sri L.* **58** 6 56N 79 58 E
Colón, *Mex.* **94** 20 48N 100 3W
Colonsay, *U.K.* **20** 56 4N 6 12W
Colorado □, *U.S.A.* **90** 37 40N 106 0W
Colorado →, *Calif., U.S.A.* **90** 34 45N 114 40W
Colorado →, *Tex., U.S.A.* **90** 28 36N 95 58W
Colorado Plateau, *U.S.A.* **90** 36 40N 110 30W
Colorado Springs, *U.S.A.* **90** 38 55N 104 50W
Colstorworth, *U.K.* **15** 52 48N 0 37W
Coltishall, *U.K.* **15** 52 44N 1 21 E
Columbia, *Miss., U.S.A.* **90** 31 16N 89 50W
Columbia, *S.C., U.S.A.* **91** 34 0N 81 0W
Columbia →, *N. Am.* **90** 46 15N 124 5W
Columbus, *Ga., U.S.A.* **91** 32 30N 84 58W
Columbus, *Ohio, U.S.A.* **92** 39 57N 83 1W
Colwell, *U.K.* **21** 55 4N 2 4W
Colwich, *U.K.* **14** 52 48N 1 58W
Colwyn Bay, *U.K.* **17** 53 17N 3 44W
Colyton, *U.K.* **16** 50 44N 3 4W
Combe Martin, *U.K.* **16** 51 12N 4 2W
Comber, *U.K.* **24** 54 33N 5 45W
Comeragh Mts., *Ire.* **25** 52 17N 7 35W
Comilla, *Bangla.* **59** 23 28N 91 10 E
Comino, *Malta* **40** 36 0N 14 20 E
Communism Pk., *U.S.S.R.* **48** 38 40N 72 20 E
Como, *It.* **40** 45 48N 9 5 E
Como, L., *It.* **40** 46 5N 9 17 E
Comodoro Rivadavia, *Arg.* **102** 45 50S 67 40W
Comorin, C., *India* **58** 8 3N 77 40 E
Comoro Is. ■, *Ind. Oc.* **73** 12 10S 44 15 E
Compiègne, *Fr.* **34** 49 24N 2 50 E
Comrie, *U.K.* **21** 56 22N 4 0W
Conakry, *Guin.* **78** 9 29N 13 49W
Concepción, *Chile* **102** 36 50S 73 0W
Conchos →, *Mex.* **94** 29 32N 104 25W
Concordia, *Arg.* **102** 31 20S 58 2W
Condover, *U.K.* **14** 52 39N 2 46W
Congleton, *U.K.* **18** 53 10N 2 12W
Congo = Zaïre →, *Africa* **80** 6 4S 12 24 E
Congo ■, *Africa* **80** 1 0S 16 0 E
Congo Basin, *Africa* **72** 0 10S 24 30 E
Congresbury, *U.K.* **14** 51 20N 2 49W
Coningsby, *U.K.* **19** 53 7N 0 9W
Conisbrough, *U.K.* **19** 53 29N 1 12W
Coniston, *U.K.* **18** 54 22N 3 6W
Coniston Water, *U.K.* **18** 54 20N 3 5W
Conn, L., *Ire.* **24** 54 3N 9 15W
Connacht, *Ire.* **24** 53 23N 8 40W
Connah's Quay, *U.K.* **17** 53 13N 3 6W
Connecticut □, *U.S.A.* **93** 41 40N 72 40W
Connecticut →, *U.S.A.* **93** 41 17N 72 21W
Connel, *U.K.* **20** 56 27N 5 24W
Connel Park, *U.K.* **20** 55 22N 4 15W
Connemara, *Ire.* **24** 53 29N 9 45W
Conon →, *U.K.* **23** 57 33N 4 28W
Cononbridge, *U.K.* **23** 57 32N 4 30W
Consett, *U.K.* **18** 54 52N 1 50W
Constance, L. = Bodensee, *Ger.* **42** 47 35N 9 25 E
Constanța, *Rom.* **43** 44 14N 28 38 E
Constantine, *Alg.* **78** 36 25N 6 42 E
Conwy, *U.K.* **17** 53 17N 3 50W
Conwy →, *U.K.* **17** 53 18N 3 50W
Cook, Mt., *N.Z.* **71** 43 36S 170 9 E
Cook Is., *Pac. Oc.* **65** 17 0S 160 0W
Cook Strait, *N.Z.* **71** 41 15S 174 29 E
Cookham, *U.K.* **15** 51 33N 0 42W
Cookstown, *U.K.* **24** 54 40N 6 43W
Cookstown □, *U.K.* **24** 54 40N 6 43W
Coolgardie, *Austral.* **66** 30 55S 121 8 E
Cootamundra, *Austral.* **70** 34 36S 148 1 E
Cootehill, *Ire.* **24** 54 5N 7 5W
Copenhagen, *Den.* **45** 55 41N 12 34 E
Coppermine, *Canada* **88** 67 50N 115 5W
Coppermine →, *Canada* **88** 67 49N 116 4W
Copythorne, *U.K.* **14** 50 56N 1 34W
Coquet →, *U.K.* **19** 55 18N 1 45W
Coquet, I., *U.K.* **21** 55 21N 1 30W
Coral Sea, *Pac. Oc.* **64** 15 0S 150 0 E
Coral Sea Islands Terr., *Austral.* **67** 20 0S 155 0 E
Corbridge, *U.K.* **21** 54 58N 2 0W
Corby, *U.K.* **15** 52 29N 0 41W
Corby Glen, *U.K.* **15** 52 49N 0 31W
Córdoba, *Arg.* **102** 31 20S 64 10W
Córdoba, *Sp.* **37** 37 50N 4 50W
Cordova, *U.S.A.* **88** 60 36N 145 45W
Corfe Castle, *U.K.* **14** 50 37N 2 3W
Corfe Mullen, *U.K.* **14** 50 45N 2 0W
Corfu = Kérkira, *Greece* **41** 39 38N 19 50 E
Corinth, G. of, *Greece* **41** 38 16N 22 30 E
Cork, *Ire.* **25** 51 54N 8 30W
Cork □, *Ire.* **25** 51 50N 8 50W
Cork Harbour, *Ire.* **25** 51 46N 8 16W
Corner Brook, *Canada* **89** 48 57N 57 58W
Cornforth, *U.K.* **19** 54 42N 1 28W
Cornwall □, *U.K.* **16** 50 26N 4 40W
Cornwall, C., *U.K.* **16** 50 8N 5 42W
Coro, *Ven.* **100** 11 25N 69 41W
Coromandel Coast, *India* **58** 12 30N 81 0 E
Coronation Gulf, *Canada* **88** 68 25N 110 0W
Corpus Christi, *U.S.A.* **90** 27 50N 97 28W
Corrib, L., *Ire.* **24** 53 5N 9 10W
Corrie, *U.K.* **20** 55 39N 5 10W
Corrientes, *Arg.* **102** 27 30S 58 45W
Corringham, *U.K.* **19** 53 25N 0 42W
Corryvreckan, G. of, *U.K.* **20** 56 10N 5 44W
Corsewall Pt., *U.K.* **20** 55 0N 5 10W
Corsham, *U.K.* **14** 51 25N 2 11W
Corsica, I., *Medit. S.* **35** 42 0N 9 0 E
Corsley, *U.K.* **14** 51 12N 2 14W
Corsock, *U.K.* **21** 55 54N 3 56W
Corton, *U.K.* **15** 52 31N 1 46 E
Corumbá, *Brazil* **100** 19 0S 57 30W
Coruña, La, *Sp.* **37** 43 20N 8 25W
Corve →, *U.K.* **14** 52 22N 2 43W
Coseley, *U.K.* **14** 52 33N 2 6W
Cosenza, *It.* **40** 39 17N 16 14 E
Cosham, *U.K.* **14** 50 51N 1 3W
Costa Rica ■, *Cent. Am.* **95** 10 0N 84 0W
Costessey, *U.K.* **15** 52 40N 1 11 E
Côte d'Or, *Fr.* **34** 47 10N 4 50 E
Cotherstone, *U.K.* **18** 54 34N 1 59W
Cotonou, *Benin* **78** 6 20N 2 25 E
Cotopaxi, Vol., *Ecuad.* **100** 0 40S 78 30W
Cotswold Hills, *U.K.* **14** 51 42N 2 10W
Cottbus, *Ger.* **42** 51 44N 14 20 E
Cottenham, *U.K.* **15** 52 18N 0 8 E
Cottingham, *U.K.* **19** 53 47N 0 29W
Coulport, *U.K.* **20** 56 3N 4 53W
Council Bluffs, *U.S.A.* **90** 41 20N 95 50W
Coupar Angus, *U.K.* **21** 56 33N 3 17W
Coventry, *U.K.* **14** 52 25N 1 31W
Cover →, *U.K.* **18** 54 14N 1 45W
Coverack, *U.K.* **16** 50 2N 5 6W
Covington, *U.S.A.* **92** 39 5N 84 30W
Cowal, *U.K.* **20** 56 5N 5 8W
Cowan, L., *Austral.* **66** 31 45S 121 45 E
Cowbridge, *U.K.* **17** 51 28N 3 28W
Cowdenbeath, *U.K.* **21** 56 7N 3 20W
Cowes, *U.K.* **14** 50 45N 1 18W
Cowfold, *U.K.* **15** 50 58N 0 16W
Cowley, *U.K.* **14** 51 43N 1 12W
Cowpen, *U.K.* **21** 55 8N 1 34W
Cowra, *Austral.* **70** 33 49S 148 42 E
Craigavon □, *U.K.* **24** 54 30N 6 25W
Craighouse, *U.K.* **20** 55 50N 5 58W
Craignish, L., *U.K.* **20** 56 11N 5 32W
Crail, *U.K.* **21** 56 16N 2 38W
Craiova, *Rom.* **43** 44 21N 23 48 E
Cramlington, *U.K.* **21** 55 5N 1 36W
Cranborne, *U.K.* **14** 50 55N 1 55W
Cranborne Chase, *U.K.* **14** 50 56N 2 6W
Cranbrook, *Canada* **88** 49 30N 115 46W
Cranbrook, *U.K.* **15** 51 6N 0 33 E
Cranleigh, *U.K.* **15** 51 8N 0 29W
Cranshaws, *U.K.* **21** 55 51N 2 30W
Cranwell, *U.K.* **19** 53 4N 0 29W
Craven Arms, *U.K.* **14** 52 27N 2 49W
Crawford, *U.K.* **21** 55 28N 3 40W
Crawley, *U.K.* **15** 51 7N 0 10W
Credenhill, *U.K.* **14** 52 6N 2 49W
Crediton, *U.K.* **16** 50 47N 3 39W
Cree →, *U.K.* **20** 54 51N 4 24W
Creeside, *U.K.* **20** 55 4N 4 41W
Creetown, *U.K.* **20** 54 54N 4 23W
Cremona, *It.* **40** 45 8N 10 2 E
Crete, I., *Greece* **41** 35 15N 25 0 E
Creusot, Le, *Fr.* **34** 46 48N 4 24 E
Crewe, *U.K.* **18** 53 6N 2 28W
Crewkerne, *U.K.* **14** 50 53N 2 48W
Crianlarich, *U.K.* **20** 56 24N 4 37W
Criccieth, *U.K.* **17** 52 55N 4 15W
Crick, *U.K.* **14** 52 22N 1 9W
Crickhowell, *U.K.* **17** 51 52N 3 8W
Cricklade, *U.K.* **14** 51 38N 1 50W
Crieff, *U.K.* **21** 56 22N 3 50W
Criffell, *U.K.* **21** 54 56N 3 38W
Crimea, *U.S.S.R.* **47** 45 0N 34 0 E
Crinan, *U.K.* **20** 56 6N 5 34W
Crinan Canal, *U.K.* **20** 56 4N 5 30W
Croaghpatrick, *Ire.* **24** 53 46N 9 40W
Croatia □, *Yug.* **40** 45 30N 17 0 E
Crocketford, *U.K.* **21** 55 3N 3 49W
Croglin, *U.K.* **18** 54 50N 2 37W
Cromarty, *U.K.* **23** 57 40N 4 2W
Cromarty Firth, *U.K.* **23** 57 40N 4 15W
Cromer, *U.K.* **15** 52 56N 1 18 E
Crondall, *U.K.* **15** 51 13N 0 51W
Crook, *U.K.* **19** 54 43N 1 45W
Crooklands, *U.K.* **18** 54 16N 2 43W
Crosby, *Cumbria, U.K.* **18** 54 45N 3 25W
Crosby, *Merseyside, U.K.* **18** 53 30N 3 2W
Crosby Ravensworth, *U.K.* **18** 54 34N 2 35W
Cross Fell, *U.K.* **18** 54 44N 2 29W
Crosshaven, *Ire.* **25** 51 48N 8 19W
Crosshill, *U.K.* **20** 55 19N 4 39W
Crouch →, *U.K.* **15** 51 37N 0 53 E
Crow Hd., *Ire.* **25** 51 34N 10 9W
Crow Sound, *U.K.* **16** 49 56N 6 16W
Crowborough, *U.K.* **15** 51 3N 0 9 E
Crowland, *U.K.* **15** 52 41N 0 10W
Crowle, *U.K.* **19** 53 36N 0 49W
Croyde, *U.K.* **16** 51 7N 4 13W
Croydon, *U.K.* **15** 51 18N 0 5W
Crudgington, *U.K.* **14** 52 46N 2 33W
Crummock Water, *U.K.* **18** 54 33N 3 18W
Cruzeiro do Sul, *Brazil* **100** 7 35S 72 35W
Cuba ■, *W. Ind.* **95** 22 0N 79 0W
Cuckfield, *U.K.* **15** 51 0N 0 8W
Cúcuta, *Col.* **100** 7 54N 72 31W
Cudworth, *U.K.* **19** 53 35N 1 25W
Cuenca, *Ecuad.* **100** 2 50S 79 9W
Cuenca, *Sp.* **37** 40 5N 2 10W
Cuernavaca, *Mex.* **94** 18 55N 99 15W
Cuiabá, *Brazil* **101** 15 30S 56 0W
Cuillin Hills, *U.K.* **22** 57 14N 6 15W
Cuillin Sd., *U.K.* **22** 57 4N 6 20W
Culiacán, *Mex.* **94** 24 50N 107 23W
Cullen, *U.K.* **23** 57 45N 2 50W
Culloden Moor, *U.K.* **23** 57 29N 4 7W
Cullompton, *U.K.* **16** 50 52N 3 23W
Culm →, *U.K.* **16** 50 46N 3 31W
Culrain, *U.K.* **23** 57 55N 4 25W
Culross, *U.K.* **21** 56 4N 3 38W
Cumaná, *Ven.* **100** 10 30N 64 5W
Cumberland Plateau, *U.S.A.* **91** 36 0N 84 30W
Cumbrae Is., *U.K.* **20** 55 46N 4 54W
Cumbria □, *U.K.* **18** 54 35N 2 55W
Cumbrian Mts., *U.K.* **18** 54 30N 3 0W
Cummertrees, *U.K.* **21** 55 0N 3 20W
Cumnock, *U.K.* **20** 55 27N 4 18W
Cumnor, *U.K.* **14** 51 44N 1 20W
Cumwhinton, *U.K.* **18** 54 51N 2 49W
Cúneo, *It.* **40** 44 23N 7 31 E
Cunninghame, *U.K.* **20** 55 38N 4 35W
Cupar, *U.K.* **21** 56 20N 3 0W
Curitiba, *Brazil* **102** 25 20S 49 10W
Currie, *U.K.* **21** 55 53N 3 17W
Curry Rivel, *U.K.* **14** 51 2N 2 52W
Cuttack, *India* **59** 20 25N 85 57 E
Cuzco, *Peru* **100** 13 32S 72 0W
Cwmbran, *U.K.* **17** 51 39N 3 0W
Cyclades = Kikládhes, *Greece* **41** 37 20N 24 30 E
Cyprus ■, *Medit. S.* **47** 35 0N 33 0 E
Czechoslovakia ■, *Europe* **42** 49 0N 17 0 E
Częstochowa, *Pol.* **43** 50 49N 19 7 E

D

Da Lat, *Viet.* **63** 11 56N 108 25 E
Da Nang, *Viet.* **63** 16 4N 108 13 E
Dacca, *Bangla.* **59** 23 43N 90 26 E
Daer →, *U.K.* **21** 55 23N 3 39W
Dailly, *U.K.* **20** 55 16N 4 44W
Daingean, *Ire.* **25** 53 18N 7 15W
Dakar, *Sene.* **78** 14 34N 17 29W
Dakhla, *W. Sah.* **78** 23 50N 15 53W
Dalbeattie, *U.K.* **21** 54 55N 3 50W
Dalian, *China* **61** 38 50N 121 40 E
Dalkeith, *U.K.* **21** 55 54N 3 5W
Dallas, *U.S.A.* **91** 32 50N 96 50W
Dalmally, *U.K.* **20** 56 25N 5 0W
Dalmatia, *Yug.* **40** 43 20N 17 0 E
Dalmellington, *U.K.* **20** 55 20N 4 25W
Daloa, *Ivory C.* **78** 7 0N 6 30W
Dalry, *U.K.* **20** 55 44N 4 42W
Dalrymple, *U.K.* **20** 55 24N 4 36W
Dalton, *Cumbria, U.K.* **18** 54 9N 3 11W
Dalton, *Dumf. & Gall., U.K.* **21** 55 3N 3 22W
Dalton, *N. Yorks., U.K.* **19** 54 28N 1 32W
Dalwhinnie, *U.K.* **23** 56 56N 4 14W
Damascus, *Syria* **57** 33 30N 36 18 E
Damerham, *U.K.* **14** 50 57N 1 52W
Dampier, *Austral.* **66** 20 41S 116 42 E
Dandenong, *Austral.* **70** 38 0S 145 15 E
Dandong, *China* **61** 40 10N 124 20 E
Dannevirke, *N.Z.* **71** 40 12S 176 8 E
Danube →, *Europe* **43** 45 20N 29 40 E
Dar-es-Salaam, *Tanz.* **80** 6 50S 39 12 E
Dar'ā, *Syria* **57** 32 36N 36 7 E
Dardanelles, *Turk.* **47** 40 0N 26 0 E
Darent →, *U.K.* **15** 51 22N 0 12 E

Dargaville, *N.Z.* 71 35 57S 173 52 E
Darién, G. del, *Col.* 95 9 0N 77 0W
Darlaston, *U.K.* 14 52 35N 2 1W
Darling →, *Austral.* 70 34 4S 141 54 E
Darling Ra., *Austral.* 66 32 30S 116 0 E
Darlington, *U.K.* 19 54 33N 1 33W
Darmstadt, *Ger.* 42 49 51N 8 40 E
Dart →, *U.K.* 16 50 24N 3 36W
Dartford, *U.K.* 15 51 26N 0 15 E
Dartington, *U.K.* 16 50 26N 3 42W
Dartmoor, *U.K.* 16 50 36N 4 0W
Dartmouth, *Canada* 93 44 40N 63 30W
Dartmouth, *U.K.* 16 50 21N 3 35W
Darton, *U.K.* 19 53 36N 1 32W
Darvel, *U.K.* 20 55 37N 4 20W
Darwen, *U.K.* 18 53 42N 2 29W
Darwin, *Austral.* 66 12 25S 130 51 E
Dasht-e Kavīr, *Iran* 57 34 30N 55 0 E
Dasht-e Lūt, *Iran* 57 31 30N 58 0 E
Datong, *China* 61 40 6N 113 18 E
Dauphin, *Canada* 88 51 9N 100 5W
Dauphiné, *Fr.* 35 45 15N 5 25 E
Davao, *Phil.* 63 7 0N 125 40 E
Davenport, *U.S.A.* 92 41 30N 90 40W
Daventry, *U.K.* 14 52 16N 1 10W
David, *Pan.* 95 8 30N 82 30W
Davis Str., *N. Am.* 89 65 0N 58 0W
Dawley, *U.K.* 14 52 40N 2 29W
Dawlish, *U.K.* 16 50 34N 3 28W
Dawson, *Canada* 88 64 10N 139 30W
Dawson Creek, *Canada* 88 55 45N 120 15W
Dayton, *U.S.A.* 92 39 45N 84 10W
De Aar, *S. Afr.* 81 30 39S 24 0 E
De Grey →, *Austral.* 66 20 12S 119 13 E
Dead Sea, *Asia* 57 31 30N 35 30 E
Deal, *U.K.* 15 51 13N 1 25 E
Dean, Forest of, *U.K.* 14 51 50N 2 35W
Dearham, *U.K.* 18 54 43N 3 28W
Dease Lake, *Canada* 88 58 25N 130 6W
Death Valley, *U.S.A.* 90 36 19N 116 52W
Deben →, *U.K.* 15 52 4N 1 19 E
Debenham, *U.K.* 15 52 14N 1 10 E
Debrecen, *Hung.* 43 47 33N 21 42 E
Deccan, *India* 58 18 0N 79 0 E
Deddington, *U.K.* 14 51 58N 1 19W
Dee →, *Scotland, U.K.* 23 57 4N 2 7W
Dee →, *Wales, U.K.* 17 53 15N 3 7W
Deeping St. Nicholas, *U.K.* 15 52 44N 0 11W
Deeping Fen, *U.K.* 15 52 45N 0 15W
Dehra Dun, *India* 58 30 20N 78 4 E
Delabole, *U.K.* 16 50 37N 4 45W
Delaware □, *U.S.A.* 93 39 0N 75 40W
Delaware →, *U.S.A.* 93 39 20N 75 25W
Delft, *Neth.* 36 52 1N 4 22 E
Delhi, *India* 58 28 38N 77 17 E
Den Helder, *Neth.* 36 52 57N 4 45 E
Denbigh, *U.K.* 17 53 12N 3 26W
Denby Dale, *U.K.* 19 53 35N 1 40W
Deniliquin, *Austral.* 70 35 30S 144 58 E
Denizli, *Turk.* 47 37 42N 29 2 E
Denmark ■, *Europe* 45 55 30N 9 0 E
Denmark Str., *Atl. Oc.* 103 66 0N 30 0W
Denny, *U.K.* 21 56 1N 3 55W
Dent, *U.K.* 18 54 17N 2 28W
Denton, *E. Sussex, U.K.* 15 50 48N 0 5 E
Denton, *Gr. Manchester, U.K.* 18 53 26N 2 10W
Denton, *Lincs., U.K.* 19 52 52N 0 42W
Denver, *U.S.A.* 90 39 45N 105 0W
Derby, *U.K.* 19 52 55N 1 28W
Derby □, *U.K.* 19 52 55N 1 28W
Derg →, *U.K.* 24 54 42N 7 26W
Derg, L., *Ire.* 25 53 0N 8 20W
Derry = Londonderry, *U.K.* 24 55 0N 7 20W
Derryveagh Mts., *Ire.* 24 55 0N 8 40W
Dervaig, *U.K.* 20 56 35N 6 13W
Derwent →, *Derby, U.K.* 19 52 53N 1 17W
Derwent →, *N. Yorks., U.K.* 19 53 45N 0 57W
Derwent →, *Tyne & Wear, U.K.* 21 54 58N 1 40W
Derwent Water, L., *U.K.* 18 54 35N 3 9W
Des Moines, *U.S.A.* 91 41 35N 93 37W
Des Moines →, *U.S.A.* 91 40 23N 91 25W
Desborough, *U.K.* 15 52 27N 0 50W
Desford, *U.K.* 14 52 38N 1 19W
Dessau, *Ger.* 42 51 49N 12 15 E
Detroit, *U.S.A.* 92 42 23N 83 5W
Deurne, *Belg.* 36 51 12N 4 24 E
Deventer, *Neth.* 36 52 15N 6 10 E
Deveron →, *U.K.* 23 57 40N 2 31W
Devizes, *U.K.* 14 51 21N 2 0W
Devonport, *N.Z.* 71 36 49S 174 49 E
Devonport, *U.K.* 16 50 23N 4 11W
Devonshire □, *U.K.* 16 50 50N 3 40W
Dewsbury, *U.K.* 19 53 42N 1 38W
Dhanbad, *India* 59 23 50N 86 30 E
Dharwad, *India* 58 15 22N 75 15 E
Dhule, *India* 58 20 58N 74 50 E
Diamantina →, *Austral.* 67 26 45S 139 10 E
Dibden, *U.K.* 14 50 53N 1 24W
Didcot, *U.K.* 14 51 36N 1 14W
Dieppe, *Fr.* 34 49 54N 1 4 E
Dijon, *Fr.* 34 47 20N 5 0 E
Dillingham, *U.S.A.* 88 59 5N 158 30W
Dinaric Alps, *Yug.* 40 44 0N 16 30 E
Dingle, *Ire.* 25 52 9N 10 17W
Dingle B., *Ire.* 25 52 3N 10 20W
Dingwall, *U.K.* 23 57 36N 4 26W
Diss, *U.K.* 15 52 23N 1 6 E
Distington, *U.K.* 18 54 35N 3 33W
Ditchingham, *U.K.* 15 52 28N 1 26 E
Ditchling Beacon, *U.K.* 15 50 49N 0 7W
Dittisham, *U.K.* 16 50 22N 3 36W
Ditton Priors, *U.K.* 14 52 30N 2 33W
Diyarbakir, *Turk.* 47 37 55N 40 18 E
Dizzard Pt., *U.K.* 16 50 46N 4 38W
Djibouti ■, *Africa* 56 12 0N 43 0 E
Dnepr →, *U.S.S.R.* 46 46 30N 32 18 E
Dneprodzerzhinsk, *U.S.S.R.* 47 48 32N 34 37 E
Dnepropetrovsk, *U.S.S.R.* 47 48 30N 35 0 E
Dnestr →, *U.S.S.R.* 47 46 18N 30 17 E
Dobrich, *Bulg.* 41 43 37N 27 49 E
Docking, *U.K.* 15 52 55N 0 39 E
Doddington, *Cambs., U.K.* 15 52 29N 0 3 E
Doddington, *Northumberland, U.K.* 21 55 33N 2 0W
Dodecanese, *Greece* 41 36 35N 27 0 E
Dodman Pt., *U.K.* 16 50 13N 4 49W
Dodoma, *Tanz.* 80 6 8S 35 45 E
Dogger Bank, *N. Sea* 26 54 50N 2 0 E
Dolgarrog, *U.K.* 17 53 11N 3 50W
Dolgellau, *U.K.* 17 52 44N 3 53W
Dollar, *U.K.* 21 56 9N 3 41W
Dolomites, *It.* 40 46 30N 11 40 E
Dolphinton, *U.K.* 21 55 42N 3 28W
Dolton, *U.K.* 16 50 53N 4 2W
Dominica ■, *W. Ind.* 94 15 20N 61 20W
Dominican Rep. ■, *W. Ind.* 95 19 0N 70 30W
Don →, *Humberside, U.K.* 19 53 41N 0 51W
Don →, *Grampian, U.K.* 23 57 14N 2 5W
Don →, *U.S.S.R.* 47 47 4N 39 18 E
Donaghadee, *U.K.* 24 54 38N 5 32W
Doncaster, *U.K.* 19 53 31N 1 9W
Dondra Head, *Sri L.* 58 5 55N 80 40 E
Donegal, *Ire.* 24 54 39N 8 8W
Donegal □, *Ire.* 24 54 53N 8 0W
Donegal B., *Ire.* 24 54 30N 8 35W
Donetsk, *U.S.S.R.* 47 48 0N 37 45 E
Dongting Hu, *China* 61 29 18N 112 45 E
Donhead, *U.K.* 14 51 1N 2 8W
Donington, *U.K.* 19 52 54N 0 12W
Donna Nook, Pt., *U.K.* 19 53 29N 0 9 E
Doon →, *U.K.* 20 55 26N 4 41W
Doon, L., *U.K.* 20 55 15N 4 22W
Dorchester, *Dorset, U.K.* 14 50 42N 2 28W
Dorchester, *Oxon., U.K.* 14 51 38N 1 10W
Dordrecht, *Neth.* 36 51 48N 4 39 E
Dorking, *U.K.* 15 51 14N 0 20W
Dornoch, *U.K.* 23 57 52N 4 0W
Dornoch Firth, *U.K.* 23 57 52N 4 0W
Dorset □, *U.K.* 14 50 48N 2 25W
Dorstone, *U.K.* 14 52 4N 3 0W
Dortmund, *Ger.* 36 51 32N 7 28 E
Douai, *Fr.* 34 50 21N 3 4 E
Douala, *Cam.* 80 4 0N 9 45 E
Douglas, *I. of M., U.K.* 18 54 9N 4 29W
Douglas, *Strathclyde, U.K.* 21 55 33N 3 50W
Douglas Hd., *U.K.* 18 54 9N 4 28W
Doune, *U.K.* 21 56 12N 4 3W
Dounreay, *U.K.* 23 58 34N 3 44W
Douro →, *Port.* 37 41 8N 8 40W
Dove →, *N. Yorks., U.K.* 19 54 20N 0 55W
Dove →, *Staffs., U.K.* 18 52 51N 1 36W
Dove Dale, *U.K.* 19 53 10N 1 47W
Dover, *U.K.* 15 51 7N 1 19 E
Dover, Str. of, *Europe* 34 51 0N 1 30 E
Doveridge, *U.K.* 18 52 54N 1 49 E
Dovey →, *U.K.* 17 52 32N 4 0W
Down □, *U.K.* 24 54 20N 6 0W
Downham, *U.K.* 15 52 26N 0 15 E
Downham Market, *U.K.* 15 52 36N 0 22 E
Downpatrick, *U.K.* 24 54 20N 5 43W
Downpatrick Hd., *Ire.* 24 54 20N 9 21W
Downton, *U.K.* 14 51 0N 1 44W
Drake Passage, *S. Oc.* 103 58 0S 68 0W
Drakensberg, *S. Afr.* 81 31 0S 28 0 E
Drammen, *Nor.* 45 59 42N 10 12 E
Drava →, *Yug.* 43 45 33N 18 55 E
Dreghorn, *U.K.* 20 55 36N 4 30W
Drenthe □, *Neth.* 36 52 52N 6 40 E
Dresden, *Ger.* 42 51 2N 13 45 E
Driffield, *U.K.* 19 54 0N 0 25W
Drina →, *Yug.* 41 44 53N 19 21 E
Drogheda, *Ire.* 24 53 45N 6 20W
Droichead Nua, *Ire.* 25 53 11N 6 50W
Droitwich, *U.K.* 14 52 16N 2 10W
Dronfield, *U.K.* 19 53 18N 1 29W
Dronning Maud Land, *Ant.* 103 72 30S 12 0 E
Drumheller, *Canada* 88 51 25N 112 40W
Drumjohn, *U.K.* 20 55 14N 4 15W
Drummondville, *Canada* 93 45 55N 72 25W
Drummore, *U.K.* 20 54 41N 4 53W
Druridge B., *U.K.* 21 55 16N 1 32W
Drymen, *U.K.* 20 56 4N 4 28W
Dubai, *U.A.E.* 57 25 18N 55 20 E
Dubbo, *Austral.* 70 32 11S 148 35 E
Dubh Artach, *U.K.* 20 56 8N 6 40W
Dublin, *Ire.* 24 53 20N 6 18W
Dublin □, *Ire.* 24 53 24N 6 20W
Dublin B., *Ire.* 25 53 18N 6 5W
Dubrovnik, *Yug.* 41 42 39N 18 6 E
Duddington, *U.K.* 15 52 36N 0 32W
Duddon →, *U.K.* 18 54 12N 3 15W
Dudley, *U.K.* 14 52 30N 2 5W
Duero →, *Sp.* 37 41 8N 8 40W
Duffield, *U.K.* 19 52 59N 1 30W
Dufftown, *U.K.* 23 57 26N 3 9W
Duisburg, *Ger.* 36 51 27N 6 42 E
Dukinfield, *U.K.* 18 53 29N 2 7W
Duluth, *U.S.A.* 92 46 48N 92 10W
Dulverton, *U.K.* 14 51 2N 3 33W
Dumbarton, *U.K.* 20 55 58N 4 35W
Dumfries, *U.K.* 21 55 4N 3 37W
Dumfries & Galloway □, *U.K.* 21 55 0N 4 0W
Dun Laoghaire, *Ire.* 25 53 17N 6 9W
Dunans, *U.K.* 20 56 4N 5 9W
Dunbar, *U.K.* 21 56 0N 2 32W
Dunblane, *U.K.* 21 56 10N 3 58W
Duncansby Head, *U.K.* 23 58 39N 3 0W
Dunchurch, *U.K.* 14 52 21N 1 19W
Dundalk, *Ire.* 24 54 1N 6 25W
Dundalk Bay, *Ire.* 24 53 55N 6 15W
Dundee, *U.K.* 21 56 29N 3 0W
Dundrennan, *U.K.* 21 54 49N 3 56W
Dundrum, *U.K.* 24 54 17N 5 50W
Dundrum B., *U.K.* 24 54 12N 5 40W
Dunedin, *N.Z.* 71 45 50S 170 33 E
Dunfermline, *U.K.* 21 56 5N 3 28W
Dungannon, *U.K.* 24 54 30N 6 47W
Dungannon □, *U.K.* 24 54 30N 6 55W
Dungarvan, *Ire.* 25 52 6N 7 40W
Dungarvan Bay, *Ire.* 25 52 5N 7 35W
Dungavel, *U.K.* 21 55 37N 4 7W
Dungeness, *U.K.* 15 50 54N 0 59 E
Dunkeld, *U.K.* 23 56 34N 3 36W
Dunkerque, *Fr.* 34 51 2N 2 20 E
Dunkery Beacon, *U.K.* 14 51 15N 3 37W
Dunkirk = Dunkerque, *Fr.* 34 51 2N 2 20 E
Dúnleary = Dun Laoghaire, *Ire.* 25 53 17N 6 9W
Dunlop, *U.K.* 20 55 43N 4 32W
Dunmanus B., *Ire.* 25 51 31N 9 50W
Dunmore Hd., *Ire.* 25 52 10N 10 35W
Dunnet Hd., *U.K.* 23 58 38N 3 22W
Dunning, *U.K.* 21 56 18N 3 37W
Dunoon, *U.K.* 20 55 57N 4 56W
Duns, *U.K.* 21 55 47N 2 20W
Dunscore, *U.K.* 21 55 8N 3 48W
Dunsford, *U.K.* 16 50 41N 3 40W
Dunstable, *U.K.* 15 51 53N 0 31W
Dunster, *U.K.* 14 51 11N 3 28W
Dunston, *U.K.* 14 52 46N 2 7W
Dunvegan, *U.K.* 22 57 26N 6 35W
Durango, *Mex.* 94 24 3N 104 39W
Durban, *S. Afr.* 81 29 49S 31 1 E
Düren, *Ger.* 36 50 48N 6 30 E
Durg, *India* 59 21 15N 81 22 E
Durgapur, *India* 59 23 30N 87 20 E
Durham, *U.K.* 19 54 47N 1 34W
Durham, *U.S.A.* 91 36 0N 78 55W
Durham □, *U.K.* 18 54 42N 1 45W
Durlston Hd., *U.K.* 14 50 35N 1 58W
Durness, *U.K.* 23 58 34N 4 45W
Durrësi, *Alb.* 41 41 19N 19 28 E
Durrington, *U.K.* 14 51 12N 1 47W
Dursley, *U.K.* 14 51 41N 2 21W
Dushanbe, *U.S.S.R.* 48 38 33N 68 48 E
Düsseldorf, *Ger.* 36 51 15N 6 46 E
Duyun, *China* 60 26 18N 107 29 E
Dvina, N. →, *U.S.S.R.* 46 61 40N 45 30 E
Dyfed □, *U.K.* 17 52 0N 4 30W
Dymchurch, *U.K.* 15 51 2N 1 0 E
Dymock, *U.K.* 14 51 58N 2 27W
Dysart, *U.K.* 21 56 8N 3 8W
Dzerzhinsk, *U.S.S.R.* 46 56 14N 43 30 E
Dzhambul, *U.S.S.R.* 48 42 54N 71 22 E
Dzungaria, *China* 60 44 10N 88 0 E

E

Eaglesfield, *U.K.* 21 55 3N 3 12W
Eagleshan, *U.K.* 20 55 44N 4 18W
Eakring, *U.K.* 19 53 9N 0 59W
Ealing, *U.K.* 15 51 30N 0 19W
Earby, *U.K.* 18 53 55N 2 8W
Eardisland, *U.K.* 14 52 14N 2 50W
Eardisley, *U.K.* 14 52 8N 3 0W
Earith, *U.K.* 15 52 21N 0 1 E
Earl Shilton, *U.K.* 14 52 35N 1 20W
Earl Soham, *U.K.* 15 52 14N 1 15 E
Earls Barton, *U.K.* 15 52 16N 0 44W
Earl's Colne, *U.K.* 15 51 56N 0 43 E
Earlsferry, *U.K.* 21 56 11N 2 50W
Earlston, *U.K.* 21 55 39N 2 40W
Earn →, *U.K.* 21 56 20N 3 19W
Earn, L., *U.K.* 20 56 23N 4 14W
Earsdon, *U.K.* 21 55 4N 1 30W
Easebourne, *U.K.* 15 51 0N 0 42W
Easington, *Durham, U.K.* 19 54 50N 1 24W
Easington, *Humberside, U.K.* 19 53 40N 0 7 E
Easington Colliery, *U.K.* 19 54 49N 1 19W
Easingwold, *U.K.* 19 54 8N 1 11W
East Anglian Hts., *U.K.* 15 52 10N 0 17 E
East Bergholt, *U.K.* 15 51 58N 1 2 E
East Brent, *U.K.* 14 51 14N 2 55W
East China Sea, *Asia* 61 30 5N 126 0 E
East Cowes, *U.K.* 14 50 45N 1 17W
East Dereham, *U.K.* 15 52 40N 0 57 E
East Fen, *U.K.* 19 53 4N 0 5 E
East Germany = Germany ■, *Europe* 42 52 0N 10 0 E
East Grinstead, *U.K.* 15 51 8N 0 1W
East Harling, *U.K.* 15 52 26N 0 55 E
East Ilsley, *U.K.* 14 51 33N 1 15W
East Indies, *Asia* 50 0 0 120 0 E
East Kilbride, *U.K.* 20 55 46N 4 10W
East Kirkby, *U.K.* 19 53 5N 1 15W
East Linton, *U.K.* 21 56 0N 2 40W
East London, *S. Afr.* 81 33 0S 27 55 E
East Markham, *U.K.* 19 53 15N 0 53W
East Moor, *U.K.* 19 53 15N 1 30W
East Retford, *U.K.* 19 53 19N 0 55W
East Siberian Sea, *U.S.S.R.* 49 73 0N 160 0 E
East Sussex □, *U.K.* 15 51 0N 0 20 E
East Wemyss, *U.K.* 21 56 8N 3 5W
East Wittering, *U.K.* 15 50 46N 0 53W
East Woodhay, *U.K.* 14 51 21N 1 26W
Eastbourne, *U.K.* 15 50 46N 0 18 E
Eastchurch, *U.K.* 15 51 23N 0 53 E
Easter Islands, *Pac. Oc.* 65 27 0S 109 0W
Eastern Ghats, *India* 58 14 0N 78 50 E
Eastleigh, *U.K.* 14 50 58N 1 21W
Eastnor, *U.K.* 14 52 2N 2 22W
Easton, *Avon, U.K.* 14 51 28N 2 42W
Easton, *Dorset, U.K.* 14 50 32N 2 27W
Easton, *Northants., U.K.* 15 52 37N 0 31W
Eastry, *U.K.* 15 51 15N 1 19 E
Eastwood, *U.K.* 19 53 2N 1 17W
Eaton, *U.K.* 15 52 52N 0 46W
Eaton Socon, *U.K.* 15 52 13N 0 18W
Eau Claire, *U.S.A.* 92 44 46N 91 30W
Ebberston, *U.K.* 19 54 14N 0 35W
Ebbw Vale, *U.K.* 17 51 47N 3 12W
Ebro →, *Sp.* 37 40 43N 0 54 E
Ecclefechan, *U.K.* 21 55 3N 3 18W
Eccleshall, *U.K.* 14 52 52N 2 14W
Ech Cheliff, *Alg.* 78 36 10N 1 20 E
Echo Bay, *Canada* 88 66 5N 117 55W
Echuca, *Austral.* 70 36 10S 144 20 E
Eck, L., *U.K.* 20 56 5N 5 0W
Eckington, *U.K.* 19 53 19N 1 21W
Ecuador ■, *S. Am.* 100 2 0S 78 0W
Edam, *Neth.* 36 52 31N 5 3 E
Eday, *U.K.* 23 59 11N 2 47W
Eddrachillis B., *U.K.* 22 58 16N 5 10W
Eddystone, *U.K.* 16 50 11N 4 16W
Ede, *Neth.* 36 52 4N 5 40 E
Eden →, *U.K.* 18 54 57N 3 2W
Edenbridge, *U.K.* 15 51 12N 0 4 E
Edenderry, *Ire.* 25 53 21N 7 3W
Edge Hill, *U.K.* 14 52 7N 1 28W
Edinburgh, *U.K.* 21 55 57N 3 12W
Edington, *U.K.* 14 51 17N 2 6W
Edmondbyers, *U.K.* 18 54 50N 1 59W
Edmonton, *Canada* 88 53 30N 113 30W
Edmundston, *Canada* 93 47 23N 68 20W
Edward, L., *Africa* 80 0 25S 29 40 E
Egersund, *Nor.* 45 58 26N 6 1 E
Egham, *U.K.* 15 51 25N 0 33W
Egmont, Mt., *N.Z.* 71 39 17S 174 5 E
Egremont, *U.K.* 18 54 28N 3 33W
Egton, *U.K.* 19 54 27N 0 45W
Egypt ■, *Africa* 79 28 0N 31 0 E
Eifel, *Ger.* 36 50 10N 6 45 E
Eigg, *U.K.* 22 56 54N 6 10W
Eighty Mile Beach, *Austral.* 66 19 30S 120 40 E
Eil, L., *U.K.* 22 56 50N 5 15W
Eildon, L., *Austral.* 70 37 10S 146 0 E
Eindhoven, *Neth.* 36 51 26N 5 30 E
Eire ■, *Europe* 25 53 0N 8 0W
El Aaiún, *W. Sah.* 78 27 9N 13 12W
El Asnam = Ech Cheliff, *Alg.* 78 36 10N 1 20 E
El Faiyûm, *Egypt* 79 29 19N 30 50 E
El Fâsher, *Sudan* 79 13 33N 25 26 E
El Gîza, *Egypt* 79 30 0N 31 10 E
El Jadida, *Mor.* 78 33 11N 8 17W
El Mahalla el Kubra, *Egypt* 79 31 0N 31 0 E
El Mansûra, *Egypt* 79 31 0N 31 19 E
El Minyâ, *Egypt* 79 28 7N 30 33 E
El Obeid, *Sudan* 79 13 8N 30 10 E
El Paso, *U.S.A.* 90 31 50N 106 30W
El Qâhira = Cairo, *Egypt* 79 30 1N 31 14 E
El Salvador ■, *Cent. Am.* 94 13 50N 89 0W
Elba, *It.* 40 42 48N 10 15 E
Elbasani, *Alb.* 41 41 9N 20 9 E
Elbe →, *Ger.* 42 53 50N 9 0 E
Elbląg, *Pol.* 43 54 10N 19 25 E
Elburz Mts., *Iran* 56 36 0N 52 0 E
Elche, *Sp.* 37 38 15N 0 42W
Eldoret, *Kenya* 80 0 30N 35 17 E
Eleuthera, *Baham.* 95 25 0N 76 20W
Elgin, *U.K.* 23 57 39N 3 20W
Elham, *U.K.* 15 51 9N 1 7 E
Elie, *U.K.* 21 56 11N 2 50W

Elishaw, *U.K.* **21** 55 16N 2 14W
Elizabeth, *Austral.* **67** 34 42S 138 41 E
Elizabeth, *U.S.A.* **93** 40 37N 74 12W
Elland, *U.K.* **19** 53 41N 1 49W
Ellen →, *U.K.* **18** 54 44N 3 30W
Eller Beck Bridge, *U.K.* **19** 54 23N 0 40W
Ellesmere, *U.K.* **18** 52 55N 2 53W
Ellesmere I., *Canada* **103** 79 30N 80 0W
Ellesmere Port, *U.K.* **18** 53 17N 2 55W
Ellice Is. = Tuvalu ■, *Pac. Oc.* **64** 8 0S 178 0 E
Ellington, *U.K.* **21** 55 14N 1 34W
Ellon, *U.K.* **23** 57 21N 2 5W
Elmira, *U.S.A.* **92** 42 8N 76 49W
Elmswell, *U.K.* **15** 52 14N 0 53 E
Eluru, *India* **59** 16 48N 81 8 E
Ely, *U.K.* **15** 52 24N 0 16 E
Emāmrūd, *Iran* **56** 36 30N 55 0 E
Embleton, *U.K.* **21** 55 30N 1 38W
Emden, *Ger.* **36** 53 22N 7 12 E
Emerald, *Austral.* **67** 23 32S 148 10 E
Emmeloord, *Neth.* **36** 52 44N 5 46 E
Emmen, *Neth.* **36** 52 48N 6 57 E
Ems →, *Ger.* **36** 52 37N 9 26 E
Enard B., *U.K.* **22** 58 5N 5 20W
Enderbury I., *Pac. Oc.* **64** 3 8S 171 5W
Enderby, *U.K.* **14** 52 35N 1 15W
Enderby Land, *Ant.* **103** 66 0S 53 0 E
Enfield, *U.K.* **15** 51 39N 0 4W
England □, *U.K.* **5** 53 0N 2 0W
English Channel, *Europe* **15** 50 0N 2 0W
Ennerdale Water, *U.K.* **18** 54 32N 3 24W
Ennis, *Ire.* **25** 52 51N 8 59W
Enniscorthy, *Ire.* **25** 52 30N 6 35W
Enniskillen, *U.K.* **24** 54 20N 7 40W
Ennistimon, *Ire.* **25** 52 56N 9 18W
Enschede, *Neth.* **36** 52 13N 6 53 E
Ensenada, *Mex.* **94** 31 50N 116 50W
Enstone, *U.K.* **14** 51 55N 1 25W
Entebbe, *Uganda* **80** 0 4N 32 28 E
Enugu, *Nig.* **78** 6 20N 7 30 E
Epping, *U.K.* **15** 51 42N 0 8 E
Epping Forest, *U.K.* **15** 51 40N 0 5 E
Epsom, *U.K.* **15** 51 19N 0 16W
Epworth, *U.K.* **19** 53 30N 0 50W
Equatorial Guinea ■, *Africa* **80** 2 0S 8 0 E
Erebus, Mt., *Ant.* **103** 77 35S 167 0 E
Erfurt, *Ger.* **42** 50 58N 11 2 E
Eriboll, L., *U.K.* **23** 58 28N 4 41W
Erie, *U.S.A.* **92** 42 10N 80 7W
Erie, L., *N. Am.* **92** 42 15N 81 0W
Eritrea □, *Eth.* **79** 14 0N 41 0 E
Erlangen, *Ger.* **42** 49 35N 11 0 E
Erne →, *U.K.* **24** 54 30N 8 16W
Erne, Lough, *U.K.* **24** 54 26N 7 46W
Erode, *India* **58** 11 24N 77 45 E
Errigal, Mt., *Ire.* **24** 55 2N 8 8W
Erris Hd., *Ire.* **24** 54 19N 10 0W
Errol, *U.K.* **21** 56 24N 3 13W
Erzurum, *Turk.* **47** 39 57N 41 15 E
Esbjerg, *Den.* **45** 55 29N 8 29 E
Esch, *Neth.* **36** 51 37N 5 17 E
Eschweiler, *Ger.* **36** 50 49N 6 14 E
Escrick, *U.K.* **19** 53 53N 1 3W
Eşfahān, *Iran* **56** 33 0N 53 0 E
Esk →, *Cumbria, U.K.* **18** 54 23N 3 21W
Esk →, *Dumf. & Gall., U.K.* **21** 54 58N 3 4W
Esk →, *N. Yorks., U.K.* **19** 54 27N 0 36W
Eskdale, *U.K.* **21** 55 12N 3 4W
Eskifjörður, *Ice.* **44** 65 3N 13 55W
Eskilstuna, *Swed.* **45** 59 22N 16 32 E
Eskimo Pt., *Canada* **88** 61 10N 94 15W
Eskişehir, *Turk.* **47** 39 50N 30 35 E
Esmeraldas, *Ecuad.* **100** 1 0N 79 40W
Esperance, *Austral.* **66** 33 45S 121 55 E
Espinhaço, Serra do, *Brazil* **101** 17 30S 43 30W
Essen, *Ger.* **36** 51 28N 6 59 E
Essex □, *U.K.* **15** 51 48N 0 30 E
Eston, *U.K.* **19** 54 33N 1 6W
Estonia ■, *Europe* **46** 58 30N 25 30 E
Etchingham, *U.K.* **15** 51 0N 0 27 E
Ethiopia ■, *Africa* **78** 8 0N 40 0 E
Ethiopian Highlands, *Eth.* **72** 10 0N 37 0 E
Etive, L., *U.K.* **20** 56 30N 5 12W
Etna, *It.* **40** 37 45N 15 0 E
Eton, *U.K.* **15** 51 29N 0 37W
Ettington, *U.K.* **14** 52 8N 1 38W
Ettrick Forest, *U.K.* **21** 55 30N 3 0W
Ettrick Water →, *U.K.* **21** 55 31N 2 55W
Eugene, *U.S.A.* **90** 44 0N 123 8W
Euphrates →, *Asia* **56** 31 0N 47 25 E
Euston, *Austral.* **70** 34 30S 142 46 E
Euxton, *U.K.* **18** 53 41N 2 42W
Evansville, *U.S.A.* **92** 38 0N 87 35W
Evercreech, *U.K.* **14** 51 8N 2 30W
Everest, Mt., *Nepal* **60** 28 5N 86 58 E
Evesham, *U.K.* **14** 52 6N 1 57W
Évora, *Port.* **37** 38 33N 7 57W
Évreux, *Fr.* **34** 49 0N 1 8 E
Évvoia, *Greece* **41** 38 30N 24 0 E
Ewe, L., *U.K.* **22** 57 49N 5 38W
Ewell, *U.K.* **15** 51 20N 0 15W
Ewhurst, *U.K.* **15** 51 9N 0 25W
Exe →, *U.K.* **16** 50 38N 3 27W
Exeter, *U.K.* **16** 50 43N 3 31W
Exford, *U.K.* **14** 51 8N 3 39W
Exminster, *U.K.* **16** 50 40N 3 29W
Exmoor, *U.K.* **16** 51 10N 3 59W
Exmouth, *Austral.* **66** 21 54S 114 10 E
Exmouth, *U.K.* **16** 50 37N 3 26W
Exmouth G., *Austral.* **66** 22 15S 114 15 E
Exton, *U.K.* **15** 52 42N 0 38W
Eyam, *U.K.* **19** 53 17N 1 40W
Eye, *Cambs., U.K.* **15** 52 36N 0 11W
Eye, *Suffolk, U.K.* **15** 52 19N 1 9 E
Eye Pen., *U.K.* **22** 58 13N 6 10W
Eyemouth, *U.K.* **21** 55 53N 2 5W
Eynsham, *U.K.* **14** 51 47N 1 21W
Eyre, L., *Austral.* **67** 29 30S 137 26 E
Eyre Cr. →, *Austral.* **67** 26 40S 139 0 E
Eyre Pen., *Austral.* **66** 33 30S 137 17 E

F

Fair Hd., *U.K.* **24** 55 14N 6 10W
Fairbanks, *U.S.A.* **88** 64 50N 147 50W
Fairfield, *Austral.* **70** 33 53S 150 57 E
Fairford, *U.K.* **14** 51 42N 1 48W
Fairlie, *N.Z.* **71** 44 5S 170 49 E
Fairlie, *U.K.* **20** 55 44N 4 52W
Fairlight, *U.K.* **15** 50 53N 0 40 E
Faisalabad, *Pak.* **58** 31 30N 73 5 E
Faizabad, *India* **59** 26 45N 82 10 E
Fakenham, *U.K.* **15** 52 50N 0 51 E
Faldingworth, *U.K.* **19** 53 21N 0 22W
Falkenberg, *Swed.* **45** 56 54N 12 30 E
Falkirk, *U.K.* **21** 56 0N 3 47W
Falkland, *U.K.* **21** 56 15N 3 13W
Falkland Is., *Atl. Oc.* **102** 51 30S 59 0W
Fall River, *U.S.A.* **93** 41 45N 71 5W
Falmouth, *U.K.* **16** 50 9N 5 5W
Falmouth B., *U.K.* **16** 50 7N 5 3W
Falstone, *U.K.* **21** 55 10N 2 26W
Falun, *Swed.* **45** 60 37N 15 37 E
Famagusta, *Cyprus* **47** 35 8N 33 55 E
Fannich, L., *U.K.* **22** 57 40N 5 0W
Fareham, *U.K.* **14** 50 52N 1 11W
Faringdon, *U.K.* **14** 51 39N 1 34W
Farnborough, *U.K.* **15** 51 17N 0 46W
Farne Is., *U.K.* **19** 55 38N 1 37W
Farnham, *U.K.* **15** 51 13N 0 49W
Farnworth, *U.K.* **18** 53 33N 2 24W
Faroe Is., *Atl. Oc.* **26** 62 0N 7 0W
Farrar →, *U.K.* **23** 57 30N 4 30W
Faslane, *U.K.* **20** 56 3N 4 49W
Fastnet Rock, *Ire.* **25** 51 22N 9 37W
Fauldhouse, *U.K.* **21** 55 50N 3 44W
Faversham, *U.K.* **15** 51 18N 0 54 E
Fawley, *U.K.* **14** 50 49N 1 20W
Faya-Largeau, *Chad* **79** 17 58N 19 6 E
Fayetteville, *U.S.A.* **91** 35 0N 78 58W
Fazeley, *U.K.* **14** 52 36N 1 42W
Fdérik, *Maurit.* **78** 22 40N 12 45W
Feale →, *Ire.* **25** 52 26N 9 40W
Feilding, *N.Z.* **71** 40 13S 175 35 E
Feira de Santana, *Brazil* **101** 12 15S 38 57W
Felixstowe, *U.K.* **15** 51 58N 1 22 E
Felpham, *U.K.* **15** 50 47N 0 38W
Felton, *U.K.* **21** 55 18N 1 42W
Feltwell, *U.K.* **15** 52 29N 0 32 E
Fenit, *Ire.* **25** 52 17N 9 51W
Fenny Bentley, *U.K.* **19** 53 4N 1 43W
Fenny Compton, *U.K.* **14** 52 9N 1 20W
Fenny Stratford, *U.K.* **15** 51 59N 0 42W
Fens, The, *U.K.* **15** 52 45N 0 2 E
Fenwick, *U.K.* **20** 55 38N 4 25W
Fergana, *U.S.S.R.* **48** 40 23N 71 19 E
Fermanagh □, *U.K.* **24** 54 21N 7 40W
Fermoy, *Ire.* **25** 52 4N 8 18W
Fernhurst, *U.K.* **15** 51 3N 0 43W
Ferrara, *It.* **40** 44 50N 11 36 E
Ferryhill, *U.K.* **19** 54 42N 1 32W
Fès, *Mor.* **78** 34 0N 5 0W
Fetlar, *U.K.* **22** 60 36N 0 52W
Ffestiniog, *U.K.* **17** 52 58N 3 56W
Fianarantsoa, *Madag.* **81** 21 26S 47 5 E
Fife □, *U.K.* **21** 56 13N 3 2W
Fife Ness, *U.K.* **21** 56 17N 2 35W
Fiji ■, *Pac. Oc.* **64** 17 20S 179 0 E
Filby, *U.K.* **15** 52 40N 1 39 E
Filey, *U.K.* **19** 54 13N 0 18W
Filey B., *U.K.* **19** 54 12N 0 15W
Filton, *U.K.* **14** 51 29N 2 34W
Fincham, *U.K.* **15** 52 38N 0 30 E
Findhorn →, *U.K.* **23** 57 38N 3 38W
Findon, *U.K.* **15** 50 53N 0 24W
Finedon, *U.K.* **15** 52 20N 0 40W
Fingest, *U.K.* **15** 51 35N 0 52W
Finisterre, C., *Sp.* **37** 42 50N 9 19W
Finland ■, *Europe* **44** 63 0N 27 0 E
Finland, G. of, *Europe* **45** 60 0N 26 0 E
Finn →, *Ire.* **24** 54 50N 7 55W
Finnart, *U.K.* **20** 56 7N 4 48W
Finnmark fylke □, *Nor.* **44** 69 30N 25 0 E
Finstown, *U.K.* **23** 59 0N 3 8W
Fionnphort, *U.K.* **20** 56 19N 6 23W
Firozabad, *India* **58** 27 10N 78 25 E
Fishguard, *U.K.* **17** 51 59N 4 59W
Fishtoft, *U.K.* **19** 52 27N 0 2 E
Fitzroy →, *Austral.* **66** 17 31S 123 35 E
Flamborough, *U.K.* **19** 54 7N 0 7W
Flamborough Hd., *U.K.* **19** 54 8N 0 4W
Flanders, *Belg.* **34** 51 10N 3 15 E
Flatey, *Ice.* **44** 65 22N 22 56W
Fleet, *U.K.* **15** 51 16N 0 50W
Fleetwood, *U.K.* **18** 53 55N 3 1W
Flensburg, *Ger.* **42** 54 46N 9 28 E
Fletton, *U.K.* **15** 52 34N 0 13W
Flimby, *U.K.* **18** 54 42N 3 31W
Flinders →, *Austral.* **67** 17 36S 140 36 E
Flinders Ranges, *Austral.* **67** 31 30S 138 30 E
Flint, *U.K.* **17** 53 15N 3 7W
Flint, *U.S.A.* **92** 43 5N 83 40W
Flint →, *U.S.A.* **91** 30 52N 84 38W
Flitwick, *U.K.* **15** 51 59N 0 30W
Flodden, *U.K.* **19** 55 37N 2 8W
Florence, *It.* **40** 43 47N 11 15 E
Flores, *Indon.* **63** 8 35S 121 0 E
Flores Sea, *Indon.* **63** 6 30S 124 0 E
Florianópolis, *Brazil* **102** 27 30S 48 30W
Florida □, *U.S.A.* **91** 28 30N 82 0W
Florida, Straits of, *U.S.A.* **95** 25 0N 80 0W
Florida Keys, *U.S.A.* **91** 25 0N 80 40W
Florissant, *U.S.A.* **91** 38 48N 90 20W
Flushing = Vlissingen, *Neth.* **36** 51 26N 3 34 E
Fóggia, *It.* **40** 41 28N 15 31 E
Folkestone, *U.K.* **15** 51 5N 1 11 E
Fontainebleau, *Fr.* **34** 48 24N 2 40 E
Forbach, *Fr.* **34** 49 10N 6 52 E
Ford, *U.K.* **20** 56 10N 5 27W
Fordham, *U.K.* **15** 52 19N 0 23 E
Fordingbridge, *U.K.* **14** 50 56N 1 48W
Forest Row, *U.K.* **15** 51 6N 0 3 E
Forfar, *U.K.* **23** 56 40N 2 53W
Formby, *U.K.* **18** 53 34N 3 4W
Formby Pt., *U.K.* **18** 53 33N 3 7W
Formosa = Taiwan ■, *Asia* **61** 23 30N 121 0 E
Formosa Strait, *Asia* **61** 24 40N 120 0 E
Forres, *U.K.* **23** 57 37N 3 38W
Fort Augustus, *U.K.* **23** 57 9N 4 40W
Fort Collins, *U.S.A.* **90** 40 30N 105 4W
Fort-de-France, *Mart.* **94** 14 36N 61 2W
Fort George, *Canada* **89** 53 50N 79 0W
Fort Lauderdale, *U.S.A.* **91** 26 10N 80 5W
Fort McMurray, *Canada* **88** 56 44N 111 7W
Fort Smith, *U.S.A.* **91** 35 25N 94 25W
Fort Wayne, *U.S.A.* **92** 41 5N 85 10W
Fort William, *U.K.* **22** 56 48N 5 8W
Fort Worth, *U.S.A.* **90** 32 45N 97 25W
Fortaleza, *Brazil* **101** 3 45S 38 35W
Forth, *U.K.* **21** 55 45N 3 42W
Forth, Firth of, *U.K.* **21** 56 5N 2 55W
Forth Bridge, *U.K.* **21** 56 0N 3 24W
Fortrose, *U.K.* **23** 57 35N 4 10W
Foshan, *China* **61** 23 4N 113 5 E
Fothergill, *U.K.* **18** 54 43N 3 30W
Fotheringhay, *U.K.* **15** 52 32N 0 28W
Foulness I., *U.K.* **15** 51 36N 0 55 E
Foulness Pt., *U.K.* **15** 51 36N 0 59 E
Foulsham, *U.K.* **15** 52 48N 1 1 E
Fountainhall, *U.K.* **21** 55 45N 2 55W
Fountains Abbey, *U.K.* **19** 54 8N 1 35W
Fovant, *U.K.* **14** 51 4N 2 0W
Foveaux Str., *N.Z.* **71** 46 42S 168 10 E
Fowey, *U.K.* **16** 50 20N 4 39W
Fowey →, *U.K.* **16** 50 20N 4 39W
Fownhope, *U.K.* **14** 52 0N 2 37W
Foxdale, *U.K.* **18** 54 12N 4 38W
Foxe Chan., *Canada* **89** 65 0N 80 0W
Foyle, Lough, *U.K.* **24** 55 6N 7 8W
Foynes, *Ire.* **25** 52 37N 9 5W
Fraddon, *U.K.* **16** 50 22N 4 55W
Framlingham, *U.K.* **15** 52 14N 1 20 E
France ■, *Europe* **34** 47 0N 3 0 E
Frankfurt am Main, *Ger.* **42** 50 7N 8 40 E
Frankston, *Austral.* **70** 38 8S 145 8 E
Frant, *U.K.* **15** 51 5N 0 17 E
Franz Josef Land, *U.S.S.R.* **48** 82 0N 55 0 E
Fraser →, *Canada* **88** 49 7N 123 11W
Fraser I., *Austral.* **67** 25 15S 153 10 E
Fraserburgh, *U.K.* **23** 57 41N 2 0W
Fredericton, *Canada* **93** 45 57N 66 40W
Frederikshavn, *Den.* **45** 57 28N 10 31 E
Fredrikstad, *Nor.* **45** 59 13N 10 57 E
Freetown, *Sa. Leone* **78** 8 30N 13 17W
Freiburg, *Ger.* **42** 48 0N 7 52 E
Fremantle, *Austral.* **66** 32 7S 115 47 E
French Guiana ■, *S. Am.* **101** 4 0N 53 0W
French Polynesia □, *Pac. Oc.* **65** 20 0S 145 0 E
Freshwater, *U.K.* **14** 50 42N 1 31W
Fresnillo, *Mex.* **94** 23 10N 103 0W
Fresno, *U.S.A.* **90** 36 47N 119 50W
Freuchie, *U.K.* **21** 56 14N 3 8W
Fridaythorpe, *U.K.* **19** 54 2N 0 40W
Friesland □, *Neth.* **36** 53 5N 5 50 E
Frimley, *U.K.* **15** 51 18N 0 43W
Frinton-on-Sea, *U.K.* **15** 51 50N 1 16 E
Frisa, Loch, *U.K.* **20** 56 34N 6 5W
Frisian Is., *Europe* **36** 53 30N 6 0 E
Frizington, *U.K.* **18** 54 33N 3 30W
Frobisher B., *Canada* **89** 62 30N 66 0W
Frodsham, *U.K.* **18** 53 17N 2 45W
Frome, *U.K.* **14** 51 16N 2 17W
Frome →, *U.K.* **14** 50 44N 2 5W
Frome, L., *Austral.* **67** 30 45S 139 45 E
* Frunze, *U.S.S.R.* **48** 42 54N 74 46 E
Fuji-San, *Jap.* **62** 35 22N 138 44 E
Fujian □, *China* **61** 26 0N 118 0 E
Fukui, *Jap.* **62** 36 0N 136 10 E
Fukuoka, *Jap.* **62** 33 39N 130 21 E
Fukushima, *Jap.* **62** 37 44N 140 28 E
Fukuyama, *Jap.* **62** 34 35N 133 20 E
Fulwood, *U.K.* **18** 53 47N 2 41W
Fundy, B. of, *Canada* **93** 45 0N 66 0W
Furneaux Group, *Austral.* **67** 40 10S 147 50 E
Furness, Pen., *U.K.* **18** 54 12N 3 10W
Fürth, *Ger.* **42** 49 29N 11 0 E
Fury and Hecla Str., *Canada* **89** 69 56N 84 0W
Fushun, *China* **61** 41 50N 123 56 E
Fuxin, *China* **61** 42 5N 121 48 E
Fuzhou, *China* **61** 26 5N 119 16 E
Fylde, *U.K.* **18** 53 50N 2 58W
Fylingdales Moor, *U.K.* **19** 54 22N 0 32W
Fyn, *Den.* **45** 55 20N 10 30 E
Fyne, L., *U.K.* **20** 56 0N 5 20W
Fyvie, *U.K.* **23** 57 26N 2 24W

G

Gabès, *Tunisia* **78** 33 53N 10 2 E
Gabon ■, *Africa* **80** 0 10S 10 0 E
Gaborone, *Bots.* **81** 24 45S 25 57 E
Gabrovo, *Bulg.* **41** 42 52N 25 19 E
Gainesville, *U.S.A.* **91** 29 38N 82 20W
Gainford, *U.K.* **19** 54 34N 1 44W
Gainsborough, *U.K.* **19** 53 23N 0 46W
Gairdner L., *Austral.* **66** 31 30S 136 0 E
Gairloch, *U.K.* **22** 57 42N 5 40W
Gairloch, L., *U.K.* **22** 57 43N 5 45W
Galápagos, *Pac. Oc.* **65** 0 0 89 0W
Galashiels, *U.K.* **21** 55 37N 2 50W
Galaţi, *Rom.* **43** 45 27N 28 2 E
Galgate, *U.K.* **18** 53 59N 2 47W
Galilee, Sea of = Kinneret, Lake, *Isr.* **57** 32 45N 35 35 E
Galle, *Sri L.* **58** 6 5N 80 10 E
Galley Hd., *Ire.* **25** 51 32N 8 56W
Gällivare, *Swed.* **44** 67 9N 20 40 E
Galloway, *U.K.* **20** 55 0N 4 25W
Galloway, Mull of, *U.K.* **20** 54 38N 4 50W
Galmpton, *U.K.* **16** 50 23N 3 32W
Galston, *U.K.* **20** 55 36N 4 22W
Galty Mts., *Ire.* **25** 52 22N 8 10W
Galtymore, *Ire.* **25** 52 22N 8 12W
Galveston, *U.S.A.* **91** 29 15N 94 48W
Galway, *Ire.* **25** 53 16N 9 4W
Galway □, *Ire.* **24** 53 16N 9 3W
Galway B., *Ire.* **25** 53 10N 9 20W
Gambia ■, *W. Afr.* **78** 13 25N 16 0W
Gamboa, *Pan.* **94** 9 8N 79 42W
Gamlingay, *U.K.* **15** 52 9N 0 11W
Gan Jiang →, *China* **61** 29 15N 116 0 E
Ganga →, *India* **59** 23 20N 90 30 E
Ganganagar, *India* **58** 29 56N 73 56 E
Ganges = Ganga →, *India* **59** 23 20N 90 30 E
Gansu □, *China* **60** 36 0N 104 0 E
Gao, *Mali* **78** 16 15N 0 5W
Gap, *Fr.* **35** 44 33N 6 5 E
Garboldisham, *U.K.* **15** 52 24N 0 57 E
Garda, L. di, *It.* **40** 45 40N 10 40 E
Gare, L., *U.K.* **20** 56 1N 4 50W
Garelochhead, *U.K.* **20** 56 7N 4 50W
Garforth, *U.K.* **19** 53 48N 1 22W
Gargrave, *U.K.* **18** 53 58N 2 7W
Garlieston, *U.K.* **20** 54 47N 4 22W
Garonne →, *Fr.* **35** 45 2N 0 36W
Garoua, *Cam.* **80** 9 19N 13 21 E
Garry →, *U.K.* **23** 56 47N 3 47W
Garsdale Head, *U.K.* **18** 54 19N 2 19W
Garstang, *U.K.* **18** 53 53N 2 47W
Garston, *U.K.* **18** 53 21N 2 55W
Garvald, *U.K.* **21** 55 55N 2 39W
Garvellachs, Is., *U.K.* **20** 56 14N 5 48W
Gary, *U.S.A.* **92** 41 35N 87 20W
Garzê, *China* **60** 31 39N 99 58 E
Gascony, *Fr.* **35** 43 45N 0 20 E
Gascoyne →, *Austral.* **66** 24 52S 113 37 E
Gaspé, Pén. de, *Canada* **93** 48 45N 65 40W
Gatehouse of Fleet, *U.K.* **20** 54 53N 4 10W
Gateshead, *U.K.* **19** 54 57N 1 37W
Gatley, *U.K.* **18** 53 25N 2 15W
Gatun, *Pan.* **94** 9 16N 79 55W
Gatun, L., *Pan.* **94** 9 7N 79 56W
Gävle, *Swed.* **45** 60 40N 17 9 E
Gawthwaite, *U.K.* **18** 54 16N 3 6W
Gaya, *India* **59** 24 47N 85 4 E
Gayton, *U.K.* **15** 52 45N 0 35 E
Gaywood, *U.K.* **15** 52 46N 0 26 E
Gaza, *Egypt* **57** 31 30N 34 28 E
Gaziantep, *Turk.* **47** 37 6N 37 23 E
Gdańsk, *Pol.* **43** 54 22N 18 40 E
Gdańsk Bay, *Pol.* **43** 54 30N 19 20 E
Gdynia, *Pol.* **43** 54 35N 18 33 E
Gedney, *U.K.* **15** 52 47N 0 5 E
Geelong, *Austral.* **70** 38 10S 144 22 E
Gejiu, *China* **60** 23 20N 103 10 E
Gelderland □, *Neth.* **36** 52 5N 6 10 E

* *Renamed Bishkek*

Gelsenkirchen, *Ger.* **36** 51 30N 7 5 E
Geneva, *Switz.* **42** 46 12N 6 9 E
Geneva, L., *Switz.* **42** 46 26N 6 30 E
Genk, *Belg.* **36** 50 58N 5 32 E
Gennargentu, Mti. del, *It.* **40** 40 0N 9 10 E
Genoa, *It.* **40** 44 24N 8 56 E
Geographe Chan., *Austral.* **66** 24 30S 113 0 E
George, *S. Afr.* **81** 33 58S 22 29 E
George Town, *Malay.* **63** 5 25N 100 15 E
Georgetown, *Guy.* **100** 6 50N 58 12W
Georgia □, *U.S.A.* **91** 32 0N 82 0W
Georgia □, *U.S.S.R.* **47** 42 0N 43 0 E
Georgian B., *Canada* **92** 45 15N 81 0W
Gera, *Ger.* **42** 50 53N 12 11 E
Geraldton, *Austral.* **66** 28 48S 114 32 E
Germany ■, *Europe* **42** 50 0N 10 0 E
Germiston, *S. Afr.* **81** 26 15S 28 10 E
Gerona, *Sp.* **37** 41 58N 2 46 E
Gerrans B., *U.K.* **16** 50 12N 4 57W
Gerrards Cross, *U.K.* **15** 51 35N 0 32W
Ghaghara →, *India* **59** 25 45N 84 40 E
Ghana ■, *W. Afr.* **78** 6 0N 1 0W
Ghaziabad, *India* **58** 28 42N 77 26 E
Ghent, *Belg.* **36** 51 2N 3 42 E
Giant's Causeway, *U.K.* **24** 55 15N 6 30W
Gibraltar, *Europe* **37** 36 7N 5 22W
Gibraltar, Str. of, *Medit. S.* **37** 35 55N 5 40W
Gibraltar Pt., *U.K.* **19** 53 6N 0 20 E
Gibson Desert, *Austral.* **66** 24 0S 126 0 E
Gifford, *U.K.* **21** 55 54N 2 45W
Gifu, *Jap.* **62** 35 30N 136 45 E
Giggleswick, *U.K.* **18** 54 5N 2 19W
Gigha, *U.K.* **20** 55 42N 5 45W
Gijón, *Sp.* **37** 43 32N 5 42W
Gilbert Is. = Kiribati ■, *Pac. Oc.* **65** 1 0N 176 0 E
Gillingham, *Dorset, U.K.* **14** 51 2N 2 15W
Gillingham, *Kent, U.K.* **15** 51 23N 0 34 E
Gilsland, *U.K.* **18** 55 0N 2 34W
Girdle Ness, *U.K.* **23** 57 9N 2 2W
Gironde →, *Fr.* **35** 45 32N 1 7W
Girvan, *U.K.* **20** 55 15N 4 50W
Girvan →, *U.K.* **20** 55 18N 4 51W
Gisborne, *N.Z.* **71** 38 39S 178 5 E
Gisburn, *U.K.* **18** 53 56N 2 16W
Gizhiga, *U.S.S.R.* **49** 62 3N 160 30 E
Gizhiga, G., *U.S.S.R.* **49** 61 0N 158 0 E
Gladstone, *Austral.* **67** 25 57S 114 17 E
Glanton, *U.K.* **21** 55 25N 1 54W
Glasgow, *U.K.* **20** 55 52N 4 14W
Glastonbury, *U.K.* **14** 51 9N 2 42W
Glemsford, *U.K.* **15** 52 6N 0 41 E
Glen →, *U.K.* **15** 52 50N 0 7W
Glen Affric, *U.K.* **22** 57 15N 5 0W
Glen Almond, *U.K.* **21** 56 28N 3 50W
Glen Coe, *U.K.* **19** 56 40N 5 0W
Glen Etive, *U.K.* **20** 56 37N 5 0W
Glen Garry, *U.K.* **22** 57 3N 5 7W
Glen Helen, *U.K.* **18** 54 14N 4 35W
Glen Mor, *U.K.* **23** 57 12N 4 37 E
Glen Moriston, *U.K.* **22** 57 10N 4 58W
Glen Orchy, *U.K.* **20** 56 27N 4 52W
Glen Spean, *U.K.* **23** 56 53N 4 40W
Glenbarr, *U.K.* **20** 55 34N 5 40W
Glendale, *U.S.A.* **90** 34 7N 118 18W
Gleneagles, *U.K.* **21** 56 16N 3 44W
Glengarriff, *Ire.* **25** 51 45N 9 33W
Glenkens, The, *U.K.* **20** 55 10N 4 15W
Glenluce, *U.K.* **20** 54 53N 4 50W
Glenmaye, *U.K.* **18** 54 11N 4 42W
Glenorchy, *Austral.* **67** 31 55S 139 46 E
Glenrothes, *U.K.* **20** 56 12N 3 11W
Glenties, *Ire.* **24** 54 48N 8 18W
Glentrool Village, *U.K.* **20** 55 5N 4 30W
Gliwice, *Pol.* **43** 50 22N 18 41 E
Glossop, *U.K.* **18** 53 27N 1 56W
Gloucester, *U.K.* **14** 51 52N 2 15W
Gloucestershire □, *U.K.* **14** 51 44N 2 10W
Gnosall, *U.K.* **14** 52 48N 2 15W
Goa □, *India* **58** 15 33N 73 59 E
Goat Fell, *U.K.* **20** 55 37N 5 11W
Gobi, *Asia* **60** 44 0N 111 0 E
Godalming, *U.K.* **15** 51 12N 0 37W
Godavari →, *India* **59** 16 25N 82 18 E
Godmanchester, *U.K.* **15** 52 19N 0 11W
Godshill, *U.K.* **14** 50 38N 1 13W
Godstone, *U.K.* **15** 51 15N 0 3W
Goiânia, *Brazil* **101** 16 43S 49 20W
Goil, L., *U.K.* **20** 56 8N 4 52W
Gold Coast, *Austral.* **67** 28 0S 153 25 E
Golden Vale, *Ire.* **25** 52 33N 8 17W
Golspie, *U.K.* **23** 57 58N 3 58W
Gomel, *U.S.S.R.* **46** 52 28N 31 0 E
Gometra I., *U.K.* **20** 56 30N 6 18W
Gómez Palacio, *Mex.* **94** 25 40N 104 0W
Gonder, *Eth.* **79** 12 39N 37 30 E
Good Hope, C. of, *S. Afr.* **81** 34 24S 18 30 E
Goodrich, *U.K.* **14** 51 52N 2 38W
Goodwood, *U.K.* **15** 50 53N 0 44W
Goole, *U.K.* **19** 53 42N 0 52W
Goondiwindi, *Austral.* **67** 28 30S 150 21 E
Gorakhpur, *India* **59** 26 47N 83 23 E
Gordon, *U.K.* **21** 55 41N 2 32W
Gorebridge, *U.K.* **21** 55 51N 3 2W
Gorey, *Ire.* **25** 52 41N 6 18W
Goring, *Oxon., U.K.* **14** 51 31N 1 8W
Goring, *W. Sussex, U.K.* **15** 50 49N 0 26W
∗ Gorki, *U.S.S.R.* **46** 56 20N 44 0 E
Gorleston, *U.K.* **15** 52 35N 1 44 E
Görlitz, *Ger.* **42** 51 10N 14 59 E
Gort, *Ire.* **25** 53 4N 8 50W
Gorzów Wielkopolski, *Pol.* **42** 52 43N 15 15 E
Gosberton, *U.K.* **19** 52 52N 0 10W
Gosford, *Austral.* **70** 33 23S 151 18 E
Gosforth, *U.K.* **18** 54 24N 3 27W
Gosport, *U.K.* **14** 50 48N 1 8W
Göteborg, *Swed.* **45** 57 43N 11 59 E
Gotha, *Ger.* **42** 50 56N 10 42 E
Gotland, *Swed.* **45** 57 30N 18 33 E
Gouda, *Neth.* **36** 52 1N 4 42 E
Goudhurst, *U.K.* **15** 51 7N 0 28 E
Gouin, Rés., *Canada* **93** 48 35N 74 40W
Goulburn, *Austral.* **70** 34 44S 149 44 E
Gourock, *U.K.* **20** 55 58N 4 49W
Governador Valadares, *Brazil* **101** 18 15S 41 57W
Gower, The, *U.K.* **17** 51 35N 4 10W
Gowna, L., *Ire.* **24** 53 52N 7 35W
Gowrie, Carse of, *U.K.* **21** 56 30N 3 10W
Goya, *Arg.* **102** 29 10S 59 10W
Gozo, *Malta* **40** 36 0N 14 13 E
Grafham Water, *U.K.* **15** 52 18N 0 17W
Grafton, *Austral.* **67** 29 38S 152 58 E
Graham Bell, I., *U.S.S.R.* **48** 80 5N 70 0 E
Graham Land, *Ant.* **103** 65 0S 64 0W
Grainthorpe, *U.K.* **19** 53 27N 0 5 E
Grampian □, *U.K.* **23** 57 0N 3 0W
Grampian Mts., *U.K.* **23** 56 50N 4 0W
Gran Canaria, *Can. Is.* **78** 27 55N 15 35W
Gran Chaco, *S. Am.* **96** 25 0S 61 0W
Granada, *Sp.* **37** 37 10N 3 35W
Granard, *Ire.* **24** 53 47N 7 30W
Grand Bahama, *Baham.* **95** 26 40N 78 30W
Grand Canyon National Park, *U.S.A.* **90** 36 15N 112 20W
Grand Cayman, *W. Ind.* **95** 19 20N 81 20W
Grand Rapids, *U.S.A.* **92** 42 57N 86 40W
Grande de Santiago →, *Mex.* **94** 21 36N 105 26W
Grande Prairie, *Canada* **88** 55 10N 118 50W
Grange-over-Sands, *U.K.* **18** 54 12N 2 55W
Grangemouth, *U.K.* **21** 56 1N 3 43W
Grangetown, *U.K.* **19** 54 36N 1 7W
Grantham, *U.K.* **19** 52 55N 0 39W
Grantown-on-Spey, *U.K.* **23** 57 19N 3 36W
Grantshouse, *U.K.* **21** 55 53N 2 17W
Grasmere, *U.K.* **18** 54 28N 3 2W
Grassington, *U.K.* **18** 54 5N 2 0W
Gravesend, *U.K.* **15** 51 25N 0 22 E
Grayrigg, *U.K.* **18** 54 22N 2 40W
Grays, *U.K.* **15** 51 28N 0 23 E
Graz, *Austria* **42** 47 4N 15 27 E
Great Abaco I., *Baham.* **95** 26 25N 77 10W
Great Australian Bight, *Austral.* **66** 33 30S 130 0 E
Great Ayton, *U.K.* **19** 54 29N 1 8W
Great Baddow, *U.K.* **15** 51 43N 0 31 E
Great Barrier Reef, *Austral.* **67** 18 0S 146 50 E
Great Basin, *U.S.A.* **90** 40 0N 116 30W
Great Bear L., *Canada* **88** 65 30N 120 0W
Great Bentley, *U.K.* **15** 51 51N 1 5 E
Great Blasket I., *Ire.* **25** 52 5N 10 30W
Great Britain, *Europe* **5** 54 0N 2 15W
Great Chesterford, *U.K.* **15** 52 4N 0 11 E
Great Clifton, *U.K.* **18** 54 39N 3 29W
Great Divide, The, *Austral.* **70** 35 0S 149 17 E
Great Dividing Ra., *Austral.* **67** 23 0S 146 0 E
Great Dunmow, *U.K.* **15** 51 52N 0 22 E
Great Falls, *U.S.A.* **90** 47 27N 111 12W
Great Harwood, *U.K.* **18** 53 43N 2 30W
Great Inagua I., *Baham.* **95** 21 0N 73 20W
Great Indian Desert = Thar Desert, *India* **58** 28 0N 72 0 E
Great Malvern, *U.K.* **14** 52 7N 2 19W
Great Massingham, *U.K.* **15** 52 47N 0 41 E
Great Missenden, *U.K.* **15** 51 42N 0 42W
Great Orme's Head, *U.K.* **17** 53 20N 3 52W
Great Ouse →, *U.K.* **15** 52 47N 0 22 E
Great Plains, *N. Am.* **82** 47 0N 105 0W
Great Salt Lake, *U.S.A.* **90** 41 0N 112 30W
Great Sandy Desert, *Austral.* **66** 21 0S 124 0 E
Great Shefford, *U.K.* **14** 51 29N 1 27W
Great Shelford, *U.K.* **15** 52 9N 0 9 E
Great Shunner Fell, *U.K.* **18** 54 22N 2 16W
Great Slave L., *Canada* **88** 61 23N 115 38W
Great Stour = Stour →, *U.K.* **15** 51 15N 1 20 E
Great Torrington, *U.K.* **16** 50 57N 4 9W
Great Victoria Desert, *Austral.* **66** 29 30S 126 30 E
Great Waltham, *U.K.* **15** 51 47N 0 29 E
Great Whernside, *U.K.* **18** 54 9N 1 59W
Great Wyrley, *U.K.* **14** 52 40N 2 1W
Great Yarmouth, *U.K.* **15** 52 40N 1 45 E
Great Yeldham, *U.K.* **15** 52 1N 0 33 E
Greater Antilles, *W. Ind.* **95** 17 40N 74 0W
Greater London □, *U.K.* **15** 51 30N 0 5W
Greater Manchester □, *U.K.* **18** 53 30N 2 15W
Greater Sunda Is., *Indon.* **63** 7 0S 112 0 E
Greatham, *U.K.* **19** 54 38N 1 14W
Greece ■, *Europe* **41** 40 0N 23 0 E
Greeley, *U.S.A.* **90** 40 30N 104 40W
Green B., *U.S.A.* **92** 45 0N 87 30W
Green Bay, *U.S.A.* **92** 44 30N 88 0W
Green Hammerton, *U.K.* **19** 54 2N 1 17W
Green Lowther, *U.K.* **21** 55 22N 3 44W
Greenhead, *U.K.* **21** 54 58N 2 31W
Greenland ■, *N. Am.* **89** 66 0N 45 0W
Greenland Sea, *Arctic* **103** 73 0N 10 0W
Greenlaw, *U.K.* **21** 55 42N 2 28W
Greenock, *U.K.* **20** 55 57N 4 46W
Greenodd, *U.K.* **18** 54 14N 3 3W
Greenore, *Ire.* **24** 54 2N 6 8W
Greenore Pt., *Ire.* **25** 52 15N 6 20W
Greensboro, *U.S.A.* **91** 36 7N 79 46W
Greenwich, *U.K.* **15** 51 28N 0 0 E
Grenada ■, *W. Ind.* **94** 12 10N 61 40W
Grenoble, *Fr.* **35** 45 12N 5 42 E
Greta →, *U.K.* **18** 54 9N 2 36W
Gretna, *U.K.* **21** 54 59N 3 4W
Gretna Green, *U.K.* **21** 55 0N 3 3W
Gretton, *U.K.* **15** 52 33N 0 40W
Grey Range, *Austral.* **67** 27 0S 143 30 E
Greymouth, *N.Z.* **71** 42 29S 171 13 E
Greystoke, *U.K.* **18** 54 39N 2 52W
Gribbin Head, *U.K.* **16** 50 18N 4 41W
Griffith, *Austral.* **70** 34 18S 146 2 E
Grimsby, *U.K.* **19** 53 35N 0 5W
Gris-Nez, C., *Fr.* **34** 50 52N 1 35 E
Grizebeck, *U.K.* **18** 54 16N 3 10W
Grodno, *U.S.S.R.* **46** 53 42N 23 52 E
Groningen, *Neth.* **36** 53 15N 6 35 E
Groote Eylandt, *Austral.* **67** 14 0S 136 40 E
Groznyy, *U.S.S.R.* **47** 43 20N 45 45 E
Gruinard B., *U.K.* **22** 57 56N 5 35W
Guadalajara, *Mex.* **94** 20 40N 103 20W
Guadalajara, *Sp.* **37** 40 37N 3 12W
Guadalete →, *Sp.* **37** 36 35N 6 13W
Guadeloupe ■, *W. Ind.* **94** 16 20N 61 40W
Guadiana →, *Port.* **37** 37 14N 7 22W
Guadix, *Sp.* **37** 37 18N 3 11W
Gualeguay, *Arg.* **102** 33 10S 59 14W
Guam, *Pac. Oc.* **64** 13 27N 144 45 E
Guangdong □, *China* **61** 23 0N 113 0 E
Guangxi Zhuangzu Zizhiqu □, *China* **61** 24 0N 109 0 E
Guangzhou, *China* **61** 23 5N 113 10 E
Guantánamo, *Cuba* **95** 20 10N 75 14W
Guaporé →, *Brazil* **100** 11 55S 65 4W
Guard Bridge, *U.K.* **21** 56 21N 2 52W
Guardafui, C. = Asir, Ras, *Som.* **73** 11 55N 51 10 E
Guatemala, *Guat.* **94** 14 40N 90 22W
Guatemala ■, *Cent. Am.* **94** 15 40N 90 30W
Guaviare →, *Col.* **100** 4 3N 67 44W
Guayaquil, *Ecuad.* **100** 2 15S 79 52W
Guaymas, *Mex.* **94** 27 59N 110 54W
Guelph, *Canada* **92** 43 35N 80 20W
Guernsey, *U.K.* **34** 49 30N 2 35W
Guestling Green, *U.K.* **15** 50 53N 0 40 E
Guildford, *U.K.* **15** 51 14N 0 34W
Guilin, *China* **61** 25 18N 110 15 E
Guinea ■, *W. Afr.* **78** 10 20N 10 0W
Guinea, Gulf of, *Atl. Oc.* **72** 3 0N 2 30 E
Guinea-Bissau ■, *Africa* **78** 12 0N 15 0W
Guisborough, *U.K.* **19** 54 32N 1 2W
Guiyang, *China* **60** 26 32N 106 40 E
Guizhou □, *China* **60** 27 0N 107 0 E
Gujarat □, *India* **58** 23 20N 71 0 E
Gujranwala, *Pak.* **58** 32 10N 74 12 E
Gujrat, *Pak.* **58** 32 40N 74 2 E
Gulbarga, *India* **58** 17 20N 76 50 E
Gulf, The, *Asia* **56** 27 0N 50 0 E
Gullane, *U.K.* **21** 56 2N 2 50W
Guntur, *India* **59** 16 23N 80 30 E
Gurnard's Head, *U.K.* **16** 50 12N 5 37W
Guyana ■, *S. Am.* **100** 5 0N 59 0W
Gwalchmai, *U.K.* **17** 53 16N 4 23W
Gwalior, *India* **58** 26 12N 78 10 E
Gweebarra B., *Ire.* **24** 54 52N 8 21W
Gweedore, *Ire.* **24** 55 4N 8 15W
Gweek, *U.K.* **16** 50 6N 5 12W
Gwennap, *U.K.* **16** 50 12N 5 9W
Gwent □, *U.K.* **17** 51 45N 2 55W
Gweru, *Zimb.* **81** 19 28S 29 45 E
Gwynedd □, *U.K.* **17** 53 0N 4 0W
Gyandzha, *U.S.S.R.* **47** 40 45N 46 20 E
Gympie, *Austral.* **67** 26 11S 152 38 E
Györ, *Hung.* **43** 47 41N 17 40 E

H

Haarlem, *Neth.* **36** 52 23N 4 39 E
Hachinohe, *Jap.* **62** 40 30N 141 29 E
Hackney, *U.K.* **15** 51 33N 0 2W
Hackthorpe, *U.K.* **18** 54 37N 2 42W
Haddenham, *U.K.* **15** 51 46N 0 56W
Haddington, *U.K.* **21** 55 57N 2 48W
Hadleigh, *U.K.* **15** 52 3N 0 58 E
Hadley, *U.K.* **14** 52 42N 2 28W
Hadlow, *U.K.* **15** 51 12N 0 20 E
Hadrians Wall, *U.K.* **19** 55 0N 2 30W
Haeju, *N. Kor.* **61** 38 3N 125 45 E
Hafnarfjörður, *Ice.* **44** 64 4N 21 57W
Hagen, *Ger.* **36** 51 21N 7 29 E
Hags Hd., *Ire.* **25** 52 57N 9 30W
Haifa, *Isr.* **57** 32 46N 35 0 E
Haikou, *China* **61** 20 1N 110 16 E
Ḥā'il, *Si. Arab.* **56** 27 28N 41 45 E
Hailar, *China* **61** 49 12N 119 37 E
Hailsham, *U.K.* **15** 50 52N 0 17 E
Hainan, *China* **61** 19 0N 109 30 E
Hainton, *U.K.* **19** 53 21N 0 13W
Haiphong, *Viet.* **60** 20 47N 106 41 E
Haiti ■, *W. Ind.* **95** 19 0N 72 30W
Hakodate, *Jap.* **62** 41 45N 140 44 E
Halberton, *U.K.* **16** 50 55N 3 24W
Hale, *U.K.* **18** 53 24N 2 21W
Halesowen, *U.K.* **14** 52 27N 2 2W
Halesworth, *U.K.* **15** 52 21N 1 30 E
Halifax, *Canada* **93** 44 38N 63 35W
Halifax, *U.K.* **18** 53 43N 1 51W
Halifax B., *Austral.* **67** 18 50S 147 0 E
Halkirk, *U.K.* **23** 58 30N 3 30W
Halle, *Ger.* **42** 51 29N 12 0 E
Hallow, *U.K.* **14** 52 14N 2 15W
Hallworthy, *U.K.* **16** 50 38N 4 34W
Halmahera, *Indon.* **63** 0 40N 128 0 E
Halmstad, *Swed.* **45** 56 41N 12 52 E
Halstead, *U.K.* **15** 51 59N 0 39 E
Haltwhistle, *U.K.* **21** 54 58N 2 27W
Hamadān, *Iran* **56** 34 52N 48 32 E
Hamāh, *Syria* **56** 35 5N 36 40 E
Hamamatsu, *Jap.* **62** 34 45N 137 45 E
Hambledon, *U.K.* **14** 50 56N 1 6W
Hambleton Hills, *U.K.* **19** 54 17N 1 12W
Hamburg, *Ger.* **42** 53 32N 9 59 E
Hämeenlinna, *Fin.* **45** 61 0N 24 28 E
Hamersley Ra., *Austral.* **66** 22 0S 117 45 E
Hamilton, *Berm.* **95** 32 15N 64 45W
Hamilton, *Canada* **92** 43 15N 79 50W
Hamilton, *N.Z.* **71** 37 47S 175 19 E
Hamilton, *U.K.* **21** 55 47N 4 2W
Hamm, *Ger.* **36** 51 40N 7 49 E
Hammerfest, *Nor.* **44** 70 39N 23 41 E
Hammersmith, *U.K.* **15** 51 30N 0 15W
Hammond, *U.S.A.* **92** 41 40N 87 30W
Hampshire □, *U.K.* **14** 51 3N 1 20W
Hampshire Downs, *U.K.* **14** 51 10N 1 10W
Hampton in Arden, *U.K.* **14** 52 26N 1 42W
Hangzhou, *China* **61** 30 18N 120 11 E
Hanko, *Fin.* **45** 59 59N 22 57 E
Hanningfield Water, *U.K.* **15** 51 40N 0 30 E
Hanoi, *Viet.* **60** 21 5N 105 55 E
Hanover, *Ger.* **42** 52 23N 9 43 E
Haora, *India* **59** 22 37N 88 20 E
Happy Valley, *Canada* **89** 53 15N 60 20W
Harare, *Zimb.* **81** 17 43S 31 2 E
Harbin, *China* **61** 45 46N 126 51 E
Hardangerfjorden, *Nor.* **45** 60 15N 6 0 E
Harewood, *U.K.* **19** 53 54N 1 30W
Haringey, *U.K.* **15** 51 35N 0 7W
Harlech, *U.K.* **17** 52 52N 4 7W
Harleston, *U.K.* **15** 52 25N 1 18 E
Harlingen, *Neth.* **36** 53 11N 5 25 E
Harlow, *U.K.* **15** 51 47N 0 9 E
Harpenden, *U.K.* **15** 51 48N 0 20W
Harrietsham, *U.K.* **15** 51 15N 0 41 E
Harrington, *U.K.* **18** 54 37N 3 55W
Harris, *U.K.* **22** 57 50N 6 55W
Harris, Sd. of, *U.K.* **22** 57 44N 7 6W
Harrisburg, *U.S.A.* **93** 40 18N 76 52W
Harrogate, *U.K.* **19** 53 59N 1 32W
Harrow, *U.K.* **15** 51 35N 0 15W
Hartest, *U.K.* **15** 52 7N 0 41 E
Hartford, *U.S.A.* **93** 41 47N 72 41W
Harthill, *U.K.* **21** 55 52N 3 45W
Hartland, *U.K.* **16** 50 59N 4 29W
Hartland Pt., *U.K.* **16** 51 2N 4 32W
Hartlebury, *U.K.* **14** 52 20N 2 13W
Hartlepool, *U.K.* **19** 54 42N 1 11W
Hartley, *U.K.* **21** 55 5N 1 27W
Hartpury, *U.K.* **14** 51 55N 2 18W
Harwell, *U.K.* **14** 51 40N 1 17W
Harwich, *U.K.* **15** 51 56N 1 18 E
Harz, *Europe* **26** 51 40N 10 40 E
Hasa, *Si. Arab.* **56** 26 0N 49 0 E
Haslemere, *U.K.* **15** 51 5N 0 41W
Haslingden, *U.K.* **18** 53 43N 2 20W
Hasselt, *Belg.* **36** 50 56N 5 21 E
Hastings, *N.Z.* **71** 39 39S 176 52 E
Hastings, *U.K.* **15** 50 51N 0 36 E
Hatfield, *U.K.* **15** 51 46N 0 11W
Hatfield Broad Oak, *U.K.* **15** 51 48N 0 16 E
Hatherleigh, *U.K.* **16** 50 49N 4 4W
Hathersage, *U.K.* **19** 53 20N 1 39W
Hatteras, C., *U.S.A.* **91** 35 10N 75 30W
Haugh of Urr, *U.K.* **21** 55 0N 3 51W
Haughley, *U.K.* **15** 52 13N 0 59 E
Hauraki Gulf, *N.Z.* **71** 36 35S 175 5 E
Hauxley, *U.K.* **21** 55 21N 1 35W
Havana, *Cuba* **95** 23 8N 82 22W
Havant, *U.K.* **15** 50 51N 0 59W
Haverfordwest, *U.K.* **17** 51 48N 4 59W
Haverhill, *U.K.* **15** 52 6N 0 27 E
Haverigg, *U.K.* **18** 54 12N 3 16W
Havering, *U.K.* **15** 51 33N 0 20 E
Havre, Le, *Fr.* **34** 49 30N 0 5 E
Hawaiian Is., *Pac. Oc.* **90** 20 30N 156 0W
Hawera, *N.Z.* **71** 39 35S 174 19 E
Hawes, *U.K.* **18** 54 18N 2 12W
Haweswater, *U.K.* **18** 54 32N 2 48W
Hawick, *U.K.* **21** 55 25N 2 48W
Hawkchurch, *U.K.* **16** 50 47N 2 56W

∗ *Renamed Nizhniy Novgorod*

Hawke B., N.Z. 71 39 25S 177 20 E
Hawkesbury Upton, U.K. 14 51 34N 2 19W
Hawkhurst, U.K. 15 51 2N 0 31 E
Hawkshead, U.K. 18 54 23N 3 0W
Haworth, U.K. 18 53 50N 1 57W
Hawsker, U.K. 19 54 27N 0 34W
Haxby, U.K. 19 54 1N 1 4W
Hay-on-Wye, U.K. 17 52 4N 3 9W
Hay River, Canada 88 60 51N 115 44W
Hayburn Wyke, U.K. 19 54 22N 0 28W
Haydon Bridge, U.K. 21 54 58N 2 15W
Hayle, U.K. 16 50 12N 5 25W
Hayton, U.K. 18 54 55N 2 45W
Haywards Heath, U.K. 15 51 0N 0 5W
Heacham, U.K. 15 52 55N 0 30 E
Headcorn, U.K. 15 51 10N 0 39 E
Heanor, U.K. 19 53 1N 1 20W
Heathfield, U.K. 15 50 58N 0 18 E
Hebburn, U.K. 21 54 59N 1 30W
Hebden Bridge, U.K. 18 53 45N 2 0W
Hebei □, China 61 39 0N 116 0 E
Hebrides, U.K. 22 57 30N 7 0W
Hechuan, China 60 30 2N 106 12 E
Heckington, U.K. 19 52 59N 0 17W
Hedmark fylke □, Nor. 44 61 17N 11 40 E
Hednesford, U.K. 14 52 43N 2 0W
Hedon, U.K. 19 53 44N 0 11W
Heerlen, Neth. 36 50 55N 6 0 E
Hefei, China 61 31 52N 117 18 E
Hegang, China 61 47 20N 130 19 E
Heidelberg, Ger. 42 49 23N 8 41 E
Heilbronn, Ger. 42 49 8N 9 13 E
Heilongjiang □, China 61 48 0N 126 0 E
Hekla, Ice. 44 63 56N 19 35W
Helensburgh, U.K. 20 56 0N 4 44W
Heligoland, Ger. 42 54 10N 7 51 E
Hellifield, U.K. 18 54 0N 2 13W
Helmond, Neth. 36 51 29N 5 41 E
Helmsdale, U.K. 23 58 7N 3 40W
Helmsley, U.K. 19 54 15N 1 2W
Helperby, U.K. 19 54 8N 1 20W
Helsby, U.K. 18 53 16N 2 47W
Helsingborg, Swed. 45 56 3N 12 42 E
Helsingør, Den. 45 56 2N 12 35 E
Helsinki, Fin. 45 60 15N 25 3 E
Helston, U.K. 16 50 7N 5 17W
Helvellyn, U.K. 18 54 31N 3 1W
Hemel Hempstead, U.K. 15 51 45N 0 28W
Hempton, U.K. 15 52 50N 0 49 E
Hemsworth, U.K. 19 53 37N 1 21W
Hemyock, U.K. 16 50 50N 3 15W
Henan □, China 61 34 0N 114 0 E
Henfield, U.K. 15 50 56N 0 17W
Hengelo, Neth. 36 52 16N 6 48 E
Hengyang, China 61 26 51N 112 30 E
Henley-in-Arden, U.K. 14 52 18N 1 47W
Henley-on-Thames, U.K. 15 51 32N 0 53W
Henlow, U.K. 15 52 2N 0 18W
Henstridge, U.K. 14 50 59N 2 24W
Henzada, Burma 59 17 38N 95 26 E
Herāt, Afg. 57 34 20N 62 7 E
Hereford, U.K. 14 52 4N 2 42W
Hereford and Worcester □, U.K. 14 52 10N 2 30W
Hermosillo, Mex. 94 29 4N 110 58W
Herne, Ger. 36 51 33N 7 12 E
Herne Bay, U.K. 15 51 22N 1 8 E
Herning, Den. 45 56 8N 8 58 E
Herstmonceux, U.K. 15 50 53N 0 21 E
Hertford, U.K. 15 51 47N 0 4W
Hertford □, U.K. 15 51 51N 0 5W
's-Hertogenbosch, Neth. 36 51 42N 5 17 E
Hesse □, Ger. 42 50 40N 9 20 E
Hessle, U.K. 19 53 44N 0 28 E
Hethersett, U.K. 15 52 35N 1 10 E
Hetton-le-Hole, U.K. 21 54 49N 1 26W
Hexham, U.K. 19 54 58N 2 7W
Heybridge, U.K. 15 51 44N 0 42 E
Heysham, U.K. 18 54 5N 2 53W
Heytesbury, U.K. 14 51 11N 2 7W
Heywood, U.K. 18 53 36N 2 13W
High Atlas, Mor. 72 32 30N 5 0W
High Bentham, U.K. 18 54 8N 2 31W
High Borrow Bridge, U.K. 18 54 26N 2 43W
High Ercall, U.K. 14 52 46N 2 37W
High Hesket, U.K. 18 54 47N 2 49W
High Pike, U.K. 18 54 43N 3 4W
High Willhays, U.K. 16 50 41N 3 59W
High Wycombe, U.K. 15 51 37N 0 45W
Higham Ferrers, U.K. 15 52 18N 0 36W
Highbridge, U.K. 14 51 13N 2 59W
Highclere, U.K. 14 51 20N 1 22W
Highland □, U.K. 22 57 30N 5 0W
Highley, U.K. 14 52 25N 2 23W
Hightae, U.K. 21 55 5N 3 27W
Highworth, U.K. 14 51 38N 1 42W
Hilgay, U.K. 15 52 34N 0 23 E
Hillingdon, U.K. 15 51 33N 0 29W
Hillsborough, U.K. 24 54 28N 6 6W
Hilo, U.S.A. 90 19 44N 155 5W
Hilpsford Pt., U.K. 18 54 4N 3 12W
Hilversum, Neth. 36 52 14N 5 10 E
Himachal Pradesh □, India 58 31 30N 77 0 E
Himalaya, Mts., Asia 60 29 0N 84 0 E
Himeji, Jap. 62 34 50N 134 40 E
Hinckley, U.K. 14 52 33N 1 21W
Hinderwell, U.K. 19 54 32N 0 45W
Hindhead, U.K. 15 51 6N 0 42W
Hindley, U.K. 18 53 32N 2 35W
Hindu Kush, Asia 57 36 0N 71 0 E
Hingham, U.K. 15 52 35N 0 59 E
Hinkley Pt., U.K. 14 50 59N 3 32W
Hinstock, U.K. 14 52 50N 2 28W
Hiroshima, Jap. 62 34 24N 132 30 E
Hispaniola, W. Ind. 95 19 0N 71 0W
Histon, U.K. 15 52 15N 0 6 E
Hitchin, U.K. 15 51 57N 0 16W
Ho Chi Minh City, Viet. 63 10 58N 106 40 E
Hobart, Austral. 67 42 50S 147 21 E
Hodder →, U.K. 18 53 57N 2 27W
Hoddesdon, U.K. 15 51 45N 0 1W
Hodge →, U.K. 19 54 14N 0 55W
Hoff, U.K. 18 54 34N 2 31W
Hoggar, Mts., Alg. 78 23 0N 6 30 E
Hog's Back, U.K. 15 51 13N 0 40W
Hohhot, China 61 40 52N 111 40 E
Hokitika, N.Z. 71 42 42S 171 0 E
Hokkaidō □, Jap. 62 43 30N 143 0 E
Holbeach, U.K. 15 52 48N 0 1 E
Holbeach Marsh, U.K. 15 52 52N 0 5 E
Holderness, U.K. 19 53 45N 0 5W
Holguín, Cuba 95 20 50N 76 20W
Holkham, U.K. 15 52 57N 0 48 E
Holland Fen, U.K. 19 53 0N 0 8W
Holland-on-Sea, U.K. 15 51 48N 1 12 E
Holme, Humberside, U.K. 19 53 50N 0 48W
Holme, N. Yorks., U.K. 18 53 34N 1 50W
Holmes Chapel, U.K. 18 53 13N 2 21W
Holmfirth, U.K. 19 53 34N 1 48W
Holmwood, U.K. 15 51 12N 0 19W
Holsworthy, U.K. 16 50 48N 4 21W
Holt, U.K. 15 52 55N 1 4 E
Holy I., England, U.K. 19 55 42N 1 48W
Holy I., Scotland, U.K. 20 55 31N 5 4W
Holy I., Wales, U.K. 17 53 17N 4 37W
Holyhead, U.K. 17 53 18N 4 38W
Holywell, U.K. 17 53 16N 3 14W
Holywood, U.K. 24 54 38N 5 50W
Homs, Syria 56 34 40N 36 45 E
Honduras ■, Cent. Am. 94 14 40N 86 30W
Honduras, G. de, Cent. Am. 94 16 50N 87 0W
Hong →, Viet. 60 20 17N 106 34 E
Hong Kong ■, Asia 61 22 11N 114 14 E
Honington, U.K. 19 52 58N 0 35W
Honiton, U.K. 16 50 48N 3 11W
Honolulu, U.S.A. 90 21 19N 157 52W
Honshū, Jap. 62 36 0N 138 0 E
Hoo, U.K. 15 51 25N 0 33 E
Hook, U.K. 15 51 17N 0 55W
Hook Hd., Ire. 25 52 8N 6 57W
Hoorn, Neth. 36 52 38N 5 4 E
Horden, U.K. 19 54 45N 1 17W
Horley, U.K. 15 51 10N 0 10W
Horn, C., Chile 102 55 50S 67 30W
Horn Head, Ire. 24 55 13N 8 0W
Horncastle, U.K. 19 53 13N 0 8W
Horndean, U.K. 15 50 50N 0 59W
Horningsham, U.K. 14 51 11N 2 16W
Hornsby, Austral. 70 33 42S 151 2 E
Hornsea, U.K. 19 53 55N 0 10W
Horsens, Den. 45 55 52N 9 51 E
Horsforth, U.K. 19 53 50N 1 39W
Horsham, Austral. 70 36 44S 142 13 E
Horsham, U.K. 15 51 4N 0 20W
Horsham St. Faith, U.K. 15 52 41N 1 15 E
Horsted Keynes, U.K. 15 51 2N 0 1W
Horton-in-Ribblesdale, U.K. 18 54 9N 2 19W
Horwich, U.K. 18 53 37N 2 33W
Hospitalet de Llobregat, Sp. 37 41 21N 2 6 E
Hotan, China 60 37 25N 79 55 E
Houghton-le-Spring, U.K. 19 54 51N 1 28W
Houghton Regis, U.K. 15 51 54N 0 32W
Hounslow, U.K. 15 51 29N 0 20W
Houston, U.S.A. 91 29 50N 95 20W
Hovd, Mong. 60 48 2N 91 37 E
Hove, U.K. 15 50 50N 0 10W
Hoveton, U.K. 15 52 45N 1 23 E
Hovingham, U.K. 19 54 10N 0 59W
Hövsgöl Nuur, Mong. 60 51 0N 100 30 E
Howden, U.K. 19 53 45N 0 52W
Howth Hd., Ire. 24 53 21N 6 0W
Hoxne, U.K. 15 52 22N 1 11 E
Hoy I., U.K. 23 58 50N 3 15W
Hoylake, U.K. 18 53 24N 3 11W
Hrádec Králové, Czech. 42 50 15N 15 50 E
Hron →, Czech. 43 47 49N 18 45 E
Huainan, China 61 32 39N 117 2 E
Huambo, Angola 81 12 42S 15 54 E
Huancayo, Peru 100 12 5S 75 12W
Huang He →, China 61 37 55N 118 50 E
Huangshi, China 61 30 10N 115 3 E
Huánuco, Peru 100 9 55S 76 15W
Hubei □, China 61 31 0N 112 0 E
Hucknall, U.K. 19 53 3N 1 12W
Huddersfield, U.K. 19 53 38N 1 49W
Hudson →, U.S.A. 93 40 42N 74 2W
Hudson Bay, Canada 89 52 51N 102 23W
Hudson Str., Canada 89 62 0N 70 0W
Hue, Viet. 63 16 30N 107 35 E
Huelva, Sp. 37 37 18N 6 57W
Huesca, Sp. 37 42 8N 0 25W
Hugh Town, U.K. 16 49 55N 6 19W
Hughenden, Austral. 67 20 52S 144 10 E
Hughes, U.S.A. 88 66 0N 154 20W
Hull, Canada 93 45 25N 75 44W
Hull = Kingston-upon-Hull, U.K. 19 53 45N 0 20W
Hull →, U.K. 19 53 43N 0 25W
Hullavington, U.K. 14 51 31N 2 9W
Hulme End, U.K. 18 53 8N 1 51W
Humber →, U.K. 19 53 40N 0 10W
Humber, Mouth of the, U.K. 19 53 32N 0 28W
Humberside □, U.K. 19 53 50N 0 30W
Humboldt →, U.S.A. 90 40 2N 118 31W
Hume, L., Austral. 70 36 0S 147 0 E
Humshaugh, U.K. 21 55 3N 2 8W
Húnaflói, Ice. 44 65 50N 20 50W
Hunan □, China 61 27 30N 111 30 E
Hungary ■, Europe 43 47 20N 19 20 E
Hungary, Plain of, Europe 26 47 0N 20 0 E
Hungerford, U.K. 14 51 25N 1 30W
Hŭngnam, N. Kor. 61 39 49N 127 45 E
Hunmanby, U.K. 19 54 12N 0 19W
Hunstanton, U.K. 15 52 57N 0 30 E
Hunter →, Austral. 70 32 52S 151 46 E
Hunterston, U.K. 20 55 43N 4 55W
Huntingdon, U.K. 15 52 20N 0 11W
Huntington, U.S.A. 92 38 20N 82 30W
Huntly, U.K. 23 57 27N 2 48W
Huntsville, U.S.A. 91 34 45N 86 35W
Hurlford, U.K. 20 55 35N 4 29W
Huron, L., N. Am. 92 45 0N 83 0W
Hursley, U.K. 14 51 1N 1 23W
Hurstbourne Tarrant, U.K. 14 51 17N 1 27W
Hurstpierpoint, U.K. 15 50 56N 0 11W
Húsavík, Ice. 44 66 3N 17 21W
Husband's Bosworth, U.K. 14 52 27N 1 3W
Huyton, U.K. 18 53 25N 2 52W
Hyde, U.K. 18 53 26N 2 6W
Hyderabad, India 58 17 22N 78 29 E
Hyderabad, Pak. 58 25 23N 68 24 E
Hynish, U.K. 20 56 27N 6 54W
Hynish B., U.K. 20 56 29N 6 40W
Hythe, U.K. 15 51 4N 1 5 E

I

Iaşi, Rom. 43 47 10N 27 40 E
Ibadan, Nig. 78 7 22N 3 58 E
Ibagué, Col. 100 4 20N 75 20W
Iberian Peninsula, Europe 26 40 0N 5 0W
Ibiza, Sp. 37 38 54N 1 26 E
Ibstock, U.K. 14 52 42N 1 23W
Icá, Peru 100 14 0S 75 48W
Iceland ■, Atl. Oc. 44 65 0N 19 0W
Ichinomiya, Jap. 62 35 18N 136 48 E
Idaho □, U.S.A. 90 44 10N 114 0W
Idar-Oberstein, Ger. 36 49 43N 7 19 E
Idle →, U.K. 19 53 27N 0 49W
Idmiston, U.K. 14 51 8N 1 43W
Idsworth, U.K. 15 50 56N 0 56W
Igarka, U.S.S.R. 49 67 30N 86 33 E
Iglésias, It. 40 39 19N 8 27 E
Iguaçu Falls, Brazil 102 25 41S 54 26W
IJsselmeer, Neth. 36 52 45N 5 20 E
Ilchester, U.K. 14 51 0N 2 41W
Île-de-France, Fr. 34 49 0N 2 20 E
Ilfracombe, U.K. 16 51 13N 4 8W
Ilhéus, Brazil 101 14 49S 39 2W
Ilkeston, U.K. 19 52 59N 1 19W
Ilkley, U.K. 18 53 56N 1 49W
Illinois □, U.S.A. 91 40 15N 89 30W
Ilminster, U.K. 14 50 55N 2 56W
Iloilo, Phil. 63 10 45N 122 33 E
Immingham, U.K. 19 53 37N 0 12W
Imphal, India 59 24 48N 93 56 E
Inari, Fin. 44 68 54N 27 5 E
Ince, U.K. 18 53 32N 2 38W
Inchcape Rock, U.K. 21 56 26N 2 24W
Inchkeith, I., U.K. 21 56 2N 3 8W
Inchon, S. Kor. 61 37 27N 126 40 E
Inchture, U.K. 21 56 26N 3 8W
Indaal, L., U.K. 20 55 44N 6 20W
India ■, Asia 58 20 0N 78 0 E
Indian Ocean 119 5 0S 75 0 E
Indiana □, U.S.A. 92 40 0N 86 0W
Indianapolis, U.S.A. 92 39 42N 86 10W
Indonesia ■, Asia 63 5 0S 115 0 E
Indore, India 58 22 42N 75 53 E
Indus →, Pak. 58 24 20N 67 47 E
Ingatestone, U.K. 15 51 40N 0 23 E
Ingleborough, U.K. 18 54 11N 2 23W
Ingleton, U.K. 18 54 9N 2 29W
Ingoldmells, Pt., U.K. 19 53 11N 0 21 E
Inishbofin, Ire. 24 53 35N 10 12W
Inishmore, Ire. 25 53 8N 9 45W
Inishowen, Ire. 24 55 14N 7 15W
Inkberrow, U.K. 14 52 13N 1 59W
Inkpen Beacon, U.K. 14 51 22N 1 28W
Inn →, Austria 40 48 35N 13 28 E
Innellan, U.K. 20 55 54N 4 58W
Inner Hebrides, U.K. 22 57 0N 6 30W
Inner Mongolia □, China 61 42 0N 112 0 E
Inner Sound, U.K. 22 57 30N 5 55W
Innerleithen, U.K. 21 55 37N 3 4W
Innsbruck, Austria 42 47 16N 11 23 E
Inny →, Ire. 25 53 30N 7 50W
Interlaken, Switz. 42 46 41N 7 50 E
Inuvik, Canada 88 68 16N 133 40W
Inveraray, U.K. 20 56 13N 5 5W
Inverbervie, U.K. 23 56 50N 2 17W
Invercargill, N.Z. 71 46 24S 168 24 E
Inverell, Austral. 67 29 45S 151 8 E
Invergarry, U.K. 23 57 5N 4 48W
Invergordon, U.K. 23 57 41N 4 10W
Invergowrie, U.K. 21 56 29N 3 5W
Inverkeithing, U.K. 21 56 2N 3 24W
Invermoriston, U.K. 23 57 13N 4 38W
Inverness, U.K. 23 57 29N 4 12W
Inverurie, U.K. 23 57 15N 2 21W
Iona, U.K. 20 56 20N 6 25W
Ionian Is., Greece 41 38 40N 20 0 E
Ionian Sea, Greece 41 37 30N 17 30 E
Iowa □, U.S.A. 91 42 18N 93 30W
Iowa City, U.S.A. 91 41 40N 91 35W
Ipoh, Malay. 63 4 35N 101 5 E
Ipswich, U.K. 15 52 4N 1 9 E
Iquique, Chile 100 20 19S 70 5W
Iquitos, Peru 100 3 45S 73 10W
Iráklion, Greece 41 35 20N 25 12 E
Iran ■, Asia 57 33 0N 53 0 E
Irapuato, Mex. 94 20 40N 101 30W
Iraq ■, Asia 56 33 0N 44 0 E
Irchester, U.K. 15 52 17N 0 40W
Ireland ■, Europe 24 53 0N 8 0W
Ireland's Eye, Ire. 24 53 25N 6 4W
Irian Jaya □, Indon. 64 4 0S 137 0 E
Iringa, Tanz. 80 7 48S 35 43 E
Irish Republic ■, Europe 25 53 0N 8 0W
Irish Sea, Europe 18 54 0N 5 0W
Irkutsk, U.S.S.R. 49 52 18N 104 20 E
Irlam, U.K. 18 53 26N 2 27W
Ironbridge, U.K. 14 52 38N 2 29W
Irrawaddy →, Burma 59 15 50N 95 6 E
Irt →, U.K. 18 54 24N 3 25W
Irthing →, U.K. 21 54 55N 2 55W
Irthlingborough, U.K. 15 52 20N 0 37W
Irtysh →, U.S.S.R. 48 61 4N 68 52 E
Irvine, U.K. 20 55 37N 4 40W
Irvine →, U.K. 20 55 35N 4 40W
Irvinestown, U.K. 24 54 28N 7 38W
Isabela, Phil. 63 10 12N 122 59 E
Ísafjörður, Ice. 44 66 5N 23 9W
Ishim →, U.S.S.R. 48 57 45N 71 10 E
İskenderun, Turk. 47 36 32N 36 10 E
Isla →, U.K. 23 56 32N 3 20W
Islamabad, Pak. 58 33 40N 73 10 E
Islay, U.K. 20 55 46N 6 10W
Islay Sound, U.K. 20 55 45N 6 5W
Isle of Whithorn, U.K. 20 54 42N 4 22W
Isle of Wight □, U.K. 14 50 40N 1 20W
Isleham, U.K. 15 52 21N 0 24 E
Islip, U.K. 14 51 49N 1 12W
Ismâ'ilîya, Egypt 79 30 37N 32 18 E
Israel ■, Asia 57 32 0N 34 50 E
İstanbul, Turk. 47 41 0N 29 0 E
Itabuna, Brazil 101 14 48S 39 16W
Italy ■, Europe 40 42 0N 13 0 E
Itchen →, U.K. 14 50 57N 1 20W
Ivanovo, U.S.S.R. 46 52 7N 25 29 E
Ivinghoe, U.K. 15 51 50N 0 38W
Ivory Coast ■, Africa 78 7 30N 5 0W
Ivugivik, Canada 89 62 24N 77 55W
Ivybridge, U.K. 16 50 24N 3 56W
Iwaki, Jap. 62 37 3N 140 55 E
Ixworth, U.K. 15 52 18N 0 50 E
Izhevsk U.S.S.R. 46 56 51N 53 14 E
İzmir, Turk. 47 38 25N 27 8 E

J

Jabalpur, India 58 23 9N 79 58 E
Jackson, U.S.A. 91 32 20N 90 10W
Jacksonville, U.S.A. 91 30 15N 81 38W
Jaén, Sp. 37 37 44N 3 43W
Jaffna, Sri L. 58 9 45N 80 2 E
Jaipur, India 58 27 0N 75 50 E
Jakarta, Indon. 63 6 9S 106 49 E
Jamaica ■, W. Ind. 94 18 10N 77 30W
Jambi, Indon. 63 1 38S 103 30 E
James B., Canada 89 51 30N 80 0W
Jammu, India 58 32 43N 74 54 E
Jammu & Kashmir □, India 58 34 25N 77 0 E
Jamnagar, India 58 22 30N 70 6 E
Jamshedpur, India 59 22 44N 86 12 E
Japan ■, Asia 62 36 0N 136 0 E
Japan, Sea of, Asia 62 40 0N 135 0 E
Japurá →, Brazil 100 3 8S 64 46W
Jarrow, U.K. 21 54 58N 1 28W
Java, I., Indon. 63 7 0S 110 0 E
Java Sea, E. Ind. 63 4 35S 107 15 E
Jedburgh, U.K. 21 55 28N 2 33W
Jedda, Si. Arab. 56 21 29N 39 10 E
Jena, Ger. 42 50 56N 11 33 E
Jequié, Brazil 101 13 51S 40 5W
Jerez de la Frontera, Sp. 37 36 41N 6 7W
Jericho, Jord. 57 31 52N 35 27 E
Jersey, I., U.K. 34 49 13N 2 7W

Jersey City, U.S.A. 93 40 41N 74 8W
Jerusalem, Asia 57 31 47N 35 10 E
Jervaulx, U.K. 19 54 19N 1 41W
Jervis Bay, Austral. 70 35 8S 150 43 E
Jhansi, India 58 25 30N 78 36 E
Jhelum →, Pak. 58 31 20N 72 10 E
Jiamusi, China 61 46 40N 130 26 E
Ji'an, China 61 27 6N 114 59 E
Jiangsu □, China 61 33 0N 120 0 E
Jiangxi □, China 61 27 30N 116 0 E
Jilin, China 61 43 44N 126 30 E
Jilin □, China 61 44 0N 124 0 E
Jima, Eth. 79 7 40N 36 47 E
Jinan, China 61 36 38N 117 1 E
Jinja, Uganda 80 0 25N 33 12 E
Jinzhou, China 61 41 5N 121 3 E
Jixi, China 61 45 20N 130 50 E
João Pessoa, Brazil 101 7 10S 34 52W
Johannesburg, S. Afr. 81 26 10S 28 2 E
John o' Groats, U.K. 23 58 39N 3 3W
Johnstone, U.K. 20 55 50N 4 31W
Johnstown, U.S.A. 92 40 19N 78 53W
Johor Baharu, Malay. 63 1 28N 103 46 E
Jönköping, Swed. 45 57 45N 14 10 E
Jonquière, Canada 93 48 27N 71 14W
Jordan ■, Asia 57 31 0N 36 0 E
Jordan →, Asia 57 31 48N 35 32 E
Jos, Nig. 78 9 53N 8 51 E
Joseph Bonaparte G., Austral. 66 14 35S 128 50 E
Jotunheimen, Nor. 44 61 35N 8 25 E
Juan de Fuca Str., Canada 90 48 15N 124 0W
Juàzeiro do Norte, Brazil 101 7 10S 39 18W
Juiz de Fora, Brazil 101 21 43S 43 19W
Juliaca, Peru 100 15 25S 70 10W
Julianehåb, Green. 89 60 43N 46 0W
Jullundur, India 58 31 20N 75 40 E
Jundiaí, Brazil 102 24 30S 47 0W
Juneau, U.S.A. 88 58 20N 134 20W
Jura, U.K. 20 56 0N 5 50W
Jura, Mts., Europe 42 46 40N 6 5 E
Jura, Paps of, U.K. 20 55 55N 6 0W
Jura, Sd. of, U.K. 20 55 57N 5 45W
Jurby Hd., U.K. 18 54 23N 4 31W
Juruá →, Brazil 100 2 37S 65 44W
Jutland = Jylland, Den. 45 56 25N 9 30 E
Jylland, Den. 45 56 25N 9 30 E
Jyväskylä, Fin. 44 62 14N 25 50 E

K

Kābul, Afg. 57 34 28N 69 11 E
Kabwe, Zam. 81 14 30S 28 29 E
Kaduna, Nig. 78 10 30N 7 21 E
Kaesŏng, N. Kor. 61 37 58N 126 35 E
Kagoshima, Jap. 62 31 35N 130 33 E
Kaifeng, China 61 34 49N 114 30 E
Kaiserslautern, Ger. 36 49 30N 7 43 E
Kaitaia, N.Z. 71 35 8S 173 17 E
Kajaani, Fin. 44 64 17N 27 46 E
Kakinada, India 59 16 57N 82 11 E
Kalahari, Africa 81 24 0S 21 30 E
Kalamazoo, U.S.A. 92 42 20N 85 35W
Kalemie, Zaïre 80 5 55S 29 9 E
Kalgoorlie-Boulder, Austral. 66 30 40S 121 22 E
Kalimantan, Indon. 63 0 0 114 0 E
* Kalinin, U.S.S.R. 46 56 55N 35 55 E
Kaliningrad, U.S.S.R. 46 54 42N 20 32 E
Kaluga, U.S.S.R. 46 54 35N 36 10 E
Kamchatka Pen., U.S.S.R. 49 57 0N 160 0 E
Kamensk Uralskiy, U.S.S.R. 48 56 25N 62 2 E
Kames, U.K. 20 55 53N 5 15W
Kamina, Zaïre 80 8 45S 25 0 E
Kamloops, Canada 88 50 40N 120 20W
Kampala, Uganda 80 0 20N 32 30 E
Kampuchea = Cambodia ■, Asia 63 12 15N 105 0 E
Kananga, Zaïre 80 5 55S 22 18 E
Kanazawa, Jap. 62 36 30N 136 38 E
Kanchenjunga, Nepal 59 27 50N 88 10 E
Kandy, Sri L. 58 7 18N 80 43 E
Kangaroo I., Austral. 67 35 45S 137 0 E
Kanin, Pen., U.S.S.R. 46 68 0N 45 0 E
Kankan, Guin. 78 10 23N 9 15W
Kano, Nig. 78 12 2N 8 30 E
Kanpur, India 58 26 28N 80 20 E
Kansas □, U.S.A. 90 38 40N 98 0W
Kansas City, Kans., U.S.A. 91 39 0N 94 40W
Kansas City, Mo., U.S.A. 91 39 3N 94 30W
Kansk, U.S.S.R. 49 56 20N 95 37 E
Kanturk, Ire. 25 52 10N 8 55W
Kaohsiung, Taiwan 61 22 35N 120 16 E
Kaolack, Sene. 78 14 5N 16 8W
Kara Bogaz Gol, Zaliv, U.S.S.R. 47 41 0N 53 30 E
Kara Kalpak A.S.S.R. □, U.S.S.R. 48 43 0N 60 0 E
Kara Kum, U.S.S.R. 48 39 30N 60 0 E
Kara Sea, U.S.S.R. 48 75 0N 70 0 E
Karachi, Pak. 58 24 53N 67 0 E
Karaganda, U.S.S.R. 48 49 50N 73 10 E

* Renamed Tver

Karakoram Ra., Asia 58 35 30N 77 0 E
Karbalā, Iraq 56 32 36N 44 3 E
* Karl-Marx-Stadt, Ger. 42 50 50N 12 55 E
Karlskrona, Swed. 45 56 10N 15 35 E
Karlsruhe, Ger. 42 49 3N 8 23 E
Karlstad, Swed. 45 59 23N 13 30 E
Karratha, Austral. 66 20 53S 116 40 E
Karsakpay, U.S.S.R. 48 47 55N 66 40 E
Karshi, U.S.S.R. 48 38 53N 65 48 E
Kāshān, Iran 56 34 5N 51 30 E
Kashi, China 60 39 30N 76 2 E
Kassala, Sudan 79 16 0N 36 0 E
Kassel, Ger. 42 51 19N 9 32 E
Katmandu, Nepal 59 27 45N 85 20 E
Katoomba, Austral. 70 33 41S 150 19 E
Katowice, Pol. 43 50 17N 19 5 E
Katrine, L., U.K. 20 56 15N 4 30W
Katsina, Nig. 78 13 0N 7 32 E
Kattegatt, Den. 45 57 0N 11 20 E
Kauai, U.S.A. 90 22 0N 159 30W
Kaunas, Lithuania 46 54 54N 23 54 E
Kavála, Greece 41 40 57N 24 28 E
Kawagoe, Jap. 62 35 55N 139 29 E
Kawasaki, Jap. 62 35 35N 139 42 E
Kawthoolei □, Burma 59 18 0N 97 30 E
Kayes, Mali 78 14 25N 11 30W
Kayseri, Turk. 47 38 45N 35 30 E
Kazakhstan □, U.S.S.R. 48 50 0N 70 0 E
Kazan, U.S.S.R. 46 55 48N 49 3 E
Kea, U.K. 16 50 13N 5 4W
Keady, U.K. 24 54 15N 6 42W
Keal, Loch na, U.K. 20 56 30N 6 5W
Kecskemét, Hung. 43 46 57N 19 42 E
Kediri, Indon. 63 7 51S 112 1 E
Keelby, U.K. 19 53 34N 0 15W
Keele, U.K. 18 53 0N 2 17W
Keeper Hill, Ire. 25 52 46N 8 17W
Keewatin, Canada 88 49 46N 94 34W
Kefallinía, Greece 41 38 20N 20 30 E
Keflavík, Ice. 44 64 2N 22 35W
Kegworth, U.K. 14 52 50N 1 17W
Keighley, U.K. 18 53 52N 1 54W
Keith, U.K. 23 57 33N 2 58W
Keld, U.K. 18 54 24N 2 11W
Kellerberrin, Austral. 66 31 36S 117 38 E
Kells = Ceanannus Mor, Ire. 24 53 42N 6 53W
Kells, Rhinns of, U.K. 20 55 9N 4 22W
Kelowna, Canada 88 49 50N 119 25W
Kelsale, U.K. 15 52 15N 1 30 E
Kelsall, U.K. 18 53 14N 2 44W
Kelso, U.K. 21 55 36N 2 27W
Kelvedon, U.K. 15 51 50N 0 43 E
Kemble, U.K. 14 51 40N 2 1W
Kemerovo, U.S.S.R. 48 55 20N 86 5 E
Kemi, Fin. 44 65 44N 24 34 E
Kempsey, U.K. 14 52 8N 2 11W
Kempston, U.K. 15 52 7N 0 30W
Ken, L., U.K. 21 55 0N 4 8W
Kendal, U.K. 18 54 19N 2 44W
Kenilworth, U.K. 14 52 22N 1 35W
Kenitra, Mor. 78 34 15N 6 40W
Kenmare, Ire. 25 51 52N 9 35W
Kenmare →, Ire. 25 51 40N 10 0W
Kennet →, U.K. 14 51 24N 0 58W
Kenninghall, U.K. 15 52 26N 1 0 E
Kenora, Canada 88 49 47N 94 29W
Kent □, U.K. 15 51 12N 0 40 E
Kentisbeare, U.K. 16 50 51N 3 18W
Kenton, U.K. 16 50 37N 3 28W
Kentucky □, U.S.A. 91 37 20N 85 0W
Kenya ■, Africa 80 1 0N 38 0 E
Kerala □, India 58 11 0N 76 15 E
Kerch, U.S.S.R. 47 45 20N 36 20 E
Kérkira, Greece 41 39 38N 19 50 E
Kermān, Iran 57 30 15N 57 1 E
Kerrera I., U.K. 20 56 24N 5 32W
Kerry □, Ire. 25 52 7N 9 35W
Kerry Hd., Ire. 25 52 26N 9 56W
Kessingland, U.K. 15 52 25N 1 41 E
Keswick, U.K. 18 54 35N 3 9W
Ketchikan, U.S.A. 88 55 25N 131 40W
Kettering, U.K. 15 52 24N 0 44W
Kettle Ness, U.K. 19 54 32N 0 41W
Kettlewell, U.K. 18 54 8N 2 2W
Keweenaw Pen., U.S.A. 92 47 30N 88 0W
Kexby, U.K. 19 53 21N 0 41W
Key West, U.S.A. 91 24 33N 82 0W
Keyingham, U.K. 19 53 42N 0 7W
Keymer, U.K. 15 50 55N 0 5W
Keynsham, U.K. 14 51 25N 2 30W
Keyworth, U.K. 14 52 52N 1 8W
Khabarovsk, U.S.S.R. 49 48 30N 135 5 E
Khaniá, Greece 41 35 30N 24 4 E
Kharagpur, India 59 22 20N 87 25 E
Kharkov, U.S.S.R. 47 49 58N 36 20 E
Khartoum, Sudan 79 15 31N 32 35 E
Khaskovo, Bulg. 41 41 56N 25 30 E
Kherson, U.S.S.R. 47 46 35N 32 35 E
Khíos, I., Greece 41 38 20N 26 0 E
Khorrāmshahr, Iran 56 30 29N 48 15 E
Khouribga, Mor. 78 32 58N 6 57W
Khulna, Bangla. 59 22 45N 89 34 E
Khulna □, Bangla. 59 22 25N 89 35 E
Khurasan, Iran 57 34 0N 57 0 E
Kibworth Beauchamp, U.K. 15 52 33N 0 59W
Kicking Horse Pass, Canada 88 51 28N 116 16W
Kidderminster, U.K. 14 52 24N 2 13W
Kidlington, U.K. 14 51 49N 1 18W

* Renamed Chemnitz

Kidsgrove, U.K. 18 53 6N 2 15W
Kidstones, U.K. 18 54 15N 2 2W
Kidwelly, U.K. 17 51 44N 4 20W
Kiel, Ger. 42 54 16N 10 8 E
Kielce, Pol. 43 50 52N 20 42 E
Kielder, U.K. 21 55 14N 2 35W
Kiev, U.S.S.R. 47 50 30N 30 28 E
Kigali, Rwanda 80 1 59S 30 4 E
Kigoma-Ujiji, Tanz. 80 4 55S 29 36 E
Kikládhes, Greece 41 37 20N 24 30 E
Kikwit, Zaïre 80 5 5S 18 45 E
Kilbirnie, U.K. 20 55 46N 4 42W
Kilbrannan Sd., U.K. 20 55 40N 5 23W
Kilcreggan, U.K. 20 55 59N 4 50W
Kildare, Ire. 25 53 10N 6 50W
Kildare □, Ire. 25 53 10N 6 50W
Kildonan, U.K. 23 58 10N 3 50W
Kilfinan, U.K. 20 55 57N 5 19W
Kilham, U.K. 19 54 4N 0 22W
Kilimanjaro, Tanz. 80 3 7S 37 20 E
Kilkee, Ire. 25 52 41N 9 40W
Kilkeel, U.K. 24 54 4N 6 0W
Kilkenny, Ire. 25 52 40N 7 17W
Kilkenny □, Ire. 25 52 35N 7 15W
Kilkhampton, U.K. 16 50 53N 4 30W
Kilkieran B., Ire. 25 53 18N 9 45W
Killala, Ire. 24 54 13N 9 12W
Killala B., Ire. 24 54 20N 9 12W
Killaloe, Ire. 25 52 48N 8 28W
Killarney, Ire. 25 52 2N 9 30W
Killarney, Lakes of, Ire. 25 52 0N 9 30W
Killary Harbour, Ire. 24 53 38N 9 52W
Killchianaig, U.K. 20 56 2N 5 48W
Killean, U.K. 20 55 38N 5 40W
Killiecrankie, Pass of, U.K. 23 56 44N 3 46W
Killin, U.K. 20 56 28N 4 20W
Killinghall, U.K. 19 54 1N 1 33W
Killybegs, Ire. 24 54 38N 8 26W
Kilmacolm, U.K. 20 55 54N 4 39W
Kilmarnock, U.K. 20 55 36N 4 30W
Kilmartin, U.K. 20 56 8N 5 29W
Kilmaurs, U.K. 20 55 37N 4 33W
Kilmelford, U.K. 20 56 16N 5 30W
Kilninver, U.K. 20 56 20N 5 30W
Kilrenny, U.K. 21 56 15N 2 40W
Kilrush, Ire. 25 52 39N 9 30W
Kilsby, U.K. 14 52 20N 1 11W
Kilsyth, U.K. 21 55 58N 4 3W
Kilwinning, U.K. 20 55 40N 4 41W
Kimberley, Austral. 66 16 20S 127 0 E
Kimberley, S. Afr. 81 28 43S 24 46 E
Kimbolton, U.K. 15 52 17N 0 23W
Kincardine, U.K. 21 56 4N 3 43W
Kindu, Zaïre 80 2 55S 25 50 E
Kineton, U.K. 14 52 10N 1 30W
King Frederick VI Coast, Green. 89 63 0N 43 0W
King Sd., Austral. 66 16 50S 123 20 E
Kingarth, U.K. 20 55 45N 5 2W
Kinghorn, U.K. 21 56 4N 3 10W
King's Lynn, U.K. 15 52 45N 0 25 E
King's Sutton, U.K. 14 52 1N 1 16W
King's Worthy, U.K. 14 51 6N 1 18W
Kingsbarns, U.K. 21 56 18N 2 40W
Kingsbridge, U.K. 16 50 17N 3 46W
Kingsbury, U.K. 14 52 33N 1 41W
Kingscourt, Ire. 24 53 55N 6 48W
Kingskerswell, U.K. 16 50 30N 3 34W
Kingsland, U.K. 14 52 15N 2 49W
Kingsteignton, U.K. 16 50 32N 3 35W
Kingston, Canada 92 44 14N 76 30W
Kingston, Jam. 94 18 0N 76 50W
Kingston, U.K. 14 51 18N 1 40W
Kingston-upon-Hull, U.K. 19 53 45N 0 20W
Kingston-upon-Thames, U.K. 15 51 23N 0 20W
Kingstown, St. Vinc. 94 13 10N 61 10W
Kingswear, U.K. 16 50 21N 3 33W
Kingswood, U.K. 14 51 26N 2 31W
Kington, U.K. 14 52 12N 3 2W
Kingussie, U.K. 23 57 5N 4 2W
Kinlochewe, U.K. 22 57 37N 5 20W
Kinlochleven, U.K. 22 56 42N 4 59W
Kinnairds Hd., U.K. 23 57 40N 2 0W
Kinneret, Lake, Isr. 57 32 45N 35 35 E
Kinross, U.K. 21 56 13N 3 25W
Kinsale, Ire. 25 51 42N 8 31W
Kinsale, Old Hd. of, Ire. 25 51 37N 8 32W
Kinshasa, Zaïre 80 4 20S 15 15 E
Kintyre, U.K. 20 55 30N 5 35W
Kintyre, Mull of, U.K. 20 55 17N 5 55W
Kippen, U.K. 20 56 8N 4 12W
Kippure, Ire. 25 53 11N 6 23W
Kirensk, U.S.S.R. 49 57 50N 107 55 E
Kirgizia □, U.S.S.R. 48 42 0N 75 0 E
Kirgiziya Steppe, U.S.S.R. 47 50 0N 55 0 E
Kiribati ■, Pac. Oc. 65 1 0N 176 0 E
Kirk Michael, U.K. 18 54 17N 4 35W
Kirkbean, U.K. 21 54 56N 3 35W
Kirkbride, U.K. 21 54 54N 3 13W
Kirkburton, U.K. 19 53 36N 1 42W
Kirkby, U.K. 18 53 29N 2 54W
Kirkby-in-Ashfield, U.K. 19 53 6N 1 15W
Kirkby Lonsdale, U.K. 18 54 13N 2 36W
Kirkby Malzeard, U.K. 19 54 10N 1 38W
Kirkby Stephen, U.K. 18 54 27N 2 23W
Kirkby Thore, U.K. 18 54 38N 2 34W
Kirkbymoorside, U.K. 19 54 16N 0 56W
Kirkcaldy, U.K. 21 56 7N 3 10W
Kirkcolm, U.K. 20 54 59N 5 4W
Kirkconnel, U.K. 21 55 23N 4 0W
Kirkcowan, U.K. 20 54 53N 4 38W
Kirkcudbright, U.K. 21 54 50N 4 3W
Kirkcudbright B., U.K. 21 54 46N 4 0W
Kirkham, U.K. 18 53 47N 2 52W
Kirkinner, U.K. 20 54 49N 4 28W
Kirkintilloch, U.K. 21 55 57N 4 10W
Kirkland Lake, Canada 92 48 9N 80 2W
Kirkliston, U.K. 21 55 55N 3 27W
Kirkoswald, U.K. 18 54 46N 2 41W
Kirkoswold, U.K. 20 55 19N 4 48W
Kirkstone P., U.K. 18 54 29N 2 55W
Kirkūk, Iraq 56 35 30N 44 21 E
Kirkwall, U.K. 23 58 59N 2 59W
Kirkwhelpington, U.K. 21 55 9N 2 0W
† Kirov, U.S.S.R. 46 58 35N 49 40 E
* Kirovabad, U.S.S.R. 47 40 45N 46 20 E
†† Kirovograd, U.S.S.R. 47 48 35N 32 20 E
Kirovsk, U.S.S.R. 46 48 35N 38 30 E
Kirriemuir, U.K. 23 56 41N 3 0W
Kirtling, U.K. 15 52 11N 0 27 E
Kirtlington, U.K. 14 51 54N 1 9W
Kirton, U.K. 19 52 56N 0 3W
Kirton-in-Lindsey, U.K. 19 53 29N 0 35W
Kiruna, Swed. 44 67 52N 20 15 E
Kisangani, Zaïre 80 0 35N 25 15 E
Kishinev, U.S.S.R. 47 47 0N 28 50 E
Kismayu, Som. 73 0 22S 42 32 E
Kisumu, Kenya 80 0 3S 34 45 E
Kitakyūshū, Jap. 62 33 50N 130 50 E
Kitchener, Canada 92 43 27N 80 29W
Kíthira, Greece 41 36 9N 23 0 E
Kitikmeot □, Canada 88 70 0N 110 0W
Kitimat, Canada 88 54 3N 128 38W
Kitwe, Zam. 81 12 54S 28 13 E
Klagenfurt, Austria 42 46 38N 14 20 E
Klerksdorp, S. Afr. 81 26 51S 26 38 E
Klondike, Canada 88 64 0N 139 26W
Knapdale, U.K. 20 55 55N 5 30W
Knaresborough, U.K. 19 54 1N 1 29W
Knebworth, U.K. 15 51 52N 0 11W
Knighton, U.K. 17 52 21N 3 2W
Knockmealdown Mts., Ire. 25 52 16N 8 0W
Knossos, Greece 41 35 16N 25 10 E
Knott End, U.K. 18 53 55N 3 0W
Knottingley, U.K. 19 53 42N 1 15W
Knowle, U.K. 14 52 23N 1 43W
Knoxville, U.S.A. 91 35 58N 83 57W
Knutsford, U.K. 18 53 18N 2 22W
Kōbe, Jap. 62 34 45N 135 10 E
København = Copenhagen, Den. 45 55 41N 12 34 E
Koblenz, Ger. 36 50 21N 7 36 E
Kodiak I., U.S.A. 88 57 30N 152 45W
Koforidua, Ghana 78 6 3N 0 17W
Kokand, U.S.S.R. 48 40 30N 70 57 E
Kokchetav, U.S.S.R. 48 53 20N 69 25 E
Kokkola, Fin. 44 63 50N 23 8 E
Kola Pen., U.S.S.R. 46 67 30N 38 0 E
Kolding, Den. 45 55 30N 9 29 E
Kolguyev, I., U.S.S.R. 46 69 20N 48 30 E
Kolomna, U.S.S.R. 46 55 8N 38 45 E
Kolwezi, Zaïre 80 10 40S 25 25 E
Kolyma →, U.S.S.R. 49 69 30N 161 0 E
Kolyma Ra., U.S.S.R. 49 63 0N 157 0 E
Komandorskiye, Is., U.S.S.R. 49 55 0N 167 0 E
Komsomolets I., U.S.S.R. 49 80 30N 95 0 E
Komsomolsk, U.S.S.R. 49 50 30N 137 0 E
Konya, Turk. 47 37 52N 32 35 E
Kópavogur, Ice. 44 64 6N 21 55W
Korce, Alb. 41 40 37N 20 50 E
Korea, North ■, Asia 61 40 0N 127 0 E
Korea, South ■, Asia 61 36 0N 128 0 E
Korea Strait, Asia 61 34 0N 129 30 E
Kōriyama, Jap. 62 37 24N 140 23 E
Korla, China 60 41 45N 86 4 E
Kortrijk, Belg. 36 50 50N 3 17 E
Koryak Range, U.S.S.R. 49 61 0N 171 0 E
Kos, Greece 41 36 50N 27 15 E
Košice, Czech. 43 48 42N 21 15 E
Kōstī, Sudan 79 13 8N 32 43 E
Kostroma, U.S.S.R. 46 57 50N 40 58 E
Kota, India 58 25 14N 75 49 E
Kota Baharu, Malay. 63 6 7N 102 14 E
Kota Kinabalu, Malay. 63 6 0N 116 4 E
Kotka, Fin. 45 60 28N 26 58 E
Kra, Isthmus of, Thai. 63 10 15N 99 30 E
Kragujevac, Yug. 41 44 2N 20 56 E
Krakatau, Indon. 63 6 10S 105 20 E
Kraków, Pol. 43 50 4N 19 57 E
Krasnodar, U.S.S.R. 47 45 5N 39 0 E
Krasnoturinsk, U.S.S.R. 46 59 46N 60 12 E
Krasnovodsk, U.S.S.R. 48 40 0N 52 52 E
Krasnoyarsk, U.S.S.R. 49 56 8N 93 0 E
Krefeld, Ger. 36 51 20N 6 32 E
Kremenchug, U.S.S.R. 47 49 5N 33 25 E
Krishna →, India 59 15 57N 80 59 E
Kristiansand, Nor. 45 58 9N 8 1 E
Kristianstad, Swed. 45 56 2N 14 9 E
Kristiansund, Nor. 44 63 7N 7 45 E
Krivoy Rog, U.S.S.R. 47 47 51N 33 20 E
Kroonstad, S. Afr. 81 27 43S 27 19 E
Krung Thep = Bangkok, Thai. 63 13 45N 100 35 E
Kruševac, Yug. 41 43 35N 21 28 E
Kuala Lumpur, Malay. 63 3 9N 101 41 E

† Renamed Vyatka
* Renamed Gyandzha
†† Renamed Yelizavetgrad

Kuala Trengganu, Malay. 63 5 20N 103 8 E
Kuangchou = Guangzhou, China 61 23 5N 113 10 E
Kuantan, Malay. 63 3 49N 103 20 E
Kucing, Malay. 63 1 33N 110 25 E
Kueiyang = Guiyang, China 60 26 32N 106 40 E
Kumanovo, Yug. 41 42 9N 21 42 E
Kumasi, Ghana 78 6 41N 1 38W
Kunlun Shan, Asia 60 36 0N 86 30 E
Kunming, China 60 25 1N 102 41 E
Kuopio, Fin. 44 62 53N 27 35 E
Kura →, U.S.S.R. 47 39 50N 49 20 E
Kurashiki, Jap. 62 34 40N 133 50 E
Kure, Jap. 62 34 14N 132 32 E
Kurgan, U.S.S.R. 48 55 26N 65 18 E
Kuria Maria Is., Ind. Oc. 57 17 30N 55 58 E
Kuril Is., U.S.S.R. 49 45 0N 150 0 E
Kurnool, India 58 15 45N 78 0 E
Kurri Kurri, Austral. 70 32 50S 151 28 E
Kursk, U.S.S.R. 46 51 42N 36 11 E
Kurume, Jap. 62 33 15N 130 30 E
Kushiro, Jap. 62 43 0N 144 25 E
Kustanay, U.S.S.R. 48 53 10N 63 35 E
Kütahya, Turk. 47 39 30N 30 2 E
Kutaisi, U.S.S.R. 47 42 19N 42 40 E
Kutch, Gulf of, India 58 22 50N 69 15 E
Kutch, Rann of, India 58 24 0N 70 0 E
Kuwait, Kuw. 56 29 30N 47 30 E
Kuwait ■, Asia 56 29 30N 47 30 E
* Kuybyshev, U.S.S.R. 46 53 8N 50 6 E
Kwangju, S. Kor. 61 35 9N 126 54 E
Kyle, U.K. 20 55 32N 4 25W
Kyle of Lochalsh, U.K. 22 57 17N 5 43W
Kyōto, Jap. 62 35 0N 135 45 E
Kyūshū, Jap. 62 33 0N 131 0 E
Kzyl-Orda, U.S.S.R. 48 44 48N 65 28 E

L

Labe = Elbe →, Ger. 42 53 50N 9 0 E
Labé, Guin. 78 11 24N 12 16W
Labrador, Coast of □, Canada 89 53 20N 61 0W
Labrador City, Canada 89 52 57N 66 55W
Laccadive Is. = Lakshadweep Is., Ind. Oc. 51 10 0N 72 30 E
Laceby, U.K. 19 53 32N 0 10W
Lachlan →, Austral. 70 34 22S 143 55 E
Lacock, U.K. 14 51 24N 2 8W
Ladock, U.K. 16 50 19N 4 58W
Ladoga, L., U.S.S.R. 46 61 15N 30 30 E
Ladybank, U.K. 21 56 16N 3 8W
Lafayette, U.S.A. 91 30 18N 92 0W
Lagan →, U.K. 24 54 35N 5 55W
Lagg, U.K. 20 55 51N 5 50W
Laggan B., U.K. 20 55 40N 6 20W
Lagos, Nig. 78 6 25N 3 27 E
Lagos, Port. 37 37 5N 8 41W
Lahore, Pak. 58 31 32N 74 22 E
Lahti, Fin. 45 60 58N 25 40 E
Lairg, U.K. 23 58 1N 4 24W
Lake Charles, U.S.A. 91 30 15N 93 10W
Lake District, U.K. 18 54 30N 3 10W
Lakenheath, U.K. 15 52 25N 0 30 E
Lakewood, U.S.A. 92 41 28N 81 50W
Lakshadweep Is., Ind. Oc. 51 10 0N 72 30 E
Lambay I., Ire. 24 53 30N 6 0W
Lamberhurst, U.K. 15 51 5N 0 21 E
Lambeth, U.K. 15 51 27N 0 7W
Lambley, U.K. 21 54 56N 2 30W
Lambourn, U.K. 14 51 31N 1 31W
Lamlash, U.K. 20 55 32N 5 8W
Lammermuir, U.K. 21 55 50N 2 25W
Lammermuir Hills, U.K. 21 55 50N 2 40W
Lampeter, U.K. 17 52 6N 4 6W
Lanark, U.K. 21 55 40N 3 48W
Lancashire □, U.K. 18 53 40N 2 30W
Lancaster, U.K. 18 54 3N 2 48W
Lancaster Sd., Canada 89 74 13N 84 0W
Lanchester, U.K. 19 54 50N 1 44W
Lancing, U.K. 15 50 49N 0 19W
Landkey, U.K. 16 51 2N 4 0W
Land's End, U.K. 16 50 4N 5 43W
Langholm, U.K. 21 55 9N 2 59W
Langness, U.K. 18 54 3N 4 37W
Langport, U.K. 14 51 2N 2 51W
Langstrothdale Chase, U.K. 18 54 14N 2 13W
Langtoft, U.K. 15 52 42N 0 19W
Langtree, U.K. 16 50 55N 4 11W
Lansing, U.S.A. 92 42 47N 84 40W
Lanzhou, China 60 36 1N 103 52 E
Laoag, Phil. 63 18 7N 120 34 E
Laois □, Ire. 25 53 0N 7 20W
Laos ■, Asia 63 17 45N 105 0 E
Lapford, U.K. 16 50 52N 3 49W
Lapland, Europe 44 68 7N 24 0 E
Laptev Sea, U.S.S.R. 49 76 0N 125 0 E
Larbert, U.K. 21 56 2N 3 50W
Laredo, U.S.A. 90 27 34N 99 29W
Largs, U.K. 20 55 48N 4 51W
Lárisa, Greece 41 39 49N 22 28 E
Larkhall, U.K. 21 55 44N 4 0W
Larne, U.K. 24 54 52N 5 50W

* Renamed Samara

Las Palmas, Can. Is. 78 28 7N 15 26W
Las Vegas, U.S.A. 90 36 10N 115 5W
Laskill, U.K. 19 54 19N 1 6W
Lasswade, U.K. 21 55 53N 3 8W
Latakia, Syria 56 35 30N 35 45 E
Latina, It. 40 41 26N 12 53 E
Latvia ■, Europe 46 56 50N 24 0 E
Lauder, U.K. 21 55 43N 2 45W
Lauderdale, U.K. 21 55 43N 2 44W
Launceston, Austral. 67 41 24S 147 8 E
Launceston, U.K. 16 50 38N 4 21W
Laune →, Ire. 25 52 5N 9 40W
Laurencekirk, U.K. 23 56 50N 2 30W
Laurentian Plateau, Canada 82 52 0N 70 0W
Laurieston, U.K. 21 54 57N 4 2W
Lausanne, Switz. 42 46 32N 6 38 E
Laval, Fr. 34 48 4N 0 48W
Lavendon, U.K. 15 52 11N 0 39W
Lavenham, U.K. 15 52 7N 0 48 E
Lawers, U.K. 21 56 31N 4 9W
Lawrence, U.S.A. 93 42 40N 71 9W
Laxey, U.K. 18 54 15N 4 23W
Laxfield, U.K. 15 52 18N 1 23 E
Laxford, L., U.K. 22 58 25N 5 10W
Lazonby, U.K. 18 54 45N 2 42W
Lea, U.K. 19 53 22N 0 45W
Lea →, U.K. 15 51 30N 0 10W
Leadenham, U.K. 19 53 5N 0 33W
Leadhills, U.K. 21 55 25N 3 47W
Leamington, U.K. 14 52 18N 1 32W
Leatherhead, U.K. 15 51 18N 0 20W
Lebanon ■, Asia 56 34 0N 36 0 E
Lecce, It. 41 40 20N 18 10 E
Lechlade, U.K. 14 51 42N 1 40W
Ledbury, U.K. 14 52 3N 2 25W
Leduc, Canada 88 53 15N 113 30W
Lee, U.K. 14 50 47N 1 11W
Lee →, Ire. 25 51 50N 8 30W
Leeds, U.K. 19 53 48N 1 34W
Leek, U.K. 18 53 7N 2 2W
Leer, Ger. 36 53 13N 7 29 E
Leeton, Austral. 70 34 33S 146 23 E
Leeuwarden, Neth. 36 53 15N 5 48 E
Leeuwin, C., Austral. 66 34 20S 115 9 E
Leghorn, It. 40 43 32N 10 18 E
Legnica, Pol. 42 51 12N 16 10 E
Leicester, U.K. 14 52 39N 1 9W
Leicester □, U.K. 14 52 40N 1 10W
Leiden, Neth. 36 52 9N 4 30 E
Leigh, Gr. Manchester, U.K. 18 53 29N 2 31W
Leigh, Hereford & Worcs., U.K. 14 52 10N 2 21W
Leighton Buzzard, U.K. 15 51 55N 0 39W
Leinster □, Ire. 25 53 0N 7 10W
Leinster, Mt., Ire. 25 52 38N 6 47W
Leintwardine, U.K. 14 52 22N 2 51W
Leipzig, Ger. 42 51 20N 12 23 E
Leiston, U.K. 15 52 13N 1 35 E
Leith, U.K. 21 55 59N 3 10W
Leith Hill, U.K. 15 51 10N 0 23W
Leitholm, U.K. 21 55 42N 2 16W
Leitrim, Ire. 24 54 0N 8 5W
Leitrim □, Ire. 24 54 8N 8 0W
Lek →, Neth. 36 51 54N 4 35 E
Lelant, U.K. 16 50 11N 5 26W
Lelystad, Neth. 36 52 30N 5 25 E
Lena →, U.S.S.R. 49 72 52N 126 40 E
Lendalfoot, U.K. 20 55 12N 4 55W
Lenham, U.K. 15 51 14N 0 44 E
Leninakan, U.S.S.R. 47 40 47N 43 50 E
* Leningrad, U.S.S.R. 46 59 55N 30 20 E
Leninsk-Kuznetskiy, U.S.S.R. 48 54 44N 86 10 E
Lennox Hills, U.K. 20 56 3N 4 12W
Lennoxtown, U.K. 20 55 58N 4 14W
Lens, Fr. 34 50 26N 2 50 E
Leominster, U.K. 14 52 15N 2 43W
León, Mex. 94 21 7N 101 40W
León, Sp. 37 42 38N 5 34W
Lérida, Sp. 37 41 37N 0 39 E
Lerwick, U.K. 22 60 10N 1 10W
Lesbos, I. = Lésvos, Greece 41 39 10N 26 20 E
Lesbury, U.K. 21 55 25N 1 37W
Leskovac, Yug. 41 43 0N 21 58 E
Leslie, U.K. 21 56 12N 3 12W
Lesmahagow, U.K. 21 55 38N 3 55W
Lesotho ■, Africa 81 29 40S 28 0 E
Lésvos, Greece 41 39 10N 26 20 E
Leswalt, U.K. 20 54 56N 5 6W
Letchworth, U.K. 15 51 58N 0 13W
Lethbridge, Canada 88 49 45N 112 45W
Letterkenny, Ire. 24 54 57N 7 42W
Leuchars, U.K. 21 56 23N 2 53W
Leven, Fife, U.K. 21 56 12N 3 0W
Leven, Humberside, U.K. 19 53 54N 0 18W
Leven →, U.K. 19 54 27N 1 15W
Leven, L., U.K. 21 56 12N 3 22W
Leverburgh, U.K. 22 57 46N 7 0W
Leverkusen, Ger. 36 51 2N 6 59 E
Lewes, U.K. 15 50 53N 0 2 E
Lewis, U.K. 22 58 10N 6 40W
Lewis, Butt of, U.K. 22 58 30N 6 12W
Lewisham, U.K. 15 51 27N 0 1W
Lexington, U.S.A. 92 38 6N 84 30W
Leyburn, U.K. 19 54 19N 1 50W
Leyland, U.K. 18 53 41N 2 42W

* Renamed St. Petersburg

Leysdown on Sea, U.K. 15 51 23N 0 57 E
Lhasa, China 60 29 50N 91 3 E
Liaodong, Gulf of, China 61 40 20N 121 10 E
Liaoning □, China 61 41 40N 122 30 E
Liaoyang, China 61 41 15N 123 10 E
Liaoyüan, China 61 42 55N 125 10 E
Liberia ■, W. Afr. 78 6 30N 9 30W
Libreville, Gabon 80 0 25N 9 26 E
Libya ■, N. Afr. 79 27 0N 17 0 E
Libyan Desert, Africa 79 25 0N 25 0 E
Lichfield, U.K. 14 52 40N 1 50W
Lichinga, Mozam. 81 13 13S 35 11 E
Liechtenstein ■, Europe 42 47 8N 9 35 E
Liège, Belg. 36 50 38N 5 35 E
Liepaja, U.S.S.R. 46 56 30N 21 0 E
Liffey →, Ire. 25 53 21N 6 20W
Lifford, Ire. 24 54 50N 7 30W
Ligurian Sea, It. 40 43 20N 9 0 E
Likasi, Zaïre 80 10 55S 26 48 E
Lille, Fr. 34 50 38N 3 3 E
Lille Bælt, Den. 45 55 20N 9 45 E
Lillehammer, Nor. 45 61 8N 10 30 E
Lilleshall, U.K. 14 52 45N 2 22W
Lilongwe, Malawi 81 14 0S 33 48 E
Lima, Peru 100 12 0S 77 0W
Limassol, Cyprus 47 34 42N 33 1 E
Limavady, U.K. 24 55 3N 6 58W
Limavady □, U.K. 24 55 0N 6 55W
Limburg □, Neth. 36 51 20N 5 55 E
Limerick, Ire. 25 52 40N 8 38W
Limerick □, Ire. 25 52 30N 8 50W
Límnos, Greece 41 39 50N 25 5 E
Limoges, Fr. 35 45 50N 1 15 E
Limpopo →, Mozam. 81 25 15S 33 30 E
Limpsfield, U.K. 15 51 15N 0 1 E
Linares, Sp. 37 38 10N 3 40W
Lincluden, U.K. 21 55 5N 3 40W
Lincoln, U.K. 19 53 14N 0 32W
Lincoln, U.S.A. 90 40 50N 96 42W
Lincoln □, U.K. 19 53 14N 0 32W
Lincoln Wolds, U.K. 19 53 20N 0 5W
Lindale, U.K. 18 54 14N 2 54W
Lingfield, U.K. 15 51 11N 0 1W
Linkinhorne, U.K. 16 50 31N 4 22W
Linköping, Swed. 45 58 28N 15 36 E
Linlithgow, U.K. 21 55 58N 3 38W
Linnhe, L., U.K. 20 56 36N 5 25W
Linslade, U.K. 15 51 55N 0 40W
Linton, U.K. 15 52 6N 0 19 E
Linxia, China 60 35 36N 103 10 E
Linz, Austria 42 48 18N 14 18 E
Lion, G. du, Fr. 35 43 0N 4 0 E
Lípari, Is., It. 40 38 30N 14 50 E
Lipetsk, U.S.S.R. 46 52 37N 39 35 E
Lisbon, Port. 37 38 42N 9 10W
Lisburn, U.K. 24 54 30N 6 9W
Liscannor, B., Ire. 25 52 57N 9 24W
Liskeard, U.K. 16 50 27N 4 29W
Lismore, Austral. 67 28 44S 153 21 E
Lismore, Ire. 25 52 8N 7 58W
Lismore I., U.K. 20 56 30N 5 30W
Liss, U.K. 15 51 3N 0 53W
Listowel, Ire. 25 52 27N 9 30W
Litcham, U.K. 15 52 43N 0 49 E
Litherland, U.K. 18 53 29N 3 0W
Lithgow, Austral. 70 33 25S 150 8 E
Lithuania ■, Europe 46 55 30N 24 0 E
Little Minch, U.K. 22 57 35N 6 45W
Little Ouse →, U.K. 15 52 25N 0 50 E
Little Rock, U.S.A. 91 34 41N 92 10W
Little Walsingham, U.K. 15 52 53N 0 51 E
Littleborough, U.K. 18 53 38N 2 8W
Littlehampton, U.K. 15 50 48N 0 32W
Littleport, U.K. 15 52 27N 0 18 E
Littlestone-on-Sea, U.K. 15 50 59N 0 59 E
Liuzhou, China 61 24 22N 109 22 E
Liverpool, Austral. 70 33 54S 150 58 E
Liverpool, U.K. 18 53 25N 3 0W
Liverpool Plains, Austral. 70 31 15S 150 15 E
Livingston, U.K. 21 55 52N 3 33W
Livingstone, Zam. 81 17 46S 25 52 E
Lizard, U.K. 16 49 58N 5 10W
Lizard Pt., U.K. 16 49 57N 5 11W
Ljubljana, Yug. 40 46 4N 14 33 E
Llandeilo, U.K. 17 51 53N 4 0W
Llandovery, U.K. 17 51 59N 3 49W
Llandrindod Wells, U.K. 17 52 15N 3 23W
Llandudno, U.K. 17 53 19N 3 51W
Llanelli, U.K. 17 51 41N 4 11W
Llanerchymedd, U.K. 17 53 20N 4 22W
Llanfair Caereinion, U.K. 17 52 39N 3 20W
Llanfair Talhaiarn, U.K. 17 53 13N 3 37W
Llanfairfechan, U.K. 17 53 15N 3 58W
Llangefni, U.K. 17 53 15N 4 20W
Llangollen, U.K. 17 52 58N 3 10W
Llanidloes, U.K. 17 52 28N 3 31W
Llanllyfni, U.K. 17 53 2N 4 18W
Llanos, S. Am. 100 5 0N 71 35W
Llanrhystyd, U.K. 17 52 19N 4 9W
Llantrisant, U.K. 17 51 33N 3 22W
Llantwit-Major, U.K. 17 51 24N 3 29W
Llanwrtyd Wells, U.K. 17 52 6N 3 39W
Llanyblodwel, U.K. 14 52 47N 3 8W
Llanymynech, U.K. 14 52 48N 3 6W
Lleyn Peninsula, U.K. 17 52 55N 4 35W
Loanhead, U.K. 21 55 53N 3 10W
Lobito, Angola 81 12 18S 13 35 E
Lochaber, U.K. 22 56 55N 5 0W
Lochans, U.K. 20 54 52N 5 1W
Lochboisdale, U.K. 22 57 10N 7 20W
Lochbuie, U.K. 20 56 21N 5 52W
Lochcarron, U.K. 22 57 25N 5 30W
Lochdonhead, U.K. 20 56 27N 5 40W
Lochearnhead, U.K. 20 56 24N 4 19W
Lochgelly, U.K. 21 56 7N 3 18W
Lochgilphead, U.K. 20 56 2N 5 37W
Lochgoilhead, U.K. 20 56 10N 4 54W
Lochinver, U.K. 22 58 9N 5 15W
Lochmaben, U.K. 21 55 8N 3 27W
Lochmaddy, U.K. 22 57 36N 7 10W
Lochnagar, U.K. 23 56 57N 3 14W
Lochranza, U.K. 20 55 42N 5 18W
Lochwinnoch, U.K. 20 55 47N 4 39W
Lochy →, U.K. 22 56 52N 5 3W
Lockerbie, U.K. 21 55 7N 3 21W
Lod, Isr. 57 31 57N 34 54 E
Loddon, U.K. 15 52 32N 1 29 E
Łódź, Pol. 43 51 45N 19 27 E
Lofoten, Nor. 44 68 30N 15 0 E
Loftus, U.K. 19 54 33N 0 52W
Logan, Mt., Canada 88 60 31N 140 22W
Logroño, Sp. 37 42 28N 2 27W
Loire →, Fr. 34 47 16N 2 10W
Lolland, Den. 45 54 45N 11 30 E
Lombardy □, It. 40 45 35N 9 45 E
Lomé, Togo 78 6 9N 1 20 E
Lomond, L., U.K. 20 56 8N 4 38W
Łomza, Pol. 43 53 10N 22 2 E
London, Canada 92 42 59N 81 15W
London, U.K. 15 51 30N 0 5W
London, Greater □, U.K. 15 51 30N 0 5W
Londonderry, U.K. 24 55 0N 7 20W
Londonderry □, U.K. 24 55 0N 7 20W
Londrina, Brazil 102 23 18S 51 10W
Long, L., U.K. 20 56 4N 4 50W
Long Beach, U.S.A. 90 33 46N 118 12W
Long Bennington, U.K. 19 52 59N 0 45W
Long Clawson, U.K. 15 52 51N 0 56W
Long Crendon, U.K. 15 51 47N 1 0W
Long Eaton, U.K. 19 52 54N 1 16W
Long I., Baham. 95 23 20N 75 10W
Long I., U.S.A. 93 40 50N 73 20W
Long Itchington, U.K. 14 52 16N 1 24W
Long Melford, U.K. 15 52 5N 0 44 E
Long Mynd, U.K. 14 52 35N 2 50W
Long Preston, U.K. 18 54 0N 2 16W
Long Sutton, U.K. 15 52 47N 0 9 E
Longford, Ire. 24 53 43N 7 50W
Longford, U.K. 14 51 53N 2 14W
Longford □, Ire. 24 53 42N 7 45W
Longforgan, U.K. 21 56 28N 3 8W
Longframlington, U.K. 21 55 18N 1 47W
Longhorsley, U.K. 21 55 15N 1 46W
Longhoughton, U.K. 21 55 26N 1 38W
Longridge, U.K. 18 53 50N 2 37W
Longton, U.K. 18 53 43N 2 48W
Longtown, Cumbria, U.K. 18 55 1N 2 59W
Longtown, Hereford & Worcs., U.K. 14 51 58N 2 59W
Löningen, Ger. 36 52 43N 7 44 E
Looe, U.K. 16 50 24N 4 25W
Loop Hd., Ire. 25 52 34N 9 55W
Lop Nor, China 60 40 20N 90 10 E
Lorca, Sp. 37 37 41N 1 42W
Lorient, Fr. 34 47 45N 3 23W
Lorn, U.K. 20 56 26N 5 10W
Lorn, Firth of, U.K. 20 56 20N 5 40W
Los Angeles, Chile 102 37 28S 72 23W
Los Angeles, U.S.A. 90 34 0N 118 10W
Los Mochis, Mex. 94 25 45N 108 57W
Lossiemouth, U.K. 23 57 43N 3 17W
Lostwithiel, U.K. 16 50 24N 4 41W
Lothian □, U.K. 21 55 50N 3 0W
Loughborough, U.K. 14 52 46N 1 11W
Loughrea, Ire. 25 53 11N 8 33W
Loughros More B., Ire. 24 54 48N 8 30W
Louisiana □, U.S.A. 91 30 50N 92 0W
Louisville, U.S.A. 92 38 15N 85 45W
Lourdes, Fr. 35 43 6N 0 3W
Louth, Ire. 24 53 47N 6 33W
Louth, U.K. 19 53 23N 0 0 E
Louth □, Ire. 24 53 55N 6 30W
Louvière, La, Belg. 36 50 27N 4 10 E
Lowell, U.S.A. 93 42 38N 71 19W
Lower Beeding, U.K. 15 51 2N 0 15W
Lower California, Mex. 94 31 10N 115 12W
Lower Hutt, N.Z. 71 41 10S 174 55 E
Lower Tunguska →, U.S.S.R. 49 64 20N 93 0 E
Lowes Water L., U.K. 18 54 35N 3 23W
Lowestoft, U.K. 15 52 29N 1 44 E
Lowick, U.K. 21 55 38N 1 57W
Lowther Hills, U.K. 21 55 20N 3 40W
Luanda, Angola 80 8 50S 13 15 E
Luanshya, Zam. 81 13 3S 28 28 E
Lubbock, U.S.A. 90 33 40N 101 53W
Lübeck, Ger. 42 53 52N 10 41 E
Lublin, Pol. 43 51 12N 22 38 E
Lubumbashi, Zaïre 81 11 40S 27 28 E
Luce Bay, U.K. 20 54 45N 4 48W
Lucknow, India 59 26 50N 81 0 E
Lüda = Dalian, China 61 38 50N 121 40 E
Ludgershall, U.K. 14 51 15N 1 38W
Ludgvan, U.K. 16 50 9N 5 30W
Ludhiana, India 58 30 57N 75 56 E
Ludlow, U.K. 14 52 23N 2 42W
Ludwigshafen, Ger. 42 49 27N 8 27 E

Lugano, Switz. 42 46 0N 8 57 E
Lugansk, U.S.S.R. 47 48 38N 39 15 E
Lugnaquilla, Ire. 25 52 58N 6 28W
Lugo, Sp. 37 43 2N 7 35W
Lugwardine, U.K. 14 52 4N 2 38W
Luing I., U.K. 20 56 15N 5 40W
Luleå, Swed. 44 65 35N 22 10 E
Lundy, U.K. 16 51 10N 4 41W
Lune —►, U.K. 18 54 0N 2 51W
Lünen, Ger. 36 51 36N 7 31 E
Luoyang, China 61 34 40N 112 26 E
Lurgan, U.K. 24 54 28N 6 20W
Lusaka, Zam. 81 15 28S 28 16 E
Luss, U.K. 20 56 6N 4 40W
Luton, U.K. 15 51 53N 0 24W
Lutterworth, U.K. 14 52 28N 1 12W
Luxembourg, Lux. 36 49 37N 6 9 E
Luxembourg ■, Europe 36 50 0N 6 0 E
Luzern, Switz. 42 47 3N 8 18 E
Luzhou, China 60 28 52N 105 20 E
Luzon, Phil. 63 16 0N 121 0 E
Lvov, U.S.S.R. 47 49 50N 24 0 E
Lyakhov Is., U.S.S.R. 49 73 40N 141 0 E
Lybster, U.K. 23 58 18N 3 16W
Lydd, U.K. 15 50 57N 0 56 E
Lydford, U.K. 16 50 38N 4 7W
Lydham, U.K. 14 52 31N 2 59W
Lyell Range, N.Z. 71 41 38S 172 20 E
Lyme Bay, U.K. 16 50 36N 2 55W
Lyme Regis, U.K. 16 50 44N 2 57W
Lyminge, U.K. 15 51 7N 1 6 E
Lymington, U.K. 16 50 46N 1 32W
Lymm, U.K. 18 53 23N 2 30W
Lympne, U.K. 15 51 4N 1 2 E
Lynchburg, U.S.A. 92 37 23N 79 10W
Lyndhurst, U.K. 14 50 53N 1 33W
Lyneham, U.K. 14 51 30N 1 57W
Lynemouth, U.K. 21 55 15N 1 29W
Lynmouth, U.K. 16 51 14N 3 50W
Lynn Lake, Canada 88 56 51N 101 3W
Lynton, U.K. 16 51 14N 3 50W
Lyons, Fr. 35 45 46N 4 50 E
Lytchett Minster, U.K. 14 50 44N 2 3W
Lytham St. Anne's, U.K. 18 53 45N 2 58W
Lythe, U.K. 19 54 30N 0 40W

M

Ma'ān, Jord. 56 30 12N 35 44 E
Maarianhamina, Fin. 45 60 5N 19 55 E
Maastricht, Neth. 36 50 50N 5 40 E
Mablethorpe, U.K. 19 53 21N 0 14 E
Macapá, Brazil 101 0 5N 51 4W
Macau ■, Asia 61 22 16N 113 35 E
Macclesfield, U.K. 18 53 16N 2 9W
McClure Str., Canada 103 75 0N 119 0W
Macdonnell Ranges, Austral. 66 23 40S 133 0 E
Macduff, U.K. 23 57 40N 2 30W
Macedonia □, Greece 41 40 39N 22 0 E
Macedonia □, Yug. 41 41 53N 21 40 E
Maceió, Brazil 101 9 40S 35 41W
Macgillycuddy's Reeks, Ire. 25 52 2N 9 45W
Machakos, Kenya 80 1 30S 37 15 E
Machala, Ecuad. 100 3 20S 79 57W
Machars, The, U.K. 20 54 46N 4 30W
Machrihanish, U.K. 20 55 25N 5 42W
Machynlleth, U.K. 17 52 36N 3 51W
Macintyre —►, Austral. 67 28 37S 150 47 E
Mackay, Austral. 67 21 8S 149 11 E
Mackay, L., Austral. 66 22 30S 129 0 E
McKeesport, U.S.A. 92 40 21N 79 50W
Mackenzie —►, Austral. 67 23 38S 149 46 E
Mackenzie —►, Canada 88 69 10N 134 20W
Mackenzie Mts., Canada 88 64 0N 130 0W
McKinley, Mt., U.S.A. 88 63 2N 151 0W
M'Clintock Chan., Canada 88 72 0N 102 0W
Macon, U.S.A. 91 32 50N 83 37W
Macquarie —►, Austral. 70 30 5S 147 30 E
Macquarie Harbour, Austral. 67 42 15S 145 23 E
Macquarie Is., S. Oc. 64 54 36S 158 55 E
Macroom, Ire. 25 51 54N 8 57W
Madadeni, S. Afr. 81 27 43S 30 3 E
Madagascar ■, Africa 81 20 0S 47 0 E
Madeira, Atl. Oc. 78 32 50N 17 0W
Madeira —►, Brazil 100 3 22S 58 45W
Madeley, Salop, U.K. 14 52 38N 2 28W
Madeley, Staffs., U.K. 18 52 59N 2 20W
Madhya Pradesh □, India 59 21 50N 81 0 E
Madīnat ash Sha'b, S. Yem. 56 12 50N 45 0 E
Madison, U.S.A. 92 43 5N 89 25W
Madiun, Indon. 63 7 38S 111 32 E
Madley, U.K. 14 52 3N 2 51W
Madras, India 58 13 8N 80 19 E
Madre, L., U.S.A. 91 26 0N 97 40W
Madre, Sierra, Mex. 94 16 0N 93 0W
Madrid, Sp. 37 40 25N 3 45W
Madurai, India 58 9 55N 78 10 E
Maesteg, U.K. 17 51 36N 3 40W
Magadan, U.S.S.R. 49 59 38N 150 50 E
Magdalena —►, Col. 100 11 6N 74 51W
Magdeburg, Ger. 42 52 8N 11 36 E
Magee, I., U.K. 24 54 48N 5 44W
Magelang, Indon. 63 7 29S 110 13 E
Magellan's Str., Chile 102 52 30S 75 0W
Maggiore, L., It. 40 46 0N 8 35 E
Magherafelt, U.K. 24 54 44N 6 37W
Maghull, U.K. 18 53 31N 2 56W
Magnitogorsk, U.S.S.R. 46 53 27N 59 4 E
Mahajanga, Madag. 81 17 0S 47 0 E
Maiden Bradley, U.K. 14 51 9N 2 18W
Maiden Newton, U.K. 14 50 46N 2 35W
Maidenhead, U.K. 15 51 31N 0 42W
Maidstone, U.K. 15 51 16N 0 31 E
Maiduguri, Nig. 79 12 0N 13 20 E
Main —►, U.K. 24 54 49N 6 20W
Maine □, U.S.A. 93 45 20N 69 0W
Maine —►, Ire. 25 52 10N 9 40W
Mainland, Orkney, U.K. 23 59 0N 3 10W
Mainland, Shetland, U.K. 22 60 15N 1 22W
Mainz, Ger. 36 50 0N 8 17 E
Maitland, Austral. 70 32 33S 151 36 E
Majorca, I. = Mallorca, Sp. 37 39 30N 3 0 E
Makasar, Str. of, Indon. 63 1 0S 118 20 E
Maker, U.K. 16 50 20N 4 10W
Makeyevka, U.S.S.R. 47 48 0N 38 0 E
Makhachkala, U.S.S.R. 47 43 0N 47 30 E
Makran Coast Range, Pak. 58 25 40N 64 0 E
Mal B., Ire. 25 52 50N 9 30W
Malabar Coast, India 58 11 0N 75 0 E
Malacca, Str. of, Indon. 63 3 0N 101 0 E
Málaga, Sp. 37 36 43N 4 23W
Malang, Indon. 63 7 59S 112 45 E
Malanje, Angola 80 9 36S 16 17 E
Mälaren, Swed. 45 59 30N 17 10 E
Malatya, Turk. 47 38 25N 38 20 E
Malawi ■, Africa 81 13 0S 34 0 E
Malay Pen., Asia 63 7 25N 100 0 E
Malaysia ■, Asia 63 5 0N 110 0 E
Maldives ■, Ind. Oc. 119 7 0N 73 0 E
Maldon, U.K. 15 51 43N 0 41 E
Malham Tarn, U.K. 18 54 6N 2 11W
Mali ■, Africa 78 15 0N 2 0W
Mallaig, U.K. 22 57 0N 5 50W
Mallorca, Sp. 37 39 30N 3 0 E
Mallow, Ire. 25 52 8N 8 40W
Malmédy, Belg. 36 50 25N 6 2 E
Malmesbury, U.K. 14 51 35N 2 5W
Malmö, Swed. 45 55 36N 12 59 E
Malpas, U.K. 18 53 3N 2 47W
Malta ■, Europe 40 35 50N 14 30 E
Maltby, U.K. 19 53 25N 1 12W
Malton, U.K. 19 54 9N 0 48W
Malvern, U.K. 14 52 7N 2 19W
Malvern Hills, U.K. 14 52 0N 2 19W
Malvern Wells, U.K. 14 52 4N 2 19W
Malvinas, Is. = Falkland Is., Atl. Oc. 102 51 30S 59 0W
Man, I. of, U.K. 18 54 15N 4 30W
Manaar, Gulf of, Asia 58 8 30N 79 0 E
Manacles, The, U.K. 16 50 3N 5 5W
Manado, Indon. 63 1 29N 124 51 E
Managua, Nic. 94 12 6N 86 20W
Manaus, Brazil 100 3 0S 60 0W
Manby, U.K. 19 53 22N 0 6 E
Manchester, U.K. 18 53 30N 2 15W
Manchester, U.S.A. 93 42 58N 71 29W
Manchuria, China 61 42 0N 125 0 E
Mandalay, Burma 59 22 0N 96 4 E
Manea, U.K. 15 52 29N 0 10 E
Mangalore, India 58 12 55N 74 47 E
Mangotsfield, U.K. 14 51 29N 2 29W
Manila, Phil. 63 14 40N 121 3 E
Manitoba □, Canada 88 55 30N 97 0W
Manizales, Col. 100 5 5N 75 32W
Manly, Austral. 70 33 48S 151 17 E
Mannheim, Ger. 42 49 28N 8 29 E
Manningtree, U.K. 15 51 56N 1 3 E
Mans, Le, Fr. 34 48 0N 0 10 E
Mansfield, U.K. 19 53 8N 1 12W
Mansfield, U.S.A. 92 40 45N 82 30W
Mansfield Woodhouse, U.K. 19 53 11N 1 11W
Mantes-la-Jolie, Fr. 34 49 0N 1 41 E
Manton, U.K. 15 52 37N 0 41W
Mantua, It. 40 45 20N 10 42 E
Manukau, N.Z. 71 37 1S 174 55 E
Manzhouli, China 61 49 35N 117 25 E
Maoming, China 61 21 50N 110 54 E
Maputo, Mozam. 81 25 58S 32 32 E
Mar del Plata, Arg. 102 38 0S 57 30W
Maracaibo, Ven. 100 10 40N 71 37W
Maracaibo, L., Ven. 100 9 40N 71 30W
Maracay, Ven. 100 10 15N 67 28W
Marajó, I. de, Brazil 101 1 0S 49 30W
Maranhão = São Luís, Brazil 101 2 39S 44 15W
Marañón —►, Peru 100 4 30S 73 35W
Marazion, U.K. 16 50 8N 5 29W
March, U.K. 15 52 33N 0 5 E
Marden, U.K. 14 52 7N 2 42W
Maree L., U.K. 22 57 40N 5 30W
Mareeba, Austral. 67 16 59S 145 28 E
Mareham le Fen, U.K. 19 53 7N 0 3W
Marfleet, U.K. 19 53 45N 0 15W
Margarita I., Ven. 100 11 0N 64 0W
Margate, U.K. 15 51 23N 1 24 E
Maribor, Yug. 40 46 36N 15 40 E
Maricourt, Canada 89 56 34N 70 49W
Marie-Galante, W. Ind. 94 15 56N 61 16W
Marília, Brazil 101 22 13S 50 0W
Maringá, Brazil 102 23 26S 52 2W
Mariupol, U.S.S.R. 47 47 5N 37 31 E
Market Bosworth, U.K. 14 52 37N 1 24W
Market Deeping, U.K. 15 52 40N 0 20W
Market Drayton, U.K. 18 52 55N 2 30W
Market Harborough, U.K. 15 52 29N 0 55W
Market Lavington, U.K. 14 51 17N 1 59W
Market Rasen, U.K. 19 53 24N 0 20W
Market Weighton, U.K. 19 53 52N 0 40W
Markfield, U.K. 14 52 42N 1 18W
Markinch, U.K. 21 56 12N 3 9W
Marks Tey, U.K. 15 51 53N 0 48 E
Marlborough, U.K. 14 51 26N 1 44W
Marlborough □, N.Z. 71 41 45S 173 33 E
Marlborough Downs, U.K. 14 51 25N 1 55W
Marlow, U.K. 15 51 34N 0 47W
Marmara, Sea of, Turk. 47 40 45N 28 15 E
Marne —►, Fr. 34 48 48N 2 24 E
Marnhull, U.K. 14 50 58N 2 20W
Maroua, Cam. 80 10 40N 14 20 E
Marple, U.K. 18 53 23N 2 5W
Marquesas Is., Pac. Oc. 65 9 30S 140 0W
Marrakech, Mor. 78 31 9N 8 0W
Marseilles, Fr. 35 43 18N 5 23 E
Marshall Is. ■, Pac. Oc. 64 9 0N 171 0 E
Marshfield, U.K. 14 51 27N 2 18W
Marske by the Sea, U.K. 19 54 35N 1 0W
Marston Moor, U.K. 19 53 58N 1 17W
Martaban, G. of, Burma 59 16 5N 96 30 E
Martham, U.K. 15 52 42N 1 38 E
Martinique, W. Ind. 94 14 40N 61 0W
Martley, U.K. 14 52 14N 2 22W
Martock, U.K. 14 50 58N 2 47W
Mary Kathleen, Austral. 67 20 44S 139 48 E
Maryborough, Austral. 67 37 0S 143 44 E
Maryland □, U.S.A. 93 39 10N 76 40W
Maryport, U.K. 18 54 43N 3 30W
Marytavy, U.K. 16 50 34N 4 6W
Masan, S. Kor. 61 35 11N 128 32 E
Maseru, Les. 81 29 18S 27 30 E
Masham, U.K. 19 54 15N 1 40W
Mashhad, Iran 57 36 20N 59 35 E
Mask, L., Ire. 24 53 36N 9 24W
Massachusetts □, U.S.A. 93 42 25N 72 0W
Massif Central, Fr. 35 45 30N 3 0 E
Masterton, N.Z. 71 40 56S 175 39 E
Masvingo, Zimb. 81 20 8S 30 49 E
Matadi, Zaïre 80 5 52S 13 31 E
Matamoros, Mex. 94 25 33N 103 15W
Matera, It. 40 40 40N 16 37 E
Matlock, U.K. 19 53 8N 1 32W
Mato Grosso □, Brazil 101 14 0S 55 0W
Matsue, Jap. 62 35 25N 133 10 E
Matsuyama, Jap. 62 33 45N 132 45 E
Matterhorn, Switz. 42 45 58N 7 39 E
Maturín, Ven. 100 9 45N 63 11W
Maubeuge, Fr. 34 50 17N 3 57 E
Mauchline, U.K. 20 55 31N 4 23W
Maughold, U.K. 18 54 18N 4 17W
Maughold Hd., U.K. 18 54 18N 4 17W
Maui, U.S.A. 90 20 45N 156 20 E
Mauna Loa, U.S.A. 90 21 8N 157 10W
Mauritania ■, Africa 78 20 50N 10 0W
Mauritius ■, Ind. Oc. 119 20 0S 57 0 E
Mawgan, U.K. 16 50 4N 5 10W
Mawlaik, Burma 59 23 40N 94 26 E
Maxwellheugh, U.K. 21 55 35N 2 23W
May, I. of, U.K. 21 56 11N 2 32W
May Pen, Jam. 94 17 58N 77 15W
Maybole, U.K. 20 55 21N 4 41W
Mayfield, Derby, U.K. 19 53 1N 1 47W
Mayfield, E. Sussex, U.K. 15 51 1N 0 17 E
Maynooth, Ire. 24 53 22N 6 38W
Mayo □, Ire. 24 53 47N 9 7W
Mazar-e Sharīf, Afg. 57 36 41N 67 0 E
Mazatlán, Mex. 94 23 13N 106 25W
Mbabane, Swaz. 81 26 18S 31 6 E
Mbandaka, Zaïre 80 0 1N 18 18 E
Mbanza Ngungu, Zaïre 80 5 12S 14 53 E
Mbeya, Tanz. 80 8 54S 33 29 E
Mbini □, Eq. Guin. 80 1 30N 10 0 E
Mbuji-Mayi, Zaïre 80 6 9S 23 40 E
Mdantsane, S. Afr. 81 32 56S 27 46 E
Mealsgate, U.K. 18 54 46N 3 14W
Measham, U.K. 14 52 43N 1 30W
Meath □, Ire. 24 53 32N 6 40W
Mecca, Si. Arab. 56 21 30N 39 54 E
Mechelen, Belg. 36 50 58N 5 41 E
Medan, Indon. 63 3 40N 98 38 E
Medellín, Col. 100 6 15N 75 35W
Medicine Hat, Canada 88 50 0N 110 45W
Medina, Si. Arab. 56 24 35N 39 52 E
Mediterranean Sea, Europe 38 35 0N 15 0 E
Medley, Canada 88 54 25N 110 16W
Medstead, U.K. 14 51 7N 1 4W
Medway —►, U.K. 15 51 28N 0 45 E
Meekatharra, Austral. 66 26 32S 118 29 E
Meerut, India 58 29 1N 77 42 E
Mei Xian, China 61 24 16N 116 6 E
Meknès, Mor. 78 33 57N 5 33W
Mekong —►, Asia 63 9 30N 106 15 E
Melanesia, Pac. Oc. 64 4 0S 155 0 E
Melbourn, U.K. 15 52 5N 0 1 E
Melbourne, Austral. 70 37 50S 145 0 E
Melbourne, U.K. 14 52 50N 1 25W
Melfort, Loch, U.K. 20 56 13N 5 33W
Melitopol, U.S.S.R. 47 46 50N 35 22 E
Melksham, U.K. 14 51 22N 2 9W
Melmerby, U.K. 18 54 44N 2 35W
Melrose, U.K. 21 55 35N 2 44W
Melsonby, U.K. 19 54 28N 1 41W
Melton, U.K. 15 52 6N 1 20 E
Melton Constable, U.K. 15 52 52N 1 1 E
Melton Mowbray, U.K. 15 52 46N 0 52W
Melvich, U.K. 23 58 33N 3 55W
Melville I., Austral. 66 11 30S 131 0 E
Melville Pen., Canada 89 68 0N 84 0W
Memphis, U.S.A. 91 35 7N 90 0W
Menai Bridge, U.K. 17 53 14N 4 11W
Menai Strait, U.K. 17 53 14N 4 10W
Menam = Chao Phraya —►, Thai. 63 13 32N 100 36 E
Mendip Hills, U.K. 14 51 17N 2 40W
Mendlesham, U.K. 15 52 15N 1 4 E
Mendoza, Arg. 102 32 50S 68 52W
Menindee, Austral. 70 32 20S 142 25 E
Menorca, Sp. 37 40 0N 4 0 E
Mere, U.K. 14 51 5N 2 16W
Mérida, Mex. 94 20 58N 89 37W
Mérida, Ven. 100 8 24N 71 8W
Meriden, U.K. 14 52 27N 1 36W
Merrick, U.K. 20 55 8N 4 30W
Merse, U.K. 21 55 40N 2 30W
Mersea I., U.K. 15 51 48N 0 55 E
Mersey —►, U.K. 18 53 20N 2 56W
Merseyside □, U.K. 18 53 25N 2 55W
Mersin, Turk. 47 36 51N 34 36 E
Merthyr Tydfil, U.K. 17 51 45N 3 23W
Merton, U.K. 15 51 25N 0 13W
Meru, Tanz. 80 3 15S 36 46 E
Mesa, U.S.A. 90 33 20N 111 56W
Mesopotamia, Asia 56 33 30N 44 0 E
Messina, It. 40 38 10N 15 32 E
Messina, Str. of, It. 40 38 5N 15 35 E
Metheringham, U.K. 19 53 9N 0 22W
Methil, U.K. 21 56 10N 3 1W
Methven, U.K. 21 56 25N 3 35W
Methwold, U.K. 15 52 30N 0 33 E
Metz, Fr. 34 49 8N 6 10 E
Meuse —►, Europe 34 50 45N 5 41 E
Mevagissey, U.K. 16 50 16N 4 48W
Mevagissey Bay, U.K. 16 50 15N 4 40W
Mexborough, U.K. 19 53 29N 1 18W
Mexicali, Mex. 94 32 40N 115 29W
México, Mex. 94 19 20N 99 10W
Mexico ■, Cent. Am. 94 20 0N 100 0W
Mexico, G. of, Cent. Am. 94 25 0N 90 0W
Miami, U.S.A. 91 25 45N 80 15W
Micheldever, U.K. 14 51 7N 1 17W
Michigan □, U.S.A. 92 44 40N 85 40W
Michigan, L., U.S.A. 92 44 0N 87 0W
Mickle Fell, U.K. 18 54 38N 2 16W
Mickleover, U.K. 19 52 55N 1 32W
Mickleton, Durham, U.K. 18 54 36N 2 3W
Mickleton, Oxon., U.K. 14 52 5N 1 45W
Micronesia ■, Pac. Oc. 64 11 0N 160 0 E
Mid Calder, U.K. 21 55 53N 3 23W
Mid Glamorgan □, U.K. 17 51 40N 3 25W
Middle Zoy, U.K. 14 51 5N 2 54W
Middleham, U.K. 19 54 17N 1 49W
Middlemarsh, U.K. 14 50 51N 2 29W
Middlesbrough, U.K. 19 54 35N 1 14W
Middleton, Gr. Manchester, U.K. 18 53 33N 2 12W
Middleton, Norfolk, U.K. 15 52 43N 0 29 E
Middleton Cheney, U.K. 14 52 4N 1 17W
Middleton-in-Teesdale, U.K. 18 54 38N 2 5W
Middleton on the Wolds, U.K. 19 53 56N 0 35W
Middlewich, U.K. 18 53 12N 2 28W
Midhurst, U.K. 15 50 59N 0 44W
Midland, U.S.A. 90 32 0N 102 3W
Midleton, Ire. 25 51 52N 8 12W
Midsomer Norton, U.K. 14 51 17N 2 29W
Midway Is., Pac. Oc. 64 28 13N 177 22W
Mieres, Sp. 37 43 18N 5 48W
Mikkeli, Fin. 44 61 43N 27 15 E
Milan, It. 40 45 28N 9 10 E
Milborne Port, U.K. 14 50 58N 2 28W
Mildenhall, U.K. 15 52 20N 0 30 E
Mildura, Austral. 70 34 13S 142 9 E
Milford Haven, U.K. 17 51 43N 5 2W
Milford Haven, B., U.K. 17 51 40N 5 10W
Milford on Sea, U.K. 14 50 44N 1 36W
Milk —►, U.S.A. 90 48 5N 106 15W
Millbrook, U.K. 16 50 19N 4 12W
Milleur Pt., U.K. 20 55 2N 5 5W
Millom, U.K. 18 54 13N 3 16W
Millport, U.K. 20 55 45N 4 55W
Milltown Malbay, Ire. 25 52 51N 9 25W
Milnathort, U.K. 21 56 14N 3 25W
Milngavie, U.K. 20 55 57N 4 20W
Milnthorpe, U.K. 18 54 14N 2 47W
Milton, Dumf. & Gall., U.K. 20 55 18N 4 50W
Milton, Hants., U.K. 14 50 45N 1 40W
Milton, Highland, U.K. 23 57 18N 4 32W
Milton Abbot, U.K. 16 50 35N 4 16W
Milton Keynes, U.K. 15 52 3N 0 42W

Milverton, U.K. 14 51 2N 3 15W
Milwaukee, U.S.A. 92 43 9N 87 58W
Minas Gerais □, Brazil 101 18 50S 46 0W
Minatitlán, Mex. 94 17 59N 94 31W
Minchinghampton, U.K. 14 51 42N 2 10W
Mindanao, Phil. 63 8 0N 125 0 E
Mindoro, Phil. 63 13 0N 121 0 E
Minehead, U.K. 14 51 12N 3 29W
Minneapolis, U.S.A. 91 44 58N 93 20W
Minnesota □, U.S.A. 91 46 40N 94 0W
Minnigaff, U.K. 20 54 58N 4 30W
Minorca = Menorca, Sp. 37 40 0N 4 0 E
Minsk, U.S.S.R. 46 53 52N 27 30 E
Minster, U.K. 15 51 20N 1 20 E
Minster-on-Sea, U.K. 15 51 25N 0 50 E
Minsterley, U.K. 14 52 38N 2 56W
Mirfield, U.K. 19 53 37N 1 54W
Mirzapur, India 59 25 10N 82 34 E
Miskolc, Hung. 43 48 7N 20 50 E
Misrātah, Libya 79 32 24N 15 3 E
Mississippi □, U.S.A. 91 33 0N 90 0W
Mississippi →, U.S.A. 91 29 0N 89 15W
Mississippi, Delta of the, U.S.A. 91 29 15N 90 30W
Missouri □, U.S.A. 91 38 25N 92 30W
Missouri →, U.S.A. 91 38 50N 90 8W
Misterton, Notts., U.K. 19 53 27N 0 49W
Misterton, Somerset, U.K. 14 50 51N 2 46W
Mitcheldean, U.K. 14 51 51N 2 29W
Mitchell →, Austral. 67 15 12S 141 35 E
Mitchelstown, Ire. 25 52 16N 8 18W
Mittelland Kanal, Ger. 36 52 23N 7 45 E
Mitumba, Mts., Zaïre 80 6 0S 29 0 E
Miyazaki, Jap. 62 31 56N 131 30 E
Mizen Hd., Cork, Ire. 25 51 27N 9 50W
Mizen Hd., Wicklow, Ire. 25 52 52N 6 4W
Mizoram □, India 59 23 30N 92 40 E
Mmabatho, S. Afr. 81 25 49S 25 30 E
Mo i Rana, Nor. 44 66 15N 14 7 E
Mobile, U.S.A. 91 30 41N 88 3W
Mobutu Sese Seko, L., Africa 80 1 30N 31 0 E
Moçâmedes = Namibe, Angola 81 15 7S 12 11 E
Modbury, U.K. 16 50 21N 3 53W
Módena, It. 40 44 39N 10 55 E
Moe, Austral. 70 38 12S 146 19 E
Moffat, U.K. 21 55 20N 3 27W
Mogadishu, Som. 73 2 2N 45 25 E
Mogilev, U.S.S.R. 46 53 55N 30 18 E
Moidart, L., U.K. 22 56 47N 5 40W
Mojave Desert, U.S.A. 90 35 0N 116 30W
Mold, U.K. 17 53 10N 3 10W
Moldavia □, U.S.S.R. 47 47 0N 28 0 E
Mole →, U.K. 15 51 13N 0 15W
Mollendo, Peru 100 17 0S 72 0W
Mölndal, Swed. 45 57 40N 12 3 E
Molokai, U.S.A. 90 21 8N 157 0W
Moluccas, Indon. 63 1 0S 127 0 E
Mombasa, Kenya 80 4 2S 39 43 E
Mona Passage, W. Ind. 95 18 0N 67 40W
Monach Is., U.K. 22 57 32N 7 40W
Monaco ■, Europe 35 43 46N 7 23 E
Monadhliath Mts., U.K. 23 57 10N 4 4W
Monaghan, Ire. 24 54 15N 6 58W
Monaghan □, Ire. 24 54 10N 7 0W
Monastir = Bitola, Yug. 41 41 5N 21 10 E
Monclova, Mex. 94 26 50N 101 30W
Moncton, Canada 93 46 7N 64 51W
Moneymore, U.K. 24 54 42N 6 40W
Monghyr, India 59 25 23N 86 30 E
Mongolia ■, Asia 60 47 0N 103 0 E
Mongu, Zam. 81 15 16S 23 12 E
Moniaive, U.K. 21 55 11N 3 55W
Monifieth, U.K. 21 56 30N 2 48W
Monkton, U.K. 20 55 30N 4 37W
Monmouth, U.K. 17 51 48N 2 43W
Monnow →, U.K. 14 51 54N 2 48W
Monroe, U.S.A. 91 32 32N 92 4W
Monrovia, Lib. 78 6 18N 10 47W
Mons, Belg. 36 50 27N 3 58 E
Montana □, U.S.A. 90 47 0N 110 0W
Montbéliard, Fr. 34 47 31N 6 48 E
Montceau-les-Mines, Fr. 34 46 40N 4 23 E
Monte-Carlo, Monaco 35 43 46N 7 23 E
Montego Bay, Jam. 94 18 30N 78 0W
Montería, Col. 100 8 46N 75 53W
Monterrey, Mex. 94 25 40N 100 30W
Montes Claros, Brazil 101 16 30S 43 50W
Montevideo, Urug. 102 34 50S 56 11W
Montgomery, U.K. 17 52 34N 3 9W
Montgomery, U.S.A. 91 32 20N 86 20W
Montluçon, Fr. 35 46 22N 2 36 E
Montpelier, U.S.A. 93 44 15N 72 38W
Montpellier, Fr. 35 43 37N 3 52 E
Montréal, Canada 93 45 31N 73 34W
Montrose, U.K. 23 56 43N 2 28W
Montserrat, W. Ind. 94 16 40N 62 10W
Moonie →, Austral. 67 29 19S 148 43 E
Moorfoot Hills, U.K. 21 55 44N 3 8W
Moose Jaw, Canada 88 50 24N 105 30W
Moosehead L., U.S.A. 93 45 34N 69 40W
Mopti, Mali 78 14 30N 4 0W
Moradabad, India 58 28 50N 78 50 E
Morar L., U.K. 22 56 57N 5 40W
Moray Firth, U.K. 23 57 50N 3 30W
Morebattle, U.K. 21 55 30N 2 20W
Morecambe, U.K. 18 54 5N 2 52W
Morecambe B., U.K. 18 54 7N 3 0W
Morelia, Mex. 94 19 42N 101 7W
Morena, Sierra, Sp. 37 38 20N 4 0W
Moreton-in-Marsh, U.K. 14 51 59N 1 42W
Moretonhampstead, U.K. 16 50 39N 3 45W
Morley, U.K. 19 53 45N 1 36W
Morocco ■, N. Afr. 78 32 0N 5 50W
Morogoro, Tanz. 80 6 50S 37 40 E
Morpeth, U.K. 19 55 11N 1 41W
Morte Bay, U.K. 16 51 10N 4 13W
Morte Pt., U.K. 16 51 13N 4 14W
Mortehoe, U.K. 16 51 21N 4 12W
Mortimer's Cross, U.K. 14 52 17N 2 50W
Morton Fen, U.K. 15 52 45N 0 23W
Morvern, U.K. 22 56 38N 5 44W
Morwell, Austral. 70 38 10S 146 22 E
Morwenstow, U.K. 16 50 53N 4 32W
Moscow, U.S.S.R. 46 55 45N 37 35 E
Moselle →, Europe 34 50 22N 7 36 E
Moshi, Tanz. 80 3 22S 37 18 E
Mossley, U.K. 18 53 31N 2 1W
Mossoró, Brazil 101 5 10S 37 15W
Mostaganem, Alg. 78 35 54N 0 5 E
Mostar, Yug. 41 43 22N 17 50 E
Mosul, Iraq 56 36 15N 43 5 E
Motcombe, U.K. 14 51 1N 2 12W
Motherwell, U.K. 21 55 48N 4 0W
Mottisfont, U.K. 14 51 2N 1 32W
Moulmein, Burma 59 16 30N 97 40 E
Moulton, U.K. 15 52 17N 0 51W
Mount Barker, Austral. 66 34 38S 117 40 E
Mount Gambier, Austral. 70 37 50S 140 46 E
Mount Isa, Austral. 67 20 42S 139 26 E
Mount Lofty Ra., Austral. 67 34 35S 139 5 E
Mountain Ash, U.K. 17 51 42N 3 22W
Mountmellick, Ire. 25 53 7N 7 20W
Mounts Bay, U.K. 16 50 3N 5 27W
Mountsorrel, U.K. 14 52 43N 1 9W
Mourne →, U.K. 24 54 45N 7 39W
Mourne Mts., U.K. 24 54 10N 6 0W
Mouscron, Belg. 36 50 45N 3 12 E
Moville, Ire. 24 55 11N 7 3W
Moy →, Ire. 24 54 5N 8 50W
Moyle □, U.K. 24 55 10N 6 15W
Mozambique ■, Africa 81 19 0S 35 0 E
Mozambique Chan., Africa 81 20 0S 39 0 E
Mu Us Shamo, China 61 39 0N 109 0 E
Mubarraz, Si. Arab. 56 25 29N 49 40 E
Much Dewchurch, U.K. 14 51 58N 2 45W
Much Marcle, U.K. 14 51 59N 2 27W
Much Wenlock, U.K. 14 52 36N 2 34W
Muck, U.K. 22 56 50N 6 15W
Mudanjiang, China 61 44 38N 129 30 E
Mudgee, Austral. 70 32 32S 149 31 E
Mufulira, Zam. 81 12 32S 28 15 E
Muine Bheag, Ire. 25 52 42N 6 57W
Muir of Ord, U.K. 23 57 30N 4 35W
Muirdrum, U.K. 21 56 31N 2 40W
Muirhead, U.K. 21 55 54N 4 5W
Muirkirk, U.K. 21 55 31N 4 6W
Mülheim, Ger. 36 51 26N 6 53 E
Mulhouse, Fr. 34 47 40N 7 20 E
Mull, U.K. 20 56 27N 6 0W
Mull, Ross of, U.K. 20 56 20N 6 15W
Mull, Sound of, U.K. 20 56 30N 5 50W
Mullet Pen., Ire. 24 54 10N 10 2W
Mullingar, Ire. 24 53 31N 7 20W
Mullion, U.K. 16 50 1N 5 15W
Multan, Pak. 58 30 15N 71 36 E
Mumbles Hd., U.K. 17 51 33N 4 0W
Munchen-Gladbach, Ger. 36 51 12N 6 23 E
Mundesley, U.K. 15 52 53N 1 24 E
Munich, Ger. 42 48 8N 11 33 E
Münster, Ger. 36 51 58N 7 37 E
Munster □, Ire. 25 52 20N 8 40W
Murchison →, Austral. 66 27 45S 114 0 E
Murcia, Sp. 37 38 20N 1 10W
Mureş →, Rom. 43 46 15N 20 13 E
Murmansk, U.S.S.R. 46 68 57N 33 10 E
Murray →, S. Austral., Austral. 67 35 20S 139 22 E
Murrumbidgee →, Austral. 70 34 43S 143 12 E
Murton, U.K. 19 54 51N 1 22W
Murwillumbah, Austral. 67 28 18S 153 27 E
Muscat, Oman 57 23 40N 58 38 E
Musgrave Ras., Austral. 66 26 0S 132 0 E
Musselburgh, U.K. 21 55 57N 3 3W
Muswellbrook, Austral. 70 32 16S 150 56 E
Mutare, Zimb. 81 18 58S 32 38 E
Muthill, U.K. 21 56 20N 3 50W
Muzaffarpur, India 59 26 7N 85 23 E
Mwanza, Tanz. 80 2 30S 32 58 E
Mweelrea, Ire. 24 53 37N 9 48W
My Tho, Viet. 63 10 29N 106 23 E
Myanmar = Burma ■, Asia 59 21 0N 96 30 E
Myddle, U.K. 14 52 49N 2 47W
Myitkyina, Burma 59 25 24N 97 26 E
Mymensingh, Bangla. 59 24 45N 90 24 E
Mynydd Du, U.K. 17 51 45N 3 45W
Mynydd Prescelly, U.K. 17 51 57N 4 48W
Mysore, India 58 12 17N 76 41 E

N

Naas, Ire. 25 53 12N 6 40W
Naberezhnyye Chelny, U.S.S.R. 46 55 42N 52 19 E
Nābulus, Jord. 57 32 14N 35 15 E
Nafferton, U.K. 19 54 1N 0 24W
Nagaland □, India 59 26 0N 94 30 E
Nagano, Jap. 62 36 40N 138 10 E
Nagaoka, Jap. 62 37 27N 138 51 E
Nagasaki, Jap. 62 32 47N 129 50 E
Nagoya, Jap. 62 35 10N 136 50 E
Nagpur, India 58 21 8N 79 10 E
Naha, Jap. 62 26 13N 127 42 E
Nailsea, U.K. 14 51 25N 2 44W
Nailsworth, U.K. 14 51 41N 2 12W
Nairn, U.K. 23 57 35N 3 54W
Nairobi, Kenya 80 1 17S 36 48 E
Nakuru, Kenya 80 0 15S 36 4 E
Nalchik, U.S.S.R. 47 43 30N 43 33 E
Nam Co, China 60 30 30N 90 45 E
Namangan, U.S.S.R. 48 41 0N 71 40 E
Namib Desert, Nam. 81 22 30S 15 0 E
Namibe, Angola 81 15 7S 12 11 E
Namibia ■, Africa 81 22 0S 18 9 E
Nampula, Mozam. 81 15 6N 39 15 E
Namur, Belg. 36 50 27N 4 52 E
Nan Shan, China 60 38 30N 99 0 E
Nanaimo, Canada 88 49 10N 124 0W
Nanchang, China 61 28 42N 115 55 E
Nanchong, China 60 30 43N 106 2 E
Nancy, Fr. 34 48 42N 6 12 E
Nanda Devi, India 58 30 23N 79 59 E
Nanjing = Nanking, China 61 32 2N 118 47 E
Nanking, China 61 32 2N 118 47 E
Nanning, China 60 22 48N 108 20 E
Nanping, China 61 26 38N 118 10 E
Nantes, Fr. 34 47 12N 1 33W
Nantong, China 61 32 1N 120 52 E
Nantucket Sd., U.S.A. 93 41 30N 70 15W
Nantwich, U.K. 18 53 5N 2 31W
Napier, N.Z. 71 39 30S 176 56 E
Naples, It. 40 40 50N 14 17 E
Nappa, U.K. 18 53 58N 2 14W
Nara, Jap. 62 34 40N 135 49 E
Narayanganj, Bangla. 59 23 40N 90 33 E
Narberth, U.K. 17 51 48N 4 45W
Narborough, U.K. 14 52 34N 1 12W
Nare Head, U.K. 16 50 12N 4 55W
Narmada →, India 58 21 38N 72 36 E
Narrandera, Austral. 70 34 42S 146 31 E
Narvik, Nor. 44 68 28N 17 26 E
Naseby, U.K. 15 52 24N 0 59W
Nashua, U.S.A. 93 42 50N 71 25W
Nashville, U.S.A. 91 36 12N 86 46W
Nasik, India 58 19 58N 73 50 E
Nassau, Baham. 95 25 0N 77 20W
Nasser, L., Egypt 79 23 0N 32 30 E
Nässjö, Swed. 45 57 39N 14 42 E
Natal, Brazil 101 5 47S 35 13W
Natal □, S. Afr. 81 28 30S 30 30 E
Nauru ■, Pac. Oc. 64 1 0S 166 0 E
Navan = An Uaimh, Ire. 24 53 39N 6 40W
Navenby, U.K. 19 53 7N 0 32W
Naver →, U.K. 23 58 34N 4 15W
Náxos, Greece 41 37 8N 25 25 E
Nazareth, Isr. 57 32 42N 35 17 E
Naze, The, U.K. 15 51 53N 1 19 E
Ndjamena, Chad 79 12 10N 14 59 E
Ndola, Zam. 81 13 0S 28 34 E
Neagh, L., U.K. 24 54 35N 6 25W
Neath, U.K. 17 51 39N 3 49W
Nebraska □, U.S.A. 90 41 30N 100 0W
Needham Market, U.K. 15 52 9N 1 2 E
Needles, The, U.K. 14 50 39N 1 35W
Negro →, Arg. 102 41 2S 62 47W
Negro →, Brazil 100 3 0S 60 0W
Negros, Phil. 63 9 30N 122 40 E
Neijiang, China 60 29 35N 104 55 E
Neilston, U.K. 20 55 47N 4 27W
Neiva, Col. 100 2 56N 75 18W
Nellore, India 58 14 27N 79 59 E
Nelson, N.Z. 71 41 18S 173 16 E
Nelson, U.K. 18 53 50N 2 14W
Nelson →, Canada 88 54 33N 98 2W
Nelspruit, S. Afr. 81 25 29S 30 59 E
Nenagh, Ire. 25 52 52N 8 11W
Nene →, U.K. 15 52 38N 0 13 E
Nepal ■, Asia 59 28 0N 84 30 E
Nephin, Ire. 24 54 1N 9 21W
Ness, Loch, U.K. 23 57 15N 4 30W
Neston, U.K. 18 53 17N 3 3W
Netanya, Isr. 57 32 20N 34 51 E
Nether Stowey, U.K. 14 51 0N 3 10W
Netherbury, U.K. 14 50 46N 2 45W
Netherlands ■, Europe 36 52 0N 5 30 E
Netley, U.K. 14 50 53N 1 21W
Netley Marsh, U.K. 14 50 55N 1 32W
Nettlebed, U.K. 15 51 34N 0 54W
Nettleham, U.K. 19 53 15N 0 28W
Neuchâtel, Switz. 42 47 0N 6 55 E
Neukirchen, Ger. 36 54 52N 8 44 E
Neuss, Ger. 36 51 12N 6 39 E
Neustadt, Ger. 36 49 21N 8 10 E
Neuwied, Ger. 36 50 26N 7 29 E
Nevada □, U.S.A. 90 39 20N 117 0W
Nevada, Sierra, Sp. 37 37 3N 3 15W
Nevada, Sierra, U.S.A. 90 39 0N 120 30W
Nevers, Fr. 34 47 0N 3 9 E
New Abbey, U.K. 21 54 59N 3 38W
New Alresford, U.K. 14 51 6N 1 10W
New Amsterdam, Guy. 101 6 15N 57 36W
New Bedford, U.S.A. 93 41 40N 70 52W
New Brighton, N.Z. 71 43 29S 172 43 E
New Brighton, U.K. 18 53 27N 3 2W
New Brunswick □, Canada 93 46 50N 66 30W
New Caledonia, Pac. Oc. 64 21 0S 165 0 E
New Castile, Sp. 37 39 45N 3 20W
New Cumnock, U.K. 20 55 24N 4 13W
New Forest, U.K. 14 50 53N 1 40W
New Galloway, U.K. 21 55 4N 4 10W
New Guinea, Pac. Oc. 64 4 0S 136 0 E
New Hampshire □, U.S.A. 93 43 40N 71 40W
New Haven, U.S.A. 93 41 20N 72 54W
New Hebrides = Vanuatu ■, Pac. Oc. 64 15 0S 168 0 E
New Holland, U.K. 19 53 42N 0 22W
New Jersey □, U.S.A. 93 40 30N 74 10W
New London, U.S.A. 93 41 23N 72 8W
New Luce, U.K. 20 54 57N 4 50W
New Mexico □, U.S.A. 90 34 30N 106 0W
New Mills, U.K. 18 53 22N 2 0W
New Orleans, U.S.A. 91 30 0N 90 5W
New Plymouth, N.Z. 71 39 4S 174 5 E
New Quay, U.K. 17 52 13N 4 21W
New Radnor, U.K. 17 52 15N 3 10W
New Romney, U.K. 15 50 59N 0 57 E
New Ross, Ire. 25 52 24N 6 58W
New Rossington, U.K. 19 53 30N 1 4W
New Siberian Is., U.S.S.R. 49 75 0N 142 0 E
New South Wales □, Austral. 70 33 0S 146 0 E
New York □, U.S.A. 93 42 40N 76 0W
New York City, U.S.A. 93 40 45N 74 0W
New Zealand ■, Pac. Oc. 71 40 0S 176 0 E
Newark, U.S.A. 93 40 41N 74 12W
Newark-on-Trent, U.K. 19 53 6N 0 48W
Newbiggin-by-the-Sea, U.K. 21 55 12N 1 31W
Newbigging, U.K. 21 55 42N 3 33W
Newburgh, U.K. 21 56 21N 3 15W
Newburn, U.K. 21 54 57N 1 45W
Newbury, U.K. 14 51 24N 1 19W
Newby Bridge, U.K. 18 54 16N 2 59W
Newcastle, Austral. 70 33 0S 151 46 E
Newcastle, U.K. 24 54 13N 5 54W
Newcastle Emlyn, U.K. 17 52 2N 4 29W
Newcastle-under-Lyme, U.K. 18 53 2N 2 15W
Newcastle-upon-Tyne, U.K. 19 54 59N 1 37W
Newcastleton, U.K. 21 55 10N 2 50W
Newent, U.K. 14 51 56N 2 24W
Newfoundland □, Canada 89 53 0N 58 0W
Newham, U.K. 15 51 31N 0 2 E
Newhaven, U.K. 15 50 47N 0 4 E
Newington, Kent, U.K. 15 51 5N 1 8 E
Newington, Kent, U.K. 15 51 21N 0 40 E
Newlyn, U.K. 16 50 6N 5 33W
Newlyn East, U.K. 16 50 22N 5 3W
Newman, Austral. 66 23 18S 119 45 E
Newmarket, Ire. 25 52 13N 9 0W
Newmarket, Lewis, U.K. 22 58 14N 6 24W
Newmarket, Suffolk, U.K. 15 52 15N 0 23 E
Newmilns, U.K. 20 55 36N 4 20W
Newnham, U.K. 14 51 48N 2 27W
Newport, Dyfed, U.K. 17 52 1N 4 51W
Newport, Essex, U.K. 15 51 58N 0 13 E
Newport, Gwent, U.K. 17 51 35N 3 0W
Newport, I. of W., U.K. 14 50 42N 1 18W
Newport, Salop, U.K. 14 52 47N 2 22W
Newport News, U.S.A. 91 37 2N 76 30W
Newport on Tay, U.K. 21 56 27N 2 56W
Newport Pagnell, U.K. 15 52 5N 0 42W
Newquay, U.K. 16 50 24N 5 6W
Newry, U.K. 24 54 10N 6 20W
Newry & Mourne □, U.K. 24 54 10N 6 15W
Newton Abbot, U.K. 16 50 32N 3 37W
Newton Arlosh, U.K. 18 54 53N 3 15W
Newton-Aycliffe, U.K. 19 54 36N 1 33W
Newton Ferrers, U.K. 16 50 19N 4 3W
Newton le Willows, U.K. 18 53 28N 2 40W
Newton St. Cyres, U.K. 16 50 46N 3 35W
Newton Stewart, U.K. 20 54 57N 4 30W
Newtongrange, U.K. 21 55 52N 3 4W
Newtonmore, U.K. 23 57 4N 4 7W
Newtown, Wales, U.K. 17 52 31N 3 19W
Newtown St. Boswells, Scotland, U.K. 21 55 34N 2 38W
Newtownabbey, Ire. 24 54 40N 5 55W
Newtownabbey □, U.K. 24 54 45N 6 0W
Newtownards, U.K. 24 54 37N 5 40W
Nha Trang, Viet. 63 12 16N 109 10 E
Niagara Falls, Canada 92 43 7N 79 5W
Niagara Falls, U.S.A. 92 43 5N 79 0W
Niamey, Niger 78 13 27N 2 6 E
Nicaragua ■, Cent. Am. 94 11 40N 85 30W
Nicaragua, L., Nic. 94 12 0N 85 30W
Nice, Fr. 35 43 42N 7 14 E
Nicobar Is., Ind. Oc. 51 9 0N 93 0 E
Nicosia, Cyprus 47 35 10N 33 25 E
Nicoya, Pen. de, C.R. 94 9 45N 85 40W

Nidd ►, U.K. 19 54 1N 1 32W
Nidderdale, U.K. 19 54 5N 1 46W
Niger ■, W. Afr. 78 13 30N 10 0 E
Niger ►, W. Afr. 78 5 33N 6 33 E
Nigeria ■, W. Afr. 78 8 30N 8 0 E
Niigata, Jap. 62 37 58N 139 0 E
Niihau, U.S.A. 90 21 55N 160 10W
Nijmegen, Neth. 36 51 50N 5 52 E
Nikolayev, U.S.S.R. 47 46 58N 32 0 E
Nikolayevsk, U.S.S.R. 49 50 0N 45 35 E
Nile ►, Africa 79 30 10N 31 6 E
Nîmes, Fr. 35 43 50N 4 23 E
Ninety Mile Beach, The, Austral. 70 38 15S 147 24 E
Ninfield, U.K. 15 50 53N 0 26 E
Ningbo, China 61 29 51N 121 28 E
Ningxia Huizu Zizhiqu □, China 60 38 0N 106 0 E
Niort, Fr. 35 46 19N 0 29W
Nipigon, L., Canada 92 49 50N 88 30W
Niš, Yug. 41 43 19N 21 58 E
Niterói, Brazil 101 22 52S 43 0W
Nith ►, U.K. 21 55 20N 3 5W
Nithsdale, U.K. 21 55 14N 3 50W
Niton, U.K. 14 50 35N 1 14W
Nizhniy Novgorod, U.S.S.R. 46 56 20N 44 0 E
Nizhniy Tagil, U.S.S.R. 46 57 55N 59 57 E
Nkongsamba, Cam. 80 4 55N 9 55 E
Nordelph, U.K. 15 52 34N 0 18 E
Nordhorn, Ger. 36 52 27N 7 4 E
Nordvik, U.S.S.R. 49 74 2N 111 32 E
Nore ►, Ire. 25 52 40N 7 20W
Norfolk, U.S.A. 91 36 40N 76 15W
Norfolk □, U.K. 15 52 39N 1 0 E
Norfolk Broads, U.K. 15 52 30N 1 15 E
Norfolk I., Pac. Oc. 64 28 58S 168 3 E
Norham, U.K. 21 55 44N 2 9W
Norilsk, U.S.S.R. 49 69 20N 88 6 E
Norman, U.S.A. 90 35 12N 97 30W
Normandy, Fr. 34 48 45N 0 10 E
Normanton, U.K. 19 53 41N 1 26W
Norrbotten □, Swed. 44 66 30N 22 30 E
Norrköping, Swed. 45 58 37N 16 11 E
Norrland □, Swed. 44 66 50N 18 0 E
Norseman, Austral. 66 32 8S 121 43 E
North Battleford, Canada 88 52 50N 108 17W
North Bay, Canada 92 46 20N 79 30W
North Berwick, U.K. 21 56 4N 2 44W
North Cape, Nor. 44 71 15N 25 40 E
North Carolina □, U.S.A. 91 35 30N 80 0W
North Cerney, U.K. 14 51 45N 1 58W
North Channel, U.K. 20 55 0N 5 30W
North Collingham, U.K. 19 53 8N 0 46W
North Dakota □, U.S.A. 90 47 30N 100 0W
North Dorset Downs, U.K. 14 50 50N 2 30W
North Down □, U.K. 24 54 40N 5 45W
North Downs, U.K. 15 51 17N 0 30 E
North Esk ►, U.K. 23 56 44N 2 25W
North European Plain 26 55 0N 20 0 E
North Foreland, U.K. 15 51 22N 1 28 E
North Hill, U.K. 16 50 33N 4 26W
North Hykeham, U.K. 19 53 10N 0 35W
North I., N.Z. 71 38 0S 175 0 E
North Minch, U.K. 22 58 5N 5 55W
North Molton, U.K. 16 51 3N 3 48W
North Petherton, U.K. 14 51 6N 3 1W
North Pole, Arctic 103 90 0N 0 0 E
North Queensferry, U.K. 21 56 1N 3 22W
North Rhine Westphalia □, Ger. 42 51 55N 7 0 E
North Ronaldsay, U.K. 23 59 20N 2 30W
North Sea, Europe 26 56 0N 4 0 E
North Somercotes, U.K. 19 53 28N 0 9 E
North Sunderland, U.K. 21 55 35N 1 40W
North Tawton, U.K. 16 50 48N 3 55W
North Thoresby, U.K. 19 53 27N 0 3W
North Tidworth, U.K. 14 51 14N 1 40W
North Tyne ►, U.K. 19 54 59N 2 7W
North Uist, U.K. 22 57 40N 7 15W
North Walsham, U.K. 15 52 49N 1 22 E
North West Highlands, U.K. 22 57 35N 5 2W
North West Territories □, Canada 88 67 0N 110 0W
North York Moors, U.K. 19 54 25N 0 50W
North Yorkshire □, U.K. 19 54 15N 1 25W
Northallerton, U.K. 19 54 20N 1 26W
Northam, Austral. 66 31 35S 116 42 E
Northam, U.K. 16 51 2N 4 13W
Northampton, U.K. 15 52 14N 0 54W
Northampton □, U.K. 15 52 16N 0 55W
Northern Ireland □, U.K. 24 54 45N 7 0W
Northern Marianas ■, Pac. Oc. 64 17 0N 145 0 E
Northern Territory □, Austral. 66 16 0S 133 0 E
Northfleet, U.K. 15 51 26N 0 20 E
Northiam, U.K. 15 50 59N 0 39 E
Northland □, N.Z. 71 35 30S 173 30 E
Northleach, U.K. 14 51 49N 1 50W
Northrepps, U.K. 15 52 53N 1 20 E
Northumberland □, U.K. 19 55 12N 2 0W
Northumberland Str., Canada 93 46 20N 64 0W
Northwich, U.K. 18 53 16N 2 30W
Northwold, U.K. 15 52 33N 0 37 E
Norton, N. Yorks., U.K. 19 54 9N 0 48W
Norton, Suffolk, U.K. 15 52 15N 0 52 E
Norton Fitzwarren, U.K. 14 51 1N 3 10W
Norway ■, Europe 44 63 0N 11 0 E
Norwegian Sea, Atl. Oc. 44 66 0N 1 0 E
Norwich, U.K. 15 52 38N 1 17 E
Noss Hd., U.K. 23 58 29N 3 4W
Nottingham, U.K. 19 52 57N 1 10W
Nottingham □, U.K. 19 53 10N 1 0W
Nouâdhibou, Maurit. 78 20 54N 17 0W
Nouakchott, Maurit. 78 18 9N 15 58W
Nouméa, N. Cal. 64 22 17S 166 30 E
Nova Scotia □, Canada 93 45 10N 63 0W
Novara, It. 40 45 27N 8 36 E
Novaya Zemlya, U.S.S.R. 48 75 0N 56 0 E
Novi Sad, Yug. 41 45 18N 19 52 E
Novocherkassk, U.S.S.R. 47 47 27N 40 5 E
Novokuznetsk, U.S.S.R. 48 53 45N 87 10 E
Novomoskovsk, U.S.S.R. 46 54 5N 38 15 E
Novorossiysk, U.S.S.R. 47 44 43N 37 46 E
Novoshakhtinsk, U.S.S.R. 47 47 46N 39 58 E
Novosibirsk, U.S.S.R. 48 55 0N 83 5 E
Nubian Desert, Sudan 79 21 30N 33 30 E
Nuevo Laredo, Mex. 94 27 30N 99 30W
Nullarbor Plain, Austral. 66 30 45S 129 0 E
Nuneaton, U.K. 14 52 32N 1 29W
Nunney, U.K. 14 51 13N 2 20W
Nuremburg, Ger. 42 49 26N 11 5 E
Nyasa, L., Africa 81 12 30S 34 30 E
Nyíregyháza, Hung. 43 47 58N 21 47 E
Nykøbing, Den. 45 56 48N 8 51 E

O

Oa, Mull of, U.K. 20 55 35N 6 20W
Oa, The, Pen., U.K. 20 55 36N 6 17W
Oadby, U.K. 14 52 37N 1 7W
Oahe L., U.S.A. 90 45 30N 100 25W
Oahu, U.S.A. 90 21 30N 158 0W
Oakengates, U.K. 14 52 42N 2 29W
Oakham, U.K. 15 52 40N 0 43W
Oakland, U.S.A. 90 37 50N 122 18W
Oakleigh, Austral. 70 37 54S 145 6 E
Oamaru, N.Z. 71 45 5S 170 59 E
Oaxaca, Mex. 94 17 2N 96 40W
Ob ►, U.S.S.R. 48 66 45N 69 30 E
Ob, G. of, U.S.S.R. 48 70 0N 73 0 E
Oban, U.K. 20 56 25N 5 30W
Oberhausen, Ger. 36 51 28N 6 50 E
Ochil Hills, U.K. 21 56 14N 3 40W
Ochiltree, U.K. 20 55 26N 4 23W
October Revolution I., U.S.S.R. 49 79 30N 97 0 E
Odense, Den. 45 55 22N 10 23 E
Odessa, U.S.A. 90 31 51N 102 23W
Odessa, U.S.S.R. 47 46 30N 30 45 E
Odiham, U.K. 15 51 16N 0 56W
Odra ►, Pol. 42 53 33N 14 38 E
Offaly □, Ire. 25 53 15N 7 30W
Offenbach, Ger. 42 50 6N 8 46 E
Ogbomosho, Nig. 78 8 1N 4 11 E
Ogden, U.S.A. 90 41 13N 112 1W
Ohio □, U.S.A. 92 40 20N 14 10 E
Ohio ►, U.S.A. 92 38 0N 86 0W
Ōita, Jap. 62 33 14N 131 36 E
Okavango Swamps, Bots. 81 18 45S 22 45 E
Okayama, Jap. 62 34 40N 133 54 E
Okazaki, Jap. 62 34 57N 137 10 E
Okehampton, U.K. 16 50 44N 4 1W
Okhotsk, U.S.S.R. 49 59 20N 143 10 E
Okhotsk, Sea of, Asia 49 55 0N 145 0 E
Oklahoma □, U.S.A. 90 35 20N 97 30W
Oklahoma City, U.S.A. 91 35 25N 97 30W
Ólafsfjörður, Ice. 44 66 4N 18 39W
Öland, Swed. 45 56 45N 16 38 E
Old Basing, U.K. 14 51 16N 1 3W
Old Castile, Sp. 37 41 55N 4 0W
Old Castle, Ire. 24 53 46N 7 10W
Old Kilpatrick, U.K. 20 55 56N 4 34W
Old Leake, U.K. 19 53 2N 0 6 E
Oldbury, Gloucs., U.K. 14 51 38N 2 30W
Oldbury, W. Midlands, U.K. 14 52 30N 2 0W
Oldenburg, Ger. 36 53 10N 8 10 E
Oldham, U.K. 18 53 33N 2 8W
Oldmeldrum, U.K. 23 57 20N 2 19W
Olekminsk, U.S.S.R. 49 60 25N 120 30 E
Olinda, Brazil 101 8 1S 34 51W
Ollerton, U.K. 19 53 12N 1 1W
Olney, U.K. 15 52 9N 0 42W
Olomouc, Czech. 42 49 38N 17 12 E
Olsztyn, Pol. 43 53 48N 20 29 E
Olympia, Greece 41 37 39N 21 39 E
Olympus, Mt., Greece 41 40 6N 22 23 E
Omagh, U.K. 24 54 36N 7 20W
Omagh □, U.K. 24 54 35N 7 15W
Omaha, U.S.A. 91 41 15N 96 0W
Oman ■, Si. Arab. 57 23 0N 58 0 E
Oman, G. of, Asia 57 24 30N 58 30 E
Ombersley, U.K. 14 52 17N 2 12W
Omdurmân, Sudan 79 15 40N 32 28 E
Ōmiya, Jap. 62 35 54N 139 38 E
Omsk, U.S.S.R. 48 55 0N 73 12 E
Ōmuta, Jap. 62 33 0N 130 26 E
Onchan, U.K. 18 54 11N 4 27W
Onega ►, U.S.S.R. 46 63 58N 37 55 E
Onega, G. of, U.S.S.R. 46 64 30N 37 0 E
Onega, L., U.S.S.R. 46 62 0N 35 30 E
Onehunga, N.Z. 71 36 55S 174 48 E
Onny ►, U.K. 14 52 30N 2 50W
Ontario □, Canada 88 52 0N 88 10W
Ontario, L., N. Am. 92 43 40N 78 0W
Opole, Pol. 43 50 42N 17 58 E
Oporto, Port. 37 41 8N 8 40W
Oradea, Rom. 43 47 2N 21 58 E
Oran, Alg. 78 35 45N 0 39W
Orange, Austral. 70 33 15S 149 7 E
Orange ►, S. Afr. 81 28 41S 16 28 E
Orange Free State □, S. Afr. 81 28 30S 27 0 E
Ord, Mt., Austral. 66 17 20S 125 34 E
Ordos = Mu Us Shamo, China 61 39 0N 109 0 E
* Ordzhonikidze, U.S.S.R. 47 43 0N 44 35 E
Örebro, Swed. 45 59 20N 15 18 E
Oregon □, U.S.A. 90 44 0N 121 0W
Orekhovo-Zuyevo, U.S.S.R. 46 55 50N 38 55 E
Orel, U.S.S.R. 46 52 57N 36 3 E
Orenburg, U.S.S.R. 46 51 45N 55 6 E
Orense, Sp. 37 42 19N 7 55W
Orford, U.K. 15 52 6N 1 31 E
Orford Ness, U.K. 15 52 6N 1 31 E
Orinoco ►, Ven. 100 9 15N 61 30W
Orissa □, India 59 20 0N 84 0 E
Oristano, It. 40 39 54N 8 35 E
Orizaba, Mex. 94 18 51N 97 6W
Orkney □, U.K. 23 59 0N 3 0W
Orkney Is., U.K. 23 59 0N 3 0W
Orlando, U.S.A. 91 28 30N 81 25W
Orléans, Fr. 34 47 54N 1 52 E
Ormesby St. Margaret, U.K. 15 52 39N 1 42 E
Ormskirk, U.K. 18 53 35N 2 53W
Örnsköldsvik, Swed. 44 63 17N 18 40 E
Oronsay, Pass of, U.K. 20 56 0N 6 10W
Oronsay I., U.K. 20 56 0N 6 14W
Orsk, U.S.S.R. 46 51 12N 58 34 E
Orton Tebay, U.K. 18 54 28N 2 35W
Oruro, Bol. 100 18 0S 67 9W
Orwell ►, U.K. 15 52 2N 1 12 E
Ōsaka, Jap. 62 34 40N 135 30 E
Osh, U.S.S.R. 48 40 37N 72 49 E
Oshawa, Canada 92 43 50N 78 50W
Oshogbo, Nig. 78 7 48N 4 37 E
Osijek, Yug. 41 45 34N 18 41 E
Osizweni, S. Afr. 81 27 49S 30 7 E
Oslo, Nor. 45 59 55N 10 45 E
Oslo Fjord, Nor. 45 58 30N 10 0 E
Osmotherley, U.K. 19 54 22N 1 18W
Osnabrück, Ger. 36 52 16N 8 2 E
Osorno, Chile 102 40 25S 73 0W
Ossett, U.K. 19 53 40N 1 35W
Ostend, Belg. 36 51 15N 2 50 E
Östersund, Swed. 44 63 10N 14 38 E
Ostrava, Czech. 43 49 51N 18 18 E
Osumi, Is., Jap. 62 30 30N 130 45 E
Oswaldtwistle, U.K. 18 53 44N 2 27W
Oswestry, U.K. 14 52 52N 3 3W
Otago □, N.Z. 71 44 44S 169 10 E
Otaru, Jap. 62 43 10N 141 0 E
Otley, U.K. 19 53 54N 1 41W
Otranto, Str. of, It. 41 40 15N 18 40 E
Ōtsu, Jap. 62 35 0N 135 50 E
Ottawa, Canada 93 45 27N 75 42W
Ottawa ►, Canada 93 45 27N 74 8W
Otter ►, U.K. 16 50 47N 3 12W
Otter Ferry, U.K. 20 56 1N 5 20W
Otterburn, U.K. 21 55 14N 2 12W
Ottery St. Mary, U.K. 16 50 45N 3 16W
Ouagadougou, B. Faso 78 12 25N 1 30W
Oujda, Mor. 78 34 41N 1 55W
Oulton, U.K. 15 52 29N 1 40 E
Oulton Broad, U.K. 15 52 28N 1 43 E
Oulu, Fin. 44 65 1N 25 29 E
Oulu, L., Fin. 44 64 25N 27 0 E
Oundle, U.K. 15 52 28N 0 28W
Ouse ►, E. Sussex, U.K. 15 50 43N 0 3 E
Ouse ►, N. Yorks., U.K. 19 54 3N 0 7 E
Outer Hebrides, U.K. 22 57 30N 7 40W
Outwell, U.K. 15 52 36N 0 14 E
Over Wallop, U.K. 14 51 9N 1 35W
Overstand, U.K. 15 52 55N 1 20 E
Overton, U.K. 14 51 14N 1 16W
Oviedo, Sp. 37 43 25N 5 50W
Owston Ferry, U.K. 19 53 28N 0 47W
Ox Mts., Ire. 24 54 6N 9 0W
Oxford, U.K. 14 51 45N 1 15W
Oxford □, U.K. 14 51 45N 1 15W
Oykel ►, U.K. 23 57 55N 4 26W
Ozark Plateau, U.S.A. 91 37 20N 91 40W

P

Paarl, S. Afr. 81 33 45S 18 56 E
Pacaraima, Sierra, Ven. 100 4 0N 62 30W
Pachuca, Mex. 94 20 10N 98 40W
Pacific Ocean 64 10 0N 140 0W
Padang, Indon. 63 1 0S 100 20 E
Paddock Wood, U.K. 15 51 13N 0 24 E
Padiham, U.K. 18 53 48N 2 20W
Padstow, U.K. 14 50 33N 4 57W
Padstow Bay, U.K. 16 50 35N 4 58W
Padua, It. 40 45 24N 11 52 E
Pagalu = Annobón, Atl. Oc. 73 1 25S 5 36 E
Paignton, U.K. 16 50 26N 3 33W
Painswick, U.K. 14 51 47N 2 11W
Paisley, U.K. 20 55 51N 4 27W
Pakistan ■, Asia 58 30 0N 70 0 E
Palawan, Phil. 63 9 30N 118 30 E
Palembang, Indon. 63 3 0S 104 50 E
Palencia, Sp. 37 42 1N 4 34W
Palermo, It. 40 38 8N 13 20 E
Palgrave, U.K. 15 52 22N 1 7 E
Palk Strait, Asia 58 10 0N 79 45 E
Palma de Mallorca, Sp. 37 39 35N 2 39 E
Palmer ►, Austral. 66 24 46S 133 25 E
Palmerston North, N.Z. 71 40 21S 175 39 E
Palmira, Col. 100 3 32N 76 16W
Pamirs, U.S.S.R. 48 37 40N 73 0 E
Pamlico Sd., U.S.A. 91 35 20N 76 0W
Pampas, Arg. 96 35 0S 63 0W
Pamplona, Sp. 37 42 48N 1 38W
Panamá, Pan. 94 9 0N 79 25W
Panama ■, Cent. Am. 95 8 48N 79 55W
Panamá, G. de, Pan. 95 8 4N 79 20W
Panama Canal, Pan. 94 9 10N 79 37W
Panay, Phil. 63 11 10N 122 30 E
Pančevo, Yug. 41 44 52N 20 41 E
Pangbourne, U.K. 14 51 28N 1 5W
Pantelleria, It. 40 36 52N 12 0 E
Papua New Guinea ■, Oc. 64 8 0S 145 0 E
Pará □, Brazil 101 3 20S 52 0W
Paraguay ■, S. Am. 102 23 0S 57 0W
Paraguay ►, Par. 102 27 18S 58 38W
Paramaribo, Surinam 101 5 50N 55 10W
Paraná, Arg. 102 31 45S 60 30W
Paraná ►, Arg. 102 33 43S 59 15W
Parecis, Serra dos, Brazil 100 13 0S 60 0W
Parepare, Indon. 63 4 0S 119 40 E
Paris, Fr. 34 48 50N 2 20 E
Parkes, Austral. 70 33 9S 148 11 E
Parma, It. 40 44 50N 10 20 E
Parnaiba ►, Brazil 101 3 0S 41 50W
Parracombe, U.K. 16 51 11N 3 55W
Parramatta, Austral. 70 33 48S 151 1 E
Parrett ►, U.K. 14 51 7N 2 58W
Partney, U.K. 19 53 12N 0 7 E
Parton, U.K. 18 54 34N 3 35W
Passage West, Ire. 25 51 52N 8 20W
Pasto, Col. 100 1 13N 77 17W
Patagonia, Arg. 102 45 0S 69 0W
Patcham, U.K. 15 50 52N 0 9W
Pateley Bridge, U.K. 19 54 5N 1 45W
Paterson, U.S.A. 93 40 55N 74 10W
Patna, India 59 25 35N 85 12 E
Patna, U.K. 20 55 21N 4 30W
Pátrai, Greece 41 38 14N 21 47 E
Patrick, U.K. 18 54 13N 4 41W
Patrington, U.K. 19 53 41N 0 1W
Patterdale, U.K. 18 54 33N 2 55W
Pau, Fr. 35 43 19N 0 25W
Paull, U.K. 19 53 42N 0 12W
Pavia, It. 40 45 10N 9 10 E
Pavlodar, U.S.S.R. 48 52 33N 77 0 E
Pawtucket, U.S.A. 93 41 51N 71 22W
Paz, La, Bol. 100 16 20S 68 10W
Pazardzhik, Bulg. 41 42 12N 24 20 E
Peace ►, Canada 88 59 0N 111 25W
Peacehaven, U.K. 15 50 47N 0 1 E
Peak, The, U.K. 18 53 24N 1 53W
Peasenhall, U.K. 15 52 17N 1 24 E
Pechora ►, U.S.S.R. 46 68 13N 54 15 E
Pécs, Hung. 43 46 5N 18 15 E
Peebles, U.K. 21 55 40N 3 12W
Peel, U.K. 18 54 14N 4 40W
Peel Fell, U.K. 21 55 17N 2 35W
Pegasus Bay, N.Z. 71 43 20S 173 10 E
Pegswood, U.K. 21 55 12N 1 38W
Pegu, Burma 59 17 20N 96 29 E
Pegu Yoma, Burma 59 19 0N 96 0 E
Pegwell Bay, U.K. 15 51 18N 1 22 E
Pekanbaru, Indon. 63 0 30N 101 15 E
Peking, China 61 39 55N 116 20 E
Peloponnese □, Greece 41 37 10N 22 0 E
Pelotas, Brazil 102 31 42S 52 23W
Pelvoux, Massif de, Fr. 35 44 52N 6 20 E
Pematangsiantar, Indon. 63 2 57N 99 5 E
Pemba, Tanz. 80 5 0S 39 45 E
Pembridge, U.K. 14 52 13N 2 54W
Pembroke, U.K. 17 51 41N 4 57W
Pembury, U.K. 15 51 8N 0 20 E
Pen-y-Ghent, U.K. 18 54 10N 2 15W
Pen-y-groes, U.K. 17 53 3N 4 18W
Penang = Pinang, Malay. 63 5 25N 100 15 E
Penarth, U.K. 17 51 26N 3 11W
Pendeen, U.K. 16 50 11N 5 39W
Pendle Hill, U.K. 18 53 53N 2 18W
Penicuik, U.K. 21 55 50N 3 14W
Peninsular Malaysia □, Malay. 63 4 0N 102 0 E
Penistone, U.K. 19 53 31N 1 38W
Penkridge, U.K. 14 52 44N 2 8W
Pennines, U.K. 18 54 50N 2 20W
Pennsylvania □, U.S.A. 92 40 50N 78 0W
Penpont, U.K. 21 55 14N 3 49W

* Renamed Vladikavkaz

Penrith, Austral. 70 33 43S 150 38 E
Penrith, U.K. 18 54 40N 2 45W
Penryn, U.K. 16 50 10N 5 7W
Pensacola, U.S.A. 91 30 30N 87 10W
Penshurst, U.K. 15 51 10N 0 12 E
Pentire Pt., U.K. 16 50 35N 4 57W
Pentland Firth, U.K. 23 58 43N 3 10W
Pentland Hills, U.K. 21 55 48N 3 25W
Penwortham, U.K. 18 53 45N 2 44W
Penza, U.S.S.R. 46 53 15N 45 5 E
Penzance, U.K. 16 50 7N 5 32W
Peoria, U.S.A. 92 40 40N 89 40W
Pereira, Col. 100 4 49N 75 43W
Perm, U.S.S.R. 46 58 0N 57 10 E
Perouse Str., La, Jap. 64 45 40N 142 0 E
Perpignan, Fr. 35 42 42N 2 53 E
Perranporth, U.K. 16 50 21N 5 9W
Perranzabuloe, U.K. 16 50 18N 5 7W
Pershore, U.K. 14 52 7N 2 4W
Persian Gulf = Gulf, The, Asia 56 27 0N 50 0 E
Perth, Austral. 66 31 57S 115 52 E
Perth, U.K. 21 56 24N 3 27W
Peru ■, S. Am. 100 8 0S 75 0W
Perúgia, It. 40 43 6N 12 24 E
Pescara, It. 40 42 28N 14 13 E
Peshawar, Pak. 58 34 2N 71 37 E
Peterborough, Canada 92 44 20N 78 20W
Peterborough, U.K. 15 52 35N 0 14W
Peterchurch, U.K. 14 52 3N 2 57W
Peterhead, U.K. 23 57 30N 1 49W
Peterlee, U.K. 19 54 45N 1 18W
Petersfield, U.K. 15 51 0N 0 56W
Petropavlovsk, U.S.S.R. 48 54 53N 69 13 E
Petropavlovsk-Kamchatskiy, U.S.S.R. 49 53 3N 158 43 E
Petrópolis, Brazil 101 22 33S 43 9W
Petrozavodsk, U.S.S.R. 46 61 41N 34 20 E
Petworth, U.K. 15 50 59N 0 37W
Pevensey, U.K. 15 50 49N 0 20 E
Pevensey Levels, U.K. 15 50 50N 0 20 E
Pewsey, U.K. 14 51 20N 1 46W
Pewsey, Vale of, U.K. 14 51 20N 1 46W
Pforzheim, Ger. 42 48 53N 8 43 E
Philadelphia, U.S.A. 93 40 0N 75 10W
Philippines ■, Asia 63 12 0N 123 0 E
Phnom Penh, Cambod. 63 11 33N 104 55 E
Phoenix, U.S.A. 90 33 30N 112 10W
Phoenix Is., Pac. Oc. 65 3 30S 172 0W
Piacenza, It. 40 45 2N 9 42 E
Piatra Neamţ, Rom. 43 46 56N 26 21 E
Picardie, Fr. 34 49 50N 3 0 E
Picardy = Picardie, Fr. 34 49 50N 3 0 E
Pickering, U.K. 19 54 15N 0 46W
Pickering, Vale of, U.K. 19 54 0N 0 45W
Pidley, U.K. 15 52 33N 0 4W
Piedmont □, It. 40 45 0N 7 30 E
Piedras Negras, Mex. 94 28 42N 100 31W
Pierowall, U.K. 23 59 20N 3 0W
Pietermaritzburg, S. Afr. 81 29 35S 30 25 E
Pilbara, Austral. 66 21 15S 118 16 E
Pilcomayo →, Par. 102 25 21S 57 42W
Pilling, U.K. 18 53 55N 2 54W
Pilton, U.K. 14 51 0N 2 35W
Pinang, Malay. 63 5 25N 100 15 E
Pinchbeck, U.K. 15 52 48N 0 9W
Pindus Mts., Greece 41 40 0N 21 0 E
Pine Bluff, U.S.A. 91 34 10N 92 0W
Pingxiang, China 60 22 6N 106 46 E
Pinhoe, U.K. 16 50 44N 3 29W
Pinjarra, Austral. 66 32 37S 115 52 E
Pinwherry, U.K. 20 55 9N 4 50W
Piotrków Trybunalski, Pol. 43 51 23N 19 43 E
Piracicaba, Brazil 102 22 45S 47 40W
Piraiévs, Greece 41 37 57N 23 42 E
Pirbright, U.K. 15 51 17N 0 40W
Pirmasens, Ger. 36 49 12N 7 30 E
Pisa, It. 40 43 43N 10 23 E
Pistóia, It. 40 43 57N 10 53 E
Pitcairn I., Pac. Oc. 65 25 5S 130 5W
Piteşti, Rom. 43 44 52N 24 54 E
Pitlochry, U.K. 23 56 43N 3 43W
Pittenweem, U.K. 21 56 13N 2 43W
Pittsburgh, U.S.A. 92 40 25N 79 55W
Pittsfield, U.S.A. 93 42 28N 73 17W
Piura, Peru 100 5 15S 80 38W
Pladda, I., U.K. 20 55 25N 5 7W
Plata, La, Arg. 102 35 0S 57 55W
Plata, Rio de la, S. Am. 102 34 45S 57 30W
Plauen, Ger. 42 50 29N 12 9 E
Plenty, Bay of, N.Z. 71 37 45S 177 0 E
Pleven, Bulg. 41 43 26N 24 37 E
Płock, Pol. 43 52 32N 19 40 E
Ploieşti, Rom. 43 44 57N 26 5 E
Plovdiv, Bulg. 41 42 8N 24 44 E
Plymouth, U.K. 16 50 23N 4 9W
Plymouth Sd., U.K. 16 50 20N 4 10W
Plympton, U.K. 16 50 24N 4 2W
Plymstock, U.K. 16 50 22N 4 6W
Plynlimon = Pumlumon Fawr, U.K. 17 52 29N 3 47W
Plzen, Czech. 42 49 45N 13 22 E
Po →, It. 40 44 57N 12 4 E
Pocklington, U.K. 19 53 56N 0 48W
Podolsk, U.S.S.R. 46 55 25N 37 30 E
Pointe-à-Pitre, Guad. 94 16 10N 61 30W
Pointe Noire, Congo 80 4 48S 11 53 E
Poitiers, Fr. 34 46 35N 0 20 E
Poland ■, Europe 43 52 0N 20 0 E
Polden Hills, U.K. 14 51 7N 2 50W
Polegate, U.K. 15 50 49N 0 15 E
Polesworth, U.K. 14 52 37N 1 37W
Polperro, U.K. 16 50 19N 4 31W
Polruan, U.K. 16 50 17N 4 36W
Poltava, U.S.S.R. 47 49 35N 34 35 E
Polynesia, Pac. Oc. 64 10 0S 162 0W
Ponce, P.R. 95 18 1N 66 37W
Pondicherry, India 58 11 59N 79 50 E
Ponta Grossa, Brazil 102 25 7S 50 10W
Pontardawe, U.K. 17 51 43N 3 51W
Pontardulais, U.K. 17 51 42N 4 3W
Pontchartrain, L., U.S.A. 91 30 12N 90 0W
Pontefract, U.K. 19 53 42N 1 19W
Ponteland, U.K. 21 55 7N 1 45W
Pontevedra, Sp. 37 42 26N 8 40W
Pontianak, Indon. 63 0 3S 109 15 E
Pontrilas, U.K. 14 51 56N 2 53W
Pontypool, U.K. 17 51 42N 3 1W
Pontypridd, U.K. 17 51 36N 3 21W
Poole, U.K. 14 50 42N 1 58W
Poole Harbour, U.K. 14 50 41N 2 0W
Pooley Bridge, U.K. 18 54 37N 2 49W
Poona = Pune, India 58 18 29N 73 57 E
Poopó, L., Bol. 100 18 30S 67 35W
Popayán, Col. 100 2 27N 76 36W
Popocatépetl, Volcán, Mex. 94 19 2N 98 38W
Pori, Fin. 45 61 29N 21 48 E
Porirua, N.Z. 71 41 8S 174 52 E
Porlock, U.K. 14 51 13N 3 36W
Porlock B., U.K. 14 51 14N 3 37W
Porlock Hill, U.K. 14 51 12N 3 40W
Porsangen Fjord, Nor. 44 70 45N 25 0 E
Port Antonio, Jam. 94 18 10N 76 30W
Port Arthur, U.S.A. 91 30 0N 94 0W
Port Askaig, U.K. 20 55 51N 6 8W
Port-au-Prince, Haiti 95 18 40N 72 20W
Port Augusta, Austral. 67 32 30S 137 50 E
Port Bannatyne, U.K. 20 55 51N 5 4W
Port Carlisle, U.K. 18 54 56N 3 12W
Port-Cartier, Canada 89 50 2N 66 50W
Port Charlotte, U.K. 20 55 44N 6 22W
Port Elizabeth, S. Afr. 81 33 58S 25 40 E
Port Ellen, U.K. 20 55 38N 6 10W
Port Erin, U.K. 18 54 5N 4 45W
Port-Gentil, Gabon 80 0 40S 8 50 E
Port Glasgow, U.K. 20 55 57N 4 40W
Port Harcourt, Nig. 78 4 40N 7 10 E
Port Hedland, Austral. 66 20 25S 118 35 E
Port Isaac, U.K. 16 50 35N 4 50W
Port Isaac B., U.K. 16 50 36N 4 50W
Port Laoise, Ire. 25 53 2N 7 20W
Port Logan, U.K. 20 54 42N 4 57W
Port Macquarie, Austral. 67 31 25S 152 25 E
Port Moresby, P.N.G. 64 9 24S 147 8 E
Port of Spain, Trin. & Tob. 94 10 40N 61 31W
Port Phillip B., Austral. 70 38 10S 144 50 E
Port Pirie, Austral. 67 33 10S 138 1 E
Port Said, Egypt 79 31 16N 32 18 E
Port St. Mary, U.K. 18 54 5N 4 45W
Port Sudan, Sudan 79 19 32N 37 9 E
Port Sunlight, U.K. 18 53 22N 3 0W
Port Talbot, U.K. 17 51 35N 3 48W
Port William, U.K. 20 54 46N 4 35W
Portadown, U.K. 24 54 27N 6 26W
Portaferry, U.K. 24 54 23N 5 32W
Portage La Prairie, Canada 88 49 58N 98 18W
Portarlington, Ire. 25 53 10N 7 10W
Porthcawl, U.K. 17 51 28N 3 42W
Porthleven, U.K. 16 50 5N 5 19W
Porthmadog, U.K. 17 52 55N 4 13W
Portishead, U.K. 14 51 29N 2 46W
Portland, Austral. 70 38 20S 141 35 E
Portland, Maine, U.S.A. 93 43 40N 70 15W
Portland, Oreg., U.S.A. 90 45 35N 122 40W
Portland Bill, U.K. 14 50 31N 2 27W
Portland, I. of, U.K. 14 50 32N 2 25W
Portnacroish, U.K. 20 56 34N 5 24W
Portnahaven, U.K. 20 55 40N 6 30W
Pôrto Alegre, Brazil 102 30 5S 51 10W
Porto Novo, Benin 78 6 23N 2 42 E
Pôrto Velho, Brazil 100 8 46S 63 54W
Porton, U.K. 14 51 8N 1 42W
Portovíejo, Ecuad. 100 1 7S 80 28W
Portpatrick, U.K. 20 54 50N 5 7W
Portree, U.K. 22 57 25N 6 11W
Portrush, U.K. 24 55 13N 6 40W
Portslade, U.K. 15 50 50N 0 11W
Portsmouth, U.K. 14 50 48N 1 6W
Portsmouth, U.S.A. 93 43 5N 70 45W
Portsoy, U.K. 23 57 41N 2 41W
Portstewart, U.K. 24 55 12N 6 43W
Portugal ■, Europe 37 40 0N 7 0W
Portumna, Ire. 25 53 5N 8 12W
Posadas, Arg. 102 27 30S 55 50W
Postbridge, U.K. 16 50 36N 3 54W
Potchefstroom, S. Afr. 81 26 41S 27 7 E
Potenza, It. 40 40 40N 15 50 E
Potomac →, U.S.A. 92 38 0N 76 23W
Potosí, Bol. 100 19 38S 65 50W
Potsdam, Ger. 42 52 23N 13 4 E
Potter Heigham, U.K. 15 52 44N 1 33 E
Potterne, U.K. 14 51 19N 2 0W
Potters Bar, U.K. 15 51 42N 0 11W
Potterspury, U.K. 15 52 5N 0 52W
Poulaphouca Res., Ire. 25 53 8N 6 30W
Poulton le Fylde, U.K. 18 53 51N 2 59W
Poundstock, U.K. 16 50 44N 4 34W
Powell, L., U.S.A. 90 37 25N 110 45W
Powick, U.K. 14 52 9N 2 15W
Powys □, U.K. 17 52 20N 3 20W
Poyang Hu, China 61 29 10N 116 10 E
Poznań, Pol. 42 52 25N 16 55 E
Prague, Czech. 42 50 5N 14 22 E
Prato, It. 40 43 53N 11 5 E
Prawle Pt., U.K. 16 50 13N 3 41W
Prees, U.K. 18 52 54N 2 40W
Preesall, U.K. 18 53 55N 2 58W
Prescot, U.K. 18 53 27N 2 49W
Preshute, U.K. 14 51 24N 1 45W
Presidente Prudente, Brazil 101 22 5S 51 25W
Presque Isle, U.S.A. 93 46 40N 68 0W
Prestatyn, U.K. 17 53 20N 3 24W
Prestbury, U.K. 14 51 54N 2 2W
Presteigne, U.K. 17 52 17N 3 0W
Preston, Borders, U.K. 21 55 48N 2 18W
Preston, Dorset, U.K. 14 50 38N 2 26W
Preston, Lancs., U.K. 18 53 46N 2 42W
Prestonpans, U.K. 21 55 58N 3 0W
Prestwich, U.K. 18 53 32N 2 18W
Prestwick, U.K. 20 55 30N 4 38W
Pretoria, S. Afr. 81 25 44S 28 12 E
Prince Albert, Canada 88 53 15N 105 50W
Prince Edward I. □, Canada 93 46 20N 63 20W
Prince George, Canada 88 53 55N 122 50W
Prince of Wales I., Canada 88 73 0N 99 0W
Prince Rupert, Canada 88 54 20N 130 20W
Princes Risborough, U.K. 15 51 43N 0 50W
Princess Charlotte B., Austral. 67 14 25S 144 0 E
Princetown, U.K. 16 50 33N 4 0W
Pripyat Marshes, U.S.S.R. 46 52 0N 28 10 E
Priština, Yug. 41 42 40N 21 13 E
Prizren, Yug. 41 42 13N 20 45 E
Probus, U.K. 16 50 17N 4 55W
Prokopyevsk, U.S.S.R. 48 54 0N 86 45 E
Prome, Burma 59 18 49N 95 13 E
Provence, Fr. 35 43 40N 5 46 E
Providence, U.S.A. 93 41 50N 71 28W
Prudhoe, U.K. 21 54 57N 1 52W
Prudhoe Bay, U.S.A. 88 70 20N 148 20W
Prut →, Rom. 41 46 3N 28 10 E
Przemyśl, Pol. 43 49 50N 22 45 E
Puddletown, U.K. 14 50 45N 2 21W
Pudsey, U.K. 19 53 47N 1 40W
Puebla, Mex. 94 19 3N 98 12W
Pueblo, U.S.A. 90 38 20N 104 40W
Puerto La Cruz, Ven. 100 10 13N 64 38W
Puerto Montt, Chile 102 41 28S 73 0W
Puerto Rico ■, W. Ind. 95 18 15N 66 45W
Pula, It. 40 39 0N 9 0 E
Pulborough, U.K. 15 50 58N 0 30W
Pulham Market, U.K. 15 52 25N 1 15 E
Pulham St. Mary, U.K. 15 52 25N 1 14 E
Pumlumon Fawr, U.K. 17 52 29N 3 47W
Pune, India 58 18 29N 73 57 E
Punjab □, India 58 31 0N 76 0 E
Punjab □, Pak. 58 30 0N 72 0 E
Punta Arenas, Chile 102 53 10S 71 0W
Punto Fijo, Ven. 100 11 50N 70 13W
Purbeck, Isle of, U.K. 14 50 40N 2 5W
Purfleet, U.K. 15 51 29N 0 15 E
Purley, U.K. 14 51 29N 1 4W
Purnia, India 59 25 45N 87 31 E
Purus →, Brazil 100 3 42S 61 28W
Pusan, S. Kor. 61 35 5N 129 0 E
Puy-de-Dôme, Fr. 35 45 46N 2 57 E
Pwllheli, U.K. 17 52 54N 4 26W
Pyŏngyang, N. Kor. 61 39 0N 125 30 E
Pyrenees, Europe 35 42 45N 0 18 E

Q

Qandahār, Afg. 57 31 32N 65 30 E
Qatar ■, Asia 56 25 30N 51 15 E
Qattâra Depression, Egypt 79 29 30N 27 30 E
Qazvin, Iran 56 36 15N 50 0 E
Qena, Egypt 79 26 10N 32 43 E
Qingdao, China 61 36 5N 120 20 E
Qinghai □, China 60 36 0N 98 0 E
Qinghai Hu, China 60 36 40N 100 10 E
Qingjiang, China 61 33 30N 119 2 E
Qiqihar, China 61 47 26N 124 0 E
Qom, Iran 56 34 40N 51 0 E
Quadring, U.K. 19 52 53N 0 9W
Quainton, U.K. 15 51 51N 0 53W
Quantock Hills, U.K. 14 51 8N 3 10W
Queanbeyan, Austral. 70 35 17S 149 14 E
Québec, Canada 93 46 52N 71 13W
Québec □, Canada 89 50 0N 70 0W
Queen Charlotte Is., Canada 88 53 20N 132 10W
Queen Elizabeth Is., Canada 103 76 0N 95 0W
Queen Maud G., Canada 88 68 15N 102 30W
Queenborough, U.K. 15 51 24N 0 46 E
Queensbury, U.K. 18 53 46N 1 50W
Queensferry, U.K. 21 56 0N 3 25W
Queensland □, Austral. 67 22 0S 142 0 E
Queenstown, N.Z. 71 45 1S 168 40 E
Queenstown, S. Afr. 81 31 52S 26 52 E
Querétaro, Mex. 94 20 36N 100 23W
Quetta, Pak. 58 30 15N 66 55 E
Quezon City, Phil. 63 14 38N 121 0 E
Qui Nhon, Viet. 63 13 40N 109 13 E
Quimper, Fr. 34 48 0N 4 9W
Quito, Ecuad. 100 0 15S 78 35W
Quorndon, U.K. 14 52 45N 1 10W

R

Raasay, U.K. 22 57 25N 6 4W
Raasay, Sd. of, U.K. 22 57 30N 6 8W
Rabat, Malta 40 35 53N 14 25 E
Rabat, Mor. 78 34 2N 6 48W
Rackheath, U.K. 15 52 41N 1 22 E
Radcliffe, Gr. Manchester, U.K. 18 53 35N 2 19W
Radcliffe, Notts., U.K. 19 52 57N 1 3W
Radley, U.K. 14 51 42N 1 14W
Radnor Forest, U.K. 17 52 17N 3 10W
Radom, Pol. 43 51 23N 21 12 E
Radstock, U.K. 14 51 17N 2 25W
Ragusa, It. 40 36 56N 14 42 E
Rainham, U.K. 15 51 22N 0 36 E
Rainworth, U.K. 19 53 8N 1 6W
Raipur, India 59 21 17N 81 45 E
Rajahmundry, India 59 17 1N 81 48 E
Rajasthan □, India 58 26 45N 73 30 E
Rajkot, India 58 22 15N 70 56 E
Raleigh, U.S.A. 91 35 47N 78 39W
Rame Head, U.K. 16 50 19N 4 14W
Rampside, U.K. 18 54 6N 3 10W
Rampur, India 58 28 50N 79 5 E
Ramree Kyun, Burma 59 19 0N 94 0 E
Ramsbottom, U.K. 18 53 36N 2 20W
Ramsbury, U.K. 14 51 26N 1 37W
Ramsey, Cambs., U.K. 15 52 27N 0 6W
Ramsey, Essex, U.K. 15 51 55N 1 12 E
Ramsey, I. of M., U.K. 18 54 20N 4 21W
Ramsey Bay, U.K. 18 54 23N 4 20W
Ramsgate, U.K. 15 51 20N 1 25 E
Rancagua, Chile 102 34 10S 70 50W
Ranchi, India 59 23 19N 85 27 E
Rangoon, Burma 59 16 45N 96 20 E
Rannoch, L., U.K. 23 56 41N 4 20W
Rannoch Moor, U.K. 20 56 38N 4 48W
Rasht, Iran 56 37 20N 49 40 E
Rath Luirc, Ire. 25 52 21N 8 40W
Rathdrum, Ire. 25 52 57N 6 13W
Rathfriland, U.K. 24 54 12N 6 12W
Rathkeale, Ire. 25 52 32N 8 57W
Rathlin I., U.K. 24 55 18N 6 14W
Rathlin O'Birne I., Ire. 24 54 40N 8 50W
Rattray Hd., U.K. 23 57 38N 1 50W
Raukumara Ra., N.Z. 71 38 5S 177 55 E
Raunds, U.K. 15 52 20N 0 32W
Raurkela, India 59 22 14N 84 50 E
Ravenglass, U.K. 18 54 21N 3 25W
Ravenna, It. 40 44 28N 12 15 E
Ravenstonedale, U.K. 18 54 26N 2 28W
Rawalpindi, Pak. 58 33 38N 73 8 E
Rawmarsh, U.K. 19 53 27N 1 20W
Rawtenstall, U.K. 18 53 42N 2 18W
Rayleigh, U.K. 15 51 36N 0 38 E
Reading, U.K. 15 51 27N 0 57W
Reading, U.S.A. 93 40 20N 75 53W
Recife, Brazil 101 8 0S 35 0W
Reculver, U.K. 15 51 22N 1 12 E
Red → = Hong Viet. 60 20 17N 106 34 E
Red →, U.S.A. 91 31 0N 91 40W
Red Deer, Canada 88 52 20N 113 50W
Red Dial, U.K. 18 54 48N 3 9W
Red Sea, Asia 56 25 0N 36 0 E
Redbridge, U.K. 15 51 35N 0 7 E
Redcar, U.K. 19 54 37N 1 4W
Redditch, U.K. 14 52 18N 1 57W
Rede →, U.K. 21 55 8N 2 12W
Redesmouth, U.K. 21 55 7N 2 12W
Redhill, U.K. 15 51 14N 0 10W
Redlynch, U.K. 14 50 59N 1 42W
Redmile, U.K. 15 52 54N 0 48W
Redmire, U.K. 18 54 19N 1 55W
Redruth, U.K. 16 50 14N 5 14W
Ree, L., Ire. 24 53 35N 8 0W
Reedham, U.K. 15 52 34N 1 33 E
Reepham, U.K. 15 52 46N 1 6 E
Reeth, U.K. 18 54 23N 1 56W
Regensburg, Ger. 42 49 1N 12 7 E
Réggio di Calábria, It. 40 38 7N 15 38 E
Réggio nell' Emilia, It. 40 44 42N 10 38 E
Regina, Canada 88 50 27N 104 35W
Reigate, U.K. 15 51 14N 0 11W
Reims, Fr. 34 49 15N 4 1 E
Reindeer L., Canada 88 57 15N 102 15W
Remscheid, Ger. 36 51 11N 7 12 E
Renfrew, U.K. 20 55 52N 4 24W
Renmark, Austral. 67 34 11S 140 43 E
Rennes, Fr. 34 48 7N 1 41W
Reno, U.S.A. 90 39 30N 119 50W
Repton, U.K. 14 52 50N 1 32W
Resistencia, Arg. 102 27 30S 59 0W
Reston, U.K. 21 55 51N 2 11W
Réthimnon, Greece 41 35 18N 24 30 E
Reykjavík, Ice. 44 64 10N 21 57W
Reynosa, Mex. 94 26 5N 98 18W

Rhayader, *U.K.* 17 52 19N 3 30W
Rheidol →, *U.K.* 17 52 25N 4 5W
Rhein →, *Ger.* 36 51 52N 6 20 E
Rheine, *Ger.* 36 52 17N 7 25 E
Rhine = Rhein →, *Ger.* 36 51 52N 6 20 E
Rhineland-Palatinate □, *Ger.* 42 50 0N 7 0 E
Rhins, The, *U.K.* 20 54 52N 5 3W
Rhode Island □, *U.S.A.* 93 41 38N 71 37W
Rhodes = Ródhos, *Greece* 41 36 15N 28 10 E
Rhodesia = Zimbabwe ■, *Africa* 81 20 0S 30 0 E
Rhodope Mts., *Bulg.* 41 41 40N 24 20 E
Rhondda, *U.K.* 17 51 39N 3 30W
Rhône →, *Fr.* 35 43 28N 4 42 E
Rhosllanerchrugog, *U.K.* 17 53 3N 3 4W
Rhossili, *U.K.* 17 51 34N 4 18W
Rhum, *U.K.* 22 57 0N 6 20W
Rhyl, *U.K.* 17 53 19N 3 29W
Rhymney, *U.K.* 17 51 32N 3 17W
Ribble →, *U.K.* 18 54 13N 2 20W
Ribeirão Prêto, *Brazil* 101 21 10S 47 50W
Riccall, *U.K.* 19 53 50N 1 4W
Riccarton, *N.Z.* 71 43 32S 172 37 E
Riccarton Junc., *U.K.* 21 55 16N 2 43W
Richmond, *N. Yorks., U.K.* 19 54 24N 1 43W
Richmond, *Surrey, U.K.* 15 51 28N 0 18W
Richmond, *U.S.A.* 92 37 33N 77 27W
Rickmansworth, *U.K.* 15 51 38N 0 28W
Ridsdale, *U.K.* 21 55 9N 2 8W
Rievaulx, *U.K.* 19 54 16N 1 7W
Riga, *Latvia* 46 56 53N 24 8 E
Riga, G. of, *Latvia* 46 57 40N 23 45 E
Rijeka, *Yug.* 40 45 20N 14 21 E
Rijswijk, *Neth.* 36 52 4N 4 22 E
Rillington, *U.K.* 19 54 10N 0 41W
Rímini, *It.* 40 44 3N 12 33 E
Rîmnicu Vîlcea, *Rom.* 43 45 9N 24 21 E
Rimouski, *Canada* 93 48 27N 68 30W
Rineanna, *Ire.* 25 52 42N 85 7W
Ringford, *U.K.* 21 54 55N 4 3W
Ringmer, *U.K.* 15 50 53N 0 5 E
Ringwood, *U.K.* 14 50 50N 1 48W
Rio Branco, *Brazil* 100 9 58S 67 49W
Río Cuarto, *Arg.* 102 33 10S 64 25W
Rio de Janeiro, *Brazil* 101 23 0S 43 12W
Río Gallegos, *Arg.* 102 51 35S 69 15W
Rio Grande, *Brazil* 102 32 0S 52 20W
Rio Grande →, *U.S.A.* 90 25 57N 97 9W
Rio Grande do Norte □, *Brazil* 94 5 40S 36 0W
Río Muni = Mbini □, *Eq. Guin.* 80 1 30N 10 0 E
Ríobamba, *Ecuad.* 100 1 50S 78 45W
Ripley, *Derby, U.K.* 19 53 3N 1 24W
Ripley, *N. Yorks., U.K.* 19 54 3N 1 34W
Ripon, *U.K.* 19 54 8N 1 31W
Risca, *U.K.* 17 51 36N 3 6W
Rishton, *U.K.* 18 53 46N 2 26W
Riverside, *U.S.A.* 90 34 0N 117 22W
Riyadh, *Si. Arab.* 56 24 41N 46 42 E
Roade, *U.K.* 15 52 10N 0 53W
Roadhead, *U.K.* 18 55 4N 2 44W
Roag, L., *U.K.* 22 58 10N 6 55W
Roanne, *Fr.* 35 46 3N 4 4 E
Roanoke, *U.S.A.* 92 37 19N 79 55W
Robe →, *Ire.* 24 53 38N 9 10W
Roberton, *U.K.* 21 55 24N 2 53W
Robin Hood's Bay, *U.K.* 19 54 26N 0 31W
Rocester, *U.K.* 18 52 56N 1 50W
Rochdale, *U.K.* 18 53 36N 2 10W
Roche, *U.K.* 16 50 24N 4 50W
Rochelle, La, *Fr.* 35 46 10N 1 9W
Rochester, *Kent, U.K.* 15 51 22N 0 30 E
Rochester, *Northumberland, U.K.* 21 55 16N 2 16W
Rochester, *Minn., U.S.A.* 91 44 1N 92 28W
Rochester, *N.Y., U.S.A.* 92 43 10N 77 40W
Rochford, *U.K.* 15 51 36N 0 42 E
Rockall, *Atl. Oc.* 26 57 37N 13 42W
Rockcliffe, *U.K.* 18 54 58N 3 0W
Rockford, *U.S.A.* 92 42 20N 89 0W
Rockhampton, *Austral.* 67 23 22S 150 32 E
Rockingham, *U.K.* 15 52 32N 0 43W
Rockingham Forest, *U.K.* 15 52 28N 0 42W
Rocky Mts., *N. Am.* 88 55 0N 121 0W
Ródhos, *Greece* 41 36 15N 28 10 E
Roding →, *U.K.* 15 51 31N 0 7 E
Roe →, *U.K.* 24 55 10N 6 59W
Roeselare, *Belg.* 36 50 57N 3 7 E
Rogaland fylke □, *Nor.* 45 59 12N 6 20 E
Rogans Seat, *U.K.* 18 54 25N 2 10W
Rogate, *U.K.* 15 51 0N 0 51W
Roma, *Austral.* 67 26 32S 148 49 E
Roma = Rome, *It.* 40 41 54N 12 30 E
Romania ■, *Europe* 43 46 0N 25 0 E
Rome, *It.* 40 41 54N 12 30 E
Romney Marsh, *U.K.* 15 51 0N 1 0 E
Romsey, *U.K.* 14 51 0N 1 29W
Rona, *U.K.* 22 57 33N 6 0W
Ronse, *Belg.* 36 50 45N 3 35 E
Roosendaal, *Neth.* 36 51 32N 4 29 E
Roper →, *Austral.* 67 14 43S 135 27 E
Ropsley, *U.K.* 19 52 53N 0 31W
Roraima, Mt., *Ven.* 100 5 10N 60 40W
Rosario, *Arg.* 102 33 0S 60 40W
Roscommon, *Ire.* 24 53 38N 8 11W
Roscommon □, *Ire.* 24 53 40N 8 15W
Roscrea, *Ire.* 25 52 58N 7 50W
Roseau, *Dom.* 94 15 20N 61 24W
Rosedale Abbey, *U.K.* 19 54 22N 0 51W
Roskilde, *Den.* 45 55 38N 12 3 E
Rosneath, *U.K.* 20 56 1N 4 49W
Ross Ice Shelf, *Ant.* 103 80 0S 180 0 E
Ross on Wye, *U.K.* 14 51 55N 2 34W
Ross Sea, *Ant.* 103 74 0S 178 0 E
Rossall Pt., *U.K.* 18 53 55N 3 2W
Rossan Pt., *Ire.* 24 54 42N 8 47W
Rosslare, *Ire.* 25 52 17N 6 23W
Rostock, *Ger.* 42 54 4N 12 9 E
Rostov, *U.S.S.R.* 47 47 15N 39 45 E
Rosyth, *U.K.* 21 56 2N 3 26W
Rothbury, *U.K.* 21 55 19N 1 55W
Rothbury Forest, *U.K.* 21 55 19N 1 50W
Rother →, *U.K.* 15 50 59N 0 40 E
Rotherham, *U.K.* 19 53 26N 1 21W
Rothes, *U.K.* 23 57 31N 3 12W
Rothesay, *U.K.* 20 55 50N 5 3W
Rothwell, *Northants., U.K.* 15 52 25N 0 48W
Rothwell, *W. Yorks., U.K.* 19 53 46N 1 29W
Rotorua, *N.Z.* 71 38 9S 176 16 E
Rotorua, L., *N.Z.* 71 38 5S 176 18 E
Rotterdam, *Neth.* 36 51 55N 4 30 E
Rottingdean, *U.K.* 15 50 48N 0 3W
Roubaix, *Fr.* 34 50 40N 3 10 E
Rouen, *Fr.* 34 49 27N 1 4 E
Rousay, *U.K.* 23 59 10N 3 2W
Rowanburn, *U.K.* 21 55 5N 2 54W
Rowrah, *U.K.* 18 54 34N 3 26W
Roxburgh, *U.K.* 21 55 34N 2 30W
Roxby, *U.K.* 19 53 38N 0 37W
Royston, *U.K.* 15 52 3N 0 1W
Royton, *U.K.* 18 53 34N 2 7W
Ruahine Ra., *N.Z.* 71 39 55S 176 2 E
Rub' al Khali, *Si. Arab.* 56 18 0N 48 0 E
Rubery, *U.K.* 14 52 24N 1 59W
Rubh a' Mhail, *U.K.* 20 55 55N 6 10W
Rubha Hunish, *U.K.* 22 57 42N 6 20W
Rudgwick, *U.K.* 15 51 7N 0 54W
Rudston, *U.K.* 19 54 6N 0 19W
Rufford, *U.K.* 18 53 37N 2 50W
Rugby, *U.K.* 14 52 23N 1 16W
Rugeley, *U.K.* 14 52 47N 1 56W
Rum Jungle, *Austral.* 66 13 0S 130 59 E
Runcorn, *U.K.* 18 53 20N 2 44W
Ruse, *Bulg.* 41 43 48N 25 59 E
Rushden, *U.K.* 15 52 17N 0 37W
Ruskington, *U.K.* 19 53 5N 0 23W
Russian S.F.S.R. □, *U.S.S.R.* 46 62 0N 105 0 E
Rutherglen, *U.K.* 20 55 50N 4 11W
Ruthin, *U.K.* 17 53 7N 3 20W
Ruthwell, *U.K.* 21 55 0N 3 24W
Rwanda ■, *Africa* 80 2 0S 30 0 E
Ryan, L., *U.K.* 20 55 0N 5 2W
Ryazan, *U.S.S.R.* 46 54 40N 39 40 E
Rybinsk, *U.S.S.R.* 46 58 5N 38 50 E
Rybinsk Res., *U.S.S.R.* 46 58 30N 38 0 E
Rydal, *U.K.* 18 54 28N 2 59W
Ryde, *U.K.* 14 50 44N 1 9W
Rye, *U.K.* 15 50 57N 0 46 E
Rye →, *U.K.* 19 54 12N 0 53W
Rye Bay, *U.K.* 15 50 50N 0 50 E
Ryhope, *U.K.* 21 54 52N 1 22W
Ryton, *Tyne & Wear, U.K.* 21 54 58N 1 44W
Ryton, *Warwick, U.K.* 14 52 23N 1 25W
Ryūkyū Is., *Jap.* 62 26 0N 128 0 E
Rzeszów, *Pol.* 43 50 5N 21 58 E

S

Saarbrücken, *Ger.* 36 49 15N 6 58 E
Saaremaa, *U.S.S.R.* 46 58 30N 22 30 E
Saarland □, *Ger.* 36 49 15N 7 0 E
Saba, *W. Ind.* 94 17 42N 63 26W
Sabadell, *Sp.* 37 41 28N 2 7 E
Sabah □, *Malay.* 63 6 0N 117 0 E
Sabhah, *Libya* 79 27 9N 14 29 E
Sacramento, *U.S.A.* 90 38 33N 121 30 E
Sacriston, *U.K.* 19 54 49N 1 38W
Saddell, *U.K.* 20 55 31N 5 30W
Saffron Walden, *U.K.* 15 52 2N 0 15 E
Safi, *Mor.* 78 32 18N 9 20W
Sagar, *India* 58 14 14N 75 6 E
Saginaw, *U.S.A.* 92 43 26N 83 55W
Saginaw B., *U.S.A.* 92 43 50N 83 40W
Sahara, *Africa* 78 23 0N 5 0 E
Saharan Atlas, *Alg.* 78 34 9N 3 29 E
Saharanpur, *India* 58 29 58N 77 33 E
Saigon = Ho Chi Minh City, *Viet.* 63 10 58N 106 40 E
St. Abb's, *U.K.* 21 55 54N 2 7W
St. Abb's Head, *U.K.* 21 55 55N 2 10W
St. Agnes, *U.K.* 16 50 18N 5 13W
St. Agnes Hd., *U.K.* 16 50 19N 5 14W
St. Agnes I., *U.K.* 16 49 53N 6 20W
St. Albans, *U.K.* 15 51 44N 0 19W
St. Alban's Head, *U.K.* 14 50 34N 2 3W
St. Andrews, *U.K.* 21 56 20N 2 48W
St. Ann's, *U.K.* 21 55 14N 3 28W
St. Asaph, *U.K.* 17 53 15N 3 27W
St. Austell, *U.K.* 16 50 20N 4 48W
St. Bees, *U.K.* 18 54 29N 3 36W
St. Bee's Hd., *U.K.* 18 54 30N 3 38 E
St. Blazey, *U.K.* 16 50 22N 4 48W
St. Boniface, *Canada* 88 49 53N 97 5W
St. Boswells, *U.K.* 21 55 34N 2 39W
St. Briavels, *U.K.* 14 51 44N 2 39W
St. Brides B., *U.K.* 17 51 48N 5 15W
St.-Brieuc, *Fr.* 34 48 30N 2 46W
St. Budeaux, *U.K.* 16 50 23N 4 10W
St. Buryan, *U.K.* 16 50 4N 5 34W
St. Catharines, *Canada* 92 43 10N 79 15W
St. Catherine's Pt., *U.K.* 14 50 34N 1 18W
St. Christopher-Nevis ■, *W. Ind.* 94 17 20N 62 40W
St. Clair, L., *Canada* 92 42 30N 82 45W
St.-Claude, *Fr.* 35 46 22N 5 52 E
St. Clears, *U.K.* 17 51 48N 4 30W
St. Columb Major, *U.K.* 16 50 26N 4 56W
St. David's, *U.K.* 17 51 54N 5 16W
St. David's Head, *U.K.* 17 51 55N 5 16W
St. Dennis, *U.K.* 16 50 23N 4 53W
St. Dominick, *U.K.* 16 50 28N 4 15W
St. Elias Mts., *Canada* 88 60 33N 139 28W
St. Endellion, *U.K.* 16 50 33N 4 49W
St. Enoder, *U.K.* 16 50 22N 4 57W
St. Erth, *U.K.* 16 50 10N 5 26W
St.-Étienne, *Fr.* 35 45 27N 4 22 E
St. Fillans, *U.K.* 21 56 25N 4 7W
St. Gallen, *Switz.* 42 47 25N 9 20 E
St. George's, *Gren.* 94 12 5N 61 43W
St. George's Channel, *U.K.* 25 52 0N 6 0W
St. Germans, *U.K.* 16 50 24N 4 19W
St. Helena, *Atl. Oc.* 118 15 55S 5 44W
St. Helena B., *S. Afr.* 81 32 40S 18 10 E
St. Helens, *I. of W., U.K.* 14 50 42N 1 6W
St. Helens, *Merseyside, U.K.* 18 53 28N 2 44W
St. Helier, *U.K.* 34 49 11N 2 6W
St-Hyacinthe, *Canada* 93 45 40N 72 58W
St. Issey, *U.K.* 16 50 30N 4 55W
St. Ives, *Cambs., U.K.* 15 52 20N 0 5W
St. Ives, *Cornwall, U.K.* 16 50 13N 5 29W
St. Ives Bay, *U.K.* 16 50 15N 5 27W
St-Jean, L., *Canada* 93 48 40N 72 0W
St-Jérôme, *Canada* 93 45 47N 74 0W
St. John, *Canada* 93 45 20N 66 8W
St. John's, *Antigua* 94 17 6N 61 51W
St. John's, *Canada* 89 47 35N 52 40W
St. John's, *U.K.* 18 54 13N 4 38W
St. Johns Chapel, *U.K.* 18 54 43N 2 10W
St. Joseph, *U.S.A.* 91 39 46N 94 50W
St. Just, *U.K.* 16 50 7N 5 41W
St. Keverne, *U.K.* 16 50 3N 5 5W
St. Kew, *U.K.* 16 50 34N 4 48W
St. Lawrence →, *Canada* 93 49 30N 66 0W
St. Lawrence, Gulf of, *Canada* 89 48 25N 62 0W
St. Leonards, *U.K.* 15 50 51N 0 34 E
St. Levan, *U.K.* 16 50 3N 5 36W
St.-Lô, *Fr.* 34 49 7N 1 5W
St-Louis, *Sene.* 78 16 8N 16 27W
St. Louis, *U.S.A.* 92 38 40N 90 12W
St. Lucia ■, *W. Ind.* 94 14 0N 60 50W
St. Maarten, *W. Ind.* 94 18 0N 63 5W
St. Mabyn, *U.K.* 16 50 30N 4 45W
St.-Malo, *Fr.* 34 48 39N 2 1W
St. Margaret's-at-Cliffe, *U.K.* 15 51 10N 1 23 E
St. Margaret's Hope, *U.K.* 23 58 49N 2 58W
St-Martin, I., *W. Ind.* 94 18 0N 63 0W
St. Martin's I., *U.K.* 16 49 58N 6 16W
St. Mary Bourne, *U.K.* 14 51 16N 1 24W
St. Mary's, *U.K.* 16 49 55N 6 17W
St. Mary's Sd., *U.K.* 16 49 53N 6 19W
St. Mawes, *U.K.* 16 50 10N 5 1W
St. Merryn, *U.K.* 16 50 31N 4 58W
St. Michael's Mt., *U.K.* 16 50 7N 5 30W
St. Minver, *U.K.* 16 50 34N 4 52W
St. Monance, *U.K.* 21 56 13N 2 46W
St.-Nazaire, *Fr.* 34 47 17N 2 12W
St. Neots, *U.K.* 15 52 14N 0 16W
St-Niklaas, *Belg.* 36 51 10N 4 8 E
St. Osyth, *U.K.* 15 51 47N 1 4 E
St. Paul, *U.S.A.* 91 44 54N 93 5W
St. Peter Port, *U.K.* 34 49 27N 2 31W
St. Petersburg, *U.S.A.* 91 27 45N 82 40W
St. Petersburg, *U.S.S.R.* 47 40 47N 43 50 E
St.-Pierre et Miquelon □, *N. Am.* 89 46 55N 56 10W
St.-Quentin, *Fr.* 34 49 50N 3 16 E
St. Stephen, *U.K.* 16 50 20N 4 52W
St. Teath, *U.K.* 16 50 34N 4 45W
St.-Tropez, *Fr.* 35 43 17N 6 38 E
St. Tudy, *U.K.* 16 50 33N 4 45W
St. Vincent and the Grenadines ■, *W. Ind.* 94 13 0N 61 10W
Saintfield, *U.K.* 24 54 28N 5 50W
Sakai, *Jap.* 62 34 30N 135 30 E
Sakhalin, *U.S.S.R.* 49 51 0N 143 0 E
Salado →, *Arg.* 102 31 40S 60 41W
Salamanca, *Sp.* 37 40 58N 5 39W
Salcombe, *U.K.* 16 50 14N 3 47W
Salcombe Regis, *U.K.* 16 50 41N 3 11W
Sale, *Austral.* 70 38 6S 147 6 E
Sale, *U.K.* 18 53 26N 2 19W
Salem, *India* 58 11 40N 78 11 E
Salen, *U.K.* 20 56 31N 5 57W
Salerno, *It.* 40 40 40N 14 44 E
Salford, *U.K.* 18 53 30N 2 17W
Salford Priors, *U.K.* 14 52 10N 1 52W
Salisbury = Harare, *Zimb.* 81 17 43S 31 2 E
Salisbury, *U.K.* 14 51 4N 1 48W
Salisbury Plain, *U.K.* 14 51 13N 1 50W
Salonica = Thessaloníki, *Greece* 41 40 38N 22 58 E
Salop = Shropshire □, *U.K.* 14 52 36N 2 45W
Salt Lake City, *U.S.A.* 90 40 45N 111 58W
Salta, *Arg.* 102 24 57S 65 25W
Saltash, *U.K.* 16 50 25N 4 13W
Saltburn by the Sea, *U.K.* 19 54 35N 0 58W
Saltcoats, *U.K.* 20 55 38N 4 47W
Saltee Is., *Ire.* 25 52 7N 6 37W
Saltergate, *U.K.* 19 54 20N 0 40W
Saltfleet, *U.K.* 19 53 25N 0 11 E
Saltfleetby, *U.K.* 19 53 23N 0 10 E
Saltillo, *Mex.* 94 25 25N 101 0W
Salto, *Urug.* 102 31 27S 57 50W
Saltwood, *U.K.* 15 51 4N 1 5 E
Salvador, *Brazil* 101 13 0S 38 30W
Salween →, *Burma* 59 16 31N 97 37 E
Salzburg, *Austria* 42 47 48N 13 2 E
Salzgitter, *Ger.* 42 52 13N 10 22 E
Samara, *U.S.S.R.* 46 53 8N 50 6 E
Samarinda, *Indon.* 63 0 30S 117 9 E
Samarkand, *U.S.S.R.* 48 39 40N 66 55 E
Sámos, *Greece* 41 37 45N 26 50 E
Sampford Courtenay, *U.K.* 16 50 47N 3 58W
Samsun, *Turk.* 47 41 15N 36 22 E
San Angelo, *U.S.A.* 90 31 30N 100 30W
San Antonio, *U.S.A.* 90 29 30N 98 30W
San Bernardino, *U.S.A.* 90 34 7N 117 18W
San Carlos, *Phil.* 63 15 55N 120 20 E
San Cristóbal, *Ven.* 100 16 50N 92 40W
San Diego, *U.S.A.* 90 32 43N 117 10W
San Fernando, *Mex.* 94 30 0N 115 10W
San Francisco, *U.S.A.* 90 37 47N 122 30W
San Jorge, G., *Arg.* 102 46 0S 66 0W
San José, *C.R.* 95 10 0N 84 2W
San Jose, *U.S.A.* 90 37 20N 121 53W
San Juan, *Arg.* 102 31 30S 68 30W
San Juan, *P.R.* 95 18 28N 66 8W
San Luis Potosí, *Mex.* 94 22 9N 100 59W
San Marino ■, *Europe* 40 43 56N 12 25 E
San Matías, G., *Arg.* 102 41 30S 64 0W
San Miguel de Tucumán, *Arg.* 102 26 50S 65 20W
San Pedro Sula, *Hond.* 94 15 30N 88 0W
San Salvador, *El Salv.* 94 13 40N 89 10W
San Salvador, *Arg.* 102 24 10S 64 48W
San Sebastián, *Sp.* 37 43 17N 1 58W
Sana', *Yem.* 56 15 27N 44 12 E
Sanda I., *U.K.* 20 55 17N 5 35W
Sanday, *U.K.* 23 59 15N 2 30W
Sandbach, *U.K.* 18 53 9N 2 23W
Sandbank, *U.K.* 20 55 58N 4 57W
Sandgate, *U.K.* 15 51 5N 1 9 E
Sandhead, *U.K.* 20 54 48N 4 58W
Sandhurst, *U.K.* 15 51 21N 0 48W
Sandness, *U.K.* 22 60 18N 1 38W
Sandown, *U.K.* 14 50 39N 1 9W
Sandringham, *U.K.* 15 52 50N 0 30 E
Sandwich, *U.K.* 15 51 16N 1 21 E
Sandy, *U.K.* 15 52 8N 0 18W
Sangli, *India* 58 16 55N 74 33 E
Sanquhar, *U.K.* 21 55 21N 3 56W
Santa Ana, *Mex.* 94 30 33N 111 7W
Santa Ana, *U.S.A.* 90 33 48N 117 55W
Santa Clara, *Cuba* 95 22 20N 80 0W
Santa Cruz, *Bol.* 100 17 43S 63 10W
Santa Cruz de Tenerife, *Can. Is.* 78 28 28N 16 15W
Santa Fe, *Arg.* 102 31 35S 60 41W
Santa Fe, *U.S.A.* 90 35 40N 106 0W
Santa Maria, *Brazil* 102 29 40S 53 48W
Santa Marta, *Col.* 100 11 15N 74 13W
Santander, *Sp.* 37 43 27N 3 51W
Santarém, *Brazil* 101 2 25S 54 42W
Santarém, *Port.* 37 39 12N 8 42W
Santiago, *Chile* 102 33 24S 70 40W
Santiago de Compostela, *Sp.* 37 42 52N 8 37W
Santiago de Cuba, *Cuba* 95 20 0N 75 49W
Santiago de los Cabelleros, *Dom. Rep.* 95 19 30N 70 40W
Santo André, *Brazil* 102 23 39S 46 29W
Santo Domingo, *Dom. Rep.* 95 18 30N 64 54W
Santos, *Brazil* 102 24 0S 46 20W
São Francisco →, *Brazil* 101 10 30S 36 24W
São José do Rio Prêto, *Brazil* 101 20 50S 49 20W
São Luís, *Brazil* 101 2 39S 44 15W
São Paulo, *Brazil* 102 23 32S 46 37W
São Roque, C. de, *Brazil* 101 5 30S 35 16W
São Tomé & Principe ■, *Africa* 73 0 12N 6 39 E
Saône →, *Fr.* 35 45 44N 4 50 E
Sapporo, *Jap.* 62 43 0N 141 21 E

Sarajevo, Yug. 41 43 52N 18 26 E
Saransk, U.S.S.R. 46 54 10N 45 10 E
Saratov, U.S.S.R. 46 51 30N 46 2 E
Sarawak □, Malay. 63 2 0N 113 0 E
Sardinia, I., It. 40 40 0N 9 0 E
Sargodha, Pak. 58 32 10N 72 40 E
Sarh, Chad 79 9 5N 18 23 E
Sarnia, Canada 92 42 58N 82 23W
Sasebo, Jap. 62 33 10N 129 43 E
Saskatchewan □, Canada 88 54 40N 106 0W
Saskatchewan →, Canada 88 53 37N 100 40W
Saskatoon, Canada 88 52 10N 106 38W
Sássari, It. 40 40 44N 8 33 E
Satpura Ra., India 58 21 25N 76 10 E
Satu Mare, Rom. 43 47 46N 22 55 E
Sauðarkrókur, Ice. 44 65 45N 19 40W
Saudi Arabia ■, Asia 56 26 0N 44 0 E
Sault Ste. Marie, Canada 92 46 30N 84 20W
Saundersfoot, U.K. 17 51 43N 4 42W
Sava →, Yug. 41 44 50N 20 26 E
Savanna la Mar, Jam. 94 18 10N 78 10W
Savannah, U.S.A. 91 32 4N 81 4W
Savona, It. 40 44 19N 8 29 E
Savonlinna, Fin. 44 61 52N 28 53 E
Sawbridgeworth, U.K. 15 51 49N 0 10 E
Sawel, Mt., U.K. 24 54 48N 7 5W
Sawston, U.K. 15 52 7N 0 11 E
Sawtry, U.K. 15 52 26N 0 17W
Saxilby, U.K. 19 53 16N 0 40W
Saxlingham Nethergate, U.K. 15 52 33N 1 16 E
Saxmundham, U.K. 15 52 13N 1 29 E
Saydā, Leb. 57 33 35N 35 25 E
Scafell Pikes, U.K. 18 54 26N 3 14W
Scalasaig, U.K. 20 56 4N 6 10W
Scalby, U.K. 19 54 18N 0 26W
Scalby Ness, U.K. 19 54 18N 0 25W
Scalloway, U.K. 22 60 9N 1 16W
Scalpay, U.K. 22 57 51N 6 40W
Scamblesby, U.K. 19 53 17N 0 5W
Scandinavia, Europe 44 64 0N 12 0 E
Scapa Flow, U.K. 23 58 52N 3 6W
Scarba, I., U.K. 20 56 10N 5 43W
Scarborough, U.K. 19 54 17N 0 24W
Scarinish, U.K. 20 56 30N 6 48W
Scarning, U.K. 15 52 40N 0 53 E
Schefferville, Canada 89 54 48N 66 50W
Schenectady, U.S.A. 93 42 50N 73 58W
Schiedam, Neth. 36 51 55N 4 25 E
Schleswig-Holstein □, Ger. 42 54 10N 9 40 E
Schwerin, Ger. 42 53 37N 11 22 E
Scilly, Isles of, U.K. 16 49 55N 6 15W
Scole, U.K. 15 52 22N 1 10 E
Scone, U.K. 21 56 25N 3 26W
Scopwick, U.K. 19 53 6N 0 24W
Scotland □, U.K. 20 57 0N 4 0W
Scranton, U.S.A. 93 41 22N 75 41W
Scremerston, U.K. 21 55 44N 1 59W
Scridain, L., U.K. 20 56 23N 6 7W
Scunthorpe, U.K. 19 53 35N 0 38W
Seaford, U.K. 15 50 46N 0 8 E
Seaham, U.K. 21 54 51N 1 20W
Seahouses, U.K. 21 55 35N 1 39W
Seamer, U.K. 19 54 14N 0 27W
Seascale, U.K. 18 54 24N 3 29W
Seaton, Cumbria, U.K. 18 54 40N 3 31W
Seaton, Devon, U.K. 16 50 42N 3 3W
Seaton Delaval, U.K. 21 55 5N 1 33W
Seattle, U.S.A. 90 47 41N 122 15W
Sedbergh, U.K. 18 54 20N 2 31W
Sedgefield, U.K. 19 54 40N 1 27W
Seend, U.K. 14 51 20N 2 2W
Segovia, Sp. 37 40 57N 4 10W
Seil, I., U.K. 20 56 17N 5 37W
Seine →, Fr. 34 49 26N 0 26 E
Sekondi-Takoradi, Ghana 78 4 58N 1 45W
Selborne, U.K. 15 51 5N 0 55W
Selby, U.K. 19 53 47N 1 5W
Selkirk, U.K. 21 55 33N 2 50W
Selsey, U.K. 15 50 44N 0 47W
Selsey Bill, U.K. 15 50 44N 0 47W
Selvas, Brazil 100 6 30S 67 0W
Selwyn Ra., Austral. 67 21 10S 140 0 E
Semarang, Indon. 63 7 0S 110 26 E
Semipalatinsk, U.S.S.R. 48 50 30N 80 10 E
Sendai, Jap. 62 38 15N 140 53 E
Senegal ■, W. Afr. 78 14 30N 14 30W
Senegal →, W. Afr. 78 15 48N 16 32W
Sennen, U.K. 16 50 4N 5 42W
Seoul, S. Kor. 61 37 31N 126 58 E
Seph →, U.K. 19 54 17N 1 9W
Sequoia Nat. Park, U.S.A. 90 36 30N 118 30W
Serbia □, Yug. 41 43 30N 21 0 E
Seremban, Malay. 63 2 43N 101 53 E
Serena, La, Chile 102 29 55S 71 10W
Sergiyev Posad, U.S.S.R. 46 56 20N 38 10 E
Serpukhov, U.S.S.R. 46 54 55N 37 28 E
Sétif, Alg. 78 36 9N 5 26 E
Settle, U.K. 18 54 5N 2 18W
Setúbal, Port. 37 38 30N 8 58W
Sevastopol, U.S.S.R. 47 44 35N 33 30 E
Seven →, U.K. 19 54 11N 0 51W
Sevenoaks, U.K. 15 51 16N 0 11 E
Severn →, U.K. 14 51 35N 2 38W
Severn Beach, U.K. 14 51 34N 2 39W
Severn Stoke, U.K. 14 52 5N 2 13W
Severnaya Zemlya, U.S.S.R. 49 79 0N 100 0 E
Seville, Sp. 37 37 23N 6 0W
Seward Pen., U.S.A. 88 65 0N 164 0W
Seychelles ■, Ind. Oc. 119 5 0S 56 0 E
Seyðisfjörður, Ice. 44 65 16N 14 0W
Sfax, Tunisia 79 34 49N 10 48 E
Shaanxi □, China 61 35 0N 109 0 E
Shache, China 60 38 20N 77 10 E
Shaftesbury, U.K. 14 51 0N 2 12W
Shahjahanpur, India 58 27 54N 79 57 E
Shakhty, U.S.S.R. 47 47 40N 40 16 E
Shaldon, U.K. 16 50 32N 3 31W
Shan □, Burma 59 21 30N 98 30 E
Shandong □, China 61 36 0N 118 0 E
Shanghai, China 61 31 15N 121 26 E
Shangrao, China 61 28 25N 117 59 E
Shanklin, U.K. 14 50 39N 1 9W
Shannon →, Ire. 25 52 35N 9 30W
Shantou, China 61 23 18N 116 40 E
Shanxi □, China 61 37 0N 112 0 E
Shaoguan, China 61 24 48N 113 35 E
Shaoyang, China 61 27 14N 111 25 E
Shap, U.K. 18 54 32N 2 40W
Shapinsay, U.K. 23 59 2N 2 50W
Shark B., Austral. 66 11 20S 130 30 E
Sharpness, U.K. 14 51 43N 2 28W
Shawbury, U.K. 14 52 48N 2 40W
Shawinigan, Canada 93 46 35N 72 50W
Shebbear, U.K. 16 50 52N 4 12W
Sheelin, Lough, Ire. 24 53 48N 7 20W
Sheep Haven, Ire. 24 55 12N 7 55W
Sheerness, U.K. 15 51 26N 0 47 E
Sheffield, U.K. 19 53 23N 1 28W
Shefford, U.K. 15 52 2N 0 20W
Shelekhov G., U.S.S.R. 49 59 30N 157 0 E
Shellharbour, Austral. 70 34 31S 150 51 E
Shelling Rocks, Ire. 25 51 45N 10 35W
Shenfield, U.K. 15 51 39N 0 21 E
Shenyang, China 61 41 50N 123 25 E
Shepparton, Austral. 70 36 23S 145 26 E
Sheppey, I. of, U.K. 15 51 23N 0 50 E
Shepshed, U.K. 15 52 47N 1 18W
Shepton Mallet, U.K. 14 51 11N 2 31W
Sherborne, U.K. 14 50 56N 2 31W
Sherborne St. John, U.K. 14 51 18N 1 7W
Sherbrooke, Canada 93 45 28N 71 57W
Sherburn, N. Yorks., U.K. 19 54 12N 0 32W
Sherburn, N. Yorks., U.K. 19 53 47N 1 15W
Shere, U.K. 15 51 13N 0 28W
Sherfield English, U.K. 14 51 1N 1 35W
Sheriff Hutton, U.K. 19 54 5N 1 0W
Sheriff Muir, U.K. 21 56 12N 3 53W
Sheringham, U.K. 15 52 56N 1 11 E
Sherston, U.K. 14 51 35N 2 13W
Sherwood Forest, U.K. 19 53 5N 1 5W
Shetland □, U.K. 22 60 30N 1 30W
Shetland Is., U.K. 22 60 30N 1 30W
Shiel, L., U.K. 22 56 48N 5 32W
Shieldaig, U.K. 22 57 31N 5 39W
Shifnal, U.K. 14 52 40N 2 23W
Shijiazhuang, China 61 38 2N 114 28 E
Shikoku, Jap. 62 33 30N 133 30 E
Shilbottle, U.K. 21 55 23N 1 42W
Shildon, U.K. 19 54 37N 1 39W
Shiliguri, India 59 26 45N 88 25 E
Shillelagh, Ire. 25 52 46N 6 32W
Shillingstone, U.K. 14 50 54N 2 15W
Shillong, India 59 25 35N 91 53 E
Shimonoseki, Jap. 62 33 58N 131 0 E
Shin, L., U.K. 23 58 7N 4 30W
Shipbourne, U.K. 15 51 13N 0 19 E
Shipdham, U.K. 15 52 38N 0 53 E
Shipley, U.K. 19 53 50N 1 47W
Shipston-on-Stour, U.K. 14 52 4N 1 38W
Shipton-under-Wychwood, U.K. 14 51 51N 1 35W
Shīrāz, Iran 56 29 42N 52 30 E
Shirebrook, U.K. 19 53 13N 1 11W
Shizuoka, Jap. 62 35 0N 138 24 E
Shkoder, Alb. 41 42 6N 19 20 E
Shoeburyness, U.K. 15 51 31N 0 49 E
Shoreham-by-Sea, U.K. 15 50 50N 0 17W
Shotts, U.K. 21 55 49N 3 47W
Shreveport, U.S.A. 91 32 30N 93 50W
Shrewsbury, U.K. 14 52 42N 2 45W
Shrewton, U.K. 14 51 11N 1 55W
Shrivenham, U.K. 14 51 36N 1 39W
Shropshire □, U.K. 14 52 36N 2 45W
Shuangyashan, China 61 46 28N 131 5 E
Siam = Thailand ■, Asia 63 16 0N 102 0 E
Sian, China 61 34 2N 109 0 E
Siberia, U.S.S.R. 50 60 0N 100 0 E
Sibiu, Rom. 43 45 45N 24 9 E
Sible Hedingham, U.K. 15 51 58N 0 37 E
Sibsey, U.K. 19 53 3N 0 1 E
Sichuan □, China 60 31 0N 104 0 E
Sicily, It. 40 37 30N 14 30 E
Sidbury, U.K. 16 50 43N 3 12W
Sidlaw Hills, U.K. 21 56 32N 3 10W
Sidlesham, U.K. 15 50 46N 0 46W
Sidmouth, U.K. 16 50 40N 3 13W
Sidon = Saydā, Leb. 57 33 35N 35 25 E
Siegen, Ger. 36 50 52N 8 2 E
Siena, It. 40 43 20N 11 20 E
Sierra Leone ■, W. Afr. 78 9 0N 12 0W
Sighty Crag, U.K. 21 55 8N 2 37W
Siglufjörður, Ice. 44 66 12N 18 55W
Sikhote Alin Ra., U.S.S.R. 49 46 0N 136 0 E
Sikkim □, India 59 27 50N 88 30 E
Silloth, U.K. 18 54 53N 3 25W
Silsden, U.K. 18 53 55N 1 55W
Silverstone, U.K. 14 52 5N 1 3W
Silverton, U.K. 16 50 49N 3 29W
Simferopol, U.S.S.R. 47 44 55N 34 3 E
Simonsbath, U.K. 14 51 8N 3 45W
Simonside, U.K. 21 55 17N 2 0W
Simpson Desert, Austral. 67 25 0S 137 0 E
Sinai Peninsula, Egypt 79 29 30N 34 0 E
Sind Sagar Doab, Pak. 58 32 0N 71 30 E
Singapore ■, Asia 63 1 17N 103 51 E
Singleton, U.K. 15 50 55N 0 45W
Sioux Falls, U.S.A. 91 43 35N 96 40W
Siping, China 61 33 25N 114 10 E
Siracusa, It. 40 37 4N 15 17 E
Sittingbourne, U.K. 15 51 20N 0 43 E
Sittwe, Bur. 59 20 18N 92 45 E
Sivas, Turk. 47 39 43N 36 58 E
Siwalik Range, Nepal 59 28 0N 83 0 E
Sizewell, U.K. 15 52 13N 1 38 E
Sjælland, Den. 45 55 30N 11 30 E
Skagerrak, Den. 45 57 30N 9 0 E
Skagway, U.S.A. 88 59 23N 135 20W
Skegness, U.K. 19 53 9N 0 20 E
Skellefteå, Swed. 44 64 45N 20 58 E
Skellingthorpe, U.K. 19 53 14N 0 37W
Skelmersdale, U.K. 18 53 34N 2 49W
Skelmorlie, U.K. 20 55 52N 4 53W
Skelton, Cleveland, U.K. 19 54 33N 0 59W
Skelton, Cumbria, U.K. 18 54 42N 2 50W
Skerries, The, U.K. 17 53 27N 4 40W
Skibbereen, Ire. 25 51 33N 9 16W
Skiddaw, U.K. 18 54 39N 3 9W
Skien, Nor. 45 59 12N 9 35 E
Skikda, Alg. 78 36 50N 6 58 E
Skipness, U.K. 20 55 46N 5 20W
Skipsea, U.K. 19 53 58N 0 13W
Skipton, U.K. 18 53 57N 2 1W
Skopje, Yug. 41 42 1N 21 32 E
Skull, Ire. 25 51 32N 9 40W
Skye, U.K. 22 57 15N 6 10W
Slaidburn, U.K. 18 53 57N 2 28W
Slaley, U.K. 21 54 55N 2 4W
Slaney →, Ire. 25 52 52N 6 45W
Sleaford, U.K. 19 53 0N 0 22W
Sleat, Sd. of, U.K. 22 57 5N 5 47W
Sledmere, U.K. 19 54 4N 0 35W
Sleights, U.K. 19 54 27N 0 40W
Slieve Aughty, Ire. 25 53 4N 8 30W
Slieve Bloom, Ire. 25 53 4N 7 40W
Slieve Donard, U.K. 24 54 10N 5 57W
Slieve Gullion, U.K. 24 54 8N 6 26W
Slieve Mish, Ire. 25 52 12N 9 50W
Slievenamon, Ire. 25 52 25N 7 37W
Sligo, Ire. 24 54 17N 8 28W
Sligo □, Ire. 24 54 10N 8 35W
Sligo B., Ire. 24 54 20N 8 40W
Sliven, Bulg. 41 42 42N 26 19 E
Slough, U.K. 15 51 30N 0 35W
Slovak Rep. □, Czech. 43 48 30N 20 0 E
Slovenia □, Yug. 40 46 0N 15 0 E
Slyne Hd., Ire. 24 53 25N 10 10W
Smederevo, Yug. 41 44 40N 20 57 E
Smethwick, U.K. 14 52 29N 1 58W
Smithfield, U.K. 18 54 59N 2 51W
Smolensk, U.S.S.R. 46 54 45N 32 0 E
Snaefell, U.K. 18 54 18N 4 26W
Snainton, U.K. 19 54 14N 0 33W
Snaith, U.K. 19 53 42N 1 1W
Snake →, U.S.A. 90 46 12N 119 2W
Snape, U.K. 15 52 11N 1 29 E
Snettisham, U.K. 15 52 52N 0 30 E
Snizort, L., U.K. 22 57 33N 6 28W
Snowdon, U.K. 17 53 4N 4 8W
Snowy Mts., Austral. 70 36 30S 148 20 E
Sobral, Brazil 101 3 50S 40 20W
Sochi, U.S.S.R. 47 43 35N 39 40 E
Society Is., Pac. Oc. 65 17 0S 151 0W
Socotra, Ind. Oc. 57 12 30N 54 0 E
Söderhamn, Swed. 45 61 18N 17 10 E
Sofia, Bulg. 41 42 45N 23 20 E
Sogn og Fjordane fylke □, Nor. 44 61 40N 6 0 E
Sognefjorden, Nor. 45 61 10N 5 50 E
Sohâg, Egypt 79 26 33N 31 43 E
Soham, U.K. 15 52 20N 0 20 E
Sokoto, Nig. 78 13 2N 5 16 E
Solapur, India 58 17 43N 75 56 E
Solent, The, U.K. 14 50 45N 1 25W
Solihull, U.K. 14 52 26N 1 47W
Solimões → = Amazon →, S. Am. 100 0 5S 50 0W
Solingen, Ger. 36 51 10N 7 4 E
Solomon Is. ■, Oc. 64 6 0S 155 0 E
Solway Firth, U.K. 18 54 45N 3 38W
Somali Rep. ■, E. Afr. 73 7 0N 47 0 E
Somerby, U.K. 15 52 42N 0 49W
Somerset □, U.K. 14 51 9N 3 0W
Somersham, U.K. 15 52 24N 0 0 E
Somerton, U.K. 14 51 3N 2 45W
Sompting, U.K. 15 50 51N 0 20W
Sondre Stromfjord, Green. 89 66 59N 50 40W
Sonning, U.K. 15 51 28N 0 53W
Sorbie, U.K. 20 54 46N 4 26W
Soria, Sp. 37 41 43N 2 32W
Sorisdale, U.K. 20 56 40N 6 28W
Sorn, U.K. 20 55 31N 4 18W
Sorocaba, Brazil 102 23 31S 47 27W
Sosnowiec, Pol. 43 50 20N 19 10 E
Sousse, Tunisia 79 35 50N 10 38 E
South Africa, Rep. of ■, Africa 81 32 0S 17 0 E
South Australia □, Austral. 66 32 0S 139 0 E
South Barrule, U.K. 18 54 9N 4 36W
South Bend, U.S.A. 92 41 38N 86 20W
South Benfleet, U.K. 15 51 33N 0 34 E
South Brent, U.K. 16 50 26N 3 50W
South Carolina □, U.S.A. 91 33 45N 81 0W
South Cave, U.K. 19 53 46N 0 37W
South China Sea, Asia 63 10 0N 113 0 E
South Dakota □, U.S.A. 90 45 0N 100 0W
South Dorset Downs, U.K. 14 50 40N 2 26W
South Downs, U.K. 15 50 53N 0 10W
South Elkington, U.K. 19 53 22N 0 5W
South Esk →, U.K. 23 56 44N 3 3W
South Foreland, U.K. 15 51 7N 1 23 E
South Georgia, Atl. Oc. 102 54 30S 37 0W
South Glamorgan □, U.K. 17 51 30N 3 20W
South Hayling, U.K. 15 50 47N 0 56W
South I., N.Z. 71 44 0S 170 0 E
South Korea ■, Asia 61 36 0N 128 0 E
South Molton, U.K. 16 51 1N 3 50W
South Orkney Is., Ant. 103 63 0S 45 0W
South Petherton, U.K. 14 50 57N 2 49W
South Petherwin, U.K. 16 50 35N 4 22W
South Platte →, U.S.A. 90 41 7N 100 42W
South Pole, Ant. 103 90 0S 0 0 E
South Ronaldsay, U.K. 23 58 46N 2 58W
South Sandwich Is., Ant. 103 57 0S 27 0W
South Shetland Is., Ant. 103 62 0S 59 0W
South Shields, U.K. 19 54 59N 1 26W
South Tawton, U.K. 16 50 44N 3 55W
South Tyne →, U.K. 19 54 46N 2 25W
South Uist, U.K. 22 57 20N 7 15W
South West Africa = Namibia ■, Africa 81 22 0S 18 9 E
South Woodham Ferrers, U.K. 15 51 40N 0 37 E
South Yorkshire □, U.K. 19 53 30N 1 20W
Southam, U.K. 14 52 16N 1 24W
Southampton, U.K. 14 50 54N 1 23W
Southampton I., Canada 89 64 30N 84 0W
Southampton Water, U.K. 14 50 52N 1 21W
Southborough, U.K. 15 51 10N 0 15 E
Southend, U.K. 20 55 18N 5 38W
Southend-on-Sea, U.K. 15 51 32N 0 42 E
Southern Alps, N.Z. 71 43 41S 170 11 E
Southern Ocean 103 62 0S 60 0 E
Southern Uplands, U.K. 21 55 30N 3 3W
Southery, U.K. 15 52 32N 0 23 E
Southland □, N.Z. 71 45 51S 168 13 E
Southminster, U.K. 15 51 40N 0 51 E
Southport, U.K. 18 53 38N 3 1W
Southwark, U.K. 15 51 29N 0 5W
Southwell, U.K. 19 53 4N 0 57W
Southwick, U.K. 15 50 50N 0 14W
Southwold, U.K. 15 52 19N 1 41 E
Sovetskaya Gavan, U.S.S.R. 49 48 50N 140 0 E
Soviet Union ■ = Union of Soviet Socialist Republics ■, Eurasia 48 60 0N 100 0 E
Sowerby, U.K. 19 54 13N 1 19W
Soweto, S. Afr. 81 26 14S 27 54 E
Spain ■, Europe 37 40 0N 5 0W
Spalding, U.K. 15 52 47N 0 9W
Spanish Town, Jam. 94 18 0N 76 57W
Sparkford, U.K. 14 51 2N 2 33W
Spean Bridge, U.K. 22 56 53N 4 55W
Speke, U.K. 18 53 21N 2 51W
Spelve, L., U.K. 20 56 22N 5 45W
Spencer G., Austral. 67 34 0S 137 20 E
Spennymoor, U.K. 19 54 43N 1 35W
Sperrin Mts., U.K. 24 54 50N 7 0W
Spey →, U.K. 23 57 26N 3 25W
Spézia, La, It. 40 44 8N 9 50 E
Spilsby, U.K. 19 53 10N 0 6 E
Spithead, U.K. 15 50 43N 1 5W
Spitzbergen = Svalbard, Arctic 103 78 0N 17 0 E
Split, Yug. 40 43 31N 16 26 E
Spofforth, U.K. 19 53 57N 1 28W
Spokane, U.S.A. 90 47 45N 117 25W
Springfield, Ill., U.S.A. 92 39 48N 89 40W
Springfield, Mass., U.S.A. 93 42 8N 72 37W
Springfield, Mo., U.S.A. 91 37 15N 93 20W
Springfield, Ohio, U.S.A. 92 39 58N 83 48W
Sproatley, U.K. 19 53 46N 0 9W
Spurn Hd., U.K. 19 53 34N 0 8 E
Sredinny Ra., U.S.S.R. 49 57 0N 160 0 E
Srednekolymsk, U.S.S.R. 49 67 27N 153 40 E
Sri Lanka ■, Asia 58 7 30N 80 50 E
Srinagar, India 58 34 5N 74 50 E

Staffa

Staffa, *U.K.* 20 56 26N 6 21W
Stafford, *U.K.* 14 52 49N 2 9W
Stafford □, *U.K.* 14 52 53N 2 10W
Staindrop, *U.K.* 19 54 35N 1 49W
Staines, *U.K.* 15 51 26N 0 30W
Stainforth, *U.K.* 19 53 37N 0 59W
Stainmore For., *U.K.* 18 54 29N 2 5W
Stainton, *U.K.* 19 53 17N 0 23W
Staithes, *U.K.* 19 54 33N 0 47W
Stalbridge, *U.K.* 14 50 57N 2 22W
Stalham, *U.K.* 15 52 46N 1 31 E
Stalingrad = Volgograd, *U.S.S.R.* 47 48 40N 44 25 E
Stallingborough, *U.K.* 19 53 36N 0 11W
Stalybridge, *U.K.* 18 53 29N 2 4W
Stamford, *U.K.* 15 52 39N 0 29W
Stamford, *U.S.A.* 93 41 5N 73 30W
Stamford Bridge, *U.K.* 19 53 59N 0 53W
Stamfordham, *U.K.* 21 55 3N 1 53W
Standish, *U.K.* 18 53 35N 2 39W
Standon, *U.K.* 15 51 53N 0 2 E
Stanford on Teme, *U.K.* 14 52 17N 2 26W
Stanhope, *U.K.* 18 54 45N 2 0W
Stanley, *Falk.* 102 51 40S 59 51W
Stanley, *Durham, U.K.* 19 54 53N 1 42W
Stanley, *Tayside, U.K.* 21 56 29N 3 28W
Stannington, *U.K.* 21 55 7N 1 41W
Stanovoy Ra., *U.S.S.R.* 49 55 0N 130 0 E
Stansted Mountfitchet, *U.K.* 15 51 54N 0 13 E
Stanwix, *U.K.* 18 54 54N 2 56W
Stapleford, *U.K.* 19 52 56N 1 16W
Staplehurst, *U.K.* 15 51 9N 0 35 E
Stara Zagora, *Bulg.* 41 42 26N 25 39 E
Start Bay, *U.K.* 16 50 15N 3 35W
Start Pt., *U.K.* 16 50 13N 3 38W
Staunton, *U.K.* 14 51 58N 2 19W
Stavanger, *Nor.* 45 58 57N 5 40 E
Staveley, *Cumbria, U.K.* 18 54 24N 2 49W
Staveley, *Derby, U.K.* 19 53 16N 1 20W
Stavropol, *U.S.S.R.* 47 45 5N 42 0 E
Stenhousemuir, *U.K.* 21 56 2N 3 46W
Sterlitamak, *U.S.S.R.* 46 53 40N 56 0 E
Stevenage, *U.K.* 15 51 54N 0 11W
Stevenston, *U.K.* 20 55 38N 4 46W
Stewart I., *N.Z.* 71 46 58S 167 54 E
Stewarton, *U.K.* 20 55 40N 4 30W
Steyning, *U.K.* 15 50 54N 0 19W
Stillington, *U.K.* 19 54 7N 1 5W
Stinchar →, *U.K.* 20 55 10N 4 50W
Stiperstones Mt., *U.K.* 14 52 36N 2 57W
Stirling, *U.K.* 21 56 7N 3 57W
Stobo, *U.K.* 21 55 38N 3 18W
Stockbridge, *U.K.* 14 51 7N 1 30W
Stockholm, *Swed.* 45 59 20N 18 3 E
Stockport, *U.K.* 18 53 25N 2 11W
Stocksbridge, *U.K.* 19 53 30N 1 36W
Stockton, *U.S.A.* 90 38 0N 121 20W
Stockton-on-Tees, *U.K.* 19 54 34N 1 20W
Stoke, *U.K.* 15 51 26N 0 41 E
Stoke Ferry, *U.K.* 15 52 34N 0 31 E
Stoke Fleming, *U.K.* 16 50 19N 3 36W
Stoke Mandeville, *U.K.* 15 51 46N 0 47W
Stoke-on-Trent, *U.K.* 18 53 1N 2 11W
Stoke Prior, *U.K.* 14 52 18N 2 4W
Stokenham, *U.K.* 16 50 15N 3 40W
Stokesley, *U.K.* 19 54 27N 1 12W
Stone, *Bucks., U.K.* 15 51 48N 0 52W
Stone, *Staffs., U.K.* 18 52 55N 2 10W
Stonehaven, *U.K.* 23 56 58N 2 11W
Stonehouse, *Gloucs., U.K.* 14 51 45N 2 18W
Stonehouse, *Strathclyde, U.K.* 21 55 42N 4 0W
Stonham Aspall, *U.K.* 15 52 11N 1 7 E
Stony Stratford, *U.K.* 15 52 4N 0 51W
Storm B., *Austral.* 67 43 10S 147 30 E
Stornoway, *U.K.* 22 58 12N 6 23W
Stort →, *U.K.* 15 51 50N 0 7 E
Stotfold, *U.K.* 15 52 2N 0 13W
Stour →, *Dorset, U.K.* 14 50 48N 2 7W
Stour →, *Hereford & Worcs., U.K.* 14 52 25N 2 13W
Stour →, *Kent, U.K.* 15 51 15N 1 20 E
Stour →, *Suffolk, U.K.* 15 51 55N 1 5 E
Stourbridge, *U.K.* 14 52 28N 2 8W
Stourport, *U.K.* 14 52 21N 2 18W
Stow, *U.K.* 21 55 41N 2 50W
Stow Bardolph, *U.K.* 15 52 38N 0 24 E
Stow-on-the-Wold, *U.K.* 14 51 55N 1 42W
Stowmarket, *U.K.* 15 52 11N 1 0 E
Strabane, *U.K.* 24 54 50N 7 28W
Strabane □, *U.K.* 24 54 45N 7 25W
Strachur, *U.K.* 20 56 10N 5 5W
Stradbroke, *U.K.* 15 52 19N 1 16 E
Stralsund, *Ger.* 42 54 17N 13 5 E
Strangford, L., *U.K.* 24 54 30N 5 37W
Stranraer, *U.K.* 20 54 54N 5 0W
Strasbourg, *Fr.* 34 48 35N 7 42 E
Stratford-on-Avon, *U.K.* 14 52 12N 1 42W
Stratford St. Mary, *U.K.* 15 51 58N 0 59 E
Strath Earn, *U.K.* 21 56 20N 3 50W
Strath Spey, *U.K.* 23 57 15N 3 40W
Strathaven, *U.K.* 21 55 40N 4 4W
Strathclyde □, *U.K.* 20 56 0N 4 50W
Strathmore, *U.K.* 23 56 40N 3 4W
Strathpeffer, *U.K.* 23 57 35N 4 32W
Strathy Pt., *U.K.* 23 58 35N 4 0W
Strathyre, *U.K.* 20 56 14N 4 20W
Stratmiglo, *U.K.* 21 56 16N 3 15W
Stratton, *Cornwall, U.K.* 16 50 49N 4 31W
Stratton, *Wilts., U.K.* 14 51 41N 1 45W
Stratton St. Margaret, *U.K.* 14 51 35N 1 45W
Streatley, *U.K.* 14 51 31N 1 9W
Street, *U.K.* 14 51 7N 2 43W
Strensall, *U.K.* 19 54 3N 1 2W
Stretford, *U.K.* 18 53 27N 2 19W
Stretton, *U.K.* 18 53 21N 2 34W
Strichen, *U.K.* 23 57 35N 2 5W
Striven, L., *U.K.* 20 55 58N 5 9W
Stromeferry, *U.K.* 22 57 20N 5 33W
Stromness, *U.K.* 23 58 58N 3 18W
Stronachlachar, *U.K.* 20 56 15N 4 35W
Strone, *U.K.* 20 55 59N 4 54W
Stronsay, *U.K.* 23 59 8N 2 38W
Stroud, *U.K.* 14 51 44N 2 12W
Studland, *U.K.* 14 50 39N 1 58W
Studley, *U.K.* 14 52 16N 1 54W
Sturminster Marshall, *U.K.* 14 50 48N 2 4W
Sturminster Newton, *U.K.* 14 50 56N 2 18W
Sturt Cr. →, *Austral.* 66 20 8S 127 24 E
Sturton, *U.K.* 19 53 22N 0 39W
Stuttgart, *Ger.* 42 48 46N 9 10 E
Subotica, *Yug.* 41 46 6N 19 49 E
Suck →, *Ire.* 25 53 17N 8 18W
Sucre, *Bol.* 100 19 0S 65 15W
Sudan ■, *Africa* 78 15 0N 30 0 E
Sudbury, *Canada* 92 46 30N 81 0W
Sudbury, *Derby, U.K.* 19 52 53N 1 43W
Sudbury, *Suffolk, U.K.* 15 52 2N 0 44 E
Suez, *Egypt* 79 29 58N 32 31 E
Suffolk □, *U.K.* 15 52 16N 1 0 E
Suir →, *Ire.* 25 52 15N 7 10W
Sukkur, *Pak.* 58 27 42N 68 54 E
Sulawesi □, *Indon.* 63 2 0S 120 0 E
Sulby, *U.K.* 18 54 18N 4 29W
Sullom Voe, *U.K.* 22 60 30N 1 20W
Sulu Sea, *E. Ind.* 63 8 0N 120 0 E
Sumatra □, *Indon.* 63 0 40N 100 20 E
Sumbawa, *Indon.* 63 8 26S 117 30 E
Sumburgh Hd., *U.K.* 22 59 52N 1 17W
Summer Is., *U.K.* 22 58 0N 5 27W
Sumy, *U.S.S.R.* 47 50 57N 34 50 E
Sunart, L., *U.K.* 22 56 42N 5 43W
Sunda Str., *Indon.* 63 6 20S 105 30 E
Sundarbans, The, *Asia* 59 22 0N 89 0 E
Sunderland, *U.K.* 19 54 54N 1 22W
Sundsvall, *Swed.* 44 62 23N 17 17 E
Sunk Island, *U.K.* 19 53 38N 0 7W
Sunninghill, *U.K.* 15 51 25N 0 40W
Sunshine, *Austral.* 70 37 48S 144 52 E
Superior, L., *N. Am.* 92 47 40N 87 0W
Sūr, *Leb.* 57 33 19N 35 16 E
Surabaya, *Indon.* 63 7 17S 112 45 E
Surakarta, *Indon.* 63 7 35S 110 48 E
Surat, *India* 58 21 12N 72 55 E
Surgut, *U.S.S.R.* 48 61 14N 73 20 E
Surinam ■, *S. Am.* 101 4 0N 56 0W
Surrey □, *U.K.* 15 51 16N 0 30W
Surtsey, *Ice.* 44 63 20N 20 30W
Sutlej →, *Pak.* 58 29 23N 71 3 E
Sutterton, *U.K.* 19 52 54N 0 8W
Sutton, *U.K.* 15 51 22N 0 13W
Sutton Bridge, *U.K.* 15 52 46N 0 12 E
Sutton Coldfield, *U.K.* 14 52 33N 1 50W
Sutton Courtenay, *U.K.* 14 51 39N 1 16W
Sutton-in-Ashfield, *U.K.* 19 53 7N 1 20W
Sutton-on-Sea, *U.K.* 19 53 18N 0 18 E
Sutton Scotney, *U.K.* 14 51 9N 1 20W
Suva, *Fiji* 64 18 6S 178 30 E
Suzhou, *China* 61 31 19N 120 38 E
Svalbard, *Arctic* 103 78 0N 17 0 E
Svendborg, *Den.* 45 55 4N 10 35 E
* Sverdlovsk, *U.S.S.R.* 46 56 50N 60 30 E
Sverdrup Is., *Canada* 103 79 0N 97 0W
Swadlincote, *U.K.* 14 52 47N 1 34W
Swaffham, *U.K.* 15 52 38N 0 42 E
Swale →, *U.K.* 19 54 5N 1 20W
Swan Hill, *Austral.* 70 35 20S 143 33 E
Swanage, *U.K.* 14 50 36N 1 59W
Swansea, *U.K.* 17 51 37N 3 57W
Swaziland ■, *Africa* 81 26 30S 31 30 E
Sweden ■, *Europe* 44 57 0N 15 0 E
Swift Current, *Canada* 88 50 20N 107 45W
Swilly, L., *Ire.* 24 55 12N 7 35W
Swindon, *U.K.* 15 51 33N 1 47W
Swineshead, *U.K.* 19 52 56N 0 11W
Swinton, *Borders, U.K.* 21 55 43N 2 14W
Swinton, *Gr. Manchester, U.K.* 18 53 31N 2 21W
Swinton, *S. Yorks., U.K.* 19 53 28N 1 20W
Switzerland ■, *Europe* 42 46 30N 8 0 E
Swords, *Ire.* 24 53 27N 6 15W
Sydney, *Austral.* 70 33 53S 151 10 E
Sydney, *Canada* 93 46 7N 60 7W
Syktyvkar, *U.S.S.R.* 46 61 45N 50 40 E
Symington, *U.K.* 21 55 35N 3 36W
Symonds Yat, *U.K.* 14 51 50N 2 38W
Syracuse, *U.S.A.* 93 43 4N 76 11W
Syrdarya →, *U.S.S.R.* 48 46 3N 61 0 E
Syria ■, *Asia* 56 35 0N 38 0 E
Syrian Desert, *Asia* 56 31 0N 40 0 E
Syston, *U.K.* 14 52 42N 1 5W
Syzran, *U.S.S.R.* 46 53 12N 48 30 E
Szczecin, *Pol.* 42 53 27N 14 27 E
Szeged, *Hung.* 43 46 16N 20 10 E
Székesfehérvár, *Hung.* 43 47 15N 18 25 E

* *Renamed Yekaterinburg*

T

Tabora, *Tanz.* 80 5 2S 32 50 E
Tabrīz, *Iran* 56 38 7N 46 20 E
Tabūk, *Si. Arab.* 56 28 23N 36 36 E
Tacna, *Peru* 100 18 0S 70 20W
Tacoma, *U.S.A.* 90 47 15N 122 30W
Tacuarembó, *Urug.* 102 31 45S 56 0W
Tadcaster, *U.K.* 19 53 53N 1 16W
Tadley, *U.K.* 14 51 21N 1 8W
Tadzhikistan □, *U.S.S.R.* 48 35 30N 70 0 E
Taegu, *S. Kor.* 61 35 50N 128 37 E
Taejŏn, *S. Kor.* 61 36 20N 127 28 E
Taganrog, *U.S.S.R.* 47 47 12N 38 50 E
Tagus = Tajo →, *Sp.* 37 38 40N 9 24W
Tahiti, *Pac. Oc.* 65 17 37S 149 27W
Taichung, *Taiwan* 61 24 10N 120 35 E
Taimyr Pen., *U.S.S.R.* 49 75 0N 100 0 E
Tain, *U.K.* 23 57 49N 4 4W
Tainan, *Taiwan* 61 23 17N 120 18 E
Taipei, *Taiwan* 61 25 2N 121 30 E
Taiwan ■, *Asia* 61 23 30N 121 0 E
Taiyuan, *China* 61 37 52N 112 33 E
Ta'izz, *Yem.* 56 13 35N 44 2 E
Tajo →, *Sp.* 37 38 40N 9 24W
Tak, *Thai.* 59 16 52N 99 8 E
Takamatsu, *Jap.* 62 34 20N 134 5 E
Takaoka, *Jap.* 62 36 47N 137 0 E
Takapuna, *N.Z.* 71 36 47S 174 47 E
Takasaki, *Jap.* 62 36 20N 139 0 E
Takeley, *U.K.* 15 51 52N 0 16 E
Takla Makan, *China* 60 39 0N 83 0 E
Talca, *Chile* 102 35 28S 71 40W
Talcahuano, *Chile* 102 36 40S 73 10W
Talgarth, *U.K.* 17 51 59N 3 15W
Tallahassee, *U.S.A.* 91 30 25N 84 15W
Tallinn, *Estonia* 46 59 22N 24 48 E
Tamar →, *U.K.* 16 50 33N 4 15W
Tambov, *U.S.S.R.* 46 52 45N 41 28 E
Tame →, *U.K.* 14 52 43N 1 45W
Tamerton Foliot, *U.K.* 16 50 25N 4 10W
Tamil Nadu □, *India* 58 11 0N 77 0 E
Tampa, *U.S.A.* 91 27 57N 82 38W
Tampere, *Fin.* 44 61 30N 23 50 E
Tampico, *Mex.* 94 22 20N 97 50W
Tamworth, *Austral.* 67 31 7S 150 58 E
Tamworth, *U.K.* 14 52 38N 1 41W
Tana, L., *Eth.* 79 13 5N 37 30 E
Tanami Desert, *Austral.* 66 18 50S 132 0 E
Tandragee, *U.K.* 24 54 22N 6 23W
Tanga, *Tanz.* 80 5 5S 39 2 E
Tanganyika, L., *E. Afr.* 80 6 40S 30 0 E
Tangier, *Mor.* 78 35 50N 5 49W
Tangshan, *China* 61 39 38N 118 10 E
Tanworth, *U.K.* 14 52 20N 1 50W
Tanzania ■, *E. Afr.* 80 6 40S 34 0 E
Tapajós →, *Brazil* 101 2 24S 54 41W
Tarābulus, *Leb.* 56 34 31N 35 50 E
Tarābulus, *Libya* 79 32 49N 13 7 E
Taranaki □, *N.Z.* 71 39 5S 174 51 E
Táranto, *It.* 40 40 30N 17 11 E
Táranto, G. di, *It.* 40 40 0N 17 15 E
Tarbat Ness, *U.K.* 23 57 52N 3 48W
Tarbert, *Strathclyde, U.K.* 20 55 55N 5 25W
Tarbert, *W. Isles, U.K.* 22 57 54N 6 49W
Tarbes, *Fr.* 35 43 15N 0 3 E
Tarbet, *U.K.* 20 56 13N 4 44W
Tarbolton, *U.K.* 20 55 30N 4 30W
Taree, *Austral.* 70 31 50S 152 30 E
Tarija, *Bol.* 100 21 30S 64 40W
Tarim Basin, *China* 60 40 0N 84 0 E
Tarleton, *U.K.* 18 53 41N 2 50W
Tarnów, *Pol.* 43 50 3N 21 0 E
Tarporley, *U.K.* 18 53 10N 2 42W
Tarragona, *Sp.* 37 41 5N 1 17 E
Tarrasa, *Sp.* 37 41 34N 2 1 E
Tashkent, *U.S.S.R.* 48 41 20N 69 10 E
Tasman B., *N.Z.* 71 40 59S 173 25 E
Tasman Sea, *Pac. Oc.* 71 36 0S 160 0 E
Tasmania □, *Austral.* 67 42 0S 146 30 E
Tatar A.S.S.R. □, *U.S.S.R.* 46 55 30N 51 30 E
Tattenhall, *U.K.* 18 53 7N 2 47W
Taunton, *U.K.* 14 51 1N 3 7W
Taupo, *N.Z.* 71 38 41S 176 7 E
Taupo, L., *N.Z.* 71 38 46S 175 55 E
Tauranga, *N.Z.* 71 37 42S 176 11 E
Taurus Mts., *Turk.* 47 37 0N 35 0 E
Tavistock, *U.K.* 16 50 33N 4 9W
Tavoy, *Burma* 59 14 2N 98 12 E
Taw →, *U.K.* 16 17 37S 177 55 E
Tay →, *U.K.* 21 56 37N 3 38W
Tay, Firth of, *U.K.* 21 56 25N 3 8W
Tay, L., *U.K.* 21 56 30N 4 10W
Tay Bridge, *U.K.* 21 56 28N 3 0W
Taynuilt, *U.K.* 20 56 25N 5 15W
Tayport, *U.K.* 21 56 27N 2 52W
Tayside □, *U.K.* 21 56 25N 3 30W
Tbilisi, *U.S.S.R.* 47 41 43N 44 50 E
Te Anau, L., *N.Z.* 71 45 15S 167 45 E
Te Aroha, *N.Z.* 71 37 32S 175 44 E
Tebay, *U.K.* 18 54 25N 2 35W
Tees →, *U.K.* 19 54 36N 1 25W
Teesdale, *U.K.* 18 54 37N 2 10W
Teesside, *U.K.* 19 54 37N 1 13W
Tegid, L., *U.K.* 17 52 53N 3 38W
Tegucigalpa, *Hond.* 94 14 5N 87 14W
Tehrān, *Iran* 56 35 44N 51 30 E
Tehuantepec, Gulf of, *Mex.* 94 15 50N 95 0W
Tehuantepec, Isthmus of, *Mex.* 94 17 0N 94 30W
Teifi →, *U.K.* 17 52 4N 4 14W
Teign →, *U.K.* 16 50 41N 3 42W
Teignmouth, *U.K.* 16 50 33N 3 30W
Tejo →, *Port.* 37 38 40N 9 24W
Tel Aviv-Jaffa, *Isr.* 57 32 4N 34 48 E
Telemark fylke □, *Nor.* 45 59 25N 8 30 E
Telford, *U.K.* 14 52 42N 2 31W
Teluk Betung, *Indon.* 63 5 20S 105 10 E
Tema, *Ghana* 78 5 41N 0 0 E
Teme →, *U.K.* 14 52 23N 2 15W
Temirtau, *U.S.S.R.* 48 50 5N 72 56 E
Temora, *Austral.* 70 34 30S 147 30 E
Temple Combe, *U.K.* 14 51 0N 2 25W
Temple Ewell, *U.K.* 15 51 9N 1 15 E
Temple Sowerby, *U.K.* 18 54 38N 2 33W
Templemore, *Ire.* 25 52 48N 7 50W
Tenbury, *U.K.* 14 52 18N 2 35W
Tenby, *U.K.* 17 51 40N 4 42W
Tenerife, *Can. Is.* 78 28 15N 16 35W
Tennessee □, *U.S.A.* 91 36 0N 86 30W
Tennessee →, *U.S.A.* 91 37 4N 88 34W
Tenterden, *U.K.* 15 51 4N 0 42 E
Teófilo Otoni, *Brazil* 101 17 50S 41 30W
Tepic, *Mex.* 94 21 30N 104 54W
Téramo, *It.* 40 42 40N 13 40 E
Teresina, *Brazil* 101 5 9S 42 45W
Terni, *It.* 40 42 34N 12 38 E
Terre Haute, *U.S.A.* 92 39 28N 87 24W
Teruel, *Sp.* 37 40 22N 1 8W
Test →, *U.K.* 14 51 7N 1 30W
Tetbury, *U.K.* 14 51 37N 2 9W
Tetlin, *U.S.A.* 88 63 14N 142 50W
Tetney, *U.K.* 19 53 30N 0 1W
Tétouan, *Mor.* 78 35 35N 5 21W
Tetovo, *Yug.* 41 42 1N 21 2 E
Tettenhall, *U.K.* 14 52 35N 2 7W
Teviot →, *U.K.* 21 55 21N 2 51W
Teviotdale, *U.K.* 21 55 25N 2 50W
Teviothead, *U.K.* 21 55 19N 2 55W
Tewkesbury, *U.K.* 14 51 59N 2 8W
Texas □, *U.S.A.* 90 31 40N 98 30W
Texel, *Neth.* 36 53 5N 4 50 E
Teynham, *U.K.* 15 51 19N 0 50 E
Thailand ■, *Asia* 63 16 0N 102 0 E
Thailand, G. of, *Asia* 63 11 30N 101 0 E
Thal Desert, *Pak.* 58 31 10N 71 30 E
Thame, *U.K.* 15 51 44N 0 58W
Thame →, *U.K.* 15 51 35N 1 8W
Thames →, *U.K.* 15 51 30N 0 35 E
Thanet, I. of, *U.K.* 15 51 21N 1 20 E
Thar Desert, *India* 58 28 0N 72 0 E
Thatcham, *U.K.* 14 51 24N 1 17W
Thaxted, *U.K.* 15 51 57N 0 20 E
The Entrance, *Austral.* 70 33 21S 151 30 E
The Grenadines, Is., *W. Ind.* 94 12 40N 61 20W
The Hague, *Neth.* 36 52 7N 4 17 E
The Pas, *Canada* 88 53 45N 101 15W
Theale, *U.K.* 14 51 26N 1 5W
Thessaloniki, *Greece* 41 40 38N 22 58 E
Thessaloniki, Gulf of, *Greece* 41 40 15N 22 45 E
Thessaly □, *Greece* 41 39 30N 22 0 E
Thetford, *U.K.* 15 52 25N 0 44 E
Thies, *Sene.* 78 14 50N 16 51W
Thimphu, *Bhutan* 59 27 31N 89 45 E
Thionville, *Fr.* 34 49 20N 6 10 E
Thirlmere, L., *U.K.* 18 54 32N 3 4W
Thirsk, *U.K.* 19 54 15N 1 20W
Thirston, *U.K.* 21 55 20N 1 34W
Thisted, *Den.* 45 56 58N 8 40 E
Thompson →, *Canada* 88 50 15N 121 24W
Thornaby on Tees, *U.K.* 19 54 36N 1 19W
Thornbury, *U.K.* 14 51 36N 2 31W
Thorndon, *U.K.* 15 52 16N 1 8 E
Thorne, *U.K.* 19 53 36N 0 56W
Thorney, *U.K.* 15 52 37N 0 8W
Thornham, *U.K.* 15 52 59N 0 35 E
Thornhill, *U.K.* 21 55 15N 3 46W
Thornthwaite, *U.K.* 18 54 36N 3 13W
Thornton, *U.K.* 18 53 52N 2 29W
Thornton Dale, *U.K.* 19 54 14N 0 41W
Thorpe, *U.K.* 15 52 38N 1 20 E
Thorpe le Soken, *U.K.* 15 51 50N 1 11 E
Thrace □, *Greece* 41 41 9N 25 30 E
Thrapston, *U.K.* 15 52 24N 0 32W
Threlkeld, *U.K.* 18 54 37N 3 2W
Threshfield, *U.K.* 18 54 5N 2 2W
Thule, *Green.* 103 77 40N 69 0W
Thunder Bay, *Canada* 92 48 20N 89 15W
Thurlby, *U.K.* 15 52 45N 0 21W
Thurles, *Ire.* 25 52 40N 7 53W
Thurmaston, *U.K.* 14 52 40N 1 8W
Thursby, *U.K.* 18 54 40N 3 3W
Thurso, *U.K.* 23 58 34N 3 31W
Tian Shan, *China* 60 43 0N 84 0 E
Tianshui, *China* 60 34 32N 105 40 E
Tiber →, *It.* 40 41 44N 12 14 E
Tiberias, *Isr.* 57 32 47N 35 32 E
Tibesti, *Chad* 79 21 0N 17 30 E
Ticehurst, *U.K.* 15 51 2N 0 23 E
Tickhill, *U.K.* 19 53 25N 1 8W
Tideswell, *U.K.* 19 53 17N 1 46W
Tientsin, *China* 61 39 10N 117 15 E
Tierra del Fuego □, *Arg.* 102 54 0S 67 45W
Tighnabruaich, *U.K.* 20 55 55N 5 13W
Tigris →, *Iraq* 56 37 0N 42 30 E

Tijuana, *Mex.* **94** 32 30N 117 10W
Tiksi, *U.S.S.R.* .... **49** 71 40N 128 45 E
Tilburg, *Neth.* .... **36** 51 31N 5 6 E
Tilbury, *U.K.* .... **15** 51 27N 0 24 E
Till →, *U.K.* **19** 55 35N 2 3W
Tillicoultry, *U.K.* **21** 56 9N 3 44W
Tilmanstone, *U.K.* .... **15** 51 13N 1 18 E
Tilt →, *U.K.* **23** 56 50N 3 50W
Timaru, *N.Z.* .... **71** 44 23S 171 14 E
Timbuktu = Tombouctou, *Mali* .. **78** 16 50N 3 0W
Timişoara, *Rom.* ...... **43** 45 43N 21 15 E
Timmins, *Canada* **92** 48 28N 81 25W
Timor, *Indon.* .... **63** 9 0S 125 0 E
Timor Sea, *E. Ind.* .... **66** 10 0S 127 0 E
Tingewick, *U.K.* **14** 51 59N 1 4W
Tintagel, *U.K.* **16** 50 40N 4 45W
Tintagel Hd., *U.K.* **16** 50 40N 4 46W
Tipperary, *Ire.* **25** 52 28N 8 10W
Tipperary □, *Ire.* **25** 52 37N 7 55W
Tipton, *U.K.* **14** 52 32N 2 4W
Tiptree, *U.K.* .... **15** 51 48N 0 46 E
Tiranë, *Alb.* .... **41** 41 18N 19 49 E
Tiree, *U.K.* **20** 56 31N 6 55W
Tiree, Passage of, *U.K.* **20** 56 30N 6 30W
Tîrgu Mureş, *Rom.* .... **43** 46 31N 24 38 E
Tiruchchirappalli, *India* **58** 10 45N 78 45 E
Tisbury, *U.K.* **14** 51 4N 2 4W
Tisza →, *Hung.* ..... **43** 46 8N 20 2 E
Titchfield, *U.K.* **14** 50 51N 1 13W
Titicaca, L., *Peru* **100** 15 30S 69 30W
Titograd, *Yug.* .... **41** 42 30N 19 19 E
Tiverton, *U.K.* **16** 50 54N 3 30W
Tizi-Ouzou, *Alg.* ...... **78** 36 42N 4 3 E
Toamasina, *Madag.* .. **81** 18 10S 49 25 E
Tobago, *W. Ind.* **94** 11 10N 60 30W
Tobermory, *U.K.* **20** 56 37N 6 4W
Tobol →, *U.S.S.R.* ... **48** 58 10N 68 12 E
Tocantins →, *Brazil* . **101** 1 45S 49 10W
Toddington, *U.K.* **15** 51 57N 0 31W
Todmorden, *U.K.* **18** 53 43N 2 7W
Togliatti, *U.S.S.R.* .... **46** 53 32N 49 24 E
Togo ■, *W. Afr.* ...... **78** 6 15N 1 35 E
Tokelau Is., *Pac. Oc.* . **64** 9 0S 171 45W
Tōkyō, *Jap.* .... **62** 35 45N 139 45 E
Tolageak, *U.S.A.* **88** 70 2N 162 50W
* Tolbukhin, *Bulg.* ..... **41** 43 37N 27 49 E
Toledo, *Sp.* **37** 39 50N 4 2W
Toledo, *U.S.A.* **92** 41 37N 83 33W
Toliara, *Madag.* ...... **81** 23 21S 43 40 E
Tollesbury, *U.K.* ...... **15** 51 46N 0 51 E
Toluca, *Mex.* **94** 19 20N 99 40W
Tom Price, *Austral.* ... **66** 22 40S 117 48 E
Tombouctou, *Mali* **78** 16 50N 3 0W
Tomnavoulin, *U.K.* **23** 57 19N 3 18W
Tomsk, *U.S.S.R.* ..... **48** 56 30N 85 5 E
Tonbridge, *U.K.* ...... **15** 51 12N 0 18 E
Tone →, *U.K.* **16** 50 59N 3 15W
Tong, *U.K.* **14** 52 39N 2 18W
Tonga ■, *Pac. Oc.* ... **64** 19 50S 174 30W
Tonga Trench, *Pac. Oc.* **64** 18 0S 175 0W
Tongue, *U.K.* **23** 58 29N 4 25W
Tonkin, G. of, *Asia* ... **60** 20 0N 108 0 E
Toowoomba, *Austral.* . **67** 27 32S 151 56 E
Topeka, *U.S.A.* **91** 39 3N 95 40W
Topsham, *U.K.* **16** 50 40N 3 27W
Tor Bay, *U.K.* **16** 50 26N 3 31W
Torbay, *U.K.* **16** 50 26N 3 31W
Torne älv →, *Swed.* . **44** 65 50N 24 12 E
Toronto, *Canada* **92** 43 39N 79 20W
Torpoint, *U.K.* **16** 50 23N 4 12W
Torquay, *U.K.* **16** 50 27N 3 31W
Torran Rocks, *U.K.* ... **20** 56 14N 6 24W
Torrens, L., *Austral.* .. **67** 31 0S 137 50 E
Torreón, *Mex.* **94** 25 33N 103 26W
Torridge →, *U.K.* **16** 50 51N 4 10W
Torridon, L., *U.K.* **22** 57 35N 5 50W
Torthorwald, *U.K.* **21** 55 7N 3 30W
Tortosa, *Sp.* .... **37** 40 49N 0 31 E
Toruń, *Pol.* .... **43** 53 0N 18 39 E
Torver, *U.K.* **18** 54 20N 3 7W
Tory I., *Ire.* **24** 55 17N 8 12W
Totland, *U.K.* **14** 50 41N 1 32W
Totley, *U.K.* **19** 53 18N 1 32W
Totnes, *U.K.* **16** 50 26N 3 41W
Totton, *U.K.* **14** 50 55N 1 29W
Toulon, *Fr.* .... **35** 43 10N 5 55 E
Toulouse, *Fr.* .... **35** 43 37N 1 27 E
Tournai, *Belg.* .... **36** 50 35N 3 25 E
Tours, *Fr.* .... **34** 47 22N 0 40 E
Towcester, *U.K.* **15** 52 7N 0 56W
Town Yetholm, *U.K.* .. **21** 55 33N 2 19W
Townsville, *Austral.* .. **67** 19 15S 146 45 E
Toyama, *Jap.* .... **62** 36 40N 137 15 E
Toyohashi, *Jap.* ...... **62** 34 45N 137 25 E
Trabzon, *Turk.* .... **47** 41 0N 39 45 E
Trail, *Canada* **88** 49 5N 117 40W
Tralee, *Ire.* **25** 52 16N 9 42W
Tralee B., *Ire.* **25** 52 17N 9 55W
Tramore, *Ire.* **25** 52 10N 7 10W
Tranent, *U.K.* **21** 55 57N 2 58W
Transcaucasia, *U.S.S.R.* **47** 42 0N 44 0 E
Transvaal □, *S. Afr.* .. **81** 25 0S 29 0 E
Transylvanian Alps, *Rom.* .... **43** 45 30N 25 0 E
Trápani, *It.* .... **40** 38 1N 12 30 E
Traralgon, *Austral.* ... **70** 38 12S 146 34 E
Trawsfynydd, *U.K.* **17** 52 54N 3 55W
Tredegar, *U.K.* **17** 51 47N 3 16W
Tregaron, *U.K.* **17** 52 14N 3 56W
Trent →, *U.K.* **19** 53 33N 0 44W

Trentham, *U.K.* **18** 52 59N 2 12W
Trentino-Alto Adige □, *It.* .... **40** 46 30N 11 0 E
Trento, *It.* .... **40** 46 5N 11 8 E
Trenton, *U.S.A.* **93** 40 15N 74 41W
Tresco I., *U.K.* **16** 49 57N 6 20W
Treshnish Is., *U.K.* ... **20** 56 30N 6 25W
Trevose Hd., *U.K.* **16** 50 33N 5 3W
Trier, *Ger.* .... **36** 49 45N 6 37 E
Trieste, *It.* .... **40** 45 39N 13 45 E
Trim, *Ire.* **24** 53 34N 6 48W
Trimdon, *U.K.* **19** 54 43N 1 23W
Trimley, *U.K.* .... **15** 51 59N 1 19 E
Trincomalee, *Sri L.* ... **58** 8 38N 81 15 E
Trinidad, *W. Ind.* **94** 10 30N 61 15W
Trinidad & Tobago ■, *W. Ind.* **94** 10 30N 61 20W
Tripoli = Tarābulus, *Leb.* .... **56** 34 31N 35 50 E
Tripoli = Tarābulus, *Libya* .... **79** 32 49N 13 7 E
Tristan da Cunha, *Atl. Oc.* **118** 37 6S 12 20W
Trivandrum, *India* .... **58** 8 41N 77 0 E
Trois-Rivières, *Canada* **93** 46 25N 72 34W
Trollhättan, *Swed.* .... **45** 58 17N 12 20 E
Troms fylke □, *Nor.* .. **44** 68 56N 19 0 E
Tromsø, *Nor.* .... **44** 69 40N 18 56 E
Trondheim, *Nor.* ..... **44** 63 36N 10 25 E
Troon, *U.K.* **20** 55 33N 4 40W
Trossachs, The, *U.K.* . **20** 56 14N 4 24W
Trostan, *U.K.* **24** 55 4N 6 10W
Trotternish, *U.K.* **22** 57 32N 6 15W
Trowbridge, *U.K.* **14** 51 18N 2 12W
Troy, *U.S.A.* **93** 42 45N 73 39W
Troyes, *Fr.* .... **34** 48 19N 4 3 E
Trujillo, *Peru* **100** 8 6S 79 0W
* Truk, *Pac. Oc.* .... **64** 7 25N 151 46 E
Trull, *U.K.* **14** 50 58N 3 8W
Trumpington, *U.K.* .... **15** 52 11N 0 6 E
Truro, *U.K.* **16** 50 17N 5 2W
Tselinograd, *U.S.S.R.* . **48** 51 10N 71 30 E
Tsimlyansk Res., *U.S.S.R.* .... **47** 48 0N 43 0 E
Tsu, *Jap.* .... **62** 34 45N 136 25 E
Tsugaru Str., *Jap.* .... **62** 41 30N 140 30 E
Tuam, *Ire.* **24** 53 30N 8 50W
Tuamotu Arch., *Pac. Oc.* **65** 17 0S 144 0W
Tuath, Loch, *U.K.* **20** 56 30N 6 15W
Tubuai Is., *Pac. Oc.* .. **65** 25 0S 150 0W
Tucson, *U.S.A.* **90** 32 14N 110 59W
Tula, *U.S.S.R.* .... **46** 54 13N 37 38 E
Tulcán, *Ecuad.* **100** 0 48N 77 43W
Tulla, L., *U.K.* **20** 56 33N 4 47W
Tullamore, *Ire.* **25** 53 17N 7 30W
Tullow, *Ire.* **25** 52 48N 6 45W
Tulsa, *U.S.A.* **91** 36 10N 96 0W
Tulua, *Col.* **100** 4 6N 76 11W
Tumaco, *Col.* **100** 1 50N 78 45W
Tummel, L., *U.K.* **23** 56 43N 3 55W
Tunbridge Wells, *U.K.* . **15** 51 7N 0 16 E
Tuncurry, *Austral.* .... **70** 32 17S 152 29 E
Tunis, *Tunisia* .... **78** 36 50N 10 11 E
Tunisia ■, *Africa* .... **78** 33 30N 9 10 E
Tunja, *Col.* **100** 5 33N 73 25W
Tunstall, *U.K.* .... **15** 52 7N 1 28 E
Tura, *India* .... **59** 25 30N 90 16 E
Turfan Depression, *China* .... **50** 42 40N 89 25 E
Turin, *It.* .... **40** 45 4N 7 40 E
Turkana, L., *Kenya* ... **80** 3 30N 36 5 E
Turkey ■, *Eurasia* .... **47** 39 0N 36 0 E
Turkmenistan □, *U.S.S.R.* .... **48** 39 0N 59 0 E
Turks Is., *W. Ind.* **95** 21 20N 71 20W
Turku, *Fin.* .... **45** 60 30N 22 19 E
Turnberry, *U.K.* **20** 55 19N 4 50W
Turnu-Severin, *Rom.* .. **43** 44 39N 22 41 E
Turriff, *U.K.* **23** 57 32N 2 28W
Tuskar Rock, *Ire.* **25** 52 12N 6 10W
Tutbury, *U.K.* **14** 52 52N 1 41W
Tuticorin, *India* ..... **58** 8 50N 78 12 E
Tuvalu ■, *Pac. Oc.* ... **64** 8 0S 178 0 E
Tuxford, *U.K.* **19** 53 14N 0 52W
Tuxtla Gutiérrez, *Mex.* **94** 16 50N 93 10W
Tuz Gölü, *Turk.* ...... **47** 38 45N 33 30 E
Tuzla, *Yug.* .... **41** 44 34N 18 41 E
Tver, *U.S.S.R.* .... **46** 56 55N 35 55 E
Tweed →, *U.K.* **21** 55 42N 1 59W
Tweedmouth, *U.K.* **21** 55 46N 2 1W
Tweedshawe, *U.K.* **21** 55 26N 3 29W
Twenty, *U.K.* **15** 52 43N 0 20W
Twyford, *Berks., U.K.* . **15** 51 29N 0 51W
Twyford, *Hants., U.K.* . **14** 51 1N 1 19W
Tychy, *Pol.* .... **43** 50 9N 18 59 E
Tydd St. Mary, *U.K.* .. **15** 52 45N 0 9 E
Tyldesley, *U.K.* **18** 53 31N 2 29W
Tyler, *U.S.A.* **90** 32 18N 95 18W
Tyndrum, *U.K.* **20** 56 26N 4 41W
Tyne →, *Tyne & Wear, U.K.* **19** 54 58N 1 28W
Tyne →, *Lothian, U.K.* **21** 55 58N 2 45W
Tyne & Wear □, *U.K.* . **19** 54 55N 1 35W
Tynemouth, *U.K.* **19** 55 1N 1 27W
Tyre = Sūr, *Leb.* ...... **57** 33 19N 35 16 E
Tyrol □, *Austria* ..... **42** 47 3N 10 43 E
Tyrrhenian Sea, *Europe* **40** 40 0N 12 30 E
Tyumen, *U.S.S.R.* .... **48** 57 11N 65 29 E
Tywardreath, *U.K.* **16** 50 21N 4 40W
Tywi →, *U.K.* **17** 51 48N 4 20W
Tywyn, *U.K.* **17** 52 36N 4 5W

U

Ube, *Jap.* .... **62** 33 56N 131 15 E
Uberaba, *Brazil* **101** 19 50S 47 55W
Uberlândia, *Brazil* **101** 19 0S 48 20W
Ucayali →, *Peru* **100** 4 30S 73 30W
Uckfield, *U.K.* .... **15** 50 58N 0 6 E
Udaipur, *India* .... **58** 24 36N 73 44 E
Uddevalla, *Swed.* ..... **45** 58 21N 11 55 E
Uddingston, *U.K.* **21** 55 50N 4 3W
Údine, *It.* .... **40** 46 5N 13 10 E
Ufa, *U.S.S.R.* .... **46** 54 45N 55 55 E
Uffculme, *U.K.* **16** 50 54N 3 19W
Ufford, *U.K.* .... **15** 52 6N 1 22 E
Uganda ■, *E. Afr.* .... **80** 2 0N 32 0 E
Ugborough, *U.K.* **16** 50 22N 3 53W
Uig, *U.K.* **22** 57 35N 6 20W
Uitenhage, *S. Afr.* .... **81** 33 40S 25 28 E
Ujung Pandang, *Indon.* **63** 5 10S 119 20 E
Ukraine □, *U.S.S.R.* .. **47** 49 0N 32 0 E
Ulan Bator, *Mong.* .... **60** 47 55N 106 53 E
Ulan Ude, *U.S.S.R.* ... **49** 51 45N 107 40 E
Ulceby Cross, *U.K.* ... **19** 53 14N 0 6 E
Ulhasnagar, *India* .... **58** 19 15N 73 10 E
Ullapool, *U.K.* **22** 57 54N 5 10W
Ullswater, *U.K.* **18** 54 35N 2 52W
Ulm, *Ger.* .... **42** 48 23N 10 0 E
Ulster □, *U.K.* **24** 54 35N 6 30W
Ulva, I., *U.K.* **20** 56 30N 6 12W
Ulverston, *U.K.* **18** 54 13N 3 7W
Ulyanovsk, *U.S.S.R.* .. **46** 54 20N 48 25 E
Ulyasutay, *Mong.* ..... **60** 47 56N 97 28 E
Umbria □, *It.* .... **40** 42 53N 12 30 E
Umeå, *Swed.* .... **44** 63 45N 20 20 E
Umtata, *S. Afr.* .... **81** 31 36S 28 49 E
Ungava B., *Canada* ... **89** 59 30N 67 30W
Ungava Pen., *Canada* . **89** 60 0N 74 0W
Union of Soviet Socialist Republics ■, *Eurasia* **48** 60 0N 100 0 E
United Arab Emirates ■, *Asia* ... **57** 23 50N 54 0 E
United Kingdom ■, *Europe* **5** 55 0N 3 0W
United States of America ■, *N. Am.* . **90** 37 0N 96 0W
Unst, *U.K.* **22** 60 50N 0 55W
Upavon, *U.K.* **14** 51 17N 1 49W
Upington, *S. Afr.* ..... **81** 28 25S 21 15 E
Upper Heyford, *U.K.* .. **14** 51 54N 1 16W
Upper L. Erne, *U.K.* ... **24** 54 14N 7 22W
Upper Volta ■ = Burkina Faso ■, *Africa* **78** 12 0N 1 0W
Uppingham, *U.K.* **15** 52 36N 0 43W
Uppsala, *Swed.* ...... **45** 59 53N 17 38 E
Upton, *U.K.* **18** 53 14N 2 52W
Upton-upon-Severn, *U.K.* **14** 52 4N 2 12W
Upwey, *U.K.* **14** 50 40N 2 29W
Ural Mts., *U.S.S.R.* ... **46** 60 0N 59 0 E
Uralsk, *U.S.S.R.* ..... **46** 51 20N 51 20 E
Uranium City, *Canada* **88** 59 34N 108 37W
Ure →, *U.K.* **19** 54 20N 1 25W
Urgench, *U.S.S.R.* .... **48** 41 40N 60 41 E
Urmia, L., *Iran* .... **56** 37 50N 45 30 E
Urmston, *U.K.* **18** 53 28N 2 22W
Uruguay ■, *S. Am.* ... **102** 32 30S 56 30W
Uruguay →, *S. Am.* .. **102** 34 12S 58 18W
Ürümqi, *China* .... **60** 43 45N 87 45 E
Usk →, *U.K.* **17** 51 37N 2 56W
Üsküdar, *Turk.* .... **47** 41 0N 29 5 E
Usselby, *U.K.* **19** 53 25N 0 21W
Ust-Kamenogorsk, *U.S.S.R.* .... **48** 50 0N 82 36 E
Ust Urt Plateau, *U.S.S.R.* .... **48** 44 0N 55 0 E
* Ustinov, *U.S.S.R.* .... **46** 56 51N 53 14 E
Utah □, *U.S.A.* **90** 39 30N 111 30W
Utica, *U.S.A.* **93** 43 5N 75 18W
Utrecht, *Neth.* .... **36** 52 5N 5 8 E
Utsunomiya, *Jap.* .... **62** 36 30N 139 50 E
Uttar Pradesh □, *India* **58** 27 0N 80 0 E
Uttoxeter, *U.K.* **18** 52 53N 1 50W
Uzbekistan □, *U.S.S.R.* **48** 41 30N 65 0 E

V

Vaasa, *Fin.* .... **44** 63 6N 21 38 E
Vadodara, *India* ...... **58** 22 20N 73 10 E
Vadsø, *Nor.* .... **44** 70 3N 29 50 E
Val d'Or, *Canada* **92** 48 7N 77 47W
Valdez, *U.S.A.* **88** 61 14N 146 17W
Valdivia, *Chile* **102** 39 50S 73 14W
Valence, *Fr.* .... **35** 44 57N 4 54 E
Valencia, *Sp.* **37** 39 27N 0 23W
Valencia, *Ven.* **100** 10 11N 68 0W
Valenciennes, *Fr.* ..... **34** 50 20N 3 34 E
Valentia Hr., *Ire.* **25** 51 56N 10 17W
Valentia I., *Ire.* **25** 51 54N 10 22W
Valladolid, *Sp.* **37** 41 38N 4 43W
Valledupar, *Col.* **100** 10 29N 73 15W
Valletta, *Malta* .... **40** 35 54N 14 30 E
Valley, *U.K.* **17** 53 17N 4 31W

Valparaíso, *Chile* **102** 33 2S 71 40W
Van, L., *Turk.* .... **47** 38 30N 43 0 E
Van Diemen G., *Austral.* **66** 11 45S 132 0 E
Vancouver, *Canada* ... **88** 49 15N 123 10W
Vancouver I., *Canada* . **88** 49 50N 126 0W
Vänern, *Swed.* .... **45** 58 47N 13 30 E
Vanua Levu, *Fiji* ..... **64** 16 33S 179 15 E
Vanuatu ■, *Pac. Oc.* .. **64** 15 0S 168 0 E
Varanasi, *India* ...... **59** 25 22N 83 0 E
Varangar Fjord, *Nor.* .. **44** 70 3N 29 25 E
Vardar →, *Yug.* ..... **41** 40 35N 22 50 E
Värmlands län □, *Swed.* **45** 60 0N 13 20 E
Varna, *Bulg.* .... **41** 43 13N 27 56 E
Västerås, *Swed.* ...... **45** 59 37N 16 38 E
Västmanlands län □, *Swed.* .... **45** 59 45N 16 20 E
Vatnajökull, *Ice.* **44** 64 30N 16 48W
Vättern, *Swed.* .... **45** 58 25N 14 30 E
Växjö, *Swed.* .... **45** 56 52N 14 50 E
Vendée □, *Fr.* **34** 46 50N 1 35W
Venezuela ■, *S. Am.* .. **100** 8 0N 65 0W
Venice, *It.* .... **40** 45 27N 12 20 E
Venlo, *Neth.* .... **36** 51 22N 6 11 E
Ventnor, *U.K.* **14** 50 35N 1 12W
Veracruz, *Mex.* **94** 19 10N 96 10W
Vercelli, *It.* .... **40** 45 19N 8 25 E
Vereeniging, *S. Afr.* ... **81** 26 38S 27 57 E
Verkhoyansk, *U.S.S.R.* **49** 67 35N 133 25 E
Verkhoyansk Ra., *U.S.S.R.* .... **49** 66 0N 129 0 E
Vermont □, *U.S.A.* ... **93** 43 40N 72 50W
Verona, *It.* .... **40** 45 27N 11 0 E
Versailles, *Fr.* .... **34** 48 48N 2 8 E
Verviers, *Belg.* .... **36** 50 37N 5 52 E
Verwood, *U.K.* **14** 50 53N 1 53W
Veryan, *U.K.* **16** 50 13N 4 56W
Veryan Bay, *U.K.* **16** 50 12N 4 51W
Vestmannaeyjar, *Ice.* . **44** 63 27N 20 15W
Vesuvius, Mt., *It.* ..... **40** 40 50N 14 22 E
Viborg, *Den.* .... **45** 56 27N 9 23 E
Vickerstown, *U.K.* **18** 54 8N 3 17W
Victoria, *Canada* **88** 48 30N 123 25W
Victoria □, *Austral.* ... **70** 37 0S 144 0 E
Victoria →, *Austral.* .. **66** 15 10S 129 40 E
Victoria, L., *Austral.* ... **70** 33 57S 141 15 E
Victoria, L., *E. Afr.* .... **80** 1 0S 33 0 E
Victoria Falls, *Zimb.* .. **81** 17 58S 25 52 E
Victoria I., *Canada* ... **88** 71 0N 111 0W
Victoria Ld., *Ant.* ..... **103** 75 0S 160 0 E
Vienna, *Austria* ...... **42** 48 12N 16 22 E
Vientiane, *Laos* ...... **51** 17 58N 102 36 E
Vietnam ■, *Asia* ..... **63** 19 0N 106 0 E
Vigo, *Sp.* **37** 42 12N 8 41W
Vijayawada, *India* .... **59** 16 31N 80 39 E
Villahermosa, *Mex.* ... **94** 17 59N 92 55W
Villefranche-sur-Saône, *Fr.* .... **35** 45 59N 4 43 E
Vilnius, *Lithuania* ...... **46** 54 38N 25 19 E
Vilyuysk, *U.S.S.R.* .... **49** 63 40N 121 35 E
Viña del Mar, *Chile* ... **102** 33 0S 71 30W
Vineland, *U.S.A.* **93** 39 30N 75 0W
Vinnitsa, *U.S.S.R.* .... **47** 49 15N 28 30 E
Virgin Is., *W. Ind.* **95** 18 40N 64 30W
Virginia □, *U.S.A.* **91** 37 45N 78 0W
Viscount Melville Sd., *Canada* **88** 74 10N 108 0W
Vishakhapatnam, *India* **59** 17 45N 83 20 E
Vistula = Wisła →, *Pol.* .... **43** 54 22N 18 55 E
Vitebsk, *U.S.S.R.* .... **46** 55 10N 30 15 E
Viterbo, *It.* .... **40** 42 25N 12 8 E
Viti Levu, *Fiji* .... **64** 17 30S 177 30 E
Vitim →, *U.S.S.R.* ... **49** 59 26N 112 34 E
Vitória, *Brazil* **101** 20 20S 40 22W
Vitoria, *Sp.* **37** 42 50N 2 41W
Vitória da Conquista, *Brazil* **101** 14 51S 40 51W
Vlaardingen, *Neth.* ... **36** 51 55N 4 21 E
Vladikavkaz, *U.S.S.R.* . **47** 43 0N 44 35 E
Vladimir, *U.S.S.R.* ... **46** 56 15N 40 30 E
Vladivostok, *U.S.S.R.* . **49** 43 10N 131 53 E
Vlissingen, *Neth.* .... **36** 51 26N 3 34 E
Vlórë, *Alb.* .... **41** 40 32N 19 28 E
Voil, L., *U.K.* **20** 56 20N 4 25W
Volga →, *U.S.S.R.* ... **47** 48 30N 46 0 E
Volga Hts., *U.S.S.R.* .. **47** 51 0N 46 0 E
Volgograd, *U.S.S.R.* .. **47** 48 40N 44 25 E
Vologda, *U.S.S.R.* .... **46** 59 10N 40 0 E
Vólos, *Greece* .... **41** 39 24N 22 59 E
Volta, L., *Ghana* ..... **78** 7 30N 0 15 E
Volta Redonda, *Brazil* . **101** 22 31S 44 5W
Volzhskiy, *U.S.S.R.* ... **47** 48 56N 44 46 E
Voorburg, *Neth.* ..... **36** 52 5N 4 24 E
Vorkuta, *U.S.S.R.* .... **46** 67 48N 64 20 E
Voronezh, *U.S.S.R.* ... **46** 51 40N 0 E
Voroshilovgrad = Lugansk, *U.S.S.R.* .... **47** 48 38N 39 15 E
Vosges, *Fr.* .... **34** 48 20N 7 10 E
Vryburg, *S. Afr.* ...... **81** 26 55S 24 45 E
Vyrnwy, L., *U.K.* **17** 52 48N 3 30W

W

Waal →, *Neth.* ...... **36** 51 59N 4 30 E
Wabash →, *U.S.A.* .. **92** 37 46N 88 2W
Waco, *U.S.A.* **91** 31 33N 97 5W
Wâd Medanî, *Sudan* .. **79** 14 28N 33 30 E
Waddenzee, *Neth.* ... **36** 53 6N 5 10 E
Waddesdon, *U.K.* **15** 51 50N 0 54W

* Renamed Dobrich

* Renamed Chuuk

* Renamed Izhevsk

Waddingham, U.K. 19 53 28N 0 31W
Waddington, U.K. 19 53 10N 0 31W
Waddington, Mt., Canada 88 51 23N 125 15W
Wadebridge, U.K. 16 50 31N 4 51W
Wadhurst, U.K. 15 51 3N 0 21 E
Wagga Wagga, Austral. 70 35 7S 147 24 E
Wagin, Austral. 66 33 17S 117 25 E
Wainfleet All Saints, U.K. 19 53 7N 0 16 E
Waipara, N.Z. 71 43 3S 172 46 E
Waitaki →, N.Z. 71 44 56S 171 7 E
Wakatipu, L., N.Z. 71 45 5S 168 33 E
Wakayama, Jap. 62 34 15N 135 15 E
Wakefield, U.K. 19 53 41N 1 31W
Walberswick, U.K. 15 52 18N 1 39 E
Wałbrzych, Pol. 42 50 45N 16 18 E
Walbury Hill, U.K. 14 51 22N 1 28W
Waldron, U.K. 15 50 56N 0 13 E
Wales □, U.K. 17 52 30N 3 30W
Walgett, Austral. 67 30 0S 148 5 E
Wallachia, Rom. 43 44 35N 25 0 E
Wallasey, U.K. 18 53 26N 3 2W
Wallingford, U.K. 14 51 40N 1 15W
Wallis & Futuna, Pac. Oc. 64 13 18S 176 10W
Wallsend, U.K. 19 54 59N 1 30W
Walmer, U.K. 15 51 12N 1 23 E
Walney, Isle of, U.K. 18 54 5N 3 15W
Walpole, U.K. 15 52 44N 0 13 E
Walsall, U.K. 14 52 36N 1 59W
Walsoken, U.K. 15 52 41N 0 12 E
Waltham, U.K. 19 53 32N 0 6W
Waltham Abbey, U.K. 15 51 40N 0 1 E
Waltham Forest, U.K. 15 51 37N 0 2 E
Waltham on the Wolds, U.K. 15 52 49N 0 48W
Walton-on-the-Naze, U.K. 15 51 52N 1 17 E
Walvis Bay, S. Afr. 81 23 0S 14 28 E
Wanborough, U.K. 14 51 33N 1 40W
Wandsworth, U.K. 15 51 28N 0 15W
Wanganui, N.Z. 71 39 56S 175 3 E
Wangaratta, Austral. 70 36 21S 146 19 E
Wansbeck, U.K. 21 55 12N 1 28W
Wantage, U.K. 14 51 35N 1 25W
Warboys, U.K. 15 52 25N 0 5W
Warburton →, Austral. 67 28 4S 137 28 E
Wardington, U.K. 14 52 8N 1 17W
Wardle, U.K. 18 53 7N 2 35W
Ward's Stone, U.K. 18 54 2N 2 39W
Ware, U.K. 15 51 48N 0 2W
Wareham, U.K. 14 50 41N 2 8W
Wark, U.K. 21 55 5N 2 14W
Warkworth, U.K. 21 55 22N 1 38W
Warley, U.K. 14 52 30N 2 0W
Warminster, U.K. 14 51 12N 2 11W
Warracknabeal, Austral. 70 36 9S 142 26 E
Warrego →, Austral. 67 30 24S 145 21 E
Warrenpoint, U.K. 24 54 7N 6 15W
Warrington, U.K. 18 53 25N 2 38W
Warrnambool, Austral. 70 38 25S 142 30 E
Warsaw, Pol. 43 52 13N 21 0 E
Warsop, U.K. 19 53 13N 1 9W
Warta →, Pol. 42 52 35N 14 39 E
Warthe = Warta →, Pol. 43 52 35N 14 39 E
Warwick, Austral. 67 28 10S 152 1 E
Warwick, U.K. 14 52 17N 1 36W
Warwick □, U.K. 14 52 20N 1 30W
Wasatch Ra., U.S.A. 90 40 30N 111 15W
Wash, The, U.K. 19 52 58N 0 20 E
Washford, U.K. 14 51 9N 3 22W
Washington, U.K. 21 54 55N 1 30W
Washington, U.S.A. 92 38 52N 77 0W
Washington □, U.S.A. 90 47 45N 120 30W
Wast Water, L., U.K. 18 54 26N 3 18W
Watchet, U.K. 14 51 10N 3 20W
Waterbeach, U.K. 15 52 16N 0 11 E
Waterbury, U.S.A. 93 41 32N 73 0W
Waterford, Ire. 25 52 16N 7 8W
Waterford □, Ire. 25 52 10N 7 40W
Waterford Harb., Ire. 25 52 10N 6 58W
Watergate Bay, U.K. 16 50 26N 5 4W
Waterloo, U.K. 18 53 29N 3 2W
Watford, U.K. 15 51 38N 0 23W
Wath, U.K. 19 53 29N 1 20W
Watlington, Norfolk, U.K. 15 52 40N 0 24 E
Watlington, Oxon., U.K. 15 51 38N 1 0W
Watton, U.K. 15 52 35N 0 50 E
Waveney →, U.K. 15 52 24N 1 20 E
Waver →, U.K. 18 54 50N 3 15W
Weald, The, U.K. 15 51 7N 0 9 E
Wear →, U.K. 19 54 55N 1 22W
Weardale, U.K. 18 54 44N 2 5W
Wearhead, U.K. 18 54 45N 2 14W
Weaver →, U.K. 18 53 17N 2 35W
Weaverham, U.K. 18 53 15N 2 30W
Weddell Sea, Ant. 103 72 30S 40 0W
Wedmore, U.K. 14 51 14N 2 50W
Wednesbury, U.K. 14 52 33N 2 1W
Wednesfield, U.K. 14 52 36N 2 3W
Weedon Bec, U.K. 14 52 14N 1 6W
Weifang, China 61 36 47N 119 10 E
Weldon, U.K. 21 55 16N 1 46W
Welford, Berks., U.K. 14 51 28N 1 24W
Welford, Northants., U.K. 14 52 26N 1 5W
Welkom, S. Afr. 81 28 0S 26 50 E
Welland →, U.K. 15 52 43N 0 10W
Wellesley Is., Austral. 67 16 42S 139 30 E
Wellingborough, U.K. 15 52 18N 0 41W
Wellington, Austral. 70 32 35S 148 59 E
Wellington, N.Z. 71 41 19S 174 46 E
Wellington, Salop, U.K. 14 52 42N 2 31W
Wellington, Somerset, U.K. 14 50 58N 3 13W
Wellow, U.K. 14 51 20N 2 22W
Wells, Norfolk, U.K. 15 52 57N 0 51 E
Wells, Somerset, U.K. 14 51 12N 2 39W
Welney, U.K. 15 52 31N 0 15 E
Wels, Austria 42 48 9N 14 1 E
Welshpool, U.K. 17 52 40N 3 9W
Welton, U.K. 19 53 19N 0 29W
Welwyn Garden City, U.K. 15 51 49N 0 11W
Wem, U.K. 14 52 52N 2 45W
Wembury, U.K. 16 50 19N 4 6W
Wemyss Bay, U.K. 20 55 52N 4 54W
Wendover, U.K. 15 51 46N 0 45W
Wenhaston, U.K. 15 52 17N 1 35 E
Wenlock Edge, U.K. 14 52 30N 2 43W
Wensleydale, U.K. 18 54 18N 2 0W
Wensum →, U.K. 15 52 35N 1 20 E
Wenzhou, China 61 28 0N 120 38 E
Weobley, U.K. 14 52 9N 2 52W
Werribee, Austral. 70 37 54S 144 40 E
Werrington, U.K. 16 50 40N 4 22W
Weser →, Ger. 42 53 33N 8 30 E
West Auckland, U.K. 19 54 38N 1 42W
West Bengal □, India 59 23 0N 88 0 E
West Bridgford, U.K. 19 52 56N 1 8W
West Bromwich, U.K. 14 52 32N 2 1W
West Calder, U.K. 21 55 51N 3 34W
West Coker, U.K. 14 50 55N 2 40W
West Fen, U.K. 19 53 5N 0 5W
West Germany = Germany ■, Europe 42 52 0N 10 0 E
West Glamorgan □, U.K. 17 51 40N 3 55W
West Grinstead, U.K. 15 50 58N 0 19W
West Haddon, U.K. 14 52 21N 1 5W
West Kilbride, U.K. 20 55 41N 4 50W
West Kirby, U.K. 18 53 22N 3 11W
West Linton, U.K. 21 55 45N 3 24W
West Lulworth, U.K. 14 50 37N 2 14W
West Malling, U.K. 15 51 16N 0 25 E
West Meon, U.K. 14 51 2N 1 3W
West Mersea, U.K. 15 51 46N 0 55 E
West Midlands □, U.K. 14 52 30N 1 55W
West Moors, U.K. 14 50 49N 1 50W
West Parley, U.K. 14 50 46N 1 52W
West Rasen, U.K. 19 53 23N 0 23W
West Schelde →, Neth. 36 51 23N 3 50 E
West Siberian Plain, U.S.S.R. 48 62 0N 75 0 E
West Sussex □, U.K. 15 50 55N 0 30W
West Tarbert, L., U.K. 20 55 58N 5 30W
West Virginia □, U.S.A. 92 39 0N 81 0W
West Wyalong, Austral. 70 33 56S 147 10 E
West Yorkshire □, U.K. 19 53 45N 1 40W
Westbourne, U.K. 15 50 53N 0 55W
Westbury, Salop, U.K. 14 52 40N 2 57W
Westbury, Wilts., U.K. 14 51 16N 2 11W
Westbury-on-Severn, U.K. 14 51 49N 2 24W
Westerham, U.K. 15 51 16N 0 5 E
Western Australia □, Austral. 66 25 0S 118 0 E
Western Ghats, India 58 14 0N 75 0 E
Western Isles □, U.K. 22 57 30N 7 10W
Western Sahara ■, Africa 78 25 0N 13 0W
Western Samoa ■, Pac. Oc. 64 14 0S 172 0W
Westfield, U.K. 15 50 53N 0 30 E
Westhoughton, U.K. 18 53 34N 2 30W
Westland Bight, N.Z. 71 42 55S 170 5 E
Westmeath □, Ire. 24 53 30N 7 30W
Weston, U.K. 14 52 51N 2 2W
Weston-super-Mare, U.K. 14 51 20N 2 59W
Westport, Ire. 24 53 44N 9 31W
Westport, N.Z. 71 41 46S 171 37 E
Westray, U.K. 23 59 18N 3 0W
Westruther, U.K. 21 55 45N 2 34W
Westward Ho!, U.K. 16 51 2N 4 16W
Wetherby, U.K. 19 53 56N 1 23W
Wetwang, U.K. 19 54 2N 0 35W
Wexford, Ire. 25 52 20N 6 28W
Wexford □, Ire. 25 52 20N 6 25W
Wexford Harb., Ire. 25 52 20N 6 25W
Wey →, U.K. 15 51 19N 0 29W
Weybourne, U.K. 15 52 57N 1 9 E
Weybridge, U.K. 15 51 22N 0 28W
Weymouth, U.K. 14 50 36N 2 28W
Whakatane, N.Z. 71 37 57S 177 1 E
Whaley Bridge, U.K. 18 53 20N 2 0W
Whalley, U.K. 18 53 49N 2 25W
Whalsay, U.K. 22 60 22N 1 0W
Whalton, U.K. 21 55 7N 1 46W
Whangarei, N.Z. 71 35 43S 174 21 E
Whaplode, U.K. 15 52 42N 0 3W
Wharfe →, U.K. 19 53 55N 1 30W
Wharfedale, U.K. 18 54 7N 2 4W
Whauphill, U.K. 20 54 48N 4 31W
Wheatley Hill, U.K. 19 54 45N 1 23W
Whernside, U.K. 18 54 14N 2 24W
Whichham, U.K. 18 54 14N 3 22W
Whimple, U.K. 16 50 46N 3 21W
Whipsnade, U.K. 15 51 51N 0 32W
Whissendine, U.K. 15 52 43N 0 46W
Whiston, U.K. 18 53 25N 2 45W
Whitburn, U.K. 21 55 52N 3 41W
Whitby, U.K. 19 54 29N 0 37W
Whitchurch, Devon, U.K. 16 50 31N 4 7W
Whitchurch, Hants., U.K. 14 51 14N 1 20W
Whitchurch, Hereford & Worcs., U.K. 14 51 51N 2 41W
Whitchurch, Salop, U.K. 18 52 58N 2 42W
White Esk →, U.K. 21 55 14N 3 11W
White Horse Hill, U.K. 14 51 35N 1 35W
White Nile →, Sudan 79 15 38N 32 31 E
White Russia □, U.S.S.R. 46 53 30N 27 0 E
White Sea, U.S.S.R. 46 66 30N 38 0 E
Whiteadder Water →, U.K. 21 55 47N 2 20W
Whitehaven, U.K. 18 54 33N 3 35W
Whitehead, U.K. 24 54 45N 5 42W
Whitehorse, Canada 88 60 43N 135 3W
Whitehorse, Vale of, U.K. 14 51 37N 1 30W
Whitekirk, U.K. 21 56 2N 2 36W
Whitesand B., U.K. 16 50 18N 4 20W
Whithorn, U.K. 20 54 44N 4 25W
Whitley Bay, U.K. 21 55 4N 1 28W
Whitney, Mt., U.S.A. 90 36 35N 118 14W
Whitstable, U.K. 15 51 21N 1 2 E
Whittington, Derby, U.K. 19 53 17N 1 26W
Whittington, Salop, U.K. 14 52 53N 3 0W
Whittlesey, U.K. 15 52 34N 0 8W
Whittlesford, U.K. 15 52 6N 0 9 E
Whitton, U.K. 19 53 42N 0 39W
Whitwell, Derby, U.K. 19 53 16N 1 11W
Whitwell, I. of W., U.K. 14 50 35N 1 19W
Whitwick, U.K. 14 52 45N 1 23W
Whitworth, U.K. 18 53 40N 2 11W
Whixley, U.K. 19 54 2N 1 19W
Whyalla, Austral. 67 33 2S 137 30 E
Wichita, U.S.A. 91 37 40N 97 20W
Wichita Falls, U.S.A. 90 33 57N 98 30W
Wick, U.K. 23 58 26N 3 5W
Wickford, U.K. 15 51 37N 0 31 E
Wickham, U.K. 14 50 54N 1 11W
Wickham Market, U.K. 15 52 9N 1 21 E
Wicklow, Ire. 25 53 0N 6 2W
Wicklow □, Ire. 25 52 59N 6 25W
Wicklow Mts., Ire. 25 53 0N 6 30W
Wickwar, U.K. 14 51 35N 2 23W
Widdrington, U.K. 21 55 15N 1 35W
Widecombe, U.K. 16 50 34N 3 48W
Widemouth, U.K. 16 50 45N 4 34W
Widnes, U.K. 18 53 22N 2 44W
Wiesbaden, Ger. 36 50 7N 8 17 E
Wigan, U.K. 18 53 33N 2 38W
Wight, I. of, U.K. 14 50 40N 1 20W
Wigmore, U.K. 14 52 19N 2 51W
Wigston, U.K. 14 52 35N 1 6W
Wigton, U.K. 18 54 50N 3 9W
Wigtown, U.K. 20 54 52N 4 27W
Wigtown B., U.K. 20 54 46N 4 15W
Wilhelm II Land, Ant. 103 68 0S 90 0 E
Wilhelmshaven, Ger. 42 53 30N 8 9 E
Wilkes Barre, U.S.A. 93 41 15N 75 52W
Wilkes Land, Ant. 103 69 0S 120 0 E
Willemstad, Cur. 94 12 5N 69 0W
Willenhall, U.K. 14 52 36N 2 3W
Willesborough, U.K. 15 51 8N 0 55 E
Williamstown, Austral. 70 37 51S 144 52 E
Willingdon, U.K. 15 50 47N 0 17 E
Williton, U.K. 14 51 9N 3 20W
Willoughby, U.K. 19 53 14N 0 12 E
Wilmington, U.K. 16 50 46N 3 8W
Wilmington, U.S.A. 93 39 45N 75 32W
Wilmslow, U.K. 18 53 19N 2 14W
Wilnecote, U.K. 14 52 36N 1 40W
Wilsons Promontory, Austral. 70 38 55S 146 25 E
Wilton, U.K. 14 51 5N 1 52W
Wiltshire □, U.K. 14 51 20N 2 0W
Wimblington, U.K. 15 52 31N 0 5 E
Wimborne Minster, U.K. 14 50 48N 2 0W
Wimmera →, Austral. 70 36 8S 141 56 E
Wincanton, U.K. 14 51 3N 2 24W
Winchelsea, U.K. 15 50 55N 0 43 E
Winchester, U.K. 14 51 4N 1 19W
Windermere, U.K. 18 54 24N 2 56W
Windermere, L., U.K. 18 54 20N 2 57W
Windhoek, Nam. 81 22 35S 17 4 E
Windrush →, U.K. 14 51 48N 1 35W
Windsor, Canada 92 42 18N 83 0W
Windsor, U.K. 15 51 28N 0 36W
Windward Passage, W. Ind. 95 20 0N 74 0W
Windygates, U.K. 21 56 12N 3 1W
Wing, U.K. 15 51 54N 0 41W
Wingham, Austral. 70 31 48S 152 22 E
Wingham, U.K. 15 51 16N 1 12 E
Winkleigh, U.K. 16 50 49N 3 57W
Winnipeg, Canada 88 49 54N 97 9W
Winnipeg, L., Canada 88 52 0N 97 0W
Winsford, U.K. 18 53 12N 2 31W
Winslow, U.K. 15 51 57N 0 52W
Winster, U.K. 19 53 9N 1 42W
Winston-Salem, U.S.A. 91 36 7N 80 15W
Winterborne Abbas, U.K. 14 50 43N 2 30W
Winterthur, Switz. 42 47 30N 8 44 E
Winterton, Humberside, U.K. 19 53 39N 0 37W
Winterton, Norfolk, U.K. 15 52 43N 1 43 E
Wirksworth, U.K. 19 53 5N 1 34W
Wirral, U.K. 18 53 25N 3 0W
Wisbech, U.K. 15 52 39N 0 10 E
Wisborough Green, U.K. 15 51 2N 0 30W
Wisconsin □, U.S.A. 92 44 30N 90 0W
Wishaw, U.K. 21 55 46N 3 55W
Wiske →, U.K. 19 54 26N 1 27W
Wisła →, Pol. 43 54 22N 18 55 E
Witbank, S. Afr. 81 25 51S 29 14 E
Witham, U.K. 15 51 48N 0 39 E
Witham →, U.K. 19 53 3N 0 8W
Withern, U.K. 19 53 19N 0 9 E
Withernsea, U.K. 19 53 43N 0 2 E
Witley, U.K. 15 51 9N 0 39W
Witney, U.K. 14 51 47N 1 29W
Witten, Ger. 36 51 26N 7 19 E
Wittersham, U.K. 15 51 1N 0 42 E
Wiveliscombe, U.K. 14 51 2N 3 20W
Wivenhoe, U.K. 15 51 51N 0 59 E
Włocławek, Pol. 43 52 40N 19 3 E
Woburn, U.K. 15 51 59N 0 37W
Woburn Sands, U.K. 15 52 1N 0 38W
Wodonga, Austral. 70 36 5S 146 50 E
Woking, U.K. 15 51 18N 0 33W
Wokingham, U.K. 15 51 25N 0 50W
Wolf Rock, U.K. 16 49 56N 5 50W
Wolfsburg, Ger. 42 52 27N 10 49 E
Wollongong, Austral. 70 34 25S 150 54 E
Wolsingham, U.K. 18 54 44N 1 52W
Wolverhampton, U.K. 14 52 35N 2 6W
Wolverton, U.K. 15 52 3N 0 48W
Wolviston, U.K. 19 54 39N 1 25W
Wombwell, U.K. 19 53 31N 1 23W
Wŏnsan, N. Kor. 61 39 11N 127 27 E
Wonston, U.K. 14 51 9N 1 18W
Woodbridge, U.K. 15 52 6N 1 19 E
Woodbury, U.K. 16 50 40N 3 24W
Woodhall Spa, U.K. 19 53 10N 0 12W
Woodhouse, U.K. 19 53 23N 1 21W
Woodley, U.K. 15 51 26N 0 54W
Woods, L. of the, Canada 88 49 15N 94 45W
Woodstock, U.K. 14 51 51N 1 20W
Wookey, U.K. 14 51 13N 2 41W
Wookey Hole, U.K. 14 51 13N 2 41W
Wool, U.K. 14 50 41N 2 13W
Woolacombe, U.K. 16 51 10N 4 12W
Wooler, U.K. 21 55 33N 2 0W
Wootton Bassett, U.K. 14 51 32N 1 55W
Wootton Wawen, U.K. 14 52 16N 1 47W
Worcester, S. Afr. 81 33 39S 19 27 E
Worcester, U.K. 14 52 12N 2 12W
Worcester, U.S.A. 93 42 14N 71 49W
Worfield, U.K. 14 52 34N 2 22W
Workington, U.K. 18 54 39N 3 34W
Worksop, U.K. 19 53 19N 1 9W
Wormit, U.K. 21 56 26N 2 59W
Worms, Ger. 42 49 37N 8 21 E
Worplesdon, U.K. 15 51 16N 0 36W
Wortham, U.K. 15 52 22N 1 3 E
Worthing, U.K. 15 50 49N 0 21W
Wotton-under-Edge, U.K. 14 51 37N 2 20W
Woy Woy, Austral. 70 33 30S 151 19 E
Wragby, U.K. 19 53 17N 0 18W
Wrangel I., U.S.S.R. 49 71 0N 180 0 E
Wrangle, U.K. 19 53 3N 0 9 E
Wrath, C., U.K. 22 58 38N 5 0W
Wrekin, The, U.K. 14 52 41N 2 35W
Wrentham, U.K. 15 52 24N 1 39 E
Wrexham, U.K. 17 53 5N 3 0W
Writtle, U.K. 15 51 44N 0 27 E
Wrocław, Pol. 43 51 5N 17 5 E
Wrotham, U.K. 15 51 18N 0 20 E
Wroughton, U.K. 14 51 31N 1 47W
Wroxham, U.K. 15 52 42N 1 23 E
Wuhan, China 61 30 31N 114 18 E
Wuhu, China 61 31 22N 118 21 E
Wuppertal, Ger. 36 51 15N 7 8 E
Würzburg, Ger. 42 49 46N 9 55 E
Wutongqiao, China 60 29 22N 103 50 E
Wuxi, China 61 31 30N 120 30 E
Wuzhou, China 61 23 30N 111 18 E
Wye, U.K. 15 51 11N 0 56 E
Wye →, U.K. 14 51 36N 2 40W
Wylye →, U.K. 14 51 8N 1 53W
Wymondham, Leics., U.K. 15 52 45N 0 42W
Wymondham, Norfolk, U.K. 15 52 34N 1 7 E
Wyndham, Austral. 66 15 33S 128 3 E
Wyoming □, U.S.A. 90 42 48N 109 0W
Wyre →, U.K. 18 53 52N 2 57W
Wyre Forest, U.K. 14 52 24N 2 24W

X

Xiaguan, China 60 25 32N 100 16 E
Xiamen, China 61 24 25N 118 4 E
Xiangfan, China 61 32 2N 112 8 E
Xiangtan, China 61 27 51N 112 54 E
Xiangyang, China 61 32 1N 112 8 E
Xingu →, Brazil 101 1 30S 51 53W
Xining, China 60 36 34N 101 40 E
Xinjiang Uygur Zizhiqu □, China 60 42 0N 86 0 E
Xuzhou, China 61 34 18N 117 10 E

Y

Yablonovy Ra., *U.S.S.R.* 49 53 0N 114 0 E
Yakut A.S.S.R. □, *U.S.S.R.* 49 62 0N 130 0 E
Yakutsk, *U.S.S.R.* 49 62 5N 129 50 E
Yamagata, *Jap.* 62 38 15N 140 15 E
Yamal, Peninsula, *U.S.S.R.* 48 71 0N 70 0 E
Yambol, *Bulg.* 41 42 30N 26 36 E
Yamuna →, *India* 59 25 30N 81 53 E
Yangtze →, *China* 60 31 40N 122 0 E
Yanji, *China* 61 42 59N 129 30 E
Yantai, *China* 61 37 34N 121 22 E
Yaoundé, *Cam.* 80 3 50N 11 35 E
Yarcombe, *U.K.* 16 50 51N 3 6W
Yare →, *U.K.* 15 52 36N 1 28 E
Yarm, *U.K.* 19 54 31N 1 21W
Yarmouth, *U.K.* 14 50 42N 1 29W
Yaroslavl, *U.S.S.R.* 46 57 35N 39 55 E
Yarrow, *U.K.* 21 55 32N 3 0W
Yate, *U.K.* 14 51 32N 2 26W
Yatsushiro, *Jap.* 62 32 30N 130 40 E
Yatton, *U.K.* 14 51 23N 2 50W
Yaxley, *U.K.* 15 52 31N 0 14W
Yazd, *Iran* 56 31 55N 54 27 E
Yealmpton, *U.K.* 16 50 21N 4 0W
Yekaterinburg, *U.S.S.R.* 46 56 50N 60 30 E
Yelizavetgrad, *U.S.S.R.* 47 48 35N 32 20 E
Yell, *U.K.* 22 60 35N 1 5W
Yell Sd., *U.K.* 22 60 33N 1 15W
Yellow Sea, *China* 61 35 0N 123 0 E
Yellowknife, *Canada* 88 62 27N 114 29W
Yellowstone →, *U.S.A.* 90 47 58N 103 59W
Yellowstone National Park, *U.S.A.* 90 44 35N 110 0W
Yemen ■, *Si. Arab.* 56 15 0N 44 0 E
Yenisey →, *U.S.S.R.* 48 71 50N 82 40 E
Yeo →, *U.K.* 14 51 10N 3 0W
Yeovil, *U.K.* 14 50 57N 2 38W
Yerevan, *U.S.S.R.* 47 40 10N 44 31 E
Yes Tor, *U.K.* 16 50 41N 3 59W
Yibin, *China* 60 28 45N 104 32 E
Yichang, *China* 61 30 40N 111 20 E
Yichuan, *China* 60 36 2N 110 10 E
Yining, *China* 60 43 58N 81 10 E
Yogyakarta, *Indon.* 63 7 49S 110 22 E
Yokkaichi, *Jap.* 62 35 0N 136 38 E
Yokohama, *Jap.* 62 35 27N 139 28 E
Yokosuka, *Jap.* 62 35 20N 139 40 E
Yonkers, *U.S.A.* 93 40 57N 73 51W
York, *U.K.* 19 53 58N 1 7W
York, *U.S.A.* 92 39 57N 76 43W
York, Vale of, *U.K.* 19 54 15N 1 25W
Yorkshire Wolds, *U.K.* 19 54 0N 0 30W
Yosemite National Park, *U.S.A.* 90 38 0N 119 30W
Yoshkar Ola, *U.S.S.R.* 46 56 38N 47 55 E
Youghal, *Ire.* 25 51 58N 7 51W
Youghal B., *Ire.* 25 51 55N 7 50W
Youlgreave, *U.K.* 19 53 12N 1 50W
Youngstown, *U.S.A.* 92 41 7N 80 41W
Yoxall, *U.K.* 14 52 45N 1 49W
Yoxford, *U.K.* 15 52 16N 1 30 E
Ypres, *Belg.* 36 50 51N 2 53 E
Ystalyfera, *U.K.* 17 51 46N 3 48W
Ythan →, *U.K.* 23 57 26N 2 0W
Yuan Jiang →, *China* 61 28 55N 111 50 E
Yucatán, Península de, *Mex.* 94 19 30N 89 0W
Yucatan Str., *Carib.* 94 22 0N 86 30W
Yugoslavia ■, *Europe* 41 44 0N 20 0 E
Yukon →, *N. Am.* 88 65 30N 150 0W
Yukon Territory □, *Canada* 88 63 0N 135 0W
Yunnan □, *China* 60 25 0N 102 30 E
Yuzhno-Sakhalinsk, *U.S.S.R.* 49 46 58N 142 45 E

Z

Zaandam, *Neth.* 36 52 26N 4 49 E
Zabrze, *Pol.* 43 50 18N 18 50 E
* Zagorsk, *U.S.S.R.* 46 56 20N 38 10 E
Zagreb, *Yug.* 40 45 50N 16 0 E
Zagros Mts., *Iran* 56 33 45N 47 0 E
Zahlah, *Leb.* 57 33 52N 35 50 E
Zaïre ■, *Africa* 80 3 0S 23 0 E
Zaïre →, *Africa* 80 6 4S 12 24 E

* *Renamed Sergiyev Posad*

Zákinthos, *Greece* 41 37 47N 20 57 E
Zambezi →, *Africa* 81 18 55S 36 4 E
Zambia ■, *Africa* 81 15 0S 28 0 E
Zamboanga, *Phil.* 63 6 59N 122 3 E
Zamora, *Sp.* 37 41 30N 5 45W
Zante = Zákinthos, *Greece* 41 37 47N 20 57 E
Zanzibar, *Tanz.* 80 6 12S 39 12 E
Zaporozhye, *U.S.S.R.* 47 47 50N 35 10 E
Zaragoza, *Sp.* 37 41 39N 0 53W
Zaria, *Nig.* 78 11 0N 7 40 E
Zeebrugge, *Belg.* 36 51 19N 3 12 E
Zeist, *Neth.* 36 52 5N 5 15 E
Zhangjiakou, *China* 61 40 48N 114 55 E
Zhangzhou, *China* 61 24 30N 117 35 E
Zhanjiang, *China* 61 21 15N 110 20 E
Zhejiang □, *China* 61 29 0N 120 0 E
Zhengzhou, *China* 61 34 45N 113 34 E
Zhitomir, *U.S.S.R.* 47 50 20N 28 40 E
Zibo, *China* 61 36 47N 118 3 E
Zielona Góra □, *Pol.* 42 51 57N 15 30 E
Zigong, *China* 60 29 15N 104 48 E
Ziguinchor, *Sene.* 78 12 35N 16 20W
Žilina, *Czech.* 43 49 12N 18 42 E
Zimbabwe ■, *Africa* 81 20 0S 30 0 E
Zion Nat. Park, *U.S.A.* 90 37 25N 112 50W
Zlatoust, *U.S.S.R.* 46 55 10N 59 40 E
Zonguldak, *Turk.* 47 41 28N 31 50 E
Zrenjanin, *Yug.* 41 45 22N 20 23 E
Zug, *Switz.* 42 47 10N 8 31 E

YUGOSLAVIA

Population 1981 census by ethnic group

Serbs	8,140,452
Croats	4,428,005
Moslems	1,999,957
Slovenes	1,753,554
Macedonians	1,339,729
Montenegrins	579,023
Albanians	1,730,364
Hungarians	426,866

Total Population (1990 est) 24,107,000

SLOVENIA
Population 1988 1,940,000
(Slovenes 90.5%)
Capital: Ljubljana

BOSNIA & HERZEGOVINA
Population 1988 4,440,000
(Moslems 39.5%, Serbs 32.0%, Croats 18.4%)
Capital: Sarajevo

SERBIA
Population 1988 9,760,000
(Serbs 66.4%)
Capital: Belgrade

CROATIA
Population 1988 4,680,000
(Croats 75.1%, Serbs 11.5%)
Capital: Zagreb

MONTENEGRO
Population 1988 632,000
(Montenegrins 68.5%, Moslems 13.4%)
Capital: Titograd

MACEDONIA
Population 1988 2,090,000
(Macedonians 67.0%, Albanians 19.7%)
Capital: Skoplje

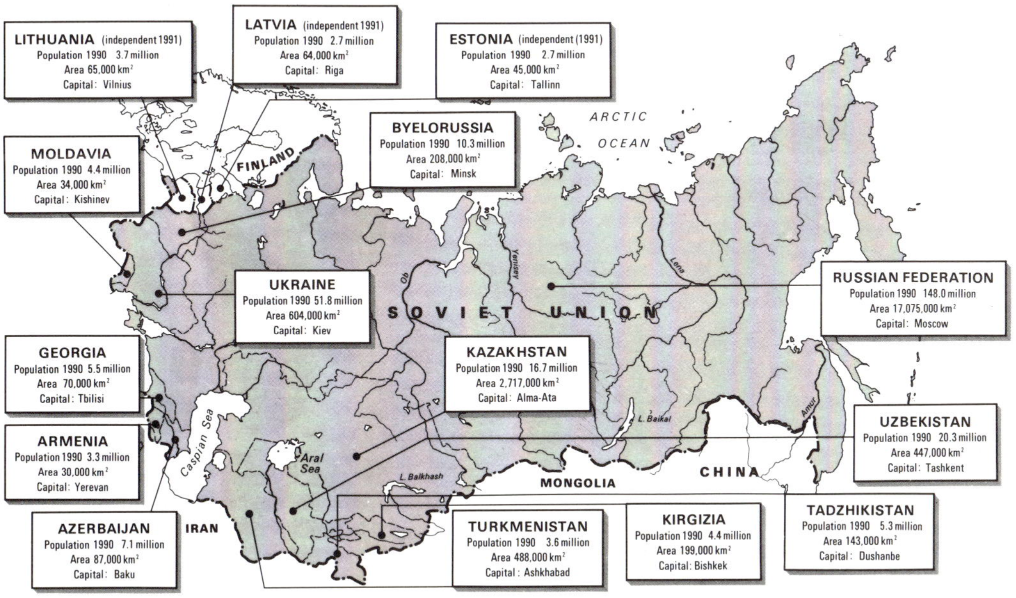

NATIONALITIES OF SOVIET UNION

Total population 1989 census 286.7 million

Russians	145.2million
Ukrainians	44.2million
Uzbeks	16.7million
Belorussians	10.0million
Kazakhs	8.1million
Azerbaijanians	6.8million
Tatars	6.6million
Armenians	4.6million
Georgians	4.0million
Moldavians	3.4million
Tajiks	3.2million
Lithuanians	3.0million
Turkmenians	2.7million
Kirghiz	2.5million
Germans	2.0million
Chuvashes	1.8million
Latvians	1.5million
Bashkirs	1.5million
Jews	1.4million
Mordovians	1.2million
Poles	1.1million
Estonians	1.0million

MAP PROJECTIONS

MAP PROJECTIONS

A map projection is the systematic depiction on a plane surface of the imaginary lines of latitude or longitude from a globe of the earth. This network of lines is called the graticule and forms the framework upon which an accurate depiction of the earth is made. The map graticule, which is the basis of any map, is constructed sometimes by graphical means, but often by using mathematical formulae to give the intersections of the graticule plotted as x and y co-ordinates. The choice between projections is based upon which properties the cartographer wishes the map to possess, the map scale and also the extent of the area to be mapped. Since the globe is three dimensional, it is not possible to depict its surface on a two dimensional plane without distortion. Preservation of one of the basic properties listed below can only be secured at the expense of the others and the choice of projection is often a compromise solution.

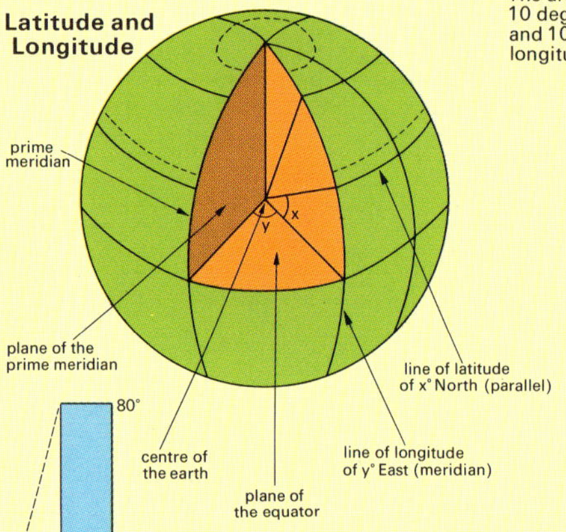

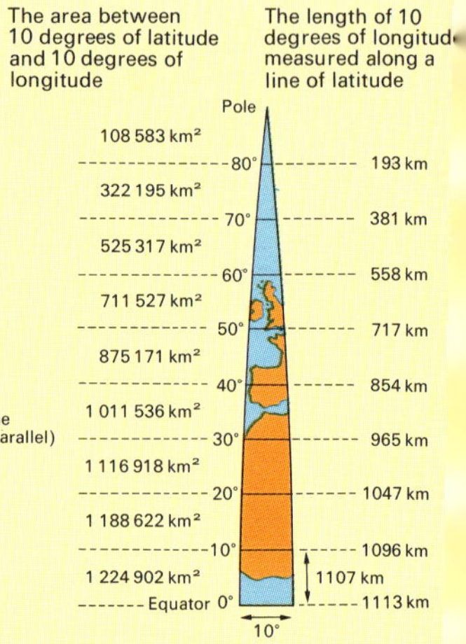

Correct Area

In these projections the areas from the globe are to scale on the map. For example, if you look at the diagram at the top right, areas of 10° x 10° are shown from the equator to the poles. The proportion of this area at the extremities are approximately 11:1. An equal area projection will retain that proportion in its portrayal of those areas. This is particularly useful in the mapping of densities and distributions. Projections with this property are termed **Equal Area, Equivalent or Homolographic.**

Correct Distance

In these projections the scale is correct along the meridians, or in the case of the Azimuthal Equidistant scale is true along any line drawn from the centre of the projection. They are called **Equidistant**.

Correct Shape

This property can only be true within small areas as it is achieved only by having a uniform scale distortion along both x and y axes of the projection. The projections are called **Conformal** or **Orthomorphic.**

In order to minimise the distortions at the edges of some projections, central portions of them are often selected for atlas maps. Below are listed some of the major types of projection.

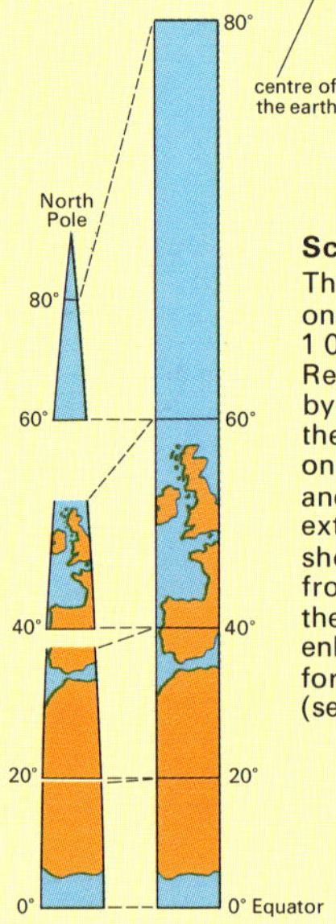

Scale Measurement

The **Representative Fraction** 1:1 000 000 means that 1 unit on the map represents 1 million on the earth. So 1 cm = 1 000 000 cm or 10 km. In SI units (the metric system) the Representative Fraction can be converted to the scale of 1 cm by moving the decimal point through five places, usually deleting the last five zeros thus :- 1: 20 000 000 – 1cm = 200 km. Scale on map projections can only be correct along specific meridians and parallels or from one or two specific points. To take an extreme example of scale distortion, the diagram on the left shows how a portion of the earth's surface, when unwrapped from around a globe (**a gore**) compares with the same area at the same equatorial scale but on Mercator's Projection. The enlargement of scale away from the equator is considerable and for this reason a variable scale for each line of latitude is given (see below).

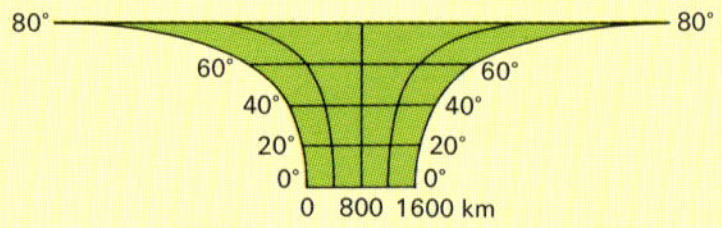

AZIMUTHAL OR ZENITHAL PROJECTIONS

These are constructed by the projection of part of the graticule from the globe onto a plane tangential to any single point on it. This plane may be tangential to the equator (**equatorial case**), the poles (**polar case**) or any other point (**oblique case**). Any straight line drawn from the point at which the plane touches the globe is the shortest distance from that point and is known as a **great circle**. In its **Gnomonic** construction *any* straight line on the map is a great circle, but there is great exaggeration towards the edges and this reduces its general uses. There are five different ways of transferring the graticule onto the plane and these are shown on the right. The central diagram below shows how the graticules vary, using the polar case as the example.

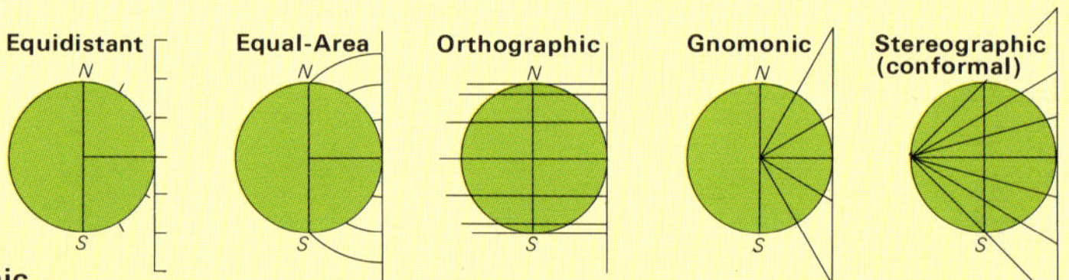

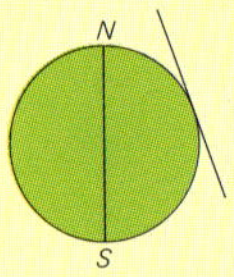

Oblique Case

The plane touches the globe at any point between the equator and poles. The oblique orthographic uses the distortion in azimuthal projections away from the centre to give a graphic depiction of the earth as seen from any desired point in space. It can also be used in both Polar and Equatorial cases. It is used not only for the earth but also for the moon and planets.

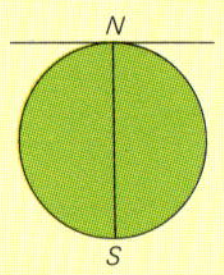

Polar Case

The polar case is the simplest to construct and the diagram below shows the differing effects of all five methods of construction comparing their coverage, distortion etc., using North America as the example.

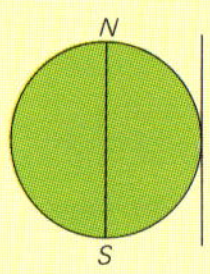

Equatorial Case

The example shown here is Lambert's Equivalent Azimuthal It is the only projection which is both equal area and where bearing is true from the centre.

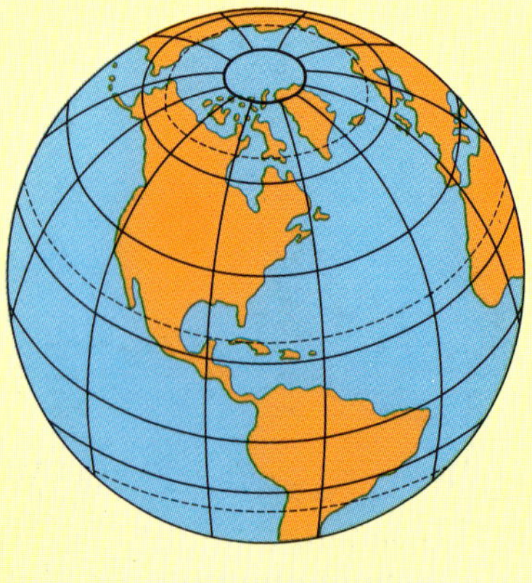

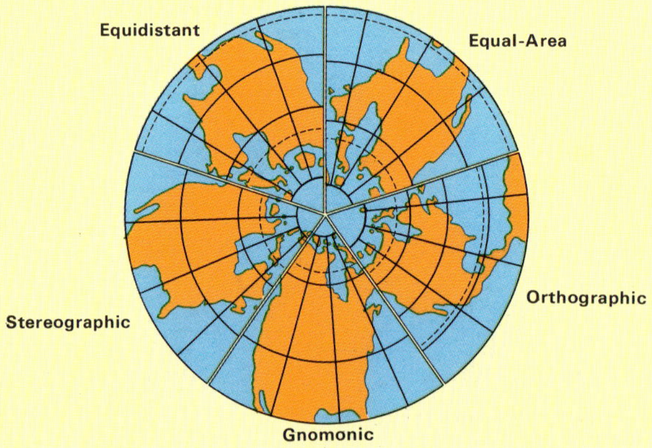

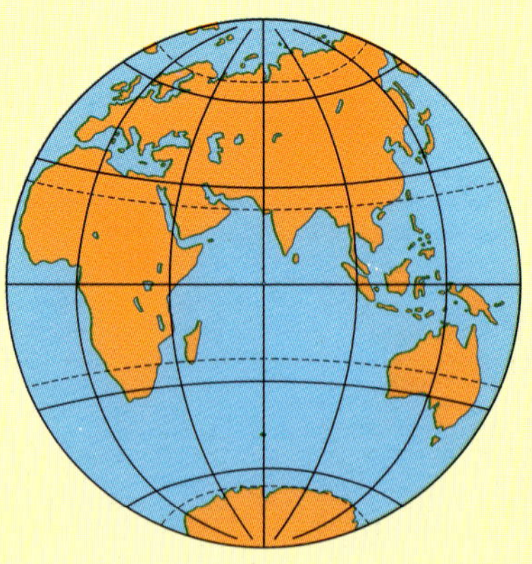

CONICAL PROJECTIONS

These use the projection of the graticule from the globe onto a cone which is tangential to a line of latitude (termed the **standard parallel**). This line is always an arc and scale is always true along it. Because of its method of construction it is used mainly for depicting the temperate latitudes around the standard parallel i.e. where there is least distortion. To reduce the distortion and include a larger range of latitudes, the projection may be constructed with the cone bisecting the surface of the globe so that there are two standard parallels each of which is true to scale. The distortion is thus spread more evenly between the two chosen parallels.

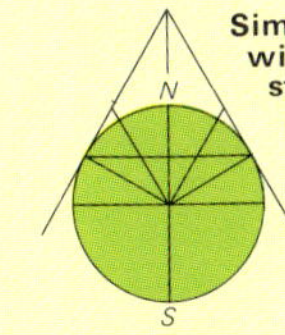

Simple Conical with one standard parallel

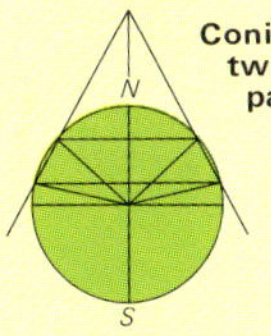

Conical with two standard parallels

Bonne

This is a modification of the simple conic whereby the true scale along the meridians is sacrificed to enable the accurate representation of areas. However scale is true along each parallel but shapes are distorted at the edges.

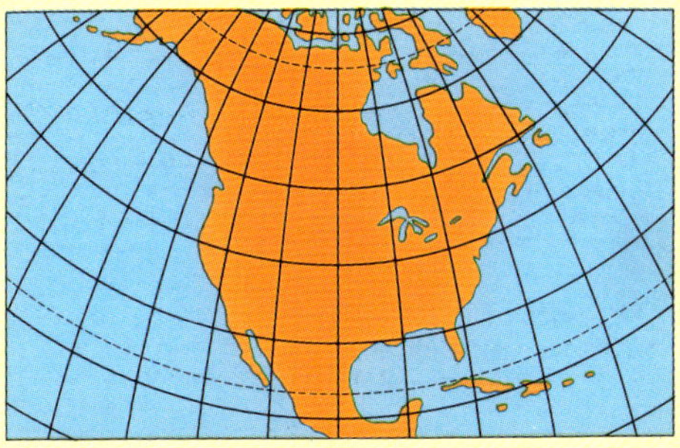

Simple Conic

Scale is correct not only along the standard parallel but also along all meridians. The selection of the standard parallel used is crucial because of the distortion away from it. The projection is usually used to portray regions or continents at small scales.

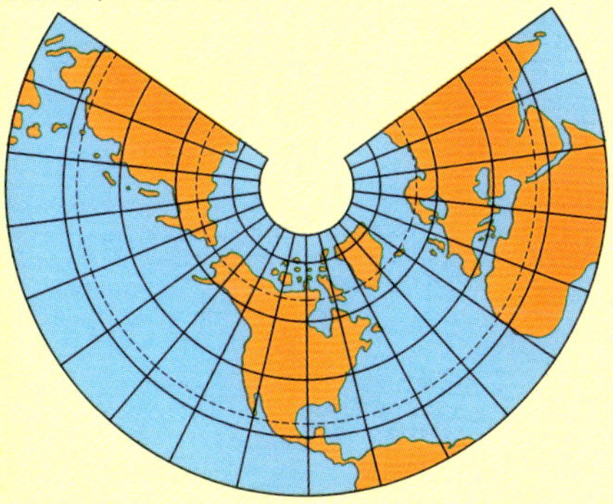

Lambert's Conformal Conic

This projection uses two standard parallels but instead of being equal area as Albers, it is Conformal. Because it has comparatively small distortion, direction and distances can be readily measured and it is therefore used for some navigational charts.

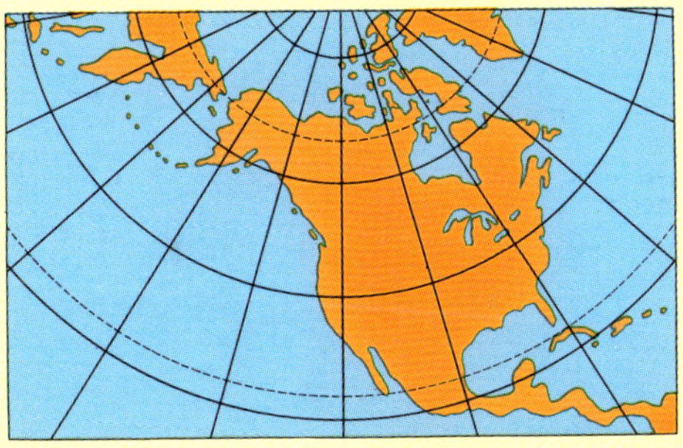

Albers Conical Equal Area

This projection uses two standard parallels and once again the selection of the two specific ones relative to the land area to be mapped is very important. It is equal area and is especially useful for large land masses oriented East-West, for example the U.S.A.

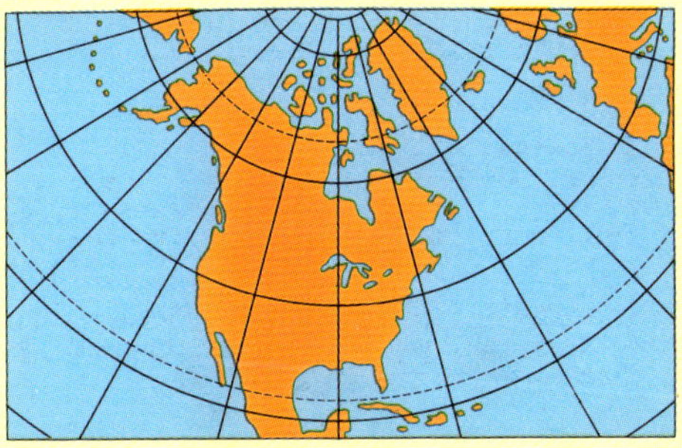

CYLINDRICAL AND OTHER WORLD PROJECTIONS

This group of projections are those which permit the whole of the Earth's surface to be depicted on one map. They are a very large group of projections and the following are only a few of them. Cylindrical projections are constructed by the projection of the graticule from the globe onto a cylinder tangential to the globe. In the examples shown here the cylinder touches the equator, but it can be moved through 90° so it touches the poles - this is called the **Transverse Aspect**. If the cylinder is twisted so that it touches anywhere between the equator and poles it is called the **Oblique Aspect.** Although cylindrical projections can depict all the main land masses, there is considerable distortion of shape and area towards the poles. One cylindrical projection, **Mercator** overcomes this shortcoming by possessing the unique navigational property that any straight drawn on it is a line of constant bearing (**loxodrome**), i.e. a straight line route on the globe crosses the parallels and meridians on the map at the same angles as on the globe. It is used for maps and charts between 15° either side of the equator. Beyond this enlargement of area is a serious drawback, although it is used for navigational charts at all latitudes.

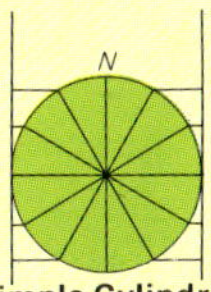

Simple Cylindrical

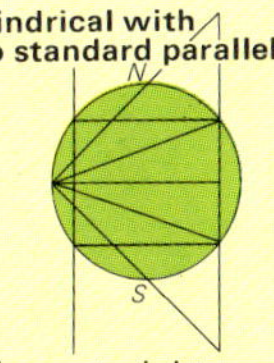

Cylindrical with two standard parallels

Mercator

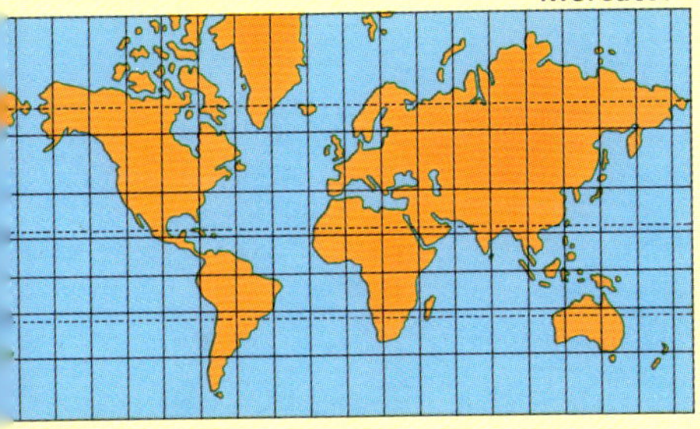

Mollweide

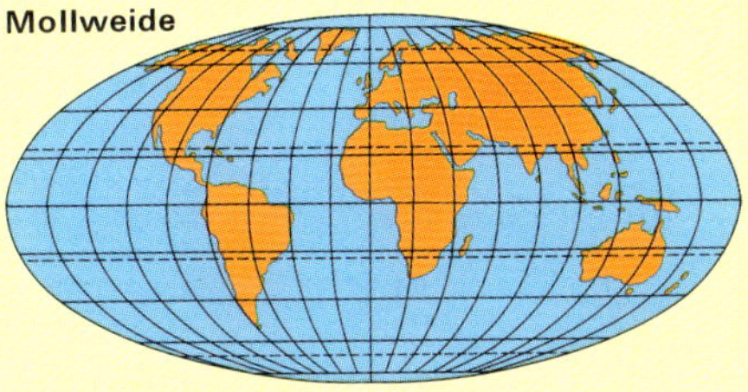

Sanson-Flamsteed

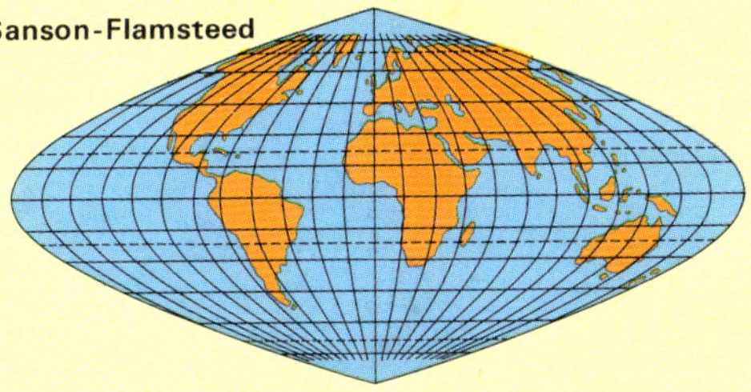

Mollweide and Sanson-Flamsteed

Both of these projections are termed **pseudo-cylindrical**. They are basically cylindrical projections where parallels have been progressively shortened and drawn to scale towards the poles. This allows them to overcome the gross distortions exhibited by the ordinary cylindrical projections and they are in fact Equal Area, Mollweide's giving a slightly better shape. To improve the shape of the continents still further they, like some other projections can be **Interrupted** as can be seen below, but this is at the expense of contiguous sea areas. These projections can have any central meridian and so can be 'centred' on the Atlantic, Pacific, Asia, America etc. In this form both projections are suitable for any form of mapping statistical distributions.

Iammer

his is not a cylindrical projection, but is developed rom the Lambert Azimuthal Equal Area by doubling ll the East-West distances along the parallels from he central meridian. Like both Sanson–Flamsteed nd Mollweide it is distorted towards its edges but as curved parallels to lessen the distortion.

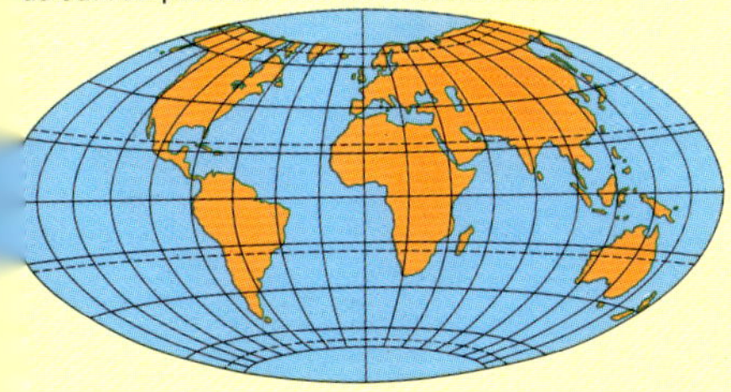

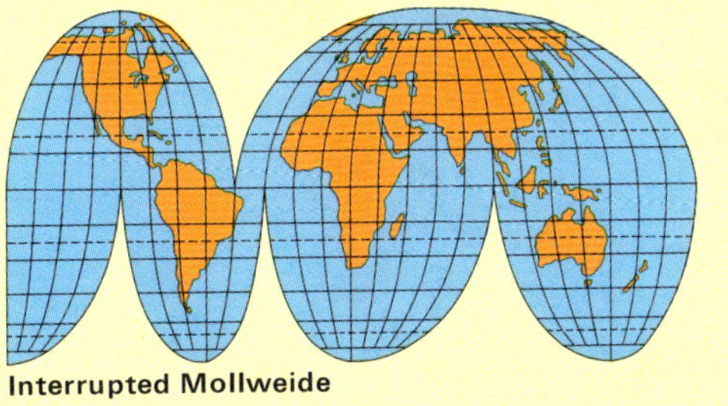

Interrupted Mollweide

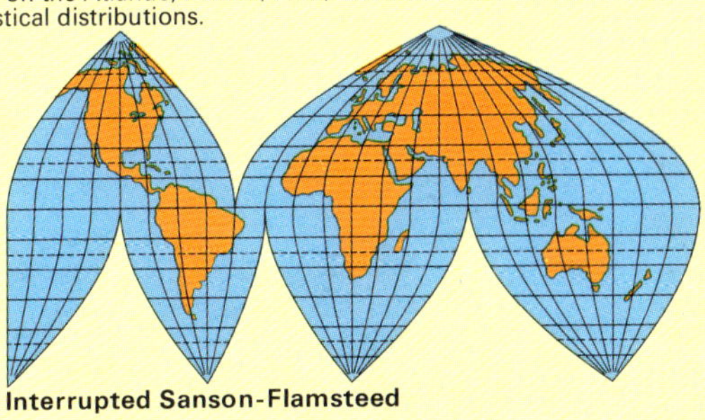

Interrupted Sanson-Flamsteed